Cassino '44

Also by James Holland

Non-fiction

FORTRESS MALTA
TOGETHER WE STAND
HEROES
ITALY'S SORROW
THE BATTLE OF BRITAIN
DAM BUSTERS
AN ENGLISHMAN AT WAR
THE RISE OF GERMANY
THE ALLIES STRIKE BACK
BURMA '44
BIG WEEK
RAF 100: THE OFFICIAL STORY
NORMANDY '44
SICILY '43
BROTHERS IN ARMS
THE SAVAGE STORM

Fiction

THE BURNING BLUE
A PAIR OF SILVER WINGS
THE ODIN MISSION
DARKEST HOUR
BLOOD OF HONOUR
HELLFIRE
THE DEVIL'S PACT

CASSINO '44

The Brutal Battle for Rome

James Holland

Atlantic Monthly Press
New York

First published in Great Britain in 2024 by Bantam
an imprint of Transworld Publishers

Published simultaneously in Canada
Printed in the United States of America

First Grove Atlantic hardcover editon:November 2024

Typeset in 11.25/14pt Minion Pro by Jouve (UK), Milton Keynes

Library of Congress Cataloging-in-Publication data is available for this title.

ISBN 978-0-8021-6384-4
eISBN 978-0-8021-6214-4

Atlantic Monthly Press
an imprint of Grove Atlantic
154 West 14th Street
New York, NY 10011

Distributed by Publishers Group West

groveatlantic.com

24 25 26 27 28 10 9 8 7 6 5 4 3 2 1

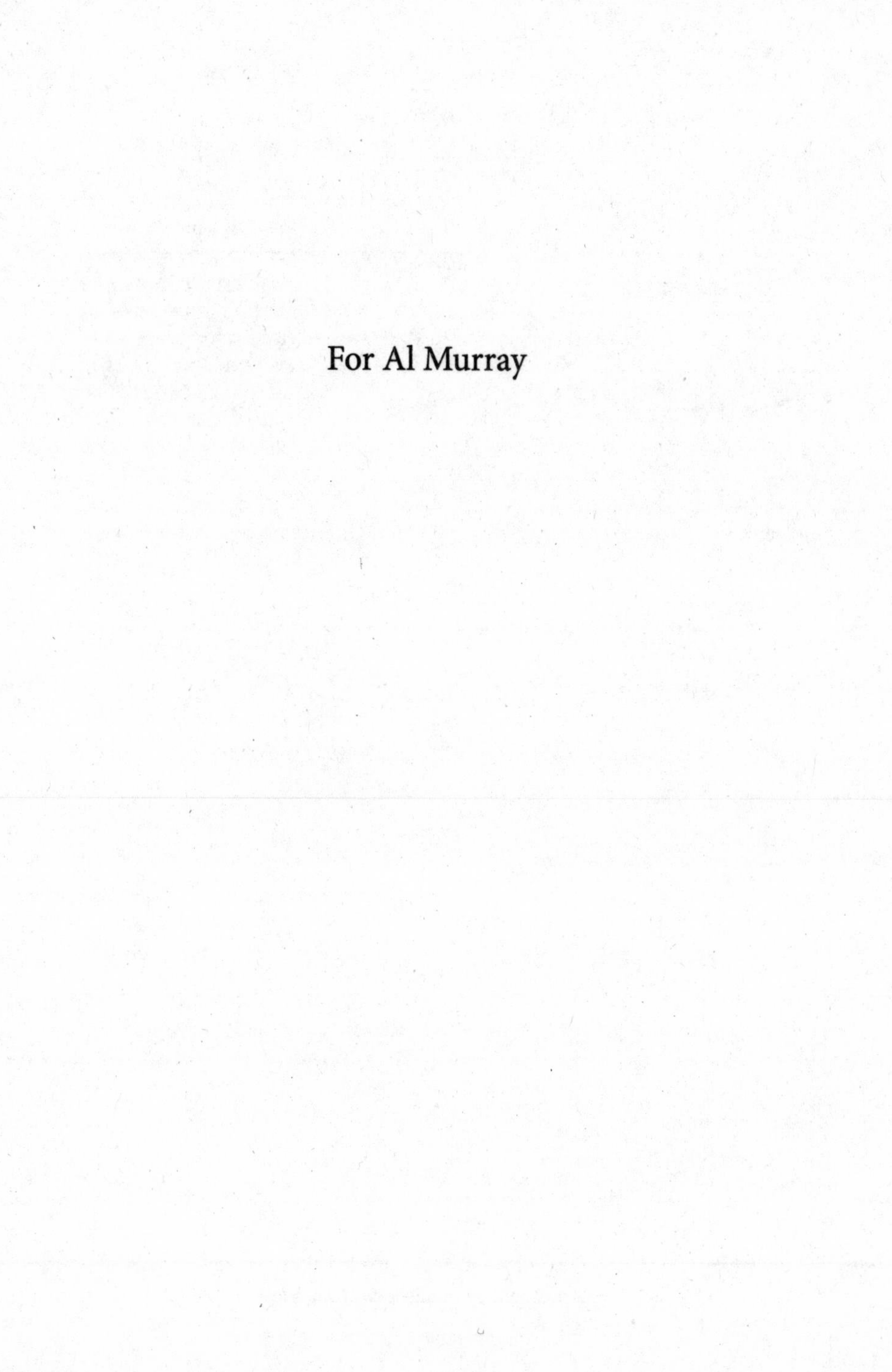

For Al Murray

'A world of shadows; of primordial gloom; of inchoate violence steeped in menace, lay all around me. I was staring down a vertiginous tunnel where all was dark and bloody, and the great wind of ultimate desolation howled and hungered. I was alone. Relentlessly alone, in a world I never knew.'

Lieutenant Farley Mowat

Contents

Part III: The Seeds of Change

Part IV: The Battle for Rome

List of Maps

Map Key

ALLIED UNITS  **AXIS UNITS** 

STANDARD MILITARY SYMBOLS

I	= Company	X	= Brigade
II	= Battalion	XX	= Division
III	= Regiment	XXX	= Corps
		XXXX	= Army
		XXXXX	= Army Group

Armoured unit   Paratroopers

OTHER ABBREVIATIONS

Alg. = Algerian
Armd = Armoured
Bde = Brigade
Bn = Battalion
Br. = British
Can. = Canadian
Cdo = Commando
CEF = Corps Expéditionnaire Français
Div. = Division
DWR = Duke of Wellington's Regiment
FBE = Folding Boat Equipment
FJD = Fallschirmjäger-Division
FJR = Fallschirmjäger-Regiment
GAK = Gebirgsarmeekorps
Gds = Guards
Ger. = German
GJD= Gebirgsjäger-Division
GR = Grenadier-Regiment
HG = Hermann Göring
Ind. = Indian
Inf. = Infantry
KSLI = King's Shropshire Light Infantry
MG-Bn = Maschinengewehr-Bataillon
NZ = New Zealand
PD = Panzer-Division
PG = Panzergrenadier
PGD = Panzergrenadier-Division
PGR = Panzergrenadier-Regiment
PIR = Parachute Infantry Regiment
PK = Panzerkorps
Pol. = Polish
Raj. Rif. = Rajputana Rifles
SSF = Special Service Force
US = United States

• 123 = Point 123

ITALY TERRAIN MAP

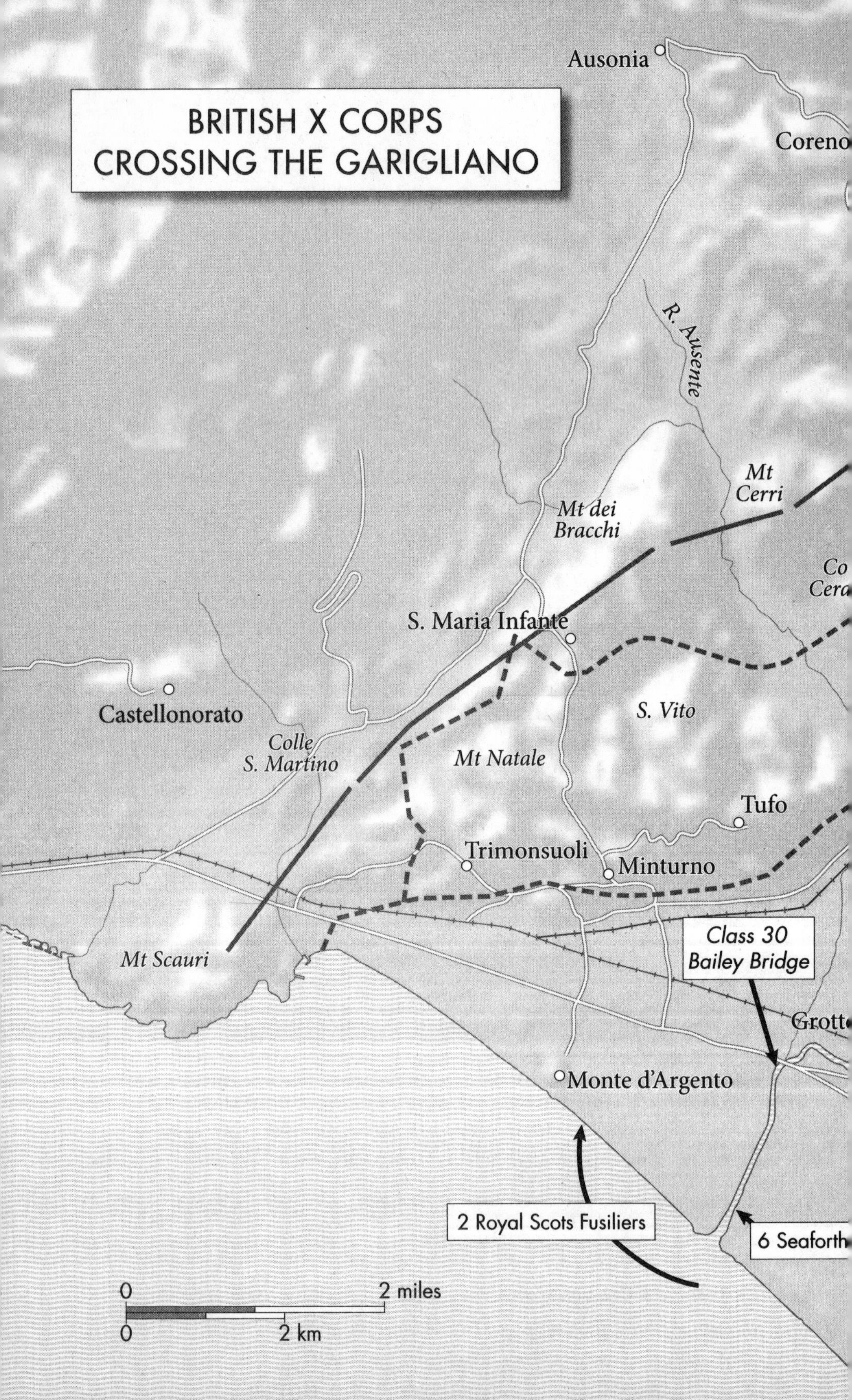

BRITISH X CORPS
CROSSING THE GARIGLIANO
Ausonia
Coreno
R. Ausente
Mt Cerri
Mt dei Bracchi
S. Maria Infante
Castellonorato
Colle S. Martino
S. Vito
Mt Natale
Tufo
Trimonsuoli
Minturno
Class 30 Bailey Bridge
Mt Scauri
Monte d'Argento
2 Royal Scots Fusiliers
0
2 miles
0
2 km

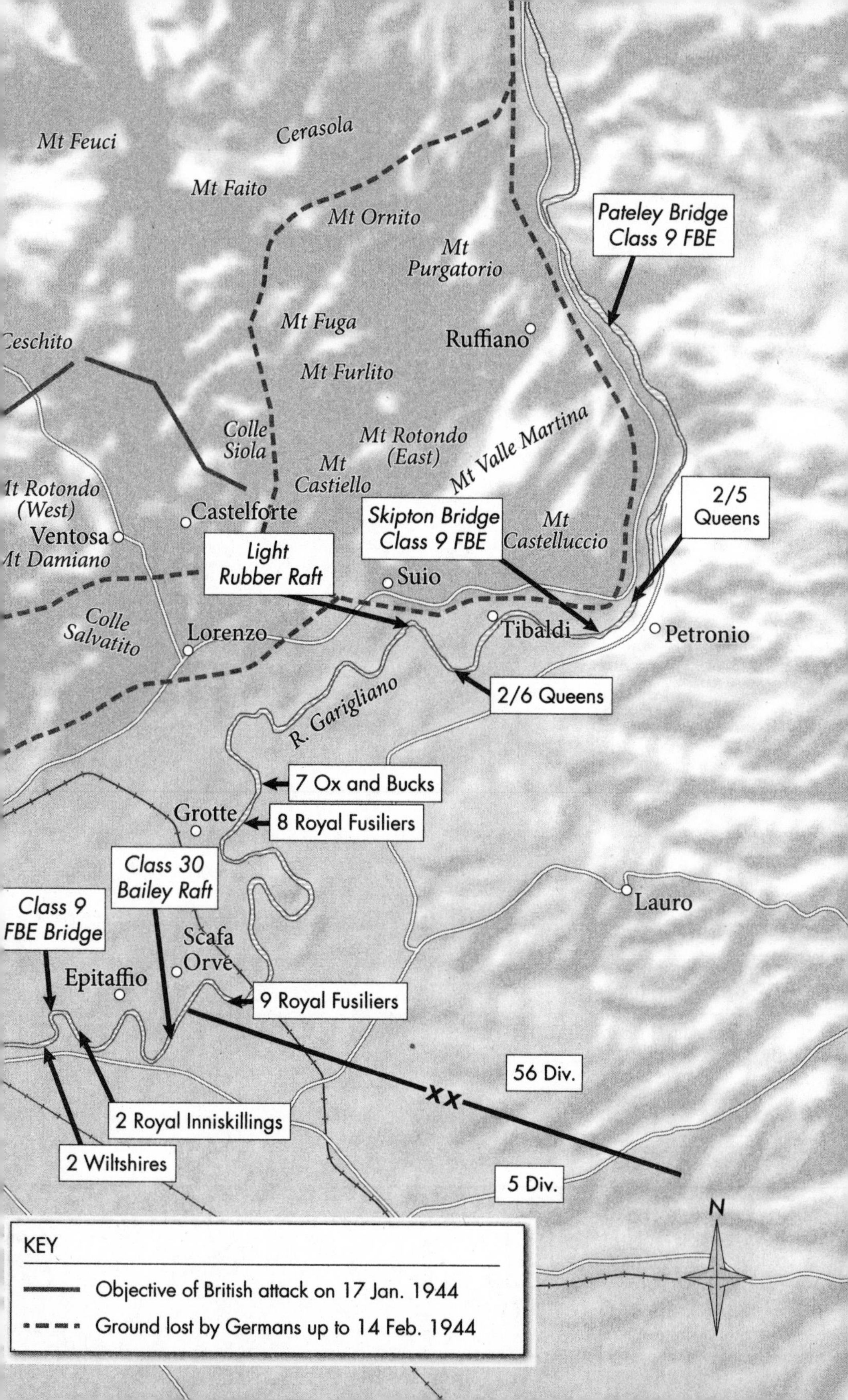

Mt Feuci
Cerasola
Mt Faito
Mt Ornito
Mt Purgatorio
Pateley Bridge Class 9 FBE
Mt Fuga
Ruffiano
Ceschito
Mt Furlito
Colle Siola
Mt Rotondo (East)
Mt Valle Martina
Mt Castiello
Mt Rotondo (West)
Castelforte
Skipton Bridge Class 9 FBE
Mt Castelluccio
2/5 Queens
Ventosa
Mt Damiano
Light Rubber Raft
Suio
Colle Salvatito
Lorenzo
Tibaldi
Petronio
2/6 Queens
R. Garigliano
7 Ox and Bucks
Grotte
8 Royal Fusiliers
Class 30 Bailey Raft
Lauro
Class 9 FBE Bridge
Scafa Orve
Epitaffio
9 Royal Fusiliers
56 Div.
XX
2 Royal Inniskillings
2 Wiltshires
5 Div.
N
KEY
Objective of British attack on 17 Jan. 1944
Ground lost by Germans up to 14 Feb. 1944

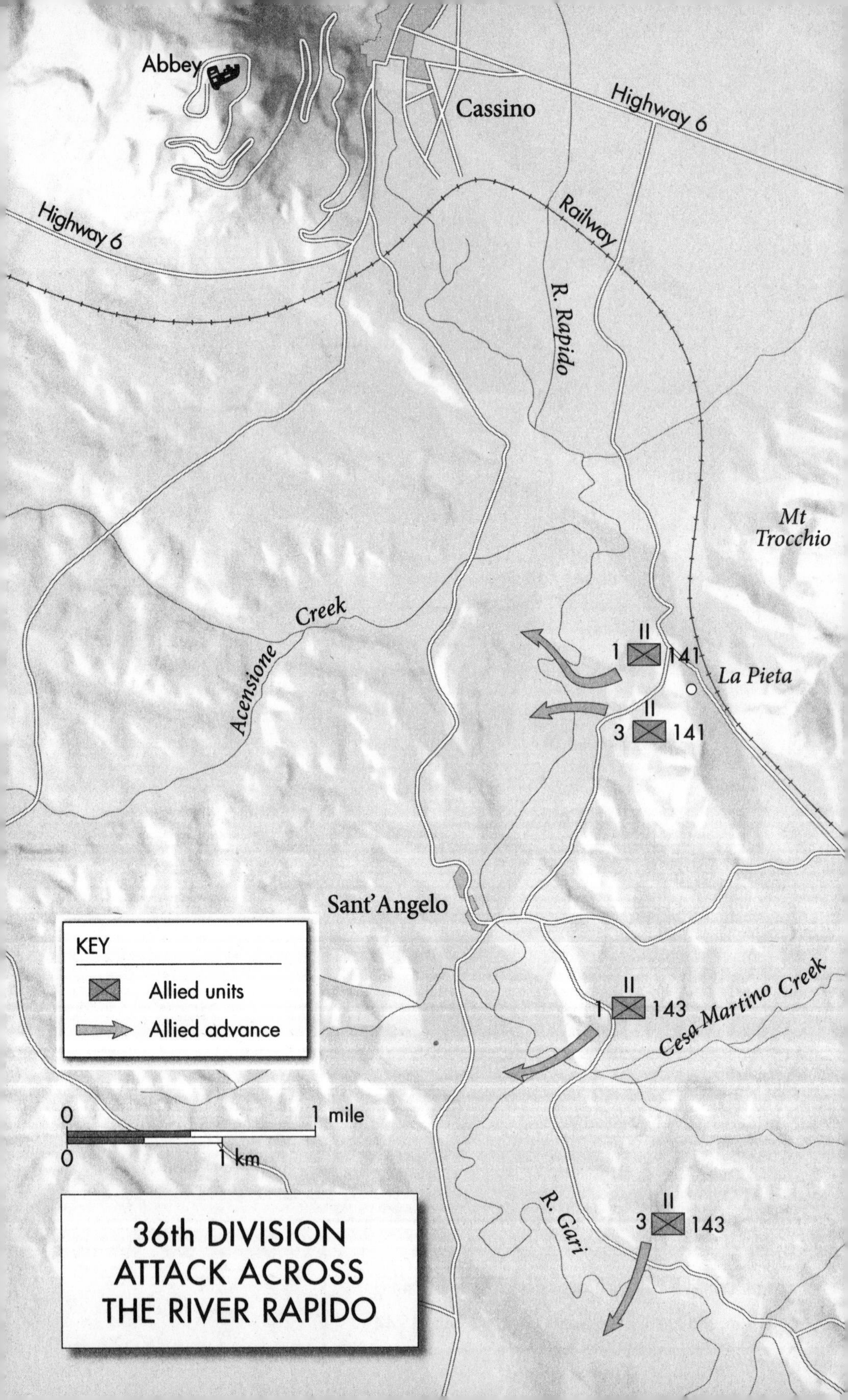
Abbey
Cassino
Highway 6
Highway 6
Railway
R. Rapido
Mt Trocchio
Acensione Creek
1 II 141
La Pieta
3 II 141
Sant'Angelo
KEY
Allied units
Allied advance
1 II 143
Cesa Martino Creek
0
1 mile
0
1 km
R. Gari
3 II 143
36th DIVISION ATTACK ACROSS THE RIVER RAPIDO

A bloodied Polish soldier following the fighting on Monte Cassino in May 1944.

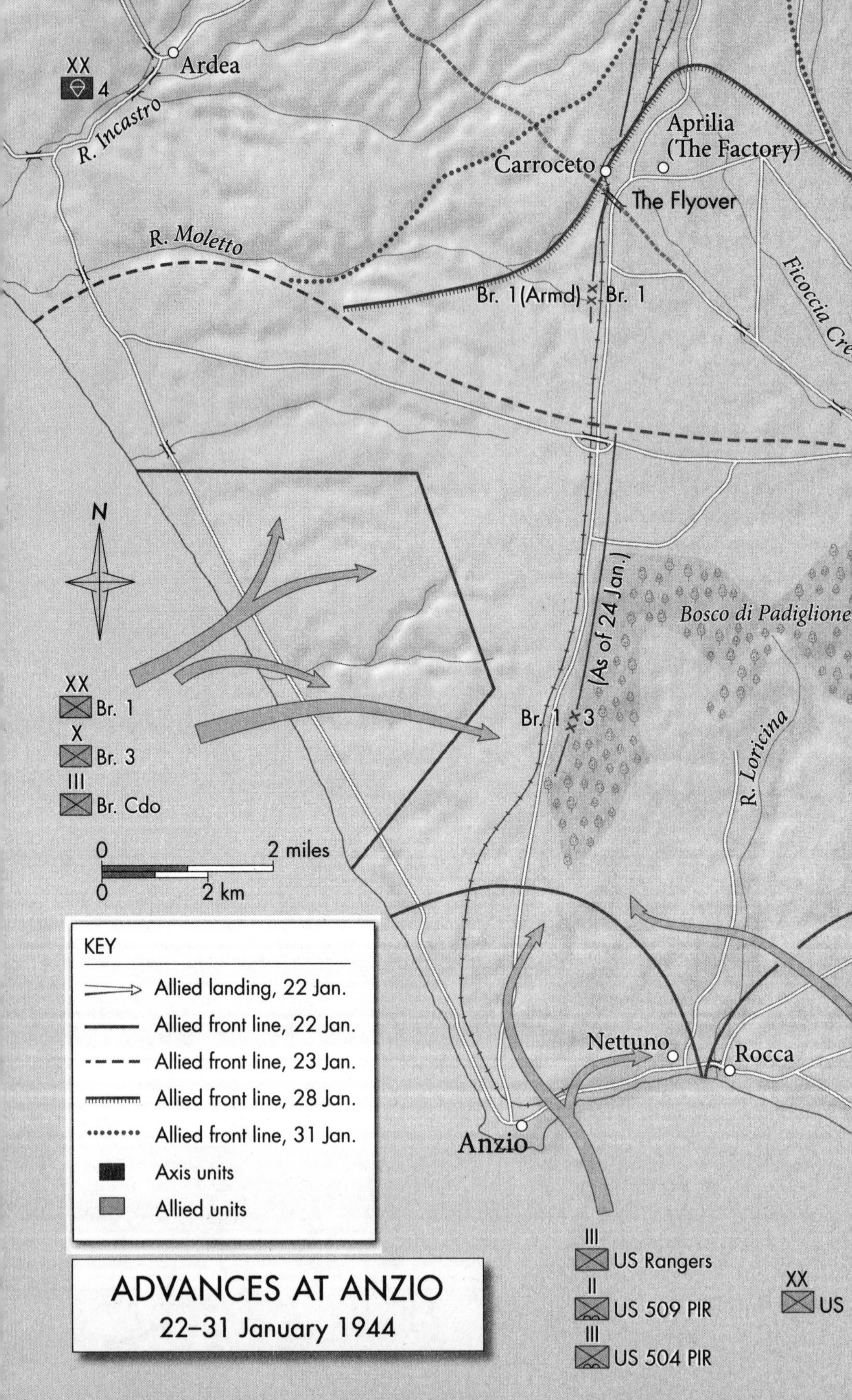
Ardea
XX
4
R. Incastro
R. Moletto
Carroceto
Aprilia
(The Factory)
The Flyover
Ficoccia Cre
Br. 1(Armd)
Br. 1
N
(As of 24 Jan.)
Bosco di Padiglione
XX
Br. 1
X
Br. 3
III
Br. Cdo
Br. 1
3
R. Loricina
0
2 miles
0
2 km
KEY
Allied landing, 22 Jan.
Allied front line, 22 Jan.
Allied front line, 23 Jan.
Allied front line, 28 Jan.
Allied front line, 31 Jan.
Axis units
Allied units
Nettuno
Rocca
Anzio
III
US Rangers
II
US 509 PIR
III
US 504 PIR
XX
US
ADVANCES AT ANZIO
22–31 January 1944

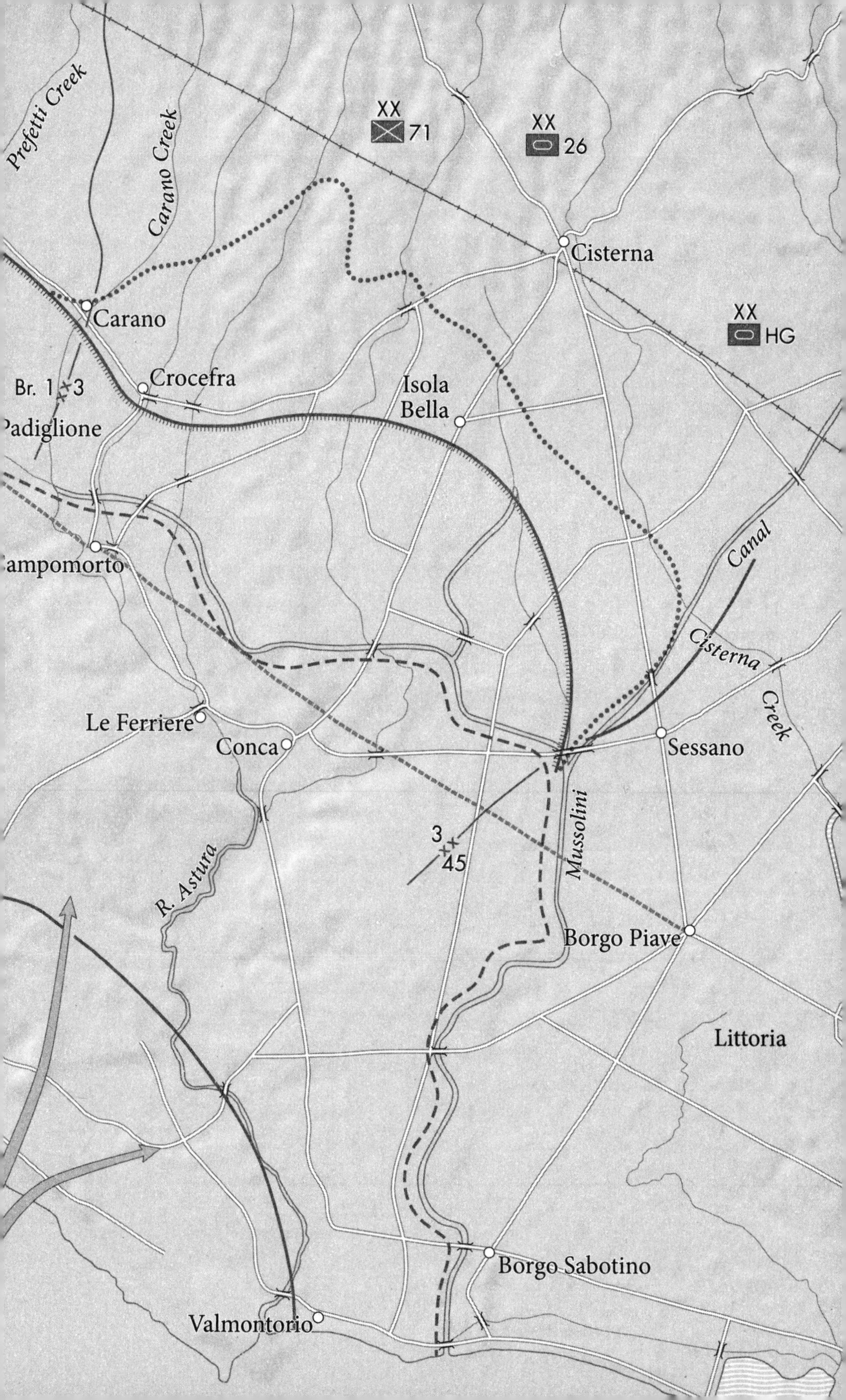

Prefetti Creek
Carano Creek
XX 71
XX 26
XX HG
Cisterna
Carano
Crocefra
Br. 1 3
Padiglione
Isola Bella
Campomorto
Canal
Cisterna
Creek
Le Ferriere
Conca
Sessano
Mussolini
3 XX 45
R. Astura
Borgo Piave
Littoria
Borgo Sabotino
Valmontorio

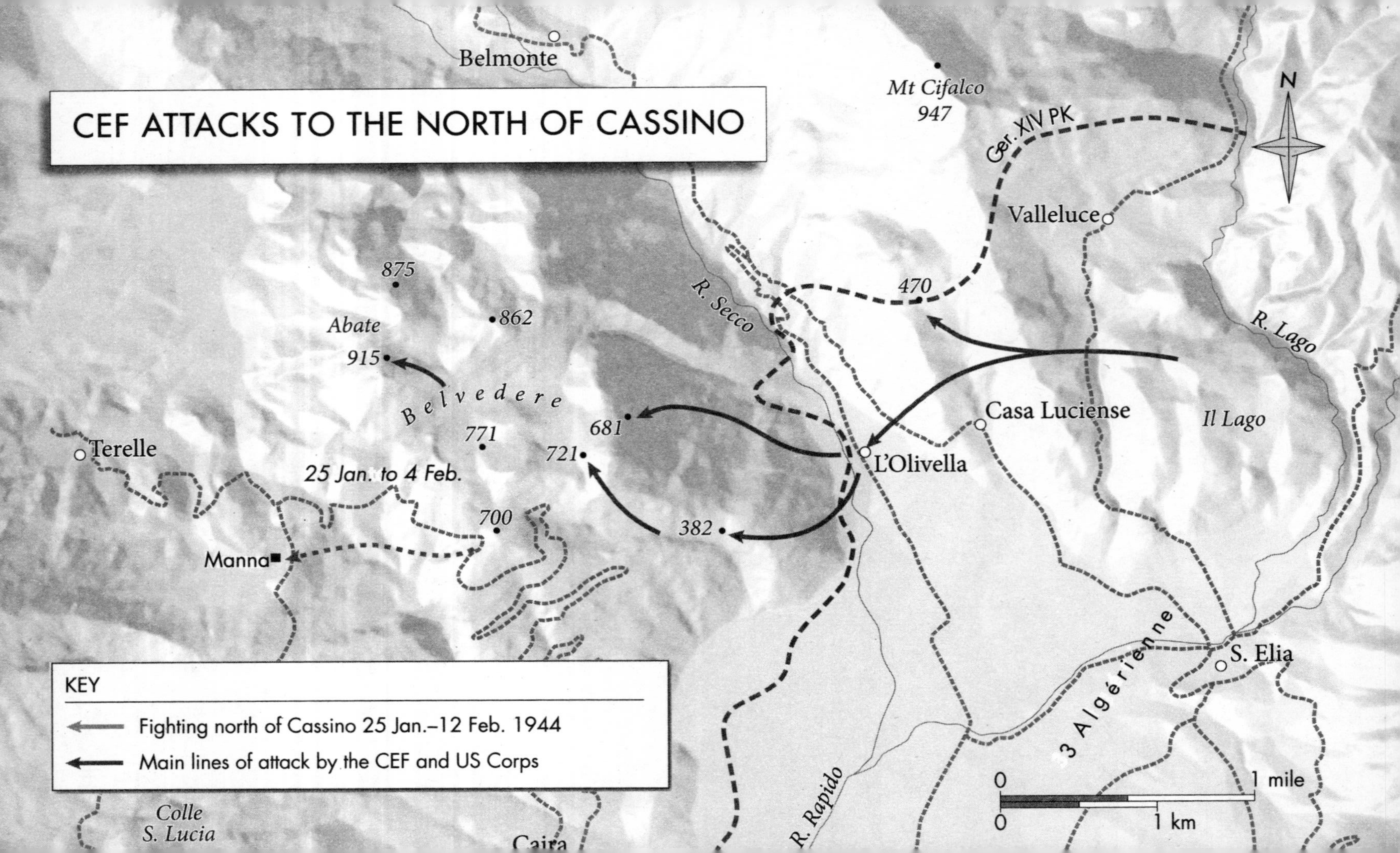
CEF ATTACKS TO THE NORTH OF CASSINO
Belmonte
Mt Cifalco
947
Ger. XIV PK
N
Valleluce
470
R. Secco
R. Lago
875
862
Abate
915
Belvedere
681
771
721
Terelle
25 Jan. to 4 Feb.
Casa Luciense
Il Lago
L'Olivella
700
382
Manna
3 Algérienne
S. Elia
KEY
Fighting north of Cassino 25 Jan.–12 Feb. 1944
Main lines of attack by the CEF and US Corps
0
1 mile
0
1 km
Colle
S. Lucia
Caira
R. Rapido

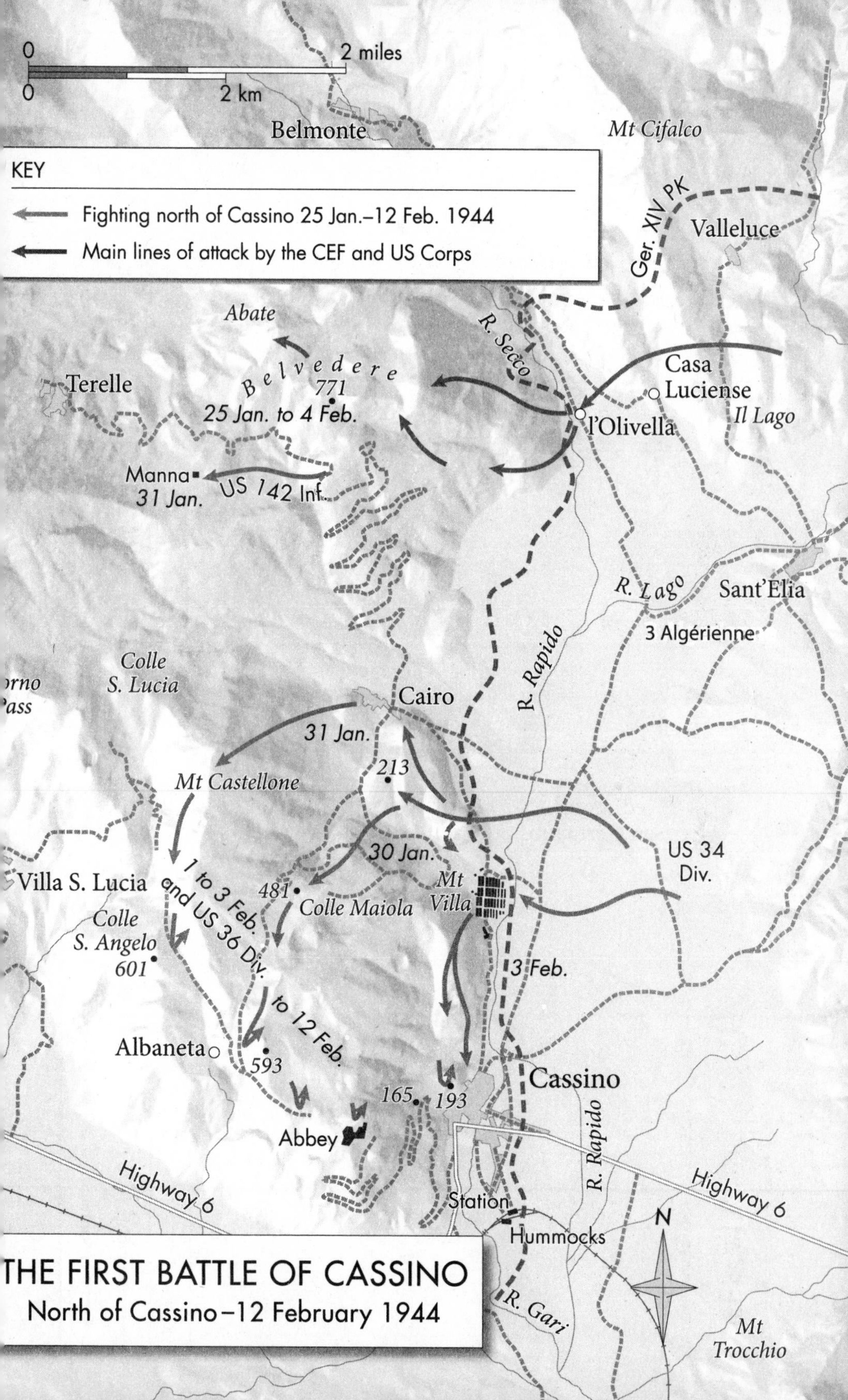

0
2 miles
0
2 km
Belmonte
Mt Cifalco
KEY
Fighting north of Cassino 25 Jan.–12 Feb. 1944
Main lines of attack by the CEF and US Corps
Ger. XIV PK
Valleluce
Abate
R. Secco
Casa
Luciense
Belvedere
771
Terelle
25 Jan. to 4 Feb.
l'Olivella
Il Lago
Manna
31 Jan.
US 142 Inf.
R. Lago
Sant'Elia
3 Algérienne
R. Rapido
Colle
S. Lucia
Cairo
31 Jan.
213
Mt Castellone
30 Jan.
US 34
Div.
Villa S. Lucia
1 to 3 Feb.
and US 36 Div.
to 12 Feb.
481
Colle Maiola
Mt
Villa
Colle
S. Angelo
601
3 Feb.
Albaneta
593
165
193
Cassino
Abbey
R. Rapido
Highway 6
Highway 6
Station
Hummocks
N
R. Gari
Mt
Trocchio
THE FIRST BATTLE OF CASSINO
North of Cassino–12 February 1944

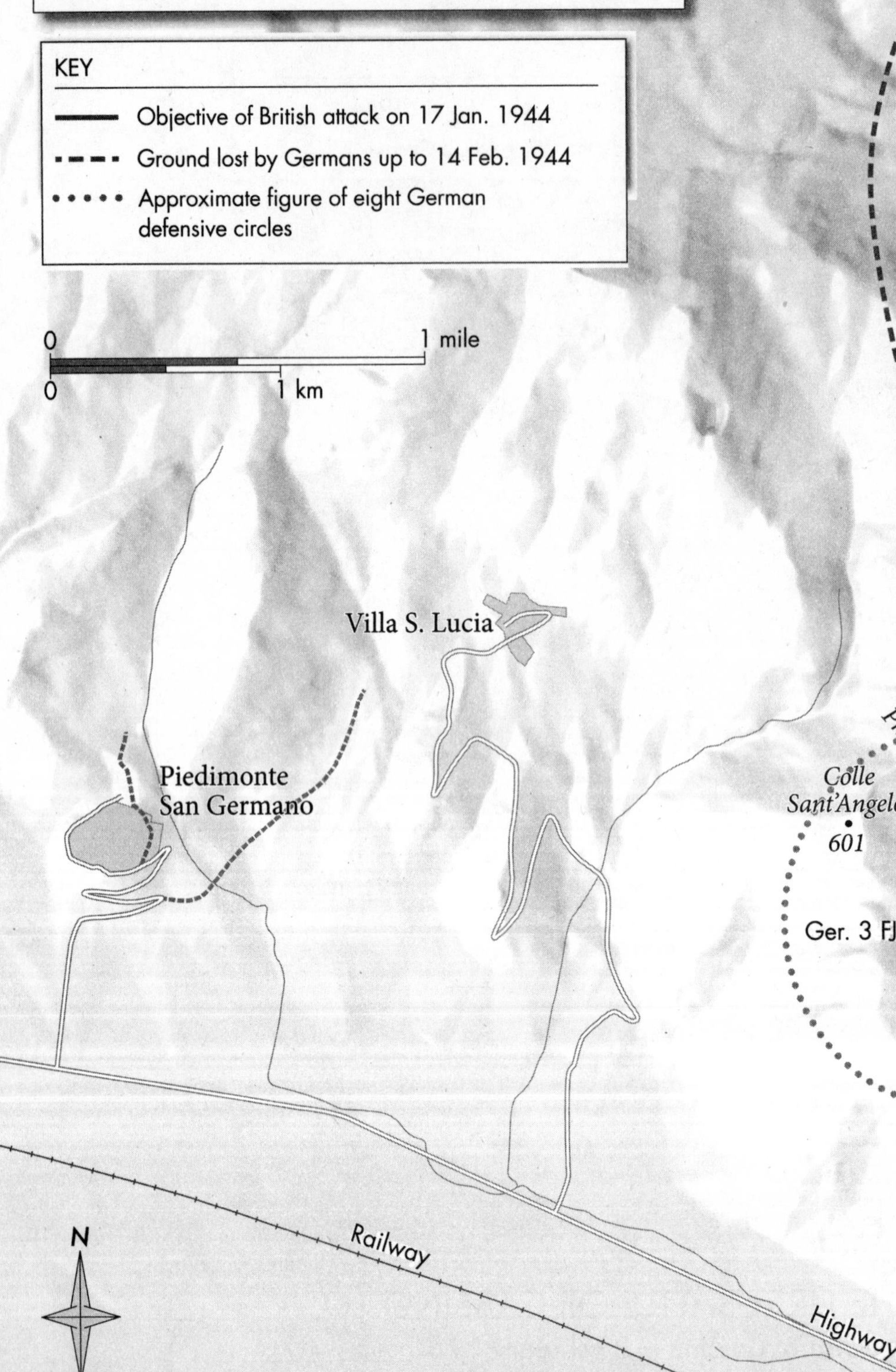

THE SECOND BATTLE OF CASSINO
KEY
Objective of British attack on 17 Jan. 1944
Ground lost by Germans up to 14 Feb. 1944
Approximate figure of eight German defensive circles
0
1 mile
0
1 km
Villa S. Lucia
Piedimonte San Germano
Colle Sant'Angelo
601
Ger. 3 FJR
Railway
Highway
N

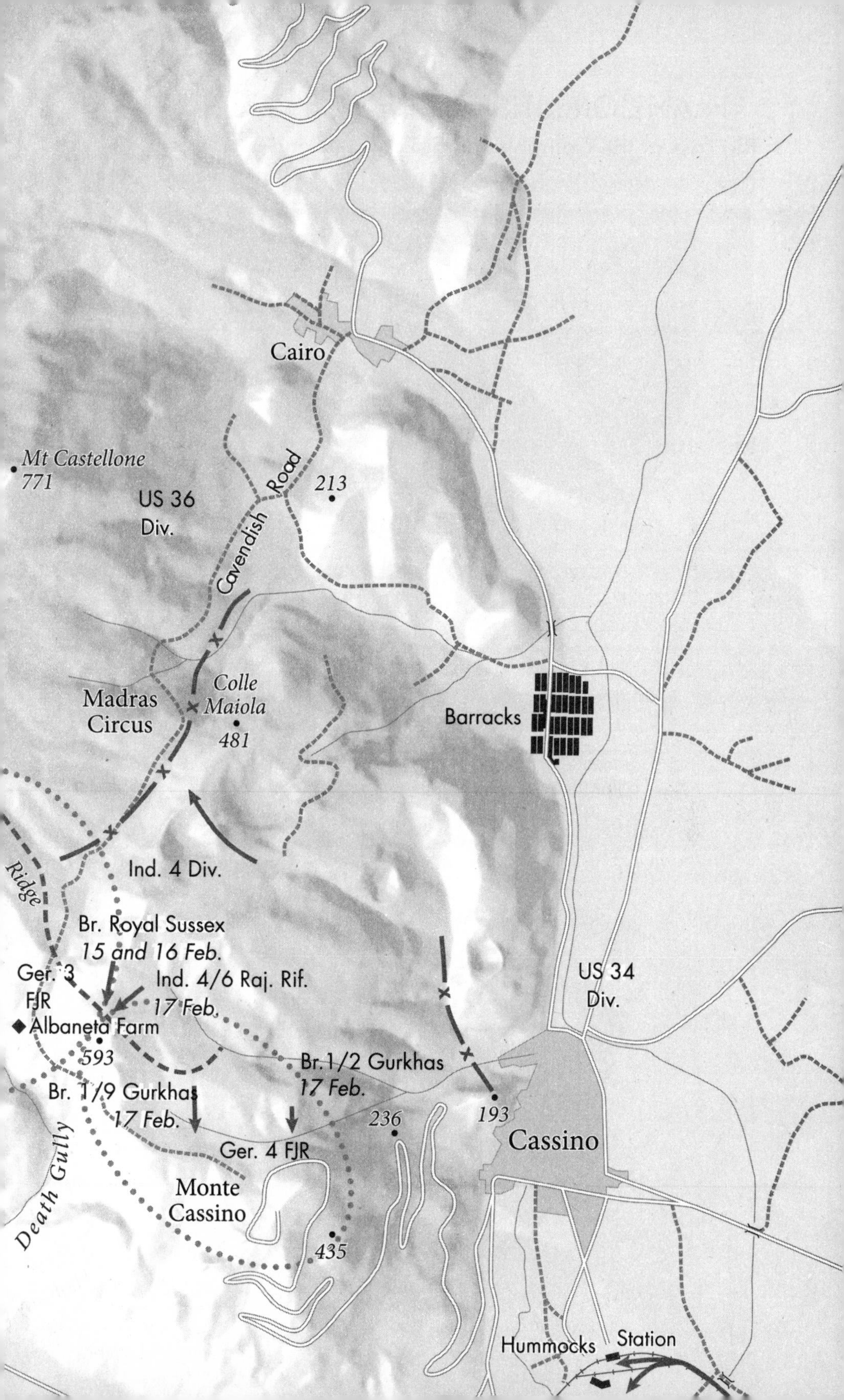

Cairo
Mt Castellone
771
US 36
Div.
Cavendish Road
213
Colle
Maiola
481
Madras
Circus
Barracks
Ridge
Ind. 4 Div.
Br. Royal Sussex
15 and 16 Feb.
Ger. 3
FJR
Ind. 4/6 Raj. Rif.
17 Feb.
Albaneta Farm
593
US 34
Div.
Br.1/2 Gurkhas
17 Feb.
Br. 1/9 Gurkhas
17 Feb.
236
193
Cassino
Ger. 4 FJR
Death Gully
Monte
Cassino
435
Hummocks
Station

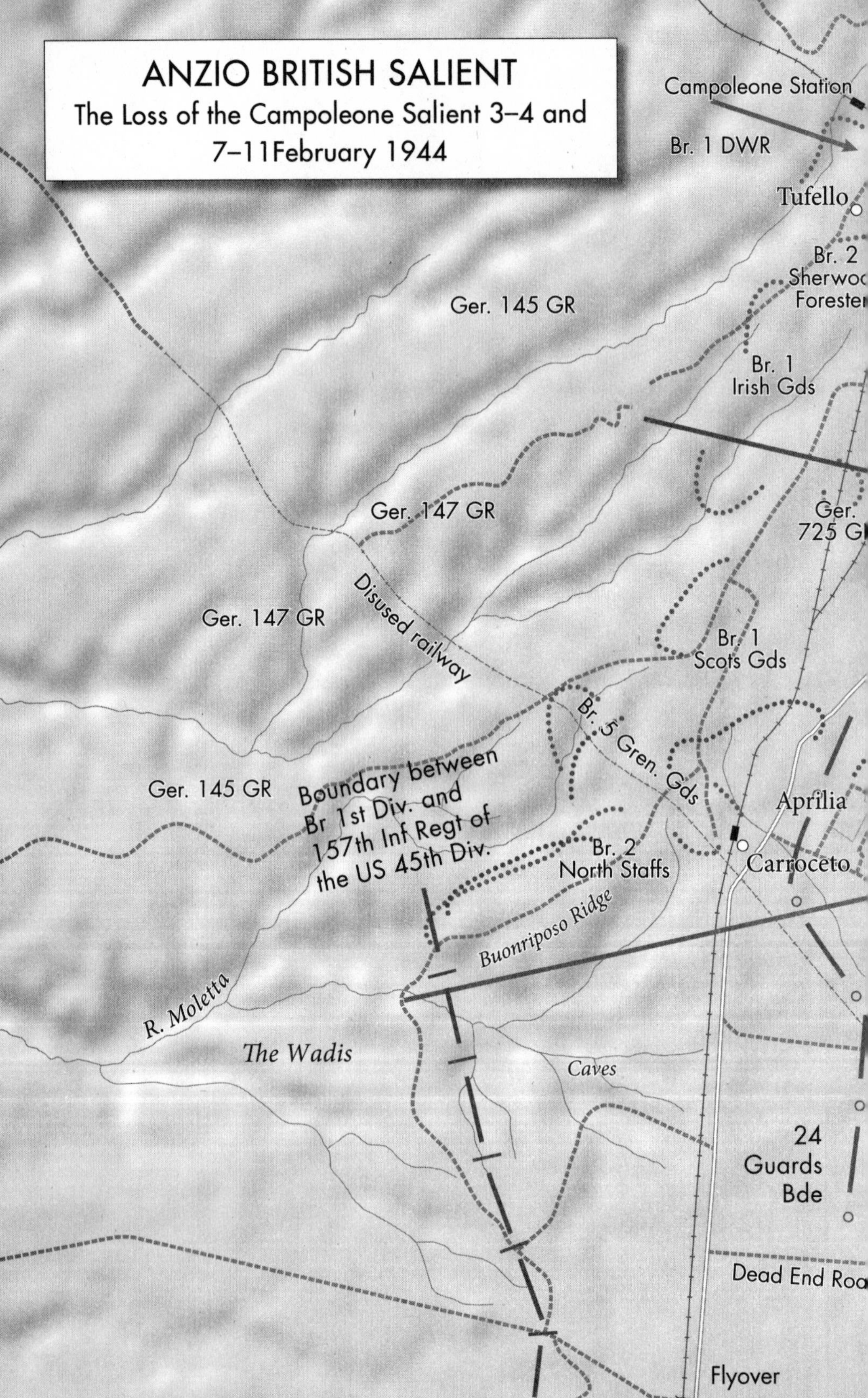

ANZIO BRITISH SALIENT
The Loss of the Campoleone Salient 3–4 and 7–11February 1944
Campoleone Station
Br. 1 DWR
Tufello
Br. 2 Sherwo
Foreste
Ger. 145 GR
Br. 1 Irish Gds
Ger. 147 GR
Ger. 725 G
Disused railway
Ger. 147 GR
Br. 1 Scots Gds
Br. 5 Gren. Gds
Ger. 145 GR
Boundary between Br 1st Div. and 157th Inf Regt of the US 45th Div.
Aprilia
Br. 2 North Staffs
Carroceto
Buonriposo Ridge
R. Moletta
The Wadis
Caves
24 Guards Bde
Dead End Roa
Flyover

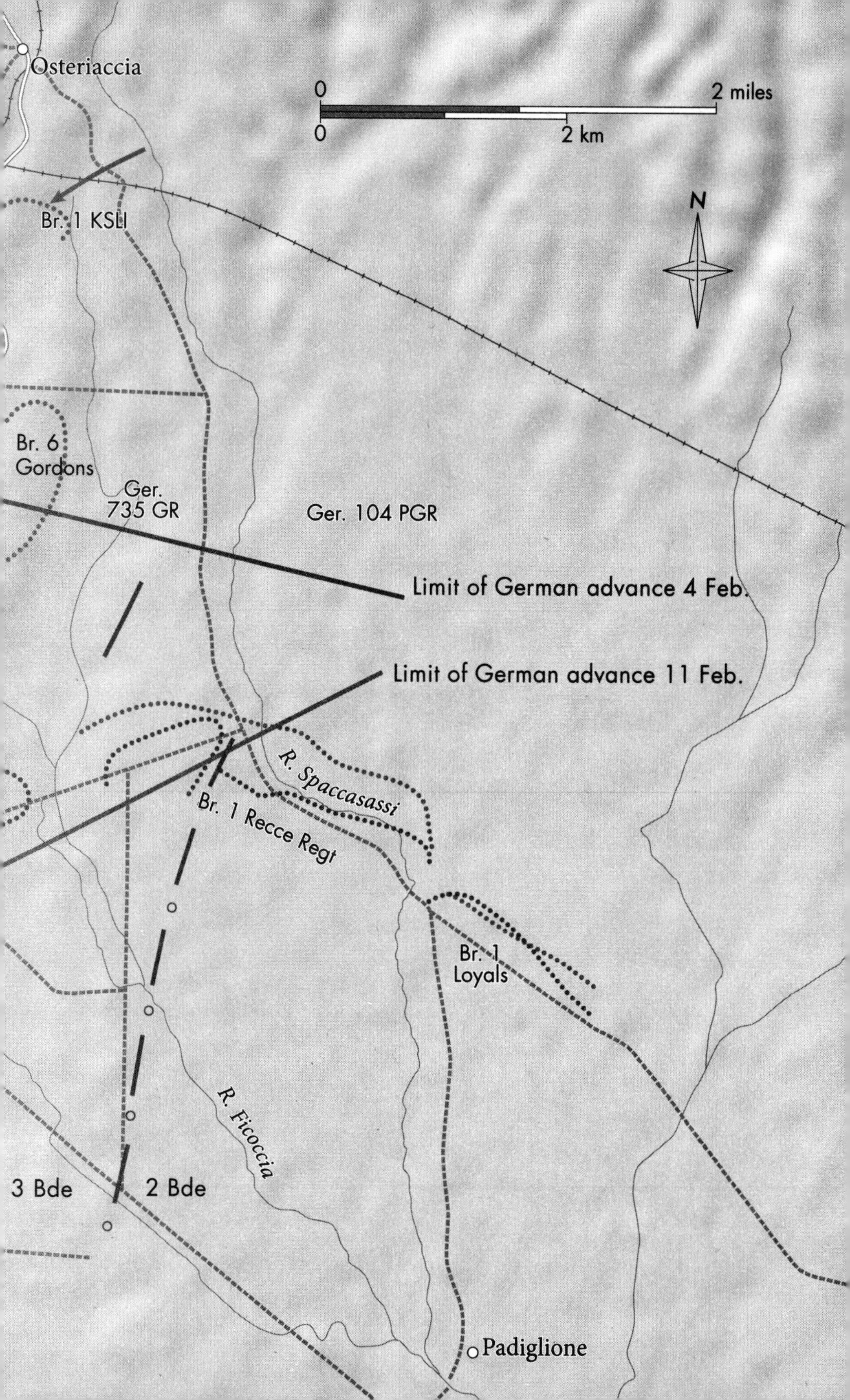
Osteriaccia
0
2 miles
0
2 km
N
Br. 1 KSLI
Br. 6
Gordons
Ger.
735 GR
Ger. 104 PGR
Limit of German advance 4 Feb.
Limit of German advance 11 Feb.
R. Spaccasassi
Br. 1 Recce Regt
Br. 1
Loyals
R. Ficoccia
3 Bde
2 Bde
Padiglione

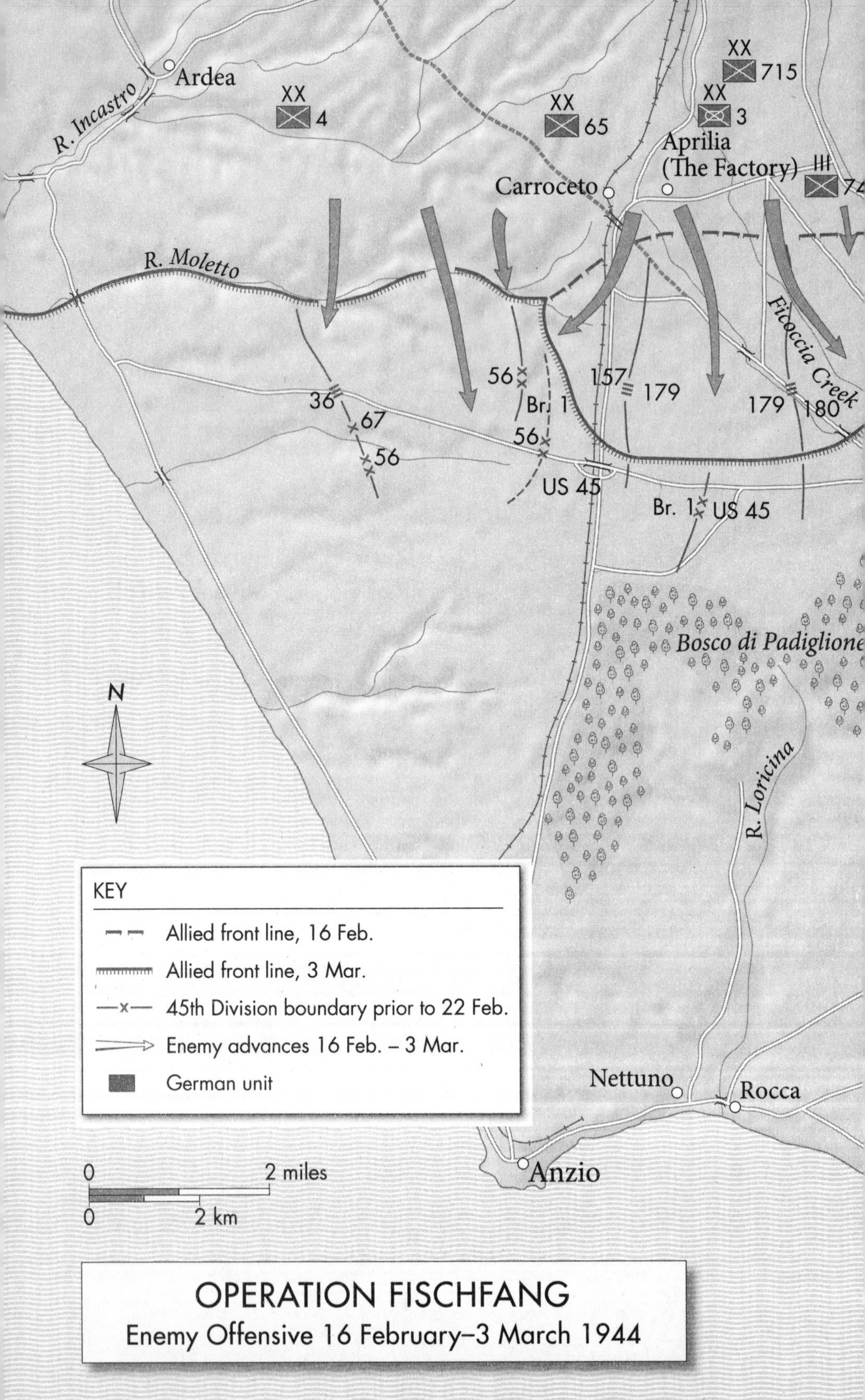

Ardea
R. Incastro
XX
4
XX
65
XX
715
XX
3
Aprilia
(The Factory)
III
Carroceto
R. Moletto
Ficoccia Creek
56
Br. 1
157
179
179
180
36
67
56
56
US 45
Br. 1
US 45
Bosco di Padiglione
N
R. Loricina
KEY
Allied front line, 16 Feb.
Allied front line, 3 Mar.
45th Division boundary prior to 22 Feb.
Enemy advances 16 Feb. – 3 Mar.
German unit
Nettuno
Rocca
Anzio
0
2 miles
0
2 km
OPERATION FISCHFANG
Enemy Offensive 16 February–3 March 1944

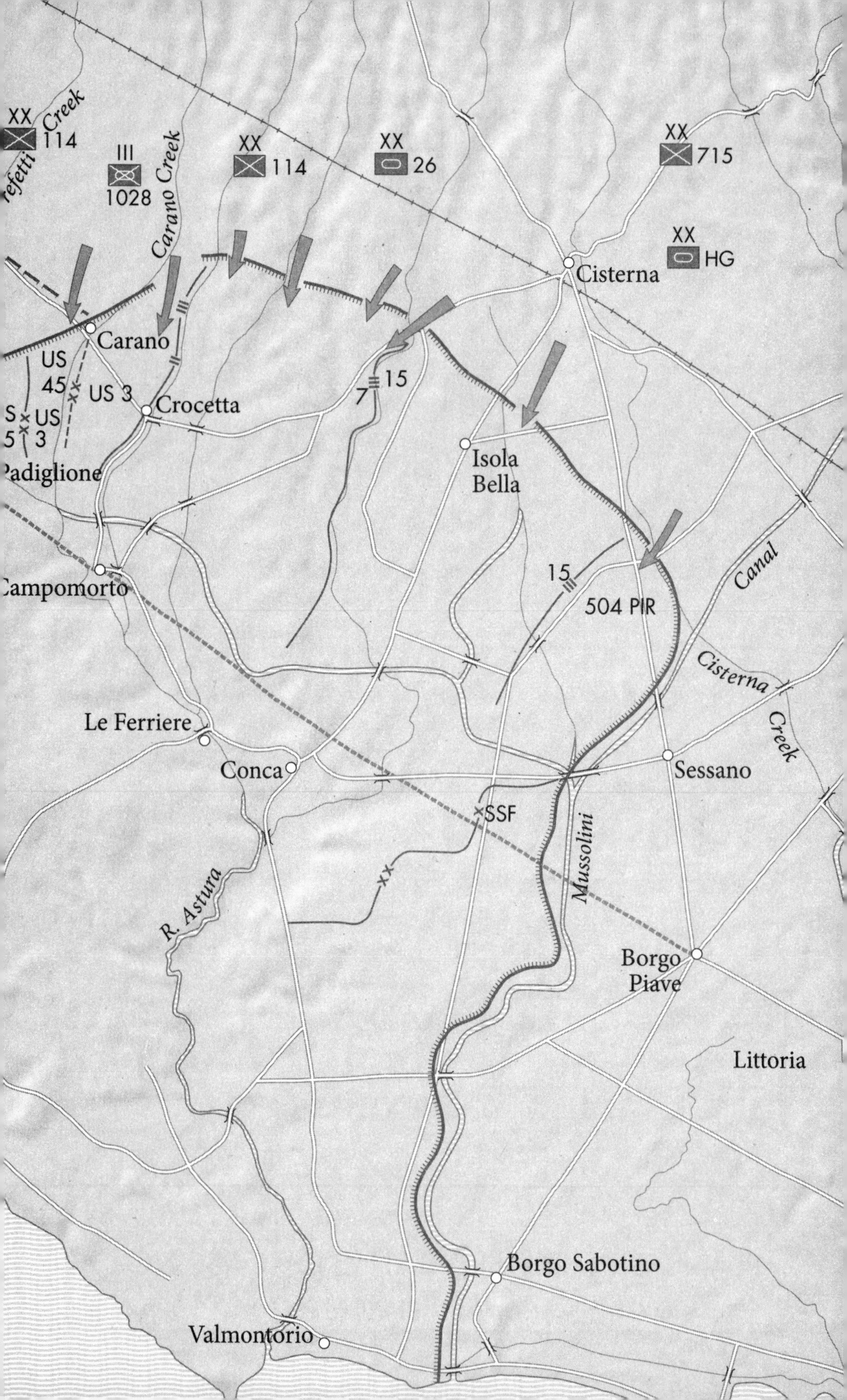

XX
114
III
1028
XX
114
XX
26
XX
715
XX
HG
Creek
Carano Creek
Cisterna
Carano
US
45
US 3
S
5
US
3
Crocetta
Padiglione
7
15
Isola
Bella
15
504 PIR
Canal
Cisterna
Creek
Campomorto
Le Ferriere
Conca
Sessano
SSF
Mussolini
R. Astura
Borgo
Piave
Littoria
Borgo Sabotino
Valmontorio

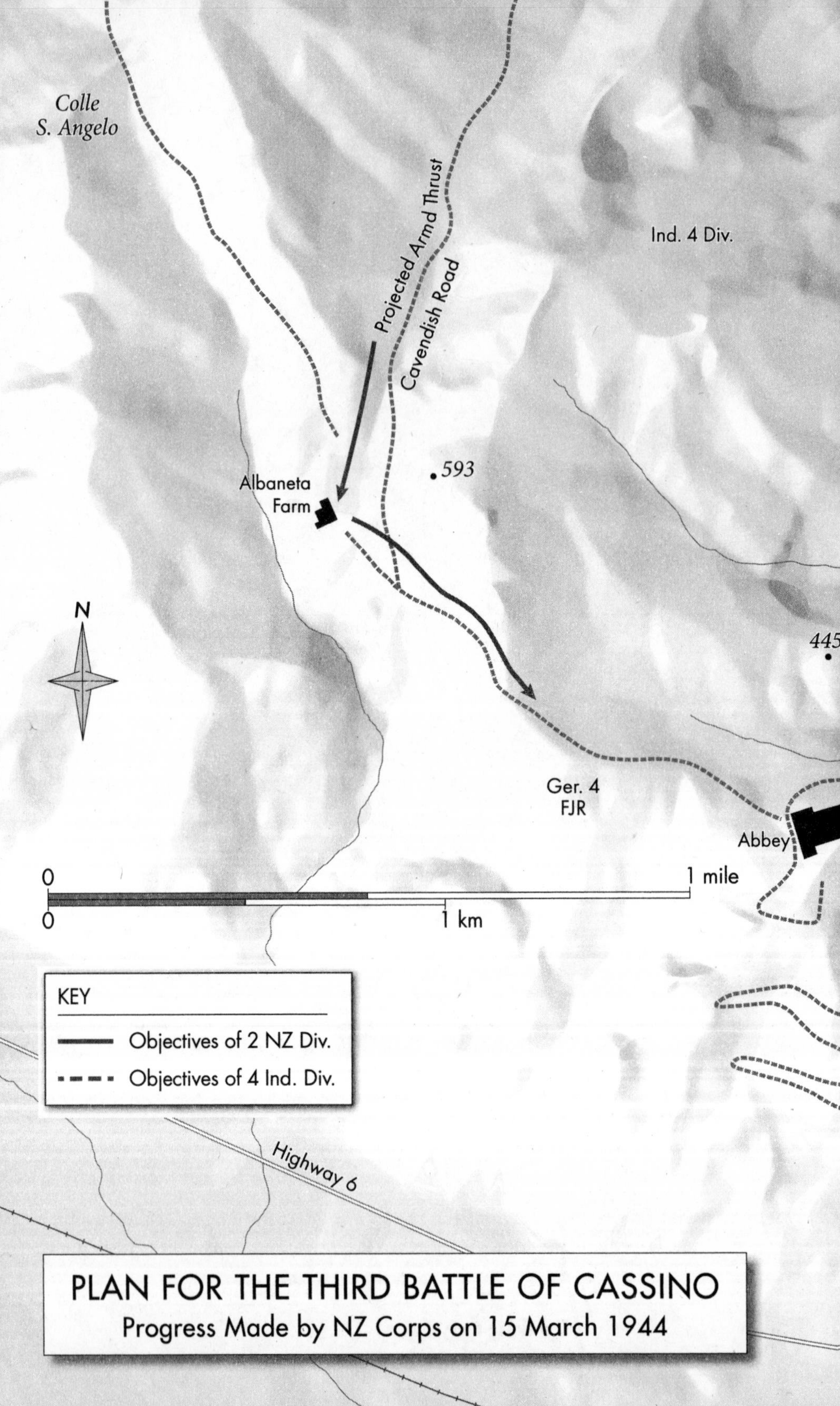

PLAN FOR THE THIRD BATTLE OF CASSINO
Progress Made by NZ Corps on 15 March 1944

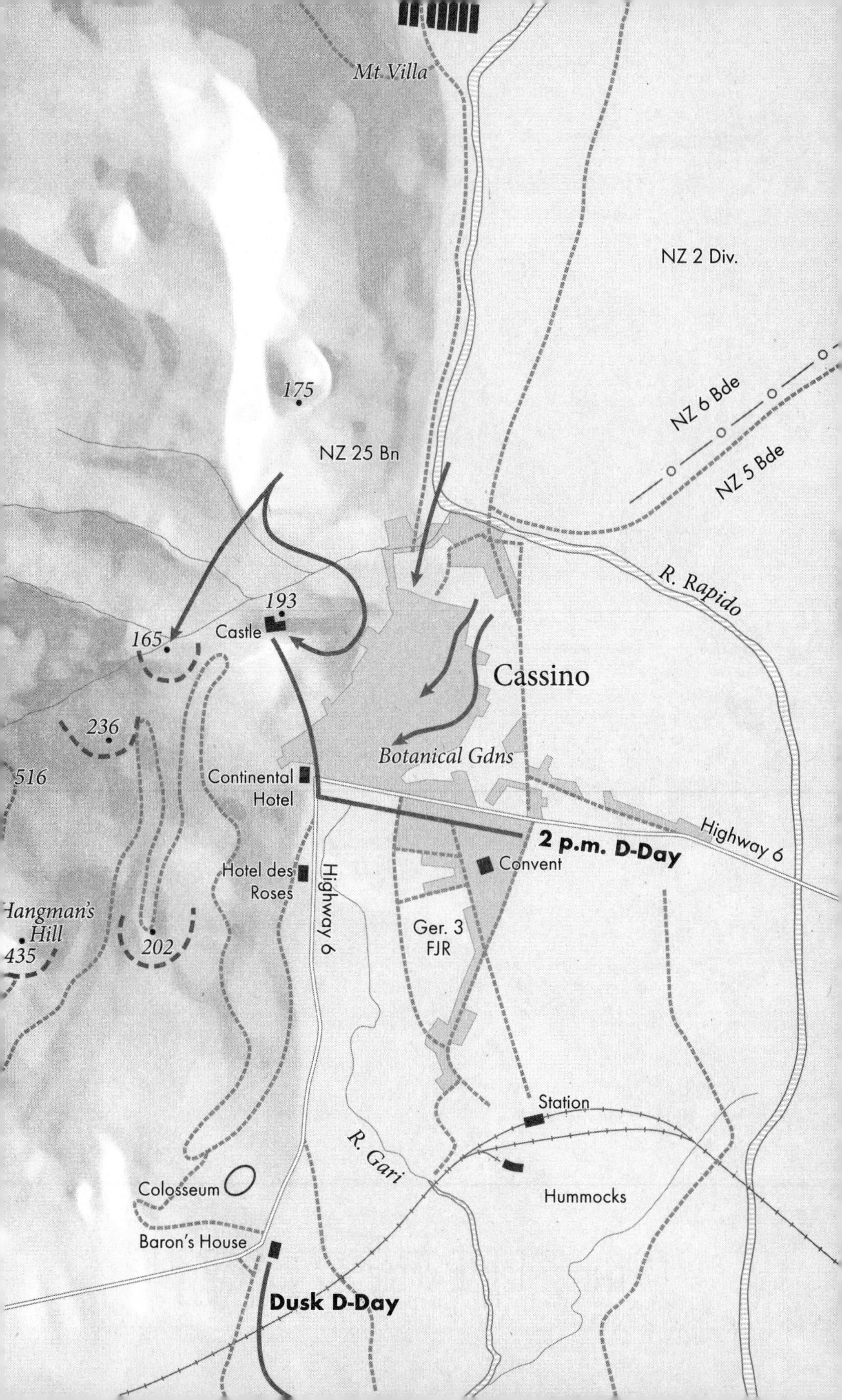

Mt Villa
NZ 2 Div.
175
NZ 6 Bde
NZ 25 Bn
NZ 5 Bde
R. Rapido
193
Castle
165
Cassino
236
Botanical Gdns
516
Continental Hotel
Highway 6
2 p.m. D-Day
Convent
Hotel des Roses
Highway 6
Hangman's Hill
435
202
Ger. 3 FJR
Station
R. Gari
Colosseum
Hummocks
Baron's House
Dusk D-Day

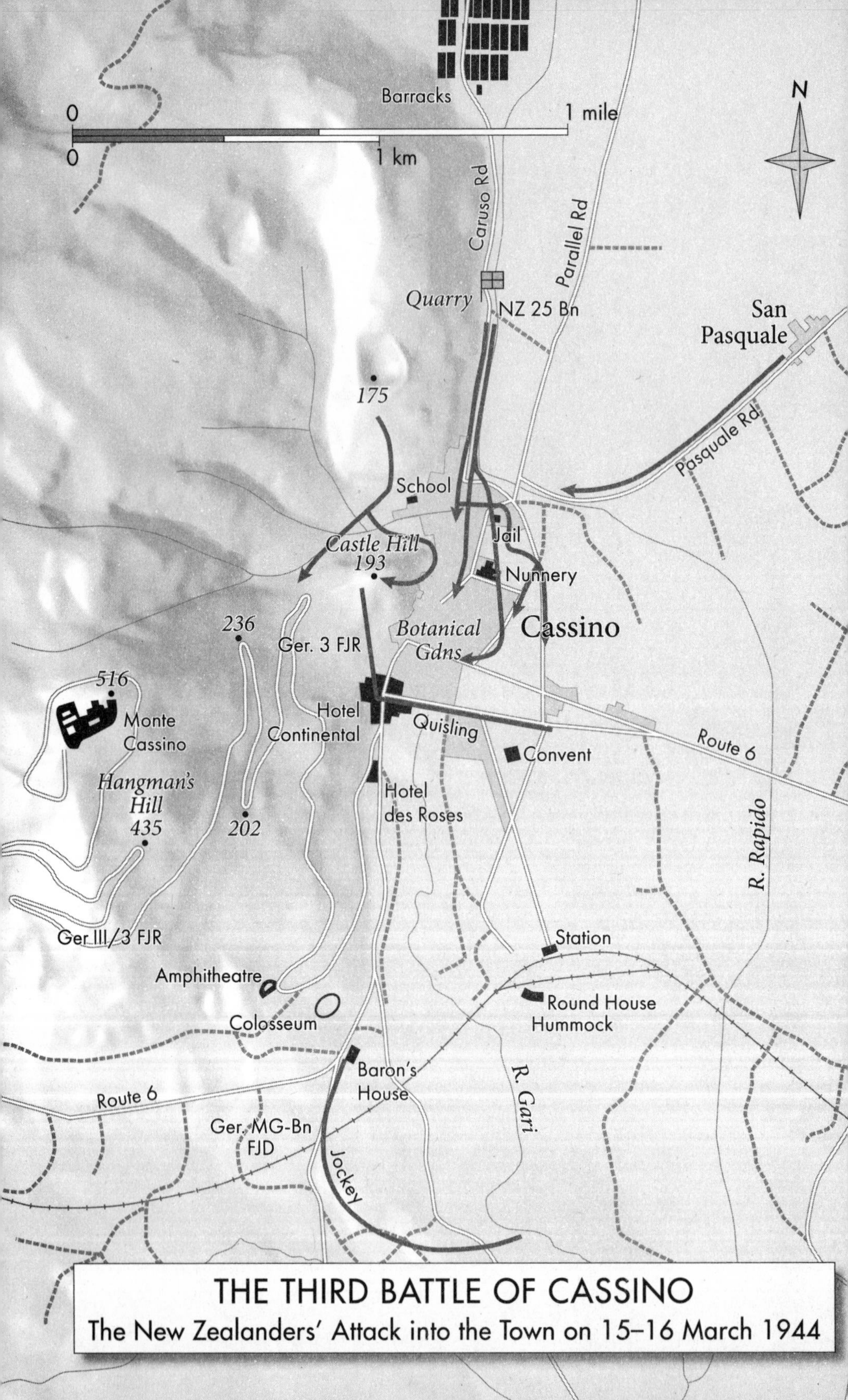

THE THIRD BATTLE OF CASSINO
The New Zealanders' Attack into the Town on 15–16 March 1944

A taped pathway clear of mines up to the ruins of the abbey, May 1944.

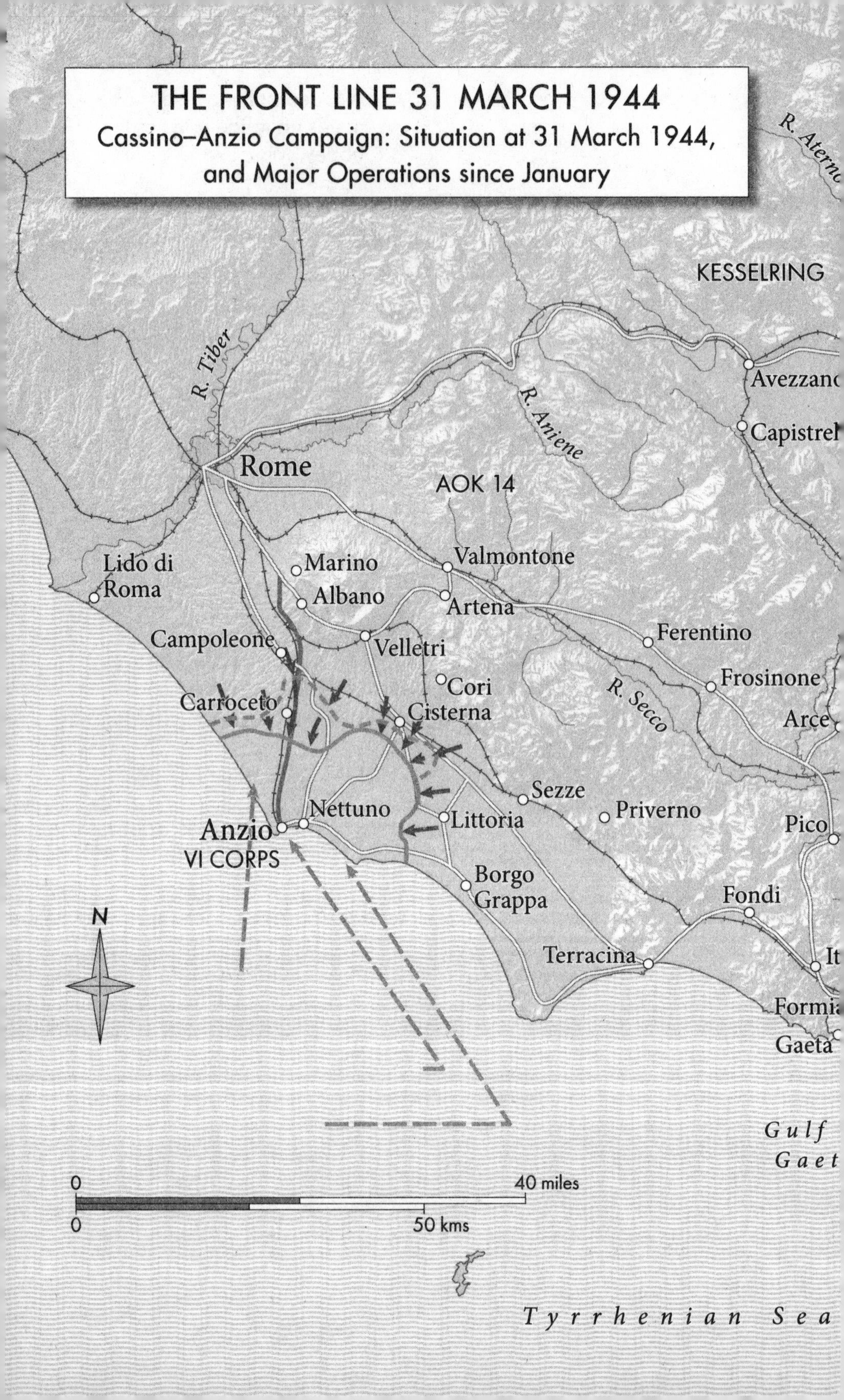

THE FRONT LINE 31 MARCH 1944

Cassino–Anzio Campaign: Situation at 31 March 1944, and Major Operations since January

R. Aterno
KESSELRING
R. Tiber
Avezzano
R. Aniene
Capistrel
Rome
AOK 14
Lido di Roma
Marino
Valmontone
Albano
Artena
Campoleone
Velletri
Ferentino
Cori
Frosinone
Carroceto
Cisterna
R. Secco
Arce
Sezze
Nettuno
Priverno
Littoria
Pico
Anzio
VI CORPS
Borgo Grappa
Fondi
N
Terracina
It
Formia
Gaeta
Gulf
Gaet
0
40 miles
0
50 kms
Tyrrhenian Sea

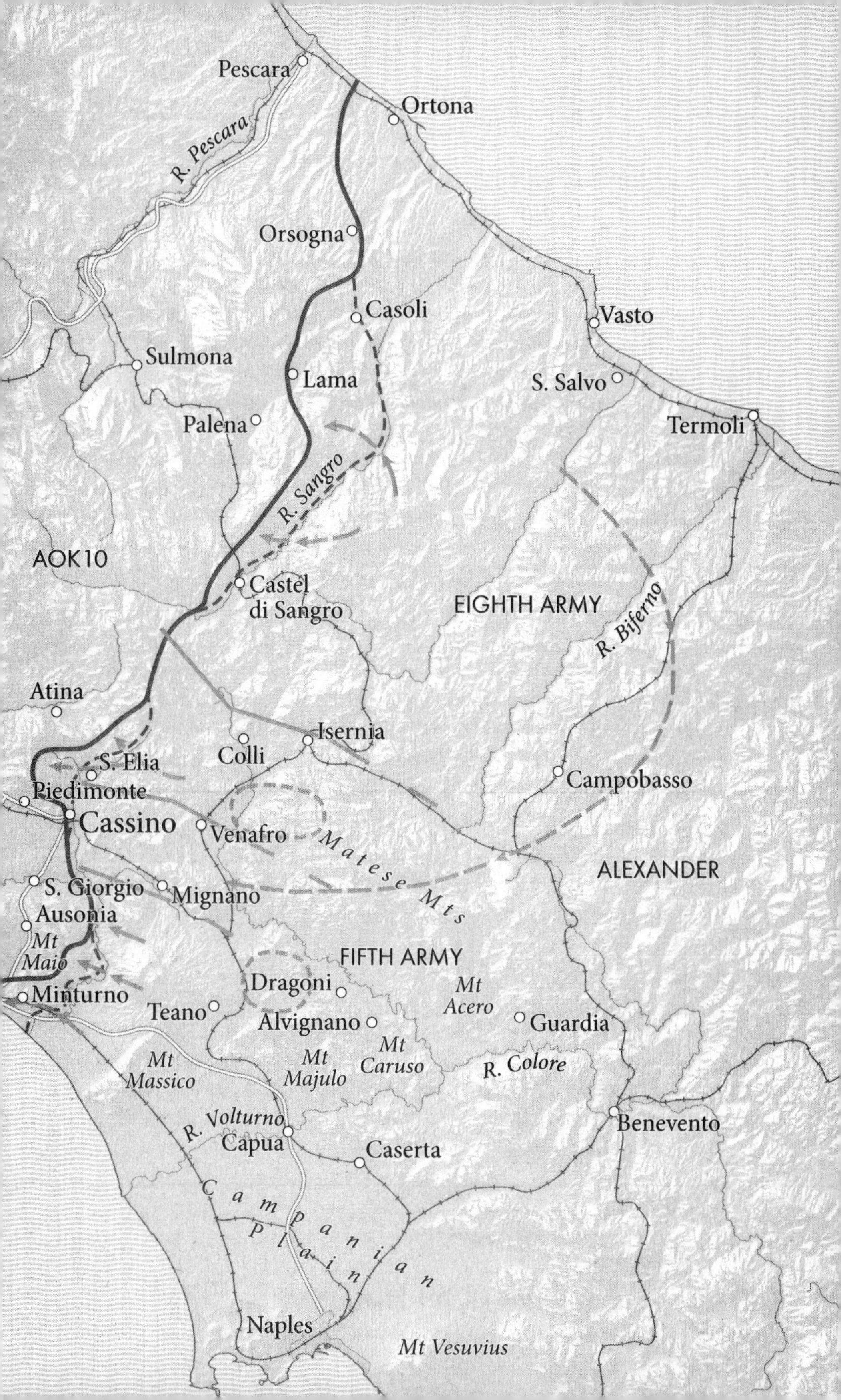
Pescara
Ortona
R. Pescara
Orsogna
Casoli
Vasto
Sulmona
Lama
S. Salvo
Palena
Termoli
R. Sangro
AOK10
Castel di Sangro
EIGHTH ARMY
R. Biferno
Atina
Isernia
Colli
S. Elia
Campobasso
Piedimonte
Cassino
Venafro
Matese Mts
ALEXANDER
S. Giorgio
Mignano
Ausonia
Mt Maio
FIFTH ARMY
Dragoni
Mt Acero
Minturno
Teano
Alvignano
Guardia
Mt Massico
Mt Majulo
Mt Caruso
R. Colore
R. Volturno
Capua
Benevento
Caserta
Campanian Plain
Naples
Mt Vesuvius

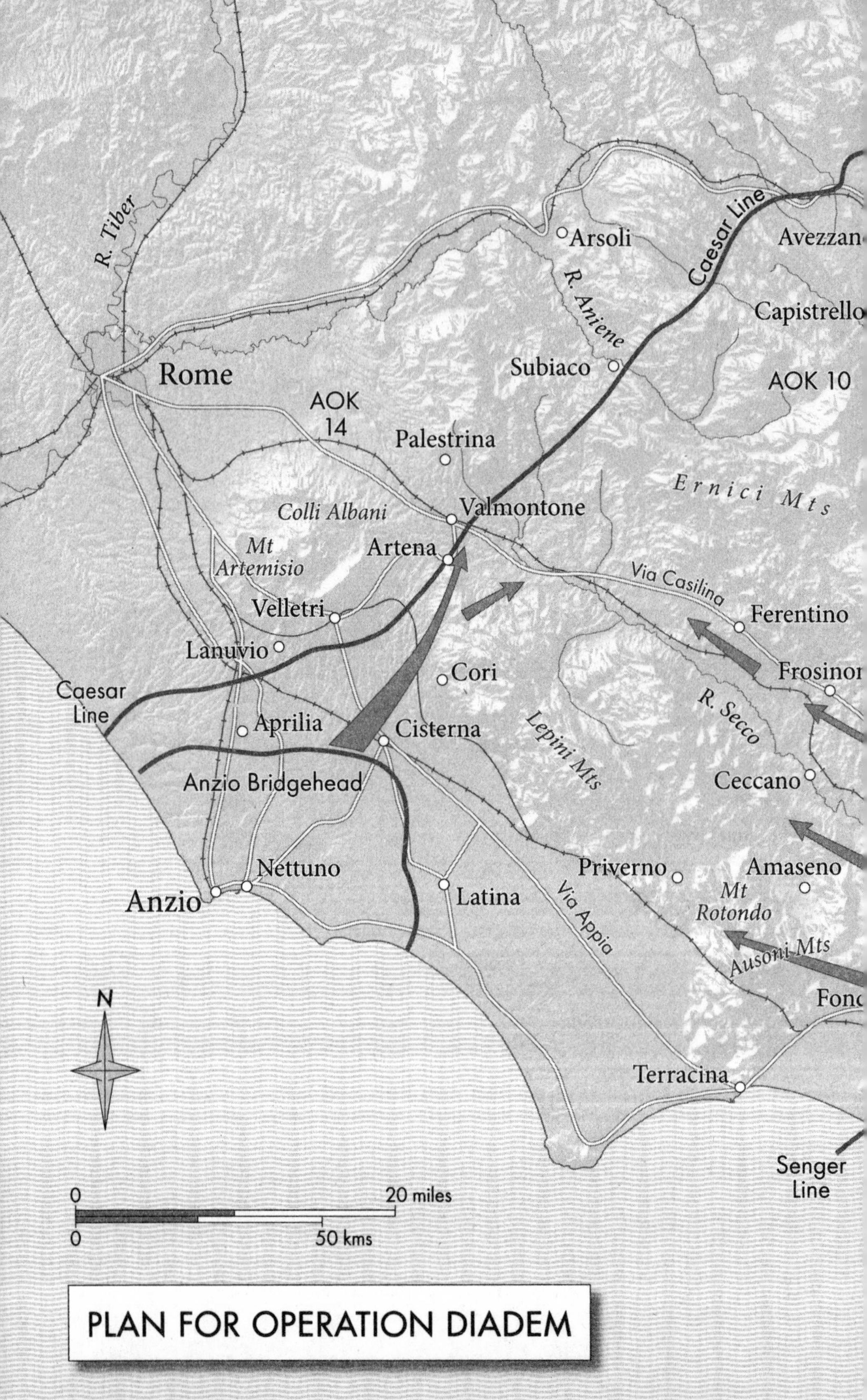

PLAN FOR OPERATION DIADEM

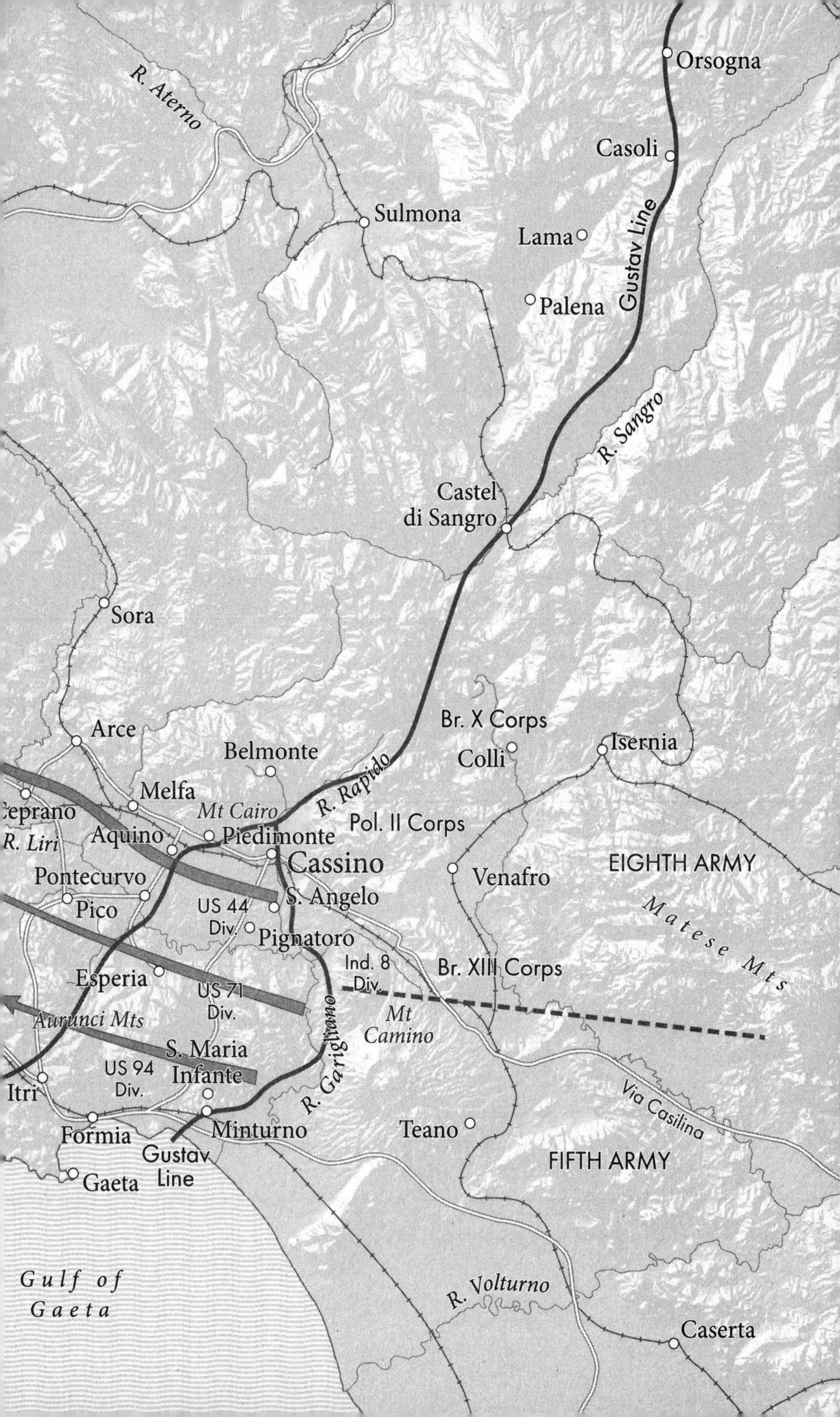

R. Aterno
Orsogna
Casoli
Sulmona
Lama
Gustav Line
Palena
R. Sangro
Castel di Sangro
Sora
Br. X Corps
Arce
Isernia
Belmonte
Colli
Melfa
R. Rapido
Ceprano
Mt Cairo
Pol. II Corps
Aquino
Piedimonte
R. Liri
Cassino
EIGHTH ARMY
Pontecurvo
Venafro
S. Angelo
Pico
US 44 Div.
Matese Mts
Pignatoro
Ind. 8 Div.
Br. XIII Corps
Esperia
US 71 Div.
Mt Camino
Aurunci Mts
S. Maria Infante
R. Garigliano
US 94 Div.
Itri
Via Casilina
Formia
Minturno
Teano
Gustav Line
FIFTH ARMY
Gaeta
Gulf of Gaeta
R. Volturno
Caserta

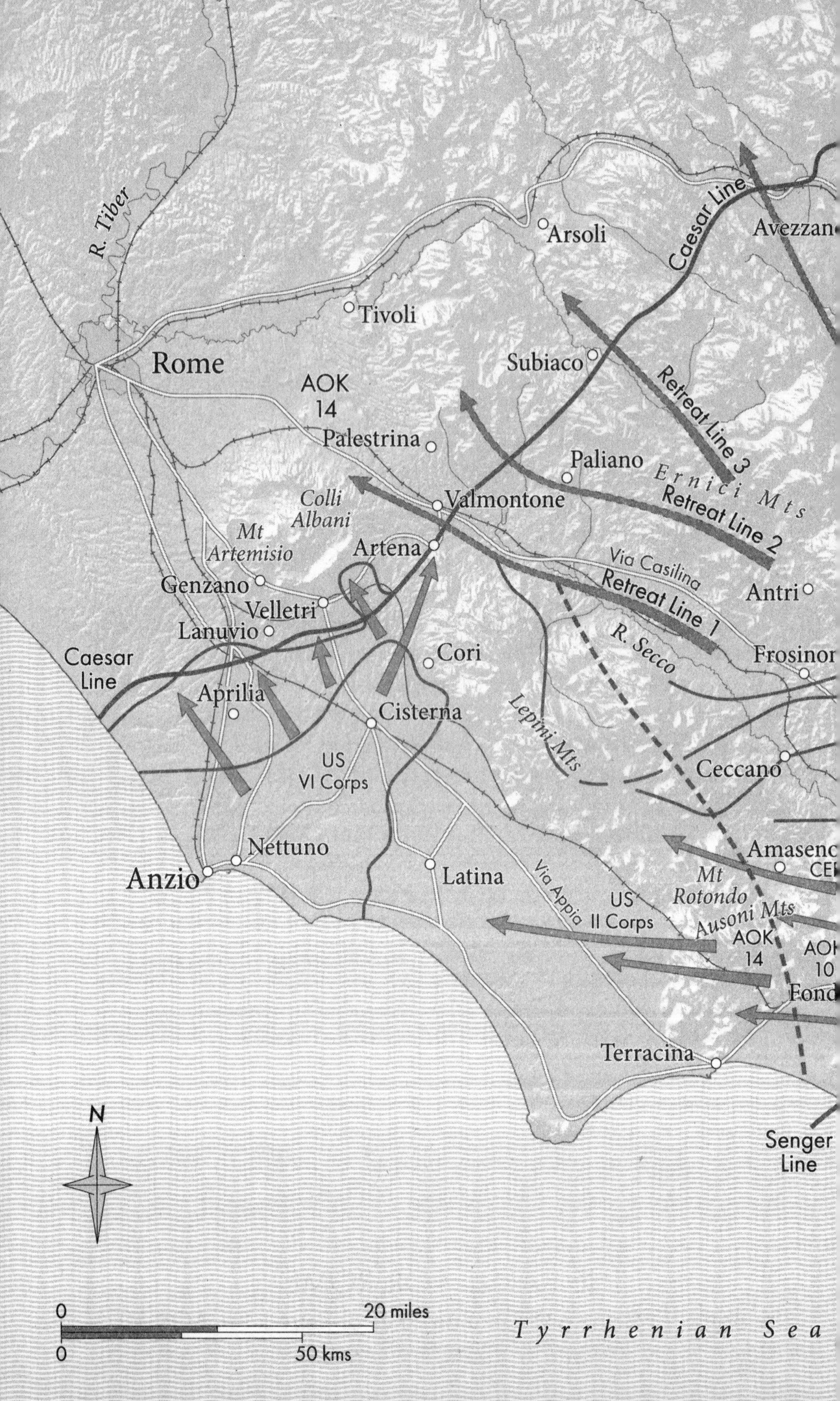
R. Tiber
Rome
Tivoli
Arsoli
Avezzan
Caesar Line
Subiaco
AOK
14
Retreat Line 3
Palestrina
Paliano
Ernici Mts
Colli
Albani
Valmontone
Retreat Line 2
Mt
Artemisio
Artena
Via Casilina
Genzano
Retreat Line 1
Antri
Velletri
Lanuvio
R. Secco
Caesar
Line
Cori
Frosinor
Aprilia
Cisterna
Lepini Mts
US
VI Corps
Ceccano
Amasenc
Nettuno
Anzio
Latina
Via Appia
Mt
Rotondo
US
II Corps
Ausoni Mts
AOK
14
AOI
10
Fond
Terracina
N
Senger
Line
0
20 miles
0
50 kms
Tyrrhenian Sea

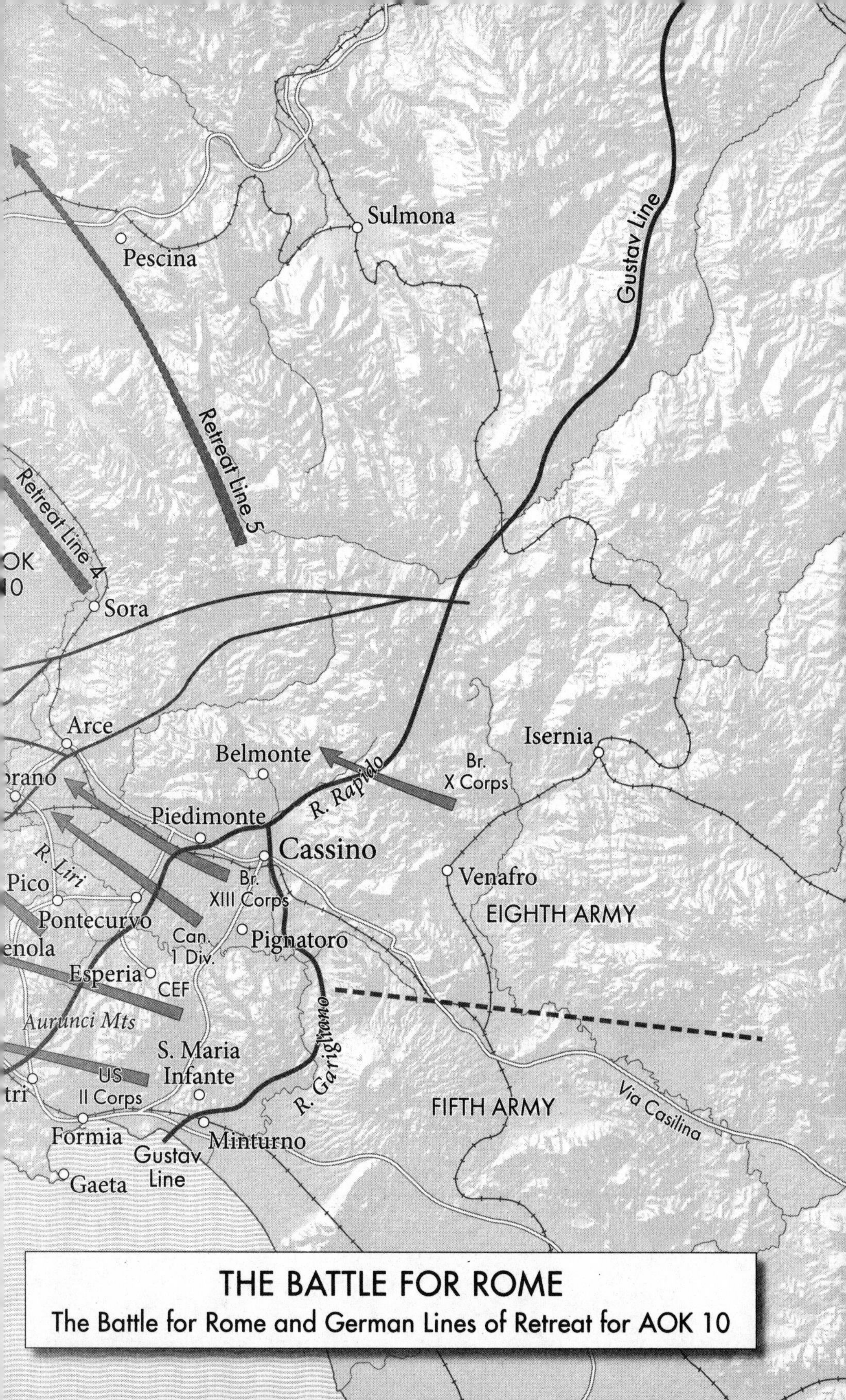

THE BATTLE FOR ROME

The Battle for Rome and German Lines of Retreat for AOK 10

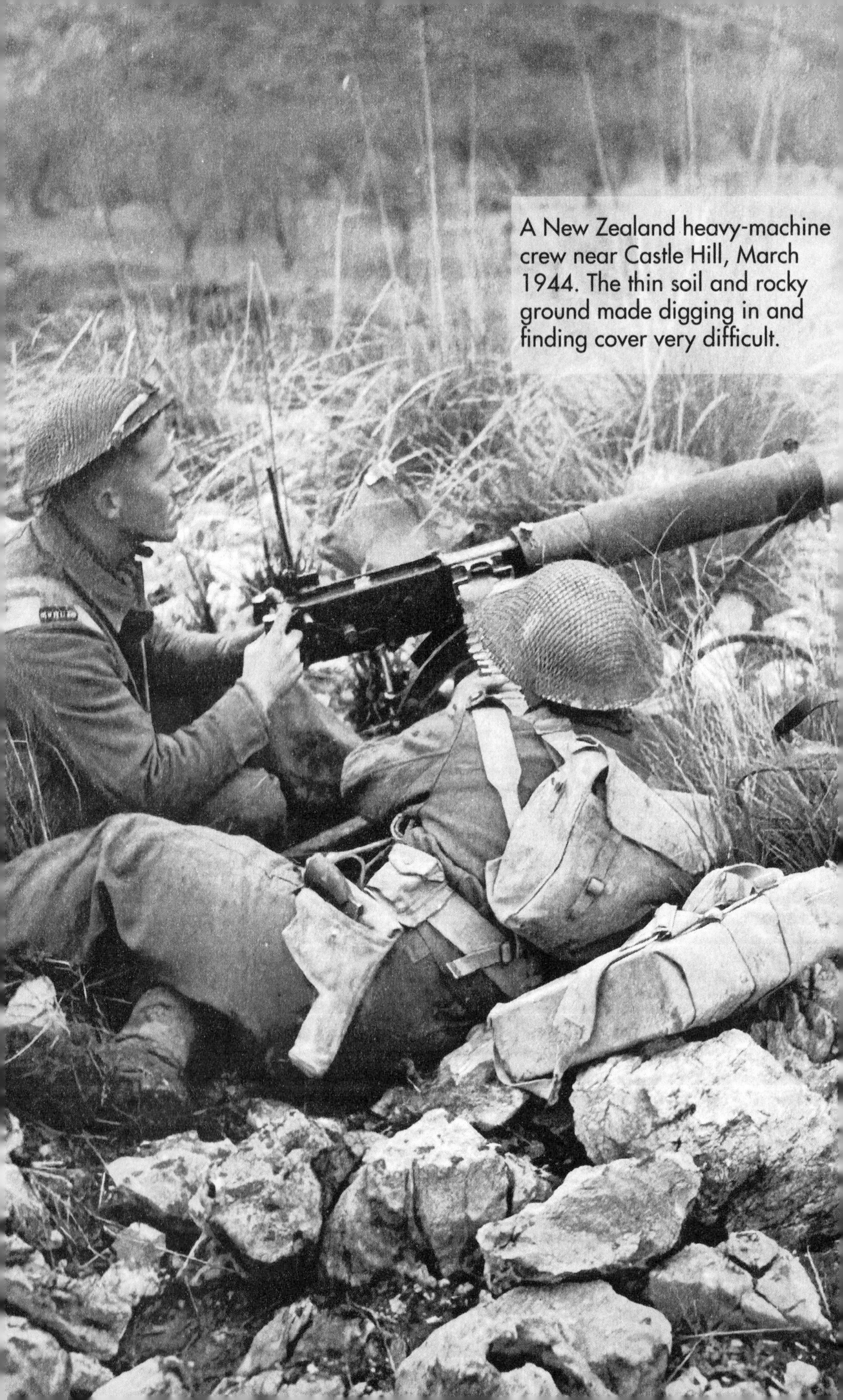

A New Zealand heavy-machine crew near Castle Hill, March 1944. The thin soil and rocky ground made digging in and finding cover very difficult.

Above: Cassino and Highway 6

Below: Cassino, November 1943

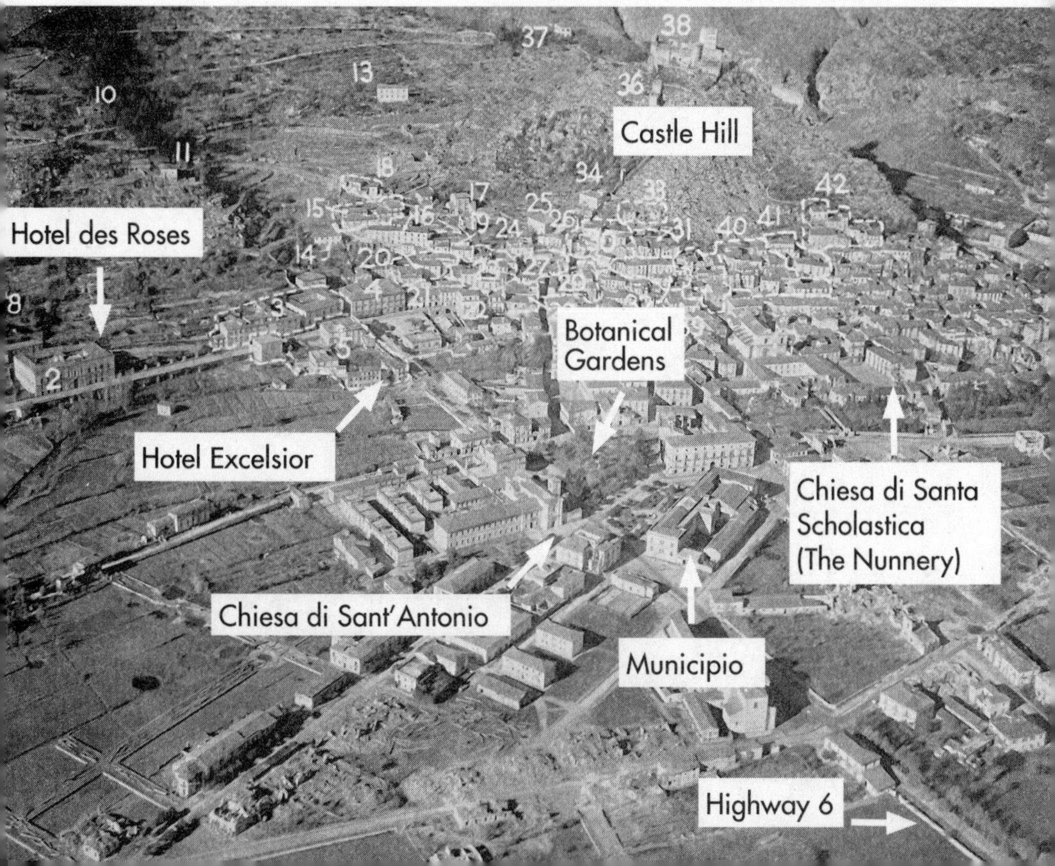

Monte Trocchio
Liri Valley
Cervaro

Monte Cassino Panorama

Overpass
Aprilia

The Factory and Overpass

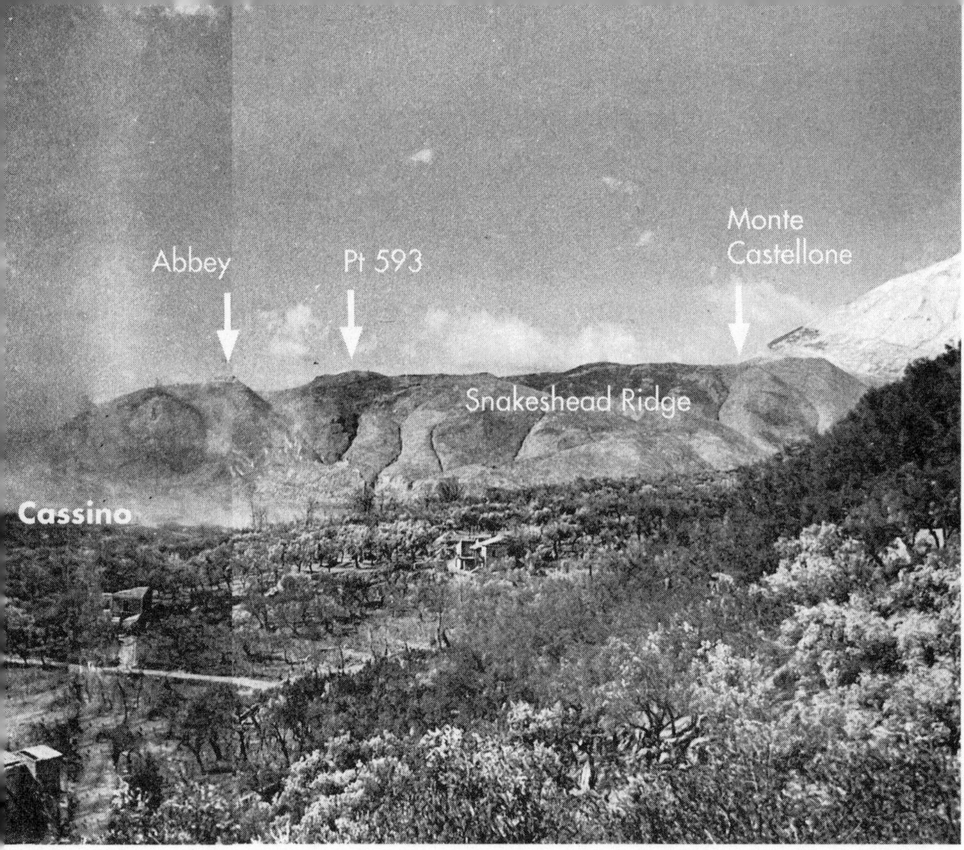

Abbey
Pt 593
Monte Castellone
Snakeshead Ridge
Cassino

The Wadis

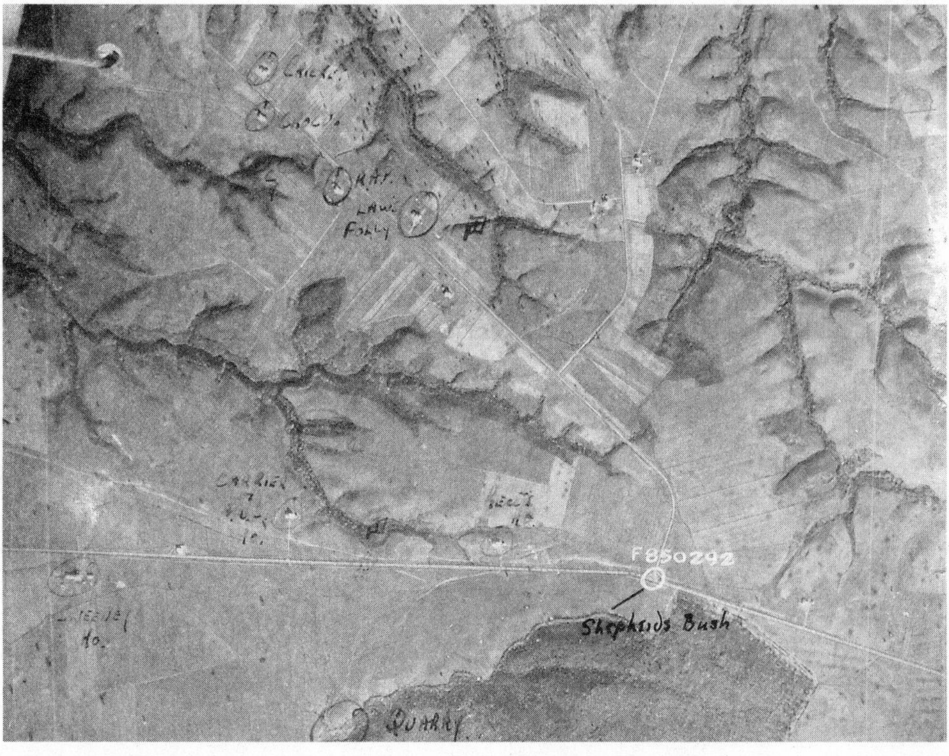

F850292
Shepherds Bush
Quarry

SKETCH MAPS OF THE MONTE CASSINO MASSIF

Prepared by Polish II Corps

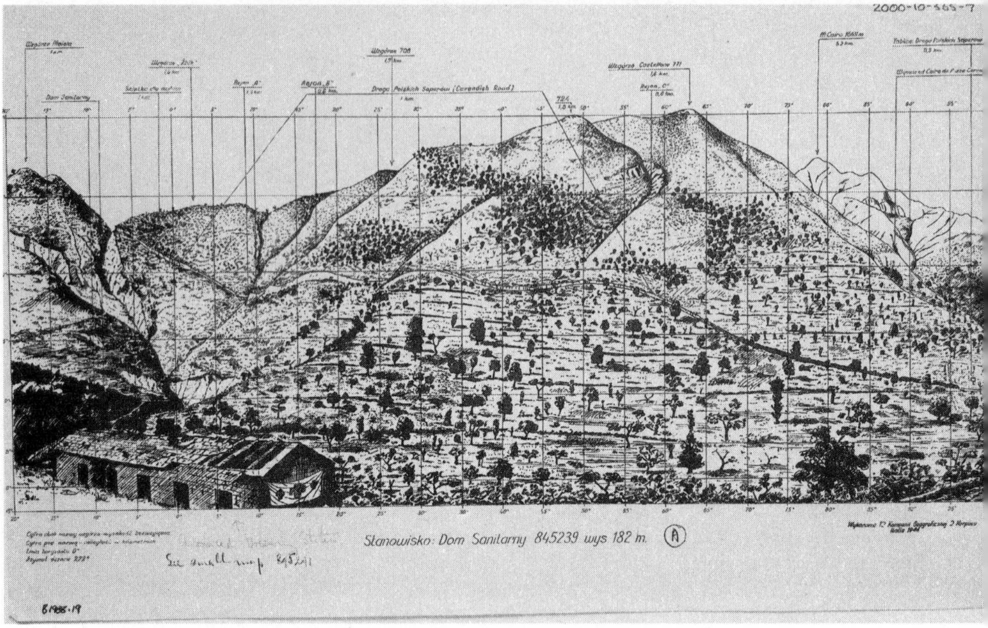

Cavendish Road

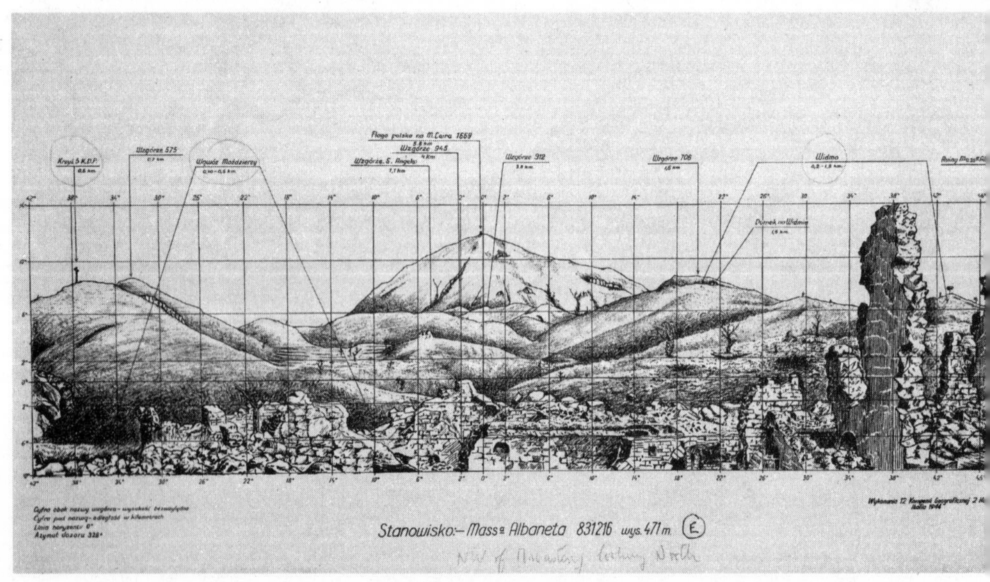

Colle Sant'Angelo from Albaneta

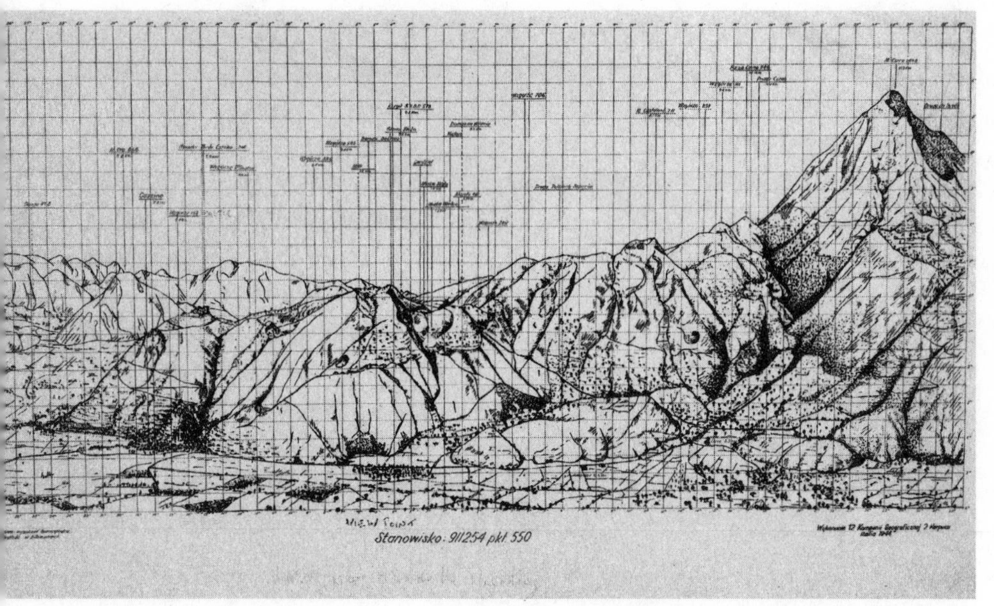

Monte Cassino Massif in Profile

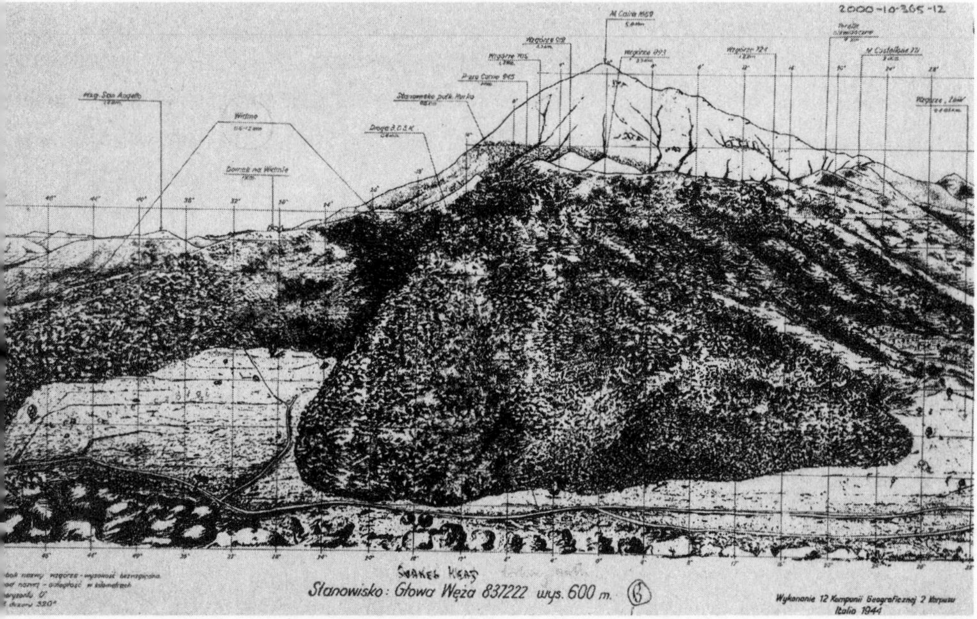

Snakeshead and Monte Cairo

A B-26 Marauder attacking railway lines during Operation STRANGLE.

Principal Personalities

American

Sergeant Maurice 'Frenchy' Bechard
Company A, 16th Engineer Regiment, 1st Armored Division

Lieutenant Harold L. Bond
Mortar Platoon, 141st Infantry Regiment, 36th Infantry Division

Sergeant Ross C. Carter
Company B, 1st Battalion, 504th Parachute Infantry Regiment

General Mark Clark
Commander, US Fifth Army

Colonel William O. Darby
Commander, Army Rangers

Captain Roswell K. Doughty
Intelligence Officer, S-2, and commanding officer of Intelligence & Reconnaissance Platoon, 141st Infantry Regiment, 36th 'Texas' Division

Lieutenant-General Ira Eaker
Commander-in-Chief, Mediterranean Allied Air Forces

Colonel Hamilton Howze
Commander, 13th Armored Regiment and later Howze Force, 1st Armored Division

Captain Klaus H. Huebner
Battalion Surgeon, 3rd Battalion, 349th Infantry Regiment, 88th Infantry Division

Lieutenant Ralph 'Lucky' Lucardi
64th Fighter Squadron, 57th Fighter Group, USAAF

Major-General John Lucas
Commander, VI Corps

Sergeant Audie Murphy
Company B, 1st Battalion, 15th Infantry Regiment, 3rd Infantry Division

Private Frank Pearce
Company C, 111th Engineer Battalion, attached to 143rd Infantry Regiment, 36th Infantry Division

Sergeant Ralph B. Schaps
Company H, 2nd Battalion, 135th Infantry Regiment, 34th 'Red Bulls' Division

Captain Felix Sparks
Commander, Company E, 2nd Battalion, 157th Infantry Regiment, 45th 'Thunderbirds' Division

Captain Robert Spencer
Commander, Company F, 2nd Battalion, 143rd Infantry Regiment, 36th Infantry Division

Lieutenant T. Michael Sullivan
Bombardier, 429th Bomb Squadron, 2nd Bomb Group, Fifteenth Air Force

Major-General Lucian Truscott
Commander, 3rd Infantry Division then US VI Corps

Lieutenant Robert A. 'Smoky' Vrilakas
P-38 pilot, 94th Fighter Squadron, 1st Fighter Group

Australian

Major Lawrence Franklyn-Vaile
1st Battalion, Royal Irish Fusiliers, 38th Irish Brigade, 78th Infantry Division

British

General Sir Harold Alexander
Commander, 15th Army Group

Brigadier Donald Bateman
Commander, 5th Indian Infantry Brigade, 4th Indian Division

Lieutenant David Cole
Battalion Signals Officer, 2nd Royal Inniskilling Fusiliers, 13th Infantry Brigade, 5th Infantry Division

Guardsman Edward Danger
5th Battalion, Grenadier Guards, 24th Guards Brigade, 1st Infantry Division

Captain Michael Doble
2nd Regiment, Royal Horse Artillery

Captain Leonard Garland
70th Field Regiment, Royal Artillery

Major Michael Gordon-Watson
Second-in-command, 1st Battalion Irish Guards, 1st Infantry Division

Lieutenant-General John Harding
Chief of Staff to General Alexander, 15th Army Group

Sergeant Norman Lewis
British intelligence officer with 312th Field Security Section

Harold Macmillan
Minister of State

Captain John Strick
Intelligence officer then D Company, 1st London Irish Rifles, 168th Brigade, 56th Division

Major-General Francis Tuker
Commander, 4th Indian Division

Corporal Harry Wilson
Cipher clerk with 8th Indian Division HQ and later 17th Indian Brigade

Lieutenant Ted Wyke-Smith
281st Field Park Company, 214th Field Company Royal Engineers, 78th Division

Canadian

Major the Reverend Roy Durnford
Padre, Seaforth Highlanders of Canada, 1st Canadian Infantry Division

French

Capitaine Jacques Denée
9ème Compagnie, 2ème Bataillon, 4ème Régiment de Tirailleurs Tunisiens, 3ème Division d'Infanterie Algérienne, CEF

Commandant Paul Gandoët
Commander, 3ème Bataillon, 4ème Régiment de Tirailleurs Tunisiens, 3ème Division d'Infanterie Algérienne, CEF

German

Feldwebel Rudolf Donth
6. Kompanie, 2. Bataillon, 4. Fallschirmjäger-Regiment, 1. Fallschirmjäger-Division

Generalleutnant Valentin Feurstein
Commander, LI Gebirgs-Armeekorps

Oberleutnant Hans Golda
Commander, 8. Batterie, Werfer-Regiment 71, 15. Panzergrenadier-Division

Hauptmann Jürgen Harder
Staffelkapitän 7. Jagdgeschwader 53, then Gruppenkommandeur of I. JG53

Feldmarschall Albert Kesselring
Oberbefehlshaber Süd

Unteroffizier Jupp Klein
2. Kompanie, 1. Pionier-Bataillon, 1. Fallschirmjäger-Division

Major Rudolf Kratzert
Commander, 3. Bataillon, 3. Fallschirmjäger-Regiment, 1. Fallschirmjäger-Division

Gefreiter Hans-Paul Liebschner
Kampfgruppe Gericke

Dr Wilhelm Mauss
Chief Medical Officer, XIV Panzerkorps headquarters

Obergefreiter Karl Müller
6. Kompanie, 2. Bataillon, 4. Fallschirmjäger-Regiment, 1. Fallschirmjäger-Division

Oberfeldwebel Felix Reimann
StuG commander in Kampfgruppe Gräser

Generalleutnant Fridolin von Senger und Etterlin
Commander, XIV Panzerkorps

Major Georg Zellner
Commander, 3. Bataillon, 44. Reichs-Grenadier-Regiment, 44. 'Hoch-und Deutschmeister' Division

Italian

Viviana Bauco
Civilian living in Ripi

Carla Capponi – 'Elena'
Member of Rome-based partisan movement Gruppi di Azione Patriottica

Count Filippo Caracciolo
Member of the Partito d'Azione based in Naples

Pasqualina 'Lina' Caruso
Civilian living in Eboli

Dom Eusebio Grossetti
Benedictine monk at the Abbey of Monte Cassino

Dom Martino Matronola
Benedictine monk at the Abbey of Monte Cassino

Pasua Pisa
Civilian living on Monte Rotondo near Amaseno

New Zealander

Lieutenant-General Sir Bernard Freyberg
Commander, New Zealand Corps

Sergeant Roger Smith
A Company, 24th Battalion, New Zealand Expeditionary Force

Polish

Lejtnant-General Władisław Anders
Commander, Polish II Corps

Lejtnant Władek Rubnikowicz
12th Podolski Reconnaissance Regiment, 3rd Carpathian Division, Polish II Corps

Isaac Akinaka

General Sir Harold Alexander

General Władysław Anders

Carla Capponi

Filippo Caracciolo

Ross Carter

Ottavio Cirulli

General Mark Clark

David Cole

William O. Darby

Mike Doble

Rudolf Donth

Roswell Doughty

Ira Eaker

General Valentin Feurstein

Lawrie Franklyn-Vaile

Paul Gandoët

Leonard Garland

Mike Gordon-Watson

Jürgen Harder

General John Harding

Klaus Huebner

Feldmarschall Albert Kesselring

Jupp Klein

Rudolf Kratzert

Ralph 'Lucky' Lucardi

General John Lucas

Harold Macmillan

Wilhelm Mauss

Audie Murphy

Władek Rubnikowicz

Ralph Schaps

General Fridolin von Senger und Etterlin

John Strick

General Lucian Truscott

Francis Tuker

Robert A. 'Smoky' Vrilakas

Harry Wilson

Ted Wyke-Smith

Note on the Text

Writing a campaign history such as this is a complicated undertaking, but although dealing with American, British, Canadian, German and Italian units across the armed services, I've tried to keep the numbers of unit names as low as possible. To help distinguish one side from another, I have used a form of vernacular – styling German units more or less as they would be written in German and likewise with the Italian units. This really is not to be pretentious in any way, but just to help with the reading and cut down on any confusion.

For those who are not familiar with the scale and size of wartime units, the basic fighting formation on which the size of armies was judged was the division. Germans had panzer divisions, which were an all-arms formation of motorized infantry, artillery and tanks; they also had Panzergrenadier divisions, which had fewer panzers – tanks – and more motorized infantry: a grenadier was simply an infantryman who was provided with motor transport to get from A to B. German infantry divisions tended to have much less motorization by 1943.

As a rule of thumb, a division was around 15,000 men, although some divisions could have as many as 20,000. Two divisions or more made up a corps, usually denoted in Roman numerals to distinguish them. Two corps or more constituted an army, and two armies or more an army group. Going back down the scales, American, German and Italian divisions were divided into regiments, while British, Canadian and New Zealand divisions were divided into brigades. Regiments and brigades were much the same, consisting of three core components which, in the case of an infantry regiment/brigade, were three battalions. An infantry battalion was around 850 men, divided into companies of some 120 men, which in turn broke down into three platoons and, finally, to the smallest formation, the ten-man squad, Gruppe, or section, depending on the nationality. I hope that this and the Glossary that follows helps.

Glossary

ACC	Allied Control Commission
AFHQ	Allied Forces Headquarters
A Echelon	immediate logistical support for a front-line unit, providing ammunition, rations etc.
AF	air force
AMGOT	Allied Military Government of Occupied Territories
AOK	Armeeoberkommando – German army command
AWOL	absent without leave
BAR	Browning Automatic Rifle – a light machine gun
B Echelon	less urgent logistical support for a front-line unit, usually based several miles behind the immediate front line
BG	Bomb Group
Bn	battalion
Bren	British light machine gun
CEF	Corps Expéditionnaire Français
CLN	Comitato di Liberazione Nazionale – the National Liberation Committee
CP	command post
DF	direct fire
DUKE	Dominion, UK and Empire forces
DUKW	an amphibious six-wheel-drive truck, pronounced 'duck'
FDL	forward defence line
Feldwebel	staff sergeant
FG	Fighter Group
FJR	Fallschirmjäger-Regiment
FOO	forward observation officer
FMCR	Fronte Militare Clandestino della Resistenza
FS	Fighter Squadron
GAP	Gruppi di Azione Patriottica, partisans operating in Rome under the command of CLN Military Council
Gefreiter	lance-corporal
GNR	Guardia Nazionale Repubblicana – National Republican Guard, a Fascist militia force of the RSI
Grenadier	private in a grenadier unit
HG	Hermann Göring
Jabo	Jagdbomber – German slang for a fighter-bomber or any low-flying Allied aircraft
Jerry	British slang for a German

Kraut	American slang for a German
LCA	landing craft, assault
LCVP	landing craft, vehicle, personnel
LCT(R)	landing craft, tank, fitted with rocket projectors
LOB	left out of battle
LSI	landing ship, infantry
LST	landing ship, tank
MAAF	Mediterannean Allied Air Forces
MACAF	Mediterannean Allied Coastal Air Force
MASAF	Mediterranean Allied Strategic Air Forces
MATAF	Mediterranean Allied Tactical Air Forces
MG	machine gun, in German Maschinengewehr
MG42	Maschinengewehr 42 – German rapid-firing light machine gun
MO	medical officer
MP	Military Police
NASAF	North African Strategic Air Forces
NATAF	North African Tactical Air Forces
NCO	non-commissioned officer
NZEF	New Zealand Expeditionary Force
Obergefreiter	corporal
OB	Oberbefehlshaber – commander-in-chief
Oberfeldwebel	sergeant-major
OKW	Oberkommando der Wehrmacht
OP	observation post
PG	Panzergrenadier – motorized armoured infantry
PIR	parachute infantry regiment
PSP	pierced-steel plating
POW	prisoner of war
RAF	Royal Air Force
RAP	regimental aid post
RCT	Regimental Combat Team
RHQ	Regimental Headquarters
RSM	Regimental Sergeant-Major
RSHA	Reichssicherheitshauptamt – Reich Security Main Office, run by the SS and incorporating all police, secret police and Nazi intelligence services
RSI	Repubblica Sociale Italiana – the Italian Socialist Republic, the new puppet Fascist state set up under Mussolini by the Germans
SD	Sicherheitsdienst – the SS intelligence agency
STD	sexually transmitted disease
SOE	Special Operations Executive
Ted	from Tedeschi – Italian for Germans
Tommy	German slang for DUKE forces
Unteroffizier	sergeant
USAAF	United States Army Air Force
Zug	German word for platoon

Prologue

THE HEADQUARTERS OF THE US Fifth Army had one of the very best addresses in all of southern Italy: the largest palace ever constructed and one that utterly dominated the otherwise rather small town of Caserta. It stood on a flat coastal plain, one of the few such areas in Italy, some twenty miles or so north of Naples, with the backdrop of the jagged ridge of the 1,800-foot-high Monte Tifata and Monte Longano rising steeply behind it – a barrier, in many ways, that hid the Bourbon royal palace from the current battle raging thirty miles to the north.

Vast it may have been, with an astonishing 1,200 rooms – more than enough to house the headquarters of several armies rather than just one – but it was not the way of Allied generals in this current war to live in luxury when the men they commanded were suffering so many privations up the line at the front. And so General Mark Clark, the Fifth Army commander, had instead made use of the nearly 300 hectares of its magnificent grounds. Here, near the mighty palace but most definitely not within it, were a collection of tents, specially adapted trucks and vehicles, sheltered by umbrella pines and camouflage nets. 'Have my camp in a new grove of trees,' he wrote to his wife, Renie, on 23 October 1943, just a week or so after moving his headquarters there. 'It's quite nice.'

Sergeant William C. Chaney was running the general's mess. A black technical sergeant, he had joined Clark's staff when the Fifth Army commander had been a lowly lieutenant-colonel and newly arrived in Washington DC to take up an instructing post at the US Army War College. When Clark had been posted to Britain as the youngest major-general in the US Army, Chaney had asked if he could go too. The pair had not been separated since. And it was Chaney who not only ran the mess but oversaw the construction of Clark's immediate encampment. 'Am having a portable hut put up about 50 yards away,' Clark wrote in the same letter to Renie, 'under a tree, where I can hold conferences when it gets cold and where we can sit in the evening and have a fire.' The idea was for it to be flat-packed into a truck if and when they moved their headquarters.

By the beginning of December he was also using this hut as a makeshift cinema. Since every day was a working day in Italy, Clark was keen to make Sundays a little different whenever possible and so had begun showing films in the hut on Sunday evenings – just for his immediate staff officers; the army commander understood as well as anyone the importance of morale. Of course, his staff were not in quite the same physical danger as front-line infantrymen, but they were not immune in a war zone, were expected to – and did – work incredibly long hours, and the pressure on all of them was considerable. The lives of many young men – and civilians of all ages, both men and women – depended on their decisions, attention to detail and assiduousness. Furthermore, most were living out of tents in one of the worst winters ever experienced in Italy.

It was impossible not to be awed by the extraordinary landscape in which they were now living and fighting. There was no view anywhere in this long, narrow peninsula that did not include mountains; even from the few flat plains, distant peaks loomed magnificently and with an immutable sense of menace. And while these immense heights were home to innumerable villages, hamlets and farming communities on their lower slopes, it was in the valleys below that most of the 40 million Italians lived, crammed into towns and cities of impossibly narrow streets and through which the few main roads, originally built in the time of the Romans, snaked their way north and south: the Via Emilia along the Adriatic coast; the Via Appia, which ran from Rome to Brindisi in the south-east heel of Italy; the Via Aurelia running down the western, Tyrrhenian coast; and the Via Casilina, which linked the cities of Naples and Rome. Ancient routes trod foot-swift, footsore, for millennia. This latter road passed through Caserta and on, north, through a narrow valley overlooked by mighty 3,000-foot peaks. It then hugged the next massif of Monte Cassino, with its sixth-century Benedictine abbey perched atop, before emerging into the wider Liri Valley that led onwards to the capital, Rome, a little over seventy miles further north.

General Clark was certainly struck by the extraordinary landscape in which he and Fifth Army now found themselves. 'Wish you could see this country,' he had written to Renie back on 19 October. 'It certainly is mountainous and difficult to fight through.' A few weeks later, he wrote again of the challenges of fighting through such difficult terrain, which so favoured the defender because the Germans could watch the Allies coming. Observers on the mountain peaks could relay to their own artillery details of Allied troops moving towards them. All roads – not least the main routes north such as the Via Casilina – could be zeroed by German guns, ready to drop shells on predetermined spots the moment the Allies tried to use them. The only way to stop this was for the Allies' own artillery to blast any suspected German positions and for the infantry to climb the mountains and prise enemy artillery observers and the infantry protecting them from these heights.

A Herculean task in any conditions, but even harder in the rain and in the increasingly cold and miserable winter. Allied armies were highly mechanized, but Clark's men had been clambering up these mountains on their own two feet and with mules to carry much of their supplies. It was the only way. And once they did crest one of the peaks they found themselves confronting an enemy that had been able to see them coming and which was already behind prepared positions, be it a stone sangar – barricade – or something more substantial. Hence the defenders held all the aces.

To make matters worse, the Allies were struggling to use their air forces. The German air force, the Luftwaffe, was by now mostly defending the Reich; its planes were few and far between in southern Italy. Allied air forces ruled the roost, but obviously only when weather conditions permitted. Overwhelming the enemy with firepower was very much the Allied way of war, designed to keep the need for, and demands on, the infantry to a minimum. Artillery would pummel the enemy from the ground while bombers and fighter-bombers would sweep in from the air, strafing targets below. At the end of November the British Eighth Army, on the eastern, Adriatic, coast, had launched an assault across the River Sangro. For once, there had been two days of clear weather, Allied air forces had been able to support the ground forces in strength, and the German 65. Division had been largely destroyed. It had made all the difference.

Frustratingly, relentless rain and heavy cloud cover had turned earthen airfields into a morass and prevented aircrew from spotting targets even if they did manage to get airborne. The Allies had worked out their way of war in North Africa and Sicily: to use mechanization, technology and immense firepower to do a lot of the hard work so that the infantry and armour – tanks – had an easier time of things. That had simply not been possible here in this wet, cold, immensely mountainous country. Rather, every yard had to be prised by the foot-sloggers, the put-upon PBI – the poor bloody infantry. Crawling up mountains, battling over the rocky terrain, wading through mud, being rained on, shot at and blasted. And when one mountain was taken, there up ahead was another. And another. And yet another. Always another bloody mountain.

The fighting in Italy was utterly, miserably relentless.

Yet this had been supposed to be an easy victory, which is why, compared with Allied forces on Sicily, for example, Clark's men, and those of Eighth Army too, were so under-resourced. When the Allies had invaded in September they had confidently expected the Germans to fall back some 200 miles north of Rome to a defensive line that ran across the peninsula from Pisa in the west to Rimini in the east. That was what a scrap of intelligence picked up the previous May had suggested, and what the Italians, former allies of Germany, had told them was still very much the German plan during their armistice negotiations back in August. Clark had expected his army to face a tough fight initially but then to meet little more than rearguard actions all the way to Rome. This was what the intelligence picture suggested and was the basis on which his superiors had backed the campaign: General Dwight D. Eisenhower, the Supreme Allied Commander in the Mediterranean, and above him the Combined Chiefs of Staff, the most senior military men in the United States and Britain. Rome by Christmas was the expectation.

Rome comfortably by Christmas.

The Allied invasion of Italy had been undertaken on this very simple presumption, and while the German Führer, Adolf Hitler, had indeed initially planned to retreat way to the north he had soon changed his mind, as was so often his wont.

In other words, an overly optimistic and very risky plan, based on hope more than concrete evidence, had been undertaken without the resources and supplies available to contest a tougher fight than expected. It wasn't a lack of manpower that was the issue, or even guns or ordnance; it was the means of getting them there, because for all the many shipyards in the United States – and Britain, for that matter – there was simply not enough shipping being produced for the demands of a truly global war: supplying the Soviet Union; sending vast amounts of aid to Chiang

Kai-shek's Nationalist Chinese Army to fight the Japanese; the Indian Army's campaign in Burma and the Americans' across the Pacific. Then there was the primary effort in Europe: the future cross-Channel invasion of Normandy, Operation OVERLORD, due to take place at the beginning of May 1944. Priority of shipping – both merchant shipping and assault shipping for landing on beaches – was for OVERLORD, not Italy. Troops were already training for amphibious assaults and readying for D-Day.

And even here, in Italy, the tyranny of OVERLORD was hampering the work of the Allied armies as efforts were under way to establish the Fifteenth Air Force at Foggia. Capturing this rare area of completely flat terrain on the eastern side of the leg had been one of the prime reasons to invade mainland Italy. From here, Allied four-engine heavy bombers could further tighten the noose around the Reich and specifically bludgeon the German aircraft industry. Clearing the skies over Normandy and a huge swathe of north-west Europe was a prerequisite for any cross-Channel amphibious assault. This was because the Allies had to hinder the Germans' ability to reinforce Normandy the moment landings were made; the success of OVERLORD was dependent on the Allies winning the race to build up decisive amounts of men and materiel in the bridgehead. The way to slow down the Germans was to bomb bridges, railways, marshalling yards and locomotives. To do so successfully required precision bombing which could only be done at low level and as long as no enemy Messerschmitts and Focke-Wulfs were hovering above them ready to pounce.

The Luftwaffe needed to be smashed, and the way to do that was by bombing factories and assembly plants, most of which were deep in the Reich, drawing fighter planes into the fight and then shooting them down. The US Eighth Air Force and RAF Bomber Command in England were doing their best, but the Foggia area was far closer to the Nazi aircraft industry in Bavaria and Austria than was England. And so what had originally been conceived as just six heavy bombardment groups operating from the Foggia airfield complex had swiftly ballooned into twenty-one – all of which were due to be operating from there by March 1944. Twenty-one bomb groups was a very heavy commitment in terms of aircrew, ground crew, maintenance, ordnance, fuel, food and a host of other facilities from tents to typewriters to technical supplies. A logistical undertaking that was competing with the ground forces for resources.

Despite Hitler's change of intention to fight it out in the south, despite the rain and increasingly challenging conditions, despite the endless mountains, rivers and mud and despite the competition for shipping space and supplies, the Allied war leaders, British and American, still expected the Allied armies in Italy to hurry up and get to Rome. And, specifically, for Fifth Army to get to Rome. That meant their eyes were not only on General Sir Harold Alexander, C-in-C of 15th Army Group in Italy, but also on General Mark Clark.

Clark was only forty-seven, young for an army commander. He stood at six foot three, which meant he towered over most of his superiors, peers and subordinates. He was handsomely lean too, and slightly hawkish. One of a comparatively few in the US Army who had seen action in the last war, in France, he had been wounded when a shell had exploded nearby. By the war's end he was a captain, a rank he kept for a further ambition-sapping sixteen years, and yet his self-belief and determination kept him going throughout that long spell in the military doldrums – and his patience paid off. In 1933, his fortunes began to change with promotion and time spent at both the US Command and General Staff College and the Army War College, which suggested he was being marked out for future high command. He was with 3rd Division by the summer of 1937, where he renewed a friendship with an old West Point colleague, Dwight D. Eisenhower, and in 1940 was promoted again, albeit still only to lieutenant-colonel, and posted as Chief of Staff to General Lesley McNair, the man appointed to completely rebuild the US Army. This was unquestionably a golden opportunity for Clark and he made the most of it, swiftly demonstrating his exceptional aptitude for planning and organization. He was smart, quick-thinking, had immense energy and resourcefulness and soon caught the eye of General George C. Marshall, who in September 1939 became Chief of Staff of the US Army, its most senior figure. In 1942 Clark, by then a brigadier-general, was sent to Britain with Eisenhower to arrange for the reception and training of US troops and to begin preparations for Operation SLEDGEHAMMER, the proposed cross-Channel invasion already being formulated at that time. After Allied efforts were redirected to North-west Africa, Eisenhower was made C-in-C with Clark as his deputy. Overseeing the planning of three separate invasion forces, two from the UK and one from the USA, was left to Clark and he did it supremely well. At the time, Operation TORCH was the largest-ever amphibious operation mounted in the history of the world – and was a terrific success for the Allies. TORCH significantly enhanced Clark's reputation, not just for its preparation and execution but also because he had risked his life by clandestinely travelling to Algeria in a submarine and secretly meeting with French Vichy officials ahead of the landings.

While his credentials as a planner and diplomat were well proven, he desperately wanted a field command and pressured Eisenhower to allow him to create, train and lead the first American army to be formed outside the United States. Fifth Army was activated on 5 January 1943, and although it was Seventh Army, under Lieutenant-General George S. Patton, that was later the first to go into action in Sicily, Fifth Army was given the lead role for Operation AVALANCHE that followed, the main assault for the invasion of mainland Italy.

Clark had been dealt a tough hand for this in an operation that set the pattern for the rest of the campaign. The invasion of Sicily, where the Allies had faced no German troops at all along the assault beaches and only two German divisions further inland, had been supported by a huge armada of 472 warships, 3,500 aircraft and 1,743 assault craft. AVALANCHE, on the other hand, in the Bay of Salerno, had been mounted with 71 warships, 670 aircraft and a mere 359 assault craft. Directly facing them and watching every move was the German 16. Panzer-Division, while a further five divisions and elements of a sixth were hurriedly sent against Clark's meagre invasion force of just four American and British divisions and a handful of US Army Rangers and British Commandos. While he was given highly effective support from further warships and air forces that were swiftly sent to Salerno, he had managed his troops deftly with skill, steely resolve and no small amount of imperturbability. AVALANCE had been a baptism of fire for a young, new army commander who had not led troops in battle since being a captain on the Western Front in 1918, let alone a multinational coalition force with all the complications and diplomacy that handling it required.

Despite a strong counter-attack by more than six German divisions, Clark – and his men – had held their nerve, forced the enemy back and won the day. Very much against the odds, AVALANCHE – always a gambler's roll of an operation – had been a success. By 27 September, the British Eighth Army, landing in the heel of the largely undefended south-east of the leg of Italy – as most German troops were at Salerno – had captured Foggia, the single most important objective of the campaign, which meant the heavy bombers would soon be on their way. Then, a few days later, on 1 October, Fifth Army had swept into Naples, Italy's third-largest city and a vital port. By the middle of the month they had faced the River Volturno, a major obstacle and one that threatened to hold them up for quite some time, partly because it was easy to defend and partly because incessant rain was severely hindering Fifth Army's ability to manoeuvre. Yet Clark's troops had got across and surged northwards until they hit the next and much more formidable defensive position, the Bernhard Line, or Winter Line as the Americans called it.

The position was formed along vast 3,000-foot-high peaks. The Via Casilina passed through here at what was known as the Mignano Gap, overlooked by the two giant sentinels of Monte Sammucro and Monte Camino, on top of which were German artillery observers surrounded by protective infantry. And it was prising the enemy off these peaks that was proving so challenging to Clark's men now that it was midwinter, cold, dark and wet. Every aspect of the Italian terrain and winter conditions favoured the enemy and yet, despite having little more than parity of infantry, his men were gaining ground. This was no small achievement in itself.

None the less, the pressure was unquestionably on Fifth Army, and specifically Clark, to deliver Rome. And imminently.

Clark was ambitious, although he was hardly unique among generals in having that character trait. He could be vain: he had adopted a studied image in which, when photographed, he liked to be wearing a standard field jacket and a field cap rather than a helmet or officer's peaked hat. It was a smart look, and he was always spick and span, but informal too, as though he were still very much one of the guys. He also preferred being photographed from his left side so that his slightly skewed nose didn't show. Again, a touch of vanity – yet something he shared with many of his peers. Clark could be moody and prone to snap, and he unquestionably had a chip on his shoulder about his comparative lack of experience. He had total faith in his own capabilities and believed he deserved the elevated position he now held, but many of his subordinates were some years older than him and most of the British commanders had a wealth of battlefield experience with which he simply could not compete. He understood the importance of being a team man, yet sometimes could not help imposing himself perhaps more than he needed to; Clark might be younger, less experienced, but he was the army commander and no one should forget it.

In truth, he had deserved his elevated position and shouldered the immense burden of high command well and stoically, was unafraid to make tough decisions, worked like the devil and had an enviable grasp of detail and an innate ability to cut through the chaff. He also understood the importance of being a visible army commander; much of his time was spent at the front line. And while he was deadly serious about war and the task facing him, he did not lack humour. 'That's one reason why I am anxious to get this thing over and get back to see you,' he wrote to his daughter, Ann, 'and have a good old laughing contest.'

There was nothing to laugh about by the second week of December 1943. Casualties had been appalling, especially since coming up against the Winter Line, and there was now more than a whiff of faltering morale; some forty men of the 34th Red Bulls Division had just deserted and headed to Naples. All had been caught and several tried and convicted for 'misconduct in the face of the enemy'. Clark had been furious and had immediately warned the divisional commander, Major-General Charles 'Doc' Ryder, to get a grip of his men. Casualties in the Red Bulls were no worse – in fact, they were marginally better – than those in the 3rd and 45th Infantry Divisions, for example, each suffering nearly 2,000 casualties since Salerno but with the number of KIA – killed in action – a little better for 34th Division.

Yet this struck at the heart of the dilemma facing Clark and his fellow senior commanders: how to motivate men and keep them going? Why should a young man from the Midwest of the United States, thousands of miles from home, keep slogging up a mountain in far-flung Italy, in December, only to risk being blasted to bits or crippled, just so they could get a few yards closer to Rome? To what end? The United States was better than any other armed forces in the world in keeping its men well fed, amply supplied with chocolate, gum, cigarettes, rest camps, mobile cinemas, Coca-Cola and even ice cream, and, most crucially, regular mail from home, despite the logistical challenges of billions of letters being dispatched all around the globe in a time of war. Yet no amount of mail or even turkey dinners at Thanksgiving could counterbalance the ghastliness of mountain fighting in winter in Italy.

And what was the point when the Allies had achieved three of the four goals for invading Italy in the first three weeks of the campaign? After all, Italy was out of the war, huge numbers of German troops had been drawn off the Eastern and Western Fronts – a big tick for OVERLORD – and the all-important strategic bomber airfields at Foggia had been taken. Only Rome eluded them, and so what? Let the Germans keep hold of it. Rome was only another stinking Eyetie city, goddammit.

It could be argued, as Winston Churchill, the British Prime Minister, had, that as Rome was a major – and ancient – capital city, its capture would have a powerful psychological benefit. Allied troops triumphantly entering Rome would offer tremendous photographs and film footage that could be shown all around the world. The Allies getting ever closer to the heart of the Reich. The vile Nazis now in irreversible retreat.

There was certainly something to be said for this view, but in truth the number-one reason for reaching Rome was because all roads led there and the Allies then desperately needed to push on beyond and create a protective buffer far ahead of the Foggia airfields. There was no point in investing in the construction of airfields, fuel pipelines and all the huge logistics of bringing twenty-one heavy bomb groups into the theatre if the Germans counter-attacked and retook the area. General Alexander concluded in early October – and the Combined Chiefs of Staff agreed – that the Allied armies in Italy needed to drive the enemy at least fifty miles north of Rome to ensure the long-term security of the airfields. In any case, by attacking, the Allies would maintain the initiative, something that was considered of vital importance now they held the southern two-fifths of the leg of Italy.

This, however, put commanders like Clark between a rock and a hard place. His masters were urging him on, desperate for Rome to be captured at the earliest moment possible and for Fifth Army to then drive on even further north, yet they had never given him sufficient resources to achieve this – not initially, when he landed his army at Salerno, and not at any point since. His men were exhausted, understrength and morale was dipping worryingly.

What was needed now, in light of the desertions, was a bit of stick and carrot, although this was a very difficult balance to strike. Yet in the first instance, having spoken personally to General Doc Ryder, Clark decided to draft a memo that he wanted to be widely circulated to all senior officers. A memo from the heart. One written with barely contained anger and frustration. The war in which they found themselves was, he admitted, a grim and bitter business, brought upon decent and kindly peoples by a rogue nation that had deliberately abandoned humanity and friendship. 'The mission of our forces is to end this war as quickly as possible,' he wrote on 12 December, 'and to do it in such a way as to prevent another such destructive world upheaval; to make it impossible for the perpetrators of this world war and the last one to repeat their crimes; to insure, in fact, that after this war the people of our country will be able to live in their chosen manner without either restriction by bandit nations abroad, or the necessity of fighting those nations periodically; in short, to win this war for keeps.'

So how, he asked, could this mission be achieved?

By crushing the Germans militarily. 'The military beating which is given to them must be so violent and terrible as to provide a permanent lesson of the folly of provoking a war with the United States. We of the Fifth Army', he continued, 'must drive our attacks into the Germans with such relentless and smashing force as to implant for all time in the minds and memories of the German Army and people an indelible respect for our military ability and power.' Only by this means, he fervently believed, would a future war be prevented. He was appalled by Nazi cruelty and ideology: the murder of so many, the looting, the disregard for civilians. Some people believed the Germans were fundamentally decent people and shouldn't be blamed for their despicable leaders; Clark did not agree. 'A nation always gets the leaders it wants and deserves,' he wrote, and because of the ruthless ambitions of their foe his soldiers had been forced to leave their homes and loved ones, head overseas and fight. Only by killing as many Germans as possible, he wrote, would they be able to return home again. Every soldier in Fifth needed to realize and understand this. 'We have not been sent here to give the Germans a fair chance. When did they ever give anyone a fair chance? We have been sent here to kill them. Our men must kill Germans as they would kill rattlesnakes or scorpions. We must DESTROY THE ENEMY wherever we find him.' Only those German troops who surrendered would be spared.

He now got to the crux of the matter. Americans, by nature, he knew, were peace-loving folk, and, of course, a huge amount was being expected of these young men now in Fifth Army's ranks. But this was all-out war and his Fifth Army forces needed to be utterly determined in their quest to beat the enemy. 'All of our personnel', he continued, 'must understand that the winning of the war is the paramount consideration of our government, and must be that of every individual who is privileged to be an American citizen; that everything else must give way to this; that the authorities directing the all-out struggle must employ our shipping and our troops in such manner as to produce the maximum effect in a global war; that scores of units at home will have their roles to play in an overall plan.'

Only by smart and persistent application of this message to the front-line troops would those thinking of desertion decide against it; troops had to understand the vital moral imperative of what they were doing. Yes, the infantry, especially, had pulled a short straw, but someone had to do this filthy job, and they had to stick at it so future generations would not have to suffer the same. 'If', he finished, 'these issues are clearly understood by the Fifth Army, nothing can stop us from reaching the goal of real and complete victory.'

A few days later, on 17 December 1943, his men finally broke through the Winter Line. Whether his note had stiffened backbones was not clear; it was more a cathartic expression of his own frustration and grim determination than anything else, but there was no doubt that this was a considerable victory in which, man for man, his American, British and, more recently, French troops had bested the Germans dug into their mountain bastions.

The trouble was, in the ruins of San Pietro, Cervaro and San Vittore and in the mud, rain and freezing cold it didn't feel much like a victory. Rome was still seventy miles away and before them, just a few miles ahead, lay the Germans' next defensive position: the Gustav Line.

And this was an even tougher nut to crack than the Winter Line that had already cost so much blood.

A US mortar team in action.

PART I

The Tyranny of Overlord

CHAPTER 1

The Storm

A STORM SWEPT IN THE New Year of 1944 in southern Italy. Lashing, torrential rain hammered down while heavy winds tore over the mountains and through the valleys. In the little village of Ripi, some fifty miles south of Rome in the Liri Valley, twenty-year-old Viviana Bauco had decided to keep a diary in the hope that before the year was out lasting peace might end the terrible war still engulfing Italy. 'The new year has been announced with a terrible cyclone,' she noted. 'An ugly omen!' Viviana suffered from progressive retinitis pigmentosa, an incurable eye disease that meant she was gradually going blind – a cruel blow for one so young. It ensured she was very dependent on her family – her father, Carlo, a registrar at the local Comune, her mother, Ines, and older sister Lucia, who worked at the Municipio in Ripi. Neither Viviana nor any of her family had much idea of what was going on but were all too aware that the war was inextricably getting closer. The sound of the guns, the concussion that made the ground shake even from twenty-five miles away; the increase in Allied aircraft overhead and the German troops stationed in the village. Viviana felt almost permanently on edge, wondering what their fate might be and whether their tiny corner of Italy would ever be left alone.

And as if the war was not bad enough, now a cyclone had whipped in through the night. She had to pray, as she did most fervently, that God would protect them.

Just a few miles away in Frosinone, one of the larger local towns of this part of southern Lazio, Oberstarzt Wilhelm Mauss was at the XIV Panzerkorps command post as his old house in Roccasecca had been bombed out back in the middle of December. Like Viviana Bauco, Mauss also wondered whether the storm was an omen and a symbol of what was to come that year. Mauss was forty-four and a colonel-doctor, the Chief Medical Officer for the corps. A learned, cultured man but convinced National Socialist, Mauss had served in the last war and then, after later becoming a doctor, rejoined the army as a surgeon and medical officer – MO – and had so far served in France and on the Eastern Front before being posted to the Mediterranean the previous summer. He had been based at XIV Panzerkorps headquarters ever since.

At the command post, he and other corps staff had listened on the radio to the German bells ringing in the New Year; the small gathering had also enjoyed some convivial drinks and then, by telephone, he had spoken to the corps commander, Generalleutnant Fridolin von Senger und Etterlin, and then tried to make a call to his wife and family back home in Hanover, western Germany, whom he missed desperately. Unfortunately, having got as far as the long-distance telephone exchange in Hanover, the storm had then brewed up and he'd been cut off. He had been so close to speaking to them, yet they had remained frustratingly out of reach.

Through the small hours, the wind had increased. Dawn on that first day of the year revealed the kind of carnage normally caused by bombs and shellfire. The telephone operator's barrack had collapsed, tents had been ripped up, tiles blown from the roofs of the houses, trees uprooted and windows smashed. Mauss could scarcely believe it, but then later that evening he witnessed a stunningly beautiful skyscape of violet and red clouds over the snowy mountains that surrounded them either side of the Liri Valley, rising like pillars over the frail blue sky. Lower, the sky glowed like liquid iron. 'May this day be a symbol for the year,' he jotted. 'From the dark-dreary clouds of the last year the redeeming storm then breaks.' Perhaps, he wondered, the tranquil scene he saw that evening would hasten in the more peaceful days that they all surely desired.

'Happy New Year,' wrote Regimental Sergeant-Major – RSM – Jack Ward in the diary he kept for his wife back home in Eastbourne on the south coast of England. 'What a start to the new year, the hardest rainstorm that I have ever seen.' A bridge just above Regimental HQ – RHQ – had been entirely washed away. Ward was forty-three, the old man of the 56th Heavy Regiment, Royal Artillery. He had joined up when he'd been eighteen, just after the end of the last war, but despite long years of service it was not until he and the rest of the regiment reached Tunisia at the back end of 1942 that he had first seen action. He'd had a skinful since – and been wounded and recovered – but although somewhat lugubrious at times, he wasn't prone to bellyaching. Rather, he continued doing his job assiduously and with as much dedication as he could and with a strong dose of fatalism. He'd much rather be back at home, but then they all would, and he had the wit to recognize that his situation was preferable to that of many others now serving in Italy. Being an RSM in a heavy artillery regiment was certainly not without danger, but the size of their guns – a big beast of a 7.2-inch howitzer – meant they were generally a few miles back from the infantry, and whenever he saw what those poor blighters had to go through he knew he had a lot to be grateful for.

While the 56th Heavy Regiment, along with the British X Corps, were part of General Clark's Fifth Army, most of the British and Commonwealth troops were serving with Eighth Army, which had famously trounced Rommel and his Panzerarmee at Alamein and later helped win the Allies all of Libya and part of Tunisia too. It was Eighth Army, under the command of the totemic General Sir Bernard Montgomery, that had invaded Sicily alongside the US Seventh Army and which, on 3 September 1943, had crossed the narrow Straits of Messina from Sicily into the toe of the boot of mainland Italy. Monty had left after Christmas, heading back to the UK to take overall command of Allied land forces in the forthcoming cross-Channel invasion of Normandy. Operation OVERLORD, planned for May that year, was the Allies' primary effort, which made Italy, despite its vast expenditure in men and materiel, a secondary theatre. Globally, Italy was even further down the pecking order of priorities, despite, this January of 1944, being the only place where the Western Allies were currently fighting the Germans on the ground.

Montgomery's replacement was General Oliver Leese, a jovial and highly experienced commander and former corps commander under Monty in the desert and in Sicily. He was, however, new as an army commander, and in the days and weeks ahead was likely have his work cut out keeping this famous warhorse of an army going with the same sense of purpose and drive; morale was a fragile beast, and Eighth Army's troops were used to being in the spotlight – Britain's most famous, most successful army had, until the end of 1943, been commanded by its most famous, most successful general. Now, suddenly, as January 1944 dawned, it found itself with a second-tier commander in the middle of winter.

And not just any old winter, but an especially savage one. Rain and wind had pummelled the western side of the leg, but in the middle, in the heart of the Abruzzo mountains, near the lonely town of Castel di Sangro, there had been very heavy snow, and Major Lawrie Franklyn-Vaile of the 1st Royal Irish Fusiliers and his men in B Company had felt the full weight of the overnight snowfall. There had been no cosy, warm bar for them or any carousing into the small hours; rather, he and his men had been posted up on to a lonely and isolated peak two days earlier.

Franklyn-Vaile was an Australian, from Melbourne, and by trade a journalist, who had moved to England before the war, married an English girl and then, when war was declared, had joined up and been posted to the 'Faughs'* – as the Royal Irish Fusiliers were known. Franklyn-Vaile was thirty-three, and so a little older than most of his fellows; he could have remained an instructor but had requested to serve overseas with the rest of the battalion to which he had grown so attached – despite being married and having a daughter now aged three years old. A wish not to be left behind, mixed with a profound sense that it was his moral duty to help defeat Nazism and Fascism, and also the age-old desire to experience war and to be tested as a man, as a soldier and as a commander had compelled him to go. He had joined the battalion late in the Sicilian campaign and had since proved a highly courageous and competent officer.

'I have never seen so much snow,' he wrote to his wife, Olive, 'in places it was waist and chest deep and what with the icy wind as well, conditions were far from pleasant.' It was certainly a contrast to his first days in Sicily when the dry heat had nearly broiled them all alive. He was, he told her, glad he'd brought his roll-top sweater with him when he'd headed off to war.

Further east, near the Adriatic coast, at 8th Indian Division HQ, Corporal Harry Wilson also woke up to discover a landscape transformed by snow. Wilson was an Irishman who had been living in Northampton in England at the start of the war and earning very little playing the piano in bars. His brother had joined the RAF, so he thought he would join up too, albeit the army rather than the air force. Slight of build but ferociously bright, he had been posted to the Royal Engineers, ended up serving in a Well-Boring Section in 10th Indian Division in the Middle East, before retraining – and passing with flying colours – as a cipher clerk. He'd been posted to 8th Indian Division the previous September and had been in

* 'Faugh' is pronounced 'fog'.

Italy with the rest of 8th Indian since October, and while he was grateful he was not in the infantry, even at Division HQ he felt he'd been quite close enough to the front.

On New Year's Eve he'd been on duty in the cipher truck, which was parked next to some oaks, with a tarpaulin stretched from the edge of the truck to the trees and under which were their foxholes. At 10 p.m. Wilson and his fellows had turned in, glad to be aboard the truck for once, and with the banshee wind howling outside. Soon after, they were roused again by Corporal Garrett telling them some V Corps ciphers needed decrypting.

'Tell them there's a bloody blizzard blowing!' yelled Corporal Spiers, one of Wilson's fellow duty clerks. But they got up and deciphered the messages anyway. They later went back to sleep only to be woken by the flapping tarpaulin, which had become loose. Cursing, they ventured out into the snow, the wind still howling, and secured it again, but others were flooded out of their foxholes. 'Only the elements were at war,' noted Wilson, 'for not a gun sounded on any front.'

It didn't last long. By the following evening the enemy guns opened up again as the sky cleared and the stars came out. Wilson was convinced Eighth Army had become bogged down and that they'd be stuck on the ridge south of Ortona and Orsogna until the ground dried out. He was spot on. That night, with his foxhole waterlogged, he took himself off to a stone shed near the farmhouse around which Division HQ was based. Five Indian soldiers were already there, desperately trying to keep a damp, smoking fire going. 'About fifty breezes played about on the flag-stones,' he noted while gazing up at the cracked stone walls and thick oak beams, each as heavy as a steamroller, sagging worryingly towards the floor.

Whether this cyclone-strength storm was considered a good or bad omen rather depended on one's perspective in life, but the New Year certainly brought with it a mixture of feelings among the many troops and civilians now caught up in this vicious war in Italy. All Major Georg Zellner could think of was home and his wife and two daughters back in Regensburg in south-east Germany. Just a brief visit was all he was asking for, but despite applying for leave several times he had been turned down on every occasion. His 3. Bataillon of the 134. Infanterie-Regiment had been temporarily assigned to 29. Panzergrenadier-Division, now holding the central stretch of the Cassino front across the mouth of the Mignano Gap. Usually part of the 44. 'Hoch-und Deutschmeister' – H-und-D – Infanterie-Division, now pulled back behind the Gustav Line to rebuild strength, 134. Regiment – Zellner's 3. Bataillon included – had been in action almost constantly since reaching the front in the middle of November and it looked likely this was not about to change. Since Fifth Army had finally smashed its way through the Bernhard Line just before Christmas, 29. Panzergrenadier-Division had been pulled back for only a short time while final preparations were made on the next major line of defence, the Gustav Line. On this first day of January, it meant Zellner had his command post between Cervaro and San Vittore, two small towns at the western end of the Monte Sammucro massif. Cervaro was a couple of miles further west than San Vittore, which was where Zellner's three infantry companies were based, and only five miles from Cassino; but whereas the huge Monte Cassino massif rose high above the latter town, both Cervaro and San Vittore were out on something of a limb – west of the former Bernhard Line but not part of the Gustav, and now the Americans were the ones with observers peering down on the Germans below.

It made Zellner feel extremely vulnerable, to say the least. He was thirty-eight years old, but a career soldier who had joined the Reichswehr aged twenty in 1926 and been posted to Regensburg, where he had been based for most of the years leading up to the war and married and raised a family. He worried about them constantly – especially since the Messerschmitt aircraft factory and an oil refinery in Regensburg had been heavily bombed the previous August. Clearly, his home city was now very much on the Allies' target list.

Zellner had already lost three-quarters of his men in the six weeks of fighting since their arrival. His companies had been used to firefight and plug gaps, and had been moved from one area of the mountains to the other. The privations had been considerable, the weather awful, the American shelling incessant, and enemy attacks by the dreaded 'Jabos' – fighter-bombers, an abbreviation of Jagdbomber – relentless whenever the skies were clear. It was hard to know what was worse: cold rain or the rain of bombs and cannon shells. Of the Luftwaffe there had been no sign.

Despite the storm, however, Zellner had slept deeply for once, total exhaustion finally catching up with him. He was not in good health – how could he be after six weeks living outside in the mountains, almost permanently wet, or in dank bunkers and cellars? 'Flatulence, heart and lung problems,' he had recorded a few days earlier. 'But I can't have time for that.' The morning was quiet, however – but almost too quiet. 'We were seized by a strange restlessness,' he noted, 'that everyone hid from each other.' Since they were on the defensive all they could do was wait for the Americans to attack. Some kind of distraction was needed; one of the men had managed to get some cuts from a dead cow and so he cooked those along with some dumplings; the meal did much to keep up spirits.

The first reports reached his command post at around midday and continued through the afternoon. All suggested the same thing: that opposite them, the Americans were moving troops forward in readiness for an attack. Then an order from Division informed them that the men of the 134. Regiment, and 3. Bataillon in particular, were at the focal point of the southern front. Well, that was tremendous news. 'Although we already knew it,' scribbled Zellner, 'it was now confirmed to us that we had to expect the worst. I suppose the magic will begin tomorrow and everyone else feels it.' The atmosphere in their bunker remained eerily quiet after their feast. 'Reidl reads,' he wrote, 'the Adj writes, Würsch sleeps, Becher sits by the fire.'

Waiting for the fire after the storm.

'Storms which assume hurricane proportions', noted the diarist at XIV Panzerkorps headquarters, 'make any large-scale operations impossible.' So while the weather wasn't much to cheer about if you were a part of B Company of the Faughs, stuck in a snowdrift on the top of a lonely mountain, nor if you were a gunner behind the lines, it was a positive blessing if you were unfortunate enough to be in the infantry on the battlefront near the town of Cassino. It meant, quite simply, you were going to be spared for that day at least, which was about as good a start to the year as any in the PBI could hope for out here in this part of southern Italy.

Yet while high winds and rain had brought the fighting to a halt, it would not be for long, as Major Georg Zellner had instinctively understood. Having finally burst through the Winter Line, Fifth Army was now continuing to bridge the gap of eight miles or so to the Gustav Line, a gap being stubbornly defended by Zellner's men among many others in XIV Panzerkorps. Orders were passed down from Fifth Army to II Corps, still manning the central part of their front. On their right was the Corps Expéditionnaire Français – the CEF – made up mostly of French North African colonial troops, while on their left were the British of X Corps. And part of II Corps were the 34th Red Bulls, the infantry unit that had been giving Clark cause for concern the previous month, although since that mass desertion there had been no further trouble.

The Americans were due to attack the following day, however, and it was the Red Bulls who would be heading straight for San Vittore and Cervaro, where Georg Zellner's battalion were positioned, while the recently arrived 1st Armored Division would be on the Red Bulls' left flank. Ralph Schaps was a buck sergeant in the 2nd Battalion of 135th Infantry, one of three infantry regiments in the Red Bulls. A squad commander in Company H, Schaps was a Minnesotan, twenty-three years old and also a veteran of Tunisia and the long slog from Salerno these past few months. The 135th had actually been out of the line since 12 December, the same day General Clark wrote his memo about the need to crush the Germans with unshakable ruthlessness, but now Schaps and his fellows were back at the front in the bitter cold and vicious wind, winding their way from the rest camp at Sant'Angelo d'Alife near Caserta, where they had been safely nestled in the lea of yet another mountain, out of harm's way.

No matter how grim life was at the front, however, nothing helped maintain morale better than receiving mail from home, and having jumped out of his truck in the San Pietro area Schaps was delighted to find a package waiting for him: a large box of Roi-Tan cigars. A small thing, but a gift that made all the difference.

General Clark himself was suffering from a severe cold – one so bad he'd even spent 30 December at the nearby 36th General Hospital in Caserta getting checked out. On New Year's Eve, although feeling better, he'd travelled down to the Officers' Rest Center, both to get a change of scene away from the front and also to visit the officers there. Since it had been an overnight stay he was still there in Sorrento, with its jagged coastline and stunning views out to sea, as the New Year dawned. There had been a small amount of fighting along the Amalfi coast back in September and this golden stretch of coast had, mercifully, survived largely unscathed. The Rest Center was perfectly positioned and large and comfortable, a former luxury hotel. It allowed those officers from the front to truly escape, relax and find themselves in a part of the country still achingly beautiful rather than battered, broken and brutalized by the violence of war.

There was, as always, much for Clark to think about, however, and just because he was in Sorrento it did not mean he was going to step away from the war even for a day. Throughout the morning of that first day of 1944, motor messengers brought dispatches from his CP at Caserta and he also discussed various matters by telephone with his trusted Chief of Staff, Major-General Al Gruenther. How to break the deadlock at the front was a conundrum facing all the senior Allied commanders in Italy. A plan had been doing the rounds for six weeks or more now to land a force from Fifth Army behind the German front line just to the south of Rome. The area chosen was a stretch of coast either side of the twin towns of Anzio and Nettuno, small fishing ports some forty miles south of the capital. From these towns the flat land of the old Pontine Marshes, reclaimed during the Mussolini era, spread out towards ever more mountains: the Lepini to the south-east and the Colli Albani – the Alban Hills – to the north. The hope was that by landing a sufficient-sized force there, the German 10. Armee would be panicked into pulling back from the Gustav Line entirely for fear of being folded up in the rear.

The issue, as always, was whether enough shipping and assault craft could be mustered to deliver a meaningful amount of men and materiel into this bridgehead. Admiral Sir Andrew Cunningham, the British C-in-C of Allied naval forces in the Mediterranean, signalled that day to tell Gruenther that all vital LSTs – landing ship, tank, the largest, 120-yard-long landing craft available – had to be released on 2 February. Operation SHINGLE, as the planned assault was code-named, was due to take place on 22 January. That meant having them for eleven days only and then they'd be off. Once again, plans were being made but without the necessary logistical support.

However, one of the developments from the Tehran Conference in early December 1943 had been the decision to mount an amphibious assault of southern France concurrently with OVERLORD, to be code-named ANVIL. This had been urged upon the Allies by Stalin, who had argued that such an assault would offer the best support for OVERLORD. Admittedly, there were sound military reasons for such an operation, but Stalin was already looking ahead to the end of the war and Soviet influence in eastern Europe and the Balkans, where in Yugoslavia the British, especially, had backed the Communist partisans under Tito. This was what made Stalin's surprise suggestion such a strategic masterstroke. Stalin also stressed that an invasion of southern France should take place at the same time as the cross-Channel invasion, while President Roosevelt wondered whether the Italian campaign should be halted now and southern France invaded ahead of OVERLORD. Such an invasion force would need a huge amount of shipping, and already there was apprehension that the Anzio operation would have a detrimental effect on ANVIL.

Leapfrogging their way with amphibious assaults all up the leg of Italy was a very obvious way for the Allies to stretch the German defences to the fullest and avoid the worst of the incredibly challenging mountainous terrain; frustratingly, they couldn't exploit this opportunity for lack of shipping.

Clark had been given the nod that he was being lined up to command the US Seventh Army for ANVIL, which would take him away from Fifth Army and Italy. This he'd been discreetly told by Eisenhower before the latter left the Mediterranean to head to London to become Supreme Allied Commander for the cross-Channel invasion. 'My guess', Gruenther noted to Clark in a personal message that day, 1 January, 'is that SHINGLE will be cancelled.' Gruenther was at Allied Forces HQ in Algiers – the North African city was still the nerve centre of the Allied war effort in the Mediterranean and he had flown over the previous day. It meant, though, that there were always a lot of moving parts. Alexander, as 15th Army Group commander – that is, overall ground commander in Italy – was in Brindisi on the southern Adriatic coast; then there was the HQ in Algiers, a major hub in Malta and still one in Sicily; Naples was now the centre for civilian affairs and another mass of desk wallahs – staff officers. 'Consensus here', Gruenther told Clark in a subsequent signal, 'is that SHINGLE should be cancelled unless Alexander and Clark can show that there will be no interference with ANVIL.'

And it was, of course, impossible to guarantee such a thing. Any amphibious operation was a major undertaking and a significant commitment. Reverses were unconscionable, which meant that, once committed, they had to continue to be backed. It was all very well saying that the crucial LSTs had to be released after eleven days and that SHINGLE must not be allowed to upset plans for the invasion of southern France in five months' time, but the enemy had a vote too. How the Germans would react could be guessed, and could even be hoped, but there were no cast-iron guarantees at all.

Such were the many levers being pulled on this first day of 1944 in Italy and the wider Mediterranean theatre. In the meantime, however, Clark was still expected to get his army through the Gustav Line as quickly as possible.

The renewed attack would begin the following morning, Sunday, 2 January 1944.

CHAPTER 2

A Cunning Plan

'ALL HELL IS BREAKING loose in San Vittore,' noted Major Georg Zellner from his cellar in Cervaro that first Sunday of the year. 'Artillery fire of all calibres for hours.' This was the prelude, the softening up before the US II Corps attack. In this terrain, in these winter conditions, it was hard to bring the normal mobility the Allies would expect to use to bear, but they could still draw upon their superior amounts of artillery. The boom of guns, the pulsing of the ground – one could physically feel it – the screech of shells whistling over, the explosion as each shell landed; the crash of falling masonry, the clatter of descending stones, brick, earth and grit. The guns continued through the night; no one at the 3. Bataillon command post got much sleep.

Good weather the next day, Monday. This meant the Jabos would be over, and so they were: in force at around 4.30 p.m., thundering in low and hammering Cervaro. Zellner and his battalion headquarters could only crouch and hope they might be spared, but it was hard not to think that a direct hit might land at any moment. Sometimes dirt fell on their heads. They were all smoking like chimneys. 'We huddle in the corners,' noted Zellner. 'Reidl climbs up and drinks cognac on an empty stomach, settles down again. Schwarzer takes a piece of wood and plays with it. He tries to sing, sometimes someone else gets up, swears, sits down again and stares into a hole.' Zellner found himself moving from one corner to another. At one point he tried to speak but his words were lost in a deafening crash nearby. Dust and smoke drifted through the room. Everyone began coughing. There was nothing they could say or do; they simply had to stay where they were, in their command post in Cervaro, and take it, just as Zellner's three companies, a short distance ahead in and around San Vittore, had to take it. They had to withstand this bombing and shelling until ordered to fall back. Eventually, Reidl got up again, ruffled his hair, drank more cognac and then said, 'Abandon all hope, you who enter the gate of horror.'

Zellner wondered whether he was going to go mad with this incessant barrage and drumming of guns. He had a desperate, overwhelming urge to relieve himself, but daren't. Eventually, though, he took some paper and went to the latrine only to realize he didn't need to go after all. 'I take my diary and write,' he recorded, 'and look at the pictures of my family. The blood and nerves are raging in my head.'

General Clark wanted to draw up to the Gustav Line as quickly as possible. The British X Corps was working its way through the mountains to the south-west and heading to the River Garigliano, but it was the US II Corps that was to push beyond the Mignano Gap – the narrow stretch that had been the key to the Bernhard Line. The giant bastions of Monte Sammucro and Monte Camino were behind them and now there was a short stretch of low, undulating terrain as Highway 6 – the Via Casilina – and the railway emerged through the Gap and met with the Rapido River Valley from the north and headed into the wider Liri Valley beyond. Barring the way were the two small towns of San Vittore and Cervaro and a series of isolated low mountains, none more than 800 feet high: Monte Porchia and the Colle Cedro to the south of Highway 6 and Colle Cicerelli and Chiaia to the north; Monte Chiaia rose between San Vittore and Cervaro. Finally, and effectively blocking the way into the Liri Valley, was Monte Trocchio, a narrow, low mountain only some 1,400 feet high with sloping shoulders and a higher central ridge. Trocchio had a distinct and significant profile and lay at right angles to the flow of Highway 6. Clark wanted it in Allied hands as soon as possible because before launching any attack on the Gustav Line he planned to put the bulk of his artillery there, as they would be protected from the all-seeing eyes of German observers on the Monte Cassino massif beyond. He could also place his own observers on top.

A few miles to the north of San Vittore, however, and effectively round the corner from the Mignano Gap, the mountains rose dramatically once again, the highest being Monte Maio, a massive peak of over 3,000 feet and taller even than Sammucro. This giant overlooked the upper Rapido Valley and was an essential mass of high ground for any future assault on the Gustav Line because Clark wanted his own observers up there, looking across the Rapido Valley towards the Monte Cassino massif. Its capture would also allow the expansion of a mountain track that would enable supplies to come forward to the edge of the Rapido Valley without German eyes watching their every move. While the French of the CEF were to push on through the mountains to the north of Maio, capturing the peak itself was given to the joint American-Canadian Special Service Force, specifically trained in mountain warfare.

The Special Service Force set out from its bivouac area in the dark of the evening of 3 January in freezing temperatures, the forward artillery observers with them struggling with the heavy radio packs through gullies thick with snow and mule tracks treacherous with ice. Major-General Geoffrey Keyes, the II Corps commander, brought up both the 36th T-Patchers' artillery to support their assault but also two battalions from the 34th Red Bulls to secure and hold the ground captured by the Special Service Force. After two days of clearing German outposts, the mountain men finally assaulted the peak of Monte Maio on the night of 6 January. Conditions were brutal: freezing, with bitter winds whipping across the exposed slopes and dark. These were not sensible conditions in which to fight; there was a reason why, in earlier times, the campaigning season had been in the summer months.

But the Allies were in a hurry. They wanted to win the war as quickly as possible so everyone could go home, and Europe – and the world – could move into a new age of peace. And in any case, here in Italy the Allied commanders were under renewed pressure to get on with things, to swiftly draw up against the Gustav Line then burst through it and link up with forces that in just a few weeks' time were to be deposited at Anzio, forty miles to the north. Despite General Gruenther's predictions on 1 January that SHINGLE, the Anzio operation, would be scrapped, it was, in fact, now very much back on again. It would have to happen quickly, though – in less than three weeks' time. Yet on Tuesday, 4 January, planning for the operation had barely begun and the finer details had yet to be worked out. With Fifth Army now engaged in battle all along the Cassino front, that was giving the staffs involved very little time to mount such a complex operation.

Shipping, or the shortage of it, was the issue forcing the Allies' hand. It had already proved the bane of the Italian campaign and was dictating the pace for the Anzio operation too.

*

That SHINGLE was back in the frame was largely down to the British Prime Minister, now recovering from his near-fatal bout of pneumonia and, convalescing in Tunis, re-energized about breaking the deadlock in Italy. Churchill had already begun thinking about the Italian conundrum when General Sir Alan Brooke, the Chief of the Imperial General Staff and Britain's most senior military figure, had visited him before Christmas on his way back from a tour of the Italian front. Brooke had been considerably disheartened by what he'd witnessed and had concluded that Fifth Army would make little progress until the ground dried, which was unlikely to be before the spring. Since the Germans had more troops in Italy than the Allies, that might well lead to the kind of reverse General Alexander had warned about back in October.

Towards the beginning of October 1943, when the Italian campaign had been only a month or so old, he had made a detailed appreciation of the situation, which had already been affected by Hitler's decision to fight for every metre rather than retreat some 200 miles north of Rome, as the Allies had expected and planned for before the invasion. As Alexander had pointed out, the Germans' quantitative superiority was likely to continue and his prediction had been spot on as there were now twenty-three Germans divisions to the Allies' eighteen at the beginning of 1944 – quite a disparity, despite the Allies' greater numbers of artillery and mastery of the skies. He worried about stagnation; his armies had done well in the winter conditions, and in terrain that so favoured the Germans, to get as far as they had, but there was clearly a risk. If the front got stuck at the Gustav Line, then the greater attrition of forces might fall on the Allies. The last thing they wanted was a fatal weakening of the Italian front just as OVERLORD was about to be launched. Even worse, the Germans might make a local counter-offensive, either to retake the Foggia airfield complex or the key port of Naples. A reverse in Italy would also have a potentially very detrimental effect on OVERLORD, because resources would have to be poured into Italy to ensure a setback did not become a disaster. The Italian campaign had been launched in the first place to assist OVERLORD; clearly, it could not be allowed to do the opposite. As a result, it was vital not to relax the pressure. Rather, they needed to push on, secure Rome – and all the roads that led to and from it – and create the buffer that kept the Germans on the back foot and ensured that Foggia, especially, remained secure.

Unlocking the Gustav Line had been foremost in Alexander's mind when SHINGLE was first put forward back in November. It had been cancelled on 20 December because Fifth Army, although through the mighty Bernhard Line, was not yet at the next line of defence, the Gustav Line, and it had been accepted that most of the shipping due for SHINGLE would have to be withdrawn by 15 January. That was simply not enough time to make SHINGLE a viable operation.

Following the Tehran Conference, the Combined Chiefs agreed that Operation ANVIL should go ahead at the same time as OVERLORD, and with whatever shipping could be made available. It was also agreed that the Italian campaign should continue and aim not only for Rome but to reach the Pisa–Rimini Line some 200 miles to the north. While General Brooke had tentatively supported ANVIL, it had occurred to him that the shipping that would have to remain in the Mediterranean as a consequence might now be used for a revived amphibious assault of Anzio first, and using a more appropriate timetable than had originally been conceived. Before heading back to the UK he planted this seed with Churchill, who, recuperating in bed and with time on his hands, now became convinced that such an operation was the panacea to unlocking the apparent deadlock in Italy.

While Brooke flew back to London, Churchill got to grips with shipping allocations. There were 246 assault craft in the Mediterranean at the end of December 1943, of which 96 were the all-important landing ships. These came in two forms: LSTs and LSIs – landing ship, infantry. Both were much the same: giant 120-yard-long vessels, as big as a destroyer, with enclosed decks, although the LST was the more important and numerous of the two; each LST was capable of carrying eighteen tanks and 217 troops but had a forward fully laden draught of just 4 feet. The LSI could take as many as 1,500 men straight on to an assault beach. They were a truly remarkable innovation and totally transformed the capabilities of the Allies, for with these landing ships, especially, and a host of other landing craft, they no longer needed a port in order to invade an island or stretch of enemy-held coast. A decent stretch of beach would do just fine.

Initially conceived by the British and then built to a joint Anglo-US design, the first purpose-built LST, HMS *Boxer*, had only been launched back in December 1942, while even the smaller assault craft such as the US-designed LCVP – landing craft, vehicle, personnel – better known as the Higgins Boat, had only been trialled in May 1941. Since the Allies had moved on to the offensive, both in the Pacific with the invasion of Guadalcanal in August 1942 and then with Operation TORCH in North-west Africa in November that same year, their entire way of war had become inextricably linked to these comparatively simple but ingenious new vessels. And for all the different varieties developed, none were more important than the landing ships, purely for the incredible amounts they could deliver directly on to a beach and the consequent economies of scale they offered.

The trouble was, because these vessels were comparatively late to the party, it was not until May 1942 that a crash-programme of landing craft production got under way in the United States. A staggering 8,719 of all kinds had been constructed by the following April, of which 214 had been landing ships, but this had come at a cost to conventional freighters and warships, which by early summer 1943 were in urgent demand once more. So production of assault shipping was wound down, although American shipyards were still producing between eighteen and twenty-two LSTs a month. The net result was that by December there were 144 LSTs in the Pacific and 138 in the European theatre for all operations, of which 105 were in the Mediterranean.

However, by 15 January 1944, 68 of those were due to head off to the UK for refit and then for training and to take part in OVERLORD. That left just 37, of which 10 were due to go for an immediate refit. A further 15 were on their way from South East Asia, no longer needed for an amphibious operation in Burma which had been scrapped – also for lack of enough assault craft. However, those 15 had already been pencilled in for an operation against the island of Rhodes in the eastern Aegean. What's more, of the 37 still left in the Mediterranean, 20 had been scheduled to transport air forces to Corsica in advance of ANVIL. So, on paper, SHINGLE was a non-starter.

Churchill, however, was undeterred. Where there was a will, there was a way. From his bed in Carthage, he had begun plotting as to how enough LSTs might be kept in the Mediterranean long enough for SHINGLE to both take place and be successful. He was desperate to unlock the apparent stalemate in Italy, partly because he had long been obsessed with capturing Rome, with all its history and symbolism as a major European capital. Yet he also wanted to push north because he had always been a champion of the Italian campaign and believed that success in that theatre would offer the greatest help to the supreme operation of crossing the Channel to Normandy. Also, Churchill believed in the Mediterranean strategy: circumstances had brought British forces into action there when the Italians, back in September 1940, had invaded Egypt. That had led to the evolution of the long North African campaign, of the failed intervention in Greece and the humiliation of Crete. It had led to triumph in Tunisia and Sicily and now progressed to Italy. From Italy, the Allies could best help Tito's partisans in Yugoslavia. And once the Po Valley had been reached, to the north of the Apennines, they could either wheel west into southern France, or right through the Ljubljana Gap into the Balkans. This latter course was what Stalin feared, but so too the Americans, who were worried that British post-war power-playing was trumping military priorities. There was some truth in this, but the Mediterranean was a theatre Churchill instinctively wanted to see right through to a triumphant conclusion, not withdraw from mid-battle.

It was on Christmas Eve 1943 that the Prime Minister first discussed the idea of resurrecting SHINGLE with Alexander and General Henry Maitland Wilson, soon to take over as Supreme Commander in the Mediterranean. The three worked late into the evening, Alexander and Wilson sitting beside Churchill's bed while he sat up in his pyjamas and an elaborate silk dressing gown. The nub of the matter was how exactly such an amphibious operation might help Allied fortunes in Italy, and the size of force that could reasonably be expected to achieve this goal. For Churchill, Rome was the great prize to be won from this exciting outflanking operation, although for Alexander it was more about spooking the Germans into withdrawing XIV Panzerkorps, now opposite Fifth Army. If a minimum of two divisions could be landed initially and a further two follow, then a corps-sized force would be planted in the German 10. Armee's western rear. This would be sufficient to threaten both their lines of supply to the Cassino front and also Rome at the same time. With the Germans caught between this pincer, with their front and rear endangered, Alexander reckoned there was a decent chance they would pull back. To achieve the full effect of the bluff, he felt it was important that the invasion force push far enough inland, off the flat coastal area and up into the Colli Albani to the south of Rome around the south-western area of the Colli Laziali. This was around twenty miles to the north of Anzio. It was, Alexander accepted, a punt, for if the Germans swiftly gathered their 14. Armee together, which was currently scattered throughout the northern half of Italy, then it would be impossible to hold such a wide bridgehead with just a single corps. However, despite extremely bitter fighting in southern Italy so far, the Germans had shown no inclination at all to send 14. Armee south. Obviously, an initial landing of three, rather than two, divisions would be preferable and would allow the best chance of success; but this, of course, all depended on what LSTs might be available.

Over the next few days, Churchill won over Eisenhower and Air Chief Marshal Sir Arthur Tedder, both soon to be heading to England for OVERLORD, as well as the British Chiefs of Staff – albeit reluctantly – and finally President Roosevelt. It was reckoned that 88 LSTs would do the trick. The operation against Rhodes was scrapped and it was accepted that the very experienced LST crews already in the Mediterranean didn't need as long for training in Britain ahead of OVERLORD as had been initially reckoned, so the 68 earmarked for the UK could linger a little longer. After considerable wrangling, the 80-odd LSTs needed were found, albeit with caveats. Thirty-three, for example, would sail for England no later than 5 February. If SHINGLE took place on, say, 20 January, that would give the Anzio operation two weeks with all those LSTs. The rest would then be packed off to dockyards in Malta and elsewhere for refitting for ANVIL. Only six would be retained for ongoing service at Anzio beyond 5 February, because OVERLORD was set in stone and sacrosanct. Nothing was allowed to disrupt those plans and SHINGLE was only agreed to on that understanding.

It all sounded simple enough, but mounting such an enterprise in less than a month and in conjunction with operations on the Cassino front was a big ask. A lot of different parts were moving all at once and involved the coordination of army, air and naval staffs. It was also based on a best guess as to how the enemy might react, but nothing more concrete than that. So far in the Italian campaign, the Allies had not proved terribly good at second-guessing German intentions.

The Allies had, since the change in British fortunes in the Western Desert in August 1942, eschewed risk as far as possible. They had won at Alamein by amassing such forces before they attacked that only one outcome was likely, and that was victory. They had done the same in Tunisia, and again in Sicily. They were planning to take the same approach for OVERLORD. Yet Italy was the exception. That General Clark's understrength Fifth Army had prevailed at Salerno had been as much down to German failings as it had been to the skill of Allied land, air and naval forces. Now, a further high-risk gamble was about to be undertaken. It was worth the risk because the alternative – continuing to try and batter through the Gustav Line – was considered even riskier. Churchill was a great one for backing madcap schemes and taking an unconventional approach; Alexander was aware of this but with SHINGLE had carefully weighed up the pros and cons. It was undeniably a big risk, but lurking at the back of his mind was the knowledge that the Combined Chiefs of Staff would not allow a catastrophe to unfold. The constraining factor for SHINGLE was shipping and, if push came to shove, he knew that a live operation would trump one still in the planning. The Anzio plan might not achieve all that was hoped but it was unlikely to be defeated. And a bridgehead at the enemy's rear would always be an asset to the main effort on the front line to the south.

Clouding any future Allied strategy in Italy was the growing belief in the minds of the US and British war leaders that the Italian campaign was not living up to its billing. This, however, was largely of their own making rather than down to Alexander, his army commanders or the men battling their way through this miserable mountainous terrain in the middle of a vicious winter. This did not mean that invading Italy had been a wrong decision, because the benefits of drawing off so many German troops into Italy and the wider Balkans and the Aegean, as well as the capture of the all-important Foggia airfields, were considerable. But had it been backed more fully earlier, when the countdown to OVERLORD had not been quite so pressing and different choices in the Pacific could still have been made, then they would also have been less likely to find Alexander's beleaguered armies struggling in the mud, mire and mountains against an obdurate enemy, and they would have been less likely to confront the logistical pickle in which they now found themselves. Nor would they have had to consider a high-risk venture made even riskier by a ridiculously tight time frame. Certainly, as General Alexander headed to see the army commander whose troops would be undertaking this 'cat-claw' venture, as Churchill was calling it, there was much weighing on his shoulders – and those of General Mark Clark too.

General Sir Harold Alexander arrived at Clark's Caserta camp at around 12.30 p.m. on 4 January, having flown into Naples from Tunis earlier that morning. Travelling regularly by plane was not without risk, was exhausting and, frankly, chewed up a fair amount of time as well, but Alexander had been shuttling back and forth across the Mediterranean and beyond like a yo-yo in recent weeks thanks to the two major strategy conferences and subsequent major changes of Allied command. Alexander had also been ill recently – not at death's door like the PM, but he had suffered a virulent bout of jaundice; front-line troops were often out of action for a couple of months with this unpleasant and debilitating disease, but

Alexander had been back on his feet within a week, such were the demands on his time and the weight of responsibility on his shoulders.

Alexander, or 'Alex' as he was widely known to his peers and superiors, was fifty-two, handsome, with pale-blue eyes, a trim moustache and crow's feet extending from his eyes; he was witty and always quick to find humour wherever it lurked. He also had considerable natural charm, spoke seven languages including German, Italian, French, Russian and Urdu, and had an unrivalled career that had seen him command troops in battle at every single rank, something that no other full general of any combatant nation could boast. He had even commanded German troops when he'd been posted to command the Baltic Landwehr in 1919 against the Russians. During the evacuation of British troops from Dunkirk in 1940 he'd been the last British soldier to leave, had conceived and developed the Battle Schools, a new approach to training, had successfully brought the Burma Corps out of Burma and into India in May 1942, had taken over as the British C-in-C of the Middle East three months later, and swiftly overseen a dramatic turn in fortunes. In February 1943, he'd been appointed Army Group commander in Tunisia and again had turned things round, this time in under a fortnight. Sicily had followed, the island being in Allied hands in just thirty-eight days, and his forces in Italy had achieved three of the four objectives for the invasion in just three weeks of fighting. Cultured, artistic and imperturbable, he was also unusual for one so senior in lacking any kind of personal ambition; rather, he merely strived to do his duty to the very best of his ability. Famously, he was known for never outwardly losing his temper or publicly swearing; calm unflappability was his style. His approach to command was to suggest rather than explicitly order, which fostered a sense of collaboration and allowed subordinates to believe they'd come up with a new idea rather than feeling they'd been ordered by their chief. There was a touch of vanity, perhaps, for he never looked anything other than immaculate and there was a rakishness to the specially made peaked cap he wore, but otherwise no other Allied commander was so widely liked or personable. For a man in his position, that was saying something.

On this Tuesday morning, however, Alexander, was, for once, not quite on peak form, which was hardly surprising considering his recent bout of illness. He was also in the midst of a changeover of his Chief of Staff. Major-General Alec Richardson was leaving him to take command of a division and his replacement, Lieutenant-General John Harding, now accompanying him to see Clark, had had a dizzying few days. Having flown from southern England on 1 January straight to Algiers, via Gibraltar, Harding had then taken a further flight to Naples the following day. No sooner had he arrived in Italy than he'd learned that his new boss had already left to see the PM in Tunis. He had then flown back to North Africa the next day, Monday 3 January, where he'd finally caught up with Alexander, joining him in key discussions about SHINGLE, and then had flown with his chief back to Naples that morning. So he was hardly on top form either.

Clark was not at all happy with the SHINGLE plan. Two days earlier, Alexander had sent a cable from Tunis in which he had warned Clark that because of the ongoing shenanigans over LSTs, there would be a maximum of 91 and a worst case of just 80. All but 6, however, were to be released by 3 February because the rest needed to be on their way to England, Corsica or shipyards by the 5th. This loss of LSTs so soon had come as a complete shock to Clark and he had immediately fired back a warning that it made the venture considerably more hazardous. 'I urgently request', he signalled to Alex, 'that you make every effort to hold adequate number of craft of SHINGLE until such time as success of the operation is assured.'

Now, on this first Tuesday of January, Alexander was here to discuss these concerns face to face. Clark believed in plain speaking, and so on Alexander's arrival with Harding and Richardson – who had not yet left – the Fifth Army commander teed off in no uncertain terms. 'We are supposed to go up there,' he said, 'dump two divisions ashore with what corps troops we can get in, with an inadequate number of craft without resupply or reinforcement, and wait for the rest of the Army to join up.' He was prepared to undertake such an operation and give it the very best chance of success, but stated frankly that it could not be done without the LSTs remaining far longer than currently planned.

Clark also then told Alexander that it was his job, as Army Group commander, to determine the size and scale of the enemy forces they might expect to oppose their landing. He also pointed out that his latest intelligence suggested the 29. Panzergrenadier-Division had just been moved from the Cassino front to a position near Rome; this, however, was not the case, although 90. Panzergrenadier-Division – or rather what was left of it, which wasn't saying much – had been pulled back from the Adriatic. Accepting these concerns, Alexander agreed to make them clear to Churchill and began drafting a cable there and then but, Clark noted in his diary, 'had a difficult time with the facts and figures.' The Fifth Army commander then supplied him with a copy of the cable he had sent him two days earlier, in which he'd pointed out that such insufficient assault shipping meant each of the divisions landed would be doing so with 1,200 vehicles fewer than expected. This, he had written and reiterated again now, would have a hugely detrimental effect on their effectiveness and ability to move inland swiftly. Nor, in the current plan, were there enough smaller assault craft to land any more than five infantry battalions and one US Army Ranger battalion; and that was simply not enough. Clark made it clear that at the very least twenty, not six, LSTs were needed for a minimum of fifteen days and probably longer. There was taking a calculated risk and there was being reckless, and as things stood Clark very strongly believed they were being the latter. As he grumbled later in his diary, those who had 'light-heartedly' decided on the SHINGLE operation had not properly understood the details of what was being demanded. Clark had a point, as the twin demands of assaulting the Gustav Line and mounting another highly hazardous amphibious operation – after Salerno – were falling on his shoulders. Furthermore, he had always been immaculate when it came to planning and staff work and had little patience with those who, in his opinion, fell short of his own high standards.

There was, though, an arrogance to Clark's sense of his own superiority. As an Army Group commander, Alexander's role was to give direction and vision but also to facilitate. At such an elevated position he could not be expected to involve himself with the minutiae, and had a Chief of Staff and further staff officers under him to provide him with such information. Had he not been in the midst of a changeover of his Chief of Staff and still recovering from jaundice, he would undoubtedly have had a firmer grip of those facts and figures. None the less, he had visited Clark to discuss his Fifth Army commander's concerns and to help resolve those, and this was precisely what he now set in motion, cabling Churchill that same afternoon. 'Certain factors have come to light', he wrote, 'which are causing grave concern, and I must therefore ask for your help and assistance.' He could, he told the PM, accept the risks of landing with just two divisions initially, so long as they were landed at full strength. He was also prepared to accept the risks of a possible strong German counter-attack, but clearly he could not countenance his troops getting sealed in at Anzio without support from the sea. Therefore, it was essential, he told the PM, that he should be allowed to keep fourteen LSTs indefinitely and a further ten for fifteen days after the landing to build up the necessary supporting strength in tanks, artillery and supplies. 'Even if this does interfere with preparations for ANVIL to some extent,' Alexander noted, 'surely the prize is worth it.' As he understood, once committed to SHINGLE, the Combined Chiefs, those ultimate arbitrators, would be compelled to support it; perhaps not to the degree he would ideally wish for, but enough to make it worth the risk.

Thirty miles to the north of Clark's camp at Caserta, the battle began again that evening, 4 January. Among those fighting along and south of Highway 6 was a battle group drawn from 1st Armored Division, and known for the battle as Task Force Allen after its commander, Brigadier-General Frank Allen, a mixture of armoured infantry equipped with armoured scout cars and half-tracks as well as two battalions of Sherman tanks and also combat engineers and artillery. The 1st Armored had served throughout the campaign in Tunisia but had not been involved in the fighting in Sicily and had been posted to Italy only in October, because it was only then that enough shipping could be found to transport them from North Africa. This was to be their first action since their arrival.

Supporting the attack was the division's entire artillery, which amounted to three field battalions each of twenty-four guns, but also a battery of the British 70th Field Regiment, part of the Royal Artillery. The British 138th Brigade were on Allen Force's left flank and would be attacking the neighbouring Colle Cedro, but while 70th Field Regiment would be supporting their own infantry, Captain Leonard Garland, normally commanding 449 Battery, had been posted as a liaison officer to Allen Force HQ on 2 January.

Garland was twenty-nine, so a little older than many of his fellows, and missed his wife, Ann, desperately. Like everyone else serving far from home, he lived for the letters and packages he received from her. Recently she'd sent him a pocket diary in which she'd written a brief note in the space for the first day of the year. 'I love you, Darling, for all the years God gives us. God bless you and keep you safe for me.' Garland had begun penning in his neat hand right away, recording his arrival at Allen Force HQ, where he'd been greeted warmly. 'They have seen action before – Kasserine – and are ready to admit mistakes and keen to avoid them,' he noted. 'Hard workers and precise gunners. Extreme politeness of introductions. Much less bad language.'

The following day, 3 January, he was taken by his new colleagues up to the front and through the Mignano Gap, the site of such brutal recent fighting. The sun was shining for once, and the air fresh and crisp; the mountains, he thought, looked quite breathtaking and he hoped that one day he and Ann might see Italy in more peaceful times. At ground level, however, the destruction was immense. They came across a dead body, which gave off a terrible stench, while trees were shattered trunks and houses demolished. Back at Allen Force HQ such unpleasant sights and smells were put to one side; Garland was experiencing American rations for the first time and with them small cultural differences, such as calling milk cream, mixing sweet hotcakes with bacon and adding fruit on to the same plate. Cigarettes were handed out liberally too. 'This sort of job suits me down to the ground,' he noted, 'but it can't last.' Nor did it; he was back with 70th Field Regiment by 5 January.

Brigadier-General Allen's plan was to send two battalions of infantry either side of the highway, each supported by a tank battalion. But ahead of the infantry, to clear the way, were men of Company A of the 16th Armored Engineer Battalion. This meant the 'Catamounts', as the battalion was known, were the spearhead of 1st Armored Division's assault. Among them was Maurice R. P. Bechard, a twenty-two-year-old T5 – a technician fifth grade – from Maine, known to his fellows as 'Frenchy'. Bechard had volunteered back in the summer of 1942 before being drafted out of a sense of duty, and, having spent a stint before that in the Civilian Conservation Corps, part of Roosevelt's New Deal initiatives, building wooden bridges and logging, had been only too happy to be posted to the engineers. Now, though, Bechard was quickly realizing that his was one of the more hazardous jobs in the army. Ahead of the attack, he and his fellows in Company A had moved a dump of equipment into no-man's-land under the cover of darkness. This included thirteen trucks of ammunition, explosives, barbed wire and mines and had been hidden behind a two-storey farmhouse. Just getting there had been unnerving as a 6th Infantry patrol had pushed on ahead of them and quickly run into a firefight with German mortars exploding just 200 yards ahead. The truck drivers had pitched in to help the Company A men unload but were jittery and all of them were only too anxious to get the hell out of there just as soon as possible.

Unloading complete, they scuttled back, but putting an ammunition dump of this size forward of the anticipated advance of Allen Force had not been the best idea, and sure enough, the following day enemy shelling scored a bullseye. 'Nothing left there but a huge hole,' noted Bechard in his diary. 'Barbed wire was everywhere.' One of the engineers had been forward to check on the dump when it blew – fortunately not close enough to get himself killed, but the blast had blown him back the best part of 100 feet. 'He was shaken up pretty bad,' added Bechard.

In the early hours of the next morning, 5 January, the Company A men were parcelled out among the leading infantry companies to clear mines, Bechard among them, supporting an attack on Monte Porchia, an 800-foot-high slug of a hill jutting from the valley floor. The infantry struggled, however. It was pouring with rain, enemy artillery, mortars and machine-gun fire pinned them down and they soon pulled back as the enemy counter-attacked, leaving scores of casualties out in the open and well short of the planned phase lines they were due to have reached. Bechard and the rest of 3rd Platoon took shelter in a dilapidated and roofless house where, with raincoats over their heads, they tucked into a round of peanut butter and jelly sandwiches that someone, somehow, had brought up from the chow truck before the attack.

By late morning the rain had stopped and a runner was needed to keep in contact with 6th Infantry, so Sergeant Mitchell Chafin 'volunteered' Frenchy Bechard. 'Sometimes,' noted Bechard, writing about himself in his diary in the third person, 'it felt like he was fighting the whole fucking war all by himself. Picks up his rifle, heads towards the line, swearing and burping peanut butter and jelly.'

While Allen Force were attacking Monte Porchia, the 135th Infantry of the 34th Red Bulls were advancing on San Vittore and towards Monte Chiaia, another block of low mountain jutting up from the valley. Sergeant Ralph Schaps and his Company H were supporting the assault on Chiaia in what was already an apocalyptic landscape: trees blasted, swirling smoke amid the rain, shell-holes and, away to the left, the shattered remains of San Vittore, a town that barely had a single building left undamaged. Schaps saw streams of German prisoners being marched back, but throughout 5 January fighting could be heard from the town. The amount of small arms being fired and the dull explosion of hand grenades told him this was a horribly close-quarter battle.

This stretch of the front was still being held by 134. Infanterie-Regiment, of which Georg Zellner's 3. Bataillon was holding San Vittore. From his command post in Cervaro, Zellner was, throughout 5 January, becoming increasingly desperate about the fate of his three companies in and around the town. All telephone and radio communications had been severed although runners from 10. Kompanie reported that the town had been penetrated and that they were involved in hand-to-hand fighting. Of 9. Kompanie there was no news. Then, Gefreiter Sitterling, a

9. Kompanie runner, suddenly appeared. They were being attacked from two sides in San Vittore, he reported. Clearly, the situation was desperate and they needed to pull back as soon as possible. With a heavy heart, Zellner ordered him to head back and give these orders to the remnants of 9. Kompanie. Zellner had a soft spot for Sitterling; the lad was just seventeen years old, blond, fresh-faced but always friendly, willing and helpful. Now, with a smile, he dashed off again. News arrived soon after that 11. Kompanie was also now fighting and had repelled one attack. Hours passed. Fighting could still be heard but there was nothing more from 9. Kompanie and Zellner began to fear the worst. 'I deploy another scouting party,' noted Zellner. 'I can't dislodge the 9th because there are no forces available. Regiment has nothing either. Night falls, still fighting in S. Vittore. Scouting party comes back. Penetration impossible.' And further depressing news: Sitterling had been found dead at the edge of the town. Dejected, Zellner and his men sat around a small fire wondering what was to follow.

He hoped the remaining men of 9. Kompanie might fight their way through, but not one man appeared. 'I can't get the 9th out of my head,' Zellner wrote on Friday, 7 January. 'The good Lt. Wünsch, the soul of a Viennese soldier, is also reported to be gone. I can't believe it.' He asked every soldier, every runner that appeared, whether they had any news of the company, but no one had. It was as though they had vanished entirely, swallowed by the hell of battle.

Meanwhile, a little way to the south, the American 6th Infantry had captured Monte Porchia on the 6th. Frenchy Bechard had followed to help clear mines. The entire area was littered with Schü-mines – simple, easily hidden and vicious anti-personnel devices designed to blow off a man's foot rather than kill him outright. The idea was that two further men would be needed to get the footless victim back to get help. Bechard was horrified by the number of dead GIs littering the slopes. Stumbling over three men killed by shell blast, he saw the skin on their faces had been burnt and rolled back with no eyelids or hair. 'Awful sight to see,' he noted. He then came across a dead German whose head had been crushed within his helmet. Bechard was so repulsed he almost passed out. Another American sergeant had been completely cut in half, sliced in two by shrapnel. Bechard then saw a 6th Infantry corporal hit by a bullet. As the man went down, clutching his guts, he shouted, 'Son of a bitch,' only to fall on his knees and trigger a Schü-mine, which finished him off. 'Scenes like these,' noted Bechard, 'one never forgets.'

Weight of fire was gradually winning the battle for the Americans, however. On 7 January, Monte Chiaia was captured and San Vittore cleared. By this time, Georg Zellner had learned that his 9. Kompanie had been destroyed, the 11th almost wiped out and his 10. Kompanie in full retreat. On the afternoon of the 7th, the enemy were so close he ordered his battalion HQ staff to destroy all their papers and get ready to fight themselves. By evening, however, men from the Fallschirm-Panzer-Division 'Hermann Göring' – HG – had helped them to hold their line with a pointless and utterly bloody counter-attack. 'Nothing is achieved,' noted Zellner. 'Another bloody day is over.'

The New Year was just a week old.

CHAPTER 3

The Tragedy Waiting to Happen

EVER SINCE FIFTH ARMY had drawn up against the Bernhard Line at the beginning of November, the troops had started to get glimpses of an extraordinary building in the distance, perched high at the end of a lengthy mountain spur. From a number of miles away it appeared to be long, low and white, sometimes even sparklingly so on the rare occasions when the sun shone. Even in a storm it stood out, a bright beacon against the dark mass of the mountain and the swirling, thunderous sky above. Now, as the Allies drew closer, it appeared like an all-seeing eye, looking down upon them, watching their every move. To the Germans too, arriving at the front for the first time, there it was, so defiantly perched, dominating the landscape for miles around. From up there, every move in the valleys below could be seen. Every truck, every tank. Every jeep.

This strange and decidedly modern-looking edifice, improbably built some 1,700 feet above sea level, was among the holiest and most venerated Christian sites in Europe. The Abbey of Monte Cassino dated back to 529 AD, founded by Benedict of Nursia, and although it had been repeatedly sacked and rebuilt over the ensuing centuries its current form had been mostly constructed in the sixteenth century. It was huge, with immense bastion walls but with galleries, courtyards and colonnades of exquisite beauty, while the abbey church itself was a celebration of the baroque: huge columns with inlaid marble, lavish gold leaf, lush frescoes. A dazzling homage to the opulence of an earlier era and to the glory of God.

Despite the garishness of the basilica, the lives of the Benedictine monks who inhabited the abbey were far more restrained. Theirs was a quiet, ascetic existence, one dedicated to prayer, learning, contemplation and work, both within and without, for the abbey was also a working farm with livestock, vineyards, beehives and olive groves. Until the previous October they had led a very self-contained life, spiritually and intellectually rich, but also one largely immune to the outside, modern world.

Then the Germans had arrived and thrown their ordered, isolated existence into disarray. Suddenly, the monks were told they were now on the front line, the massif on which the abbey perched being part of a defensive line that was to be built from one side of Italy to the other. And because the end of the Monte Cassino massif overlooked the main road to Rome, this made the outcrop on which the abbey was perched, with its unrivalled views, the single most important feature of the entire defensive position the Germans had called the Gustav Line. The Most Reverend Father Abbot, Gregorio Diamare, was seventy-eight and for all his piety and scholarship had discovered he was tragically ill-prepared to deal with the calamity now befalling them. Ingratiating German art scholars, in SS uniform, encouraged him to hand over all of the abbey's considerable treasures for safe-keeping. Father Gregorio had agonized over whether he could trust the Germans, in the end offering a number of works of art and manuscripts into their hands but secretly burying and hiding a fair proportion of the abbey's riches too. A number of civilians had been sheltering at the abbey once the Allies had started to regularly bomb Cassino town; but periodically the Germans would show up and insist that these desperate people would have to leave. The upheavals had often brought the ageing Father Abbot to tears; nothing in his life had prepared him for the fate now befalling his flock and which threatened the abbey itself. He felt so ill-equipped to know what to do for the best, but it was all too horribly clear that the front was inching its way closer and that the defensive line built by the Germans, which ran over their normally isolated mountain home, was about to face the storm of war. 'May God forgive our failings,' noted Dom Eusebio Grossetto on the last day of 1943, 'and reward us for these days of great and meritorious trial.'

Dom Eusebio was thirty-three years old, both a monk and priest at the abbey and one of the Father Abbot's closest companions and advisers. He had been faithfully keeping a diary ever since the Germans had first arrived in October, recognizing that these were both extraordinary and disturbing times for the abbey and its small community. Now, as the New Year dawned, praying might offer some solace but there was little doubt the battle was getting closer; artillery fire had continued through much of the night on 4 January and increased the following day when at least twenty-five shells had screamed over Monte Cassino. That same day, the regular German interpreter had arrived to see the Father Abbot and told him that the army command no longer recognized the 300-metre exclusion zone around the abbey and that all civilians, without exception, were to be evacuated immediately. The Father Abbot and the monks were also advised to leave for Rome without delay, and the interpreter further announced that all the abbey's animals were to be compulsorily purchased. Later that morning three trucks arrived, and by one o'clock had rounded up the abbey's staff and sheltering civilians and driven them away. Only the invalids being tended by the monks and members of their dependent families, now gathered in the lower infirmary, remained. Even that had caused heated arguments with the Germans, who only conceded when the Father Abbot pointed out the impossibility of transporting them in their condition. The Germans vowed to return with an ambulance. 'It is impossible', noted Dom Eusebio, 'to describe what a terrible day this was for our little community . . . accompanied the whole time by an intense artillery barrage which continued until midday.'

The following day the Father Abbot told the Germans that he and his monks would not leave the abbey nor sell them their animals, protesting against what had taken place and the Germans' change of attitude; after all, they had reiterated their promise to uphold an exclusion zone only a few weeks earlier on 12 December. Despite the Father Abbot's protestations, some of the sick were taken away that day. 'All were weeping,' noted Dom Eusebio. Those who remained were critically ill. Eventually, on 7 January, the three families still in the infirmary were given belated permission to remain, but that same day more trucks arrived to take away most of the animals regardless: fourteen cows, thirty-five sheep, ten lambs and their donkeys, for which they were paid less than the value of two cows. A further eighty-eight sheep were taken away two days later, on 9 January; all that remained were a small handful of chickens, goats, pigs and a couple of donkeys, all of which were brought into the abbey itself since their fields had now been occupied by troops. 'It is a real Noah's Ark,' wrote Dom Eusebio. Two Feldgendarms were posted to guard them, and by Monday, 10 January German troops had completely surrounded the abbey and occupied a cave directly beneath the bastions.

The monks felt like prisoners. That same day, one of their sick, a thirteen-year-old girl called Lucia Verrechia, died; she was the daughter of their cook. Dom Eusebio had to prepare the casket himself; he had now become the abbey's undertaker. 'We are still very fearful for our immediate future,' noted Dom Eusebio, 'and can see no ray of hope at present.'

Down below, the battle to draw up to the Gustav Line was all but over. The Special Service Force had secured Monte Maio and the twin towns of San Vittore and Cervaro – now utterly wrecked – and the surrounding hills were also in US hands. South of Monte Porchio the British had also cleared Colle Cedro, where after his brief secondment to Task Force Allen Captain Leonard Garland had been operating as a forward observation officer – a FOO – a particularly hazardous occupation as it meant being very close to the front and the one person, above any other on the battlefield, that the enemy wanted to obliterate. Being a FOO was not for the faint-hearted. By 10 January, the only feature still in German hands to the south of the Rivers Rapido and Garigliano was Monte Trocchio. To get this far had been another costly battle, though; Allen Force alone had lost 66 men dead and 379 wounded and several hundred missing. To make matters worse, there had been a further 516 non-battle casualties, mostly trench foot and exposure cases. Leonard Garland had lost a couple of friends in the fighting too. 'Howard Maughan killed,' he noted on 4 January, 'wife is expecting.' Three days later he added, 'Tony Gray killed outright.' The battle had not even been the main event – merely a preliminary operation before the assault on the Gustav Line. Frenchy Bechard was utterly exhausted after nearly a week of mine-clearing and fighting. 'Cleared a lot of trails for mines and booby traps,' he scribbled on 8 January, 'many times under shells and mortar fire.' When they eventually got back to their bivouac area the Red Cross truck was waiting for them with coffee and donuts, but many of the men were so tired they passed out in their tents without bothering to eat. The next day he was defusing yet more booby traps, many of which had been attached to the bodies of dead GIs waiting to be buried. What a terrible time it was to be in this part of Italy.

And even more awful if one was German infantry. Georg Zellner's battalion had been decimated in these first days of January. The remnants were now holding what was called the Cervaro Line, or the Gustav Outpost Line, which ran through the shattered town and along the foot of the mountains opposite Monte Cassino. It was an even more hopeless position than that around San Vittore because the Americans could now look down on them more clearly. The line ran southwards along Monte Trocchio, which was an admittedly significant feature that blocked the advance to Cassino town, but the Germans had not a hope of holding it, and whatever gains there were to be had from denying it to the Americans for a few days longer were going to be more than offset by the losses they would suffer in defending it. The Gustav Line was waiting behind them, three months in the preparation, an incredibly strong position and one that was no longer going to be significantly improved by a week's further tinkering.

In the evening of 8 January, Zellner received seventy replacements, which equated to two platoons, or half a company. 'Young lads,' he noted, 'no combat experience. All right, they'll be split up. The Regiment calls as usual. The line must be held to the last drop of blood. My answer is yes, we can't let ourselves be beaten to death.' Later that evening they sat by the fire, the guns booming, and tried to work out when the Americans would be at the door. Probably the following day, they reckoned. 'The food carriers arrive,' he added, 'there's mail and then another day is over.' The next day two new lieutenants arrived, both thirty-eight years old and with no experience of combat at all. At the start of the war it had taken well over a year to become an officer, and cadets – Fahnenjunker – had to serve as non-commissioned officers first and prove their leadership skills and battlefield courage. This might be for three-quarters of a year and was then followed by an intense eight-week stint at Kriegsschule and then a more specialized Truppenschule. Those days had long gone. The new men who presented themselves to Georg Zellner were both lawyers and utterly shocked by what they were discovering at the front; it was not how they'd imagined war to be at all. How much use they would be was questionable; Zellner sighed wearily and posted them to his stripped-out companies. More useful was a company from the HG-Division, which was placed under Zellner's command. Such a move was a terrible way to manage troops, however, and spoke of the dire straits the 134. Regiment found itself in, because splitting up units from other divisions risked damaging unit cohesion and further affecting morale. Firefighting with penny packets – a company here, a battalion there – was an appallingly inefficient way to fight. It was a totally unsustainable way to manage front-line troops.

One of the new arrivals, however, did instantly prove something of a fillip. Gefreiter Hebeler had been assigned to Zellner's command post and in no time was regaling them with stories of his complicated love life. Although married, his wife had a child with another man, while he also had a baby with a different girl. Not to be outdone, his sister, also married, had a child by a man who was not her husband, while Hebeler's father had six children out of wedlock. 'Despite his coarseness,' jotted Zellner, 'he is a blessing for us. He has an uncomplicated view of life. Without inhibitions, he constantly tells us about his love stories, which makes us laugh.' They all needed that.

The brief interlude in the fighting soon came to an end, however, with a renewed American attack on 12 January. The new boys, both the officers and the replacements in the ranks, were flung into the battle with predictable results. Hill 190 was lost, then so too 186, but in time-honoured fashion the 3. Bataillon men were expected to counter-attack, which they did, despite Zellner reporting to Regiment the increasingly desperate situation. Their own artillery opened up but fell short, almost on top of them. An American prisoner was brought in who complained about the war, cursing those at the top who wanted to continue fighting. 'So the madness continues,' noted Zellner. By last light on 13 January he feared they were surrounded, but at 2 a.m. on the 14th, orders came through to pull back across the upper Rapido Valley to Cassino. That was not going to be easy as American artillery had every crossing point zeroed. At 3 a.m. Zellner led the battalion staff out to begin the two-mile journey. 'First, I take a deep breath, think about my family, and then we set off,' he wrote. 'It's going to be a gauntlet. Panting, we reach the hairpin bend.' A shell screamed over, and Zellner took a dive as the missile whammed all too close by. Grit, stones, smoke, Zellner and his men gasping and cursing, then laughing at their commander's goal-keeping dive – back in the day, in happier times before the war, Zellner had been the keeper for Regensburg. They rushed on. Up ahead was the bridge, a terrible pinch point, but they all managed to sprint across, only for Zellner to trip over some telephone wire and fall headlong into a ditch. More shells screeched in; one man was badly wounded, but an ambulance sped towards them, scooped up the injured man and hurtled off again. Otherwise, no one was about as they approached the town; Zellner worried he'd misunderstood the order and they'd have to go back. Pioniere were laying mines. A vehicle appeared – yes, they were in the right place after all, and would now be heading back to Castrocielo, some miles to the rear. Relief. As they sped through the town in the moonlight, Zellner spotted creepy figures pressed against the walls. 'They are the ones occupying the position. Poor people,' he noted, then added, 'What do you mean, poor people? Tomorrow or the day after tomorrow it will be our turn again.'

CHAPTER 4

Meddling Madness

COMMANDING ALL GERMAN TROOPS in Italy was Generalfeldmarschall Albert Kesselring, fifty-seven years old, a born optimist, Hitler loyalist and a man of wide experience, not least of fighting against the British and Americans. Quick to smile, outwardly genial and lacking the stiffness of many of the old Prussian military aristocracy that still held sway within the Wehrmacht, he was nicknamed 'Smiling Albert'. Kesselring was the son of a schoolteacher from Bavaria and had risen extraordinarily high for someone of his background, but had reached field marshal in the Luftwaffe rather than the army; despite having originally been with the artillery during the First World War, he had joined the Luftwaffe at its inception in 1935 having been Reich Commissariat for Aviation before that. He'd even briefly been Chief of Staff of the Luftwaffe before commanding an air fleet during the Polish campaign and throughout the summer of 1940. Since then, he'd commanded on the Eastern Front before being posted to the Mediterranean at the end of 1941. He'd been in this theatre ever since, first as Oberbefehlshaber Süd, commander of German forces in the south and then, following the loss of Sicily, as commander-in-chief of Heeresgruppe Südwest– Army Group South-West.

It was largely because of Kesselring that German troops were still fighting – and being slaughtered – in this corner of Italy, seventy-odd miles south of Rome. Hitler had originally planned that Feldmarschall Erwin Rommel, Kesselring's immediate subordinate for much of the North African campaign, should command German forces in Italy, and on Rommel's advice had planned to withdraw all his troops well to the north of Rome, along the Pisa–Rimini Line, where the mountains ran uninterrupted from coast to coast. Rommel argued that, providing defences were well prepared, this would be the best place to defend indefinitely without the Italian peninsula sucking up an ever-increasing number of troops they could ill afford to divert from other theatres. Having experienced growing Allied air power at first hand in North Africa, he also thought supplying the front at this position across the leg of Italy would be considerably simpler because lines of supply and communication would be that much shorter.

Rommel's thinking was pretty sound, although with the Allies' devotion to strategic air power, the flat terrain around Foggia was an obvious area the Germans would do well to safeguard. Over the summer of 1943, however, when the German high command was actively planning for such time when the Italians inevitably made peace with the Allies, the importance of Foggia was not given much, if any, consideration. At any rate, Hitler had been planning to withdraw his troops north of Rome, just as Rommel had suggested, on 9 September 1943 – the very same day Mark Clark's Fifth Army landed in the Bay of Salerno. This meant the invasion fell on Kesselring's turf, because as commander of German forces in the south he had eight divisions around Rome and to the south at that time. Rather than hurriedly pulling back, however, he had kept one lightly armed division to guard Rome and directed the rest to head quickly for Salerno. Only 1. Fallschirmjäger-Division had been left to cover the entire south-east of Italy, although Hitler had personally intervened and insisted that a part of this division also be sent to stiffen the backbones of several others then heading to Salerno. Of all the various formations in Italy, 1. Fallschirmjäger were the least appropriate to defend such a large area on their own and at half-strength; despite being all German and all volunteers, and despite considering themselves a cut above other units, they were, as airborne troops, lightly armed and lacking heavy weapons. Light rearguard actions, demolitions and liberal mine-laying was the limit of what they could expect to achieve. This would not hold up stronger enemy forces for long should push come to shove.

Kesselring had hoped it would not come to this. Rather, his plan had been to throw the Allies back into the sea at Salerno, then turn south and systematically clear the British from the boot of the peninsula. Yet by throwing all his eggs into one basket at Salerno – and failing to defeat the attackers – he had left the back door open. The British were able to land troops straight into the southern ports of Taranto, then Brindisi and Bari without any need for the all-precious landing craft. Foggia had fallen in a trice, so handing the Allies one of their prime objectives for the campaign and Kesselring thus losing any chance of clearing the southern part of Italy in the future.

Bizarrely, despite this failure and hopeless misjudgement, Hitler had been rather impressed, which spoke loudly about the Führer's woeful shortcomings as a military commander. At any rate, Hitler now decided not to retreat to the Pisa–Rimini Line as had been planned but ordered Kesselring to fight for every metre south of Rome instead. That they had abandoned the all-important Foggia airfield complex and lost arguably the single most important strategic area of all of Italy still did not appear to cross either Hitler's mind or those of the OKW – the Oberkommando der Wehrmacht, the German General Staff – or indeed Kesselring. This made little sense, because Hitler had always been obsessed with the Southern Front and particularly anxious not to jeopardize the oilfields of Ploeşti in Romania, the only source of real, rather than synthetic, fuel Nazi Germany could call upon. Protecting this was one of the prime reasons he had invaded Crete back in May 1941, had insisted on resupplying Tunisia so heavily and fought in Sicily. To hand over one of the prime goals for the Allies so limply was astonishingly careless and short-sighted. Ploeşti was now a closer target for the Allied heavy bombers than it had been, and for handing this gift to their enemies and failing to kick Fifth Army back into the sea Kesselring was rewarded with command of all of Italy and Rommel packed off to take charge of the Atlantic Wall instead.

By January 1944, Kesselring had two armies under his command, AOK – Armeeoberkommando – 10, now moving back behind the Gustav Line and commanded by Generaloberst Heinrich von Vietinghoff, and AOK 14, reactivated only in November with Generaloberst Eberhard von Mackensen as commander-in-chief. Kesselring's arsenal of divisions was, in these first weeks of January, in something of a state of flux, with 29. and 90. Panzergrenadier and also the HG-Division due to be pulled into reserve for refitting. More, though, were on their way to Italy, including 114. Jäger-Division and also 16. SS Panzergrenadier-Division, only recently formed and stationed in Hungary, but promised to Kesselring for Italy. On paper this gave him twenty-three divisions to the Allies' eighteen, but he didn't feel he could send them all to the southern front. There were worries about the security of the vital Brenner Pass route through the Alps from Austria, but also deep paranoia that the Allies would launch a series of amphibious outflanking operations. The coast around Rome and further north, near the naval port of La Spezia, seemed to Kesselring and his staff the most likely areas and so two divisions were kept on standby near the capital and three in the north, between Livorno and Genoa. La Spezia was more than 300 miles north of the current front line, yet since the Allies had occupied Corsica the previous September it was, theoretically, within range of Allied fighter cover. Having experienced the vast armada the Allies had used for Sicily, especially, Kesselring convinced himself his enemy had an abundance of shipping they could draw upon should they choose to use it. He was not really wrong about this; it was just that the Allies had chosen not to use such riches in Italy. The global nature of the war meant they had to prioritize.

Kesselring's caution kept AOK 14 and its eight divisions north of Rome, but that still left fifteen for AOK 10 along the southern front. And seven of those were in XIV Panzerkorps' area, guarding the Liri Valley, which gave it the strength of an army all on its own; the British Eighth Army at this time, for example, had just six divisions, of which two had not even reached the front. Numbers of divisions, however, could be deceptive and both von Vietinghoff at AOK 10 and Generalleutnant Fridolin von Senger und Etterlin, commander of XIV Panzerkorps, now had a number of badly understrength divisions with which to defend the Gustav Line. That they faced a manpower shortage was in part due to their own – and Kesselring's – mismanagement of their front-line forces and also because of meddling by the Führer.

Kesselring's decision to fight aggressively at Salerno rather than pull back north of Rome might have led to him besting Rommel and winning command of all of Italy, but it also ensured that the Hitlerian spotlight had been glaringly turned upon him and his forces now battling south of Rome. Hitler frequently changed his mind but also often took unwanted, and detailed, interest in particular battlefronts and Italy had certainly fallen under his capricious eye – even more so since December, when his forces had been fighting Fifth Army just to the south of Cassino on the Bernhard Line and Eighth Army on the Adriatic at Ortona and Orsogna. The overall message coming from Hitler was invariably the same: fight – and die – for every metre. No one was allowed to pull back without his say-so. He even sent General Alfred Jodl, Chief of the Operations Staff at the OKW, to Italy to discuss with Kesselring the Führer's plans for further defences in Italy. It had been von Senger who had first suggested building a secondary line from Monte Cassino to Piedimonte, a little to the north-west of Cassino and out into the Liri Valley, but, as discussed by Jodl and Kesselring on 4 January, this was now to be further developed and called the 'Hitler Line'. Another secondary position, the River Foro Line, was also to be constructed to cover Pescara on the Adriatic coast. Two days later, with Jodl having now flown back, Kesselring ordered unwavering defence. This command was issued at the very moment Fifth Army was hammering the Germans around San Vittore and Monte Maio. It was why Georg Zellner had ended up pointlessly losing most of his battalion.

So Hitler issued his instructions never to give ground and Kesselring endorsed them, which meant that corps and divisional commanders then had to ask permission to withdraw rather than making up their own minds based on the situation as they saw it. This extended further down the line. Zellner was telling his regimental commander that his forward companies were being destroyed, but the commander of 134. Regiment no longer had the authority to act on a battalion commander's advice. Rather, a regimental commander had to refer it up the chain to division, division to corps, corps to army, and army to Kesselring. Kesselring then had to put in a call to the OKW. The German Army of the Blitzkrieg years had never been stymied like this; commanders were told to think on their feet, make quick decisions and were sufficiently trained and experienced to be trusted to make those decisions. As in any army, men who did well were promoted, men caught short were fired. Those days, however, were long over. 'The superiors have no freedom,' noted Zellner wearily. 'Everything has to be approved by the Führer.'

On Tuesday, 11 January, Oberstarzt Wilhelm Mauss walked in on a heated telephone conversation between von Vietinghoff, General Fries – the neighbouring LXXVI Panzerkorps commander – and von Senger over the latest front-line dispositions. Von Senger wanted to pull back behind the Gustav Line but von Vietinghoff would not – or could not – authorize such a move. Mauss understood that the situation always looked very different from the rear – and especially from Hitler's Wolf's Lair headquarters in East Prussia – than it did at the front. It was not the first tug of war over front lines that he'd witnessed. 'The higher commanders especially', he wrote, 'live in fear of the Führer.' All events at the Italian front fell under Hitler's eyes and he demanded to be informed about every detail and would then repeatedly intervene. 'So every little adjustment to the front', Mauss added, 'needs exhaustive negotiation and reasoning.' It was absolutely no way to fight a battle, let alone a war.

The consequence of this meddling from the very top – and Kesselring's zealous determination to follow the Führer's instructions – was the cruel and militarily reckless wastage of front-line units. A rule of thumb was that 20–30 per cent of casualties in a single unit – whether platoon, company, battalion or regiment – would be the point at which it was pulled back and replaced by fresh troops. This was sensible military practice as it ensured a strong cadre of experienced troops – troops used to operating with one another and who could then maintain unit cohesion. It wasn't just about morale, but also about understanding and trust; it was human nature that men who knew one another, and understood each other, would operate as a better team than a bunch of strangers cobbled together. Yet German front-line units were regularly expected to keep fighting with 80 per cent losses and more. It was madness, and the only way to keep units functioning was by plugging gaps, firefighting and taking from Peter to feed Paul. It was why a regiment from 44. Infanterie-Division had been attached to 29. Panzergrenadier-Division, and why a company of the HG-Division had, in turn, been attached to Georg Zellner's 3. Bataillon of 134. Regiment.

And what could possibly be achieved by fighting in the hinterland between the Bernhard and Gustav Lines? Without the natural and prepared defences of a well-sited position such as was now ready just a couple of miles behind, the German infantry manning this nothing-terrain could expect only one outcome: slaughter. Allied superiority in artillery, especially with forward observers on the recently captured high ground behind them, and the weight of firepower that gave them, was always going to win the day, and especially when, on clear days – and there had been a few this past week – the Allies could then also bring their overwhelming air superiority to bear. Just a couple of months earlier, 29. Panzergrenadier-Division in the centre and 15. Panzergrenadier to the north had both been better than average formations, well equipped and with a strong spine of experienced troops. Now they had become decimated and the losses suffered in this first week or so of January 1944 were especially pointless. Their misguided sacrifice had achieved nothing.

Not everyone was having such a terrible time, however, for there were sections of the front stretching across the peninsula where there was little or no fighting. General Alexander had realized during the brutal battles of December, when both Eighth Army on the Adriatic and Fifth Army on the Tyrrhenian coasts had been fighting simultaneously, that the best chances of the Allies reaching Rome lay with focusing efforts solely on Fifth Army's front. Alex usually favoured a two-fisted approach to battle, attacking with a first punch to draw off as many enemy troops as possible, then striking hard with a second thrust elsewhere. In Italy, in winter, on the other hand, and with a chance to break into the Liri Valley offering, he felt, the best chances of success – especially with SHINGLE in the offing – he decided to regroup his forces, moving divisions from Eighth Army to Fifth, and, in agreement with General Leese, placing Eighth Army on the defensive. New units were also arriving which would be given to Leese. The 4th Indian Division, for example, had now reached Italy, hugely experienced and trained in mountain warfare, which made its comparatively late arrival from North Africa a bit puzzling. A quick glance at Italy's terrain should have put it first on the team sheet for the initial invasion. Also soon to arrive would be the Polish II Corps, which was completing training in Palestine and was due to be shipped to Italy in February. A second Canadian division, the 5th Armoured, was also now on the scene. Alexander's concerns about a potential reversal, with a strong counter-attack from the Germans, was looking less likely with every passing week. The upshot for those in Eighth Army was a comparatively easier time of things, for the time being at any rate. There would be no repeat of the terrible battles of November and December in the immediate future.

This was good news for the men of the Canadian 1st Infantry Division, who'd fought a protracted and particularly brutal battle to win the small coastal town of Ortona throughout much of December. Major Roy Durnford, padre to the Seaforth Highlanders of Canada, was still busy with the after-effects of this battle and had spent the first few days of 1944 visiting the wounded, writing endless letters of condolences and holding several services of both thanksgiving and commemoration. Nor were they entirely out of the fire because, while the battle was over, the enemy were still slinging over shells. 'Shelled all night long,' he noted in his diary on 3 January. 'My house faces the enemy worse luck. Shrapnel hit walls.' A few days later, on 7 January, they found a Christmas tree in the wreckage of the town left by the Germans. 'Sorry we can't stay to put mistletoe on,' one of the retreating Fallschirmjäger had written on a board beside it, 'but we'll make it hot for you in the hills.' This had made Durnford think back a couple of weeks to the Christmas they'd spent in the town; he'd delivered one service after another to each of the Seaforths' companies.

And he remembered the Italian woman he had seen who'd had her arm shot off as she'd been carrying her baby. She went mad. They'd gone a little deranged in Ortona, if truth be told.

Durnford was actually an Englishman by birth – he'd grown up in Somerset in the West Country – but had emigrated to Vancouver in British Columbia and become a priest, volunteering for the Canadian Army Chaplain Service early in the war. Although now forty, he was coping with the conditions all right, but what he'd witnessed so far had wrenched his heart over and over although never challenging his faith. His was important work: to lead church services but also to provide pastoral care, solace, a shoulder to cry on, and be a link between the men and home. The numbers of letters he'd written already were legion.

And it was also his task to bury the dead so that the men did not have to. Much of that first and second week of January was spent tramping the battlefield looking for the missing, locating hastily dug graves so they could be transferred to the new cemetery at the southern edge of the town. Padres like Durnford were worth their weight in gold to the men at the front.

A little further inland to the west, the snow had melted on the ridge that ran between the villages of Sant'Apollinare and San Martino to the south of Ortona. At 8th Indian Division HQ, Harry Wilson and his friend Ken had discovered some caves overlooking the valley ahead of them just below the HQ farmstead, and quickly bagged them for ciphers. They were warmer than any half-destroyed stone shed or foxhole, were dry and, most importantly of all, appeared bombproof, which was just as well as sporadic shelling was still hurtling over and causing plenty of casualties. On 3 January, thirty-two Indian troops had been killed when a salvo of Nebelwerfer rockets screamed in. A sudden salvo had then whooshed into Division HQ in the early hours of the 7th, wrecking the officers' mess, blowing up telephone lines and splattering a number of vehicles with shrapnel. What amazed Wilson was how this intermittent artillery fire seemed to barely register with the local Italians. There were a handful of farms around them on the ridge and the men would continue working in the fields, the women in their homes and the children romping around apparently as carefree as ever. On 9 January, some enemy Focke-Wulfs thundered over and dropped single bombs, and while Wilson ran for his slit trench several local children hid behind a hayrick, which they mistakenly considered ideal cover. None of them had the sense to get down on the ground. One of the girls glanced across at Wilson and, putting her hands together in prayer, mouthed, 'Me af-reed.'

'So am I,' Wilson called back.

Still holding the German front line, around eight miles to the north-west, were 3. Fallschirmjäger-Regiment and other various units from 1. Fallschirmjäger-Division, among them the Pionier-Battalion. Unteroffizier Jupp Klein, one of the platoon commanders in 2. Kompanie, had been posted from the centre of the line in the mountains near Castel di Sangro to the Ortona–Chieti front at the end of December and he and his men were now on the Foro Line beneath the ridge-top village of Tollo. In the side of the hill, overlooking the valley that snaked its way to the coast in front of them, the villagers had dug a number of shelters into the soft sandstone, which had since been enlarged by the Germans into three- or four-man bunkers. One night, soon after taking over these positions, Klein had been startled by a sudden thud. He had first wondered whether it had been a dud Canadian shell but, hurrying out to investigate, realized it had been the sound of one of the shelters collapsing. Frantically, he and his comrades tried to dig the three men free, but by the time they'd cleared the stone, soil and sand they had already suffocated. Klein could hardly believe it; he'd served long years with these men. Each had fought on the Eastern Front, in Crete, in Sicily and here in Italy. To be killed by an accident such as this seemed especially cruel.

A few days later they were posted again, this time to Ripa, near Chieti, where they managed to find a winery in which to base themselves and with far safer cellar vaults, and that was something. Strengthening of the Foro Line, as per Hitler's direct instructions, was their prime role and this meant laying ever more mines. Klein soon found himself acting company commander as no sooner had they settled in at Ripa than Leutnant Kabinger, the company commander, was struck down with malaria. Klein was an old hand, though, and as about experienced at laying mines as anyone in the Wehrmacht, so he and his men got on with the job, working long days but knowing they had safe quarters, and plenty of wine to drink, each night.

After a few days, however, Kabinger's replacement arrived. Oberleutnant – First Lieutenant – Römberg was supposedly very experienced yet immediately insisted that Klein's layout of the minefields would have to be changed.

'Nothing can be changed,' Klein retorted; he'd had his orders as to where they were to be placed.

'I don't mean the location of the minefields,' Römberg replied. 'They have been predetermined, but my orders are to change the spacing of the mines to 2.5 metres.'

Klein was flabbergasted. He explained that this was strictly forbidden because a closer pattern risked ignition transmission. Römberg, however, insisted such instructions only applied to Italian box mines and argued that Allied tanks could easily create a clear lane if mines were spaced 5 metres apart. Klein was appalled, and after telling him that he would not take responsibility for the consequences was relieved of his platoon and given the job of marking up the mines on a map instead. Unteroffizier Johannsen of 2. Platoon took over overseeing the laying of the minefields, now at Römberg's prescribed distance of just 2.5 metres.

A couple of days later, Klein and his squad were busy marking up the minefields when there was a sudden and huge detonation nearby, the force blasting him over. Quickly getting back on to his feet, he was at first blinded, but his vision then quickly returned as a hazy cloud swirled from the ground around him. Then he heard one of his men shout to him. He answered back and began moving towards him when suddenly a body landed beside him, completely naked. It was one of Johannsen's men, blown sky-high by the blast and thudding, dead, back on to the ground. The black cloud of smoke was rising around them and again he heard someone calling his name. He recognized it as Unteroffizier Pape. 'Here!' Klein replied, hurrying over through torn and now desolate ground. As he reached his friend Pape called out, 'Jupp, shoot me dead!'

Then Klein saw him and was horrified. Both of Pape's arms and legs had been almost entirely ripped off, linked only by threads of sinew, each limb a bloody pulp. The rest of his body was covered in splinters and trembling with shock and pain. Klein could understand why his friend wanted a bullet to the head, but he couldn't do it – not in cold blood. Instead, he told him he would get help and ran to find some medics. Pape, though, died before they could reach him.

It soon became clear that in all, five minefields had been detonated – and all of them ones sown too close together. Eight men had been killed and a further fourteen seriously wounded.

'Look what you've done!' Klein snarled at Römberg.

'What do you expect?' Römberg replied. 'If you want to make an omelette, you've got to crack a few eggs.'

In his rage, Klein found himself gripping his pistol and only refrained from pulling it on Römberg by the urgent need to help the wounded, of whom Johannsen was one. Later, Klein was summoned by Hauptmann Frömming, the battalion commander, who barked at him that he'd been reported for threatening an officer. Only then did Klein tell him that Römberg had given the order to space the mines half the normal distance apart. Frömming was incredulous and demanded that Klein tell him everything, chastising him not for threatening Römberg but for not coming to him earlier. It was the last they saw of Römberg; he was fired and Klein reinstated as acting company commander. It didn't bring back the dead or the wounded, however. Even on a quiet part of the front, danger and death were never very far away.

For all the wrangling by the senior German commanders on the Cassino front, von Senger was able to pull the last of his troops back behind the Gustav Line overnight on 15–16 January. When troops of the 34th Red Bulls, supported by a regiment of the 36th Texan Division, now back at the front, assaulted Monte Trocchio on the morning of 16 January they found this low mountain abandoned.

From the saddle either side of Trocchio's crest, the Americans could look out over the Liri Valley beyond, a promised land that stretched for more than thirty miles away to the north. Beyond that, further than the distant blue mountains, lay Rome. The sun shone that day and the valley looked remarkably peaceful. A few miles away, however, the Monte Cassino massif rose above the valley and over the town of Cassino beneath it; perched on its outcrop was the abbey, glinting in the sunlight – mocking them rather than offering any spiritual solace. And immediately to their front, not a mile away, snaked the River Rapido as it flowed into the larger Garigliano, which in turn wound its way through the mountains all the way to the sea, some fifteen miles to the south.

Furious, frantic planning was now going on among the various Fifth Army headquarters. SHINGLE was due to take place in just six days' time. First, though, General Clark intended to get his men along the Cassino front across these two rivers. No one, least of all Clark, was expecting it to be easy.

CHAPTER 5

The Garigliano

SINCE DECEMBER, HQ of the 56th Heavy Regiment, RA, had been based at Sparanise, a small bashed-up town well to the south of the Mignano Gap, where, back in December, the big guns had been supporting the British X Corps attacks on Monte Camino and the Special Service Force's assault on the neighbouring Monte la Difensa. Since then, two of their twelve-gun batteries had been sent up to San Clemente, supporting the British 46th Division on the southern edge of the Mignano defile. Now, though, the whole regiment was in the process of moving up to the village of Lauro, a fifteen-mile drive along rough dirt roads, or *strade bianche*, as they were known, that led them up and down low ridges, past the long 1,500-foot high Monte Pecoraro and on beyond to the rolling, undulating folds left by the eruptions of Roccamonfina, an extinct volcano that dominated this corner of south-west Italy. Lauro, their destination, was built either side of a single road that ran along a low ridgeline towards the flat coastal plain where the River Garigliano finally met the sea.

RSM Jack Ward was in reasonably good spirits, not least because he'd received lots of news from home, always a vital ingredient for the morale of front-line troops. Letters 106, 108 and 109 from his wife, Else, had arrived in a bundle at the beginning of the month plus one from his son, Michael, and then two more from Else, Numbers 112 and 113. Two of them had taken just six days to reach him, a new record. He was also thrilled to learn that the parcel of gifts he had sent had reached home before Christmas. 'Has been a grand day,' he noted cheerfully on 8 January, 'having frost with plenty of sun, don't mind the cold. I feel warm but

I am wearing the thickest vests and leather jerkin. So long as the rain holds, we can keep smiling on.'

Ward drove up to Lauro three days later to see how the men were progressing with digging gun pits. Because the ground was less mountainous, fewer folds could hide their guns, so digging out large scrapes into which the big guns could be rolled was important. Camouflage netting had to be draped around them, stocks of ammunition brought up, as well as rations and other supplies. The BL 7.2-inch was a beast of a gun that could hurl a 202-pound high-explosive shell – more than a tenth of a ton – some ten miles, but the gun itself also weighed 10 tons, and this made it tricky to move around, especially on rough roads over which increasing numbers of other, mostly heavy, vehicles had already passed and with the ground still sodden from rain, thawing snow and renewed downpours. Moving a modern, highly mechanized army at all in Italy was problematic. Moving it in winter, during a time of excessive rainfall, was even more so. Even so, at Lauro he found a hive of activity and the gun pits nearly finished. From the new RHQ near the village, Ward looked out over the surrounding countryside as it gently dropped down to the Garigliano. In the distance the land rose again in a series of jutting hills that climbed into the Aurunci Mountains, white-capped with snow in the distance. Quite a long stretch of low ground on their side of the river – perhaps two and a half miles – and beyond, almost directly overlooking the Garigliano, were the hill villages of Suio and Castelforte. 'Jerry country,' as Jack Ward called it. He moved up with the rest of RHQ and the regiment's guns on the night of 15 January, using the cover of darkness to hide their arrival ready for the battle that was due to launch in two nights' time. Just after 11 a.m. the following morning, 16 January, all guns were in position and the regiment was ready. 'Think that is going to be a sticky run,' noted Ward, 'plenty of action by the look of things.'

Further to the north, the 70th Field Regiment, RA, was also getting ready for the forthcoming battles. The 70th used 25-pounders, the staple field gun of the Royal Artillery, and a highly versatile weapon that fired a mixture of high-explosive – HE – and armour-piercing – AP – solid-shot rounds of 87.6mm diameter up to around seven and a half miles. It was unique in having a circular firing platform which was slung beneath while travelling, but which could be easily dropped to the ground and on to which the two wheels would fit, allowing the crew to then use it to quickly turn the gun through a full 360 degrees should they wish to. A crew could fire up to eight rounds a minute if needed, although three to four rounds per minute was more normal practice.

Captain Leonard Garland was now back with his 449 Battery; the only reason he'd been posted first to Allen Force HQ and then as a FOO was because his guns were all being recalibrated back at the Fifth Army workshops at Castel Volturno, some thirty-five miles to the south. With the amount these guns were being used the barrels soon wore out, so regular maintenance work was essential. Now, though, the entire regiment of twenty-four guns was back together ready to support 46th Division's planned crossing of the Garigliano at the southern edge of the Liri Valley. Garland was depressed about the news of his friend Howard Maughan, killed on 5 January while serving with 71st Field Regiment. 'We often discussed our chances when we were instructors,' he noted. 'Return of the old query: what divine purpose can be behind such a tragedy?' A devout man himself, Garland still wanted to believe there was some higher purpose for the mayhem in which they now found themselves. These were the same questions being asked by Dom Eusebio and the monks up at the abbey on Monte Cassino.

Artillery was a vital part of the Allied armies in Italy and the Allied way of war, and amounted to 22 per cent of the make-up of both Eighth and Fifth Armies. It was not just the number of guns that was superior to anything the Germans could bring to bear; it was also the weight of fire, both in terms of numbers of shells and the ability of the long tail of Allied forces to repair, recalibrate and completely build afresh new barrels at workshops behind the lines. The plan was always to pummel the enemy, and especially key positions, as heavily as possible and, whenever the weather allowed, from the air as well before any attack by the infantry. None the less, while the weight of artillery certainly increased the effectiveness of any Allied assault, it could only achieve so much. Men huddling in caves, cellars or in a number of hastily constructed concrete bunkers were largely immune unless, perhaps, unlucky enough to receive a direct hit by a heavy-calibre shell. Even those in earth foxholes tended to be safe from all but a direct hit. Yet artillery was fired to smash minefields, dislocate enemy lines of supply, hamper reinforcements and, most of all, simply to encourage the enemy to keep their heads down while Allied infantry moved forward.

Even so, taking ground was incredibly difficult and costly in lives. This was because defending was much, much easier than attacking. When defending, one could lie in wait and, if well positioned, look down on the enemy. And it didn't require an awful lot of training or many men to sit in the hills watching an advance and fire machine guns and mortars at the oncoming troops. Barbed wire, millions of cheap mines of various kinds – from anti-personnel to bigger anti-tank – and booby traps were the enemy's first line of defence. Gaps would be left which would then canalize the attackers into areas already zeroed beforehand – this meant that lines of fire and coordinates on a map had already been worked out, so that when the enemy appeared in this zone they could be swiftly cut down. Carefully placed observation posts – OPs – with men equipped with superb optics and linked with radios and field telephones could then direct this fire of all kinds: artillery out of sight, mortars closer to hand, and many machine guns equally well placed so they could provide interlocking fields of fire. The earlier model, MG34, and the now pretty much standard MG42 had terrific cyclical rates; the MG42 could spit out twenty-three bullets a second. This meant its barrels might quickly overheat and it was never very accurate even when first fired, but accuracy wasn't the point. Spewing a huge amount of lead over a specific area was the aim. In this it was lethally effective.

And it was why launching any such attack in Italy, in winter, when tank and mobile fire support as well as that from the air was so limited, was particularly lethal for the attacking infantry. Yet it was the infantry, the PBI, that were about to shoulder the lion's share of the Allies' next multi-pronged attacks to try and unlock the Gustav Line. And then get to Rome.

'Operation SHINGLE is on!' noted General Clark in his diary on 8 January. 'At least 25 LSTs will be available for the follow-up, thus assuring an opportunity for re-supply and the bringing in of supporting corps troops.' Clark had already decided that his VI Corps, under Major-General John Lucas, would be sent to Anzio and that the proven 3rd Infantry Division would make up the initial American contribution along with the Ranger Force. Alexander had insisted it be a joint venture – he didn't want the Americans bearing all the responsibility – and so allocated the 1st Infantry Division, recently arrived in Italy and at full strength, to be the second division in the initial assault. The 45th

Thunderbirds and parts of 1st Armored Division were also lined up to be among the follow-up forces.

The next day, 9 January, a major planning conference was held at Clark's HQ involving all the senior commanders. Alexander explained that Churchill had secured the extra commitment of landing ships and more besides. This had been easier to accomplish than might have been the case ten days earlier because General Montgomery had already ripped up earlier plans for OVERLORD and dramatically increased the scale of the operation. Even at the Tehran Conference, the Combined Chiefs of Staff had conceded that the cross-Channel invasion might take place closer to 1 June 1944 than 1 May, but Monty's initial re-examination of the assault plan, still being worked on back in England, suggested more time would be needed. OVERLORD was rapidly heading into June. That took a little bit of pressure off SHINGLE – albeit not very much.

While Clark was cheered by this, he was not by Alexander's insistence that SHINGLE be launched on 22 January. This did not allow Clark enough time for a landing rehearsal, which he believed was needed. Even a delay of two days, to the 24th, would make a difference, Clark pleaded, but Alex was not to be budged: the concessions on the LSTs had been granted to Churchill by the President and Combined Chiefs on the understanding that no operation in Italy should further jeopardize the launch date of OVERLORD, so it was out of Alexander's hands. Alex warned that while SHINGLE would get a maximum air effort, Allied air forces would also be needed over the Cassino front. There was also the capricious nature of the weather to consider. He further warned Clark against taking too many vehicles, which might clog exits and roads initially, but promised swift follow-ups instead. He also announced that four liberty ships, the standard Allied ocean-going freighter, would be available to be beached and could be considered expendable should it come to it.

Once the conference was over, everyone left except Alex, his new Chief of Staff, General John Harding, Clark and Al Gruenther, Clark's own Chief of Staff. Clark asked Alex what he really thought of ANVIL, the proposed summer invasion of southern France. That it might never take place was his answer. Alex told them he thought it a great mistake not to exploit success in Italy. His reasoning was this: that for all the merit of invading southern France, vast armed forces were already in place in Italy. The logistical challenges of moving divisions across the Mediterranean had already been considerable – the late arrival of divisions from North Africa being a case in point. Why start afresh? He also believed, as did Churchill, that the greatest benefit to OVERLORD and the overall strategy against Nazi Germany would be achieved by pushing ever closer to the Reich from the south, with the flexibility they would also have once they reached the Po Valley between the Apennines and the Alps. There were arguments for reducing Italy to a defensive front, but with shipping so stretched and with so much committed to Italy already, both on the ground and in terms of the Fifteenth Air Force, there were also good reasons for continuing the campaign ahead of ANVIL.

Clark himself was also keen to remain in Italy, even though he'd been earmarked to command Seventh Army for the operation in southern France. 'He did not wish to be withdrawn from his Fifth Army command,' noted his stenographer, 'and be left in some planning command when the war ended and thereby miss a chance to march into Germany at the head of his Army.'

Alexander and Harding had returned to their own digs before calling in again later for a convivial drink. Alex asked Clark whether he might accompany Clark in a PT boat – a small, fast, motor-torpedo boat – during SHINGLE, so long, he added, as he would not be in the way. 'I'd be delighted,' Clark told him. Afterwards, though, once Clark was alone with Gruenther, he told his Chief of Staff that he thought Alexander 'was a peanut and a feather duster'. This was a metaphor of Clark's own making and meant to imply that Alex was out of his depth and rather a lightweight senior commander. It was both unfair and unnecessarily waspish, although Clark would never have made such a remark beyond a private conversation with Gruenther. The comment was committed to his diary in order to cover his back should things go wrong, but it also revealed the chip he had on his shoulder about his comparative lack of command experience compared with Alexander, something he felt keenly despite his firm belief in his own capabilities. Clark and Alexander got on well, regardless of this mean-spirited line, yet they were very different characters. Clark called a spade a spade and liked plain speaking; Alex, on the other hand, could be perfectly resolute when he felt such an approach was required, but his manner was outwardly gentle, relying on charm and inference. It was not his way to bark. During the conference he had said, 'I'm frightfully keen for a diversion and for a Commando to crack into the outskirts of Rome.' This was effectively an order, but said in such a way that he was asking Clark instead. When Clark replied that such a plan might dissipate the landing craft they did have, Alexander pressed the point. 'I feel certain,' he told him, 'that it would frighten Kesselring and keep Rome garrisoned by the Germans.' In other words: make it happen.

Most of all, however, Clark's catty comment revealed the extraordinary pressure he was under and the immense responsibilities he faced. His Fifth Army was now huge, containing four substantial corps, all recently reinforced. Alexander had given him the plum role in the Italian campaign, with Eighth Army now taking the back seat. Clark commanded Americans, Brits, Canadians, French, Algerians, Moroccans and Tunisians in his truly polyglot force and expectations were high: a major two-fisted assault on the enemy, currently separated by the sea and only a few days. Alexander had issued some very specific orders: to draw up to the Gustav Line both in the centre, through the Mignano defile, and to the north where the CEF had taken over from VI Corps, and to the south in the British X Corps' sector that ran down to the coast. Then he was to mount a series of river crossings: X Corps near the sea over the Garigliano and also further north at the southern edge of the Liri Valley, and II Corps to strike across the Rapido* ahead of Monte Trocchio. A couple of days after, SHINGLE was to be launched. Multiple thrusts, different parts of the front, a major amphibious assault to the north, and not much preparation time.

The weary divisions already battered and bloodied by the fighting since Salerno had had little opportunity to properly refit and recover. Clark had already survived Salerno – and by the skin of his teeth. AVALANCHE had lacked shipping, been short of air cover, and had not had enough warships. He and his men had pulled it off, but seeing Alexander, unruffled and imperturbable as ever when he was the commander on the ground trying to keep control of all these different levers, irked him. It was no wonder he was feeling the strain a little; the stakes were incredibly high. Had he stopped to think about it, he might have considered that the burden of responsibility was every bit as great, if not greater, for Alexander; but Alex managed to wear this a little lighter than his Fifth Army commander. After all, he'd had more experience, which took Clark's

* The Americans of 36th Division and II Corps always referred to the river here as the Rapido when actually it had already become the Garigliano at this point. In the interests of consistency, I've stuck with the American name.

vexation full-circle again. That evening, with so many balls to juggle, it was understandable that Clark should feel on edge; if he was sounding and acting peevish, in the circumstances he could probably be forgiven.

Despite the pressure he was under, by evening on Sunday, 16 January, both Clark and Alexander had cause to feel reasonably pleased. The French were making progress in the mountains north of Cassino, the kind of operation for which these colonial troops were well trained. Monte Maio had been secured; and breaking out of the Mignano defile, the US II Corps had managed to take Trocchio and draw up to the Gustav Line. The stage was thus set for the next phase, although Clark was concerned that his longest-serving divisions were overworked and understrength. Back on 11 January, he had sent an urgent cable to General Devers in Algiers for more infantry, demanding 4,000 replacements, 2,500 immediately. He recommended taking them from the 85th and 88th Divisions, now newly in theatre but not yet deployed. 'Advise action taken,' was the response that same day.

It was the British of X Corps that were to make the very first breach of the Gustav Line, however. Clark wanted the British to cross the Garigliano near the coast, drawing as many German troops from the centre of the line as possible. Lieutenant-General Sir Dick McCreery, the corps commander, intended to strike at four different places concurrently, right on the coast with 5th Division, newly switched from Eighth Army, and with 56th Division a little inland at Suio and Castelforte. An artillery barrage using most of the corps' guns would get the ball rolling in 56th Division's sector on the evening of the 17th. The hope was that under the cover of darkness, the troops would be able to cross the river in rubber boats and get far enough inland while sappers hurriedly made a series of pontoon bridges, over which heavier reinforcements of tanks and mobile firepower could then be poured.

Among the infantry now getting ready for the crossing were the 1st London Irish Rifles, one of the three battalions in 168th Brigade in 56th Division. After a brief stint out of the line, the London Irish had moved back up to positions looking down towards the River Garigliano on New Year's Day, basing themselves around the village of Corigliano. This lay on one of the low volcanic ridges running down from the Roccamonfina volcano and was a couple of miles north-east of Lauro, where Jack Ward and the 56th Heavy Regiment were now based. The London Irish had fought throughout Sicily when part of 50th Division and had had a pretty torrid time since joining 56th Division, landing at Salerno, fighting their way north across the Volturno, and then taking part in the December battle for Monte Camino.

For the first couple of weeks since reaching this sector their task had been to keep a watch for enemy patrols across the river but also to conduct night and even daylight reconnaissance patrols themselves, trying to prise as much information about German dispositions as possible. The undisputed battalion master of patrol work was Captain John Strick, who had on several occasions taken it upon himself to dress in civilian clothes and wander down the road from Corigliano, pretending to be Italian and casually wandering along the riverbank.

Strick was twenty-five, lean-faced, fair-haired and looked both younger than he was and more like an embryonic don than an aggressive infantry officer. The son of a First World War general, he had been brought up in the Devon countryside, then packed off to Wellington College, an English boarding school where he had proved too slight, small and lacking coordination to do well at games, but had done rather better at his lessons. A year at the London School of Economics had followed, but he then abandoned economics and instead won a place to read history at King's College. As well as having a love of history, he was also an aspiring poet and writer, taking it upon himself to edit the London Irish Rifles' regimental magazine, *The Ordinary Fellow*. Strick also enjoyed travelling and during his university holidays had visited France, Switzerland and even Nazi Germany. He had joined up through conviction, before the war, was commissioned, and, with the battalion, headed first to Iraq and then to Sicily for Operation HUSKY. There, in the Catania Plain, the battalion had had a particularly tough fight. The men had all been exhausted, with no or little sleep for two nights when they'd been ordered to attack across a stretch of the plain with no artillery support at all to take an enemy strongpoint known as Bottaceto. Suddenly, enemy machine guns had opened up and the LIR had found themselves caught in the open with no cover. 'We lost very many but captured it,' Strick had written to his mother just before Christmas, by which time he had reckoned it was safe to tell her all. 'I was hit in the first moment.' Fortunately, his batman – his soldier-servant – Jack Hargreaves was beside him. It had not been a serious head wound but had bled profusely. Bullets had been spraying all around them, but miraculously they had not been hit and, once bandaged up, Strick had led his men forward and driven the Germans out.

Since their arrival in Italy he had taken over the Carrier Platoon but had also set up X Platoon, or the Battle Patrol as it was also known. This was entirely irregular but consisted of sixteen NCOs and other ranks, always the same men, whom he would lead on night patrols and recces. They were an odd bunch. There was Jack Hargreaves, never far from his side, while one of the men had run a ladies' hairdressing salon before the war and another NCO was a graduate of University College, Dublin. 'Drink has been his problem,' Strick had written to his mother on New Year's Eve, 'but otherwise a delightful character. Here we all are – a sort of Commando really, though, of course, we get neither their publicity nor pay.' Strick's motivation in continually risking his neck in this brave but decidedly highly risky way was partly for the thrill of it, but also a subconscious way of proving himself; because of his lack of sporting prowess, it thrilled him that former rugger captains in his battalion now treated him with respect.

At any rate, X Platoon's adventures had helped the battalion add a number of features to their maps ahead of the attack across the river: hiding places, German strongpoints, minefields and more. Not all patrols had been successful, however. On the night of 11 January, they'd attempted to cross the Garigliano in rubber boats under the cover of darkness, part of a larger raid across the river by 168 Brigade; the plan had been to destroy any enemy outposts and hopefully capture some prisoners, but the water levels in the river had been high, the current very swift, and Strick's platoon were unable to get across. Sergeant Budd had tried, his boat had capsized and he'd been swept away, never to be seen again.

'I have only time to write a short note,' Captain David Cole had written to his parents on 16 January, the eve of X Corps' attack in the south. 'The war rolls on, with plenty more to look forward to. Fortunately, in battle, part of me goes into a sort of anaesthetised trance! I hope the anaesthetic will not fail me before the whole bloody business is over!' Cole tried to put a cheery spin on things in his letters home, yet this time couldn't help betraying his nerves about the upcoming battle. Aged just twenty-three, he was the Signals Officer in the 2nd Inniskillings, part of 5th Division, now operating to the south of the 56th, and the radio link between the attacking companies and the commanding officer, Lieutenant-Colonel Joseph O'Brien Twohig.

Cole had come ashore with the 2nd Inniskillings – or Skins, as they were known – in Sicily as a green and untested junior officer. He had been studying history at Cambridge University when he decided to interrupt his studies to join up. Studious, bespectacled, with a neat moustache and a pipe often thrust in his mouth, he was another, like John Strick, for whom soldiering was not an obvious career choice. Yet these extraordinary times required ordinary – and even unlikely – people to do their bit. Cole had survived Sicily, won a promotion and had then been among the very first Allied troops into Italy, crossing the Straits of Messina with the rest of 5th Division back on 3 September 1943. What an age ago that seemed now.

Everything about the forthcoming attack, however, told Cole that they were in for a rough time. Based at the small village of Fasani, their advance to the River Garigliano was around four miles across flat, open plain. The crossing point itself was as much as 50 yards wide over a river still very full with the recent rain and melting snow from the mountains and flowing at pace. From the far side there was a further two miles or so over completely flat ground to the Minturno Ridge and another, lesser river crossing over the Ausente, which flowed into the plain between the Minturno Ridge of hills and the larger, more dominating Colle Ceracoli and Monte Damiano beyond.

Therefore, both 56th and 5th Division's crossings looked extremely challenging, to say the least. The floodplains had been laid with as many as 40,000 mines of various types. Enemy observers dotted the high ground in well-hidden OPs. Mortar pits and MG – machine-gun – posts had also been sited all along the German lines. Further inland, where 56th Division were due to cross, the stretch of completely flat and exposed ground was only around a mile or so, but on the far, northern side of the river there was a brief area of floodplain before the hills rose sharply. In other words, the enemy would be looking right down upon them. It was hoped that a very heavy artillery barrage, to which the 56th Heavy Regiment would be contributing, would keep the enemy's heads down and, combined with the darkness of the night assault, would give the attackers a chance to quickly get across both the river and the plain and then, using the cover of the rising ground, push on into the hills and the German positions.

A few miles to the south, however, the floodplain was much wider as the Garigliano neared the sea. The plan for 5th Division was to cross at three places: two to the north of the main Highway 7 – the old Roman Via Appia – and one to the south, with a further, small amphibious operation out to sea. The 2nd Inniskillings were to be crossing north of Highway 7, on a stretch where the river curled and snaked.

Opposite them was 94. Infanterie-Division, comparatively new to the front and, like so many in XIV Panzerkorps, a phoenix division, re-formed from scratch following its annihilation at Stalingrad; although at pretty much full strength, it was not reckoned to be of especially high calibre. The overall aim for this British two-division attack was to smash through the Gustav Line, climb into the hills and then down into the Ausente Valley to Ausonia, some nine miles away, by evening of D-plus 1, i.e. the second day of the attack. This would then allow the British to push on into the Liri Valley and get in behind the German positions while the Germans were busy fighting the Americans at the mouth of the valley. With the French pressing the enemy to the north of Cassino, a secondary attack by 46th Division at the southern side of the Liri Valley and, of course, SHINGLE, this combined, multi-pronged attack, Alexander and Clark hoped, would prove too much for XIV Panzerkorps.

There were other grounds for cautious confidence. Both divisions had been in position opposite the Garigliano since the end of December. Active patrol work – not least by men like John Strick and his X Platoon – had given the British a clear understanding of the terrain and enemy dispositions. The 56th Division had also been involved in the Volturno crossing back in October and had learned hard lessons. Training exercises at night using boats had been carried out on the Volturno in the run-up to the attack. Guns had been brought up, such as those of the 56th Heavy Regiment, and sited carefully. So too stocks of ammunition. The boats to be used in the initial crossings had also been carried forward and hidden over the preceding three nights. Minefields on the southern side had been cleared.

And yet, despite all these preparations, Cole felt sick to his core. All day on that Monday, 17 January he tried to convey an impression of easy insouciance, smiling, chatting, packing and repacking his haversack and stuffing his pockets with aspirin, boiled sweets and matches for his pipe. His softer sensibilities he pushed to one side. Anaesthetizing himself, as he'd written to his parents, was the only armour he had.

At 4 p.m. they marched out, the day already darkening. Bagpipes were being played, their mournful, reedy notes fading hauntingly as the trucks rumbled out on the start of their journey. Through quiet hamlets and farmsteads, the few Italians he glimpsed along the way were oblivious that a major battle was about to be unleashed. In the flat river valley an evening mist shrouded their advance. That was good but added to the feeling of impending doom. It was dusk by the time they halted. Out they clambered. A short walk down the Via Appia – how many had walked this road before, Cole wondered – and then they turned down a track, D Company leading and Cole and his men with Advanced HQ following.

Tension in the air. Muffled talk. Nervous laughter. Faces taut. Minutes passed. At one minute to nine o'clock – 21:00 hours – Cole glanced at his watch then gazed at the looming mass of hills silhouetted against the night sky. The CO whispering to Jim Bradley, the adjutant. One of his signallers blowing into the microphone of his radio set. The creak of a drum of telephone wire being unwound on its spindle.

The London Irish Rifles were in reserve for the attack, which meant that Captain John Strick could watch the opening barrage from the battalion area at Corigliano, perhaps five miles as the crow flies from where David Cole was waiting by the riverbank. It began suddenly, 9 p.m. on the nose, a sheet of bright light then flickering explosions on the hills beyond. Strick thought the Bofors cannons, firing tracer, were rather like leisurely red and white fireworks. 'In the distance, one could see great golden sparks shoot up where the shells landed on the hills,' he noted. 'The noise was deafening as we were right in front of a battery.'

A little to the south-west, RSM Jack Ward was also watching the barrage. One year earlier to the day, he realized, they had landed in Algeria. Now, here they were in Italy and hopefully starting the battle for Rome. 'Time is now 10.15pm,' he jotted, 'and I have just been to the top of the lane and I saw shells bursting on the far side of the river.' Fires had started around the battlefront and he found himself wondering how the PBI were getting on.

Down on the Garigliano, David Cole had also seen and heard the barrage – a deafening roar and twinkling flashes in the hills. He'd felt it too. The dull ripple of fire retorted around the hills and made the ground tremble. Shells whined, screamed and whooshed over them while the hills were speckled with flashes of orange, bursting shells. Away to their right, to the north, machine-gun tracer spat in lazy lines across the open river plain. But there was no barrage in their sector; 5th Division was to assault silently, without artillery support. It was sometimes considered that the benefits of attacking with surprise could outweigh the destructive element of a barrage ahead of an attack, especially, if, as in this case, it was being mounted alongside a noisy assault on the flank.

The first troops, a single platoon, managed to swiftly get across only for a nearby enemy machine gun to open fire from a lone farmhouse. This was quickly subdued, but moments later, as D and A Companies began crossing in their boats, German artillery opened up, shells whooshing and screaming in, crashing into the riverbanks and the river itself. Two boats were hit, troops laden with equipment falling into the fast-flowing water. From the southern bank, David Cole heard the cries of men against the thunder of exploding shells, struggling with the weight and current. Others were pulled from the bank but in a matter of moments A Company alone had lost over thirty men and two officers.

The enemy barrage now crept southwards to where the rest of the battalion was still assembled for the crossing. Suddenly three shells screeched in, sucking the air around them and whamming into the Advanced HQ area. Cole was lying prostrate in the grass next to the riverbank alongside Barks and Paddy Campbell, two of his Signals Platoon men, as one of the shells landed just yards from them. A blast of hot air, bitter, choking smoke and steel shrapnel hissing and fizzing past them. A pause, a gasp. Still alive.

'I think Paddy's hit, sir,' said Barks.

They both looked at Campbell, who had been lying between them. There was no obvious mark on him but no signs of life either. Cole could scarcely believe it; he and Paddy Campbell had served together since Sicily. He felt consumed by both shock and grief as, with Barks, they gently pulled the control radio set from Campbell's lifeless shoulders. Cole became a punch-drunk automaton, dazed, stumbling, trying to gather his platoon. The ground was now pitted with increasing numbers of craters as ever more shells continued to thunder around them. Darkness to blinding light, figures briefly lit up, then shadows once more. Air thick with smoke and the stench of explosive. Ground pulsing. And the noise: a deafening, senses-hammering thunder. Four boats had been lost and seven damaged. Soaked men, many of them wounded, clung to the riverbank.

News drifted in, but A Company, although across the river, had lost radio contact entirely. Word arrived that Henry Macrory had been killed during the crossing, a former adjutant and a friend of Cole's. At 11.30 p.m., with the moon now up, a decision was made to abandon their current crossing point and move to that of the Wiltshires instead, half a mile to the south; the reports were that their sister battalion in 13th Brigade were now mostly across and making good progress. Much to his relief,

Cole, along with his Signals Platoon and Advanced HQ, all managed to reach this quieter crossing unscathed, and by 4 a.m. all had got across. News gradually filtered in. Major John Nixon of B Company had reached the edge of the Mignano Ridge as planned, and so now C Company and Advanced HQ all began to move forward from the river too. However, because they had used the Wiltshires' crossing they now had to move diagonally across an area not cleared of mines. An eerie silence had fallen on the valley; the German guns were briefly silent and all that could be heard was occasional small arms. And no mines detonated. That was a relief, and by just before 5.30 a.m. they'd reached the starting point for the assault on the ridge looming 800 yards away. That was just as well, because that was when the barrage was due to begin: an all-out hammering of the ridge first and then a creeping barrage behind which both the Wiltshires and the Skins were due to advance.

Right on cue, over 100 guns opened fire. The ridge in front was punctured by bursting flashes of explosions, the din immense; Cole felt his knees weaken, his thoughts blunted. Then they were moving forward through blasted orchards and past stone sheds, barns and farmhouses. Machine-gun tracer stabbing the air around them, fizzing, zipping, whining. Cole's face was cold with sweat, his stomach struggling to keep pace with his feet. Advanced HQ paused at the edge of the last orchard before the hills rose above the plain. Men from the Cheshire Machine Gun Battalion and mortarmen pushed past. Cole saw men falling, hit by bullets and shrapnel.

Then in a split moment all sound ceased and he was conscious of floating in the air then landing with a sudden jolt. He heard no sound, felt nothing, only blackness. Slowly, he opened his eyes. Prostrate on the ground, he felt for his haversack. His hand touched lumps of what felt like suet. Below his knees, his battledress was soaked in blood. But thank God – his feet and legs were still there. A choking, gagging rawness on his throat. Dim light now, swirling smoke, figures reeling away. Then beside him he saw Jim Bradley, the adjutant to whom he'd been speaking moments before, in pieces. And close by half of a second body, intestines slick and oozing, just feet away. It was this man's blood that covered Cole. To his left, a single boot with a foot still protruding. Other lumps of flesh. His eyes were absorbing these horrors but were utterly immune, shock being the protective shield.

He knew he had to get up and find his men, and particularly the command radio. Clambering to his feet, he stumbled about then spotted Paddy Campbell's replacement lying on the ground, the wireless still strapped to his back. Bending over him, Cole saw the man no longer had a face. The entire front of his head had been sliced off, blood gulping thickly from the mess. Barks was beside him now and together, slippery blood on their hands, they pulled the radio off the dead man's shoulders. Numbly, Cole then put the blood-smeared headphones on his head, made some adjustments to the set and, despite the shell bursts and mortars and deafening phantasmagoria of the battle, heard a crackling voice in his ears: 'Connaught! Connaught! Connaught!' The signal that C Company had successfully crossed the River Ausente. Looking around, stumbling, he found the CO, sitting quietly under a tree, blood on his neck, and reported the news.

'Good. Good. Anything from B?'

'We're trying to get through to B, sir,' Cole replied.

Five men had been killed and seven seriously wounded by the one shell that had blown Cole off his feet. Quickly, though, miraculously, Advanced HQ began to function once again. The ability of decent, gentle men like Cole to gather their wits amid such carnage was astonishing. Messages started to come through. C Company was on the ridge. Then so too was B Company, who had got round a minefield and followed them up, joining them in well-constructed trenches recently occupied by the Germans. By the time dawn crept over the valley and hills the battalion had gained its objective and created a bulge 800 yards wide in the Gustav Line.

Nor were they alone. By first light, ten battalions from both divisions were successfully across the Garigliano and throughout that day they significantly expanded their bridgeheads. On the coast, 17th Brigade had run into trouble with the particularly deep minefields there, while half of the amphibious assault landed on the southern, not northern side of the river mouth. Chaos, but enough men moving forward. At the river, engineers frantically continued building bridges – a combination of Type 9 and Type 30 Bailey bridges, the former for infantry only, the latter for vehicles and even tanks. So, in terms of progress and objectives, not so bad after all.

David Cole spent the day digging in at the edge of the orchard, some 800 yards from the rising Minturno Ridge ahead of them but still in radio communication with B and C Companies up on the hills beyond. A Company had been largely decimated – not a single officer or NCO had survived the night; a lance-corporal named Banton had led the surviving twenty or so survivors back across the river – not two dozen out of the more than 100 that had begun the attack. Sporadic enemy shelling was directed at the engineers bridge-building behind them, while twice during the morning Luftwaffe fighter-bombers thundered over low and dropped bombs on the sappers.

As dusk fell once more, both divisions prepared to renew their assault. In 56th Division's area it was now time for 168th Brigade to attack, which meant that Captain John Strick and the London Irish would be entering the battle. Further north, 46th Division were also due to make a crossing that night. David Cole knew little of this, however. He'd spent much of the day in a state of semi-permanent shock. It was impossible for his brain to process what he had experienced, what he'd seen. His battledress still covered in blood, but now dried and stiff. His face and hands roughly washed, but underlyingly filthy. As the light faded, Harry Christie, one of the C Company officers, arrived with a trudging procession of prisoners. Cole thought they looked every bit as exhausted, filthy and dishevelled as their own troops did, as though, no longer burdened by the impossible task of trying to defend the Third Reich, they had become both ordinary-looking and innocuous.

Cole clambered out of his trench to speak to his friend.

'A pretty scruffy lot,' Christie said, glancing back at the prisoners, then noticed the row of freshly dug graves. Cole told him what had happened and who had been killed. Christie was silent for a moment then said, 'The fun has gone out of this war.' Then, without another word, he walked on.

Earlier that afternoon, General Alexander visited Clark, learned that the Garigliano attack was going well, then headed on to visit Dick McCreery at X Corps Tactical HQ to hear more about the state of play from the corps commander. In tow were John Harding and Alex's American Chief of Staff, Major-General Lyman Lemnitzer. 'Battle in progress for crossing of Garigliano River,' noted Harding later that evening. 'Marvellous view across valley with shells falling on far hillside. All going satisfactorily.'

Necessarily, battles were often reduced to lines and arrows on a map, drawn in different-coloured crayons and described in terse, easy-to-decode cables or pithy summaries. After all, it was the most efficient and effective way of passing on information. It also protected commanders from the unpalatable scenes playing out in the maelstrom of battle; it was hard enough sending young men to fight as it was without dwelling on thoughts of dismembered limbs and shattered lives. Yet there was also something rather awful about reducing these sacrifices to a generalization or a roughly drawn arrow. The 2nd Skins had lost a third of their number: drowned, shot, blasted, cut to globs of flesh or completely atomized. Their experiences had been repeated all along the two-division front, some battalions less so, others even worse. So, too, those front-line units of the German 94. Division. Harry Christie had been right. There was nothing fun about this. It was a bloody, brutal beast of a war and not least here, in this corner of southern Italy.

And it was about to get even worse.

CHAPTER 6

The Plight of the People

FIFTH ARMY'S MULTI-PRONGED SERIES of attacks designed to smash through the Gustav Line was now well under way. On Tuesday, 18 January, while the British X Corps were trying to expand their bridgehead across the Garigliano, General Mark Clark was holding an off-the-record press conference in his hut at his encampment in the grounds of the Palazzo Reale in Caserta. Seventeen war correspondents, photographers and public relations officers all gathered around, all of whom were being attached to various ships and units for the major new operation against the Germans. Clark could not yet tell them where this blow was due to fall or when, but it was to be the hardest strike by Fifth Army since Salerno. After giving a brief outline of current operations – the French to the north of Cassino, the British to the south – he told them these were preludes to weaken the centre of the line before a major assault by the US II Corps. Was this designed to hasten the fall of Rome, one of the correspondents asked? 'Every operation the Fifth Army undertakes is designed to speed the day when Allied troops enter Rome,' Clark replied. Another asked how long it might be until Rome was taken and when forces currently facing the Germans might be expected to hook up with the amphibious assault he'd just been briefing them about. Clark told them he hoped within two weeks.

There were still many plans to be ironed out, however. Clark's focus was now firmly on the SHINGLE operation and he had left detailed planning of II Corps' river crossing of the Rapido in the hands of General Keyes and his staff and to Major-General Fred Walker, the 36th Division's commander, and his team. Instead, Clark was now considering a number of other issues, such as how to deploy the 504th PIR – Parachute Infantry Regiment – into Anzio, and whether it should it be dropped by air or landed by sea. This three-battalion unit was part of 82nd Airborne; the rest of the division had gone back to the UK in preparation for OVERLORD, but Clark had been allowed to retain this now highly experienced unit in his Fifth Army. He knew they would prove invaluable at Anzio. A decision over the 504th had still not been made when Alexander arrived at 11.30 a.m. on the 18th with Harding and Major-General Lyman Lemnitzer. Alex was driving his jeep himself, speeding in rather fast and then halting in front of the aides' tent a little too suddenly for comfort, not that he looked remotely fazed by this. At any rate, he was able to report that X Corps were continuing to make progress and that Sherman tanks were now being ferried across the river mouth. The outlook for X Corps' operation was reasonably bright, although there was still no bridge across any part of the river despite ceaseless work by the sappers. This meant that apart from the Shermans being ferried by sea into the bridgehead, the British were dependent on rafts to bring over anti-tank guns, vehicles and ammunition, and that was inevitably a slow process. Also, the leading battalions had suffered badly. Reserve brigades were being brought up and a number of Shermans and antitanks were ferried over, but after twenty-four hours the leading infantry units now up in the hills were a long way still from Ausonia, the original objective for the operation. Much would depend on how the follow-up forces fared, how quickly the bridges could be got across the river and, of course, most importantly of all, on how the Germans reacted.

All the senior German commanders had been taken by complete surprise by X Corps' attack and immediately recognized the danger it posed. Generalleutant Fridolin von Senger had visited 94. Division on 17 January and, climbing up on to the hills above the Garigliano, had realized it was a position with both strength and weakness. The Mignano Ridge, above the town of Minturno, was a triangular hill mass; there was a valley directly behind it to the west before the ground rose up into the Aurunci Mountains. The coast and the sea were to the south, and the Ausente Valley was on the third side of the triangle to the north-east. North of the Ausente Valley was another mass of hills, the largest of which were Monte Damiano and Monte Fuga, the latter nearly 2,000 feet high. The artillery of 94. Division were behind these hills, both in the Ausente Valley and along the coast, and so long as von Senger's infantry held the high ground overlooking the Garigliano and his artillery observers could look down on the enemy, all would be well. On the other hand, if they were to be driven off, then the enemy would hold the all-important heights and this would mean that his artillery in the Ausente Valley and down on the coast would be effectively blind, while the enemy would now have the benefits of the high ground instead; so whatever they lost would also be the Brits' gain.

As he had looked around that day, he had realized that if 94. Division was attacked simultaneously along the coast and across the Garigliano, they would potentially be in a lot of trouble. The Ausente Valley would most likely be overrun, Ausonia captured, and the enemy would be able to get into the Liri Valley and roll up the Gustav Line from the flank – exactly as Alexander and Clark had planned. Generalmajor Bernhard Steinmetz, the division's commander, whom von Senger regarded highly, was similarly concerned. 'He saw things as they were in reality,' noted von Senger, 'that is, he knew that in effect the division was faced with a mission impossible to fulfil.'

Von Senger was fifty-two, a devout Catholic, former Rhodes Scholar and a career cavalry officer. A highly cultured and learned man, he was no admirer of Hitler and had been convinced, back in December 1941, when the army had failed to take Moscow, that Germany could no longer win the war. Despite this, like so many of his fellow senior commanders, he continued to do his duty and serve as a general commanding many thousands of troops to the best of his ability, reasoning with himself that he was impotent to do anything and that refusing to fight – or something more drastic – would achieve nothing and endanger his family.

And so, after hearing the news of the British attack the night before, that morning, 18 January, he hurried to Steinmetz's command post once again, his hunch of the previous day having proved unwelcomely prescient. Monte Damiano was in British hands and so too the heights of the Minturno Ridge. From Steinmetz's command post he put through a call to Kesselring rather than his army commander, von Vietinghoff, and urged the field marshal to urgently send the two divisions now in army group reserve. Kesselring had sent 90. Panzergrenadier-Division to the Rome area in case of an outflanking move from the sea that he was convinced was surely coming soon. The 90th had been largely destroyed at Ortona the previous month but a glut of replacements had brought it back up to some kind of strength. Then, only a few days earlier, the overused and battered 29. Panzergrenadier-Division had also been moved back. These two were Kesselring's army group reserve, albeit they'd only just been given this dubious honour. Von Senger now asked Kesselring to send them urgently down to rescue Steinmetz's beleaguered men. This, he told him, was absolutely necessary if they were to save the Gustav position. He also knew that Kesselring would do as he suggested as the field marshal always backed tenacious resistance over retreat. 'He was, after all,' noted von Senger in his diary, 'an advocate of holding out at any cost.'

He most certainly was, determined to fulfil Hitler's orders. With a fair wind, Kesselring, ever the optimist, expected to keep the Allies at bay indefinitely along the Gustav Line. His only real worry was a landing from the sea, but he had troops in place to deal with such an eventuality. So, as von Senger had rightly predicted, Kesselring ordered them to move right away. 'I am convinced', he told von Vietinghoff emphatically, 'this is the greatest crisis that we have yet experienced.' There were other troop movements too. North of Rome was I Fallschirmjägerkorps, which was now ordered to hurry to the south of the city in place of 90. and 29. Panzergrenadier, while a further four artillery battalions were also sent southwards. As if that wasn't enough, three battalions from the HG-Division, still due to leave Italy at the beginning of February, were also ordered to move hurriedly to bolster Steinmetz's men.

That same night, X Corps renewed its attacks against the weakening 94. Division while, under the cover of darkness, the engineers continued to try and get a vehicle bridge over the Garigliano. Among those now about to cross the river into the bridgehead were the 1st London Irish Rifles. Captain John Strick was struggling with a bad cold, caught off one of his fellow officers on his return from leave, and he was tired from both that and a protracted lack of sleep. Down at the river, because no bridge had been put across yet, there was a queue of infantry waiting to get over in boats and on the raft ferry that had been set up. Strick was freezing; there had been some discussion about whether to wear greatcoats or not, but the CO had eventually decided they would be too restrictive and cumbersome to wear in battle. Strick was cursing this decision. He didn't see why they couldn't simply be dumped later.

Eventually they got across in boats, then on the far side followed the white tape that showed a path through the minefields. Walking for perhaps a mile, the battalion then paused, and Strick and his X Platoon found an empty stable; despite the cold and the flagstone floor he fell asleep immediately. It was around 1 a.m. when he was woken and told to report to the CO, Lieutenant-Colonel Ian Good. Wearily he trudged off. Good wanted him and his platoon to investigate Castelforte. This was a long, narrow village built into a low bulging ridge beneath Monte Damiano to the south and Monte Fuga to the north. The village, full of narrow streets and alleyways and densely packed buildings, climbed as the ridge rose so that it looked down over the Garigliano, not half a mile ahead. The peaks either side were now reportedly in Allied hands but Castelforte itself was something of an unknown quantity; reports suggested it was empty of Germans, but there was only one way of finding out for certain and that was to send a patrol to investigate. This was to be Strick's X Platoon.

He and his men set off at once. It was a fair distance of several miles to Castelforte. The moon was up, casting a creamy glow over the hills and the river valley. They passed B and C Companies, now holding positions taken over from the Ox and Bucks, who had captured them the previous evening. On they pressed, away from the valley and towards the village. The road wound its way steeply as it climbed up on to the ridge past terraced olive groves and then, a short way further on, was the edge of the village and the first outlying buildings and homesteads. The air was still, the only sound their own movement, hobnail boots on the dirt road. Strick had intended to reach a hairpin bend that marked the start of the main part of the village and then turn off and get round the village cross-country; certainly, walking up the road, the first few houses now on either side, made him nervous and on edge, yet they couldn't possibly investigate them all. Then, as they reached a bend in the road, he heard something and called his men to a halt. A click. That was all. On his left. Then silence again. He left Sergeant Murphy with the Bren group of four men to guard a crossroads, took the rest of the patrol and began carefully investigating each of the houses after all; that click he'd heard had made him twitchy. Then from one they heard voices and, after thinking for a moment, decided to force entry. With men either side of him and a Tommy gun at the ready, he opened the front door only to discover some twenty Italians packed into the room. An old man greeted them and explained that there were so many in the house because some of them had had their homes destroyed. The Germans, he said, had moved out the day before but they had sown many mines – although, he told Strick, who could speak Italian, the main road into the village was clear.

This was a clear warning and yet now, having left the Italians and rejoined Murphy, to head straight up the main road into the heart of the village seemed suicidal. If Germans were occupying the place, there would be nowhere to run – just buildings on either side. It was now the early hours of the morning, the moon still shining down on a rare clear night. Above them the hills loomed while ahead all they could see was the dark mass of the village. Strick needed to try and think clearly. Suddenly they heard the sound of a column of troops away to their right, heading up towards the village. This made no sense; there was no road or track in that direction – or least nothing on the map he'd been issued. He and Sergeant Murphy stalked up the road a little way and tried to listen. An occasional voice, but whether it was English or German they couldn't tell.

This convinced Strick that they must head round the village to their left. So far, they had just come across a handful of dwellings and the main part of the village was still 200 yards or so up ahead, but just off the road was an olive grove and beyond that an embryonic orchard with lines of young saplings. Strick now divided the patrol into two, Sergeant Murphy leading one half and he the other. For some reason he himself could not answer he placed Private Pile, the Bren-gunner, behind him and Jack Hargreaves in third place, whereas up until that point his batman had always been right behind him. Strick set off with his half of X Platoon and Murphy with his, but they'd only walked a short way when there was a sudden explosion behind him. 'I shot about eight foot through the air,' wrote Strick, 'thinking as I went, I suppose this is a mine.' Landing heavily, he lay on his back for a moment, then managed to get to his feet and staggered back to see what had happened. Apart from bruising and some cuts he reckoned he was all right, but Pile lay moaning on the ground. As the men gathered around the wounded man, they discovered he'd lost a foot and that both legs had been broken. A Schü-mine that had done for him. Despite his horrific injuries, Pile remained both conscious and surprisingly spirited.

Strick quickly rallied the others from Murphy's patrol, who thought an attack had begun and were ready to fire, when they all heard another explosion a little distance away and a burst from a German Schmeisser. They took Pile back a little way and applied a tourniquet to his footless leg, then suddenly heard voices again. 'My nerves were in pieces,' scribbled Strick, 'and it was then I suddenly realised that Sgt Murphy was missing. I was horrified to find I could not go back again and my head was going round.' One of his corporals, a man whom Strick had always thought a decent fellow but not much of a soldier, volunteered to lead a search party, which meant heading out into the potentially mine-strewn orchard. Meanwhile, some of the others managed to find a ladder, which they used as a makeshift stretcher for Pile. They waited, nerves taut, for the others, but when, thankfully, they eventually reappeared it was without Murphy, of whom they had found no trace. With a heavy heart, Strick decided they should head back. It seemed clear to him that Castelforte was still occupied – the voices, the sound of a column and shots from a submachine gun all pointed to this. Strick hated to leave Murphy, but what else was he supposed to do? So they set off, Strick hobbling beside Pile on the ladder, and every piece of ground and blade of grass looking deadly to him now.

Eventually reaching C Company in one piece, Pile was put on to a proper stretcher and Strick had his wounds bandaged. 'I kept breaking into tears,' he wrote, 'which was alarming.' More tears followed when he eventually reached Advanced HQ. 'The CO was very kind and fatherly, thanking me for what we had tried to do,' Strick added. 'The hysterical fits came on for about 2 hrs, after which I was OK.' Even so, although his physical wounds were all superficial, the MO prescribed a stint with B Echelon or hospital, and Strick chose the latter. 'Have no news of the Sgt,' he wrote to his mother in an extraordinarily frank letter. 'He was a personal friend and I do not think after this I can face that sort of job again.' In his diary he wrote of the awful feelings of guilt he felt over Murphy. 'It is terrible,' he wrote, 'what blast can do to one.'

'Discipline tightens,' noted Sergeant Audie Murphy. 'Night and day, we spend hours executing new tactics against a supposed enemy. In full battle gear, we wade to our hips in sea water and crawl through the marshes on our bellies. Our clothes are crusted with mud and salt.' Murphy was part of Company B in the 1st Battalion of 15th Infantry, one of the three regiments in the US 3rd Division. The 3rd was one of those earmarked for SHINGLE; it had not been involved in the Salerno landings, nor had the British 1st Division, so they were now being put through their paces on the flat coastline just to the north of Naples. Murphy had been newly promoted to staff sergeant even though he was still only eighteen and with his youthful dark good looks certainly appeared no older. Yet in many ways he was far older than his years or looks suggested. The son of sharecroppers from Hunt County, Texas, his father had abandoned his family of eleven siblings when he'd been young. Aged ten, he'd quit school and begun working full-time as a cotton picker to help support his family; he also developed considerable skill with a hunting rifle to put extra food on the table. His mother died when he was thirteen and at sixteen, using falsified papers, he signed up for the army. So Murphy knew a thing or two about resilience and how to look after himself. Since the division had landed in Sicily, he'd repeatedly proved himself as both a superb soldier and a leader of men. He had deserved his promotions despite his youth.

Now he and the men were in dark moods. He might have volunteered for this war, but he'd quickly realized it was a grim, dirty business. They all felt as though they were being prepared for the slaughter. Fights were being picked with the base troops, of whom there seemed impossibly large numbers in and around Naples. Generally, Murphy and his platoon were quick to snap. Rumours buzzing around didn't help: some said they would be heading to England for the invasion of France. Others said it was a new beachhead in Italy. Southern France was also in the mix. No one knew for sure. Uncertainty gnawed.

An Italian man called Drago had latched on to their company, a chancer, unnoticed by the brass but tolerated by the men because he was promising them girls. Rumours abounded that they would all soon be given passes into Naples, so Drago became even more popular. Murphy himself had been dreaming of being with a girl. Not any old woman, but a young, beautiful and innocent girl who, in his imagination, was called Maria. They would make love but it would be perfect and he would feel both loved and looked after. It was, he knew, only a dream, but the passes to Naples then became a reality and Drago was promising that he could find whatever women they wanted. Plans were made; rendezvous agreed.

First, though, Murphy had a day to kill, so he and his old squad pals found themselves in a café in the heart of the city. An American paratrooper, drunk, was asleep at one table. Three British soldiers then came in, one with a dog, and sat down nearby.

'No dogs,' the waiter told them.

'Eh?' said the Tommy who held the leash. 'The dog? No, no. 'E's a good bloke.' The soldier turned to the dog and said, 'There is no beer. But if it's wine you want, speak, lad.'

The dog barked.

The waiter continued to protest but the Tommies insisted, and when one of them stood up menacingly the Italian gave in. A bottle of wine was brought and four glasses, three for the men, one for the dog, who lapped his tumbler happily.

Some time later, after the Tommies had left, two women came in, thick with make-up and lipstick. One had a scar on her forehead, the other several gold teeth. Introductions were made and Murphy's pal, Martin Kelley, called them over. The girl with the gold teeth eyed Murphy intently then ran a hand through his hair. 'He is a babe,' she said. 'He is too young for soldier.' Murphy angrily flung her hand away. 'Get away before I break your neck,' he snapped. He couldn't understand his anger but he felt dirty, debased. This woman was not the Maria of his imagining.

Later, Murphy left them all and went to meet Drago as planned. It was dusk but soon he was being hassled by a *scugnizzo,* a young street urchin. 'Hey, Joe!' the boy called out. Did he want eggs? Beef steak? A nice girl?

'No,' Murphy replied.

'Fine type girl. *Seexteen*.'

Murphy eventually gave him some chocolate and told him to scram. He didn't want an underage girl and he had no cigarettes; he was unusual in neither smoking nor touching drink. As darkness shrouded the city he met up with Drago as planned, who led him to a house – a simple, family home shared by a middle-aged couple and their eighteen-year-old daughter. Introductions were made and Murphy emptied out a number of tins of food from his musette bag, then stood there awkwardly, unable to speak Italian. He was tempted to leave when Drago left but something kept him there. The mother and father eyed him, the father defiant, the mother delighted with the tins he'd brought. The girl was called Maria, as in his imaginings, but she was not the girl of his dreams, even though she was pretty and delicate enough. Her hair was in braids and shone in the low light of the house. She wore an old dress, barely to her knees, and sandals. Hunger and despair marked her, however. 'Already shadows dance in the hollows of her cheek,' he noted, 'and her eyes have the tiredness of age.' She was thin, too. Far too thin. For a while they all sat round the kitchen table, the girl saying nothing and Murphy trying to translate what the father said with the help of his dictionary. It seemed they had had a son but he had been killed in North Africa. The war was bad. Mussolini a treacherous man. The Germans arrogant and vicious. Murphy understood that he was expected to take the girl to a quiet place; it was what her hungry, poverty-stricken parents were expecting too, but somehow he couldn't bring himself to do it. Instead, Maria suggested they play a makeshift board game with dice and some old buttons. Murphy readily agreed; what a surreal situation he had found himself in.

It was evening and suddenly the air raid siren droned. Maria's parents hurriedly grabbed coats and blankets and, speaking quickly in Italian, urged him to come with them. Murphy shook his head – he only had one night in Naples and he was not going to spend it in an air raid shelter. The siren continued to wail and after a heated argument Maria led her parents to the door, almost pushed them out and then returned to Murphy. Only then did he discover that she spoke some English after all. Sitting opposite one another, the only light that of a single candle, they heard the sound of anti-aircraft guns opening, then falling bombs. The house rocked with the explosions and the candle flickered. Then, blowing it out, she stood up and asked him for his hand. The gunfire was deafening. More bombs fell, closer this time, but Murphy wasn't too bothered; after the front line it was nothing to get too excited about, but her hand tightened in his and as he put his hands around her he could feel her body trembling. 'I kiss her full on the mouth,' he wrote. 'The trembling stops.'

Some time later, before the all-clear, he fell asleep, only to be woken by her telling him he must go quickly. The raiders had finally passed and her parents would soon be back. He could see she had been crying. As he left he promised to return and that he'd write to her.

'No,' she told him. 'A soldier never writes; never come back. Eet ees not the first time.'

Italian women were selling themselves throughout southern Italy, not just Naples. The British 1st Division had landed at Taranto back in December then moved up the Adriatic Canosa, close to the small port town of Barletta. Guardsman Edward Danger and some of his fellows in the 5th Grenadier Guards ventured into the town, where they were immediately accosted by small boys pimping for their sisters and shouting 'ficky-fick, Johnny!' at every serviceman they saw. Four of Danger's pals followed one of these boys home. The family lived in two rooms: the mother and father, two daughters, both around twenty, and the boy. Danger's mates were astonished to discover that the father was the master of ceremonies. His two older daughters took off two of the lads into the spare room. 'Mother accommodated the third member of the party,' noted Danger, 'and for the fourth member, they eventually produced a girl of about twelve.'

The Allies had embarked on this war to rid the world of the tyranny of Fascism, Nazism and ultra-nationalism, and yet the morality of their mission had begun to blur. It was, even by the standards of the day, appalling that young Allied troops were able to take advantage of the terrible poverty and hunger now ravaging Italian citizens. A culture prevailed in the ranks that made such behaviour acceptable; yet that prostitutes were descending on Allied troops in Naples and Barletta, and young girls like Maria were offering themselves for a few cans of beans, corned beef and tinned fruit was because of the appalling state into which much of southern Italy, but especially the towns and cities such as Naples, had fallen. War had swept into this nation of 40 million like a hurricane and brought with it destruction on an unprecedented scale.

Some areas had remained thankfully unscathed – much of rural Italy, through which the armies had only briefly passed, and even stretches such as the Amalfi coast had avoided the typhoon of war rolling up the leg of Italy. But not so Naples, the most densely populated city in Europe before the war, when it had been home to some 900,000 people. It was still reeling from the terrible damage wrought first by Allied bombers, who had visited the city over 200 times and on 180 occasions in the first nine months of 1943, and then by the Germans. Under Kesselring, retreating troops had been carrying out a scorched-earth policy, deliberately trying to create a humanitarian catastrophe in an effort to delay the Allied advance and force them to divert much-needed resources to the Italian population. The electricity system had been destroyed, so too the water system; the docks had also been blown up. Streets were filled with rubble and ruined buildings; there were also shortages of everything and disease spread rapidly in a city where sanitation was no longer possible. The Allies had swiftly repaired the docks and got running water and electricity working again, but Naples had been starving and still was by the start of the New Year. Not only had the city's infrastructure taken such a hammering but so had the wider communications network in the south; even what food could be produced was almost impossible to distribute. By the start of 1944, in the south, 75 per cent of Italy's pre-war trains had been destroyed, 85 per cent of its railway carriages and 90 per cent of its trucks and lorries. Furthermore, 87.5 per cent of its merchant fleet had been sunk and was now lying at the bottom of the Mediterranean.

The Allies had plenty of vehicles, but these were needed for the battle at the front; the task of the military was to win the war as quickly as possible with the fewest casualties, which in Italy was already proving very challenging. Of course, the Allies knew they had a responsibility to help the civilian population, but the British had not asked Italy to declare war on them back in June 1940, so to a very large extent it was considered that Italy's problems were entirely of its own making. Food was provided and distributed but it was never enough, especially not in the cities; even in the countryside it was hard to grow food in winter, and especially during one as bad as the current one was proving to be. A further problem was the shortage of working men. Millions were now in prison camps in England, Canada and the United States, and working as slave labour in Germany. The Allies had also demanded 180,000 men to be employed as manual labour and a further 45,000 for use in military rear areas. They were paying them, but a pittance, and very often taking them away from their homes. The Italians had also been ordered to hand over any Italian currency that the Allies might require and to honour Allied military-issued lire. Control of banking and business had also been placed in Allied hands, as well as any foreign exchange and overseas trade. Southern Italy, already ruined by a terrible war it had been ill-equipped to fight and unable to afford, had been stripped bare.

The Allies had imposed the Allied Military Government of Occupied Territories – known by its acronym, AMGOT – and pledged to distribute around 2,000 calories per person per day, but this had not been achieved, largely due to the immense pressures on shipping and the time it was taking to get infrastructure up and running again. Most civilians in Naples, for example, were having a good day if they scavenged a quarter of that. Since the Allies' arrival, inflation had rocketed by 321 per cent, largely because desk wallahs back at AFHQ in Algiers had set the exchange rate based on the Italian lire that had been used in East Africa back in 1941. An element of carelessness, encouraged by a streak of vindictiveness for the misery caused by Italy's warmongering, had pervaded the way these staff officers had planned AMGOT for Italy. As a consequence, a civil servant now working in Naples might expect around 5,500 lire a month, but this was the equivalent of less than $20.* A postman earned just 450 lire – a little over a dollar.

In Eboli, nineteen-year-old Pasqualina Caruso and her family were struggling to survive. 'Economically in Italy,' she noted in her diary, 'things are going from bad to worse. We are starving. There is little food and what there is, is at an exaggerated price and it is impossible to buy it.'

* Around $440 in 2024.

The family were Neapolitans, but Lina – as she was known – and her mother and three sisters had moved to Eboli the previous year to escape the bombing raids, only to find themselves in the midst of the Allied invasion and the battle that followed. Her father had initially remained in Naples as the Chief Secretary of the State Railways, which were now functioning in a limited capacity, albeit primarily on behalf of the Allies. Although a civil servant, his salary was still a pittance in the current exchange rate. Bread was scarce because the mills were still not working and flour could not be effectively distributed. A loaf, Lina noted, cost between 80 and 130 lire per kilo, pasta 100 lire and olive oil 120. Potatoes were the cheapest food at 20–30 lire per kilo, but they were heavy, didn't go very far and were, like everything else, scarce.

Her father had recently joined them in Eboli but needed to get back to his job, and so on 15 January her parents and her sisters Flora and Nella decided to all return to Naples in the hope that in the larger city they might find more food as well as work; it was a major port, after all. Lina and her older sister Rosetta planned to remain in Eboli a little longer, but accompanied their parents and sister to the station at around 9.30 a.m.; since there was no timetable any more, it was a case of turning up and waiting until a train appeared. The station was crowded, as was the train when it eventually appeared. Lina could scarcely believe it: people were crammed into the carriages, on to the roofs, on the links, the running boards and clinging to the windows. There was no way her family could board it and so they decided to wait for the freight train instead. Lina went off with Rosetta to try and find some food, managing to buy some watery ricotta for 40 lire and a couple of apples for 10 lire. When they returned to the station it was 3 p.m. and her mother, father and sisters were still waiting. Eventually, exhausted and fed up, they abandoned their plans and trudged back up the hill with their luggage once more.

It was probably just as well because Naples was struggling as wretchedly as ever. Norman Lewis was an intelligence officer in the 312th Field Security Section, a unit of a single officer and eleven NCOs, of whom Lewis, a sergeant, was one. On paper they were part of the Intelligence Corps, but in practice their role was to act as linguists and to bridge the gap between the military and civilian population. Lewis had come ashore at Salerno back in September, but he and his fellows in the 312th FSS had been posted to Naples the moment the Allies had swept in on 1 October and had been based there ever since, battling, without much success, to help the local population. It had been an uphill struggle, the challenges seemingly insurmountable and made worse by the indifference of many of the AMGOT staff and the rising corruption and growing black market that was filling the political void left by, first, the collapse of Fascism and then the collapse of Italy as a whole.

At the beginning of January, Lewis found himself trying to suppress a spate of telegraph wire-cutting that was playing havoc with military communications. Phone lines that worked one day did not the next, as Italians crept out in the night, cut the line and then sold the copper on the black market. Colonel Edgar E. Hume, the Chief AMGOT officer in Naples, had ordered a clampdown, which had prompted a renewed drive by the Military Police. 'As usual,' noted Lewis, 'the small people who cut the wire bear the brunt of the offensive, but no attempt is made to track down the traders who buy and sell the copper.' In nearby Afragola, a suburb to the north of the city, Antonio Priore, a scrap dealer about seventy years old, was stopped by the MPs as he wheeled his handcart through the streets. Searching his wares, they found several lengths of copper wire. He insisted it was German wire and he'd cut it because in broadcasts the Allies had urged Italians to do just that, but they arrested him and flung him in a cell in Poggioreale in the centre of Naples. Lewis was informed and sent to see him the following day. He found the old man, thin and decrepit, shivering in his cell, utterly bewildered as to why he'd been arrested and worried about his wife. He assumed Lewis had come to take him home. 'Be nice to get back home to the old woman,' Priore told him. 'I didn't like to think of her in that house all on her own last night. Can't get about too well any more.'

Lewis did not have the authority to free him but did instead drive over to Afragola to check on the old man's wife. He had considerable difficulty finding the place and was eventually directed through waterlogged fields to a small shack. It was raining and bitterly cold but inside he found the old lady, shrivelled in her bed under a pile of rags. 'Starving cats, rats, leaking roof, a suffocating smell of excrement,' noted Lewis. 'Not the slightest sign of food anywhere.'

Lewis took himself off to see the *brigadiere* of the local Carabinieri, the Italian military police. The commandant was struggling to keep any kind of order at all. 'He was suffering from daily gunfights between rival gangs,' wrote Lewis, 'bandits, pillaging army deserters, vendettas, kidnappings, mysterious disappearances, reported cases of typhus, the non-arrival of his pay and the shortage of supplies of every kind, including ammunition.' He was also dumbfounded that Lewis should be concerned about the fate of an old woman. If he was so worried about her, the *brigadiere* said to him, why not simply release the old man?

From the Carabinieri, Lewis went to the local MPs and suggested they send the stolen wire to Signals for examination. The captain admitted it was German wire all right; that wasn't the point. German wire was now Allied wire, so the key question here was when it was cut. The cuts looked quite fresh. Back at his own HQ in Naples, Lewis recommended that Priore be immediately released, but was told it was nothing to do with him and to mind his own business. 'So Priore would be brought to trial in a week's time,' he jotted, 'or maybe two weeks, or even three weeks, depending on pressure of business in the courts. Meanwhile the wife would die alone in their shack.'

The shortage of men and of jobs, combined with a profound lack of food and rampant inflation, meant the black market thrived, mostly with the exchange of stolen Allied supplies, which already accounted for around 75 per cent of all available food. For all too many women, left behind by the men as they'd gone off to war or been bundled into trucks and packed off to Germany, there was only one way of feeding themselves and their children, and that was through prostitution. Naples was pullulating with troops, both base troops and those on leave from the front and now training for Anzio. Italian doctors informed the American medical services that by January 1944, at least 50 per cent of 'available women in Italy' had some form of sexually transmitted disease. In populous areas such as Naples, between 95 and 100 per cent of prostitutes had some form of venereal disease, a staggering proportion.

This was a horrific situation. Desperation, poverty and starvation had led these women to prostitute themselves. Drago was not the only pimp hanging around 3rd Infantry Division – so too were women in their hundreds who had descended on their encampment, and that of the British 1st Division, sneaking through the barbed wire, disguising themselves as laundresses and setting themselves up in the nearby caves. Every day, truckloads of women were being rounded up and delivered into the custody of the local Carabiniere, who promptly released them again. American authorities thought the only way to deal with this was to maintain continuous education for the troops, issue prophylactics as widely as possible and bring in known prostitutes for examination and treatment.

Yet if it was reckoned that half of Italian women were prostituting themselves and that nearly all of them were now thought to be suffering from STDs, then the Allies were clearly dealing with a huge – and unmanageable – number. Back in December, the latest Fifth Army medical statistics showed that 92 in every 1,000 men were suffering from an STD – almost one in ten – and although most of those were not front-line infantry, the danger of considerable numbers of afflicted women descending on 1st and 3rd Divisions was potentially a big problem and one that was taken very seriously.

The tragedy, though, was that Fifth Army MOs were looking at this from the perspective of how to keep their men fit and healthy and able to fight, rather than considering the catastrophe that so many women were making themselves ill, not to mention humiliating and degrading themselves, because of a situation that was, in large part, of the Allies' own making. If they more swiftly improved infrastructure, brought in more food, prioritized the civilian population further and took measures to drastically reduce inflation the situation would rapidly improve. And so would the health of the troops. Yet again, though, the pressure to press on with the war, to get to Rome and to ensure that nothing got in the way of OVERLORD meant that Italian civilians would continue to play second fiddle – if not third or fourth – to the perceived greater needs of supplying and maintaining the Allied armies at the front. And after all, a major offensive was already starting seventy miles to the north.

CHAPTER 7

The Largest Air Force in the World

GENERAL MARK CLARK WAS acquiring a number of new neighbours in Caserta. First, General Alexander and his staff of 15th Army Group moved into the Palazzo Reale from their previous HQ near Bari on 17 January; this made sense now that the main emphasis of the campaign lay in Fifth Army's sector in the west. Then, on 20 January, it was the turn of the Mediterranean Allied Air Forces – MAAF. Having such a palace as the new letterhead address might have seemed grand, but the Palazzo Reale was not in the best shape and, as the air staff discovered, they were sharing their new digs with 180 years of accumulated fleas. None the less, Lieutenant-General Ira Eaker, the new C-in-C of the MAAF, was able to write to Robert Lovett, the US Assistant Secretary of War for Air, that he was now established in Italy. 'At 8 o'clock on Thursday morning, the 20th,' Eaker wrote, 'the MAAF HQ officially opened.' They were now in business, close to the front, cheek by jowl with Alex's Army Group and with Clark's Fifth Army HQ, which was exactly where they needed to be. It was a considerable fillip for Allied ground operations because it marked a moment of new clarity and focus in which Italy and the southern Reich, rather than the wider Mediterranean, were now the prime focus of air operations in the theatre.

The MAAF – or 'Maff' as it was widely known – had been created only on 10 December, part of a shake-up of the now enormous air commands throughout the Mediterranean. But at the end of the year there had also been a change of command too, with Tedder and Spaatz, the MAAF's first commander and deputy, heading back to the UK for OVERLORD. In their place, in a reversal of nationalities, Eaker of the US Army Air Force took over as C-in-C, while Air Marshal Sir John Slessor of the RAF arrived as his deputy.

Eaker was forty-seven years old, the same age as Clark, and had come from commanding the US Eighth Air Force in England through a great crisis in the late summer and autumn of 1943. Eaker had been one of a number of leading airmen between the wars, of whom General Henry 'Hap' Arnold, C-in-C of the US Army Air Forces, and Tooey Spaatz, now in England as C-in-C of the US Strategic Air Forces, were two others, who devoutly believed in the primacy of daylight precision-bombing. It had been their conviction before the war that tight formations of heavily armed four-engine bombers would, collectively, be well defended enough to see off any potential enemy fighter attack. Morally and pragmatically, they also believed that daylight bombing, using stunning new science such as the Norden bombsight over a clear target, would enable very accurate and therefore more efficient bombing: the more accurately bombs were dropped, the fewer would be needed to destroy a specific target and the less collateral damage would be caused.

Such theories had been cruelly exposed in a series of raids deep into the Reich when fighter escorts had not had the range to stay with the bombers. On 17 August 1943, the very same day the Allies completed the conquest of Sicily and the Italians and Allies opened face-to-face negotiations for Italy's armistice for the first time, 315 heavy bombers from the Eighth had attempted to hit aircraft and ball-bearing production plants in Regensburg and Schweinfurt. It had been a massacre, as four times as many Luftwaffe fighter planes had intercepted them at various points along the way and 60 of them had been shot down, a further 11 had to be scrapped and 164 were damaged, some badly so. In other words, 75 per cent of those that flew had been hit. At the beginning of October they tried a series of similar deep-penetration raids over the course of a week, culminating in 'Schweinfurt II' on 14 October. It became known as 'Black Thursday' as a further 60 of the attacking force were destroyed. In seven days, the Eighth had lost 148 heavy bombers.

Clearly, even Flying Fortresses needed fighter escorts all the way to the target and back; what's more, visual bombing was often not possible, especially in winter because of the amount of cloud over Europe. Where Eaker had been quite correct, however, was that destroying the

Luftwaffe was of paramount importance and should be the Strategic Air Forces' primary target. The reasons were twofold. First, enemy fighters, not anti-aircraft guns, were the bombers' most deadly enemy. Destroy them and bombing would become a lot simpler and less costly. Second, the Allies needed control of the airspace over much of north-west Europe before they could even consider launching OVERLORD. Eaker had conceived and championed Operation POINTBLANK, the planned systematic destruction of the Luftwaffe, which had been signed off by the Combined Chiefs the previous June. It was the prospect of continuing POINTBLANK from Italy, and so further tightening the noose of the combined bomber offensive around Nazi Germany, that had been the key factor, above all, in convincing the Combined Chiefs that the Allies should invade Italy in the first place back in September. The disasters of August and October had prompted the urgent acceleration of moving heavy bombers to the Foggia area; the US Fifteenth Air Force had been formed on 1 November 1943, two weeks after Black Thursday, and the number of bomb groups earmarked for the Fifteenth increased from a modest six to a whopping twenty-one.

There was a sense, certainly felt by Eaker, that he'd been demoted upstairs by being moved to the MAAF. Perhaps a fresh pair of hands had been needed, yet General Jimmy Doolittle, his replacement, also took over at the Eighth the very moment fortunes were changing. A long-range fighter had been found in the Merlin-powered P-51 Mustang and the Eighth's bomber force was also starting to increase in size exponentially. At any rate, Eaker was a good, decent man, had an intellect's mind for strategy and was, a bit like Alexander, both conspicuously charming and liked by all. His deputy, John Slessor, was another intellectual as well as being dynamic and charismatic, and had recently transformed the RAF's Coastal Command into an Atlantic War-winning operation. The two were friends and complemented one another well.

And both charm and clear, strategic thinking would be needed at the MAAF. For all the concerns about the shortage of shipping, the MAAF was currently the world's largest-ever air command, and included not only 321,439 American, British and DUKE – Dominions, UK and Empire – men and women, but also a staggering 12,598 aircraft of which 4,323 were operating in combat units. It included the Mediterranean Allied Strategic Air Forces – MASAF – of which the US Fifteenth Air Force was a part; also the Tactical Air Forces – MATAF – and the Coastal Air Forces – MACAF. While this led to a lot of very similar acronyms, under these headings were the heavies and their fighter escorts of the US Fifteenth Air Force, the fighters and twin-engine medium bombers of the US Twelfth Air Force and the RAF's Desert and Balkan Air Forces. Most of these, by January 1944, were in Italy. While cloud, rain and the miserable weather often came between planning and reality, when the skies cleared the ground forces could and did expect to see large numbers of fighters, fighter-bombers and medium bombers over the front.

The truth was, since the final phase of the Tunisian campaign Allied air forces had totally dominated in the Mediterranean, had been instrumental in the final victory in North Africa in May 1943 and had played a critical role in the Sicilian campaign and at the start of the battle for Italy during those far-off days of azure-blue skies and sunshine. The Mediterranean had been a proving ground, particularly for the development of tactical air power directly supporting ground operations. Many of those pioneers, both RAF and USAAF, had been transferred to the UK and would be playing a key role in the run-up to and during OVERLORD, but the MAAF commanders now running the show were all highly experienced and extremely competent. The ground forces might have been struggling against the terrain and determined German defence, but the Allied air forces were in a class of their own.

Over the past year the Luftwaffe had been utterly hammered, losing more than 6,000 aircraft between November 1942 and October 1943. At the same time, RAF Bomber Command's all-out strategic air offensive against Germany had been launched in early March 1943 and had been followed by the growing strength of the Eighth Air Force too, for all its crises along the way. German aircraft production had since switched to producing predominantly fighters and most of these were now in the Reich, although Luftflotte II remained in northern Italy, primarily to try and intercept the increasing numbers of heavies operating out of the Foggia area.

Among those now starting to fly regularly once more was Lieutenant T. Michael Sullivan, a B-17 Flying Fortress bombardier in 429th Bomb Squadron, part of the 2nd Bomb Group – BG. From Elgin, Illinois, Sullivan was still only twenty years old and had joined the 2nd BG back in October, when they'd been based in Algiers. They had moved to Foggia after several false starts due to bad weather on 10 December and since then it had seemed as though every other mission had been scrubbed for the same reason. And it wasn't just the weather over the target but the conditions on the ground. There were no asphalted runways on the Foggia airfields, only pierced-steel plating, which was better than nothing, but even so these flat, dirt airfields rapidly flooded and became bogged very quickly too. There had been no flying on 1 January because of the storm, nor on the 2nd. Sullivan and his crew had flown on the 3rd, hitting a ball-bearing plant in northern Italy, another POINTBLANK target. His ship had been out of commission on the 4th, bad weather scrubbed another mission on the 5th, they flew on the 7th but cloud covered the target. And so it went on. It had been frustrating, to say the least.

Recently, however, the weather had improved a little and since 15 January the Fifteenth Air Force had been bombing targets in northern Italy every day as part of the pre-SHINGLE air plan, designed to hammer German lines of communications and hamper their efforts to supply the front. Sullivan and his crew bombed the marshalling yards at Poggibonsi, between Siena and Florence, on the 15th. 'Flak heavy, intense and extremely accurate,' he scribbled in his diary. '15 holes in our ship.' The next day he was detailed to fly as bombardier with a new crew as 'Sad Sack' had not yet recovered from its splintering over Poggibonsi. They bombed the Luftwaffe airfield at Villorba, near Venice. 'Completely destroyed target,' he noted. 'No fighter opposition.' Sullivan had rarely flown three missions in three days, but with SHINGLE around the corner a maximum air effort had been demanded and so on the 17th he'd flown to Prato, north of Florence, and bombed the marshalling yards there. Once again, he felt confident they'd smashed the target good and proper; as bombardier, he wanted to hit it every time. And yet again there had been no enemy fighters to be seen; he simply couldn't understand it. 'They are going to hit us one of these days,' he jotted. 'Highly successful raid. No 17s lost for a change.' Prato had been a milk run, and perhaps because it had been such a piece of cake Sullivan had flown yet again, a fourth day on the trot, and this time with his old crew back in 'Sad Sack.' The target had been the Certaldo marshalling yards, another town near Florence, all part of the plan to make it as difficult as possible for the Germans to reinforce the south. 'Easy mission,' he noted. 'Blew hell out of all military targets in area.'

Also now at Foggia were the 1st Fighter Group – FG – who had moved to Salsola, one of the many airfields in the complex, on 8 January. Captain Robert 'Smoky' Vrilakas had been on leave on the island of Capri at the time but rejoined his squadron, the 94th, four days later at their new home. Vrilakas, a second-generation American-Greek, had been serving in the Mediterranean since July and was finally nearing the end of his tour of duty – one that had seen him fly all over the central Mediterranean and even into the southern Reich, escorting bombers. The 1st FG flew the P-38 Lightning, a twin-engine, twin-boom fighter plane that was surprisingly agile, very quick and armed to the hilt. With two, rather than one, engines it lacked the manoeuvrability of a single-engine fighter, but it did have incredible range and, with a 20mm cannon and four .50-calibre machine guns, certainly packed a punch. And it was quick, as its name suggested, operating at over 400 mph if needed. That could be very useful in a melee; certainly, Vrilakas had no complaints with his aircraft.

Vrilakas was less impressed with Salsola, however. All around the airfield were wrecked German aircraft, which he was fascinated to see, but the place was a quagmire. They were living in four-man tents, heated by a stove rigged up using an oil drum, which was hazardous to say the least. Because of the mud they walked everywhere on duckboards, which soon became slick with mud too. Runway drainage wasn't very effective, and while landing and taking off, large puddles always had to be negotiated.

Vrilakas's first mission back from leave was as a bomber escort to Bolzano, a key town in the South Tyrol through which the main road and rail link to and from the southern Reich ran. It was a four-hour trip during which they had to dodge heavy flak but no enemy fighters. A greater danger was from the wear and tear they were now experiencing on their aircraft. The supply chain in Italy was the problem – the shortage of shipping was affecting the maintenance of aircraft too. Parts were being scrounged and cannibalized from other aircraft, but for the pilots these shortages added a very unwanted layer of extra risk. 'We would often start out with a full squadron of twelve aircraft,' noted Vrilakas, 'and have as many as four be forced to turn back.'

Despite these mechanical concerns, the Allied air forces were certainly making themselves felt. Oberst Wilhelm Mauss at XIV Panzerkorps headquarters was all too aware of how the recent days' raids had been hampering efforts. As wonderful as the recent weather had been, it was making the military situation very difficult. 'The opponent's aircraft can romp around just as they like,' he noted. 'Ever again they keep destroying the railway lines, with supplies always getting stocked up. A railway station is barely repaired when another one cannot be used or is ruined again.'

What a difference clear skies made.

'Extensive enemy movements observed opposite left wing of 15 Pz Gren Div,' recorded the AOK 10 war diary on 17 January, 'where the enemy has crept up to the river bank.' The Ic staff at AOK 10 – the intelligence section – concluded that American divisions must be preparing for a major attack in the area south of Cassino. If so, that meant an attempted river crossing into the sector of 15. Panzergrenadier-Division and 44. Infanterie-Division.

Back at the front and resuming his role within 15. Panzergrenadier was Oberleutnant Hans Golda. An Austrian from Vienna, Golda had been one of the lucky few to have been granted some leave over Christmas and he had relished the chance to see his wife and baby son. Golda commanded the 7. Batterie of Werfer-Regiment 71, which operated five-barrelled rocket mortars. 'Nebelwerfer' literally translated as 'fog launcher' and had originally been designed to provide smoke, used for masking attacks, but had quickly been developed to fire high-explosive warheads. The Nebelwerfer 42, with which Werfer-Regiment 71 was equipped, was quite a beast: five 210mm tubes that could fire high-explosive rockets nearly five miles. And when these rockets were fired, one after the other in quick succession, they screamed and whined as they sped low through the sky. The Allied troops named them 'moaning meanies', akin to the scream of a dive-bombing Stuka. Nebelwerfers were both lethal and terrifying to hear.

Golda was pleased to see his boys again, to whom he felt a deep and rather avuncular connection. A sentimental fellow who tended to wear his heart on his sleeve, he was quick to laugh, enjoyed the simple things in life and had established a strong esprit de corps within his battery. He treated his men as well as he could, always watched their backs but expected devoted loyalty in return. He'd only been gone less than a fortnight but, as he was well aware, that was a long time at the front, and several old friends were missing on his return, not least Gefreiter Beecken, a giant of a fellow and former baker who had not only helped provide the men with extra rations but who had been one of the ever-present characters too. 'Faithful as a child,' Golda had noted, 'a man such as I have rarely known.' But Beecken had been badly wounded in the arm and was gone. Obergefreiter Gomm had been killed while trying to blow up a tree. 'He was completely torn to pieces,' wrote Golda, 'so he didn't suffer anything the poor boy!' Golda felt these losses keenly. Others might have been able to harden their hearts but not he.

The batteries were deployed separately, which meant each had a considerable amount of autonomy. Golda had to report to the regiment for orders and instructions, but for the most part he was left alone to get on with the job in hand, which was supporting the grenadiers – infantry – up ahead around the village of Sant'Angelo in Theodice, which stood on a low bluff overlooking the River Rapido. This current position had been occupied in the middle of December and was, Golda, thought, well sited just ahead of the village of Pignataro Interamna and beneath a low ridge a couple of hundred yards long. On the left-hand side, deep in the slope, they had dug bunkers, propped by wood joists and beams; on the right of the ridge was Golda's own bunker. On the brow of this little rise stood a farmhouse, under which they had built another bunker. Zigzagging trenches linked the bunkers to the launchers, while behind them, alongside the main village road, was the cemetery. And towering above them, looking down from above, was the abbey, white against the dark mass of Monte Cassino and the huge Monte Cairo towering behind.

Golda had only been back a few days when the American artillery opened up and pounded them almost without let-up. For the next ten days or so he and his men barely left their bunkers; he noted that several of those who dared, for reasons of necessity, were wounded as they used the latrines. They lived by the meagre light of home-made lamps using tightly rolled paper as a wick soaked in fuel in a bottle, which worked all right but was very smoky. All of them were filthy, and every time the shelling resumed with particular intensity they found themselves crouching, steel helmets on, waiting for the end. An end which, thankfully for Golda and his men, never came; they had dug their bunkers well. Outside, meanwhile, the lush, rolling valley turned into a desolate lunar landscape: the earth ripped up, the trees torn to shreds, the houses nothing but ruins.

On 18 January, 134. Regiment, now with 44. Division once more, was posted back to the front and Major Georg Zellner and his 3. Bataillon found themselves close to Hans Golda's battery at Pignataro, less than three miles due west from the Rapido at Sant'Angelo in Theodice. It really was ridiculous how quickly battered and bruised divisions such as these were expected to turn round and face the onslaught once again. Four days was all 134. Regiment had been given, and Georg Zellner had been put on standby after just two. Not that he had found the chance for a rest as restorative as he'd hoped. Rather, the time to himself had given him long hours in which his mind had whirred. 'Personal life creeps into your soul, into your thoughts,' he had written in his diary, 'and makes your heart beat faster than when at work. What is my fate? That's how it sounds in your ears. If a shell tears you apart, then it's over. The agony is over.' But then another part of his mind told him to shut out such thoughts, that he wanted to live. What about a wound? Or being captured? But he didn't wish to be behind wire either. He found himself thinking about all the seventeen-year-olds buried at the crossroads, then of his little girl, his daughter back home in Regensburg. Good thoughts of home, then sadness, then dark thoughts again – death, which would make everything the same and take away his worries. These thoughts – they were impossible to control. He simply wanted the war to end and to get back home.

A summons to the regiment on the 16th warned of deployment overnight on the 18th. Instructions from on high: the men needed to be re-educated; they needed to believe in National Socialism and in final victory. Some officers in the division had been shot for being drunk. 'When do you actually not get shot?' Zellner had asked. Everyone had laughed, but it was hardly a laughing matter. On his shoulders lay the task of rebuilding the battalion yet again – but how, when they were never given enough replacements and when all the old-timers, men who actually knew how to fight, had gone? Further grumblings from higher up the food chain: that young replacements were not fighting well because they no longer believed in victory. Wrong. They weren't fighting well because they had received almost no training, were still teenagers and were not prepared for the horrific violence and assault on their every fibre they experienced the moment they reached the front line. Zellner asked for leave but it was, of course, refused. Instead he was promised a quiet section. He knew what that meant: it was a euphemism for being flung into the fire. There was no quiet section.

They had moved up on the afternoon of the 18th, his battalion still woefully understrength but reinforced with teenagers who looked like the children they were. When he had seen the Cassino Valley for the first time back in November he had said to himself, 'God have mercy on those who are deployed in this valley.' Now, he thought, it is us. Through Pontecorvo, a ghost town, rubble and destroyed buildings, and a stench of rotting corpses. Zellner felt sick. He was riding ahead on his motorcycle and at the edge of the town, blinded by artillery smoke, collided with a car and was hurled into a ditch. Miraculously, he was unhurt save for a few scratches and bruises. 'Outrageous luck,' he noted. Even the bike was all right. The battalion rendezvoused at the cemetery behind Golda's battery, then he and Schwarzer, one of his officers, went to look for a command post and found a mill house on the Cassino road. It was still occupied but they requisitioned it and told the family to head back, clear of the front. 'What a shame,' noted Zellner. 'Children, women, old men.'

By 8 a.m. on the 19th everything was in place, only for heavy enemy artillery fire to crash in around them. The result: yet more dead and wounded in his battalion.

From Cassino town at the edge of the Monte Cassino massif to the north to the village of Sant'Apollinare on the southern side, where the mountains climbed once again, the distance as the crow flies was five miles. Along here flowed the Rapido until it met with the River Liri in front of Sant'Apollinare and became the Garigliano, these two rivers now merged and flowed all the way to the sea, ten miles or so to the south-west. From the top of Monte Trocchio the Liri Valley, stretching away to the north-west, looked largely flat and innocuous, but that was deceptive because apart from occasional stretches of floodplain either side of the rivers, this was an area of softly rolling, undulating countryside with plenty of small ridges, bluffs, folds and hillocks. The village of Sant'Angelo was roughly in the middle of the mouth of the Liri Valley, halfway between Cassino and Sant'Apollinare, and in front of the series of hills recently captured by the Red Bulls and particularly 1st Armored, which meant guns could be deployed behind them.

The intelligence picture of the German defences here was fairly sobering, and had been released by Fifth Army's G2 – intelligence staff – on 12 January. Artillery in depth, including mortars and Nebelwerfers – this included Hans Golda's battery – then, closer to the Rapido, outposts, barbed-wire entanglements and mines, with trees and vegetation cleared for uninterrupted fields of fire. Towering over the entire stretch was the ever-watching Monte Cassino massif, on top of which were German observers. Subsequent patrol work and captured enemy troops confirmed that the line here was held by 129. Panzergrenadier-Regiment to the north of Sant'Angelo and a reconnaissance battalion and part of 104. Panzergrenadier-Regiment to the south.

There was no question that breaking through these prepared defences, especially with a fast-flowing river to cross first, was going to be extremely challenging. On the other hand, so was crossing the Garigliano, which was much wider, had deeper fields of fire on the far side and more pronounced hills from which German troops could look down on any attackers. Crossing the Volturno the previous October had also been a challenge when both river and terrain around it favoured the defender. Nor had climbing up the 3,000-foot-high Monte Sammucro and Camino been a cakewalk. Far from it; in many ways it had been something of a miracle that both had eventually fallen at all. That they had done so had been because of the immense weight of Allied artillery and the dogged determination of the infantry, despite the scale of the challenge and the horrendous mountain terrain over which they were fighting. Up there in the mountains, where the soil was almost non-existent, mortars and shells were doubly lethal because there was no earth to absorb the missiles and plenty of flying, razor-sharp pieces of rock to add to the shrapnel blast. At least in the Liri Valley the rich, waterlogged soil could soak up much of the explosive effect of mortars and artillery shells.

And no matter how many guns the Germans could bring to bear, it was nothing like as many as those of the US II Corps. The plan, in a nutshell, was this: to bring together as much artillery as possible, including all attached to 36th Division, all of 1st Armored and some of the Red Bulls. There was to be armour on standby to offer both close fire support during the crossing and exploit success. The infantry were to get across at night, in darkness and behind plenty of smoke. They would then push forward and take out the enemy outposts, forward mortar and MG positions, and then push on. No one was denying it would be costly in lives, but it did not look impossible. In fact, General Keyes, the II Corps commander, had swollen the Texan Division substantially, providing two tank battalions which were specifically attached to the division and no fewer than twelve extra field battalions of artillery to add to the four already part of the T-Patchers' arsenal, so sixteen in all. This included 120 155mm long-toms, and also two further tank destroyer battalions of high-velocity anti-tank guns and an anti-aircraft battalion to be used in a ground role. In total, that amounted to 371 field guns. There were also two chemical battalions providing smoke, four companies of bridging engineers and the 13th Armored Regiment of some 150 Shermans, attached from Combat Command B from 1st Armored Division.

Major-General Fred Walker, commander of the 36th T-Patchers, was fifty-six years old, a decorated soldier from the First World War and now, in January 1944, the oldest divisional commander in the US Army. Back in the early 1930s he had been an instructor at the US Army War College, where he'd taught not only Omar Bradley, now commanding US First Army as it prepared for OVERLORD, but also Mark Clark. If Walker found it a little awkward to have been leapfrogged by one of his students, he never said, and so far had led the 36th very well indeed, first at Salerno, then fighting their way north and, back in December, bursting through the mighty Bernhard Line at San Pietro and Monte Sammucro. Although Walker had not been given specific orders for the Rapido assault until 16 January, he had known early in December that a crossing was in the planning and was aware early in the New Year that it was almost certainly going to be his division carrying it out. As a result he'd given considerable thought to how it might be achieved.

His conclusion was that it could not. He did raise his concerns with both Clark and Keyes, his corps commander, but they rightly pointed out that Italy was full of rivers, they'd crossed plenty of them already and getting over the Rapido and Garigliano was something they simply had to do if they were going to get to Rome. Walker accepted that, but suggested a better option would be to cross the Rapido further to the north, between the Monte Maio massif and Monte Cassino. Yet, as Clark and Keyes pointed out to him, that would not bring them into the Liri Valley, but rather the Gustav Line at Monte Cassino, which looked an even more formidable proposition. Nor would it be possible to coordinate an attack there with X Corps' operations in the south.

Walker had convinced himself that there had not been a single instance in history where an attack had been successful when made across an unfordable river and covered by the enemy's main line of resistance. Yet that was exactly what had happened when Fifth Army crossed the Volturno and when Eighth Army had crossed the Rivers Biferno, Sangro and Moro. It was also what X Corps had achieved when they crossed the Garigliano. Clearly, Walker had got himself into something of a lather about the operation. The T-Patchers had been through the ringer, but then so had all the divisions that had landed back in September. It had been brutal for all of them and the casualties, roughly as appalling in each, were testimony to this.

Divisional commanders played very important roles, however. They set the tone, and the culture. The attitude of the commander – aggressive or cautious, spick-and-span or casual – filtered down through the staff to the regiments, the battalions, companies, platoons and squads. The trouble with harbouring such profound reservations was that these started to prey on a commander's mind, cloud judgement and then spread, osmosis-like, down through the division. Such fears were then in danger of becoming a self-fulfilling prophecy. Walker first noted in his diary the impossibility of the task back on 8 January. At the time, the division had still been out of the line and Walker had not been anywhere near Sant'Angelo. He'd had maps and photos, but nothing more. Nor, at that stage, had he been told what assets he was going to be given, or that his division would be so considerably swollen for the operation. And nor had he known then that it would be the third assault off the rack, following behind X Corps' strike across the Garigliano to the south and after 46th Division's crossing towards Sant'Apollinare. It had been a little early, to put it mildly, to throw in the towel so soon.

Meanwhile, 46th Division had been preparing their own crossing, due to be carried out the night before the T-Patchers in an effort to draw off enemy troops in this sector. This southern part of the Liri Valley was also held by 15. Panzergrenadier, just as it was across the whole five-mile stretch to Cassino. Clark had wanted the Brits to throw everything they had at it, but there were only sufficient boats to send one brigade and so Major-General 'Ginger' Hawkesworth opted for two crossing points, a battalion each, about a mile or so from Sant'Apollinare at a tiny village called Sant'Ambrogio. The objective was for 128th Brigade to get across and secure a low ridge overlooking both the Garigliano and the Liri; the two rivers met about a mile to the north. Once on this low ridge, a second brigade would follow and push towards Sant'Apollinare.

Preparations went well. Infantry moved up to the river apparently unseen and even the bridging equipment was brought up as planned. Supporting these moves was the 70th Field Regiment, who were joining in with the rest of the division's artillery to hit known enemy mortar and artillery positions. Captain Leonard Garland's battery had been involved in these 'strafes'. 'Everything tickety-boo,' he noted in his diary, 'except my frame of mind: a sort of steady depression.' He put it down to being in the line too long. Clearly, someone in the regiment had recognized that Garland needed a rest, because having established his OPs on the morning of the 18th he was told he was being given some leave. 'Felt guilty about going,' noted Garland, 'but army training too strong to allow me to refuse more than once!'

It meant Garland missed the battle, which was launched, as planned, on the night of 19 January. A fog was lying over the river which brilliantly masked the attacking force and not a squeak was heard from the enemy. Complete surprise had been achieved. Everything was looking good for the attack until the first men began getting into the boats. Only then did they realize that the river was both higher and flowing considerably faster than it had been earlier in the day. Unbeknown to them, the Germans had just opened the sluice gates of an irrigation dam much further up the Liri, presumably primarily aimed at making life more difficult for the British further to the south. At any rate, wire cables sent across the river snapped; repeated attempts to get another vital cable across, which could be used to help steady the boats, also failed. A number of other boats were swept away and several more smashed. Time and again, efforts were made to get cables across at both crossing points but all attempts failed. Several men tried to swim but simply could not get across, so strong was the current. Hawkesworth had no choice but to suspend the operation for the night, which Clark then cancelled for good the following day. 'The failure of the attack of the 46th Division,' noted Clark on the morning of the 20th, 'was quite a blow.' He thought it was because Hawkesworth had not flung enough men into the crossing, but in this he was mistaken; it was entirely because of the dramatically increased flow of the river and all the more frustrating because they had achieved total surprise and would have very likely seized their objective. On the other hand, while 46th Division could no longer help the Americans in their planned crossing, it did mean they could now be diverted to helping the rest of X Corps, who were still fighting to the south.

The battle had dramatically increased in scale and tempo as the British continued to expand their bridgehead. 'We are still doing well,' noted RSM Jack Ward, 'although Jerry, as usual, is fighting every inch of the way.' The regiment's big guns were still firing and the house they were using as their RHQ kept shaking with every boom; they spent much of their time clearing bits of plaster off their maps. 'News has just come through that Minturno has been captured by our troops,' he added that same day, 19 January. 'Good work.' Later that day, Trimonsuoli, a little further along the coast on the Via Appia, was also taken.

Up on the Minturno Ridge, the 2nd Inniskillings were still holding their part of the slope that overlooked the Ausente Valley. They'd been heavily counter-attacked, but with the help of the artillery had managed to drive the Germans back again. Casualties, however, were mounting, including David Cole's friend Harry Christie, who had been killed in his trench by splinters when a shell hit a nearby tree. Cole was devastated;

they all were. Christie had already won a DSO and MC, was loved by all and had been something of a legend in the battalion. In just thirty-six hours, the Skins had lost a third of all their officers and NCOs.

Follow-up battalions were being flung into the battle, however, and armour too. At dusk on the 19th, Cole had been in his trench when he heard a rumble begin behind them, which grew as darkness fell and then increased as, in the early hours, the first Class 30 Bailey bridge was finally opened. Tanks, anti-tank guns and carriers began pouring across the river in a constant stream, as did a further brigade of infantry.

Yet Kesselring was now pouring troops of his own into the battle. The 29. Panzergrenadier, barely rested, were reaching the southern front and hurrying down the Ausente Valley up over Monte Damiano towards Castelforte. The equally beleaguered 90. Panzergrenadier were also sent down the Via Appia, while in the entirely typical way in which mixtures of units were flung together, parts of the HG and even the reconnaissance battalion of 44. Division were also urgently sent south. Finally, Kesselring also ordered 1. Fallschirmjägerkorps into the Garigliano battle too.

Alexander's plan had been to draw German troops away from the Anzio area ahead of SHINGLE. So far, despite the failure of 46th Division's crossing, the Germans appeared to be falling for the ruse hook, line and sinker.

CHAPTER 8

The Rapido

IN THE DAYS RUNNING up to the Rapido operation, Captain Roswell K. Doughty had been sending out his I & R – Intelligence and Reconnaissance – men each night on forays across the river, lowering rubber boats, paddling over then scrambling up the far side and under the cover of darkness scouting around trying to learn what enemy outposts were there. The I & R Platoon was something unique to American regiments and was made up of eighteen enlisted men and one officer, whose task was to learn whatever they could about the enemy by whatever means. This meant patrol work behind enemy lines, interrogation of prisoners, talking to civilians and, of course, simple observation. They were the eyes and ears for the regiment, expected to know as much as possible about the enemy and pass that on to the regimental commander and his staff. Captain Doughty was thirty-three, married with two children and from Boston, Massachusetts, not Texas. He was a college graduate, sharp as a tack and possessed a healthy dose of cynicism, and since joining the division back in 1942 had commanded the I & R Platoon of the 141st Infantry, one of three regiments, along with the 142nd and 143rd, that made up the infantry arm of the Texas Division. Doughty was unafraid to stand up to superiors he knew to be wrong, and while this had sometimes landed him in trouble, the regiment had learned to trust him and value the work that he and his I & R Platoon undertook. Doughty and his men had been actively patrolling the area between Sant'Angelo and a couple of miles to the north, which was where 141st Infantry were due to cross, two battalions leading the way and the third remaining in reserve. Interestingly, though, they'd discovered very little in the way of enemy opposition in and around Sant'Angelo itself.

Walker's plan was to launch the assault at 8 p.m. on the 20th, three hours after sunset, which would give his men some eleven hours of darkness. While the 141st were to cross to the north, the 143rd would assault in two places, the first a little over half a mile south of Sant'Angelo and the second a mile further on. At 12 to 15 yards the river was a fraction of the width of the Garigliano further to the south. In theory, this made it far simpler to bridge; the Bailey bridge was like a giant Meccano set and could be comparatively easily assembled on one side and then pushed across, although the first wave of infantry were to be using a combination of rubber inflatable boats and specially made plywood craft that could carry between six and twelve men each. The engineers would follow up with Bailey catwalks, which would be floated as a pontoon bridge. Class 30 Baileys were then to be put across overnight with the division's engineers laying down perforated-steel plating – PSP – so vehicles could cross the rather waterlogged open fields of the floodplain either side. The Bailey bridge classification number referred to the tonnage it could take at one time, so a Class 30 could cope with a 30-ton vehicle such as a Sherman tank. Getting fire support – tanks and anti-tank guns – over as quickly as possible and then vehicles to resupply the infantry was vital if the bridgehead across was to be successfully maintained then enlarged.

Walker's gloom and sense of impending disaster was growing as the moment to launch the attack grew ever nearer. During the day he was visited by Ginger Hawkesworth, who apologized profusely for not having got across the Garigliano. The failure of 46th Division was not necessarily a harbinger, however. The excess flow at their crossing point had been caused by the Liri, so although the Rapido was flowing reasonably fast, it hadn't prevented patrols like those of Doughty and his men nipping across without too much difficulty. And, of course, the Rapido was a quarter of the width of the Garigliano. It did mean, however, that the British had been unable to draw off German troops. There was no sugar-coating that fact. Hawkesworth wished him the very best of luck, but Walker, now reading catastrophe into every word and expression, sensed the British general had grave doubts.

What worried Walker most of all was that, once across, the darkness meant troop leaders would struggle to exercise effective control of their men. He also worried that the artillery support would be ineffective because observers would not be able to see in the dark and so would be resorting to map firing only. Nor did he see how they could effectively keep the enemy defenders down – those mortar positions and MG posts that he feared could play havoc. 'There were no satisfactory answers,' he noted. 'Though I felt we were undertaking the impossible.'

There were solutions to all of these conundrums, but Walker was no longer able to see them for all the knots he'd tied himself into. He would have done well, for example, to have visited Dick McCreery and X Corps and also Major-General Douglas Graham of 56th Division and Major-General Philip Gregson-Ellis of 5th Division, who had just completed crossings with similar challenges. But he did not. The answer was that artillery could fire on fixed targets; while pummelling known enemy artillery positions, those Germans in question would be cowering in their dugouts. Hans Golda and his men would not be firing their Werfers while they were being shelled. So an intense barrage to begin with, followed by concentrations of fire would, in theory, help keep enemy artillery subdued. Second, Walker had plenty of tank support, which could be brought up and which, rather than hanging around for a bridge to be opened, could be firing both machine-gun and 75mm main gun support. As countless observers had discovered, Allied and German machine guns rarely fired at the same time. He also had a battalion of anti-aircraft guns, M45 Quadmounts. These were towed and highly manoeuvrable mounts of four .50-calibre machine guns, which were certainly not going to be needed to shoot down the Luftwaffe but which could provide immense suppressing fire if used in a ground role. Yet although Walker had been thinking about this operation for the best part of three weeks, neither the armour nor the Quadmounts were part of his assault plans. Rather than trying to work out solutions he had allowed himself to find only further reasons why the mission was surely doomed.

There were certainly logistical challenges, not least the large number of mines that had been laid by the Germans on both sides of the river but especially on the eastern, American side. Most of these, however, were on the floodplain that ran down to the east bank of the Rapido. This meant sweeping mine-free tracks between the road and the river and then marking those cleared paths with white tape. There were ways of minimizing this challenge, though, because a road wound its way southwards, roughly following the route of the river and at a distance of between 500 and just a few yards from the riverbank. So it made sense to cross where the distance between the river and the road was narrowest. Roads and approach tracks were generally easier to sweep for mines than open ground because of the canalizing effect of their parameters; if a road was, say, 6 yards wide, then so long as that strip was clear of mines, traffic could safely pass. The trouble with a field was that the whole area had to be cleared, or alternatively paths swept and then marked with tape; but tape could easily shift or get broken. With no tracks from the road to the river, marking such paths was the only viable option. The infantry would have to pass down them carrying their boats with them – but in the dark. Clearly, the greater the distance between the road and the riverbank, the higher the chances were of that final advance to the river going awry.

To help clear these mines, Clark had added two extra engineer battalions from Fifth Army. Frenchy Bechard had spent much of the 20th clearing mines from the road to the river's edge at one of the crossing points south of Sant'Angelo, where 143rd Infantry were due to cross, and marking the paths with white tape. The crossing points of the 143rd were well chosen where the distance from the road to the river was short and so fewer mines had to be cleared; at the northern crossing point of the 143rd, the distance was between 15 and 50 yards only. The same could not be said for the crossing point of the 141st, however. This was to be either side of a pronounced S-bend bulging towards the enemy, with the main effort by two battalions on the northern side of the bend and a feint by 2nd Battalion to the south of it. Yet, despite Doughty's recce work, this crossing point was just a little too close to the bluff on which Sant'Angelo was perched for comfort, and also more than 800 yards from the road. Sweeping paths through a depth of half a mile was considerably harder and more time-consuming than one of 50 yards. It would also be far riskier for the infantry carrying their boats towards the river. Why the regimental staff chose to cross there was hard to fathom. It made no sense at all.

Inevitably, just about everything that could go wrong did go wrong. Another thick mist hung over the river, which had not been predicted or planned for, even by the doom-mongering General Walker. Laying down smoke for the actual crossing of the river was one thing, but mixing this with an already thick fog so that no one could see anything much at all was quite another. Meanwhile, the lead battalions of the 141st to the north of Sant'Angelo reached their assembly areas without any great difficulty, not least because the engineers had also been widening the approach roads the past few nights and the mist was by the river, not over the higher ground to the east. Most of the assault boats had been brought up and hidden behind the railway embankment, which snaked north-west about three-quarters of a mile from the crossing point. When the attack battalions reached here, however, they discovered that a number of the boats had been damaged and wrecked by enemy shellfire. This prompted a frantic rearrangement of which troops were allocated to the boats that were still intact. They set off a little late, huffing and puffing with all the kit – and boats – they were carrying, but in the fog the guides escorting the lead company got lost and so everyone had to turn round and start again, which was no easy matter in the dark while carrying an assault boat. Men and boats bumped and crashed into one another, and the noise of this fiasco was heard by the enemy who then brought down artillery fire which killed the company commander and several others. The shelling also destroyed much of the minefield tape so that they were soon straying from the path, with disastrous consequences; more men and boats were lost to mines. Engineers were also trying to hurriedly bring up footbridges, but one was discovered to have been damaged already so was abandoned, another was destroyed crossing the minefield and a third wrecked by a shell. The fourth was successfully put across the river, however, and two companies managed to get over to the far side, followed by men of a third, only for heavy German mortar and shellfire to force them to abandon the crossing. Engineers also desperately tried to get an 8-ton infantry bridge across, but the weight of enemy fire was so great that by 4 a.m. they had to abandon this too.

Captain Roswell Doughty was in the I & R CP, which he'd set up in a small house on a little hill next to the Chiesa della Pietà just off the southern end of Monte Trocchio. Although a little exposed on the ridge, this gave him a front-row view of the regiment's crossing. The noise had been incessant all night, beginning with the opening barrage using the full weight of the combined Allied guns. Initially, the barrage had concentrated on known enemy strongpoints picked from aerial reconnaissance and patrol work and then, after half an hour, moved back in 100-yard shifts. Doughty had seen the sprinkle of explosions, dim orange flashes through the river fog and smoke that had been laid down. The ground shook, the air was thick with smoke and the bitter, cloying stench of explosives. The entire valley seemed to be rocking with the immense weight of this fire.

German gunners, emerging from their bunkers, had soon begun firing back, however, and although most of their fire was directed at the crossings, they were also targeting the forming-up positions on the American side, which made Doughty's CP far from immune. 'We heard machine-gun bullets rattling off the walls,' he noted, 'mortar shells "cramped" close by, and artillery dug deep holes around us.' Fortunately, no one was hurt, even though several shells hit the house, blowing wood and stone past them. Much to Doughty's relief, their basement bunker held firm.

By the early hours, it was already clear that in the northern sector of the 141st the attack had failed. Lead companies of 1st Battalion had got across but were now reported to be coming under heavy fire. Contact was then lost as telephone cable was repeatedly cut. The thick fog, made worse by the smoke, meant that those on the far side became disorientated, horribly exposed, and soon found themselves pinned down and rapidly running short of ammunition. Casualties were mounting alarmingly. Doughty then got a call from Lieutenant-Colonel Aaron Wyatt, acting commander of the 141st, ordering him to hurry to the railway station at Fontanarosa, less than a mile to the south. This was the assembly area for 141st Regiment's attack. The message: to halt any further attempts to cross. It was now too late.

Doughty took a couple of his men and hurried down to the road that ran parallel to the railroad track. The fog was now very thick but enemy shells kept screeching over with a low howl and then exploding with a dim flash. The spectral heavy mist and dull glow of explosions made Doughty wonder if he were walking through hell. The station was also under fire, so having transmitted the colonel's orders he and his men paused to take shelter before scurrying on to the divisional CP behind Trocchio.

To the south, meanwhile, the northern crossing point for 143rd Infantry had gone reasonably well, with all of 1st Battalion across by 5 a.m., but this was where the road and the minefield were shallowest. Further south, however, at the second crossing point, not one rifleman had got across. The engineers had become lost in the fog, stumbling off the cleared paths and into the minefield, destroying most of the boats and killing and injuring a number of men. Confusion reigned; leadership and cohesion broke down in the fog, the smoke and amid the relentless shelling and mortaring. It was hard to see more than a few paces ahead, yet flashes of light pulsed through the shroud, shells screamed in, immense eruptions of stone, grit and earth were hurled into the air along with razor-sharp, white-hot shards of metal fizzing and hissing lethally in a deadly arc. The *brrrrrppp* of enemy machine guns, screams of men, cloying smoke and the stench of burning added to the total sense of disorientation caused by the fog. Doughty had thought he was walking through hell; the 143rd men certainly did too.

By first light, there were just two bridgeheads – one to the south and another to the north of Sant'Angelo; but pinned down, going nowhere, with almost no cover to speak of, rapidly running low on ammunition and with little prospect of reinforcement, the acting battalion commander, Major David Frazier, decided to pull his remaining men back across the river. The night attack had been a fiasco.

It had been horrendous for the German defenders too. Major Georg Zellner was only a couple of miles west of the Rapido and found the barrage and relentless shelling all through the night, combined with the screaming of Hans Golda's Nebelwerfers nearby, almost unbearable. 'We can't stay awake and we can't rest,' he jotted. 'We don't know what to do at all. You lie down, get up again, smoke a lot.' He could hardly comprehend how many shells the Americans were able to send over.

By morning, a clearer picture of what had happened reached his command post. It seemed two companies of Americans had managed to get across the river but in his sector they'd been pushed back; this was 1st Battalion of the 141st Infantry. In the lull Zellner went up to the battlefield to see things for himself. More than 200 American prisoners were brought in, a number of them wounded. He was dismayed, however, to discover civilians were still living in their homes during the middle of this carnage. A young man accosted him and his men and asked for a spade. His sixteen-year-old sister had been torn apart by a shell and he wanted to bury her. 'We help him,' noted Zellner. 'Prisoners are still moving about. It gets quieter.'

Heavy fighting was still continuing to the south on the Garigliano and more troops were being committed to the battle there, but the situation was now looking far better here, on the Cassino front. Von Senger, for one, had cause to be pleased with his forces in this sector. 'Strong enemy assault detachments, which have crossed the river in the sector of the 15. Panzergrenadier-Division,' noted the AOK 10 war diary, 'are annihilated.'

General Clark had known that the Rapido crossings would be costly and had admitted as much to his diary, but had felt compelled to press ahead in order to hold as many German troops at the Cassino front as possible ahead of SHINGLE. After all, battles were not won without spilling blood. General Keyes had briefed him on the current situation on the Rapido and told him he'd ordered Walker to attack again that afternoon at 4 p.m. 'I have talked with Keyes,' Clark noted, 'and not only yesterday but today directed him to bend every effort to get tanks and tank destroyers across promptly.' That was the key: without them the infantry were doomed.

The tanks, however, were going nowhere. Walker had a battalion of Shermans, which meant around fifty, but they were waiting in a wood to the south of Monte Trocchio. The three battalions of Shermans from 1st Armored were still at Mignano, eight miles away. Lieutenant-Colonel Hamilton Howze, commander of 13rd Armored Regiment, earmarked for the attack, had sent liaison officers to watch the action carefully. They had reported back to him that the attack had been poorly mounted. Howze had hurried to see for himself and was horrified to discover that the divisional armour was sitting idle. Looking at the riverbank he saw the dykes either side, raised anti-flood mounds, which he reckoned would have offered ideal hull-down positions. The idea was to manoeuvre a tank so that only its turret showed and from there offer fire support both with its main gun and with two Browning machine guns. Getting these into position required planning and coordination but should have been within the capabilities of the divisional staff, and while other vehicles could not have crossed the floodplain without PSP, the tanks, with their tracks, could have done. They could also have positioned themselves hull-down on the eastern side of the raised road, from where they would have had a slightly elevated position. Howze was thirty-five, the son of a general, and had gained considerable combat experience in Tunisia where the division had taken many knocks but learned much as well. 'It would have been the most beautiful defilade,' he noted, 'because they could have just hung their guns across the bank and tank commanders, with the benefit of their field glasses, could have been watching the hills on the far side.' As Howze toured the battlefront, his exasperation mounting, he spoke to two of the battalion commanders. He asked them what the artillery fire plan had been. Neither knew. They'd had no idea. That meant nor had the company commanders or any of the men. Howze could not believe what he was hearing. Again and again he found himself scratching his head and wondering why the armour had not been brought forward. 'It was', he noted, 'an ideal place to use tanks in over-watching fire in support of infantry on the far side of an obstacle.'

Nor was there any sign of the Quadmounts. What a difference they could have made. Four .50-calibre machine guns firing a little under 600 rounds per minute each packed a heck of a punch and, like the tanks, could have been used to suppress enemy machine-gunners and offer cover for the attacking infantry.

They were not called up for the second attack either, which, unsurprisingly, slipped in schedule from a 4 p.m. daylight assault to a second night attack, this time launched at 9 p.m.

Many of the difficulties that had confronted the first attack hampered the second attempt as well. Boats collapsing, insufficient bridging, mines, weight of enemy fire. Even so, all troops that could now be committed were, including those reserve companies that had been held back the previous evening. Lieutenant Robert F. Spencer, a twenty-eight-year-old farm boy from Washington, Indiana, had just a few days before found himself becoming the commander of Company F of the 2nd Battalion, 143rd Infantry. The previous commander, a young captain, had fallen ill, leaving just three second lieutenants – himself, King and Zebroski. The battalion CO had appointed Spencer to fill the sick captain's shoes. It was indicative of the shortage of troops still afflicting the T-Patchers that Spencer found himself in this situation. The division had been decimated in the four long months since they'd landed in the first wave at Salerno, particularly so while slogging their way to capturing Monte Sammucro and San Pietro back in December. Plenty of replacements had come through but they had not been enough to completely fill the ranks, particularly not those of the officers who, proportionally, had been hardest hit. It also meant that there were now an awful lot of greenhorns in the Texas Division for whom the Rapido was their first combat action.

Spencer had been up at 143rd Regiment's staging area the previous evening and had heard the firing going on all night; he'd *felt* it going on too, the entire ground beneath his feet trembling. 'Imagine my consternation,' he noted, 'when I learned that the initial attack had failed with the attacking unit suffering extremely heavy casualties.' That evening he was called to a briefing by the regimental officers. They were, Spencer could see, visibly upset but still insisting they had to attack again. They simply had to break through the German lines. Failure could not be tolerated.

This was a terrifying situation for all. No one fancied heading into the jaws of what appeared to be certain death. Spencer and his men now had most of the night to contemplate their turn at being flung into the meat grinder because it wasn't until the early hours, before dawn, that he was told to get his men ready as they were next to cross the river.

The river mist, combined with smoke once again, made visibility extremely limited as they crossed the road, following the white tape into the unknown. Artillery still boomed and screamed overhead while at the river crossing itself enemy mortars were raining down with horrible regularity. Machine guns and small arms also chattered close by. Leading the way, Spencer managed to get across a small footbridge and once his men were over he urged them forward, stumbling through the carnage of craters, past the dead and on through the fog. Then, suddenly before them, German wire entanglements. But there was a gap from a shell blast. With help from 1st Sergeant Jones he was able to expand it so they could all pass through.

They pushed on blindly, with no sense of space, into a surreal and ultra-violent never-world, the sound of battle drumming. On through the smoke and mist and mayhem. Then more Americans. The preceding company. Or rather, the remains of them; their casualties were so numerous that the rest had dug in and were now squatting in their foxholes and refusing to move. Despite this Spencer pressed on, although he soon became disorientated. Mortars continuing to crash around him. German machine guns raking the flat floodplain. Shells screaming over. The cries of men – and now, as he stumbled forward, the realization that he had lost contact with part of his company. Then he bumped into a fellow lieutenant – what a place to meet – from a different unit and together they began urging the men forward, yelling at them to keep going, not stop. To stop meant certain death. Germans were shouting – he could hear them over the din, their voices horribly real, jarring, but how close by he could not tell. He felt anxious, and the cold and the darkness and the fog added to the terrible feeling of not knowing what could happen next or where.

Something then struck him on the head, felling him instantly. He was unconscious for a moment – or maybe longer – but when he came to he felt sick, dazed and scared, lying out there, not knowing how badly he was injured. His head throbbed. But Sergeant Jones was beside him again, bandaged his head as best he could and offered to try and find him some stretcher-bearers. Spencer declined – safer to make his own way back. He told Jones to leave him and look after himself. An unknown GI squatted beside him and asked him if he could have his Tommy gun. Spencer figured he wouldn't need it any more so handed it over.

Dawn crept over the battlefield. There was little let-up in the firing but he now spotted an irrigation ditch that seemed to be leading towards the river. Slowly he crawled towards it and tumbled in, down into a foot of ice-cold water. Inching his way along it, Spencer suddenly came up against another entanglement of wire. He saw a gap a little way along, up on the flat; but there was heavy fire going on and in his trench he was safe. He had to work up the courage to move. Deep breath, hope for the best. He crawled out on all fours, pushed his way through the gap and then back down into the ditch again.

On he crawled until – miracle – he reached the river and saw the footbridge over which they'd initially crossed just a short distance away. It was partially submerged because some of the flotation tanks had been hit, but he crawled there, keeping as low as he could; no point in blowing his chances through carelessness and impatience now he was so close. At the half-sunken bridge he once again found himself having to work up his nerve: he knew he was not steady enough to walk and so would have to crawl, but that meant holding on tight to the edges of the bridge on all fours, through the icy water. Forcing himself to move, he inched on to the platform and into the water, gripping the edges and moving carefully, slowly, a little at a time. These felt like the longest minutes of his life, the short stretch an eternity.

But, inch by inch, he made it, and with the last of his energy and his head still spinning hauled himself up the bank and staggered clear. There he met one of the other company commanders, who looked at this wet, bloodied, mud-caked figure incredulously. 'My God, Spencer,' he said, 'what happened?'

Spencer told him then was helped to the aid station. He'd been lucky, but his men less so: most dead, wounded and taken prisoner. Company F had headed down to the river the previous evening with 140 enlisted men and three officers. By midday on the 22nd, all three officers had been wounded and only fifteen men managed to get back again to the safety of the eastern side. The company had been effectively destroyed.

Frenchy Bechard had been one of the many engineers down at the 143rd's crossing point trying to get a bridge across, but the fast flow of the water and the intense enemy shelling had made it impossible. 'Lost one officer, Sgt R J Young, and four men of the 1st Platoon,' he noted. 'Also, the Krauts had re-mined the area we had cleared the night before.' That had been on the far side. Throughout the next day, the 22nd, they made another attempt to bridge the river, their work shrouded by smoke pots, which blocked the enemy's vision but also theirs, as Sergeant Chafin, Bechard's platoon commander, discovered. On the far side the sergeant was walking towards a group of men, thinking them GIs, only to discover they were a German patrol. 'Slowly, he walked away from them,' jotted Bechard. 'He's no dead hero.'

The second attack failed as surely as the first had done. Not a single vehicle had got across and although many more men had headed over into the bridgehead and even advanced as much as 800 yards, without support the infantry were doomed.

Later, at 1.05 p.m., Bob Spencer's battalion commander sent the following signal to his regimental commander, Colonel William H. Martin: '1) We had 50% casualties from mortar and small arms fire. 2) Did our best to evacuate all to near side river – some captured. 3) Far side of river no longer in our hands. 4) Our defense consists of small separated groups in attempted all around protection – slowly being wiped out.'

Captain Doughty had spent the second day and night at Fontanarosa Station, which had become the main aid post and the place from which he could grill survivors and feed information back to RHQ. On the second morning he had sent one of his men, Charlie Lane, down to the river to learn what the bridging situation was. 'He came back through the smoke and reported a holocaust,' noted Doughty. 'The battalion that crossed the river was caught between barbed wire entanglements in front of the German positions and the river. They had dug in shoulder-to-shoulder but their small area was swept by all kinds of fire and many were being killed or wounded with little hope of moving forward or backward.' And no vehicle bridge had been successfully put across.

The attack was abandoned that evening, Walker's worst fears realized. There was no doubt he'd been dealt a cruel hand, but there was no reason it should have been the tragic fiasco it was. Better planning would have seen his assault include not just the divisional armour and attached tank destroyer battalions but Colonel Howze's 13th Armored Regiment too; that would have offered him 250 Sherman tanks and 100 anti-tank guns. None of these – not one – took part in the battle. The Allied way of war was to use as much firepower as possible to lessen the burden on the infantry, so how could he possibly have squandered such enormous fire support for them? The anti-aircraft Quadmounts should have been used;

there was no point in having assets added for the attack if they were then to sit idle, especially these particularly superb and valuable pieces of weaponry. The siting of the crossing points, bar one, made no sense whatsoever; a mile further north of 141st Infantry's crossing point, for example, the floodplain was less than 200 yards in depth, a quarter of the distance they had been attempting to cross. That battalion and company commanders had no knowledge of the artillery fire plan that was supporting them was unforgiveable. Night attacks, especially across a river, were unquestionably difficult and complicated, which was why no man involved should have too much information. The unexpected fog was a case in point. It was disorientating but it worked against the enemy as well, and hindered not only American artillery observers but German ones too. Clinical study of the terrain beforehand would have helped the infantry – this was the kind of message that came down from the top and which should have been drummed into every man. Instead, Bob Spencer was essentially clueless about what he and his men were doing and where they were heading when they set off into the fire. It was all very well being told that failure was not an option, but they needed to know what success looked like first and how it was to be achieved.

It was as though, in his despair about the task given him, Walker had become unable to separate the wood from the trees. Rather than trying to find solutions to the immense challenge that faced his division, he had convinced himself they did not exist. In this he was wholly wrong. The plan had not been for his division to drive all the way to Rome but to punch a hole, which, in combination with the battle raging on the Garigliano and the landings at Anzio, might have been enough to persuade Kesselring to withdraw his troops along the Cassino front and so save a huge number of lives and misery. And punching a hole, though difficult, was not the impossibility Walker believed it was – not if the support he'd been given had been properly used. Whether this would have actually made Kesselring, the Hitler loyalist, pull back will never be known, but the attack cost the T-Patchers a comparatively modest 143 killed from six attacking battalions – an average of 24 per battalion of 850 men – as well as 663 wounded and 875 missing, most of whom were now POWs and heading back to Germany to spend the rest of the war in prison camps.

On the plus side, the area around Rome was now almost entirely empty of German troops.

CHAPTER 9

SHINGLE

'I LEARN FROM THE RADIO that Ciano and his other colleagues from the Grand Council were shot in Verona,' noted Filippo Caracciolo in his diary. 'I cannot get over the horror of this news.' Count Galeazzo Ciano had been Foreign Minister under Mussolini before and during the war; he had also been Il Duce's son-in-law. Suave, urbane and fiercely intelligent, he had been an ardent Fascist but also very against the war; Ciano had had a far greater geopolitical understanding than Mussolini and had recognized, from the outset, that war for Italy would lead to catastrophe and ruin. By the time the Allies had invaded Sicily the previous July, Italy had been on its knees. Financially, morally, spiritually. Ciano had been part of the Fascist Grand Council that had voted to depose Mussolini on 25 July, a decision ratified by the King the following day. Fearing he'd be arrested by the new Badoglio government, Ciano and his wife, Edda, and their three children had fled to Germany. However, after Mussolini was sprung from captivity by German airborne troops on 11 September, the Germans reinstalled the former dictator as head of the new Repubblica Sociale Italiano – RSI – and with a new capital, the tiny town of Salò on Lake Garda. The South Tyrol and Istria were annexed into the Third Reich and what remained of northern Italy became a puppet state, with an ageing, mostly unmotivated Mussolini nominally head of state but in reality nothing but a Nazi stooge, while leadership of the Fascist Party was run by the charismatic young pretender Alessandro Pavolini.

As for Ciano, he was handed over to the new Fascists the moment Mussolini had been put back in power, and promptly arrested for treason. At the urging of the Germans and supported by Pavolini, Ciano and six others from the Grand Council, all in prison in the north, were given a show trial on 8 and 10 January. All were found guilty, five sentenced to death and the sixth given thirty years. Those executed had been tied to chairs and shot in the back the following day.

There had been a sense of shock throughout Italy at the news, but mixed sympathies. Caracciolo was no Fascist; in fact, long before Mussolini's overthrow, he had been working for the underground Partito d'Azione – Action Party – and had had a series of clandestine meetings with Allied secret intelligence agents, not least Allen Dulles of the OSS, the Office of Strategic Services, but also with the British Special Operations Executive – SOE. Yet Caracciolo felt great empathy for Edda, whom he also knew quite well, and was sorry that Ciano had died in such a murderous way. 'I recall my relations with him,' he noted, 'and his many friendly sides. Also, the vanity, the sensuality, the love of power that misled him.' Caracciolo felt Ciano had been a tormented figure, caught between what he knew was right and the lure of power. 'See it is difficult,' added Caracciolo, 'to act in a straight line.'

He was, in many ways, reflecting his own dilemmas and those of the democratic parties in Italy, no longer existing underground in the south but still doing so in the north. After the dominance of Fascism, these differing political parties had come together to form the Comitato di Liberazione Nazionale – CLN. All six parties were vehemently anti-Fascist. The largest was the Communists, but there were also the Socialists – once a major force in Italy before the Fascists took power; the Christian Democrats; the Liberals; the Labour Democrats; and the Partita d'Azione, of which Caracciolo was a leading member. They were united in their desire to see democracy return and also a viable new government to run Italy, but that was about all they agreed on. The Communists, Socialists and the Partita d'Azione, for example, were every bit as anti-monarchist as they were anti-Fascist, while the Liberals were still very much royalist to their core. The President of the CLN was Ivanoe Bonomi, a former Socialist prime minister before Mussolini seized power back in 1922, and now leader of the Labour Democrats. Already seventy and a political figure of a bygone age, he was, inevitably, the compromise choice.

Caracciolo was forty years old, lean, handsome and debonair, and a member of one of the most prominent families ever to have lived in Naples. Duke of Melito since the age of three, in 1938 he had also become the eighth Prince of Castagneto, which brought with it the post of

Patrician of Naples. A multi-linguist who spoke French, German and English fluently, he also had a doctorate in economics and during the 1930s had held a series of diplomatic roles despite having never been a Fascist. Since the Allies had reached Naples he had been trying to use his diplomatic skills and influence to try and thrash out a deal that would see a change of government; he believed, as many in the CLN did, that the Badoglio government needed to be overthrown. Certainly, it had no democratic legitimacy. The Allies were quite prepared to see the back of Badoglio, but the CLN were not collectively willing to take power while the King remained on the throne. They were hardly being unreasonable. After all, Vittorio Emanuele III had backed Mussolini, backed the war and had run out on his people on 9 September, fleeing Rome to save his skin. He was not a worthy monarch. And while the Americans were all for forcing his abdication, Churchill and the British had been anxious to keep Vittorio Emanuele in power for the time being, not particularly because Britain was a monarchy too but because the Italian armed forces served the King. The Italian Navy and Merchant Navy – what was left of it – were cooperating very well and efficiently on sea and on shore, in the docks and workshops. The Italian Army was being retrained and, if not currently fighting, was at least on the Allied side. Almost all embassies around the world had also rallied to Vittorio Emanuele. 'We are not sure what would be the effect on all these people', noted Harold Macmillan, the British Minister of State, 'of an abdication which was *not* voluntary, but enforced.'

Macmillan was the key Allied political figure now in Italy. A former Guardsman who had been badly wounded in the last war – he still walked with a slight limp – he had turned to politics and was something of a rising star of the Conservatives but also the coalition government. He had brought considerable good sense and diplomacy to the complex political situation in the Mediterranean with his handling of French North Africa when the Allies had invaded back in November 1942; and he had dealt with de Gaulle, the Free French leader, with equal tact and dexterity. The previous August, Macmillan had also helped draw up the armistice terms for the Italian surrender and, since then, played one of the key roles in advising the Badoglio government as well as Eisenhower. With his spectacles, buck teeth and moustache he looked more like a schoolteacher than a serious political player, and there was no doubt that this rather innocuous appearance proved both disarming and very effective. Although unquestionably charming and naturally affable, he was also ferociously bright, extremely shrewd and politically very savvy. These attributes had served him well in the often Machiavellian and extremely complicated world of coalition warfare in the Mediterranean, and he had been rewarded by being elevated to the post of UK High Commissioner for the Advisory Council for Italy and Political Advisor to the Supreme Allied Commander, to name but two of his current titles.

Governance of Allied-occupied Italy had been somewhat evolving since the landings the previous September. Although the King and Badoglio had remained in nominal power, the whole of Italy had come under the authority of AMGOT. What had been agreed at the end of the year, however, was that control of much of southern Italy and Sicily should be handed back to the Italians, albeit with indirect, rather than direct, control by the Allies. Supervising this indirect form of government would be the Allied Control Commission (ACC). The differences between this set-up and that of Mussolini in the RSI with his German masters were paper-thin, however, as the ACC retained total authority over the Italian armed forces, resources and finances. Even so, the aim was to enable the Italians, certainly at a local and day-to-day level, to govern and rule themselves. As for the question of the King, for the moment this was to be parked too. The CLN and pre-Fascism political figures such as Count Sforza could rail all they liked, but until Rome fell, the Allies had agreed, Vittorio Emanuele would be keeping his crown.

Yet AMGOT and the ACC were not the only groups involved, because in addition there was also the Advisory Council, there to provide gentle guidance to Badoglio and his ministers and to the newly formed Control Commission. Established at Stalin's suggestion back in December, it included one member from Britain – Macmillan, of course – the United States, the Soviet Union and also the Free French. It was completely unnecessary, but agreed as a placatory gesture to the Russians now they were friends for the duration of the war. It was, though, yet another move by Stalin as he looked ahead to the post-war landscape with designs on Italy as a future Communist state.

The Allies were naturally alive to such machinations, but the New Year had in any case dramatically increased British influence in Italy, for not only were the navy and ground force commanders British, so too was General 'Jumbo' Maitland Wilson, the new Supreme Allied Commander, who had taken over from Eisenhower. Furthermore, under the new system, largely drawn up by Macmillan, General Noel Mason-MacFarlane, formerly British Governor-General of Gibraltar, was to be the head of both AMGOT and the ACC. It made sense for one man to be chief of both, Macmillan had argued, because many issues, such as the supply to civilians of food, clothing and housing, were the same problem whether just behind the lines or in the rest of southern Italy. Macmillan had also ensured that Mason-MacFarlane's HQ staffs were to be amalgamated. It had taken a huge amount of work – cajoling, bartering, placating and also just in terms of paperwork – but by Thursday, 20 January Macmillan had the final draft of the new plans for AMGOT and the ACC agreed, typed and ready for signing. 'I am hopeful', he noted, 'that in due course *so far as organisation is concerned*, we shall be on the road to solving some of our problems.'

After lunch he had driven up from Naples to Caserta to see Generals Wilson and Alexander, armed with the draft of the agreement but also drafts of the army orders to be issued by both generals in respect of what, administratively, remained in their power, and also a draft telegram for Wilson to send to the Combined Chiefs. Both signed readily, delighted that progress was being made. 'Everything', noted Macmillan, 'was agreed.' His relief was palpable.

It had been a dizzying few weeks for General John Harding since joining Alexander's staff. He'd had to get himself up to speed in very quick order, arriving in the middle of a raft of major operations, all of which involved numerous conferences, visits and, of course, paperwork. Harding was forty-seven, the same age as Clark and Eaker, and was a career soldier, a Gallipoli veteran of the last war, who had spent much of this current conflict in the Middle East and North Africa; he'd been right-hand man to General Richard O'Connor in the first, triumphant battles against the Italians in the Western Desert and had a deserved reputation as a highly efficient and perceptive staff officer, but also as a fearless fighting commander; he'd already accumulated an MC, DSO and bar. At Alamein he'd commanded 7th Armoured Division, the Desert Rats, before being wounded near Tripoli in January 1943, which cost him three fingers on his left hand. Fortunately, however, he was right-handed and, having been earmarked to command VIII Corps in Normandy, was then posted to Alexander's staff instead. Harding had been won over by Alex's charm, calm and grasp of the many complex strands facing him as an Army Group commander, while his chief was quickly coming to appreciate Harding's clarity of thought and attention to detail. The most successful generals were always a double act with brilliant Chiefs of Staff; Harding and Alexander had not really known one another three weeks earlier, but so far, so good. The new team appeared to be gelling.

On the 19th they'd headed south to visit the assault divisions for SHINGLE; Harding had been shocked by what he'd seen as they'd driven through Naples. 'Very depressing,' he had noted. 'Extensive bomb damage. Sordid and squalid in most parts. People looked underfed, ill-clothed and generally dejected. Hordes of them about, couldn't help feeling sorry for them.' Both divisions appeared to be in a confident mood, even though 3rd Division had had a disastrous rehearsal the day before in which forty-three DUKWs – a type of six-wheel amphibious truck – and a mass of artillery had been lost after the navy released them much too far out to sea.

Then there had been two final high-level conferences and SHINGLE was given the go-ahead as the weather, so capricious in Italy, looked favourable. 'It's a difficult gamble,' noted Harding, 'but the omens are good. Do hope we pull it off.' He was back at Caserta on the 21st, disappointed to hear the news from the Rapido. 'Whole 5 Army plan lacks concentration to my mind,' he wrote, 'but enemy seems to be swallowing the bait and putting in his resources piecemeal to plug holes in his line.' This was certainly true: elements of no fewer than five German divisions were now fighting on the Garigliano front and more were on their way as I Fallschirmjägerkorps hurried southwards. 'SHINGLE set off OK,' Harding added. 'Great good fortune with the weather so far.'

Three naval task forces set sail from Naples in five groups and included 5 cruisers, 24 destroyers and a number of other gunships and support vessels. The invasion fleet had also amassed 420 assault craft of various kinds, including 51 LSTs and 46 LSIs, making 97 landing ships in all, more than had originally been hoped for. Among those on board one of the LSIs was Guardsman Edward Danger of the 5th Grenadiers. Tall, slightly gangly and naturally rather diffident, Danger had been an insurance clerk in Surrey in civilian life and, as a meticulous fellow, had been posted to the Grenadiers as No. 4 Company clerk. This was far from being a cushy number, however, as he'd discovered in Tunisia; being company clerk meant being where Company HQ was and that was invariably directly in the firing line. However, so far he'd not had a scratch and very much hoped his good fortune would continue on this next venture.

Theirs had been a lengthy train journey from the Adriatic over the leg by train to Salerno, and then on to Gragnano to the south-west of Naples. The journey, only 100 miles or so, had taken a day and a half due to frequent stops. Danger had been shocked by the number of refugees clinging to the carriages despite the biting cold and obvious hazard; these hapless civilians crowded the troops the moment they pulled into a station. Danger and his fellows would throw them food and cigarettes, over which there was then a mad rush. 'We were horrified at such poverty,' he noted. 'I found out afterwards that they were refugees from a typhus outbreak in Naples.' Typhus had certainly been rampant in the city, but many were now roaming the countryside because they were homeless, lacked jobs and were starving.

The following days had been spent getting ready with training exercises, loading vehicles and receiving new kit: leather jerkins, Mae West life vests, the issuing of rations and so on. Now, though, late morning on the 21st, they were on their way, steaming out of Naples harbour having boarded the previous evening. Immediately, Danger and his mates had gone on the hunt for food and were pleasantly surprised to learn that there was enough aboard to last seven days. They were not going to go hungry on the run-up to Anzio.

Their LSI then later formed up with others and from around 5 p.m. began to steam for Anzio. On the landing ship's deck, Danger was able to look out and see the fleet as it moved out of the Bay of Naples. It was an imposing sight: two outer lines of LSTs and then two inner lines of LSIs that seemed to stretch for miles and, beyond these lines, the escorting warships. He and his friends smoked, ate excess amounts of rations and brewed endless cups of tea as they headed northwards at a steady 10 knots or so, the sea thankfully remaining calm.

Aboard the command ship, USS *Biscayne*, was Major-General John P. Lucas, just turned fifty-four but looking a lot older with snow-white hair, grey-flecked moustache, spectacles and invariably a pipe sticking out of his mouth. An artillery man by trade, he had been in the Mediterranean a while, first as Eisenhower's deputy, then, for Sicily, effectively General George S. Patton's sidekick at Seventh Army. Widely liked and trusted for his intelligence and good judgement, he had taken command of VI Corps at Salerno after his predecessor had been found wanting and been fired by Clark. Since then he had got his corps across the Volturno and battled the mud, mountains and misery with the best of them; his corps had played a key part in helping to crack the Winter Line.

A humane man who cared deeply about the men in his charge and keenly felt the burden of responsibility, he was not, however, an aggressive commander, despite his previous proximity to Patton, and had been chosen for SHINGLE primarily because of the two American corps in the line, his was the one least heavily employed at the time the Anzio operation had been given the green light. 'We have every confidence in you,' Alexander had told him after their first planning conference. 'That is why you were picked.' Rather than feeling flattered, this had somewhat put the wind up Lucas.

None the less, he now had a stronger force under him than had first seemed likely. Although the British 1st Division had not been in action since the assault on the island of Pantelleria back in June, and was unknown to the Americans, 3rd Infantry was probably the pick of Clark's infantry divisions and led by one of the most dynamic and charismatic divisional commanders in Italy, Major-General Lucian K. Truscott. Furthermore, Lucas's invasion force had been swollen by the Commandos of Special Service Brigade, as had been requested by Alex, and the Ranger Force that included not only three battalions of Ranger special forces but also a battalion of the 509th and the entire 504th Regiment. What had been designed as a two-division landing was, in effect, more like three in terms of fighting troops allocated.

Lucas went aboard the *Biscayne* at 3 p.m. on the afternoon of the 21st, aware that in less than twelve hours, at 2 a.m. on Saturday, 22 January, his first troops were due to be coming ashore on the beaches either side of Anzio. Lucas had very mixed thoughts about SHINGLE, thoughts that continually fluctuated. When he'd first heard he was up for the job, the entire plan had seemed madcap to him: not anything like enough shipping, not enough time for training and rehearsal, a G2 intelligence picture that looked as though half the enemy forces in Italy were only a stone's throw away, and over-optimistic thinking from the higher brass that was at odds with those who had actually fought in this wretched terrain the past few months. Yet the shipping situation, to an extent, had been substantially improved, a large number of German forces had, as promised, been drawn away from the Anzio area, and reports from the air forces were also encouraging. Some 4,000 tons of bombs had been dropped on rail targets since the start of the month and 1,885 on German airfields; the Allies appeared to be masters of the air and certainly, between coming aboard *Biscayne* and sitting down to write his diary that evening, Lucas had not seen a single enemy aircraft at all. The very latest intelligence picture also suggested that the Germans had not the slightest idea of what was heading their way.

On the other hand, the lack of training time had been worrying. There had been the fiasco with 3rd Division's rehearsals near Salerno and the 1st Division exercise Lucas had watched had also been poor. This worried him; if the navy couldn't land the troops properly in a peaceful training exercise, how the heck would they manage when under enemy fire? He reckoned he'd been given three weeks to do what would normally be expected to take three months. That was an exaggeration, but there was no denying the rushed nature of the operation. Everything in Italy was now being carried out in a hurry: major assaults against incredibly challenging defensive positions; timetables that made no allowance for bad weather, sudden unexpected fog or equally unexpected increases in river flow. And major amphibious assaults mounted with a quantity of shipping that everyone knew, in their heart of hearts, despite the positive chat, was insufficient for the task. From Alexander all the way down, the withdrawal of a large part of their supply capacity for Anzio in a fortnight was hovering over them. That knowledge didn't make commanding generals on the spot feel tremendously gung-ho. Yet nothing was allowed to interfere with the OVERLORD timetable. The Combined Chiefs had wanted Italy, had sanctioned it, but had done so with the potential prizes it might offer clouding the hard reality of a truly global strategic strain in which shipping, or rather the shortage of it, was the overriding constraint. There were plenty of tanks, even plenty of troops, guns, ammunition, rations, bombers, fighter planes, medical supplies and bridging equipment. There just weren't enough assault vessels in the Allied arsenal and, especially, not enough of that most precious commodity of all: landing ships.

And as a result, General Johnny Lucas was sitting in his cabin that evening with a massive knot of anxiety in his stomach, wondering what the hell lay in store and trying to convince himself all would be OK. 'I think we have a good chance to make a killing,' he jotted in his diary, then added, 'I have many misgivings but am also optimistic. I struggle to be calm and collected . . .'. He just wished the 'higher levels' were not so over-optimistic. 'The Fifth Army is attacking violently towards the Cassino line,' he added, 'and has sucked many German troops to the south and the high command seems to think they will stay there. I don't see why. They can still slow us up there and move against me at the same time.' Time would tell soon enough who was right.

*

At midnight, the davits on HMS *Royal Ulsterman*, a former River Clyde ferryboat, swung out to sea lowering the LCAs into which men from 6615th Ranger Group were already loaded. Among them was Colonel William O. Darby, still only thirty-two years old and both the founder and commander of the Army Rangers. Ambitious, energetic and tenacious, and with plenty of charm besides, Darby had passed out of West Point back in 1933 and been sent to Britain in early 1942 as aide to the divisional commander of the 34th Red Bulls, the first US troops to be shipped across the Atlantic. Darby had soon felt restless in what was a staff role, but salvation was at hand. General Marshall, the American Chief of Staff, was anxious to form a Commando-style force and had sent the then Colonel Lucian Truscott to the British Combined Operations HQ, to which the Commandos were attached, to look into the matter.

Truscott reported back to Marshall that he thought setting up a similar formation within the US Army would be a good idea. This was what Marshall wanted to hear, but to keep things separate he chose a different name, opting for 'Rangers' after Rogers' Rangers from the pre-Revolutionary force. With the Red Bulls being the only American troops in Britain at the time, the first recruitment drive had to be drawn from their numbers and Darby was given the task of getting this dynamic new force into being. It was exactly what he'd been waiting for and grabbed the chance with both hands. His criteria were strict: those applying had to be bright, fit young men who were willing to use their initiative and think on their feet, attributes not required of drafted troops. They needed to quickly establish a strong esprit de corps and want to be part of a new special and elite unit. To a man, they would be volunteers and would have to be interviewed by Darby first. Those lucky chosen few had then been packed off to Scotland for intensive training with the Commandos.

It had been the *Royal Ulsterman* that had brought the Rangers to Arzew in Algeria for their very first combat mission during TORCH back in November 1942, which Darby felt augured well for this current operation. Since that first landing in North-west Africa they had repeatedly proved their worth: in Tunisia, leading from the front in Sicily, and again during the Salerno invasion, securing vital passes and, more importantly, holding on to them. They'd grown too, and under Darby's command now were the 1st, 3rd and 4th Battalions as well as the 509th Parachute Infantry Battalion. Perhaps unsurprisingly, he had a close working relationship with General Truscott. Such bonds were not essential but they certainly helped, particularly in an ambitious amphibious operation such as this one.

It was very much Darby's way to lead from the front and so his were among the first two battalions now circling out at sea, waiting for the rest of the force to form up from the three transports that had brought them to the coast off Anzio. And then they were away, on the far left-hand flank of 3rd Division, who were due to land a couple of miles to the south of Nettuno, Anzio's neighbouring town. Darby's force, however, was to head straight into Anzio and secure both towns; on D-Day for Sicily they'd dashed ashore and swiftly taken the town of Gela despite heavy resistance from the Italian defenders. Lucas wanted and expected them to repeat this task. From his LCA, Darby could see the lights of vehicles moving along the shore and into the town, seemingly untroubled. A good sign. On they surged, the sky clear, with not an enemy aircraft to be either heard or seen. Picking up the first guide light, then the second, they closed towards the town, then Darby spotted the pier at Anzio away to his left and the guide boat bobbing up and down on the slight swell, the crew waving them on.

Then, around ten minutes before they were due to hit the shore, one of the LCT(R)s suddenly opened up from out to sea off 3rd Division's landing beaches. These were landing craft specially adapted to saturate the shore with a staggering 972 rockets, each with a 7-pound high-explosive warhead. Firing in clusters, they screamed in towards the shore, but while it was hard not to marvel at such a sound and sight, Darby was worrying where their supporting LCT(R) had got to. This prompted some anxious moments; the last thing he wanted was for them to hit the beach then get smothered by their own rockets.

He need not have worried; it never showed up at all and the LCAs reached the beach right on schedule at 2 a.m. Down went the ramp, but instead of hearing enemy machine guns and the explosions of mortars and shells, there was nothing – no firing at all. The Rangers had landed completely unopposed and exactly where they'd asked to be, on the southern edge of Anzio. 'I had laughingly said that when I got out of my boat in the centre of the flotilla,' noted Darby, 'I wanted to be at the front door of the casino. The navy put me down the exact spot.' One German soldier appeared but was immediately cut down, then so too was a second as the Rangers began fanning out through Anzio. Darby had hated having to split his force but the lack of landing craft ensured there would be two lifts. He kept expecting to see Germans suddenly appear, but what resistance there was continued to be light and very scattered. The second wave were not long in arriving, however, and these turned towards neighbouring Nettuno, a short distance to the south of Anzio. In the meantime, Darby established his CP in the casino, the art nouveau Paradiso sul Mare, set up communications with the Ranger representative still aboard *Royal Ulsterman*, and then ordered his men to spend the remaining hours of darkness getting ready for the inevitable enemy counter-attack he felt was sure to come. Both Anzio and Nettuno were now in Allied hands. It was barely 8 o'clock in the morning.

At 3.05 a.m., the first reports from Anzio started to reach Fifth Army HQ at Caserta, followed a few minutes later by the coded signal 'FOGGIA NEW YORK ALBANY CHICAGO OMAHA KANSAS CITY', which, decoded, ran as 'Landings appear to be proceeding on schedule. First troops have hit beach. No reports from landings yet. Troops have started to land on yellow beach, red beach and green beach.' Very quickly it became clear that the Allies had achieved complete surprise because nowhere along the invasion front did the assaulting infantry meet any opposition of note. The 3rd Division came ashore and troops of 30th Infantry, one of its three regiments, pushed inland to the north, while 3rd Regiment's recce troop hurried towards the Mussolini Canal, about five miles inland, to seize four bridges.

To the north of Anzio, 1st Division also landed totally unopposed, the only difficulty being a sandbar that hadn't been marked. This part of the coastline was desolate – low dunes, pine trees and barely a building to be seen. Of the enemy there was not a sign. The first ashore landed by 2.45 a.m., a little delayed by the sandbar. By 5.30 a.m. the first field regiment had landed, and by 8.30 a.m. was firing its 25-pounders. Because of the comparative paucity of landing craft, units were shuttled in with the LCAs scuttling back and forth to the parent ships. Edward Danger and the 5th Grenadiers and been due to land at 7 a.m., but delays had backed up and it wasn't until after 9 a.m. that they finally came ashore, by which time the beach was alive with activity and hubbub. Sappers were already toiling with strips of roadway, bulldozers clearing paths through the dunes and hauling jeeps and trucks out of soft sand where they had become stuck; and, miraculously, a pier had also already been run out so that LSTs could open their bows and unload vehicles directly on to the pier end. For all the mishaps of rehearsal, the landings themselves were going as close to clockwork as possible. Danger and his mates had been eating almost non-stop since getting aboard and, determined not to waste the excess rations on board, had stuffed every pack and pocket with as much as possible. 'All those who could lift anything', he noted, 'were carrying sacks of assorted eatables and it quite broke one's heart to leave so much grub aboard.'

Generals Alexander and Clark had left Caserta early, headed to the coast and, transferring to PT boats, had arrived at USS *Biscayne*, now anchored three and a half miles offshore, at around 9 a.m. General Lucas gave them a briefing; he'd scarcely been able to believe his eyes when he'd stood on the bridge earlier and seen no machine-gun fire nor any other from the beach. He'd expected a fight, just as they all had, despite the optimistic intelligence picture. Having been briefed, the generals and their party headed to the shore, Clark grabbing a jeep and speeding down the coast to see Truscott and 3rd Division, Alexander to see 1st Division. It was around 11 a.m. when Alex paused by the beach where the 24th Guards Brigade were coming ashore. Thirty-three years earlier, in 1911, he had joined the Irish Guards on passing out of Sandhurst and had fought with them throughout the First World War; now, the 1st Battalion was coming ashore on the beaches north of Anzio. He looked immaculate, as he always did, in an Irvin sheepskin flying jacket, breeches and boots and his trademark bespoke peaked cap. Pausing by a young officer of an anti-tank platoon as the lieutenant emerged soaking from the sea, Alex said, 'You look extremely scruffy.'

'Sir!' said the lieutenant, saluting smartly.

By now some occasional enemy shelling had opened up, but as several shells screamed in and landed far too close for comfort Alex neither flinched nor paused, but instead brushed off the soil that pattered down as he strode on.

Clark, meanwhile, was delighted to see so much activity: columns of vehicles rolling off the makeshift piers, and LCIs – landing craft, infantry, half the length of landing ships – at the shoreline, disgorging ever more men, vehicles and weaponry. Wire netting was being rolled out on to the shore, bulldozers were clearing paths and vehicles speeding along the coast as though they'd been there weeks, not a few hours. This was the unrivalled Allied, and especially American, industrial and technological machine at work. SHINGLE might not have been as powerfully backed as Alexander, Clark and his generals might have wished, but it was demonstrating a degree of military muscle with which the German armies in

Italy could never hope to compete. A new approach to unloading had also been devised by Truscott's staff that aimed to dramatically speed up the process: rather than load crates on to ships and then unload them again into waiting tenders and vehicles on shore, trucks would be loaded to the gunwales and simply drive off. The landing craft would then turn round and head back to Naples, where more loaded vehicles would be waiting. Meanwhile, DUKWs were shuttling supplies directly from liberty ships a little further out to sea.

The 504th PIR reached Anzio that afternoon and, after all the debate about whether to drop them by air, in the end they were brought in from the sea like everyone else. Among their number was Sergeant Ross S. Carter, part of Company C in the 1st Battalion. Carter had turned twenty-five on 9 January, and although an NCO was a university graduate with a degree in history. With blond, wavy hair, blue eyes and slightly protruding ears, Carter was smart, quick-witted and one of the early volunteers for the 504th, the original regiment of the 82nd Airborne. He also knew a thing or two about self-reliance, having funded his way through university working on a dairy farm and mostly sleeping in the barn there with the cows. He'd served in North Africa, had parachuted into Sicily and Salerno the previous September, and was among a cadre of battle-hardened paratroopers who'd served and survived the 504th's already long haul through the war.

The deck of their LCI was crammed with troopers ready to disembark when a Luftwaffe bomber swooped over and dropped a bomb that exploded just a little way off the bow. Although it wasn't a direct hit, the blast lifted the LCI clear out of the water and whammed it back down again. Shrapnel spattered the sides and a huge spume of water rose above them, drenching all the men aboard in a shower of oily seawater. This was one of only a few minor incursions by the Luftwaffe, however. Allied air forces had mounted cover over the beaches all day while fighter sweeps had screened far and wide; for the most part any enemy aircraft that had tried to get through were turned back or shot down. In the air, at any rate, Eaker's men ruled supreme.

Of greater danger to the paratroopers had been getting off their LCI, because when they did finally start disembarking they discovered they were too far out and ended up wading on to the beach, some up to their necks, some completely submerged for a few steps. Jumping out of an aircraft was a cakewalk compared with this. 'Wet, cold, miserable, mad, disgusted and laughing,' noted Carter, 'we crossed a level space into a wood, hung our clothes on the bushes and began to get settled for our brief stay.'

By the end of the day, General Lucas was feeling immensely relieved. There had been almost no opposition, unloading was continuing far faster than he could have possibly hoped, and even the port of Anzio was open after wrecks had been swiftly cleared away. It meant the landing ships could now unload directly on to the quayside. Some 36,000 men and 3,000 vehicles were already ashore and that figure was rising by the hour. Casualties had been lighter than anyone had dared hope: 13 killed, 97 wounded and 44 missing.

The fighting to the south, so mixed in its results, had drawn off enemy troops just as Alexander and Clark had hoped. The Germans had been caught out, wrong-footed by the timing and location of this assault. It was now up to Lucas and his force to try and exploit this success. British troops had already sent patrols eight miles out but if they were to reach the all-important high ground of the Colli Laziali they needed to move faster, with greater urgency and with as many men and as much materiel as possible.

Because neither Adolf Hitler nor Feldmarschall Albert Kesselring had any intention of leaving the Anzio area under-defended for long. A great opportunity for both sides beckoned.

CHAPTER 10

Rapid Response

UP AT THE ABBEY, the monks and those civilians still allowed by the Germans to be sheltering there had been continuing to make the best of the bewildering and frightening situation they now found themselves in. Starved of information and with little understanding of modern warfare, they had been guilty at times of trying to second-guess the meaning of what they saw and heard. A few days earlier, for example, a mule had been seen entering one of the caves underneath the abbey's bastions and reappearing soon after, fully laden. Perhaps, Dom Eusebio and others had wondered, this meant the Germans were pulling out?

It meant no such thing, of course. A day later, a woman down in the town below had been killed by a shell and a number of others wounded, including a girl of just twenty months, so she was hurriedly brought up to the abbey to be tended and looked after. Splinters had struck her still-soft skull. 'Her brain', noted Dom Eusebio with despair, 'was leaking out of the hole caused by the shrapnel.'

The monks had asked the Vatican to intervene and demand that the Germans move their positions clear of the abbey, but on 18 January letters had arrived telling them that official hands in Rome were tied. 'Only God can save us,' wrote Dom Eusebio. All hope had been further dashed by the opening barrage of the Texas Division's attack on the Rapido. Dom Eusebio had watched from the monks' corridor. It had seemed to him as though the entire valley had erupted in a long line of flame. Even up there, on Monte Cassino, the abbey had shaken; they had all felt it, the reverberations trembling the very mountain on which the abbey was built.

The following morning, at 5 a.m., they were awoken by a frantic knocking on the main door into the abbey. It turned out to be the gatekeeper; his son was desperately ill. Dom Agostino hurried out to try and help the boy, but he died half an hour later. Then an American shell hit the basilica, entering through a glass window. Heavy dust covered everything, the confessionals were damaged, marble was chipped and a large painting by Luca Giordano was shredded. Was this the beginning? It was just so hard to know what to think, how to react. Later that day, Dom Eusebio found himself making a coffin for the little boy and as he did so several more shells from the valley below burst over the abbey. 'A diabolical noise,' he noted, 'and creating fear that was no less diabolical.' In the evening, the porter began to feel ill.

Shellfire continued to scream overhead and occasionally land all too close for comfort during the next day and night. Windows were getting shattered by the blast and to be on the safe side they held Mass in the Crypt and ate their meals in a windowless stone storeroom. Two days later, 22 January, even Dom Eusebio had to admit he'd been feeling under the weather and struggling to keep on his feet. Being all cooped up there together in the abbey, and then in windowless, airless rooms and, in Dom Eusebio's case, tending to the corpses of those who had died of illness, it was perhaps hardly surprising – even for someone still as young, fit and healthy as he was.

Casualties from the recent fighting had been pouring into Fifth Army's hospitals. Lieutenant Bob Spencer was sent to the 36th General Hospital in Caserta. On arrival he was cleaned up, given a bed, and in due course a surgeon visited and told him he would be all right. 'You've had a slight fracture,' he told Spencer, 'you've had concussion, and you have a severe scalp injury.' Some skin grafts were going to be necessary or else he would have a bad scar on his head for life. Spencer had one operation but was told he would need a second. For the time being, however, he was safe, out of the firing line, and would be for a number of weeks to come.

Also in hospital was John Strick, at the 103rd British General Hospital at Nocera, and while fighting continued along the Cassino front and troops were coming ashore at Anzio he was having a lazy and also rather monotonous day, so much so that he decided to resume his diary. Strick had aspirations to be a published poet and had found something of a mentor in Harold Nicolson, the MP, publisher and writer. Strick and Nicolson had corresponded regularly; Nicolson had encouraged him to keep writing and had intimated that it might be possible to publish a collection of his poetry. At any rate, taking up his pen again, he jotted that only two on his ward were really ill – a Norwegian sea captain who had been wounded during the Bari raid by the Luftwaffe back in December, and a Commando lad. The others were all mostly convalescent cases. Strick, though, still felt listless and sick in mind. He was suffering from recurring visions: of the banks of the Garigliano and of Sergeant Budd being swept away, and of the night patrol in Castelforte. He wondered how he could have acted so rashly as to have left the road. 'At first I was inclined to discount the "bomb-happy" explanation myself,' he scribbled, 'but in view of my four breakdowns I begin to wonder and must try and see a psychologist.' He was also haunted by the fate of Sergeant Murphy, with whom he had shared so much and whom he considered a friend. 'How terrible', he added, 'if he had died from loss of blood.'

The losses had to be replaced somehow, some way. Germany, with a pre-war population of over 80 million, had managed to keep the conveyor belt running by combing the population for ever-younger and ever-older recruits. The twenty- to thirty-year-olds had all gone a long time ago, which was why Georg Zellner was being fed seventeen-year-olds and middle-aged lawyers. The pool of able-bodied men had been increased by drawing on the occupied territories, particularly from Ukraine, Poland, the Baltic States and other countries in eastern Europe. These were mostly placed into 'Ost' – east – battalions and generally treated as low-grade cannon fodder. Germany was starting to scrape the barrel, though, one of the reasons why Mark Clark had exhorted his men to kill – or take prisoner – as many as possible.

Britain, with a population of under 50 million, had an even smaller pool to draw from than Germany, although very sensibly had tried to use industry and mechanization and especially air power to minimize the number of front-line troops, so that while Germany had over 300 infantry divisions, Britain had planned to have no more than 36 active divisions. It could, however, also call on the Dominions and its empire, which was why there were Canadian, New Zealand, Indian and now South African divisions in Italy serving under the British flag. There was also an entire corps of Polish troops recently arrived in Italy, also British-trained, -armed and -equipped – men who had refused to accept Nazi rule and who were determined to fight on.

The United States had a population similar to that of the USSR, but was now committed to fighting globally and on multiple fronts, which is where the Soviet Union differed. Stalin had just one front with which to contend; the USA had many fronts and multiple theatres, and its manpower had to be split between the army, navy and air forces. New American army divisions were still forming and earmarked to be shipped overseas, but existing units needed to be replaced. Some companies within the 36th Texas Division, for example, had suffered more casualties since landing at Salerno on 9 September than there were men allocated to them. Nor was that unique to the Texas Division; it was a similar story across the board. Italy was proving a terrible meat grinder of front-line infantry units, and that was the case no matter which side one was on.

So although there were many reasons for the urgency to hurry up and get the war done and dusted, one of them was the rate at which all the major combatant nations were getting through the available manpower. There was, though, a balance to strike, because the harder commanders pushed their men, the greater were the casualties. OVERLORD was dictating the pace in Italy, but the alternative for the Allies was to do nothing, call off any further offensives and wait for better weather and longer days when their overwhelming air power could achieve more, the strain on the PBI would be less, and a breakthrough would be the inevitable consequence of several months of building up men and supplies. The risk, however, was that the Germans would do the same, reinforcing existing, badly depleted divisions in Italy but not drawing off any more from France, Germany and elsewhere. So in a way, Allied troops had to lose their lives and limbs in Italy in order for fewer to lose their lives and limbs in Normandy.

One of those arriving in Italy as a replacement junior officer – the class of soldier on both sides suffering the most – was 2nd Lieutenant Harold L. Bond, a twenty-two-year-old college graduate from Boston, Massachusetts, and like Bob Spencer before him and even Roswell Doughty another New Englander, with no connection to Texas whatsoever. He'd volunteered out of conviction ahead of his draft because he believed Hitler and Nazism were evil and needed to be stood up to. But the impassioned ideals with which he'd signed up were now confronting the brutal reality of his situation: that he was heading to one of the more dangerous locations on the planet at this current time and in one of the most life-threatening roles.

Bond had actually reached the division on the afternoon before the Rapido attack was due to begin, his journey north a bewildering experience of wrecked towns, numerous Bailey bridges and an endless stream of vehicles, with jeeps darting in and out of the line to overtake laden trucks. He also noticed that as they neared the front, the faster everyone seemed to drive. Then he heard the guns booming and without warning spied his first dead German, left on the side of the road with a hideous stomach wound, the corpse ugly, swollen and dirty, and past which every vehicle seemed to hurtle with no more regard than if it had been a dead bird or rabbit. Bond then learned the reason for the speed: here, as they neared Monte Trocchio, German observers could see the road and enemy gunners would often try and shell it. The driver enjoyed Bond's obvious revulsion. 'A dead Kraut,' he said, 'is a good Kraut.'

They eventually pulled into a dirt track that led to the CP of 141st Regiment, a cluster of battered farm buildings behind Trocchio. Bond was greeted by an ageing colonel, who told him he should be proud to have been assigned to the 'Fighting 36th' and even more proud to be in the 141st, which back in the day had fought at the Alamo.

'You know,' the colonel told him, 'the three most difficult military operations are the invasion of a defended coast, attacking up a mountain, and crossing a river which is covered by enemy fire.' He explained they had already overcome the first two and were about to attempt the third. Seeing Bond's horrified expression, he added, 'I won't send you down there tonight because there might be some Germans in the way.'

Bond spent the next two days at the farmhouse, listening to the terrifying sounds of the battle raging on the far side of Trocchio and wondering when he might suddenly be ordered to join the regiment. Eventually, he was told he wouldn't be assigned in the middle of the battle, because as a new officer he'd only be in the way and get himself killed. Instead he spent the time kicking his heels and watching the stream of people who came in and out. One such person was a dishevelled and exhausted young lieutenant who, Bond learned, had been placed under arrest for abandoning his men on the far side of the river. The officer told Bond that half his company had been killed or wounded and the remainder were isolated and cut off, and so he decided to swim back across the river to get help because he knew he was a good swimmer and didn't like to risk his men doing this. As soon as he had reported to the battalion commander he'd been charged with deserting them. Over and over, he told Bond, 'But I'm a good swimmer. I was the one to go.' He was certainly a physically strong-looking fellow. Bond said nothing, for what could he say? 'You don't know what it was like over there,' he then told

Bond. 'Germans everywhere, mortar shells crunching down in front of us and behind us, the screams of the wounded men . . . '.

It wasn't until 22 January that Bond was finally driven to his newly assigned unit, 3rd Battalion of the 141st Infantry Regiment. Dropped off in the yard of a stone house with his kit, he was confronted by four exhausted infantrymen trying to get warm in the weak winter sunshine. None even looked at him. Inside the main room was full of soldiers. A fire was smouldering and filling the room with smoke. Bond spotted a captain, who seemed be both in charge and the senior officer there at the battalion CP. Stepping over between the troops, he reached the captain, who was unshaven and looked as exhausted as the rest. Bond told him he'd been posted to the battalion. 'What in Christ's name did they do that for?' he snarled. 'As if I haven't got enough trouble with the goddamn river crossing, they have to send me a new officer now.' Bond would have to wait, he told him, until he had a better idea of where he could best be used. He then asked him what was he trained for. Bond mumbled something about mortars, thinking he might be able to manage this better than a rifle platoon. The captain said he would have to see, then told him to wait. Bond stepped back out into the yard and saw properly, for the first time, the abbey, perched high on the Monte Cassino massif, looking surprisingly bright on this January afternoon. The sun even reflected some of the glass windows, which dazzled in the sunshine. 'Like a lion it crouched,' noted Bond, 'dominating all approaches, watching every move made by the armies down below.'

Meanwhile, Oberst Wilhelm Mauss was trying to improve the medical services of his teams in XIV Panzerkorps. For some time he'd wanted to provide specialist mountain training for the medical unit of each division, so that they could be better equipped to assist those wounded in the terrain in which the men were fighting. Frustratingly, although there was a specialist mountain medical school at St Johann in the Austrian Alps, he could not spare the men and send them up there for the course. Instead, he had repeatedly asked that instructors from St Johann be sent to the Cassino front. Finally this had been agreed and the first course had run from 16 January with the medical staff of 44. Division, some fifty medical grades and stretcher-bearers taking part. New equipment had also been sent to him, including cables on which stretchers could be pulleyed and back saddles for mules which held stretchers. 'The cable railway is especially impressive,' noted Mauss, 'by which deep ravines can be crossed with a thick steel cable and all this with light and very primitive means.' It would, he hoped, shorten the transportation of the wounded by hours, which would mean saving many lives. This new equipment was to be deployed immediately, he noted with satisfaction, and not before time.

Then came the news of the Allied landings at Anzio. 'Yesterday passed full of tension,' Mauss noted on 23 January. 'Our blocking forces are moving forward from all sides.' So they were. As soon as von Vietinghoff heard the news of the Anzio landing, he recommended they do exactly as the Allies had hoped and pull back. He was not alone. Generaloberst Eberhard von Mackensen, commander of AOK 14, based in Verona in northern Italy, was of the same mind and believed the only way to save the German Army in Italy was to withdraw AOK 10 north. It was certainly questionable whether continuing to fight south of Rome made much military sense, and allowing front-line divisions to be splintered and farmed out piecemeal until only 20 per cent or less of fighting troops were still standing was not a recommended way of managing forces. However, there was no denying Kesselring's extraordinary capacity to both think clearly and act decisively in a moment of deep crisis such as the one in which his forces now found themselves. Kesselring, though, was having none of it, despite the protestations of his two army commanders.

Kesselring had been awoken early on the 22nd and had immediately invoked Case RICHARD, the prepared plan of action should the Allies make a landing south of Rome. There were other plans for different landings north of Rome and elsewhere, but the news of the landings had reached him via a corporal of a small number of German railway engineers based at Anzio, who had immediately sped off on his motorbike to desperately look for a German unit of some kind. The first soldier he'd seen was a young officer of 200. Panzergrenadier-Regiment, en route to join his unit. This young Leutnant passed on the news to the German commander at Albano Laziale, who then rang through to Rome and then to Monte Soratte. There were no German tactical headquarters in Anzio, Nettuno or for miles around. After dressing quickly, Kesselring hurried to the large briefing room where he met his Chief of Staff, General Siegfried Westphal. This was a room carved into the side of Monte Soratte, a long, razorbacked mountain that rose out of the Tiber Valley north of Rome, and part of an extensive bunker complex originally built by the Italians in the late 1930s.

As Kesselring, Westphal and a number of bleary-eyed staff officers poured over maps the Feldmarschall said, 'We have a problem,' and then added, 'but not an insurmountable one.' Westphal reckoned there were perhaps 800 German troops all told in the wider area around Anzio. Kesselring recognized that their first task was to block all routes into Rome and get as many troops as possible to contain the Allied bridgehead as quickly as possible. General Max Ritter von Pohl, commander of the Luftwaffe's air defence of Rome, was instructed to move all his flak units into easily defendable positions in the hills south of the city, while 4. Fallschirmjäger-Division, still mostly north of Rome despite the I Fallschirmjägerkorps move south, was also to head to the area without delay.

Kesselring's tendency to fling penny packets into the fray actually worked in his favour on this occasion because errant Kampfgruppen – battle groups – from divisions now fighting on the Garigliano front were still reasonably close; one such group from 29. Panzergrenadier was based at Velletri, for example, only twenty miles from Anzio and a stone's throw from the Colli Laziali, the prime Allied objective. Kesselring also decided to reverse his orders to I Fallschirmjägerkorps, still en route to the Ausente Valley, and instructed General Alfred Schlemm to about-turn and get to the Anzio area as fast as he could and take command.

A call was also put through to Hitler's headquarters at the Wolf's Lair at around 6 a.m. Needless to say, the Führer immediately ordered an overwhelming counter-attack and insisted that immense resources should be poured into Italy to ensure this happened. AOK 10, still based in the north, had been nominally under the direct authority of the OKW, but was now handed over to Kesselring; von Mackensen had little time for the field marshal, which was one of the reasons why he was grumbling about being sent south. An infantry division was ordered to move immediately from southern France to south of Rome. The 114. Jäger-Division was sent from the Balkans, three independent regiments were posted south too, while new and recovering divisions in Italy were also told to pack up and get moving to the Anzio area. These included 65. Infanterie-Division, which had been destroyed on the Sangro but which had been rebuilt immediately with Osttruppen, old men and teenagers; a further infantry division; and the recently formed 16. Waffen-SS Panzergrenadier-Division.

Kesselring also ordered his troops along the Garigliano to break off the attack and go on to the defensive, accepting that while they had not been able to push the British back across the Garigliano, after four days of heavy fighting there was no longer much threat of the Tommies breaking into the Liri Valley. Effectively, stalemate had been achieved and that was good enough, Kesselring reckoned, for the time being. Finally, recognizing that the Adriatic front was reasonably stable too, he pulled out 26. Panzer and a handful of units from 1. Fallschirmjäger from that stretch of the line, and a handful of battalions from the HG and 3. Panzergrenadier and 71. Infanterie-Division from AOK 10. Von Vietinghoff was not happy but Kesselring was deaf to his concerns.

All these orders had been issued by early afternoon on that first day. With Hitler's direct assistance Kesselring was amassing a huge force, way larger than Lucas's corps. Already by midday, the first lead units of 29. Panzergrenadier had begun to form blocking positions on the few roads heading in and out of the bridgehead.

Also speeding to the front was Kampfgruppe Gericke, the southernmost unit of 4. Fallschirmjäger-Division, which, on the morning of 22 January, had been stationed a little north of Rome. They were now ordered to head south, across the city, out the far side on the Via Appia and turn straight down the Via Anziate, the main road to Anzio that splintered right off Highway 7 at the edge of the Colli Laziali. They were only a battalion-strong, so fewer than 1,000 men, but Kesselring wanted them there as soon as they could humanly manage it – not to counter-attack but, in the first instance, just to block the road and make sure the Allies did not push past and take the high ground of the hills.

Gefreiter Hans-Paul Liebschner and his comrades had just been finishing breakfast that morning when the alarm was given for the battalion to hurriedly pack up and head south. It took them no more than a couple of hours to get ready, so that by mid-morning Liebschner was sitting in the back of a troop lorry, heavily laden with ammunition, driving southwards. Such journeys were always fraught because of the number of Allied Jabos seemingly roaming at will. Several times their column had to pull off the road, but fortunately for them they were not hit and were able to continue on their way. Liebschner found it a frightening and unnerving experience. No one had said where they were going or why they were heading there. They drove past the Colosseum, a landmark Liebschner had always wanted to see – but not like this, sitting on a wooden bench in the back of truck and spending more time looking for Jabos than playing the tourist.

Liebschner was eighteen, from Liegnitz in Lower Silesia, and the son of an income tax collector. As a child he'd joined the Jungvolk, enjoyed every minute, and had then been every bit as keen on the Hitler Jugend, so that by the time he was seventeen he had been desperate to join up and fight for Führer and Fatherland. Just five days after his seventeenth birthday he was on his way to a training unit in Austria to become a fighter pilot. From there, he and his fellow recruits had been sent to France to receive basic military training before initial flying training began. After the Hitler Jugend, Liebschner had found this undemanding, but once they were eventually sent to flying school it soon became clear that due to the shortage of fuel he would not be doing much flying any time soon. This concerned him because he was desperate to get into the action and worried that if he waited for flying training the war might be over before he was even qualified. So, being young and impetuous, he transferred to the Fallschirmjäger. To begin with this went well; he found the training tough and challenging and was singled out to become a machine-gunner. However, at his pre-jump medical he was told he had a heart condition and so was prevented from making his first airborne jump. He could not understand it; he'd never had any trouble with his heart and had always led a very active life. But there had been no arguing with the medical officers.

Training standards were shifting, though, and by this stage of the war there were few opportunities in which anyone in the Wehrmacht imagined paratroopers would be required to jump. Furthermore, there was neither the fuel nor transports from which to do so. So, having heard in November that 4. Fallschirmjäger-Division was being formed in Italy purely as ground troops, Liebschner applied, was accepted, and by Christmas was heading to Perugia, where he joined Kampfgruppe Gericke and was soon made company runner of the MG Kompanie.

It was dark by the time they de-bussed and were given the briefest of briefings: the enemy had landed and they were to probe southwards down the Via Anziate. Although heavily laden with ammunition and small arms, paratroopers were lightly armed and lacked any kind of heavy firepower. Their role, therefore, was to try and make contact with the enemy without getting involved in a major firefight. Liebschner was armed with a sub-machine gun, revolver, field glasses and a bicycle, but as the battle group headed southwards along the dark, empty road Allied shells started whistling over, prompting them all to jump clear and dive for the ditches. Liebschner soon began to curse his bicycle; he couldn't imagine ever using it, so asked the Feldwebel what he should do with it.

'No idea, Liebschner,' the Feldwebel replied. 'You signed for it, you are responsible for it.' Eventually Liebschner decided to ditch it beside a large tree a little further on, making the most of the darkness to mask this abandonment of vital Wehrmacht equipment. Perhaps, he told himself, he would pick it up again if they ever came back that way. For now, though, he knew he was well shot of it.

The speed of the German response to the Allied invasion was, by any reckoning, extremely impressive. Odds and sods, replacement companies, battalions here, artillery units there – all were urgently sent forward, and by nightfall on that first day as many as 20,000 German troops were in a rough ring all around the bridgehead, holding key nodal points such as towns like Cisterna and Mussolini's tiny new model town, Aprilia, astride the Via Anziate. Guns were moving into positions in the Colli Laziali and Colli Albani. General Schlemm had set up his headquarters and was now commanding the defence until von Mackensen arrived and took over. Leading units from not only 4. Fallschirmjäger but also 3. Panzergrenadier, the HG-Division and 29. Panzergrenadier were all now reaching this new front.

In the meantime the Allies had been busy unloading, establishing a beachhead perimeter and preparing for the counter-attack Lucas and all his subordinates knew must surely arrive. American patrols had pushed towards Littoria to the east and to Cisterna, the largest town in the area, which lay twelve miles to the north-east, and a further reconnaissance patrol had been ordered to head to Velletri, twenty miles north and lying at the foot of the Colli Albani. None of these patrols had reached their destinations; a recce troop of the 3rd Division had run into some Germans between Cisterna and Littoria and been captured. Other patrols had stopped short of their destinations; Velletri had seemed altogether too far for a light patrol on D-Day. The British, meanwhile, had set off north through the largely uninhabited and flat countryside on the Via Anziate through a dense forest called the Bosco di Padiglione until, emerging again, they reached a large concrete flyover which crossed both the road and the railway line that ran alongside and which was marked on their maps as 'Campo di Carne' – the field of meat. The name was curiously fitting for an area that seemed eerily empty, wild and abandoned and which had so little to recommend it.

This coastal region south of Rome had been a desolate area of salt bogs which had been notorious breeding grounds for malarial mosquitoes. From 1930 onwards, a huge works project began here. Much of the scrub pine forest had been cleared, irrigation ditches dug and a larger waterway constructed: the Mussolini Canal, which ran roughly north to south, three miles east of Cisterna and down to the sea about ten miles east of Anzio. A second stretch of the canal, at roughly right angles from the west, joined the main part of the waterway six miles north of the coast. A raft of new towns had been built such as Littoria and Aprilia, but while the draining of the marshes had been completed by the war, Mussolini's grandiose plans for the area had not. The Flyover that British patrols reached on the afternoon of 22 January had been constructed, but not the road running either side. It looked exactly like the incomplete building project it was: an isolated concrete bridge in the middle of nowhere. Barely a house could be seen, although in the distance, emerging from the flat plain, was a cluster of buildings the British assumed must be an industrial plant of some kind. In fact it was Aprilia: a church, a town square and statue, a Casa del Fascio and a handful of houses. As a symbol of Fascist public works projects it had little to recommend it, for it stood forlorn and isolated in a largely featureless plain. The British troops who first spied it named it 'the Factory'.

The Allies held a loose bridgehead, known as the Beachhead Line, roughly eight miles or so deep. The American, eastern half was based along the Mussolini Canal. Lucas called this waterway 'a prime tank trap.' German troops had travelled as much as sixty miles in the first twenty-four hours, almost ten times as far as the Allies had moved from Anzio. No massed charge for the hills had been ordered by Lucas or by anyone else, only patrols, nor was there one during the next couple of days that followed. Instead Allied troops consolidated the bridgehead, furiously digging slit trenches around blocking positions, the Americans creating a defined perimeter along the two stretches of the Mussolini Canal and generally readying themselves for the long haul. Clark ordered rapid reinforcements and on 24 January the first of the 45th Thunderbirds' three regiments arrived; this was followed by the rest of the division as well as much of 1st Armored. For all the anxieties of Clark and Lucas, especially about landing understrength, SHINGLE had always been more than a mere two-division assault, and in the ensuing days VI Corps was rapidly swelling further. Allied intelligence on German intentions was limited; a counter-attack was expected and Lucas's prime concern was to ensure that whenever that blow fell and with whatever forces the Germans could muster, his corps would not be flung back into the sea. Unbeknown to him, however, far more German forces than he had imagined *were* massing.

But only light enemy forces had reached Anzio at this time. A strong thrust to the hills was still there for the taking.

German Fallschirmjäger prisoners being led back by New Zealand troops on the road north of Cassino towards Caira.

PART II

Missed Opportunities

CHAPTER 11

The Distant Hills

BENITO MUSSOLINI MIGHT HAVE been reinstalled as head of the RSI in the north of Italy, but no one could doubt who was really running the show. Italy was occupied by the Germans and treated very much as such, which meant regarding Italians mostly with utter contempt and bleeding the country dry while openly maintaining a veneer of friendly alliance. Kesselring was in charge of the German armed forces in Italy while effective control of the administration of the occupied half of the country was in the hands of Obergruppenführer Karl Wolff, former Chief of Staff to Heinrich Himmler, the head of the SS, and liaison officer between the SS and the Führer. In terms of rank he had equal billing with Ernst Kaltenbrunner, the head of the Reich Security Office, and was second only to Himmler himself. Wolff was a smooth-talking charmer and a highly intelligent senior Nazi but utterly ruthless, unscrupulous and decidedly lupine. The German ambassador to the RSI was Rudolf Rahn, an Iago figure who hovered around Mussolini as his political 'advisor'. The former Duce, a shadow of his earlier bombastic self, had almost no room at all for manoeuvre.

It was Wolff who had drawn up the measures and terms under which the RSI operated, which were restrictive to say the very least. The RSI was even denied the right to an economic trade policy of its own, while the factories of the industrial north were taken over by Albert Speer, the Nazi Armaments Minister. Food, so desperately needed in Germany, was siphoned off at the expense of ordinary Italians. German war-related costs in Italy were also expected to be paid by the Italians of the north to the tune of 10 billion lire each month, which was around \$3 million – a huge sum in 1944. Manpower had been creamed off just as much as material assets. The disbanded armed forces were now mostly toiling in Germany as enforced labour, but many able-bodied men in Italy were also swept up into Organisation Todt, or OT, the Nazi labour organization, whether by voluntary, coerced or compulsory means. Families were often ripped apart in the process. It was Italian labourers who had carried out most of the defensive work along the Gustav Line and it was mainly Italian labour that was also preparing a series of further defensive belts across Italy, not least the Pisa–Rimini position.

Mussolini had been desperate to create a new Italian Army and eventually Hitler conceded, albeit against the advice of the OKW, and allowed him to raise four divisions, which he felt might be useful, not as front-line troops but as coastal guards and behind the lines. Somewhat dampened but not deterred, Mussolini issued a conscription order for all those born in 1923, 1924 and 1925. By the beginning of 1944, some 50,000 had responded to Mussolini's call to arms, but this was obviously very small beer indeed when compared with the fifty-six divisions that had been dismantled by the Germans back in September.

In any case, those young Italians still willing to fight for Germany and Fascism generally signed up to the GNR, the Guardia Nazionale Repubblicana – the Fascist militia – or to the SS police battalions; recruitment in these militias was four times that of Mussolini's National Republican Army. Inevitably, however, many did not wish to work for Nazi Germany, nor be recruited in a new army or militia. Most, for the time being, did their best to dodge the recruitment drives, ignored call-up papers or hid when the press-gangs were on the march. Others decided to fight clandestinely and over the winter had begun to form themselves into partisan organizations. By November 1943, the Communists, part of the CLN, had set themselves up in Milan with Luigi Longo in command; he, like many others vowing to take the fight to the Nazi-Fascists, had fought in the Spanish Civil War. Ferruccio Parri, a Socialist partisan and political activist, also made contact with the SOE in Berne, Switzerland. Generally, the Allies were wary of irregular troops, but Parri quickly found favour, not least because he was not a Communist. The first arms drop arrived six weeks after these talks had taken place, while funds were also starting to be given to the partisan leadership. Furthermore, the CLN, while an open organization in the south, had established itself as a structured organization in the north as well, albeit under the moniker CLNAI – for *alte Italia*, the north. 'Today it can be stated that all partisans are under a single powerful and well-organized leadership,' ran an article in a Swiss newspaper back in November. 'Since 1 November all activities have been directed by the National Committee of Liberation.' It was an article read with interest both by the Foreign Office back in London and by the OSS. As the Allies were discovering with both the French Resistance and with the partisans in the Balkans, the better structured and centralized a resistance organization was, the more effective it was too. It paid to help them – and to play a part in controlling them as well.

In Rome, partisan organizations had emerged very swiftly following Germany's crushing of the popular insurrection of 9–10 September, although there were three main factions. One was the Fronte Militare Clandestino della Resistenza, the FMCR, a right-wing monarchist organization led by the aristocratic Colonnello Giuseppe Cordero Lanza di Montezemolo. Another was the Communist Bandiera Rossa – the Red Flag – but the largest was the Gruppi di Azione Patriottica, known more simply as GAP, backed by the CLN and run and organized by the CLN's Military Council. In recent months they had been increasingly active: targeting Fascists initially, then assassinating German officers, setting off bombs and making life as difficult for the occupiers as they possibly could. In the early hours of 22 January, the Military Council received a radio cable from the Allied Command. 'The hour has arrived for Rome and all Italians to fight in every possible way and with all forces,' it ran. 'Sabotage the enemy. Block his roads of retreat. Destroy his communications to the last wire. Strike against him everywhere continuing the fight indefatigably, without thought of political questions, until our troops have arrived. Notify all bands and parties.'

Among those Gappisti to be given new instructions on the back of this call to arms were Carla Capponi and her boyfriend Rosario Bentivegna, two key partisans in GAP Centrale. Carla – code-named 'Elena' – lived in the heart of the city with her mother in a flat near Trajan's Column. Twenty-four years old, she came from a left-wing anti-Fascist family; her father, a former mining engineer, had refused to join the Fascist Party, his career suffering as a consequence, and, posted far from home, he had died in a mining accident in 1940. Carla had never forgiven the Fascists for this. Having helped those fighting against the Germans in Rome in September, she had then met Bentivegna and become an increasingly active partisan. In December Elena had even carried out her first assassination, shooting dead a German staff officer and stealing vital plans that revealed details of power and communications grids which linked the flak sites around Rome.

On 22 January, both Elena and Bentivegna – code-named 'Paolo' – were instructed to meet Carlo Salinari, code-named 'Spartaco', at the Caffè Greco near the Spanish Steps. Elena had not been there since saying goodbye to her then boyfriend, who was heading off to war in Greece – a war from which he did not return; she had learned he'd been killed. Now, though, more than three years later, Spartaco was sitting opposite her and telling her that GAP Centrale was to be redeployed around the edge of the city. Paolo was to become commander of the new Zone VIII with Elena as his deputy, and they were to relocate in Centocelle, a Fascist-built suburb that lay between the Via Casilina and the Via Appia, the two key roads heading out of Rome to the front.

They were to leave immediately, although Paolo and Elena asked permission to carry out one last attack in central Rome that was planned for that very day. Perhaps foolhardily, Spartaco assented. Sure enough, that afternoon, from the parapet of a building overlooking the Via Cavour, they waited for a German fuel truck that passed through the route as regularly as clockwork and threw grenades on to it. The truck blew up in a ball of flame and swirling smoke, killing the driver and guards and bringing traffic to a standstill.

Once again, they had got away with it.

These were hectic days for the Fifth Army commander, with two fronts to contend with and different operations now going on all at once. Early on the 23rd he had a sobering meeting with Generals Walker and Keyes, where the full extent of the T-Patchers' failure to get across the Rapido was made clear. Clark had known that the crossing would be costly, but it had been one of those tough decisions army commanders had to make at times, and there was no question that, collectively, the series of assaults had massively helped the landings at Anzio. 'Some blood had to be spilled on either the land or the SHINGLE front,' he noted, 'and I greatly preferred that it be on the Rapido, where we were secure, rather than at Anzio with the sea at our back.'

Yet while the landings at Anzio had succeeded far better than he had dared hope, the key now was to try and capitalize on that success, which meant continued pressure around Cassino. The French of the CEF had also been pushing through the mountains to the north without let-up, but Clark now wanted to use them in a coordinated assault with the 34th

Red Bulls on to the Monte Cassino massif. The Red Bulls were to attack across the upper Rapido Valley then up on to the massif a couple of miles north of Cassino, while the French would change direction and assault Monte Belvedere and Abate, yet another 3,000-foot peak, but which stood below the mighty Monte Cairo, 6,000 feet high and the largest mountain for miles. The Red Bulls were to begin their attack on the night of 24 January, the French early the following morning. At the same time, the T-Patchers, using 142nd Infantry, the one regiment that had not been flung to the wolves in the Rapido battle, were to make a feint attack north of Sant'Angelo and just south of Cassino, with the weaponry of 1st Armored's Combat Command B to help.

The weather had turned again on the 24th, with strong winds, cloud and driving rain, which meant the battering ram along the Cassino front would be swinging into the wall of the Gustav Line once again with limited air support. The tantalizing promise of this breakthrough, and the perceived need to make progress ahead of OVERLORD, was driving the entire January offensive.

The attacks on the Cassino front, however, were designed to be launched hand in glove with strikes out of the Anzio bridgehead towards the hills south of Rome – high ground that could be seen rising up in the distance even from the coast. While Clark was beetling from Keyes's CP to that of McCreery and then to Général Alphonse Juin – the commander of the CEF – demanding urgent maximum effort, very little aggressive action was taking place from the Anzio bridgehead. Rather, Lucas was concentrating on making sure his defensive ducks were lined up in a row and that he had sufficient men and materiel ashore with which to launch a major drive to the hills.

General Lucas was now ashore permanently and based in an Italian barracks near Nettuno. He was aware of the need to push on and had ordered Truscott to 'advance on Cisterna', which the 3rd Division had done, although they still hadn't taken the town. The British were also pushing northwards. 'I must keep in motion', he noted on the 24th, 'if my first success is to be of any value.' He was absolutely right about that, but it was also clear that Lucas's idea of keeping in motion wasn't necessarily the same as Alexander's or even Clark's. There was, furthermore, a difference in military parlance between advancing 'on' and advancing 'to', a distinction Lucas himself had been very mindful of when he'd received his written orders for SHINGLE from Clark back on 12 January. Under the subtitle 'MISSION', Lucas had been told 'a) To seize and secure a beachhead in the vicinity of Anzio' and to 'b) Advance on COLLI LAZIALI'. Lucas understood that to 'advance on' meant 'move in the direction of', which was not quite the same thing as being instructed to swiftly strike and capture an objective. It was perhaps odd that he didn't question this because in the planning conferences both Alexander and Clark had been unequivocal about the need to press on and get to the high ground of the Colli Laziali as quickly as possible. After all, this was the driving concept behind SHINGLE: that by doing so, by bluffing the Germans into thinking that both Rome and AOK 10's rear were threatened, they would be encouraged to pull back from the Gustav Line.

However, Lucas's written orders had been issued ten days before SHINGLE's launch and at the time no one knew how many enemy troops might still be in the area. Orders had to be written with the knowledge that was available at the time of writing, which was why, on 12 January, the emphasis had rightly been on securing the beaches and ports and establishing a beachhead first. In the event, however, the landings had gone almost entirely to plan, which then gave Lucas the opportunity to use his initiative and make a concerted effort to get his troops far further forward than they had been so far. It was hard to imagine a field commander such Patton or Rommel still sending only small and tentative reconnaissance patrols forty-eight hours after a landing of such complete tactical surprise.

Meanwhile, to the south, the fighting along the Garigliano front had continued at a ferocious pace, even though Kesselring had pulled back I Fallschirmjägerkorps and ordered them to hurry to Anzio instead. At that moment, the three German divisions still in the line had been planning a coordinated massed counter-attack to push the British off both the Minturno Ridge and the high ground above Castelforte and Suio around Monte Damiano. However, 29. Panzergrenadier was also then pulled back and ordered to head to Anzio, as well as 94. Infanterie-Division, by now already badly mauled and in some disarray. That had left just General Baade's 90. Panzergrenadier, which had been hurriedly arriving in dribs and drabs, but which then unleashed the heaviest counter-attack yet on the British positions around Monte Damiano.

At the 56th Heavy Regiment's CP, RSM Jack Ward had never experienced anything like it. Their own guns had been booming without let-up;

they'd sent thousands of shells over, yet the Germans were still firing back. 'As I write I can hear the shells hurtling outside,' he wrote. 'Our office is shaking to pieces.' He had heard from some of the infantry he'd spoken to that it had been the hardest battle they'd yet fought. In an effort to help the infantry on Damiano, they'd established an OP up there so as to better direct fire against the enemy. Those on the OP had soon found themselves being mortared almost incessantly. Three men were wounded, so replacements and a stretcher party of six were sent up to fetch them. 'The battle is still fierce,' noted Ward, 'Jerry is putting in counter-attack after counter-attack. We're holding him but it's hard going.' Word reached HQ that several of the men at the OP were now suffering from shell shock. One of them, Gunner Terry Milligan, had been wounded in the right leg, suffered something of a mental as well as physical collapse and was stretchered off the hill. Rather like John Strick a few days before him, he was unable to stop weeping. 'I'm sitting in an ambulance', wrote Milligan, 'and shaking, an orderly puts a blanket round my shoulders, I'm crying again.'

Milligan had come under particularly intense mortar fire, but on the evening of 23 January the Damiano Ridge position had been restored in part due to the heroics of Private George Mitchell of the 1st Scottish Borderers, who had single-handedly stormed a German MG nest, shooting one German gunner and bayonetting another, and had then charged the rest of the position. As his section caught up, another enemy machine gun opened fire, so Mitchell single-handedly attacked that as well, killed both gunners, then forced the rest of the astonished Germans to surrender. But one of the surrendering Germans, when Mitchell wasn't looking, picked up a rifle and shot him in the head, killing him instantly.

On the far side of the Ausente Valley from Damiano, the Inniskillings were still dug in and holding their part of the ridgeline and occupying what had been German positions; these included a dugout 15 feet underground and a series of connecting trenches, although David Cole was stuck in a small and filthy slit trench. From here he had watched warships out to sea shelling German positions and, from time to time, had a grandstand view of Allied fighter-bombers sweeping over and hammering the enemy. At night, beyond Monte Damiano, they'd seen the guns firing along the Rapido too, flickering in the sky. Their own positions were shelled repeatedly, something which Cole never got used to. 'Familiarity', he noted, 'bred not contempt but quicker reflexes and increasing horror.' He had lost count of how many lucky escapes he'd had, which only reminded him how close he was – how close they all were – to death. Casualties had continued to mount.

On the afternoon of 24 January, 56th Division had attempted to push on down the right-hand side of the Ausente Valley, following a cable from Clark to McCreery urging him to continue attacking. Infantry and tanks had subsequently set off together behind yet another immense barrage. They made no progress at all: deep minefields, well-directed enemy fire and miserable weather ensured that they soon ground to a halt. Cole had watched it from his slit trench, tanks trundling like mechanical toys, troops dashing from one ditch to another and the wispy smoke from the shells bursting around them. The truth was that both sides had, by this time, shot their bolt. The Garigliano battle had succumbed to stalemate, the British still stubbornly clinging to the ridges but the Germans equally stubbornly refusing to pull back from the far side. And Castelforte, where John Strick's patrol had come unstuck, remained in German hands, the troops moving around in what had since become little more than rubble.

Nor was it only British troops that were breaking down. Hans-Paul Liebschner and the men of Kampfgruppe Gericke had been ordered to fan out to the west side of the Via Anziate while the newly arrived lead battle group from 3. Panzergrenadier occupied Aprilia. Having ditched his bicycle, Liebschner was walking down a track with Unteroffizier Kreuzer, a veteran of the Eastern Front. Kreuzer and he had become friends while they'd briefly been in Perugia, both having transferred from a Luftwaffe field division. Like Liebschner, Kreuzer had no parachute jumps to his name, and because of this the other sergeants didn't really consider him to be one of them. Liebschner rather looked up to him – a man of proven combat experience – yet as Allied shells started screaming overhead and they got ever closer to the enemy, Kreuzer began to complain of stomach pains. Then, spotting a small bridge, he sat down beside it and broke down in convulsive sobs. 'I tried to pull him up,' noted Liebschner, 'but he would not, or was unable, to move. His nerves had given out.' Some of those passing him gave words of encouragement, others called him a coward. Liebschner tried to jolt him out of his despair but it was no use. Something deep inside Kreuzer had snapped. Eventually, Liebschner was ordered to leave him.

They had yet to make any direct contact with the enemy, but as they tentatively moved west of the Via Anziate they found themselves suddenly in a very different landscape, no longer a flat, reclaimed coastal marsh but instead an area that rolled and undulated and which was scored by numerous gullies and channels. Some were just a few feet deep, others as much as 20 or 30, cut into the clay by the flow of streams and rivers running down from the distant hills towards the sea, and lined by trees and bushes and tangled thorns. One of their patrols eventually drew some enemy fire, so they hastily pulled back and began digging in. 'As far as I could make out,' noted Liebschner, 'our company seemed to be the only unit in the whole wide world around us.'

The 504th PIR were now holding a stretch of the Mussolini Canal to the north. The canal itself was only 20 or so feet wide, but either side of it were huge 30-foot-high anti-flood dykes set back from the edge of the canal and about 100 yards apart. Company C of the 1st Battalion placed half a dozen men in outpost houses, several hundred yards apart, which overlooked the canal – a natural defensive position if ever there was one. Yet while it was all very well digging in, the point was obviously to push out as quickly and as far as possible, and so a couple of nights after they'd landed, Lieutenant Horace A. Warlock, the Company C commander, and Staff Sergeant Frank L. Dietrich called for five further volunteers to head across the canal on a recce patrol.

Sergeant Ross Carter agreed to go. 'What are we looking for, lieutenant?' he asked.

'We're looking for trouble,' Warlock replied, 'any kind of trouble.'

It was around 8 p.m. that night when they headed across the canal in boats, then down a track that led, nearly 2,000 yards to the north, to the Via Appia, Highway 7, which crossed roughly east–west ahead of them. It was night-time and dark, but their eyes soon adjusted and faint shapes could be picked out, especially in this flat terrain where men and objects would be dimly silhouetted against the sky. Eight hundred yards further on they paused and listened to some Germans digging in near a grove of trees, then stealthily pressed on. Carter was up front, leading the patrol, and halted them 100 yards short of the Via Appia before heading on alone to the road. He soon discovered a series of well-prepared outposts – holes dug in the ground with ammunition boxes, shovels and jackets left beside them and telephone wire running out of each. Hurrying back, he reported to Lieutenant Warlock, who ordered them all to now cut across to the road but clear of the enemy foxholes.

Off they all moved again, only for a guttural voice to call out 'Halt!' just a short distance from the Via Appia. All seven paratroopers hit the deck. Twice more the German called out and then a machine gun opened fire. To the paratroopers' surprise, the bullets were not aimed anywhere near them. 'Obviously,' noted Carter, 'someone else farther to the left was annoying the uneasy sentinel.' A firefight opened up which the patrol used to wriggle into a ditch beside the road. Soon after, a panzer or some kind of assault gun rumbled up to the far side of the road and opened fire, the projectile whooshing over their heads. Then a truck pulled up and a number of men got out and began digging in noisily not 50 yards from them. Dark figures could be seen running about. The panzer moved with grinding gears and fired again. The firing quietened down and after a little while a lone German walked towards them, clearly to answer the call of nature. One of the men silently stepped up and cut the man's unsuspecting throat, dropping him quietly to the ground, an action that was passed down from man to man in whispers until it reached Carter too.

'Lieutenant,' he whispered to Warlock, 'are we still looking for trouble?' Before Warlock could reply, the sound of marching hobnailed boots came down the road and they saw four men tramp past in perfect rhythm, then halt a little way beyond and fire a white flare, which hissed into the air and burst with a crackle, casting a glow of light over the area. Fortunately, the patrol was hidden from view by a bend in the ditch, but clearly they were in a very precarious situation. The enemy, they knew, would be looking for a patrol sneaking back, so Carter suggested they wait for the flare to die down, then march down the road themselves as though they owned it. Warlock agreed. 'OK,' he said. 'Lead off, We're right behind you.'

'We German-stepped,' noted Carter, 'our guts and saliva frozen, up the ditch road to a little bridge, which we crossed and then continued down the main road till we reached the prepared positions.' So far so good, but then they saw the four Germans who had earlier walked past them, one now leaning on a machine gun and staring at them. The paratroopers walked straight on, careful in their rubber-soled boots to keep on the dirt because they made a different sound to hobnails on gravel. On they walked, unchallenged, heading for the comparative cover of a wood just up ahead. Carter's heart was in his mouth when he spotted a German emerge from the wood just as they approached it and felt for his weapon, but the man headed off, unsuspecting, and so they kept on, reached the canal, crossed back over and made it to safety. 'By God,' noted Carter, 'we'd done the kind of thing the story books tell about! We shook each other's clammy hands and kidded about the condition of our baggy pants.'

While Allied air forces still dominated the skies over Anzio, they no longer had mastery. 'Four ships knocked out yesterday,' noted Lucas. 'A couple of destroyers and a hospital ship. The dirty swine.' In fact, a Luftwaffe formation of fifty-five bombers had made for Anzio, and while half the force had been driven off by Allied fighters, twenty-one had got through and using Fritz-X, a radio-controlled guided aerial torpedo, sunk HMS *Janus* and damaged the *Jervis*; fewer than half of *Janus*'s crew were rescued as she went down in just twenty minutes. Allied fighters were slaughtering these bomber formations, but they kept coming all the same. A formation of more than forty bombers thundered over at dusk that same day; fifty-two came later and in the darkness damaged a further destroyer and minesweeper, while the *St David* – the hospital ship – was sunk and its sister ship, the *Leinster*, hit and set on fire.

This was an effort by the Luftwaffe it could not hope to sustain, but was part of Hitler's orders for an all-out drive to kick the Allies back into the sea. Fighters were also being sent south, including Jagdgeschwader 77 and 53, which had several months earlier been posted to the north to protect the southern Reich but also to keep their machines safe from marauding Allied fighters. The III Gruppe of Jagdgeschwader 53 – III/JG53 – were suddenly ordered to fly south on 24 January, to Orvieto near Lake Bolsena in southern Umbria. The move, however, turned into something of a fiasco. The Gruppe commander, Major Franz Götz, had become ill in the night and so was grounded, while of the three Staffeln – squadrons – only 7. Staffel made it to Orvieto as the other two ran into bad weather and had to turn back. Hauptmann Jürgen Harder and his fellow pilots in 7. Staffel touched down at Orvieto on their own and then discovered no one there had been expecting them. It was hard enough having to lead the Staffel against superior numbers of enemy, but at Orvieto Harder had found himself having to sort out meals and accommodation, as well as fuel and maintenance for their Messerschmitts. 'Now', he wrote to his wife a couple of days later, 'I have things in order and the men are being fed and things are taking their course.'

Harder was twenty-five, from Swinemünde, a Baltic port in East Prussia, and had joined the Luftwaffe back in 1939, although it was not until March 1941 that he had completed his training and been posted to JG53, the fighter wing he'd served with ever since. The war had been hard on

Harder and his family. His older brother Harro had also been a fighter pilot but had been killed over England in August 1940, while his younger brother, Rolf, had been a gunner and had lost his life the previous March. So far, however, Jürgen had managed to stay alive, not least because following his brother Rolf's death he'd been taken off flying duties, although he continued to command the Staffel from the ground. Now, though, at this advanced stage of the war, he was back flying again; he was needed because those new pilots coming through had barely 100 hours in their logbooks, whereas Harder now had hundreds of hours and thirty-nine victories to his name. That was the kind of experience and skill that was in very short supply in the Luftwaffe these days.

Harder and his squadron had quickly been ordered into the fray, flying their first mission over Anzio almost immediately and then, after refuelling and rearming, a second. 'They were very difficult missions,' he told his wife, 'for there are always Spitfires over the beachheads at all altitudes.' As soon as they neared the beachhead they were swamped by superior numbers of Allied aircraft, which meant they spent all their fuel trying to avoid being pounced on and never seemed to have a chance to line up a decent target. 'Unfortunately,' he told her, 'we have too few aircraft and so our attacks have little effect.'

The Rangers were now dug in just to the south of the Factory, or Aprilia as the Fascists had named it. Colonel Darby could see this curious cluster of red-tiled buildings and the distant hills south of Rome rising up from the plain eight or so miles away. It was certainly easy enough to dig foxholes, which they'd all done in quick order, and Darby was grateful for his hole in the ground because by 24 January German artillery fire was starting to whoosh over fairly regularly. The Rangers now had the battalion of the 509th PIR on their right and the British on their left, the other side of the Via Anziate. Like everyone, it seemed, Darby was waiting for the enemy to counter-attack but in the meantime had been sending out patrols to gauge enemy strength and positions. Occasionally he'd even spotted German patrols scuttling about in the distance, tiny figures jumping from one drainage ditch to another. It had all been rather surreal. Back in November and December, they'd spent more than forty days up a mountain; this flat, open plain could hardly be more different.

One patrol from Company A, part of 1st Battalion, had reached the edge of the Factory but had seen it was occupied, they reckoned by at least a company, and reinforced with three or four tanks. Other self-propelled guns had also been spied on the road north of the town. These were StuGs, tracked vehicles with a high-velocity anti-tank gun but without a rotating turret. Another patrol spotted German troops laying mines near the tiny cluster of buildings marked as Padiglione. This was a mile or two to the east on their right. His Rangers also ran into a fifteen-man enemy patrol slinking around some farm buildings, but after both sides exchanged a few shots they each hurriedly withdrew. It was as though neither side wanted to fight – not yet, at any rate.

Orders did reach Darby that night, however, instructing him to move his men and take hold of an irrigation ditch that ran from the Factory to Padiglione. Sending his 4th Battalion and the paratroopers, they attacked at first light and immediately drew a spattering of machine-gun fire. But behind his forward troops were the anti-tank guns of a tank destroyer battalion who made light work of the enemy resistance. The ditch was swiftly taken – and held.

The British had also pushed forward on 25 January, with the Guards Brigade ordered to take the Factory. Leading the way were the 5th Grenadier Guards, who set off up through the Bosco di Padiglione along Via Anziate, No. 1 Company leading after what Edward Danger noted had been a hectic night of preparation. Danger and the Battalion HQ followed, pausing by the Flyover at the Campo di Carne. The ground here was tilled either side of the road all the way to the Factory, so a surprise flank attack was out of the question. To the east stretched a vast area of farmland dotted with squat modern farm buildings, while up ahead was the strange huddle of buildings of Aprilia, looking ever more like the Factory it had been christened. 'And behind that', noted the Grenadiers' diarist, 'loomed the great bulk of the Colli Laziali, which commands the approaches to Rome from the south and east.' The Grenadiers now split themselves into small battle groups, the first with Guardsmen in tracked carriers, supported by three Shermans and sappers in scout cars; the second with anti-tank guns, a mortar detachment and some Vickers heavy machine guns.

This proved too much for the defenders, an outpost of around 150 men of 3. Bataillon from 29. Panzergrenadier. Despite some heavy fighting, the Factory was cleared by dusk with over 100 enemy troops taken prisoner. Many of these, it seemed, came from a recent reinforcement draft, of whom twenty were Alsatians forcibly conscripted and only too happy to give any information asked for. Edward Danger reached the Factory, already looking very battle-worn, that evening with the rest of Battalion HQ and set up shop in a basement garage. 'I made a start sorting out the casualties,' he noted, 'and it took me the best part of the night.' The total losses were eight killed, although that rose to thirteen, including two officers, and a further fifty wounded.

So far these modest advancements had been won fairly easily, but there were still no instructions from VI Corps HQ ordering a stronger thrust north. Meanwhile, the distant hills loomed, rising up from the plain – close enough, but still tantalizingly out of reach.

'6 Corps virtually unopposed,' noted General John Harding in his diary on the 24th. 'Wish they could get on quicker. Am afraid we shall miss our chance unless they are really lucky.' He was aware that Kesselring was still collecting his forces and knew that although there had been no enemy counter-attacks yet, it was only a matter of time; this was why he felt it was so important to strike quickly, to break up the German forces as they arrived and before they had a chance to dig in or reconnoitre. Before they gained their balance.

As it happened, General Mark Clark was having much the same thoughts. He'd been heading from one corps and division to another along the Cassino front, impressing upon his generals the utmost urgency and the need to drive his men hard in an effort to break the deadlock and to give SHINGLE the best possible chance of success; and yet this same message did not appear to be getting through to Lucas. He was troubled by the lack of detailed words from his VI Corps commander and fired off an irritated cable with a raft of questions, from enemy strength estimates to unloading capacity to his intentions for immediate operations. 'Lucas must be aggressive,' Clark noted in his diary. 'He must take some chances.'

Alexander was of the same mind and asked Clark to join him at the bridgehead on Tuesday, 25 January. Clark rather took exception to this. 'He apparently feels as though he is running the show,' he grumbled. 'Not much I can do about it.' Lucas had groused to his diary in much the same way when Clark had announced he was setting up an Advanced CP at Anzio; neither liked having a superior breathing down their neck. The fact was, however, that Alexander *was* running the show, not Clark. The stakes were enormous, the Fifth Army commander had a huge amount to deal with just on the Cassino front alone, and Alex was not convinced that Lucas was being anything like as aggressive as he needed to be; it did not seem that Clark was pushing him hard enough. So he wanted to visit the bridgehead again and see for himself what was going on. As theatre commander, that was not only his right, it was clearly what was needed too.

Alex was planning to head there by fast destroyer, but the weather had once again closed in and the winds were strong. Doubting they would ever manage to get safely ashore, Clark decided to fly in his Piper Cub instead, an arguably much riskier option but one that paid off as he touched down around 10.30 a.m., commandeered a jeep and sped off to VI Corps HQ. Alexander, meanwhile, travelled with his American Chief of Staff, General Lemnitzer, and a small party that included the American journalist Cy Sulzberger, the thirty-one-year-old foreign correspondent for the *New York Times*.

Sulzberger spent much of the journey out on the bridge with Al Gruenther, Clark's Chief of Staff, watching high plumes of spray as they scythed through the swell. 'One after another,' noted Sulzberger, 'we passed swaying, heaving convoys heading up to the beachhead.' Alexander, Gruenther told Sulzberger, was very friendly, pro-American and a good listener; there was no hint of the cattiness Clark had noted in his diary. They were, Gruenther told him, very disappointed with the Rapido assault but delighted with the surprise they had achieved at Anzio, the result of their command of the skies. 'Nevertheless,' Gruenther added, 'the Germans have been very skilful. They have already brought reinforcements up to the high ground and are massing there.' Despite the roll of the ship, they all sat down to a lunch of roast beef and Yorkshire pudding. Sulzberger was amused to discover that Alexander was currently reading Schiller's poetry – in German. 'I asked him why,' wrote Sulzberger, 'and he said he thought he had better polish up his German; he would be needing it one of these days.'

Despite Clark's fears, Alexander – and Gruenther – did make it ashore, visiting Lucas at around 1.30 p.m. 'What a splendid piece of work,' he told Lucas, having seen the rate of build-up. LSTs were now able to line up in rows of eight, side by side, bows open, in Anzio harbour. They could be unloaded and pulling out again within just three hours. Guns were already dug in around the bridgehead, covered in camouflage netting and firing away at distant targets. The Chief then toured the front. As always, Alex wore his peaked cap with its red band round it. Cy Sulzberger, still in tow, asked him whether this wasn't rather drawing attention to himself. Possibly, Alexander told him, but he wanted the men to see their commander up at the front line; the red band on his cap advertised the fact.

Lucas's prime concern, he made clear, was maintaining the build-up of men and materiel and ensuring that the precious landing ships were not withdrawn too soon. He felt that a ten-mile perimeter after three days had been good going. 'I must keep my feet on the ground and my forces in hand and do nothing foolish,' he jotted. 'This is the most important thing I have ever tried to do and I will not be stampeded.' Alexander, however, was not at all impressed by this overly cautious approach. He had accepted that a drive to the Colli Albani might not fool the Germans into pulling back from the Cassino front, but the whole point of SHINGLE had been to give it a go – and swiftly. Now, on D-plus 3 – and despite the weather that day – the Allies had unloaded considerably more than had been expected and had had a far easier ride than had ever been imagined. Lucas, however, was readying himself for a counter-attack, not a series of regimental-strength thrusts to the hills.

On the eve of SHINGLE, Alexander had sensed that a great opportunity lay in their hands. The chance to make a decisive drive from the bridgehead – if ever it had been possible – was, however, rapidly running out.

CHAPTER 12

Belvedere

THE PREVIOUS NIGHT, 24 January, it was the turn of the Red Bulls to launch a new and major assault, this time across the upper Rapido Valley. On the eastern side of the valley, opposite Cassino, were the shattered remains of Cervaro and, a little to the north, the village of San Michele and beyond that Sant'Elia. They were roughly two miles across the largely flat central part of the valley, down which the Rapido flowed, before the Monte Cassino massif rose up like an immense wall of rock. This was the edge of the Gustav Line and part of the strongest stretch of the German defences. The Rapido itself had been dammed and its course diverted, so that while its riverbed was little more than a soggy, muddy trickle the rest of the valley here was now badly waterlogged and appeared impassable to vehicles. Needless to say, it had also been sown with plentiful mines. Any attackers would have to cross this boggy plain, scramble over a number of irrigation ditches and over the riverbed, 12 feet or so deep, and then clamber over the next stretch of open ground to the edge of the mountains, which was covered in yet more mines and a mass of wire entanglements. And this waterlogged ground, the mines and the wire all had to be negotiated in full view of the Germans, who had bulldozed every building, every bush, hedge and tree so they now had a clear field of fire. This appeared to be a tougher proposition than where the T-Patchers had attempted to cross the Rapido. About a mile and a half due north of Cassino town, on the ledge of ground above the western side between the river and the mountains, there were the remains of twenty single-storey barracks blocks, smashed by bombs and shellfire but originally built by the Italians, into which the Germans had built a series of concrete pillboxes hidden by the debris of the wrecked buildings. Above, on the slopes directly overlooking the valley, were further MG and mortar pits and observers. As a defensive position it was strong, to say the very least.

General Doc Ryder, the commander of the Red Bulls, decided he would attack with two thrusts, the first crossing the Rapido Valley, striking at the barracks, then turning south into Cassino. The second thrust would cross a little to the north near the village of Caira then climb up round the back of Monte Cassino to Monte Castellone, which formed a long curving ridge between the abbey and the giant Monte Cairo. Ryder hoped to then push on down into the Liri Valley on the other side of the massif, cutting Monte Cassino off at the head. Like most such plans it looked logical enough on paper, but as the T-Patchers had discovered on the Rapido, attacking the enemy's main defensive strongpoint, and at night, and in winter, was far from straightforward.

Be that as it may, they'd been ordered to strike here and so at 10 p.m. the Red Bulls' attack jumped off with 133rd Infantry moving out across the boggy valley behind the usual artillery barrage and supported by two battalions of Sherman tanks. Attached to 133rd Infantry was the 100th 'Nisei' Battalion, mostly from Hawaii and made up entirely of Japanese-Americans. As the Hawaiian Provisional Infantry Battalion they'd been sent to Oakland, California, for training and had quickly proved to be outstanding recruits. Renamed the 100th Battalion, they'd been shipped to Algeria in August 1943 and their commander given the choice of being assigned guard duty or posted to Italy. Lieutenant-Colonel Farrant L. Turner had volunteered them for combat duty, and as an orphan unit they had been attached to the 34th Red Bulls. Doc Ryder had been both glad to have them and mightily impressed with their fighting spirit and esprit de corps.

One of those who had willingly volunteered to serve had been Sergeant 'Isaac' Fukuo Akinaka, thirty-two years old and the son of Japanese immigrants who had reached Hawaii more than forty years earlier. He'd been nicknamed Isaac at school; it was a name he liked and used on his army papers; it was also another way of identifying himself as both an American and a Christian, for although his parents practised Shinto he had joined the Mormon Church and had even been ordained. Akinaka had reached Italy as a technical sergeant in the Communications Platoon but had since retrained as a medic, a job that dovetailed well with both his faith and his determination to do his duty as a proud second-generation American.

The 100th Battalion had been on the left, southern, side of the attack, but the assault soon got bogged down, the 30-ton tanks sinking in the morass and even the men struggling across the waterlogged ground amid the carnage wrought by shelling, mortars and machine-gun fire. By around 5 a.m., however, most of the attacking infantry had managed to reach the eastern side of the Rapido riverbed. Here, ahead of it, were a couple of irrigation ditches and then a stone wall on the river's eastern bank, while beyond, on the far side, the riverbed rose far higher so that the western side, right up to the barracks and to the foot of the massif, was on a kind of shelf. It meant that those crouching in the irrigation ditches or behind the wall were largely safe from sweeping enemy machine-gun fire. Sergeant Akinaka found himself taking cover in one of the irrigation ditches, soaked to the bone. Ahead of him was a tree stump, but as dawn crept over the valley he discovered that every time he tried to move, bullets hissed past either side of the stump. He was stuck there, cold, wet and frustrated. Like most of those taking part in the Red Bulls' attack.

Meanwhile, in the early hours of the 25th, as the Red Bulls were struggling to get across the Rapido riverbed, the French were preparing to launch their attack on Monte Belvedere. This had been ordered by Clark primarily to draw off troops from the Red Bulls' attack, yet what he was asking them to do was every bit as challenging as what had been expected of the 36th T-Patchers. Général Juin, the commander of the CEF, had given the task of storming Belvedere to Général Joseph de Monsabert's 3ème Division Algérienne. 'Storming the Belvedere!' de Monsabert had exclaimed. 'Who could have thought of such a thing?' As de Monsabert had pointed out, his men would have to cross two rivers and climb up and down several mountains with a final ascent of nearly 3,000 feet, all the while being overlooked by the enemy on Monte Cifalco, let alone on Belvedere itself. What's more, to attack Belvedere they had to pivot 90 degrees from their current axis of advance, which was not easy; men had to be shifted, by night, across mountain tracks slick with ice; guns had to be manoeuvred into different positions so they could support the infantry; ammunition and supplies brought forward, ground reconnoitred – and all this in just two days. That was not long at all, especially not when operating in the mountains.

The northern end of the Rapido Valley was an especially difficult terrain in which to fight – one of immense mountains, narrow valleys, plunging ravines and stubborn rocky knolls. From the northern end of the upper Rapido Valley, it seemed at first to the untrained eye that there was a solid wall of mountains, but actually two rivers merged here to form the Rapido, one, the Lago, dropping quite steeply from the north and the other, the Secco, cutting down through a narrow, steep-sided valley from the town of Atina, five miles to the north-west and past the small village of Belmonte and hamlet of L'Olivella. Belvedere, a mountain spur jutting out like a giant sentinel beneath Monte Cairo, overlooked the mouth of the Secco Valley, which was only around 500 yards wide at that point. The course of the Gustav Line dropped down from Belvedere, across the narrow Secco Valley floor and climbed up to Monte Cifalco, which marked the start of a long, razor-backed ridge well over 3,000 feet high that led all the way to Atina. Juin's troops had been intending to advance on Atina with this ridge as their axis, but now had to drop down into the mountain valley of the Lago then climb up on to the end of the Cifalco massif, before dropping down again into the valley floor of the Secco, cross over to the other side and climb up nearly 3,000 feet again to reach Monte Belvedere and the summit behind it, Monte Abate. To make matters worse, Monte Cifalco was still in German hands. In other words, enemy troops would be looking down on them from two giant peaks either side of the Secco Valley.

The shock troops for the attack had already had to trek up to Il Lago, a knoll 1,200 feet high that was hidden from the prying eyes of the Germans on Monte Cifalco. It had been hard work just getting there and most of the men were wet from having to cross the Lago and from the drizzling rain that had begun to form into a mountain fog by first light on the 24th. Even so, Commandant Paul Gandoët, commander of the 3ème Bataillon, felt his men were equal to the challenge. 'The battalion', he noted in his pocketbook, 'is morally and physically ready.'

Gandoët was just a few days shy of his forty-second birthday and had spent the past twenty-four years in the Armée d'Afrique; he'd fought in the Rif War, in Syria in the late 1920s and had still been in North Africa, in Tunis, during the German attack on the west in 1940. An unfailing optimist, always quick to laugh and both respected and much loved by his troops, he was also determined to fight for France, to help rekindle some honour after the defeat of 1940. He had imbued in his men, both Frenchmen and North Africans, a deep sense of duty and esprit de corps – a spirit that also cut across the entire regiment and even division. Most felt it keenly: a sense of pride in their unit and in what and whom they represented in the CEF; as Juin had said to de Monsabert, they had to do this job. 'Honour', he told him, 'is engaged.'

Mules were desperately needed, but it had not been possible to bring them over the mountains in time. 'Decision:' noted Gandoët, 'one big meal will be served on the night of the 24th–25th, then everyone will leave with a K-box (one third daily ration), a container of water, a tent canvas, a saltire blanket, and the maximum of ammunition for machine-gun, mortars and grenades. The loading for each man is unbelievable.'

Moving the artillery had been a monumental task too. 'This is demented! It's impossible!' Colonel Radiguet de la Bastaïe, commanding the divisional artillery, had raged to de Monsabert; and yet somehow they had managed to move all the 105s and 155s from the valley around Acquafondata to the Sant'Elia basin in time. This had meant each artillery piece, with gun tractor and ammunition trucks, crawling along the widened Acquafondata track – a journey less than three miles as the crow flies but four times that on the ground, round hairpins, along precipices and on a road barely able to cope with the weight of traffic. And at night. Yet by dawn on the 24th they were almost all there and being dug into position. It had been an astonishing logistical achievement.

At 5.30 a.m. on the morning of 25 January, the French attack was about to jump off. More artillery had been brought over from the corps' reserves, as well as some Sherman tanks and tank destroyer anti-tank guns, now waiting out of sight in the Sant'Elia basin. Gandoët had placed his command post beneath a knoll marked as Point 502, which overlooked the small monastery of Casa Luciense. From here he could look across at Belvedere and see down into the Secco Valley but also maintain a clear view of the southern end of the Monte Cifalco spur. Daylight was coming. The sky to the east began to perceptibly lighten, but low cloud hid the summit of Belvedere and, behind them, Cifalco. That was good: a better screen than the best smoke shells could ever manage.

Gandoët's 3ème Bataillon was to play the lead role in the initial assault, with the 2ème Bataillon taking the left side of Belvedere once the attempted ascent began. There were many challenges facing them, but the closeness of the terrain, the narrow Secco Valley mouth and the steep sides of Belvedere might actually work to their advantage. Gandoët had spotted a ravine running down from a lip below the summit of Belvedere which, he reckoned, might well shield men from view. However, on the other, Cifalco, side of the valley was a jutting spur, marked as Point 470 on the map and known locally as Monte La Propaia. It was a kind of rounded balcony overlooking the Secco Valley and directly opposite Belvedere. Aerial photographs showed it to be heavily defended – which was confirmed by the capture of prisoners the previous night, all men from the 131. Regiment of 44. Infanterie-Division. Clearly, an already difficult task would become impossible while Point 470 remained in German hands. The plan, then, was for Gandoët's 9ème Compagnie to assault 470 at 6 a.m., following a twenty-minute artillery barrage. Meanwhile, his 10ème and 11ème Compagnies would move down into the Secco Valley, take the hamlet of L'Olivella with the support of the armour and begin their ascent once Point 470 was in 9ème Compagnie's hands. Then, on the left, Commandant Berne's 2ème Bataillon would also cross the Secco at L'Olivella and climb to the left of the ravine, again using the spurs and folds of the mountain to hide them from the summit. The 3ème Régiment was then to take over Point 470 and the 9ème Compagnie would join the rest of the battalion on Belvedere.

Commanding the 9ème Compagnie was thirty-year-old Capitaine Jacques Denée, another pre-war soldier who, like Gandoët, had always served with the Armée d'Afrique rather than the Armée Métropolitaine back in France. Early that morning he had approached Gandoët and, taking out his wallet, pulled out a photograph. It was a picture of his wife, and he asked Gandoët to look after it for him. 'I will succeed,' he assured the commandant, then added, 'I will surely be hit . . . but I will see her again.' Gandoët reassured him. Capturing Point 470 was a big deal, but, he promised, they would take it as easily as a knife going through butter.

Denée had briefed every man, wristwatches had been synchronized and now, with them all assembled beneath Point 502, he ran through their task one more time. A silent walk down the slopes from 502 the moment the barrage began – and as quickly as possible. If anyone was injured no one was to stop to help – that would come later. It was essential that they all kept moving, heading straight for the summit of Point 470. 'My friends,' he told his men, 'the long-awaited morning has arrived. Be worthy of the Ninth. Good luck to everyone.'

Denée was without his batman, Tirailleur Mohammed Tahar, who had slipped on the climb up to 502 during the night and broken his arm, but the chaplain, Padre Alfred Bérenguer, agreed to be by Denée's side every step of the way and now, in the last moments before the attack, moved among the men offering blessings to all of them, Christian and Muslim alike. For the Muslims, a simple tap on the shoulder was enough; a gesture of reassurance if nothing else.

5.40 a.m. Suddenly, immense noise erupted around the mountains and through the valley. Great lights from the Sant'Elia basin, purple and orange flickering over the lower slopes of the mountain. Above, the shelf of mist reflected copper, but beyond, pulsing dimly through the cloud, was a yellow incandescence. Beneath their feet, the ground trembling. From Gandoët's command post visibility was now reduced to almost nothing by the swirling smoke mixing with the cloud and fog. Choking vapours stagnated on the cold air. Tanks already began moving out, towards L'Olivella, where they knew the Germans had built bunkers into the ruins of the houses. Then a formation of B-26 Marauders, twin-engine bombers, droned over to drop their loads on to Belvedere, disappearing into the cloud, and the sound of their engines was soon drowned out by the guns still firing.

A scene of desolation spread down the upper Rapido Valley, where the Red Bulls were still attempting to cross the Rapido. Not a single building to be seen remained untouched. The flashes of the guns, the smoke, the ceiling of cloud, the sharp, acrid tang on the cold morning air. And for all this firepower, for all the shells screaming over, tanks firing and bombs being dropped, it was still men – French, Moroccan, Algerian and Tunisian – who would have to cross this cursed ground and prise the enemy out of positions that were only too easy to defend.

By the time the barrage ended, at precisely 6 a.m., Denée's men were hidden behind the trunks of olive trees, squatting against the walls of the terraces at the foot of Point 470. Above them sinister silhouettes of trees, now just blasted stumps, stood out against the early light of the sky. Drizzle began to fall. Up on high, Cifalco still lay hidden by the sheet of cloud.

This was the moment.

Denée now stood up, pointed his officer's cane towards the summit of the hill and began to run forward up the slopes. The others followed, jumping up from their hiding places, leaping over the walls of the terraces, but then a moment later came the buzz of the enemy's machine guns and the *vlouf* of mortars. Angry, scything hisses of shards of stone and metal. A mine triggered and exploded. Cries, screams. Men falling. The whoosh of mortars, and, a hundredth of a second before the impact, a sucking of air. Stomachs tightening but adrenalin keeping the men going forward amid the carnage of so much flying steel and rock.

Briefly, the attack stalled as Denée and his men took shelter in a fold of land hidden by the summit. 'This is a mission of trust, Denée,' Gandoët had told him. 'The success of the attack rests on you.' It was now 6.30 a.m.

Soon after, Monte Cairo and Cifalco started to emerge as the cloud gradually dispersed. German counter-battery fire rang out and an artillery duel began, huge geysers of stone and grit erupting on the mountain slopes each side of the valley. Denée took this moment to renew 9ème Compagnie's assault. 'Onwards!' he shouted, and now they were all up again, the North Africans yelling, '*La Allah ihl! La Allah ihl!*'

What were the men thinking at this moment as they ran, clambered, upwards into the fire? Fear in the pit of the stomach, senses blunted by the shock of explosions, flashes of light, fizzing, zipping bullets and slivers of rock, ears blocked, blind fury, animal rage, stumbling over the rocky ground, men falling, flesh sliced, limbs severed. Around the summit, stone sangars and behind them machine guns, mortars and men with rifles, all looking down as 9ème Compagnie scrambled up the slopes towards them.

Denée suddenly remembered what Gandoët had said to him earlier about the attack being as easy as a knife going through butter. But now, he thought, the butter had hardened into a rock of machine guns. He knew he had to get them to the top and from there they could hurl grenades, sweep over and clear the rest with bullet and bayonet. A machine-gunner near him was hit but he saw Sergent Gibou grab the weapon and continue firing, but then, as he leaped forward, he was hit too, a terrible strike across his stomach, and he fell. Again the attack stalled, but as Denée lay sheltering, gasping, catching his breath, he knew that every minute they paused could cost the lives of many others. Lying beside him was Padre Bérenguer, so Denée handed him his cane and then took his German carbine off his back, a small rifle but easy to handle. He'd taken it from a prisoner in Valleluce the previous day, along with the man's belt and ammo pouches. He looked down at the buckle and read *Gott mit uns*. He prayed God was now with him and his men, not the Germans.

From his command post on Point 502, Gandoët was joined by Colonel Jacques Roux. It was after 7 a.m. and Gandoët had been trying to follow the progress of his lead companies through the smoke, mist and haze. He was anxious. Relief troops from the 3ème Régiment had not yet arrived from Il Lago; they had been due before the attack had been launched. It meant there were no follow-up troops at all at present. He was more concerned about his 9ème Compagnie, however. Now that the cloud was dispersing and the morning light becoming stronger he could see bodies on the slopes, the flashes of exploding mines, and hear the crackle of uninterrupted small-arms fire. Roux asked him where the rest of his battalion was.

'Already departed, Colonel, to attack L'Olivella,' Gandoët told him. 'We couldn't wait any longer, the artillery preparation was finished. Taken or not, Hill 470 is being hard fought for at the moment by Denée. The Boches over there surely can't take care of anything else. If we have a chance, one alone, to climb the Belvedere, it's while their attention is elsewhere. We have to take advantage of it.'

Colonel Roux agreed he'd made the right call. Down in the Secco Valley, Gandoët's 11ème Compagnie were currently clearing L'Olivella, each bunker taken out by tank, grenade and liberal use of Tommy guns. Now, though, Gandoët's command post began to be shelled, so both he and Roux took cover while the artillery liaison officer made radio contact with the gunners in the Sant'Elia basin and requested renewed fire towards Monte Cifalco. Moments later, French shells were whooshing over and Cifalco once again disappeared behind a wall of detonations and smoke.

It was now a little after 8 a.m. and the 9ème Compagnie were close to the summit of Point 470, creeping around the edge and using rocks and the folds and small spurs in the ground to inch their way closer. Capitaine Denée now leaped up again from his latest place of shelter then immediately exclaimed, 'Oh, the bastards!' and dropped to the ground. An immense punch to the chest, and his first thought was that he'd been hit by a stone thrown with incredible force. Sergent Charbonnier crouched down beside him. 'The bastards!' Denée exclaimed again. 'They're throwing rocks now!' Then a moment of doubt, and he felt his jacket but found no blood. His breath was short and he was wheezing badly, but he now knew he had to get up again and make one last charge to the summit. Back on his feet, he saw Lieutenant El Hadi beside him and together with Charbonnier moved forward again only for another blow to hit him, this time in the legs. Again he buckled, feeling as though he'd been cut in two. As he tried to get up again his legs wouldn't move, and he still had a deep burning sensation in his chest. Suddenly men were gathering round him but he urged them on – no one was to stop for the wounded, remember!

But Lieutenant El Hadi Ben Kacem Ben Battab, a Tunisian from Kairouan, squatted beside him and Denée now told him to take over command of the company. 'I'm screwed,' Denée gasped, then called for the radio set he'd been carrying but which had fallen from his shoulders when he'd collapsed. 'This is Denée,' he mumbled into the receiver to Gandoët. 'I'm injured . . . objective will be taken. I'm passing command to Lieutenant El Hadi.'

El Hadi touched Denée's shoulder then leaped up and, urging his men, fired, began surging towards the summit, the men around him shouting and scrambling up the slopes, and moments later they were in among the first of the German defenders; grenades were being hurled, bayonets thrust, rifles snapping and machine guns barking. Suddenly an explosion, men falling, but El Hadi still ran up the slope even though the blast had ripped off his forearm and with it his revolver. Still yelling as blood covered his jacket, his men swept past and cleared the top of the hill in a vicious hand-to-hand melee. With his mutilated arm and blood-soaked jacket El Hadi had become a kind of living totem, and suddenly the surviving Germans were fleeing, running down the far slopes of the hill. Yet in this moment a series of bullets tore into El Hadi's chest. Felled, he tried to get up but crumpled again. Tirailleur Barelli crouched beside him. El Hadi wanted to know they had taken the summit. Yes, Barelli told him. 'So quickly, fire the flare,' El Hadi told him. Barelli took the flare pistol from El Hadi's haversack and fired. It fizzed up into the air and burst red, crackling as it slowly descended. It was the signal that Point 470 was finally in their hands.

It was now 10.30 a.m.

On the other side of the valley, the men of 11ème Compagnie under Lieutenant Raymond Jordy had managed to clear L'Olivella and begun their scramble up what they were now all calling the 'Gandoët Ravine'. To begin with they made surprisingly good progress, but soon came up against sheer rock faces and stretches that were very difficult to scale. The trouble was that the moment they moved from the deep fissure of the ravine they came under fire from two pillboxes above. One was soon silenced by four tirailleurs climbing round its flanks and then hurling grenades, but the one on their left proved more problematic. It was eventually taken out by men of the 2ème Bataillon, who had been climbing on a wider approach to the left of the ravine.

Meanwhile, the summit of Point 470 had been twice counter-attacked and twice the enemy had been repulsed. On the first attempt the Germans had been cleared, only for the mortally wounded Lieutenant El

Hadi to try and raise himself up and shout, '*Vive la France!*' before collapsing once more, his life slipping away. The survivors were then pinned to the hill by enemy artillery fire. At around 4.30 p.m., with dusk approaching, Gandoët moved his command post down to the monastery at Casa Luciense, from where he was better able to see what was going on. He'd not been there long when a number of men came hurrying down the slopes from the direction of Point 470. Gandoët stopped one of them and asked where on earth they were running to, then realized it was Sergent Ahmed of 9ème Compagnie, covered in blood and clutching his damaged hand. Ahmed frantically explained that he and sixteen others were the only men still standing in the company. All the officers – Denée, El Hadi – were gone.

Gandoët realized that this was a fateful moment. There was still no sign of the 3ème Régiment, due to relieve them, and his own command post radio had been destroyed by the earlier enemy shelling. His 11ème Compagnie was now at Point 681, just below the summit of Belvedere, but 10ème Compagnie was near the bottom of the valley near L'Olivella and expecting to be counter-attacked at any moment; 9ème Compagnie had been lost. The danger was that 10ème Compagnie would be counter-attacked in the valley now that Point 470 had been overrun for good. If that happened, Jordy's men would be left stranded beneath Belvedere. Gandoët then saw one last figure emerge, running, from the murk of the dusk – the eighteen-year-old Aspirant Couthures, one of the battalion's officer candidates. Couthures still had a revolver in his hand but he was weeping with despair. Recognizing that the situation on Point 470 needed to be salvaged and quickly, Gandoët gathered some of 10ème Compagnie, the men at his command post and the remaining men from 9ème Compagnie and led a charge back up the hill towards Point 470. He did not have enough men to clear the summit, but most of the lost ground was retaken; certainly, it was enough to secure a hold on the southern sides of the slopes.

From the valley floor Belvedere looked like an enormous peak but its summit, hidden from below, was actually the remains of a volcano, encircled by a number of bluffs; the French called these high points *pitons*, and on their maps they were marked as dots with numbers beside them: Point 700 to the south, Point 862 to the north; Point 681 where Lieutenant Jordy and his 11ème Compagnie were clinging. The highest, though, did have a name: Monte Abate, and it was this that was the objective for

Colonel Roux's 4ème Régiment. Beyond Abate, however, was a high mountain plain before the massif rose once again to the giant peak of Monte Cairo. Nestling on this plain was the village of Terelle, accessed by a winding track, full of hairpins, that climbed up from the village of Caira on the Rapido Valley floor and then skirted past Belvedere. While Jordy's men had been ascending the ravine the 2ème Bataillon had climbed on a wider, more southerly approach; and while German attention was kept on these attackers, the 3ème Régiment de Spahis Algériens had been working their way up the hairpin road to Terelle in armoured cars. By late afternoon they had taken Points 700 and 771. They were swiftly counter-attacked, as was the German way, but with darkness falling the Spahis dug in on Point 721, alongside the 2ème Bataillon and with Jordy's men just a stone's throw away on Point 681. It was astonishing to think what they'd achieved here, just a few miles north of Cassino; they'd punched a hole in the Gustav Line and scaled more than 2,000 feet, and with the promised reinforcements and the arrival of mule trains to bring up supplies there was every chance they would be able to prevail and clear Abate the following day. Even so, as Commandant Gandoët headed back down to Casa Luciense that evening, with the rain starting to fall once more, he knew his situation remained extremely precarious.

A little to the south, the Red Bulls had managed to get men from all three attacking battalions over the riverbed and establish small bridgeheads, although the wire entanglements had held them up considerably and their situation seemed almost as perilous as that of the French. What a day of terrible fighting it had been; but darkness had now fallen once more on the mountains, and with this shroud the battle had quietened down. Occasional shelling continued, the odd crack of small arms rang out and even a hiss and crackle of a flare, but both sides were exhausted. The French held on to much of Point 470 and were clinging to the lip below Belvedere, and the Red Bulls had a toehold on the western side of the Rapido. The Germans, meanwhile, were desperately trying to firefight and patch the holes in the line; von Senger's men were reeling from the combined onslaught that over the past week had hammered his positions from the sea all the way to the mountains overlooking the Secco Valley. Both sides needed reinforcements, and urgently, for the day's fighting had come at an appalling cost.

CHAPTER 13

Cisterna

Capitaine Jacques Denée had spent long hours drifting in and out of consciousness. Shivering, lying there on the slope of Point 470, and wet too from the rain, he was sure he was close to death – so close that he felt as though Death was standing over him, waiting for him. Denée knew he had to stay awake; he didn't want to die on a mountainside, only thirty years old. He didn't want to leave his wife. Then, as dusk had been falling, he had seen Padre Bérenguer crouching beside him and telling him he was going to get help.

Unbeknown to Denée, the priest had been shot himself; he had been disturbed by a German as he'd been giving the wounded absolution and despite pointing out his Red Cross armband the soldier had fired. He was not dead, but wounded, and slowly Bérenguer managed to crawl back across the rocky ground between the bodies of the dead and find Denée once more. By this time, Denée was bitterly cold. He'd heard the dying talk of it, an all-consuming shroud that swept over them in their last moments. And now Bérenguer was beside him once more but could offer no help other than absolution.

'God is waiting for you, Capitaine,' Bérenguer told him.

'Yes,' mumbled Denée. 'Kiss my wife for me. Goodbye.'

Yet it seemed that Death had not quite taken Denée after all, because following Gandoët's counter-attack both the captain and Padre Bérenguer were found and stretchered back to safety. Denée had not been hit by a stone at all, but by a bullet just above his heart, and then by shell splinters in his legs. He'd been lucky – they both had been, found in the nick of time. Neither would have lasted another hour without aid, let alone the night.

By the morning of Wednesday, 26 January, troops from the 3ème Régiment had arrived to take over Point 470, which allowed Gandoët to move the rest of his battalion to join Lieutenant Jordy and the men of 11ème Compagnie, still clinging to Point 681, the lower lip of Belvedere. Gandoët had been given the 1er Bataillon's 2ème Compagnie to make up for the losses of the destroyed 9ème but he could still muster only around 300 men – all of whom were frozen with cold, wet and with empty stomachs. For all the brilliance of the two-day preparation for the attack, the supply chain was now suffering badly, for there was still no sign of any mules or rations. That one meal on the evening of 24 January seemed a long time ago now, and the K-rations had been eaten more than twenty-four hours earlier.

It was now Gandoët's chance to climb the ravine that bore his name. As he quickly discovered, the chasm only partially hid the climbers, requiring quick dashes across open stretches. 'In small groups of four or five,' he noted. 'The enemy's fire doesn't stop. Men lie down, jump up, spin, crawl, run. So it goes.' The climb was also extremely physically challenging, each man clambering up a stretch at a time. 'Lower your head under the brows, look for holes to infiltrate, mark a pause behind a rock,' wrote Gandoët, 'then leave again, and arrive up there with the ammunition. Heavy machine guns, mortars, shells, radio, everything goes up slowly but surely.' They had reached the twin points on the lip of Belvedere, 721 and 681, by 2 p.m.; Capitaine Goiffin and his 2ème Compagnie joined Gandoët half an hour later.

Gandoët's orders from Colonel Roux and Général Joseph de Monsebert were to push on, come what may, and take the three high points of Belvedere to the north-west: Points 862, 875 and 915, Monte Abate. These three peaks all circled another long-extinct volcano and so surrounded a second, higher bowl. They needed to make these assaults in leaps, each step secured before the next one, but now that they firmly held the lower lip, Lieutenant Jordy's company, strengthened by that of Lieutenant Bouakkaz, were to capture 862 first, a peak of enormous rocks, and from there move along a craggy pass to the summit of Monte Abate. However, because Belvedere was an extinct volcano, this meant descending into the bowl then ascending again. Up here, at least, there was some cover – from rocks, from folds in the ground, from jagged spurs and small fissures and ravines, and also from stone walls long ago built into the bowl.

The Germans were behind stone sangars around the peaks but much of the time did not have the angle of fire. It meant the 3ème Bataillon men had a chance. Gandoët watched them set off, following their progress anxiously. His men seemed rather like worms, he thought, slithering here and there, darting from rock to rock, a dash and then a pause. 'Firing, bursts, bayonets, forward!'

Incredibly, Jordy and his men did manage to take Point 862, the startled Germans stunned to find the French had managed to scale such a peak. Later, in the early hours of Thursday, 27 January, Major Berne's 2ème Bataillon managed to secure Abate itself, attacking from the other side. Once again, however, casualties had been heavy. Lieutenant Bouakkaz, a Tunisian, was yet another junior officer killed in the fighting; he had vowed to his men that he would be the first man to the peak, but when he was cut down, just short, three of his men carried his lifeless body and placed it there, his promise upheld. Yet Gandoët's battalion was being stripped bare. What's more, their situation was as precarious as ever. 'Men would like to eat,' noted Gandoët, 'there is nothing to eat. They would like to drink; there is nothing to drink . . . We will hold on, but only so long as tomorrow there is food and ammo arrives!'

Meanwhile, General Doc Ryder had tried to get the Red Bulls' attack going again on the 27th. Behind yet another barrage, 168th Infantry were now sent across the open valley to the north of the barracks, but with two battalions of Sherman tanks following the raised road across the waterlogged valley. The road was extremely muddy and badly churned up, but Ryder hoped that if they advanced behind a rolling artillery barrage, they might just have a chance. Then the infantry were to clamber up a rounded hill – Point 213 – just to the north of the barracks and south of the village of Caira. Clear this hill, Ryder reckoned, and then his men would be able to push into the village and use the narrow valley immediately south of the hill to start the climb up on the massif.

The 1st Battalion of the 135th had also been ordered to cross the river overnight south of the barracks, so that by first light there were even more infantry on the far side ready to expand the bridgeheads if and when the tanks got across. The plan was more or less successful. Three Shermans got across a very narrow bridge the Germans had inexplicably left intact on the causeway leading across the river to Caira. Several other tanks became bogged, and although engineers hastily built a corduroy road from logs, the first Sherman to try and use it tore it up into a splintered mess. Another tank did manage to get across, however, and the four Shermans now on the western side quickly made all the difference, churning up anti-personnel mines, blasting enemy strongpoints and destroying wire entanglements. What a different story these battles might have been had the Allies been able to use the full weight of their air forces and mechanized firepower. All four tanks had been knocked out by early afternoon but they had enormously helped the infantry, whose numbers were just beginning to bite chunks out of the German defences at the base of the massif. By dusk, men of the 168th were digging in around the base of Point 213, while 135th Infantry were pushing south towards the edge of Cassino town.

The 100th Nisei Battalion was also trying get more men across the river, just to the south of the barracks. The battalion commander had been wounded, so Major Dewey, Executive Officer – second-in-command – of 133rd Infantry, took over temporary command. Dewey was then wounded in turn as he hurried to the river wall on the eastern side of the river. It was Isaac Akinaka who was called to help, but patching him up was no easy matter, as although it was now night-time, flares were constantly being sent up and machine guns were sweeping the area, bullets fizzing and hissing horribly close to their heads. Then, just as Akinaka was finishing bandaging the major, another wounded officer crawled on top of a mine and blew himself up, the blast knocking Akinaka backwards. Fortunately he was not seriously hurt, but endless mines, machine guns, mortars and artillery created a lethal cocktail made infinitely worse by the cold and the morass of the wide-open valley floor. The Red Bulls could not clear those lower hills of the massif soon enough.

While the valleys and mountains north of Cassino were now heavy with the thunderous roar of battle, there was still not a huge amount of action within the Anzio bridgehead. 'Trying to put some ginger into the battle,' noted General Harding. 'With Chief to see Clark. Hope he'll get a move on.' Now that Alexander and Clark were living cheek by jowl in the grounds of the Caserta palace, face-to-face conversations were considerably easier, although at present, in these tense and anxiety-filled days, the Fifth Army commander was looking past the benefits of this and instead interpreting it as interference. At any rate, Alex told Clark that he was worried by how long it was taking Lucas to launch an attack from Anzio. 'I am too,' noted Clark, 'and have been for about 48 hours.' Clark had already sent the entire 45th Thunderbirds Division and also most of the 1st Armored Division to help stiffen Lucas's resolve, and told Alexander that he planned to head up to Anzio the next day and stay for several days, personally ensuring that Lucas's forces undertook an all-out coordinated corps attack supported by tanks. Alexander, Clark noted, was completely satisfied with this plan. While Clark sniped in his diary about Alex and even the Prime Minister watching over him, he thought it entirely justified that he should do the same to Lucas.

That same day, Lucas was also jotting down his thoughts. His CP, where he was also sleeping, was a house between Anzio and Nettuno, and although it had its own bathroom, water came from a storage tank on the roof which had quickly run dry. There were four bedrooms and a large living room on the second floor with views all the way to the Colli Albani twenty miles away, his corps' objective – but an objective that might as well have been 100 miles away, it still seemed so out of reach to him. A touch of siege mentality was creeping over Lucas. He was fully aware that the Germans were massing their forces somewhere out there beyond the plain, and to add to his growing sense of discomfort increasing numbers of Luftwaffe bombers and fighter-bombers were getting through the screen of the Allied fighters and flak gunners. A raid the previous evening had been followed by another first thing that morning, 28 January. 'Considerable damage done,' he noted, 'trucks destroyed, ammunition blown up, people killed, but the port is still operating, thank God!' He had gone down there to see the damage for himself and it had certainly looked a mess: smashed buildings, rubble on the streets, debris on the quaysides, twisted metal and burnt-out vehicles, craters right on the harbour front and numerous fires burning, the thick black smoke a beacon for future raiders. '11.14. A bomb just fell outside my window,' he added. 'There goes the rest of the glass.' He decided thereafter to sleep in the capacious cellar beneath the building while further cavities were hastily being dug. This, though, only added to the sense of being pegged into the bridgehead.

Clark duly arrived soon after, although he had been lucky to do so. First, the coxswain on his storm boat hit a sandbar and they took on a lot of water, soaking all on board, including the general. Eventually, though, they managed to reach the waiting PT boats and get going, only to find themselves under attack by a minesweeper seven miles from Anzio who mistook them for enemy S-boats. One 40mm shell hit the deckhouse only about 5 feet from Clark, and a second right under the stool on which he was sitting. All three naval officers on board were hit by splinters. Four of the men were bleeding profusely and the deck was becoming swamped with their blood; Ensign Donald had had an artery in his leg severed; another had had his kneecap blown away. Fortunately, the minesweeper swiftly realized its error and stopped firing, and they sped on and pulled alongside a hospital ship. That, however, was not the end of Clark's adventures because they finally reached Anzio just as another enemy air raid began. Clark and his party quickly clambered ashore, where jeeps hurriedly pulled up and whisked them off to Lucas's CP.

This time Clark did not mince his words and ordered Lucas to launch an attack by Sunday morning, 30 January, at the latest, pointing out that only by bold and aggressive action could SHINGLE fulfil its aims. Delay now, he stressed, would only allow the enemy to build up ever-greater forces opposite them. In fact Clark did not stay at Anzio that day, although his Advanced CP was set up. Instead he returned to his main CP, which he had that day ordered to be moved away from Caserta to the small village of Presenzano, more than twenty-five miles to the north but far closer to the Cassino front.

Lucas, however, was unapologetic about his lack of drive. 'I think more has been accomplished than anyone had a right to expect,' he noted. 'This venture was always a desperate one and I could never see much chance for it to succeed.' As had been the case with Fred Walker and his Texas Division at the Rapido, General Lucas had rather tied himself in knots by an increasing fear of failure. He had convinced himself he would never have enough troops with which to launch a successful all-out assault from the beachhead – he couldn't attack until the rest of the Thunderbirds had arrived, then until the latest shipment pulled into port, or more tanks had reached him or more shells and guns; but by then the enemy would have increased in strength, so he would then need even more. There would always be a reason to remain on the defensive rather than grab the initiative. Yet by 29 January, seven days into the operation, he had 356 tanks, 12,350 vehicles and 61,000 troops. The Germans could only dream of such mechanization and firepower. Clark, however, had now given him a date: an all-out attack by Sunday, 30 January – and quite right too.

It was not a good state of affairs that the commander on the ground had never believed in the operation. His status had allowed him a voice before SHINGLE had been launched and yet, like Walker, he'd aired a few concerns but otherwise allowed himself to go along with an operation in which he had little faith. He could have refused; he would have lost his job, but better that, and to have had the courage of his convictions, than lead thousands of young men into a major assault in which he had little confidence. Conversely, having accepted the mission, he should have thrown himself into it and done all in his power to fulfil its aims. Whether his scepticism was justified or misplaced was not the point. Doc Ryder's Red Bulls and Juin's CEF were hurling themselves into the fray at Cassino and were closer than anyone knew to securing a breakthrough. Lucas should have already unleashed the wildcat; that, after all, had been the whole point of his mission.

Certainly, General von Senger was increasingly concerned about the situation along his front. The Allied attacks were relentless, hammering every stretch of the line, it seemed. No sooner was one crisis averted, one breach plugged, than another appeared. Just as General Clark understood the importance of cutting into the Liri Valley, von Senger was every bit as aware of its vulnerability. The French attack, especially, seemed to have struck at a particularly weak part of the line, for this was held by the understrength 44. Division. As soon as he'd heard about the CEF's attack he had hurried down to Belmonte from his headquarters at Roccasecca to see 191. Regiment, actually part of 71. Infanterie-Division and the only unit from it to have reached the front. It was bridging a gap between the 44. H-und-D, who were up on Belvedere and holding the line along the Monte Cassino massif, and 5. Gebirgsjäger-Division on Monte Cifalco – which meant it was now bearing the brunt in the Secco Valley and up around Point 470. Oberst Mathes's command post was in a cave, and because of the booming French guns von Senger struggled to make himself heard. Looking at the grenadiers now manning the line, he also realized with a sinking heart that these men were utterly inadequate compared with the French troops opposing them. None of them had had any training in mountain warfare, and frankly very little training at all.

So it seemed he could not expect too much from the newly arriving units of 71. Division, nor had he been impressed by the 44. H-und-D either; he'd deployed it up on the massif because it seemed like the safest place to tuck it out of the way. After the December battles and the fighting earlier in the month, each battalion in the H-und-D-Division had been left horribly understrength; but he also felt the regimental commanders were too inexperienced. 'The commander of the 44. Infanterie-Division', he noted tersely, 'had not been fortunate in his choice of regimental commanders.' That the talent pool was extremely shallow does not appear to have been considered by von Senger. And if the division wasn't cutting the mustard, that was because it was full of young and ageing grenadiers who had been flung into the fray without adequate training. It was hardly the fault of men like Zellner and his superiors.

Von Senger understood, though, that the H-und-D would be unable to make a prolonged defence of the massif and so needed urgent reinforcing. His number-one go-to man in a situation like this was General Ernst-Günther Baade, currently commanding the battered 90. Panzergrenadier at the southern end of the line near Minturno. Sensing the British offensive there had run out of steam, he now ordered Baade to hurriedly move north with the remains of his division and take over the southern end of the Monte Cassino massif. None the less, it was a risk. Privately, von Senger thought it time to pull back to the Caesar position, already being prepared just to the south of Rome but which ran across the peninsula like the Gustav Line; as things stood, he was losing a battalion a day. The risk of the Allies making a decisive breakthrough seemed increasingly likely.

So with the assault by the CEF looking especially threatening, another frantic round of new troop deployments got under way. Major Georg Zellner and his 3. Bataillon of 134. Regiment had just been posted to the hills above Sant'Ambrogio, opposite the British 46th Division, when suddenly orders arrived for them to urgently pack up and move to the mountains overlooking Belmonte in the Secco Valley. Although this stretch of line was held by their parent 44. Division, Zellner was told he was to come under the command of 191. Grenadier-Regiment, which was normally part of 71. Infanterie-Division; however, this division was not fully at the front and so, as was very much the way in these patch-and-mend, firefighting times, had been temporarily attached to the 44. H-und-D-Division. This meant that Zellner's battalion, which two days earlier had been ordered to plug a hole and so had been detached from both regiment and division, was now transferring back to the 44. but under the command of a regiment entirely unknown to them and from a different division altogether. Notions of unit cohesion and morale were clearly playing second fiddle to the urgent need to simply seal a gap and prevent a catastrophic breakthrough. It was indicative, however, of just how desperate the German situation on the Cassino front now was.

Zellner's men were to walk to San Giorgio, a six-mile tramp round the base of the mountains on the southern side of the Liri Valley, and from there they would be taken by truck. Cursing, they packed up and set off, darkness now falling. As they passed through Sant'Apollinare the village was shelled, but they managed to duck down each time a missile hurtled over, then dash on a bit further. It was a pitch-dark night as they emerged out of the village and walked cross-country, clambering over fences, tripping into ditches, the only light coming from shell bursts behind them. It was 2 a.m. on the 26th when they reached San Giorgio but the promised trucks didn't arrive until 6 a.m., by which time the faint streaks of dawn were spreading over the valley. 'We set off dead tired,' noted Zellner. 'I don't care about anything else. So, we're going back into the shit.' Five hours later, at 11 a.m., having trundled across the valley to Roccasecca, then climbed up over the mountains in a wide circle to Atina and down the Secco Valley road, they reached Oberst Mathes's command post at Belmonte, where Zellner was told his battalion was to hurry up and attack immediately towards L'Olivella. Then there was a delay – reason not given – so they had a brief respite. Instead, they attacked at 4 p.m. that afternoon.

As they moved down the road, the French artillery fire grew stronger. A black cat ran out in front of Zellner and his men. Shells hurtled over, they all lay down, the shells exploded, they got up and moved on until they reached the staging area – the jump-off point. Immediately, another shell whooshed in, a splinter from which hissed by and tore Zellner's wind-smock. Orders issued: 11. Kompanie to move on the hill marked K8 on the map, 9. Kompanie to take Point 290 then on to 389. 10 Kompanie to stay put. 'It's a mess,' noted Zellner. 'No enemy intelligence, no artillery, no liaison and being told the terrain is tank-proof. Oberst Mathes is clueless.' Most of Zellner's men were barely men at all but ill-trained teenagers who had arrived at Pignataro just a few days earlier. Despite this, K8 was taken and fifty-two Moroccans captured, but 9. Kompanie was struggling on Point 290. Then enemy tanks rumbled forward down the valley and Zellner watched his 11. Kompanie get shot to pieces. At 6 p.m., in the darkness, 10. Kompanie was then flung into the fray.

By the evening of Thursday, 27 January the situation on Belvedere and in the Secco Valley below was critical for both sides, although by dawn the following morning the Germans had snatched back control of L'Olivella and the valley crossing point to Belvedere. However, at 6 a.m. the French then counter-attacked heavily with more Sherman tanks and just two hours later Zellner's battalion had been routed for the second time in as many weeks. His battalion, which should have had around

900 men at full strength, had been only a third of that number when they'd reached Belmonte, so had already been horrendously weakened. 'Of 320 men only I, my adjutant and 18 men are left,' jotted Zellner. 'It is a crying shame.' Twenty men! That was a little over 2 per cent of what it should have been. Yet this tiny force continued to cling on to Point 290 despite him telling Mathes that it could not possibly be held by fewer than twenty men.

Up on Belvedere, German forces counter-attacked with greater success, taking advantage of the isolated state of the French tirailleurs, swamping their positions all at once, attacking from the north towards Points 862 and 681 and from the direction of Terelle towards Abate. Major Berne, the commander of the 2ème Bataillon, was killed in the fighting, while Commandant Gandoët frantically pulled together what troops he could: the survivors of the 10ème Compagnie and the remnants of Berne's 2ème Bataillon. Entrenched in what had been German sangars and scrapes in the ground, Gandoët's men held on, sometimes fighting the enemy attacks at the point of bayonet. At 12.40 p.m. he received an SOS message from Lieutenant Jordy, still clinging on to Point 862. Against his orders from de Monsabert, Gandoët instructed Jordy to pull back; so long as they held the lip at 681 and 721, he hoped they might be able to hang on, although key to their chances was the arrival of supplies of food, water and ammunition. In the meantime, he drew all the available men together – it was better to be a concentrated force than one spread thinly – and radioed to the artillery for as much support as possible.

When Lieutenant Jordy reappeared, he was in tears. To have given so much to take that peak only to lose it again – it was the bitterest of pills. That afternoon they had to listen to one of their younger soldiers, Lorraine Bianco, calling plaintively for his mother from his shallow foxhole where he squatted, badly wounded. '*Maman, maman*.' Neither Gandoët nor any of his men could do anything to save him – not with shells and mortar rounds crashing on their positions. Bianco had escaped occupied France, made his way to North Africa and had been determined to fight for his country. Now, on this lonely, bleak mountain in an otherwise unremarkable corner of Italy, he was crouched in his shallow foxhole, wounded, frozen, hungry, thirsty and alone as his life gradually slipped away. By nightfall he was dead.

Darkness once again shrouded the mountain. With still no sign of any supplies arriving, Gandoët ordered his men to steal out into no-man's-land and search all the wounded and dead for weapons and ammunition.

The harvest brought them a few sub-machine guns and some precious ammunition, but without supplies they were finished.

The French were imposing German levels of self-sacrifice on their hold of Belvedere, although had supply lines been functioning better, a lot of the losses still being taken might well have been avoided. Yet, as Georg Zellner was experiencing all too tragically in the Secco Valley below, von Senger was also flinging ever more troops into holding this part of the line. Général de Monsabert was following the orders of Juin, who was following orders from Clark, who was trying to fulfil the demands that had been placed on Alexander by the British Prime Minister and the Combined Chiefs. Von Senger was following orders from von Vietinghoff and Kesselring, who had Hitler breathing down his neck. It was very easy, from a distance nowhere near Italy, to look at numbers of divisions and lines on a map and announce the need for stout defence or a new attack; but Hitler was making these demands from a bunker in East Prussia, while Churchill was recuperating at No. 10 in London. Neither could possibly comprehend the desperate fighting going on over these mountains, or the utter insanity of throwing so many lives away over a peak that registered no more significance on a map than a dot and the figure of its height above sea level in metres.

Somehow, throughout 28 January Gandoët's men held on to the lower lip of Belvedere even though no one had eaten for three days, had barely a thimble of water each to drink, and despite repeated attacks by the Germans. They were, however, well dug in behind sangars, rocks and scrapes in the ground, and supported by the firing of some 10,000 shells from the guns in the valley below. Then, at dusk, a miracle: Sergent-Chef Santaner arrived with two mules. He'd begun with sixteen but the rest had been killed on the way up; now, though, they had a resupply of grenades and machine-gun ammunition. That was something. But they still had no food.

And then, as darkness fell once more, word arrived that Colonel Roux, the regimental commander, had been killed. Hot on the tails of this shocking news came orders for them to retake Point 862 the following morning. A further company from the 3ème Régiment was on its way; the 1er Bataillon was to attack Point 711 at the same time. At 7 p.m. the reinforcement company arrived but, after the fighting of the past couple of days, had been reduced to just thirty-five men, one machine gun and a mortar.

Gandoët had spent the night trying to work out how to reach Point 862. The answer, he hoped, was to send small groups of men crawling forward to take out the four German machine guns that were currently preventing them from moving very far. The attack jumped off at 7 a.m., with the Americans of 142nd Regiment, not used during the Rapido crossing, now driving on Terelle to the south of Belvedere and the remnants of the 1er and 3ème Bataillons attacking from the southern side of the peaks. Fortunately for Gandoët's men, this was enough to draw away the Germans from Point 862. With the French artillery pounding one side of the peak and preventing any German reinforcements, and their one heavy machine gun giving covering fire, Jordy's men were able to creep forward towards the first enemy bunker, hurl grenades through the embrasure and then follow up with their sub-machine guns and rifles. This they repeated three more times and in so doing managed to snatch back the summit.

Even so, it was now being held by a thread. At Point 771, the 1er and 3ème Bataillons were counter-attacked and pushed off again. A well was discovered on the north side of Point 862 so that Gandoët's men could finally get a proper drink, but there were just handfuls of men left, and even after taking weapons and ammunition from dead and captured Germans they had nothing like enough to hold the peak for long. Repeatedly, Gandoët requested urgent reinforcements and eventually he received a reply from Général de Monsabert: 'Prisoners say that in front of us are weakened troops; redouble your energy and tenacity; I have you bracketed by artillery; free yourself with the bayonet.'

This was hardly the signal any of these utterly exhausted, famished, broken men needed to hear. Gandoët told his men to make the most of the dark and collect as many weapons and rounds as possible and to pray and hope for the best.

And then: salvation. At around 7 p.m. on Saturday, 29 January, a convoy of twenty-six mules reached them. 'Food and ammunition,' noted Gandoët. 'We *will* be able to hold on.'

General Lucas had decided to attack along two axes. The plan was for the British to head up the Via Anziate and capture Campoleone Station and for the Americans to take Cisterna. These were the two first objectives before striking onwards to Albano and even Valmontone, astride the Via Casilina. General Ronald Penney, the commander of the British 1st Division, intended for the Scots Guards and Grenadier Guards to lead the charge on Campoleone Station, although on 28 January tragedy had struck the Grenadiers. The four company commanders and four other officers had set out in jeeps to join the Scots Guards' position about a mile north of the Factory. Unfortunately, they took a wrong turn and ran straight into German outposts. While trying to escape, four officers, including three company commanders, were killed. At the Grenadiers' CP in the Factory, Corporal Edward Danger was stunned by the news; they all were. They'd lost 130 casualties since landing, and with three out of four company commanders now dead they were withdrawn from the battle plans and replaced by the Irish Guards instead.

It was, though, Colonel Darby's three Ranger battalions who were the first troops to be getting the great offensive under way. They'd all known something was afoot when, two days earlier, they'd been pulled back from their positions next to the British to the south of the Factory, and sure enough, the following day, 29 January, Darby had been briefed for what was going to be the first major attack from the bridgehead. The role of the Rangers was to advance overnight to within a couple of miles of Cisterna and attack the town an hour before the main assault the following morning. From Truscott's 3rd Division, 7th Infantry were going to be attacking on the Rangers' left and 15th Infantry on their right, with a tank battalion following behind them. The road from Nettuno and Conca ran north-east to Cisterna, while another road ran north-west, with the town at the apex of the triangle. The Rangers were to use this triangle for their advance – the 1st and 3rd Battalions would sneak up along an irrigation ditch known as the Fosso di Pantano, while the 4th Battalion and Rangers HQ would follow behind up the road from Conca and clear and hold a series of farm buildings called Isola Bella, a couple of miles south-west of Cisterna, then push on and join the rest.

The Rangers had set off once night had fallen in a confident mood, armed with two bandoliers of ammo each and grenades stuffed in their pockets, and accompanied by their old friends of the 83rd Chemical Mortar Battalion, with whom they'd shared the heights of Monte Corno on the Bernhard Line for much of the previous November. They also had plentiful amounts of sticky grenades and bazooka hand-held anti-tank rocket launchers. Intelligence suggested that Cisterna was only lightly held.

At midnight they were about four miles south and due to split up for their close advance on the town, so Darby held a final commanders' conference and told them to keep radio silence until they'd passed an imaginary line that ran east–west through the Isola Bella farmstead.

His HQ, accompanying 4th Ranger Battalion, was hooked in by radio and wire to 3rd Division. The three battalions now split off, the 1st and 3rd disappearing into the pitch-dark night and cutting across fields to take the Pantano ditch. In no time at all they had simply melted from Darby's view.

The 4th Battalion, meanwhile, began advancing down the Conca–Cisterna road, but they'd barely gone half a mile when they began running into resistance: dug-in enemy troops either side of the road, shots from houses they passed and then a roadblock made by two smashed jeeps and an Italian truck. Calling up a couple of tanks, they soon cleared the roadblock but already alarm bells were ringing: the intelligence picture had not reported any such enemy outposts or obstacles. Clearing these also sucked up time, so that 4th Battalion had still not reached Isola Bella by the time the 1st and 3rd Battalions were due to attack.

At 7 a.m. 1st Battalion broke radio silence, as planned, Lieutenant-Colonel Jack Dobson reporting that they were now in an open field 800 yards south of Cisterna but with three StuGs giving them trouble. The 3rd Battalion was strung out just to the east of them, while soon afterwards the lead companies of 4th Battalion, with some mortars and tank destroyers to help, were fighting heavier than expected enemy troops dug in around the Isola Bella farmstead. A tragedy for the Rangers was rapidly unfolding. Caught in the apex of the triangle and out of radio contact with 4th Battalion and any armoured support, the two leading battalions had walked straight into a trap – one that was rapidly closing around them as a German battle group of Fallschirmjäger and armoured troops neatly encircled them with greater firepower than the lightly armed Rangers could hurl back. The Rangers had known they'd walked past a few outposts and a Nebelwerfer battery, but they had had no idea, in the inky darkness, that they'd infiltrated past many more enemy troops than that. News began flooding in on the radio and none of it was good. Colonel Dobson was reported wounded and the commander of 3rd Battalion killed. Darby was frantically sending messages back asking for urgent reinforcements, but by 8.30 a.m. two entire battalions had reported by radio that they were entirely surrounded. And in risk of annihilation.

The men of the 504th PIR, meanwhile, had jumped off with their attack to the east of the beachhead around 1 a.m. that same morning, 30 January, with Sergeant Ross Carter's platoon taking the lead in Company C, which was in turn leading the whole of 1st Battalion. Carter reckoned it had never been easier to kill and capture Krauts than it was that night. 'They seemed too dazed to fire,' he noted, 'except very spasmodically. It was a rare opportunity.' At one point in the early hours, they were attacking a house occupied by the enemy when a Sherman rumbled and squeaked up beside them.

'Boys, that house is my meat,' the tank commander yelled down at them, 'and I'll tear it down for you.' The first armour-piercing round went straight through it and the second struck right in the middle. Moments later, between shouts of '*Kamerad!*', twenty Germans stumbled out and surrendered. The paratroopers pushed on and came across a battery of light 20mm flak guns. One German poked his head out and got a bullet through the forehead for his trouble, but otherwise the enemy remained hidden until Carter remembered a western he'd read where the hero shot the bad guys by ricocheting bullets off a rock. Noticing the gun mounts were above ground, he opened fire, bouncing his bullets off the curving metal and into the gun pits. After a few rounds a terrified face appeared, arms aloft, followed by twenty-nine others. Soon afterwards they were leapfrogged by 2. Battalion.

The 504th were too far away to help the beleaguered Rangers, however. Rather, the only realistic chance of rescue lay in the hands of 15th Infantry, part of 3rd Infantry Division, who were attacking on the Rangers' right flank. None of the men in Sergeant Audie Murphy's platoon, however, were feeling particularly good about their attack that morning and they probably got going too late to save them in any case. Murphy had only returned to the platoon the previous day, having spent a week in hospital with a renewed bout of malaria – he'd first caught it back in Sicily – and on recovering rejoined his men, only to learn that two of his great pals had been killed: Fife, a Cherokee Native American, and Joe Sieja, a second-generation Pole, who'd been blown to bits by a shell. No one was talking about getting to Valmontone, however. As far as Murphy understood matters, their aim now was to expand the bridgehead to try and push the enemy artillery out of range of Anzio and Nettuno. Company B of 1st Battalion were to clear a section of Highway 7 that ran between Terracina and Cisterna.

They advanced in squads along the flanks of a dirt track. The sun was shining and Murphy felt the fear creeping inside him, marching with him, every step of the way. 'In the heat of battle it may go away,' he noted. 'Sometimes it vanishes in a blind, red rage that comes when you see a friend fall. Then again you get so tired that you become indifferent. But when you are moving into combat, why try fooling yourself.' The fear was in him, tying his guts in knots. He knew that someone would be killed this day; it was inevitable. 'But the question keeps pounding through the brain,' he wrote, 'this time will I be the one that gets it?'

The German lines were more than a mile away but scouts were prowling cautiously in front of the rest of the infantry. Their own artillery was firing ahead of them and then suddenly it tailed off, right at the moment they began walking over the churned-up ground the rolling barrage had plastered earlier. This was the worst moment, Murphy knew – just before the enemy opened up. Despite the artillery doing their best, he knew the Germans were out there, up ahead. Waiting. Scouts waved them forward. Then suddenly, from hidden positions, light flak wagons opened fire, the kind that should have been used on the Rapido. One of the scouts was hit, his upper body disappearing in a shower of red. Automatic fire burst out from a dozen places. Branches and leaves ripped as bullets hissed, fizzed and zipped. Two men were squirming, caught in the open, trying to wriggle clear, but the bullets followed them. 'The bodies writhe like stricken worms,' wrote Murphy. 'The gun fires again. The bodies relax and are still.'

'Where are our goddam tanks?' cried out Martin Kelly, one of the old-timers in his platoon. 'They're never here when we need them.' They all opened fire, shooting blindly. Murphy dragged himself into a shallow ditch beside Mason, another of his men. He was trying to shoot a German who was sniping at them when suddenly the shriek of an incoming shell filled the air and landed close by with an immense wallop, the force of which lifted Murphy into the air and slammed him back down again. 'My brain whirls; my ears ring with the noise of a hundred bells. Greasy black smoke drifts over the earth; and the stench of burnt powder fills my nostrils.' He yelled at Mason, then wriggled up towards him only to realize that the eyes staring at him were lifeless, that blood was oozing from his nose and mouth and that his neck was broken. Murphy removed Mason's helmet, closed his eyes and straightened his head. An image of himself talking to Mason's mother entered his head. He tapped his forehead with his fist; he needed to blank out such thoughts.

He crawled over to Kelly just as the tanks arrived and began pounding and spraying bullets with their machine guns. A number of Germans tried to flee but in their panic simply exposed themselves as easy targets. Murphy and his men shot them all, each one crumpling to the ground.

*

By this time, however, it was afternoon on that fateful Sunday, 30 January, and all over for the 1st and 3rd Rangers. Repeated calls for help were transmitted but 15th Infantry were making no progress at all and could not reach them. Audie Murphy and the rest of Company B had barely made any ground at all. Nor had anyone else. It was difficult attacking a well-dug-in enemy over ground as flat as a billiard table. Almost as hard as attacking up mountains. Colonel Darby had kept in contact with his men for as long as he could. By late morning, a captain had been commanding both battalions – the most senior officer left. Overwrought and weeping, he was unable to speak clearly so Darby called for one of his sergeants, a tough New Yorker from Brooklyn. 'Some of the fellows are giving up,' the sergeant told Darby. 'Colonel, we are awfully sorry. They can't help it because we're running out of ammunition. But I ain't surrendering. They are coming into the building now . . .' Then there was a loud double crash on the radio and it went dead. By around 2.30 p.m., a sergeant-major of 3rd Battalion reported that he was going to destroy his radio and called off. That had been it: just 6 out of 767 made it back; 122 had been killed and 639 taken prisoner. It was a disaster: two battalions of the finest troops in the US Army destroyed. The 4th Battalion fought on, capturing 250 enemy troops around Isola Bella, but then withdrew later that evening, just as the 3rd Division men had pulled back too. The British had fared better, the Guards Brigade pushing on down the Via Anziate and very nearly reaching Campoleone Station, but it had been a day of bitter disappointment for the Allies and a triumph for General von Mackensen's AOK 14.

That night it was Darby's turn to break down and weep. He blamed himself; he'd exhorted them to fight on, but had he been with the forward battalions he reckoned he might have withdrawn them far earlier. Command could be a lonely job. 'The strain of a thing like this is a terrible burden,' General Lucas had noted in his diary a few days earlier. 'Who the hell wants to be a general?'

Back at the 15th Infantry lines, Audie Murphy and his fellows were not getting much sleep that night as the guns continued to boom. 'Cheerless rumours have spread,' he noted. 'Our men have been beaten back over the entire front. The day has but served to deplete our forces. We attack again tomorrow . . .'

CHAPTER 14

So Close Yet So Far

CARLA CAPPONI – ELENA – HAD NOW JOINED Paolo in Centocelle on the south-west edge of Rome. The suburb was built around the Via Casilina – Highway 6 – so it really was a key part of the city for the GAP partisans to control. Both Elena and Paolo were surprised by the extent to which they ruled the roost in this neighbourhood. In fact, on Paolo's arrival he had given a stirring speech to an assembled crowd of some 150 people in the main piazza. When the Carabiniere then drove up and asked them to disperse, Paolo went over to them and pointedly refused, telling the officer that the partisans were now in charge. They immediately drove off again, but the following day returned and struck a deal. If Paolo's group wanted to meet they promised to keep away, but otherwise would patrol as normal. The officer then suggested that Paolo and some of his partisans might even like to join them at a police shooting range where they could train. The curfew was disregarded and for the most part German police troops as well as the Carabiniere kept well clear.

Yet while the Gappisti in Centocelle were able to move and operate at will, German control of central Rome remained as tight, if not tighter than ever. In charge of the Sicherheitsdienst – SD, the SS intelligence agency, – in Rome was SS-Obersturmbannführer Herbert Kappler. Kappler was thirty-six years old, from Stuttgart, a Party member since 1931 who had joined the SS back in 1933. He had graduated from its leadership school in Berlin as a criminal commissioner and became part of the SD, later helping with the deportation of Austrian Jews following the Anschluss, the annexation of Austria, in 1938. He had then been sent, in September 1943, to Rome to specifically oversee the round-up of Italy's

Jews. After sending more than 1,000 to Auschwitz, however, he had made Rome's surviving Jewish elders collect 50 kilos of gold – most of which they borrowed from the Vatican. Since then, most of Kappler's time had been spent on anti-partisan operations. In this he was also helped by Pietro Koch, an Italian Fascist who ran an RSI-backed special police unit dedicated to hunting partisans, and now, at the beginning of February 1944, Pietro Caruso, the new *Questore* – Chief of Police – in the city. Both men were not only ardent Fascists but also only too willing to collude with Nazi anti-Semitism, and together were determined to stamp down very hard on the growing number of partisan activities.

One of those arrested by Kappler's men was thirty-eight-year-old Ottavio Cirulli, a cobbler by trade but also a committed Communist and member of the Bandiera Rossa, who since the capture of Rome on 10 September had been distributing anti-Fascist propaganda, helping to hide British agents and also stealing and storing weapons and ammunition. In December he been involved with spreading leaflets in Rome's cinemas, but when four of his team were caught at the Principe movie house the trail then led to Cirulli. Arrested, he was flung into the Regina Coeli Prison. Along with ten others, he was tried on 28 January and sentenced to death. That he had a wife, as well as five children aged thirteen to just a few days old, cut no ice at all. There was to be no clemency in this cruel time.

Cirulli wrote a last letter to his wife, Anna. 'My dear love,' he scribbled, 'unfortunately this was my destiny. While I write, I feel the worst pain of my life. Anna, my love, look after our beautiful darling children . . . I kiss you and I will think of you until my last breath.' At 11 a.m. on 2 February, Cirulli and the ten others sentenced with him were bundled into a truck. It raced through the city, on through Trastevere to the barracks at Via di Bravetta. There they were ordered out and led to an embankment where there were soldiers, German officials, the prison director and a doctor. The first five prisoners were blindfolded, led to a set of chairs fixed to the ground by stakes and made to sit down with their backs to the platoon. The sentence was read out and the order to fire was given, each man shot in the back of the head. The next six, Cirulli included, were killed the same way.

To make the tragedy worse, Cirulli's oldest daughter, Maria, had visited the prison the previous morning to bring her father's clean laundry, but was told he'd been deported. Fearing the worst, his wife went to the prison the following day, 2 February, accompanied by friends. 'Look,' she was told, 'they shot your husband this morning.' They handed back his belongings: a musical score he'd been studying, some English books, his coat and the keys to his cobbler's shop.

Meanwhile, the six parties of the CLN were trying to shape a political future for Italy by convening a congress in Bari, a gathering they had wanted to take place back in December but which the Allied Military Government had refused to allow. The creation of the ACC had, however, changed the landscape, and while Naples remained in AMGOT hands, Bari no longer was and so permission was granted for the Congress to go ahead in that city. Since the Allies had resolved to hand back control of much of southern Italy to the Italians, the need for a resolution of their own had become more urgent; yet getting consensus from six very different political parties and ideologies was not easy.

Attending was Filippo Caracciolo, who had been part of many lengthy discussions with a number of the key players in the Partita d'Azione ahead of the Congress. The big sticking point was the future of the King and the monarchy. Badoglio, still Prime Minister, had appointed Generale Pietro Gazzera as Extraordinary Commander of Bari for the duration of the Congress; Gazzera had been a minister under Mussolini. A limit of ninety delegates had also been imposed, with no public attendance allowed at all. 'The harbingers of the Congress are daunting,' noted Caracciolo. Nor was he much impressed by Gazzera. 'His actions spread a climate of agitation.' The following day, Caracciolo presided over a session with his Partita d'Azione colleagues full of bickering, discontent, claims and recriminations, largely over who was going to Bari to represent the party and who would be staying behind. 'The thankless task,' he noted, 'of distributing the few entrance cards attributed to the Partita d'Azione falls to me.'

The Congress opened on Friday, 28 January in the Piccinni Theatre in Bari, in a somewhat febrile atmosphere. Caracciolo found himself quite moved by the occasion, and while he was hopeful for a resolution he was not overly optimistic that one would be agreed. 'Words so far,' he noted, 'nothing but words and a lot of uncertainty.' Two titans of Italian politics lined up to speak were Benedetto Croce, lawyer, philosopher, anti-Fascist and Liberal; and Count Carlo Sforza, a former diplomat and minister who had exiled himself throughout the Fascist era. 'A breath of grandeur blows into the busy room,' Caracciolo noted when Croce began to speak, 'and a long, thunderous ovation fills the theatre when he finishes speaking.' Debate continued into the afternoon, when it became clear that the Christian Democrats were threatening to shipwreck a resolution that had been proposed by the Partita d'Azione and endorsed by the Communists and Socialists: to draw up a joint bill of indictment against the King and make the CLN the representative assembly of Italy, which would immediately form a government. Away from the Congress, Caracciolo worked into the night with Croce, Sforza and others to draft a new resolution acceptable to the Christian Democrats and at 3 a.m. it was done. Four hours later, at 7 a.m. on that second day, they were already having further discussions with the Socialists and Communists, and at 8.30 a.m. all parties met; but still the Christian Democrats baulked. More feverish discussions and compromises ensued, and then, at 10.30 a.m. on 29 January, a resolution was finally agreed by all: a new government, but only after the liberation of Rome and the abdication of the King without the dissolution of the monarchy. Back in the Piccinni Theatre the formalities were agreed. 'All those called to speak aloud said "yes",' noted Caracciolo, 'and this fills my soul with profound joy.'

The vast majority of Italians, however, simply wanted to keep their heads down and get on with their lives. Viviana Bauco, still at the family home in Ripi in the Liri Valley, spent much of her time living in a state of terror. There was no one to explain what was happening, what they might expect, or how to react; rather, they were caught in a kind of no-man's-land in which they'd been completely abandoned by the state, the normal structures of life having fallen away. On 29 January, Allied planes thundered over and bombed the village; Viviana had been with her friend Maria at the time. 'How to describe the feelings of fear today?' she wrote. 'It seemed even more scary to me because I was not with my family.' The following day the nuns at the abbey left, believing it was no longer safe for them to stay. For most Italians, however, there was nowhere else to go, other than to take to the mountains; but that, of course, brought a host of other risks and challenges. On 6 February Viviana turned twenty-one. It should have been a great moment in her life, but she felt no joy at all. 'The sad events of the war,' she wrote, 'the uncertainty of tomorrow – they make me forget my youth. What a bad era I was born in!'

The monks of Monte Cassino were finding life at the abbey even more troubling and terrifying. Surrounded by troops dug in just beneath the bastion walls and with the sound of battle now all too close, they were aware that the fighting was almost at their door. 'We pray that the wrath of God may soon pass,' noted Dom Eusebio, 'because it is breaking us.' Civilians from the mountain farms, from Terelle and even from the town below were now coming daily to their doors, asking for food and shelter;

those German commanders who had earlier insisted that civilians should not remain in the abbey appeared to have moved on – or perhaps those in charge on the mountain simply had other things to worry about. One morning, after matins in the Father Abbot's room, he told the other monks a story which he admitted he had never recounted to anyone before. Some years earlier, he had visited Nocera dei Pagani and stayed overnight at the Sanctuary of Sant'Alphonso dei Ligouri. While in his room he distinctly heard someone weeping, who, between sobs, called out, 'Monte Cassino! Monte Cassino! Monte Cassino!' as though in lamentation. 'This story made a very strong impression on us,' noted Dom Eusebio. 'Father Abbot has linked this mysterious weeping to the destruction of Monte Cassino and is interpreting this voice as a premonition.'

The Father Abbot was recovering from his bout of illness, but not so Dom Eusebio, who was feeling increasingly ill. On 27 January he noted that all the mountains seemed to be smoking like volcanoes, then took to his bed with a temperature. Two days later it had risen to 39 degrees Celsius and Dom Martino Matronola took over the writing of his diary. 'A night broken by the sounds of shells exploding in the area below our shelter,' wrote Dom Martino a few days later. 'The *raganella* shells are still flying over the abbey. Massive artillery barrages.' Heavy shellfire and machine-gunning continued almost perpetually now. 'Our former "neutral zone"', wrote Dom Martino, 'was nothing more than a diplomatic cover story.'

'My head will probably fall in the basket,' jotted General Lucas on 2 February, 'but I have done my best. There were just too many Germans here for me to lick and they could build up faster than I could.' He had called off the offensive on the evening of the 31st; after all, although the British now held an extended finger-like salient up the Via Anziate, little progress had been made. There was no sugar-coating the failure. Both Alexander and Clark were up at the bridgehead, conferring with their commanders. Alex, with Harding in tow, busied himself touring the front, talking to as many senior officers as possible, from Lucas to the divisional commanders to every battalion CO. For Harding, this was his first time right on the front line since he'd been wounded in North Africa and he was pleasantly surprised to discover that he was no more frightened of shellfire than he had been before he'd been hit. That, however, was pretty much the only cause for cheer. Lucas was apologetic but told them his mission had always been an impossible one, which was not what they wanted to hear. 'Lucas is an old woman,' jotted Harding, 'and the whole thing lacks drive and direction.' Alexander then drew up a new plan, which was to reinforce the British salient and for 3rd Division to build up its reserves directly behind the front line – armour, tank destroyers, artillery and ammunition – and then to attack again and at least straighten out the bridgehead in line with the British salient. Alexander and Harding hoped this plan would be swiftly put into effect, but unbeknown to them Lucas had already ordered his entire front on to the defensive in preparation for a German counter-attack that now seemed imminent – a decision made without recourse to Alexander or Clark, even though both were present at the bridgehead. Of course, the order could have been countermanded, but that would expose senior leadership at loggerheads and badly risk morale; what could not be countenanced now was a major reversal. So Lucas's order stood. Alexander, though, was extremely disappointed and suggested to Clark it was time to relieve his VI Corps commander.

Clark was not happy either, although he didn't sack Lucas. 'I have been disappointed for several days by the lack of aggressiveness on the part of the VI Corps,' he noted on 30 January. He did not now think a drive for the Colli Laziali had been realistic, but he understood the need to secure vital nodal points and dramatically increase the depth of the bridgehead. 'Reconnaissance in force with tanks,' he added, 'should have been more aggressive to capture Cisterna and Campoleone. Repeatedly, I have told Lucas to push vigorously to get those local objectives. He has not insisted upon this with the division commanders.' Nor was he impressed to find that more than half the available armour was currently supporting the British left flank to the west of the Via Anziate. This was the terrain where Hans-Paul Liebschner and Kampfgruppe Gericke were operating – the strange landscape of scored riverbeds the British had already nicknamed the 'Wadis' from their days in North Africa. It was hardly ideal tank country, and there was no question they would have been put to better use supporting Truscott's men, not least because the British infantry had their own armour support. The destruction of the Rangers had also been a bitter blow, and one that he felt was entirely avoidable. 'This was a definite error of judgement,' he wrote, 'for the Rangers do not have the support weapons to overcome the resistance indicated.' Darby's men had only been sent there in the first place because Cisterna was believed to be lightly held, but Clark had a point. With some 350 tanks and half that number again of anti-tank guns, the sensible approach was to use combinations of all-arms: infantry, supporting armour, reconnaissance troops and, of course, artillery, creeping forward and clearing strongpoints one at a time. The Rangers had been destroyed for lack of firepower; regardless of the intelligence picture, it paid to go in hard, especially since the Allies were not lacking these assets.

Lucas's head probably should have rolled, as he'd expected, but the Rangers debacle had led Clark to question the judgement of Truscott too, deservedly highly regarded and the only person who could have realistically taken over. Nor did sacking corps commanders reflect particularly well on the army commander; after all, if a corps commander was sacked, didn't that suggest an error of judgement that he'd been appointed in the first place? Whether VI Corps could have ever held the Colli Laziali was really not the issue. Striking quickly, and hard, had been the entire point of the landing in the first place: a giant, elaborate bluff to encourage the Germans to pull back. Alexander had always made it clear that it might not work, but it had been agreed from the very top of the Allied chain of command that it was worth the punt. That had been Lucas's mission and yet he'd prevaricated at every turn, consumed by a growing siege mentality. Could it have worked? Possibly. High ground was the king of the battlefield, after all. From there, Highway 7 could have been blocked. Offshore naval guns could have provided fire support, air power dropped supplies. The aim, though, was never to support an isolated battle group. Rather, it was to force the hand of the Germans on the Gustav Line. Perhaps Kesselring could never have been persuaded, but the pressure on him to do so might have been greater had the Allies reached the Colli Laziali, as Lucas had been instructed.

At any rate, had Lucas sent as many forces as possible in the first twenty-four to forty-eight hours of the invasion, there was every reason to think they would have got there. The point was this: whether it would have worked or not was hardly the issue. His mission was to try, something he'd never wanted to do and never believed in. Clark was surely right that, at the very least, stronger efforts should have been made earlier to clear Campoleone and Cisterna. That hadn't happened either. And by the time Lucas had been bulldozed into finally making an attack, it was too late. It was no wonder Alexander and Clark were feeling frustrated. So much effort had been put into this combined, multi-pronged offensive; so many lives sacrificed in an attempt to break the deadlock. And it really had come so close to succeeding – closer than either man realized. On Belvedere and on the Cassino massif, understrength German units were desperately trying to hold on. In the south, along the Garigliano front, 94. Division was once again fending for itself, battered, depleted, a shadow of what it had been.

Although Lucas's men were now on the defensive at Anzio, and dreams of striking out to the distant hills had now vanished with the stark realities of the situation in which they found themselves, it wasn't all bad news, because the current all-out Allied effort in Italy was profoundly benefiting OVERLORD. At the OKW, still based at the Wolf's Lair in East Prussia, there had been much consternation about where and when the main Allied invasion blow might occur. At the start of the year the presumption was that it would come early, most probably in the Pas-de-Calais. Hitler was aware that the success of such an invasion would be decisive for the outcome of the war and so it made sense to clarify some strategic priorities. It was precisely for this reason that Feldmarschall Erwin Rommel had proposed pulling back to the Pisa–Rimini Line the previous autumn. Certainly, at a time when German resources were ever more limited and demands on those immense, tough decisions needed to be made, and in their current parlous state they had to work out where their greatest threats lay. Those were in the east and especially, at the start of 1944, the west, because the western Reich was where Germany's industrial heartland lay and where most of its coalfields – and those of France – were located. Without coal, which was used both for making synthetic fuel and powering the Reichsbahn – the German railway on which most of their transport depended – they were finished. Quite simply, if western Germany was overrun by the Allies, the war was over.

So reinforcing the front south of Rome was of very limited strategic value. As Kesselring was well aware, they were only holding on by the skin of their teeth along the Cassino front and von Senger, especially, needed urgent reinforcement. Limited forces could probably hold the Allies at bay in the Anzio bridgehead, but Hitler, egged on by General Jodl, decided that the best way to counteract the threat of an invasion in the West was to kick the Allies back into the sea at Anzio. 'If we succeed in dealing with this business down there,' Hitler pronounced, 'there will be no further landing anywhere.' Achieving such a goal only had a remote chance of being successful if considerably more troops were sent to the southern Italian front. And therein lay the rub, because those extra troops had to come from Germany and from the western front, so weakening German strength in the west.

The most senior Allied politician in Italy, Harold Macmillan, had not attended the Congress of Bari and had instead spent the time working out the legal terms for the transfer of power from AMGOT to the ACC, which required regular consultation not just with General Mason-MacFarlane and General Jumbo Wilson but also with Alexander, of whom he had become very fond. On 29 January, between Alex's trips to Anzio, Macmillan had accompanied him on a tour of the Cassino front in the Chief's open-top Ford V8. They called on Juin and General Keyes and climbed a hill from which they could see the battle playing out in the upper Rapido Valley. Macmillan was fascinated to observe Alexander's technique of suggestion rather than directly ordering. 'These are put forward with modesty and simplicity,' he noted. 'But they are always so clear and lucid that they carry conviction. It is a most interesting (and extremely effective) method.' He was realizing too that Alex liked to talk of other things as much as possible – politics, ancient art, Roman antiquities, country life. 'He hates war,' Macmillan noted.

Yet as January gave way to February, the Allies were far closer to a breakthrough than Alexander or any of the senior Allied commanders realized; but, as had already proved the case so often in Italy, they just did not have quite enough troops to land the killer punch. Général Juin, for example, had only ever been able to use one of his two divisions on Belvedere because his Moroccan division was holding the right of the line and facing the Germans on the Monte Cifalco massif. Gandoët and the survivors up on Belvedere had managed to hang on to Monte Abate and the entire Belvedere mountain feature for good. They were in a brilliant position to drive on round the southern side of the mighty Monte Cairo and decapitate the Monte Cassino massif there and then, especially now that the T-Patchers' 142nd Regimental Combat Team* were driving towards Terelle on their left flank. The trouble was, the Algerian division had understandably now shot its bolt, having lost half its strength; even

* A Regimental Combat Team – RCT – was an entire three-battalion infantry regiment but with artillery, engineers and heavy weapons attached, making it, in theory, a more balanced formation of all-arms.

though supplies had reached them in the nick of time, they no longer had the strength to push any further.

This was a great shame, because the back door to the entire Cassino position was suddenly open and there to be ruthlessly exploited. Not only had von Senger appreciated that the situation north of Cassino was dire, so too had von Vietinghoff and even Kesselring. The H-und-D-Division was barely functioning; by the beginning of February, 134. Regiment, to which Georg Zellner's III. Bataillon belonged, could barely muster 260 men. That amounted to about two companies and just 8 per cent of full strength; a three-battalion regiment such as 134. should have had a complement of 3,250 men. The 131. Regiment, to which Zellner's battalion had been attached, had only 430 men left, so a little over 13 per cent. These units had been utterly decimated, so it was no wonder von Senger now privately believed it was time to fall back to the Caesar position just to the south of Rome.

Yet despite these catastrophic losses, Kesselring was not to be budged. The 5. Gebirgsjäger-Division on the Cifalco massif thinned out and shifted troops up the other side of the Secco Valley to face the French. General Baade's 90. Panzergrenadier – likewise at a fraction of full strength – was also now moving up on to the southern end of the massif. In addition, Kesselring's favourite fire-brigade unit, 1. Fallschirmjäger-Division, was on its way in typically piecemeal fashion. Even this unit, however, had already sent a battalion to Anzio, and at full strength could call on little more than 3,000 men; it was supposed to have been more than 17,000 men-strong, so was under 18 per cent of strength. It had never been so depleted, but Kesselring had repeatedly refused General-leutnant Richard Heidrich's entreaties to send it back to southern France to re-equip and retrain.

In other words, XIV Panzerkorps looked spent, and there was now a golden opportunity for the Allies to capitalize on the relentless battering of the line by Fifth Army since the start of the year. They needed to move quickly, and their best chance of success was probably to dramatically reinforce the 142nd RCT, still on loan while Fred Walker's battered other two regiments absorbed the latest round of replacements, which was continuing its drive towards Terelle. They were certainly well placed to do this because overnight on 29–30 January, the Red Bulls had taken Point 213 overlooking the upper Rapido Valley and then, the following night, had taken the village of Caira too, the ideal stepping stone for sending the rest of the division up on to this far wider route across the massif. Neither General Doc Ryder nor General Keyes nor Clark for that matter, who at this point was at Anzio, spotted this opportunity, however. Rather, they decided to continue with the route they had always planned to take ever since launching the Red Bulls' assault back on 24 January: to push up on to the Monte Cassino massif to the south of Monte Cairo and from there to drop down into the Liri Valley.

So on 1 February Doc Ryder launched his renewed attack, unaware of just how tantalizingly close they were to a really decisive breakthrough. The 133rd Infantry were to push south into Cassino town, while the 168th would hold Hill 213 and the narrow valleys either side leading up on to the mountains. The 135th Infantry, meanwhile, was to take Monte Castellone, the highest point of a long, slithering ridge that ran from one side of the massif to the other immediately south of Monte Cairo. The T-Patchers of the 142nd RCT, meanwhile, would merely watch the backs of the Red Bulls from the Terelle region.

Sergeant Ralph Schaps was among those in 135th Infantry now heading up into the mountains. He and the rest of 2nd Battalion had been involved in holding the line north of the T-Patchers, to the rear of Cassino, but had then been pulled out before their deployment on the mountain. Schaps had been ready for a couple of days' break; it had been their first rest in three weeks. Hot showers, clean clothes, some decent chow and mail and, much to Schaps's delight, another package of cigars from home too.

Now, though, on the night of Monday, 31 January they marched five miles to the upper Rapido Valley and crossed over in the dark, ready to jump off the following morning at 6.30 from the bottom of the gorge to the south of Hill 213. Schaps and the rest of 2nd Battalion were to try and clear Point 451, Colle Maiola, the lower knoll on a second curving ridge that led to Calvario, 'Calvary Hill' – Point 593 on the map – which directly overlooked the abbey. Meanwhile, 3rd Battalion was to clamber up Monte Castellone. There were goat tracks up on to the mountain but the lower slopes especially, closer to the valley floor, were very steep in places. 'The terrain was extremely tough,' noted Schaps. 'There were gullies, crevices and out-croppings, some scrub and growth and some bushes that had needles that would penetrate your clothes.' The rocky, rough terrain did offer some cover but Schaps, for one, found it was very easy to lose one's bearings up there. It was also an incredibly hard climb for soldiers laden with ammunition, weapons, ration packs and canteens of water, especially since none of them had slept the night before.

Artillery boomed, shells screeched over and exploded somewhere up ahead on the massif, but the men of the 135th were lucky that morning because there was a thick mist once again that shrouded the mountain and hid them from the watchful eyes of the enemy. As a result, they swiftly overran the German outposts on the way up, PFC Chuck Bussey single-handedly charging and clearing a machine-gun nest after their lead scout was hit.

Having secured the first knoll on their climb, 2nd Battalion saw off several counter-attacks, brought up more supplies and then, once it grew dark, hunkered down for the night. The following day, Schaps's squad were climbing a particularly steep part of the ridge and his men were becoming strung out. Pausing on a ledge of rock for the rest to catch up, he was joined by his friend, Rosey, over thirty, and so one of the older men. Since he was loaded down with two boxes of ammo, Schaps told him to pause and catch his breath, a suggestion Rosey gratefully accepted. He then pulled out a tin of fruit and some cookies which he shared with Schaps while the others joined them, one by one. Once the last had climbed past them, Schaps got up and continued, Rosey behind him. Moments later, a mortar shell hissed down and hit the ledge where they'd just been sitting. Schaps looked around but couldn't see his friend – only dust, debris and smoke. Schaps hollered down for him and had begun to climb back down, fearing the worst, when Rosey reappeared, covered in dust. 'Bastards!' he exclaimed. 'Almost got me!' He'd been lucky; the shell had landed nearby, but because of the steepness of the mountain there most of the blast had spread out and down. It had been a close shave.

By nightfall that day, 3rd Battalion were on Monte Castellone and the 2nd on Colle Maiola, their objectives taken. So far the Red Bulls had done well. With more supplies brought up overnight there was every reason to believe they could push on the following day, 2nd Battalion having been ordered to clear the remaining ridge that led to Point 593 but also the narrow mountain plain around Albaneta Farm, which stood on a low saddle between the two ridges. Meanwhile, 3rd Battalion was to continue along the Castellone Ridge to Colle Sant'Angelo. By then they would be looking right down on to the Liri Valley, their breakthrough very nearly complete.

By 1 February, General Baade had managed to move the headquarters of his 90. Panzergrenadier-Division up to the Cassino front. His disparate units from the Garigliano and from the Anzio bridgehead had been brought back together, and although severely understrength were now in the process of taking over positions on the Monte Cassino massif from the 44. H-und-D-Division. It had been the H-und-D that had borne the brunt of the attacks by both the CEF and Red Bulls and by this stage its 131. Regiment, which had faced the French, had been destroyed – literally, it had ceased to exist. A manpower count of AOK 10 on 3 February gave the entire 134. Regiment a little over 400 men and 132. Regiment, which had confronted the Red Bulls at the foot of Monte Cassino and now up on the massif, just 400. That was the full extent of the entire division's fighting strength: 800 men in a division that should have had 15,000. It was why the Americans had had a comparatively easy time of things getting up on to the massif.

Changeovers of troops always created a hiatus and the Red Bulls had also benefited from this; two of Baade's battalions were starting to move up on to the mountain just as 135th Infantry attacked, although they were hardly faring any better. One of its regiments could muster around 550 men, another 430, along with 220 pioneers and 90 in the reconnaissance battalion – so around 1,300 in all. Not even 10 per cent of full strength. The best-placed division was 5. Gebirgsjäger, operating at around 50 per cent strength, but collectively AOK 10 was in a truly parlous position. The army had been decimated by the fighting of the past few months. Had General Ryder known this and been able to fling everything into the attack, the Americans might well have broken through. As it was, the H-und-D-Division had been left to hold the northern stretch of the massif, 132. Regiment shifting northwards, so also changing positions. This was why an even greater opportunity for an American breakthrough lay in the Terelle sector. Both Keyes and Doc Ryder continued to be blind to this incredible opportunity.

Instead, Baade was able to reinforce the Colle Maiola Ridge with the first arrivals from 1. Fallschirmjäger-Division. This was 3. Bataillon of the 3. Fallschirmjäger-Regiment commanded by Major Rudolf Kratzert, forty-five, who had been awarded the Knight's Cross and was one of the most experienced officers in the division. He'd also been one of the lucky ones to be given some leave at Christmas, but had come back from Vienna on 7 January to discover that his battalion had been in further fighting north of Ortona. Even after his return they were bombed and strafed almost daily and attacked by fighting patrols. Needless to say, the losses had not been replaced, so that when he received orders on 1

February to hurriedly move to Cassino he had just four officers and 236 men; he should have had 1,000.

They left San Silvestro on the Adriatic coast at 8 p.m. on 1 February, driving all night in trucks through the mountains and down valleys, on their way to the western side of the peninsula. The journey took the best part of twenty hours, but the following afternoon Kratzert presented himself at Baade's command post, a smoke-filled cave near Castrocielo. On maps spread out on a table, Baade pointed out Colle Maiola. This, he told Kratzert, was the danger point. His grenadiers had tried repeatedly to push the Americans off the ridge but to no avail. He wanted Kratzert's men to head up there and finish what his men had been unable to do.

Kratzert set off with his troops right away, climbing up from the Liri Valley that same night. A deep ravine ran all the way up from the Via Casilina to the mountain pastures around Albaneta Farm, and from there he led his men up a track on to the ridge which ran from Point 593 at the Liri Valley end down to Colle Maiola at the other. Setting up two machine-gun positions on the higher part of the ridge to give covering fire, he then took the rest of his men down towards Maiola. It was another cold night, the air misty and murky, and all he had was his map; in all other regards this was entirely new terrain for him and his men. Then an American outpost opened fire and suddenly grenades were being hurled. That morning he and his men pushed Ralph Schaps and the rest of 2nd Battalion back a few hundred yards, but then the Red Bulls' artillery was called up, smothering the ridge, and Kratzert was forced to pull back in turn, but now in line with the rest of Baade's men on the massif. 'The area was strewn with dead bodies,' noted Schaps, 'most of them German.'

That might have been so, but Kratzert and his men were just the vanguard. More paratroopers were on their way. What's more, Baade had started to work out how to best defend this mountain landscape of strutting knolls and plunging ravines with the minimum amount of men and maximum effect. The chance for a decisive breakthrough by the Americans was slipping away with every passing day.

CHAPTER 15

The Battle of the Thumb

CAPTAIN JOHN STRICK HAD recovered well from his physical wounds and was due to be heading back to his battalion on 2 February, so long as Jack Hargreaves, his batman, could get down in a truck and pick him up. He felt the time he'd had for reflection and for reading had been valuable. 'I only hope', he added, 'my nerves are not going to let me down in whatever new fields of responsibility may lie ahead.' He had particularly enjoyed the last few days as he'd felt well enough to get up and leave the hospital and so had taken himself off on a couple of trips. Nocera Inferiere, he felt, had rather lived up to its name – 'a straggling, dirty place' – and as it was his first day out he had felt a little shaky on his legs. That had been on the Saturday. Then on Sunday, 30 January, as Lucas's attack at Anzio had been playing out, Strick had taken himself off for a walk up the hill behind the town to see the castle perched up there. Finally, on the last day of the month, he'd visited Pompeii, hitching a ride down in an army truck. He'd toured the ancient ruins with a couple of American soldiers on leave who he thought were 'not bad, intrinsically'. Strick had, though, been rather shocked by some of the more graphic murals. 'Life in those days had reached a high pitch of socialism,' he noted a little pompously, 'with communal bakeries, baths (some of the inlaid mosaic is remarkable). Houses of ill-fame were much in evidence.' Later, he had taken himself off to the main hotel and treated himself to a plate of pasta and some wine, which made him rather tipsy, then after buying some trinkets and souvenirs managed to get a lift all the way back in a 46th Division truck.

By 4 February he was back with the battalion whether he was mentally fit for duty or not – or rather, what was left of the battalion, because most of them had already set sail for Anzio; all of 168th Brigade had been posted there – the rest of 56th Division would be following soon. 'I only missed them by a day,' he noted, 'and am not altogether sorry as I hardly feel up to it yet.' This meant that for the time being, at any rate, he had joined the battalion's rear party and was billeted in a house near Naples. Jack Hargreaves was in a place next door and they were waiting for some others to return from leave or recovered wounds and then they would be on their way to Anzio too. 'Life, if it goes on like this will be extremely easy,' noted Strick, 'but I don't suppose it will.'

The move of 168th Brigade was part of another reshuffling of troops now taking place on both sides. The Germans needed desperately to hold the line at Cassino and destroy the bridgehead at Anzio, but for the Allies the situation was the very opposite: it was now vital for them to hold the line at Anzio and destroy the Gustav Line at Cassino. General Clark was still determined to break through north of Cassino, and since his forces were so very close to achieving this he was right to think it was within their grasp. The trouble was, the 45th Thunderbirds were now at Anzio, the 36th T-Patchers were still recovering and the 142nd RCT was already in action; the CEF was spent and the Red Bulls were already fighting on the massif. The only solution was once again to milk Eighth Army over on the Adriatic. There, the Canadians were holding the coastal stretch alongside 8th Indian and the New Zealanders were having a comparatively quieter time of things. Also ready for deployment was 4th Indian Division, which had reached Italy in December and was trained for mountain fighting, the only British unit to be so. Its commander, Major-General Sir Francis Tuker, was also one of the very best divisional commanders in the theatre. Having survived the First World War, Tuker had briefly considered giving up the army to become an artist but had stuck with his first chosen profession, remaining in the Indian Army and seeing action in Iraq, Assam and northern Iran as well as border operations along the North-West Frontier and Waziristan. Tuker was a great student of warfare – both ancient and modern – and had spent much time during the 1930s thinking about the shape future wars might take. Yet he had largely come up against a wall of indifference; the inter-war Indian Army took enormous interest in sports, pig-sticking and its social life, with some colonial policing thrown in for good measure, but was certainly not a breeding ground of creative thought. The British Army had not been much better; Tuker had been shocked, for example, at the poor standards of teaching during a year at Staff College in England in 1925. Certainly, putting one's neck on the line by expressing ideas on tactical developments was widely viewed as dangerously bad form. Tuker had got round this by writing articles in august defence journals such as the *Royal United Services Institute Journal* under the pseudonyms 'John Helland' and 'Auspex' – a classical reference entirely lost on the majority of his peers. He once published a piece early in the 1930s on the use of combined air power and armoured forces – exactly as later used by the Germans in the Blitzkrieg years.

He did, however, become the Director of Training for the Indian Army and many of his infantry training methods were adopted by GHQ India for general use. With the coming of the war he was given command of a division in India, then took over 4th Indian at the end of 1941, by which time it was already in Egypt. While his division was waiting in reserve he had toured the front in Libya and realized that the planned Gazala Line, fifteen miles ahead of the fortress of Tobruk, was likely to lead to disaster. He strongly suggested to Lieutenant-General Neil Ritchie, then commander of the British Eighth Army, that Tobruk could be easily made impregnable and used as a springboard for attacking and defeating Rommel's Panzerarmee Afrika. This was ignored by both Ritchie and General Claude Auchinleck, then C-in-C Middle East. The Gazala Line was turned at the end of May 1942 and Tobruk surrendered on 21 June, arguably the nadir of the British Army so far in the war.

Whenever Tuker was allowed a voice and able to do things his way, British fortunes improved. At Wadi Akarit, in early April 1943, his 4th Indians turned the Axis line by assaulting through the mountains and coming round the back of the enemy positions. Towards the end of the Tunisian campaign he was given free rein to devise and execute Operation STRIKE, the battle to break through very strong German positions in the Medjerda Valley. Battles very rarely go entirely according to plan, but STRIKE did: a massive all-arms, supremely well-executed assault that was coordinated with MATAF and also used high-velocity heavy anti-aircraft guns in a ground role for the first time. STRIKE was all over in twenty-four hours, the path to Tunis laid wide open and the campaign finished a week later. It was also Tuker who accepted the Axis surrender from Generaloberst Hans-Jürgen von Arnim.

So why 4th Indian had been languishing ever since, unused in this most mountainous of countries, was bizarre to say the least. Montgomery did not care for Tuker – too clever and know-it-all by half for his liking; and there was no question that Tuker was seen as an outrider and a nonconformist and treated with a certain amount of suspicion as a result. He would surely have overcome this if he'd been as diplomatically astute as he was tactically so, and not quite so ready to reveal his exasperation and frustration; yet there was no doubt that the Allies had missed a trick in not bringing his division into the fray earlier.

They were, though, now on their way to Cassino, albeit subordinated to the New Zealanders, because Alexander had just created the New Zealand Corps under Lieutenant-General Sir Bernard Freyberg VC. It was not the first time this had happened; Freyberg had been given command of all Allied troops on Crete back in 1941 – disastrously so – and again in January 1943 in Tunisia, which had been much more successful. Freyberg was as brave as a lion, had won his VC in the First World War when he'd been wounded multiple times, was a personal friend of Churchill's and had a devotion to duty that was second to none. On the other hand he was not, by any reckoning, an intellectual, or indeed a great thinker and tactician like Tuker. Politically, however, with New Zealand punching massively above its weight in this war, it was inconceivable that the New Zealanders would play second fiddle to Tuker and 4th Indian; nor could the creation of a new corps really be avoided, as to have taken either V or XIII Corps from Eighth Army would have left it structurally off-balance. At any rate, two new divisions, fresh and at pretty much full strength, were now on their way across the leg of Italy, the new corps reinforced by a further eight field regiments of artillery. They could not arrive soon enough.

Yet with 168th Brigade on its way to Anzio and the rest of 56th Division soon to follow, General McCreery's X Corps was suddenly being thinned out a little as the grand juggling of troops continued. Those still dug in on the ridges and hills continued to push and probe, but they seemed unable to find a way to winkle the shattered 94. Division out of Castelforte and the remainder of the hills and peaks beyond. The front had become one of incessant artillery duels and active patrolling as the British desperately tried to find weak spots they might exploit and then force a breakthrough. Still in the line was the 56th Heavy Regiment, albeit further back than most with the immense range their big 7.2-inch guns could fire. 'Have not yet taken Castelforte,' noted RSM Jack Ward lugubriously on 1 February, 'in fact Jerry has counter-attacked from that position. We are gaining some ground on the right flank.' This was where 46th Division were now pushing through the mountains north of the village of Suio and immediately west of the Garigliano; they'd extended the line by several miles, clearing Monte Furito, Monte Fuga and Monte Ornito. A few days later, Ward reported that they were now gaining ground to the north-east of Castelforte around Monte Damiano, which had stubbornly remained in German hands. 'But the town has yet to fall,' he added. 'I could see our shells falling on there yesterday and any minute now we are going to have a shoot at a church tower, thought to be a Jerry OP.'

Captain Leonard Garland and 70th Field Regiment had been shifted southwards to support the ongoing operations of X Corps around Castelforte. He was now back commanding 449 Battery, his mood lurching from despair one moment to renewed optimism the next. 'Nostalgia not nearly as sharp as it was,' he noted, following the arrival of a package of books and photographs from his wife, Ann, 'replaced by a numbness to events and a deep seated confidence in future victory.' Incredibly, 70th Field Regiment had fired a staggering 100,000 shells in a little over two months; the CEF artillery had sent over 158,000 shells during their attack on Belvedere. How could they possibly lose with such an advantage in firepower? They couldn't, of course, but eventual victory, although certain enough, remained somewhere in the future, and how long that would be, and what road would take them there, was far less knowable. After all, they'd all thought they'd be in Rome before Christmas – and yet here they were. On 2 February Garland's spirits were given a further fillip by the news that he'd received an MC – a gallantry medal that was awarded very sparingly – but then a few days later he received a rather sad and wistful letter from Ann. 'Wonder why,' he noted, 'and what I can do about it, apart from going home?'

This war was demanding a huge amount from the mostly young people expected to fight it. Garland and his wife had married on 17 December 1942; she was a FANY – First Aid Nursing Yeomanry – and they'd met, fallen in love and married while he'd still been based in England. She was from Sunbury in Surrey, he from London, and they'd married at the King's Chapel in the Savoy Hotel on The Strand in London, had a honeymoon of one night, then a further night at the barracks in Aldershot – a 'hellish place' – then that had been it: after thanking her for marrying him, he'd said goodbye at 8.10 a.m. on Monday, 21 December 1942. He'd taken the train to Liverpool, boarded a troopship and sailed to North Africa and the war in the Mediterranean. Now, a little over a year since they'd last seen each other, he was on a hillside in southern Italy and she driving an ambulance in Falmouth in Cornwall.

They missed each other desperately. Memories, letters and the promise of being together again some sunny day often did more to tantalize than provide solace. She'd just sent him a scarf – her scarf – and he could smell her scent on it. 'Poor scarf,' he wrote, 'if it was led to believe it had found a good job caressing your dear neck it's in for disillusionment now: it's going to find it a rough life, and dirty.' But he was thrilled with it – a tactile link to her, which although a poor substitute for her arms was none the less a powerful aid to his imagination. 'Though often I dare not let my imagination wander too freely about you, Ann,' he added, 'it hurts a lot at times.'

He wrote to her about the battery CP, from where he was writing. Officers self-censored their letters so could write more freely than other ranks. His CP, he told her, was a rectangular hole in the ground about 4–5 feet deep and covered by a tent. To one side they had excavated a bit more and created a fire pit – it was blazing warmly as he wrote. 'By stepping outside on a bank,' he added, 'I can see in the bright moonlight across the valley a great mountain mass, the peaks gleaming silver with recent snow and the foothills sprinkled from time to time with the flashes from the bursts of our own shells.' Harassing fire from their own guns continued throughout the night, the ground trembling with every salvo and bits of earth crumbling from the edge of the dugout. Jerry, he told her, did not get much sleep. One of his fellow officers, Mike Frewer, was sat beside him, also writing a letter and also wearing a scarf sent from home; behind him next to the fire was their signaller reading *Picture Post*, a weekly British magazine, while an assistant signaller was thumbing a copy of *Reader's Digest*. 'Scattered around are our instruments and books, maps and protractors and intermingled mugs and plates, hats, letters, scraps of paper.' The air was heavy with the smell of woodsmoke and oranges. And yet, he told her, no matter where he was, he could shut out all other thoughts and think only of her. 'For me,' he wrote, 'however lousy the weather or depressed my mood, you are always there to beckon to a brighter, finer future – a good, peaceful, loving future. Ours.'

The 70th, however, were soon to be on the move again, posted back up to the southern side of the Liri Valley opposite Sant'Apollinare as the battle along the Garigliano ran out of steam. Casualties among all three British divisions in X Corps had been horrendous, but the Germans couldn't defend equally strongly everywhere, and with Baade's 90. Panzergrenadier being pulled out to Monte Cassino and General Schlemm's I Fallschirmjägerkorps being sent back to Anzio, only the very mauled 94. Infanterie-Division remained opposite the British. The progress of 46th Division had been all well and good, but the main opportunity still lay down through the Ausente Valley to Ausonia, the back door into the Liri Valley to the south.

The stumbling block, however, had been Monte Damiano and Castelforte, which, despite the very best efforts of 56th Division, simply hadn't yet been unlocked. This overlooked the Ausente Valley, so until this hill mass was cleared, the line was stuck. Back on 26 January, 5th Division had been lined up for another assault down the valley and the 2nd Inniskillings earmarked to take the lead in clearing a key peak on their southern side. Captain David Cole had been fearing the worst and had started to think his luck must surely run out, but when 56th Division again found themselves unable to clear Damiano the attack was called off – much to Cole's enormous relief. On 1 February, Cole wrote to his parents, his disillusionment all too obvious; after all, they'd been in the line for two weeks and although the enemy counter-attacks had lessened, the shelling was still heavy and every day they were losing more men. The battalion had been stripped bare by the fighting, while around them they were now confronted by a desolate landscape. 'The fields below us,' he wrote, 'which were once pleasantly green, are now brown and pocked with a thousand craters. The few houses within sight have been smashed to pieces. The roads are cratered and the verges littered with burnt-out trucks and new graves. We live in our trenches on the hillside through mist, drizzle and damp cold. It is strange how companionable the earth becomes. Cold clay seems comfortable against the cheek. A snail settles amicably on one's equipment; and insects set up houses inside one's clothes.'

The Commandos of the Special Service Brigade had been sent to bolster the bottom end of the line, but it was not enough and with no spare division – or armour and artillery to go with it – unfolding the Gustav Line here was another goal that was still tantalizingly out of reach.

Adolf Hitler had fired off a new directive to Kesselring on 28 January, demanding the 'Battle for Rome' be fought to the last man and declaring it one of vital and decisive importance. 'The battle must be hard and merciless,' he stated, 'not only against the enemy but against all officers and units who fail in this decisive hour.' This was clearly a warning shot to any of his generals wanting to indulge in talk about retreating to a new line. Despite the Führer's threats, however, General von Mackensen did offer a less hysterical appreciation to Kesselring on 3 February. The son of a First World War field marshal, von Mackensen was the epitome of a Prussian aristocratic general, with his head shaved at the sides and back, a monocle, permanent frown and always immaculate in his appearance. He had become deeply disillusioned with the leadership and loathed Kesselring, whom he regarded as a middle-class Luftwaffe popinjay largely unqualified for the post of commander-in-chief in Italy. A foil to Kesselring's unbridled optimism, von Mackensen was as little enthused about fighting at Anzio as Lucas was, and since reaching the beachhead a week earlier had seen nothing to alter his view that the best and only sensible course of action was to pull back to the Gothic Line, now under construction between Pisa on the west coast and Rimini on the Adriatic. None the less, he'd been given his orders, and he did now have more than 95,000 troops under his command, admittedly of very varying quality, and with more coming too from Germany and France. From 800 troops on 22 January to nearly 100,000 was quite a speedy build-up, from whichever angle one looked at it.

Despite this numerical superiority, however, von Mackensen was far from convinced that he could kick the Allies back into the sea as things stood, despite Hitler's exhortations. His plans for a counter-attack had also been thrown by the Allies' own attack on 30 January, so instead he intended to regroup his forces and, to begin with, straighten out the British salient up around Campoleone. Further developments would depend on how that operation panned out and what further reinforcements were sent to him.

His first line-straightening operation began late on the afternoon of 3 February with the Kampfgruppe Pfeifer moving to attack the western flank of the salient and Kampfgruppe Gräser, made up from units of 3. Panzergrenadier and the newly arriving 715. Infanterie-Division, fresh from France, attacking the eastern side. The attack on the salient had already been postponed once after Allied bombers had dropped nearly 200 tons of bombs on German ammunition dumps and supply lines on 1 and 2 February. Now, though, on the afternoon of the 3rd, the weather was filthy – freezing-cold and wet – and von Mackensen wanted to postpone the assault again. Kesselring was having none of it, however; bad weather meant little Allied air cover, which, as far as he was concerned, was an advantage that outweighed the disadvantages of operating in the wet.

That was all very well, but attacking in the rain was problematic, as the Allies had repeatedly discovered; the mud, the wet, the misery all conspired against the men trying to make progress. Hans-Paul Liebschner, still in the wadi country to the south-west of Campoleone with Kampfgruppe Gericke, was soaked through, as they all were. Food hadn't come through to their positions in this strange, rolling landscape of steep, narrow gullies and they were exhausted too; there hadn't been much chance for sleep the past few days because of the incessant artillery fire. What's more, much of the attacking force in Kampfgruppe Pfeiffer came from units of 64. Infanterie-Division, last seen in action over on the Adriatic when, at the end of November, it had been annihilated by Eighth Army and Allied air power. Yet here it was, miraculously built up again in just two months almost from scratch, but now mostly consisting of troops even less well trained and motivated than those in its previous iteration.

None the less, German artillery was meting out the kind of pummelling normally dished up to the Germans by the Allies, and the British infantry battalions, from 3rd Brigade at the top of the thumb-like salient to the 24th Guards at the neck, were strung out in their salient. And although dug in, they were hardly in the best defensive positions because they occupied a very narrow line either side of the railway line and the Via Anziate, with their backs to one another, and being assaulted from both sides.

The length of this thumb sticking up was only around three miles in length and no more than a few hundred yards wide. Holding the line in the middle on the western side were the 1st Irish Guards – Alexander's old regiment – with the 1st Duke of Wellington's on their right, Scots Guards on their left, and the 6th Gordon Highlanders at their back. Temporarily commanding the Irish Guards was Major Michael Gordon-Watson, thirty years old and a former Oxford University history graduate. Gordon-Watson had joined the army back in 1934 after signing up for the Territorial Army and enjoying it enough to decide to make a career of it. He had been posted to the 1st Battalion soon after and had subsequently seen action in Palestine, where he'd won the first of two MCs. Since the start of the war he'd served in Norway in 1940, where he'd won his second MC, and then in Tunisia before the battalion had been posted to Italy with 1st Division at the end of 1943. Forthright, adventurous and a natural leader of men, Gordon-Watson now found himself needing to draw on all his vast experience as the battalion prepared to face the first major German onslaught on the bridgehead.

Gordon-Watson held an 'O' group at 9.50 p.m. for his company commanders and the attached mortars and company from the Middlesex Machine Gun Regiment. 'O' stood for 'orders', and such a gathering was a simple briefing and a chance to talk through plans and expectations. Mortars and artillery concentrations had been worked out for various locations and were known as 'SOS' and 'DF' – direct fire – targets. The idea was that via a simple radio and field telephone message, a request for one of these concentrations could be ordered and delivered swiftly. OPs had also been set up because most of Gordon-Watson's men were on a low, undulating ridge immediately west of the railway line. All in all, he felt reasonably happy that he and his battalion were ready for whatever the Germans might hurl at them.

The enemy's attack began with an intense five-minute barrage, which the Micks – as the Irish Guards were known – weathered easily enough. Recognizing that this was the prelude to an attack, Gordon-Watson then ordered up the prearranged SOS and direct-fire tasks from the supporting mortars and artillery, all of which duly screamed, whistled and screeched over. A second five-minute enemy barrage followed but fell behind them, and soon after that, from his CP down by the railway line, he received various radio messages from No. 3 Company, on the left, southern part of their front, that hundreds of Germans, at least one battalion in strength, were advancing towards them. One of his platoon commanders, Lieutenant Hall, was shot in the liver but managed to crawl to the Scots Guards' lines, while his machine-gunners, including Vickers teams attached to him from the Middlesex Regiment, mowed down the attacking Germans in waves. Despite this, the enemy continued pressing forward, and at 11.15 p.m. Captain McInerney, commanding 3 Company, reported his position as having being overrun. 'And this,' noted Gordon-Watson, 'was the last I heard of him.'

With one of his companies lost, the situation was clearly serious, to say the least, as there was now a gap in the lines between the Micks' positions and the Scots Guards to their left and south. The danger was that the enemy would cut in behind them and that everyone to the north, including the three battalions of 3rd Brigade, would be encircled and wiped out. Gordon-Watson immediately contacted Brigade HQ and asked for some Shermans to be with them by first light; he was confident he could hold the enemy at bay until then because in their attack on 3 Company the Germans had set fire to a haystack. 'This acted as a permanent parachute flare,' noted Gordon-Watson, 'and each time the Germans formed up for an attack in the light of those flames they were plastered by the gunners of the Scots Guards and the machine-gunners of the Middlesex Regiment with us.'

Gordon-Watson was still anxious about enemy troops infiltrating them, however. Flares were sent up regularly, but he worried they might exhaust their arsenal before dawn. He was also concerned that the Germans might be creeping along the railway track towards his CP, which was by the bridge that crossed over the track. To counter this he ordered up the Carrier Platoon to surround his CP and positioned his best Bren-gunner, Sergeant McConnell, in an ideal position under a knocked-out enemy 88mm gun where he had both great views and was well hidden. Finally, he also called up two M10 tank destroyers with instructions for them to liberally use their machine guns as well as their 3-inch main anti-tank guns.

Despite the proximity of the attackers, Gordon-Watson remained confident that once dawn came they would soon be able to clear up the situation. A section of 3-inch mortars also seemed to have gone missing – presumably taken prisoner – but he had been assured by Brigade that the tanks he'd called for were on their way – and a whole squadron, which meant nineteen in all. 'So, with this news,' noted Gordon-Watson, 'one felt perfectly happy that the whole situation could be retrieved in a matter of hours.' Four further M10s also arrived before dawn and so began a duel, with Sergeant McConnell on his Bren gun firing from the knocked-out 88mm, Corporal Carr firing from the house next to the railway bridge, and the tank busters all trying to knock out the four or five German machine-gunners who had appeared overnight on their western part of the line.

The Shermans arrived but were caught up with the Gordons behind them on the eastern side of the road, and so offered no immediate help to the Micks. To clear up enemy MG posts, Gordon-Watson really needed the help of these tanks – there seemed to him to be no point in wasting valuable lives by sending infantry against them when the tanks were so close and would, he hoped, soon be available. Yet as the morning developed, the chatter of small arms ringing out above the incessant boom of artillery, suddenly a number of German tanks – Panzer IVs and Tigers – began to appear from the north. This seemed quite a major new threat, but the M10s, tucked in behind the railway bridge, did manage to knock out three Tigers and one Panzer IV and there was not much sign of further German armour pushing southwards.

Defending a thumb-shaped salient like the one the Guards and 3rd Brigade were still trying to hold was a confusing and disorientating business. Bullets, mortars and shells seemed to be coming from every direction. German machine guns had a much faster rate of fire than the Bren and other Allied machine guns – often more than double – and made a sawing *brrrrrppp* sound rather than a more steady *rat-a-tat*. Mortars were comparatively short-range and low-velocity and could be very hard to anticipate, as the sucking sound they generated as they came in could only be heard for a couple of seconds before they landed and detonated. They could also come in very quick succession; it was possible to load and fire an 80mm mortar, for example, every three seconds. Artillery shells shrieked as they passed through the air and could be heard for far longer than a mortar – and the bigger the shell, the louder their air-sucking shriek. Whether one heard them, though, rather depended on what else was going on. Nebelwerfers screamed and moaned. Together, the sound of all this different ordnance was immensely loud. The ground trembled, men quickly became deafened; acoustic shock was not uncommon – the ears simply shutting down and unable to convey the din to the brain. The air was often thick with the sharp stench of explosive and smoke; it caught in the back of the throat, made eyes sting, made the heart pound. And this was all happening here, in this narrow corridor in the Anzio Plain, in winter time, in the rain and the cold, with the ground – already slick with mud – made so much worse by being increasingly churned up. The landscape was largely flat to the east, but there were strange ridges and gullies west of the road; the railway sat perched on an embankment, while round about were tracks and farm buildings – so cover of sorts, but moving around was difficult because anyone who did so was invariably spotted almost immediately. A person who could be seen was a person who could be cut down.

As the day wore on, the situation seemed caught in the balance. Gordon-Watson's battalion were clinging to their positions despite 3 Company having been overrun, but the promised tanks were still further south fighting with the lower part of the Gordons' line and the Recce Regiment next to them. Up ahead, the Dukes, King's Shropshire Light Infantry – KSLI – and Foresters of 3rd Brigade were also still holding the tip of the salient despite the threat of being pinched out by German armour.

And then there was a sudden turn in the battle. 'About this time,' noted Gordon-Watson, 'one of the biggest tragedies and most disgraceful things I have ever seen occurred.' It was early afternoon and to the south he could see the Shermans and infantry bringing in as many as 100 prisoners, but at the same time, at the northern end of the Gordons' position, an even larger number of men were surrendering to the enemy. Gordon-Watson was dumbfounded. He could think of no reason why they should do this. 'No one was more surprised than the Germans,' he wrote. 'It seemed to us that the Germans would have been only too delighted to have been taken prisoners themselves.'

Gordon-Watson desperately tried to rectify the position but with 3 Company gone, and No. 1 and No. 2 Company already a composite, he really didn't have enough manpower. What was needed were those tanks, but despite his repeated calls on the radio they still didn't move up the road. In no time, he saw German MG teams moving into the now empty Gordons' positions; so, getting hold of a couple of Brens, he and Guardsman Montgomery got themselves into a decent position and poured fire on to the new arrivals, as well as on a Tiger crew bailing out. They also shot up some more enemy troops as they tried to occupy a house on the far side of the railway. 'This little episode,' he noted, 'brought back the fire quite sharply but definitely made one feel better.'

Even so, it was clear that he now needed to move his Battalion HQ a little out of harm's way as it was by the bridge opposite the abandoned Gordons' positions. He did, though, still have the support of the Vickers machine-gunners of the Middlesex Regiment; these weapons, first developed before the last war, were mounted on a tripod and water-cooled and could keep up a steady rate of 450–500 rounds per minute. Certainly, the Vickers crew helped save the battalion that day. Gordon-Watson had seen them slaughter a mass of enemy the previous night in the light of the burning haystack and now watched as some 150 ill-trained Germans from 65. Division were caught trying to form up; they were skittled ruthlessly. The Middlesex men also pinned down and knocked out at least seven MG posts; while those on the German MG42 could only fire short bursts and had to repeatedly switch red-hot barrels, the Vickers could keep pounding away all day so long as there were belts of ammunition to be fed into them. Gordon-Watson reckoned they must have killed at least 200 enemy troops.

Even so, by mid-afternoon it was clear they had no choice but to escape south because they were now being attacked on both sides and the M10s had long since pulled back for rearming and refuelling, which had left the Micks and the Middlesex machine-gunners rather on their own. Enemy shells were raining down on them, so too mortars, and machine guns were pouring bullets into their positions too. One single shell from an enemy 105mm killed an entire section of ten men. However, just as all seemed lost, reinforcements then turned up. The 168th Brigade from 56th Division had arrived that morning and the London Scottish were sent straight up the Via Anziate and into the fray, this time with the Shermans accompanying them. This allowed No. 4 Company to join in, and in so doing they captured 150 enemy troops while the London Scottish swiftly retook the positions lost by the Gordons. The battered troops of Kampfgruppe Pfeiffer had had enough and pulled back, which allowed 3rd Brigade, stranded and in danger of being encircled, the chance to pull out overnight. 'The battle', wrote Gordon-Watson three days later, 'became very fluid at this time and all that we can say is that we must have killed, wounded or captured a very large number of Germans.'

That was true enough, but the two British brigades in the salient had been hammered too. By dawn on the 5th the Irish Guards could muster only 270, a long way short of the 845-strong they should have been; the story was much the same for the other five battalions holding the salient. General Penney now very sensibly ordered a new front line that ran through Aprilia roughly west–east and out on to the Buonriposo Ridge, slightly south-west of the Factory, and which stood at the head of the wadi country. It meant both that the salient had been largely reduced and that the Battle of the Thumb was over.

CHAPTER 16

Point 593

LATE ON THE AFTERNOON of 3 February, the new commander of 2nd Battalion of the 135th, Lieutenant-Colonel Jerome Kessner, joined the Company H men up on Colle Maiola on the Monte Cassino massif. The battalion was attempting to make a reasonably firm base up there, having been pushed back a couple of hundred yards by Major Rudolf Kratzert's men. Sergeant Ralph Schaps had just used triangulation to establish precisely where they were. Pinpointing their positions was important, partly because they needed to feed accurate coordinates and map grid references to the artillery, but also so that they could liaise with other units of the 135th. Schaps was asked by Lieutenant Baker to show Kessner their position on the map but the colonel told him he was wrong, that they weren't on Maiola but instead were holding Point 593. Schaps protested as forcibly as his rank would allow but Kessner was having none of it. They were, he insisted, on 593.

This was a bad mistake, and hard to explain, because Point 593 lay at the southern end of the ridge, a long hill that was already being renamed 'Snakeshead'. Point 593 – 'Calvary Hill' – was the single most important feature of the entire massif because although it wasn't the highest spot, its position at the end of the ridge dominated the area. From here, to the south-east, one could look down on the saddle that dropped away to the fields farmed by the monks at the abbey. The ground then rose a little again to the promontory at the end of the massif on which the abbey itself stood, but from Point 593 one was looking across and down at the abbey perhaps half a mile away. To the north was Monte Castellone, which continued in a long ridge towards Colle Sant'Angelo but also forked, a spur of the ridge – soon to be renamed 'Phantom Ridge' – running down towards Albaneta. Colle Sant'Angelo was also half a mile away. The southern end of Point 593 then dropped very dramatically – almost vertically – 200 feet or so; directly beneath was a track and blasted out of the rock were caves in which German troops – and ammunition – were entirely protected. The track led round the base of Point 593 to another area of mountain pastures and to the Albaneta Farm, also belonging to the abbey. This included the Masseria Albaneta, a large stone dwelling, and another cluster of buildings 200 yards away. Between this valley of pastures and the two ridges of Snakeshead and Colle Sant'Angelo was a deep and comparatively narrow ravine that ran down to the Liri Valley floor and the Via Casilina. All these features could be seen with an all-round 360-degree sweep from Point 593, and even more so now because, as part of the early preparations for the defence of this key spot, every tree and every bush had been cleared. Monte Cassino had become an outcrop of bare ridges, with thin soil and nothing more than low, thorny scrub.

It was because of Point 593's unique vantage point that General Baade had made it the focal point for his defence of the massif. The idea was to use it as the apex of a figure-of-eight, with two rough circles of defensive posts meeting there. To the north-west of Point 593 the circle dropped down into the pastures around Albaneta, up to Colle Sant'Angelo, then down again into the ravine – a haven for mortars – before circling back up to the foot of the cliff face beneath this key apex point. To the south-east the line ran along Snakeshead Ridge for a stretch then dropped down into the saddle before rising up to the foot of the bastions of the abbey; the road from the town offered particularly good vantage points back across the saddle to Snakeshead from its final corner. The line then ran along the northern side of the abbey before working up the southern slopes beneath Point 593. The two circles were interconnected, with strongpoints of machine-gun posts all around each, mortars hidden in crevices and out of sight to the rear and in the ravine. It meant the Germans could give enfiladed fire from any point – in other words, any Allied troops trying to pierce these two circles could expect to be fired on from more than one direction. It also meant that anyone trying to take and hold Point 593 would then have bullets and mortars poured on to them from both the abbey hill and Colle Sant'Angelo, while observers on both these neighbouring high points could also direct artillery and mortar fire on to any spot – Point 593, the saddle running up to the abbey, or around Albaneta – the moment any kind of incursion was made.

As Baade was well aware, this skilful siting of his defences meant that those holding these positions around the two circles didn't need to be elite troops. They just needed to be able to direct fire and fire a machine gun. What's more, the standard German machine gun by early 1944, the MG42, was not designed to be accurate. Rather, its main function was to offer a huge weight of lead – bullets spraying about all over the place at a rate of twenty-three per second – in an arc. Anyone caught by multiple cones of bullets coming from these weapons from differing directions would very quickly be pinned to the ground; this would then allow mortars to paste the same area. If any Allied troops were still able to move they could then be finished off with hand grenades, sub-machine guns and the new assault rifles that had been issued to the H-und-D and 1. Fallschirmjäger. These had been developed by Hugo Schmeisser and were halfway between a standard rifle and the shorter-range sub-machine gun; they could fire at a rate of around 500–600 rounds per minute and took a curving thirty-round magazine that slotted underneath the breech. This was the world's first assault rifle and, unlike most German weaponry, it was made from stamped metal rather than machined steel, was decidedly rough and ready, but for the kind of ranges troops were operating on up in the mountains was ideal. Whereas the effective range of a sub-machine gun such as the MP40 was really only about 20 yards, the MP44 could be used reasonably accurately at 75–100 yards.

The really key point about the figure-of-eight defence around Point 593 was, however, that it required comparatively few men to hold it, which was just as well because Baade did not have very many. A machine-gun team was two men. An 80mm mortar, three men. Troops were needed to lug ammunition around and follow up attacks, but maintaining the defences required neither special skill nor huge numbers, and the only way the Allies would be able to overwhelm Point 593 – and the entire massif – would be by crushing more than 50 per cent of both defensive circles at the same time. To do that they needed to understand how the system was laid out. The 135th Infantry, now clinging to half of Snakeshead Ridge and Monte Castellone, had no idea about these defensive rings, however.

Nor did the 2nd Battalion commander, Colonel Kessner, even know where his men were. It's hard to understand how he could possibly have got this wrong; after all, their maps showed contours, but he was not to be told otherwise. This meant that 168th Infantry, moving up on the left flank of the 2nd 135th, were preparing to attack across the saddle that lay between Snakeshead and the abbey, believing that Point 593 was in American hands. It was not.

Commandant Paul Gandoët and the survivors of his mixed force of men from the shattered 4ème Régiment de Tirailleurs Tunisiens were finally relieved on the night of 3–4 February after ten nights of almost no sleep and ten days of combat in which the regiment had been decimated. Bodies still littered the slopes of Monte Abate and Point 862, yet for all the losses, for all the tragedy that had played out, these survivors felt a very real sense of pride too; French honour had been at stake. French honour had, they believed, been restored.

They climbed down off the mountain the following morning, slowly heading along the ravine they had climbed up nine days earlier. Signs of the fighting were everywhere: burnt vegetation, rocks still stained with blood, abandoned weapons, helmets and other detritus. Rocks shattered by shell blasts. By the time they were down in the valley an evening mist was forming, which was helpful because they still had to cross 500 yards of ground that was under the watching eye of German observers on Cifalco. Gandoët paused a moment with Lieutenant Jordy, who was the only other officer still standing. Incredibly, Jordy had not suffered so much as a scratch, and now that they all knew they'd made it there was a sudden lightness to their step; exhaustion, for the moment at any rate, was forgotten. Together, Gandoët and Jordy discussed which route to take across the mouth of the Secco Valley and they decided to split into two groups. Gandoët and Jordy were among those taking the left-hand course; the first stretch was to the remains of a shepherd's house 300 yards away, then the second to the edge of Sant'Elia. It was agreed that the second column would not move until the first had gone at least 100 yards.

They walked calmly but then, 50 yards or so from the shepherd's house, Jordy said, 'Sir, let's run.'

'Run if you like,' Gandoët replied. 'But not me.'

Jordy took off, but at that moment the familiar air-sucking whoosh filled their ears then shells crashed around them. Gandoët was knocked off his feet by the blast; his wrist was struck but as he staggered to his feet he hurried towards the sheepfold and there saw Jordy, lying on the ground, his body convulsing. Gandoët crouched down but moments later the young lieutenant was dead. The doctor, Ravelonanosy, had also been wounded, another of his men killed, and then he heard his name being called and Gandoët turned to see it was Gacem Ben Mohammed, lying against the embankment having been thrown by the blast. Both his legs had been ripped from him and Gandoët gazed at him, aghast, his pink flesh burnt and blistered. The rifleman looked at his commander then fumbled for his field dressing and handed it to him. 'Take it, my commander,' said Ben Mohammed. 'You don't have to die.' Numbly, Gandoët took it from him. Then Gacem Ben Mohammed died too.

Gandoët and the last survivors made it to the aid post where, after having had his wrist treated, he swiftly discharged himself. Unbeknown to him, however, he was suffering from a fractured femur and eye socket as well as concussion. Yet he knew he'd been one of the lucky ones. Belvedere and Point 470 had cost his battalion alone every one of his officers, forty non-commissioned officers and 363 tirailleurs killed or wounded. What a meat grinder the Cassino front had become.

Up on the massif, Doc Ryder paused his men for a couple of days as it had become painfully clear that a handful of infantrymen creeping along the crest of an exposed ridge were not going to get very far without considerably greater amounts of firepower. More ammunition, more men and more supplies were brought up on to the mountain. The weather up there was terrible: icy-cold, with a whipping wind, occasional snow and rain much of the rest of the time. Nebelwerfer batteries hidden by the abbey and in 'Death Gully' – the narrow gorge that ran down to the valley floor from Albaneta – regularly pounded the American positions with 'screaming meanies', clusters of five or six 280mm mortars, whining in and shattering the rocks around them. The trouble was, although there were folds in the ground and plenty of rocks, it was next to impossible to dig down. The blast effect of each mortar, Nebelwerfer or artillery shell was made worse because there was only one way for the shrapnel and thousands of razor-sharp shards of rock to go, and that was outwards. One could crouch and shelter behind rocks but it was impossible to get oneself below ground up there. It made the men horribly exposed – both to the brutal weather and even more to the brutal enemy fire.

More Fallschirmjäger units were now heading to Cassino, including Kampfgruppe Schulz. Oberst Schulz's 1. Regiment, which had been sent to firefight at Anzio, had fought in the Allied attack of 30 January, but on 3 February began hurriedly heading to Cassino instead. That day it numbered around 320 men, so 10 per cent of full strength. Kratzert, however, having halted the advance of 2nd Battalion of the 135th Infantry, now hastily sent men up on to Colle Sant'Angelo and Phantom Ridge under the cover of darkness on the night of the 4th to take over positions there from the H-und-D-Division and stop the advance of the 3rd 135th Infantry. He also moved his command post down to Albaneta, which he renamed the 'Kastelli'. Up on the ridges, the H-und-D troops couldn't hand over their positions quickly enough; Kratzert thought they seemed like men abandoning a sinking ship.

Dawn on 5 February revealed their new position; from Albaneta he had clear views to Monte Castellone, Colle Sant'Angelo and Phantom Ridge as well as up towards Snakeshead Ridge and Point 593. On the other hand, the farm buildings stood so conspicuously alone on this low saddle that the moment the Americans realized they were there they could expect to be hammered by Allied artillery. It was also slightly worrying to see an American patrol walk past the ruins having come down from Phantom Ridge; fortunately for Kratzert, the Americans did not know they were there, but he had also assumed that his men, whom he'd posted up there, would have seen them first and shot them or taken them all prisoner. Albaneta soon came under enemy artillery fire and Kratzert realized that, no matter how good the views, it was far too exposed for a command post. Even though it was still daylight, Kratzert and his ordnance officer, Oberleutnant Teske, decided to recce for an alternative location but were shot at by an American machine-gunner. Although Kratzert was unscathed, Teske was hit and soon after bled to death. This tragedy confirmed what Kratzert had already feared: that the Americans had far more of the massif in their hands than he'd at first appreciated.

This, and the preceding days, were when the golden opportunity to break through presented itself to the Allies: when the defenders on Monte Cassino were still mostly made up from the H-und-D-Division, when Baade's figure-of-eight had yet to be applied, when units such as Kratzert's were trying to do too much with the very small numbers they had available. Even more vulnerable was the line further to the north; there, beyond Belvedere and towards Terelle, the mountain mass was higher above the valley floor and wider too, but once up there it was far easier ground on which to fight with few of the hidden crevices and gullies that were such a feature of the Monte Cassino massif. Perhaps more importantly, nor were there any Fallschirmjäger or men from 90. Panzergrenadier stepping into the weapons pits and hidden crags.

That very narrow window was rapidly closing, however. While Kratzert set up a new command post in the cellar of the Masseria Albaneta, a Fallschirmjäger MG-Bataillon reached Monte Cassino and began slotting into posts of the south-east circle on the figure-of-eight, around Monastery Hill up around the abbey. Because of Colonel Kessner's mistake, 3rd Battalion of the 168th Infantry, now arriving on the left flank of Ralph Schaps and the rest of the 2nd 135th, attacked across the saddle, believing Point 593 was in American hands as Kessner had insisted was the case. The 3rd 168th lost 165 men, cut down with brutal efficiency by the newly arrived Fallschirmjäger machine-gunners. The mistake cost Kessner his job.

Meanwhile, the 2nd 135th were pushing on along Snakeshead and by the afternoon of 6 February were on the slopes either side, just a stone's throw from the peak and the end of the ridge. Now, though, the figure-of-eight began to make itself felt, with machine-gun fire and mortars pouring in from Monastery Hill beneath the abbey but also from Kratzert's men down below at Albaneta, his mortars in Death Gully and his machine-gunners up on the Colle Sant'Angelo and Phantom Ridge. Colonel Ward, the commander of 135th Infantry, had sent up cooks, drivers, supply troops and others to bolster his rapidly depleted companies at the coalface. Even Major Don Landon, the new 2nd Battalion commander, was fighting up there alongside Ralph Schaps and the rest of his men. At one point, as dusk was falling, the Red Bulls stormed the end of Snakeshead Ridge, shooting from the hip, bayonets fixed to rifles, in what became very close-quarter fighting. Schaps was knocked to the ground by a rifle butt in the jaw and lost a couple of teeth but managed to get up again. 'There was a lot of screaming and cursing,' he noted, 'as we were not going to let the Goddam Krauts push us off the hill.' Schaps had reached an adrenalin-fuelled zone where he no longer felt any fear but instead a visceral hatred of the enemy. Their frenzied determination paid off. 'Finally,' he wrote, 'the Krauts seemed to disappear.' As night fell the fighting died down and Schaps and his fellows took over the German positions around Point 593. They were now looking out over the Liri Valley and almost directly down on to the Via Casilina.

One of his fellows found a bottle of brandy abandoned by the Germans, which Schaps swilled around his mouth. After spitting out some blood and more chipped pieces of tooth, he took a couple more slugs and started to feel better. He could hardly believe he'd just been involved in hand-to-hand combat. The dead were now strewn all over the ridge, while the white limestone rock was becoming blasted and shattered. This did, at least, give the Red Bulls something with which to hastily build small stone sangars. In Company H, Lieutenant Baker had been wounded and was replaced overnight by a new officer, fresh to combat. 'He was a gung-ho type who couldn't wait to kill the enemy,' noted Schaps. 'We told him that he would get plenty of chances first thing the next morning.' Despite these warnings, the lieutenant decided to head out on a night recce of the position all on his own. He simply disappeared in the night; the following morning there was no sign of him.

Meanwhile, General Baade realized that the loss of Point 593 was potentially catastrophic. For his defensive system to work he really needed more men to fill positions around both circles. Von Senger was also so concerned to learn that the Americans could now see the Via Casilina that he decided he had to speak out, and formally urged Kesselring to pull them back to the Caesar position. His forces had been so reduced by the recent fighting that they were now holding on by a thread, and with the Allies almost within touching distance of the Liri Valley it seemed madness to keep fighting when they could pull back, reorganize themselves and bring both AOK 14 and AOK 10 side by side across the peninsula just to the south of Rome. However, in light of Hitler's warning of 28 January against any officers who failed to show the right determination to keep fighting, von Senger was taking quite a risk. Fortunately for von Senger, Kesselring was not about to snitch on one of his senior corps commanders to the Führer; but nor was he going to acquiesce. 'This proposal,' noted von Senger tersely, 'was not approved.' The desperate plugging of gaps, shifting of troops, and flinging broken, battered combat units no longer fit for battle into the fray over and over again would continue, but this time they would be thrown on to the Monte Cassino massif. There would be no pulling back.

While the 135th Infantry were up on the massif, the 133rd Regiment, meanwhile, were pushing south, past the wrecked barracks that were now in their hands and into Cassino. On the afternoon of 3 February, two leading infantry companies and a platoon of five Shermans reached the first houses, clearing them one at a time. Urban fighting was a particularly difficult business. Every street was largely without cover for those attacking and with ideal fields of fire for those defending. The defenders had numerous protected firing positions, hiding places and potential ambush sites. Fighting in towns was necessarily close-quarters, casualties were always high and the strain on the nerves – with every step bringing potential mortal danger – particularly severe. Apart from dense woods or jungle, there was no other combat environment in which horizons were so limited; keeping any kind of control on what was going on was very difficult indeed. The Canadians, during the Ortona battle in December, had recognized they needed the firepower of tanks to get into a street, but tanks were also very vulnerable to short-range anti-tank weapons, such as the new Panzerfaust, rather like the American bazooka, and to grenades being lobbed from above. The Canadian infantry had developed a technique known as 'mouse-holing': infantry would burst into a house, work their way up, blast a hole in the next building in the terrace, then work their way down and continue again. The effectiveness of such techniques took time to spread, but the terraced streets of Ortona were not replicated in Cassino, where most buildings, especially at the edge of town, stood alone, unattached to their neighbours.

Instead, the technique adopted by Companies I and K of 133rd Infantry was to approach each building with a squad of men, half approaching the building while the others, and the Shermans, gave covering fire. Those near the house would lob grenades into the lower rooms, wait for the explosion then storm in. Any surviving Germans in the building would have to be on the floors above, so those giving cover outside would fire rifle grenades in through the upper windows, which would force the enemy within to go down a floor where they'd then be promptly killed or taken prisoner. This approach carried them to the first crossroads in town, but they increasingly came under fire. The third tank clattering in was hit, which then prevented the escape of the first two. With their route back out now blocked, they decided to hammer the buildings ahead with their main guns and machine guns while the infantry stormed two buildings on the far side of the crossroads. The trouble was, they were under fire from Castle Hill, which directly overlooked them, and were confronting increasingly heavy resistance. What's more, they'd attacked on a narrow axis, and as they inched forward they left men stationed in each of the buildings they'd cleared. This meant their numbers were thinning; the further they pushed into the town the more they began to run short of infantrymen. Really, they needed to swamp one end of the entire town, clearing each part completely. Instead, only Companies I and K had been sent forward and that was nothing like enough. With no reinforcements anywhere to be seen, overnight they pulled back out again, the tanks managing to inch past the Sherman that had been knocked out earlier.

This in turn meant they would have to start all over again the following day. It wasn't a very effective or efficient way to try and clear the town.

General Mark Clark had headed back up to his Forward CP at Anzio on 6 February. 'Heavy fighting continues on the Cassino front,' ran a signal he received that night from Al Gruenther back at his Main HQ. '135 Regiment is near monastery. Ryder has hopes of surrounding it this afternoon.' This was decidedly more cheering news; at long last, it looked as though his repeated bludgeoning of the Gustav Line was about to achieve a major breakthrough. Gruenther did report, however, that Keyes reckoned the Red Bulls needed the full weight of the Texas Division to help get them over the line. He suggested bringing the troops now facing Terelle southwards to support the Red Bulls. Keyes and Ryder were still blind to the much, much easier axis of advance the Terelle front offered. Clark agreed to this move; after all, it sounded like a breakthrough was imminent and it always paid to exploit potential success. And right now he was at Anzio, so was dependent on the counsel of his Chief of Staff and his commanders on the ground.

What's more, although the situation at Anzio seemed to him to be fairly well in hand, there was still much that concerned him. Shipping was an ongoing source of considerable worry now that most of the LSTs had left the theatre. A consequence was a shortage of ammunition and rations, and artillery was limited to twenty-five rounds per gun per day until a special shipment from the United States arrived – due on 3 March. General Penney had lost a number of anti-tank guns as well as troops; Truscott was also short of 2,400 men. On the other hand, he was pleased to see the work going on to prepare a series of three defensive lines: the immediate front, an intermediate one, and what was being called the Canal Line – based along the Mussolini Canal.

What was clear to all, however, was that any thought of going on the offensive and striking to the hills had long gone. Lucas had already put the entire corps on to a defensive footing, but there was now a widespread atmosphere of besiegement – and this despite an enemy attack against 3rd Division on the evening of the 6th that had got nowhere, a small victory that should have given the defenders a bit of confidence. Rather, Lucas decided that the Allies' task in the immediate term was to dig in and make sure the Germans were unable to throw them back into the sea. Such a defensive mindset, however, at a time when the war's overall outcome was no longer supposed to be in doubt, was not doing morale much good. 'A doomlike quality hangs over the beachhead,' noted Audie Murphy. 'Just what it is I cannot say, but it is everywhere.' It was in the wind, in the rain, in the mud that got into everything, and in the growing number of cases of trench foot. 'And, above it,' he added, 'it is in the eyes of the men.' He was now platoon sergeant despite still being only nineteen; Murphy was far too young to be so disillusioned and world-weary yet he couldn't help himself. There had been no thrill in promotion.

Hans-Paul Liebschner and his comrades were finding the Anzio front every bit as depressing, although he was relieved he'd survived the salient battle – one in which he'd been involved in four separate assaults on just one day alone. On a number of occasions he'd been ordered to take prisoners back to Kampfgruppe Gericke headquarters and had been struck by how exhausted and defeated they had looked. 'With their arms above their head,' he noted, 'and huddled together for self-protection, only their dull eyes in grey faces gave some indication that they were still under the living.' Yet the battle had cost Kampfgruppe Gericke dearly as well.

He and the rest of the battle group were still holding the line a couple of miles to the west of the Via Anziate, opposite the recently arrived 45th Thunderbirds. The artillery fire seemed incessant, they were living in holes in the ground, insufficient rations were reaching them so he and his comrades were always hungry and they were all suffering from chronic sleep deprivation. The losses, too, were debilitating. He was still struggling to clear the first dead bodies he'd seen from his mind. As a company runner, he'd been hurrying through one of the wadis soon after reaching the front and had spoken briefly to some young lads manning a mortar, teenagers just like he was. A short while later, he came back through to find they'd all been killed. 'They were all huddled around,' he noted, 'all dead, and looking a fearful sight because they were really all blown to pieces.'

Then, on the morning of 8 February, it began to rain – and really hard, in slanting streaks. Liebschner and his comrades were soaked to the skin. So too was Audie Murphy and his platoon. Their whole area quickly turned to a sea of mud, pulling at their feet like quicksand. They began scooping out the water with their helmets but quickly gave up. Then heavier than usual enemy shelling began. When a shell landed close by, the soft walls of the dugouts crumbled, prompting furious renewed digging to clear the morass. On the other hand, while rain meant there was no flying on either side, it also meant enemy armour wouldn't be getting very far either. From an Allied perspective, that was very much to the good because the previous evening, 7 February, von Mackensen had renewed his attack, and once again it was down the Via Anziate.

'3.10am,' Lucas had noted in his diary in the early hours of the 7th. 'The dope is that the German will attack with all his strength at 4am. I am as ready as I can be. I hope it is enough. I must not lose.' He was not a man sounding flush with confidence. Near to his headquarters an ammunition dump was on fire and making a heck of a racket as ordnance was exploding. Enemy artillery was also shelling Anzio and Nettuno again, although Lucas was struggling to tell which was the sound of fresh shells whooshing over and which was the ammo dump still exploding. In fact, the Germans did not attack until later that evening and it was directed at the British 1st Division astride the Via Anziate. They had, however, been given some updated intelligence on this thanks to a captured prisoner cheerily telling them chapter and verse.

The 5th Grenadier Guards had avoided the worst of the fighting when the Germans had first attacked the salient but were now very much in the line on the Buonriposo Ridge to the immediate west of the Via Anziate and the Factory. It was under this ridge, in ancient Roman quarries, that the Irish Guards had sheltered on the evening of 4 February. Battalion HQ, however, was now down a gully shaped rather like a question mark, and accessed gradually until the sides were as high as 25 feet. It meant they were well out of sight and largely protected from anything other than a direct hit. Edward Danger had been given twenty-four hours' rest behind the lines and had returned to Battalion HQ to discover that it had moved to this new location, but also to the news of the imminent enemy attack that same night – so everyone was rather braced, with three days' worth of rations stockpiled and the forward companies all ready – standing to – waiting in their foxholes.

Dusk fell, then darkness. Then, at 9 p.m., an enemy barrage began, the air heavy with the racket of screeching, whistling, then exploding shells. Soon afterwards the first enemy attacks began on the Grenadier Guards' front. It appeared to be largely an infantry attack by Kampfgruppe Pfeiffer, drawn from the reborn 65. Division, and it was directed at the Buonriposo Ridge, where the North Staffordshires and 5th Grenadiers were holding the line. To begin with, both battalions took a heavy toll on their attackers, but as the night wore on the Germans increasingly seemed to be everywhere in a fight that was both confusing and terrifying. Visibility depended on flares and explosions, but these flashes of light were sporadic. Shells and mortars were exploding, small-arms fire ringing out, and it was freezing-cold. From a foxhole it was difficult to know who was who. In the gully, Edward Danger was hearing the radio messages coming through from the forward companies and getting something of a running commentary. A German force had broken through the North Staffs on the Grenadiers' left and then a report arrived from No. 4 Company warning of Germans now in their area. This was concerning because 4 Company were in reserve, and so suggested that Nos 1 and 3 had already been overrun. At 11.04 p.m. 4 Company reported Germans all around, then the North Staffs warned that their forward companies had been overrun and surrounded. How many had been killed, wounded or taken prisoner was not clear. The Irish Guards, in reserve and still sheltering in the caves, were urgently asked to send what they could to help the North Staffs, but after the fighting of three days earlier were still woefully depleted.

'Do you realise that I have sent all I have got away now?' Major Mike Gordon-Watson told the Brigadier over the radio net.

'Well, draw in your horns, recall the interception unit,' Brigadier Malcolm Erskine told him.

'I will draw in my horns as you politely call it, and I will leave the carrier patrol out.'

'OK – this will leave you a little something.'

'Then thank God for a little something – there are fifty very unpleasant gentleman down this road somewhere.'

It was reassuring that even in these desperate moments, commanders in the Guards Brigade were not losing their sense of humour. Edward Danger was listening to these exchanges as well as further signals from the Grenadiers' 1 and 3 Companies, each becoming ever more desperate. One of those captured was Lieutenant Paul Freyberg, of 1 Company, the son of General Freyberg, now commanding the New Zealand Corps. Fortunately, most of 4 Company managed to pull back in the melee and confusion and reached Battalion HQ in the gully, as did a company of the 504th PIR, led by Lieutenant La Riviere, who told them all calmly that his boys would deal with any Krauts that came their way. This composite force was deployed either side of the gully while Battalion HQ was moved back out of the northern end and made ready to defend the southern part. The situation was both confused and decidedly critical for the British. On the far side of the Via Anziate, Kampfgruppe Gräser had also begun attacking the Factory, grenadiers storming southwards supported by assault guns and tanks. Among those were Oberfeldwebel Felix Reimann and crew in their StuG, *Lucy*, rumbling forward into the heart of the shattered remains of Mussolini's model town. 'Every time our gun fired,' he noted, 'a few more bricks would fall onto us with a clang.' The ruins of the Factory were now being defended by the London Irish; John Strick had even more reason to be glad he'd missed the first boat to Anzio.

By the early hours, German troops had reached the edge of the gully and were lobbing grenades down into the chasm, but the Grenadiers held on, in no small part thanks to the help of the American paratroopers. 'At daylight,' noted Danger, 'Jerry could be seen entrenched about 50 yards from us. Here we sat for the whole long day while Jerry fired everything he had at us, including the kitchen sink.'

Yet it wasn't only the Germans hurling everything they had. So too were the Allies, including from the combined firepower of four cruisers out to sea that bombarded Kampfgruppe Gräser throughout the morning, hurling salvos of 5-inch shells relentlessly. Then, later in the morning, the rain briefly cleared and Allied bombers thundered over. For Felix Reimann and his crew it was three hours of never-ending hell. 'There is nothing worse than waiting to be killed,' he recalled, 'but that is what we had to do.' It seemed a miracle to him that he survived the day; he and his crew were among the lucky ones, for the bombs and naval shells seemed to be obliterating everything around them. The brutal reality of attacking was that the moment troops did so, they had to emerge from their places of camouflage and comparative safety and advance over open ground. This was the reason for attacking at night, but having taken ground during the hours of darkness, they then had to remain where they were or risk losing it again. The price, however, was being pummelled by offshore naval guns and Allied bombers.

The fighting continued through the day. Lucas had sent up some light Stuart tanks and the whole 3rd Battalion of the 504th to help; part of the Buonriposo Ridge was retaken, but then the Germans renewed their attacks again after dusk. Edward Danger had been given a rifle and was poised ready at the edge of the gully, contemplating that being both sodden and frozen was possibly worse than waiting for the Germans. Then an order came for a withdrawal and so they all hurriedly loaded up their carriers, the only vehicles capable of escaping the icy lake in the gully, and scuttled away out of the far end under the cover of a smokescreen and the darkness of the night to the comparative shelter of a railway embankment – this was from a disused line that cut across the railway running north and the Via Anziate. In other words, they now had a large earthen mound behind which they could take cover from any attack from the north. Even so, not long after they'd reached this position, the Grenadiers' CO, Lieutenant-Colonel Arthur Huntington, was shot in the heart as he stood by the RAP – regimental aid post. He was killed instantly.

That same morning, 9 February, Kampfgruppe Gräser also renewed their attack on the Factory. They'd been very badly mauled in the fighting but had been bolstered by a regiment of 715. Infanterie-Division. The London Irish had now been pushed back to the southern edge of the rubble. Felix Reimann and his StuG were part of the attacking force. That morning he was ordered to pull out from their position of cover to support a renewed assault through the north of the wrecked town. They were firing on the move, Reimann scanning ahead, eyes peeled for danger. The gun of a StuG could traverse its gun barrel a little but it wasn't a tank; as it did not have a rotating turret it was more vulnerable when on the move because it could only really fire in one direction. Reimann was still carefully watching the northern edge of the town when suddenly there was a blinding flash of light on their right-hand side and a massive explosion. Blinded by the flash, he could hear the terrible screams of his crew as they burned to death. Somehow he managed to get out and collapsed on the ground, unconscious. Medics picked him up but he was the only survivor – his StuG had been destroyed by a British anti-tank round he'd never seen coming.

The London Irish pulled out of the remains of the Factory that morning, which meant that the only British troops north of the railway embankment by nightfall on the 9th were the Scots Guards at Carroceto. 'There is a fucking great German tank sitting outside my door,' the adjutant of the Scots Guards signalled to Brigade the following morning, 'demolishing my house brick by brick.' They asked for help, but with the rest of the line now back behind the embankment there was little point in vainly holding on to Carroceto, so the Scots Guards also pulled back that day. The British 1st Division had been devastated by the battles of the past week. The Grenadier Guards, for example, had lost 50 per cent; the Irish Guards 40 per cent. The figures were similar across all eleven battalions that had been involved. The London Irish now had just 40 per cent; they desperately needed John Strick and the other promised reinforcements.

As it happened, John Strick was on his way the following day, 10 February. He had enjoyed his week since being released from hospital. He'd been reading plenty of poetry and had been particularly struck by a line by the poet Alun Lewis. Life, Strick mused, could be broken by war and by time, but as Lewis had written from a hospital bed in Poona a year earlier, 'love survives the venom of the snake.' The journey to Anzio was to be Strick's fourth time back into the fray. 'I have lost the old keenness,' he jotted in his diary, 'no use pretending – it's gone. The intimate deaths, the hair-breadth escapes, the strange faces and absences – the lack of respite – it is too much.' He was aware that the battle at Anzio looked as sticky as any he'd been involved with and he found his thoughts shifting between fatalism, concerns about his nerves and a deep wistfulness.

Strick and a few other officers spent their last day in Naples. He had a sketch of himself done by a street artist, they enjoyed a convivial lunch with an orchestra playing 'Lili Marlene' and other old favourites, then went to see a performance of *Madama Butterfly*. Not a bad day in all, and one that would have to sustain them as they headed once more back to the front and the promise of battle.

CHAPTER 17

The Meat Grinder

THE MONKS AT THE abbey were feeling more vulnerable than ever now that the battle for the mountain had begun. Dom Eusebio was still struggling with a raging fever so Dom Martino continued writing the diary in his absence. More stray shells were hitting the abbey and the walls were being regularly raked by machine-gun fire, mostly from Allied weapons but from German artillery too. On 5 February, for example, a German shell struck the infirmary and another hit the Benefactor's Cloister between the well and the church entrance; the famous bronze doors were badly damaged. Dom Martino had also been spotting plenty of German troop movements, including a machine-gunner next to the well outside the abbey walls. 'At one point,' he noted, 'I saw signalling from German medical orderlies near the well and two German soldiers took an injured man towards Colle d'Onofrio.' There were several small stone houses and farm buildings there; Colle d'Onofrio was a low ridge that rose from the saddle between the abbey and Monte Calvario – what the American troops now called Snakeshead Ridge.

Later that same morning, several dozen women appeared, banging on the door, weeping and pleading to be allowed in. The Father Abbot agreed to open the doors and allow them to come inside and take refuge, but as they did so a much larger crowd of civilians poured in after them. The monks did what they could, clearing rooms from the carpenter's workshop and the space below the Biblioteca Monumentale, the porter's lodge, the postroom and the Curia corridor. 'Among the refugees,' added Dom Martino, 'there were, unfortunately, some people of bad reputation and pillagers. May God be with us!' Over and over, the monks warned the people that they were not necessarily safe in the abbey and also asked them not to go wandering around the cloisters. 'A waste of breath!' noted Dom Martino. The shelling began again in the afternoon. One man was killed by the main well in the courtyard; two women by a blast in the Prior's Cloister. A boy died in the Bramante Cloister. Dom Martino had stopped counting how many shells hit the abbey, but it was a rapidly increasing number. Then, in the evening, a German medical officer arrived asking whether they had any room for the wounded. 'We gave him the S. Agata guesthouse,' recorded Dom Martino.

So it continued. No one in the abbey was getting much sleep, while the building itself was suffering increasing amounts of damage. Dom Martino had taken to making a tour of inspection each morning after saying Mass in the Crypt. Chunks of plaster littered all parts. 'The Anglo-American gentlemen,' he wrote, 'have treated Monte Cassino like a ploughed field and it looks here just like any other place they have given their special treatment.' On the afternoon of the 9th, a German medical captain visited to look at all their sick. He thought Dom Eusebio was not suffering from influenza, but more likely paratyphoid, which was more serious. Later that same afternoon, three more civilians were killed as they collected water from the well. 'That well,' noted Dom Martino sombrely, 'will be known as the "Well of Death".'

Meanwhile, the battle continued at Anzio. 'Have spent the morning trying to do something about the mess on the British front,' noted General Lucas on 9 February. 'The situation is very serious. I have had to put a regiment of the Corps reserve in the line which leaves me very little to meet what may come against us in the near future.' He thought 1st Division seemed very knocked to pieces and in worse shape than he felt they ought to be. What he had not done was make a visit up to the front to see General Penney or any of the forward units; his cellar CP near Nettuno was hardly the best place from which to judge the situation. He might as well have been in a villa twenty miles behind the lines if he wasn't prepared to venture out and see what was going on for himself.

Lucas now had his infantry units manning a connected front line and engineers and service troops helping to prepare the two further lines of defence. Almost all his armour, at this stage, was well behind the line, operating as a mobile reserve. Because the distances were comparatively small in the big scheme of things, hurriedly moving them when the need arose should not have been very challenging; and there is no doubt that there had been a golden opportunity here to wallop the enemy with a giant fist of a counter-attack that might well have given the cautious von Mackensen plenty to think about. The reduction of the thumb north of Carroceto was very much the hors d'ouevre for von Mackensen's main effort, so to have stopped it dead in its tracks would have been just the kind of bold move an aggressive commander with a smidgen of imagination should – and would – have instigated immediately.

After all, Lucas had known the German attack there was coming; in fact, he'd had an entire day to get ready. Penney had been repeatedly asking for support, but had initially been sent a company of paratroopers, and then eventually seven light tanks and the rest of 3rd Battalion of the 504th PIR. By no reckoning was that overwhelming support. A decent proportion of the 380 tanks now in Lucas's corps, mostly in General Ernest N. Harmon's 1st Armored Division, were doing absolutely nothing whatsoever while 1st Division's infantry battalions were being decimated. The same was true for his arsenal of M10 tank destroyers and other anti-tank weaponry. Some of the light flak units would have made short work of the German infantry had the mindset not been quite so defensive; they were hardly needed for anti-aircraft duty in the appalling weather. Combine this amount of mobile firepower with the offshore naval guns, and the German battle groups sent to capture the Factory and Carroceto, most of whom were badly trained conscripts, would have been annihilated. 'Lucas does not go into details,' Clark had groused to his diary back on 7 February. 'I urged him to designate Harmon as his Tank Destroyer and Tank Officer to coordinate the whole defense. He apparently has no mobile tank destroyer unit to rush from place to place as the situation requires it.' Clark had even told Lucas to use his anti-aircraft guns in an anti-tank role. Yet Lucas had neither ordered them to be used in this way nor sent his armour into the fray. Instead, he'd moaned in his diary that he was losing 800 men a day at current rates of attrition.

The United States had developed a truly incredible arsenal of weaponry. The frustration about operating in the mountains was that mobile anti-tank guns, tanks and light flak could rarely be brought to bear, but that was not the case here. Huge logistical efforts had been made to give Lucas a significant amount of armour and other weaponry that would act as a major force multiplier for the infantry. As had been the case at the Rapido, this materiel superiority and immense amount of firepower had not been used when it was both needed and, for once in Italy, where it could have been very effectively deployed. When, on 9 February, Lucas had signalled to Clark to tell him he was worried about the battle raging on the British front, Clark cabled him straight back. 'I feel you can stop most anything', he replied, 'with the 350 tanks you have.' Clark was not wrong.

Lucas finally called on Penney on 10 February, by which time it was far too late. Even then he made no effort to talk to the brigade or battalion commanders or take a look at the lie of the land. Instead, he told Penney to counter-attack the following day with the help of the Thunderbirds' 179th Infantry Regiment. There was still no suggestion that a mass of armour was on offer. Penney was a devout Christian and a highly experienced soldier who had just lost half his infantry capability because his requests for assistance had gone largely unheeded; he was understandably incensed. 'No operational appreciation,' he noted, 'no orders, no intention, no objective, no nothing.' Penney had thought Lucas's disinterest, lack of foresight and even lack of empathy not just a travesty but a tragedy too. Lucas's unwillingness to listen to Clark and to adopt anything other than a deeply unimaginative and defensive mindset had led to unnecessary loss of life, numerous casualties, an entirely avoidable tactical defeat and a missed opportunity to strike back hard at the enemy. When 179th Infantry attacked the following day, 11 February, they did so still without the tanks that had been vaguely promised and didn't get very far at all. Yet another chance to wrench back the initiative from the Germans was lost.

At the Cassino front, preparations were under way for the next phase of the fighting. McCreery was going to lose the rest of 56th Division, which was heading to Anzio. Alexander had suggested they might be a direct swap for the battered 1st Division, but Clark was outraged at the thought; all his divisions were tired and suffering from manpower shortages and he had no intention of treating 1st Division any differently to 3rd Division or any of his others for that matter. After sleeping on it, Alex acquiesced. The move prompted McCreery to put the Garigliano front on to the defensive, though, just as the Germans had already done. The fighting there had brought both sides to a stalemate.

It was clear that the Red Bulls were fast becoming a busted flush and that the exhausted T-Patchers and CEF also needed some urgent relief. The 2ème Division Algérienne had been decimated and the 4ème Régiment de Tirailleurs Tunisiens destroyed, which meant that until his replacements arrived, Juin effectively had one functioning division. Commandant Paul Gandoët, still recovering from his wound, was soon to be leaving Italy; he'd received a request to join the staff of Général Jean de Lattre de Tassigny, who was building up the French 2ème Armée in North Africa. It was precisely because of the battering of the CEF and II Corps that Alexander had created the New Zealand Corps and brought them over to the Cassino front, and why he had asked Freyberg to prepare plans for their employment. This had ruffled Clark's feathers a little, and with some justification; the New Zealand Corps were now attached to Fifth Army, and as Army commander he felt it important that he should be part of the planning discussions the moment Freyberg came under his command. He had a point. Yet, be that as it may, there was no doubt that a fresh pair of eyes – and an experienced pair of eyes to boot – were much needed in this sector. Fifth Army had been looking at the double-lock defensive system around Cassino since the beginning of November. They'd busted their way through the first lock, the Bernhard Line, but, having been hammering away at the outlying defences and then the Gustav Line itself for over a month, there was no doubt they were now struggling to see the wood for the trees.

It was why the keen mind of General Francis Tuker was so very welcome. He'd reached the Cassino area ahead of his 4th Indian Division towards the end of January and had immediately busied himself visiting the front and talking to his fellow commanders, not least Général Juin, who told him Fifth Army was wasting its time hammering against the strongest part of the line. There was, Juin told him, a much easier route through to the Liri Valley by exploiting the gains the French had made on Belvedere and on towards Terelle and from there striking down to the valley at Roccasecca. Having seen the ground for himself, Tuker was very much of the same mind. He also scoured the intelligence reports of II Corps and the CEF, which included a wealth of information: details of new enemy weaponry, translations of captured diaries, summaries from prisoner-of-war interrogations, weather reports, estimations of enemy casualties, summaries of operations and details of any new enemy unit discovered in the area. These G2 summaries really were remarkably detailed and Tuker rightly concluded that the mountain area around Monte Cairo was not only defended by a comparatively small number of lower-grade troops, but also that the defences there were far less well developed, with fewer constructed emplacements – either concrete, stone or blasted cave.

He also believed that an assault over the Rapido in the Liri Valley at similar crossing points to those of the T-Patchers around Sant'Angelo was a far better option than continuing to batter the Monte Cassino massif. Although very aware of the T-Patchers' attempt to cross ten days earlier, he felt that failure had been down to a lack of planning and poor coordination of fire rather than being the wrong idea in principle. What he was suggesting was the kind of assault Walker could have undertaken had he used armour, anti-aircraft weapons in a ground role and a mass of artillery softening up enemy positions not for half an hour but for days ahead and, crucially, firing in concentrations. This meant aiming a mass of artillery to fire on one fixed area, then moving on to the next and the next. It was certainly a more effective way of saturating ground than each battery firing straight ahead. Crucially, he suggested this be carried out in conjunction with an attack through the mountains south of Monte Cairo and north of Monte Castellone. 'We considered this to be a big undertaking,' he noted, 'but within the resources of the New Zealand, 4th Indian and 78th Divisions, because the Army artillery would have full play for all natures of gun from heavy to field.'

General Freyberg was entirely behind these plans and happy to absorb the confidence emanating from Tuker and his staff. Because of the hasty nature in which the New Zealand Corps had been created, Freyberg had not been given a corps staff, so he was dependent on his New Zealand Division staff and that of 4th Indian to make do. It didn't matter too much because Tuker and his team brought immense clarity of thought and a forensic eye for detail. Or rather, it didn't until tragedy struck on 2 February, when Tuker fell ill while at Juin's headquarters. Struck by a sudden and dramatic flare-up of rheumatoid arthritis, a debilitating disease that had blighted him periodically, his driver got him back to his caravan where he collapsed. This was a cruel blow. Prostrate on his bed and in profound pain, he none the less refused to go to hospital until he had seen Freyberg. The corps commander arrived on 3 February; again Tuker stressed that a direct attack would be a terrible mistake and urged him to pursue an assault further north, preferably in conjunction with an attack across the Rapido in the manner he'd outlined. Freyberg assured him he would do as he suggested. Tuker also said that if he had to temporarily relinquish the division, then Freyberg should do all he could to get Major-General Tom 'Pasha' Russell, currently commanding 8th Indian Division on the Adriatic. Again, Freyberg assured him he would do his level best to see that this happened. In acute and debilitating pain, Tuker was taken by ambulance to the MDS – Main Dressing Station – the following day and from there to the Fifth Army hospital at Caserta.

At this point, 4 February, Tuker had to relinquish direct command, but instead of getting Pasha Russell to take temporary command Freyberg appointed Brigadier Harry Dimoline, the 4th Indian artillery commander, instead. This was an inexplicable decision, especially at this critical time. Dimoline was a pre-war Territorial – part-time soldier – and had been a fine divisional artillery commander, but he was a gunner through and through and had no experience at all of commanding Indian infantry, let alone in action. Nor did he have the authority or force of character to be able to argue 4th Division's corner in the upcoming battle. It was an appointment made by Freyberg without sufficient understanding of the division now in his command; why he chose Dimoline is not clear, because the infantry brigade commanders had far greater experience of commanding fighting troops and were entirely wedded to Tuker's way of thinking. Brigadier Donald Bateman, for example, commanding 5th Brigade, was both older and senior to Dimoline, had worked closely with Tuker on the plans and understood how they might work. He, too, had urged the New Zealand staff to ask for Pasha Russell to take over. This suggestion had been ignored.

Clark finally held a planning meeting with Freyberg at his headquarters in Presenzano on 4 February, at which Keyes and Juin had also been present. At this Freyberg presented Tuker's plan, yet without the 4th Indian Division commander there he started to flounder in the face of Keyes's obvious anger. Keyes was exhausted; he'd not had much sleep in recent weeks, and hearing Freyberg suggest a further crossing of the Rapido had made his blood boil. This was where Freyberg's fundamental shortcomings revealed themselves. His VC, his friendship with Churchill, the respect he rightly deserved, as well as his position as New Zealand's most senior soldier did not alter the fact that every man should only be promoted to the level of his capabilities. Commanding a division was the upper reach of Freyberg's, and a corps most definitely a step too far. He simply didn't have the clarity of thought and intellect to be able to argue his case. Rather, he needed Tuker, who would have been able to stand his ground and press their case better than anyone else present. At the very least, it might have made Clark – and Keyes – pause for thought.

Instead, Clark concluded that the New Zealanders should assault south of Cassino once the Red Bulls had Monte Cassino, a not unreasonable assumption at that time, and that Juin's French should go all out for

Terelle, aiming to reach the Liri Valley at Roccasecca – which chimed with Tuker's suggested approach.

Over the course of the next few days, however, the situation dramatically changed, not least because there had been no breakthrough on Monte Cassino. On 8 February, Clark then met with Alexander and Harding. It was clear to them that the Red Bulls had shot their bolt, so instead of using the New Zealand Corps to burst into the Liri Valley as had been hoped, they decided 4th Indian should replace the Red Bulls on the massif and the New Zealand Division in the town. There was no suggestion of a crossing at Sant'Angelo or of abandoning the current line of attack on Monte Cassino. This decision was then passed on to Freyberg.

At this stage, Freyberg was entirely within his rights to suggest an alternative approach on the lines that Tuker had outlined but he was not a confident senior commander, had no real experience of mountain warfare, and without Tuker to stiffen his resolve found his arguments weakening. He was also worried that there were not enough mules for the task Tuker had proposed, and in any case the more he looked at the map, the more he began to think a continuation of the direct assault was the best approach after all. The Americans were already there, and from the map it was only a very short distance over which the fresh and experienced troops of 4th Indian Division would have to attack. Furthermore, Keyes and Walker had been badly scarred by the Rapido experience and were dead set against such a move across the Rapido as Tuker was advocating. At no point, however, had either reflected on that experience and drawn the conclusion which Tuker had: that it had been a badly fought battle. Sadly, Freyberg had never been particularly good at fighting his own corner.

Meanwhile, Clark was still hopeful that a breakthrough on Monte Cassino was imminent. Despite the exhaustion of his infantry, Doc Ryder renewed his effort on 8 February, this time, however, an all-out effort using all three regiments of the Red Bulls. After all, they were so close to the breakthrough, the Liri Valley and the Via Casilina being within spitting distance. Just one last all-out effort and the whole of the Gustav Line would surely fold. Yes, II Corps was exhausted, but some further lives lost now might save much more blood that would be spilled if they let the enemy off the hook.

Nor was the fighting happening only in the mountains, because down below the 133rd had been continuing their attack on the town, assaulting both the northern edge and Castle Hill at the same time. The ruins of the medieval castle stood on a jutting knoll nearly 600 feet above the northern part of the town, on a hairpin bend of the road leading up to the abbey. Clearly, holding this hill that so dominated the town was vital. After several days in which 133rd Infantry took the castle then lost it again it was the turn of the 100th Nisei Battalion, who on the morning of 8 February, under the cover of smoke, began moving out from the barracks area for the renewed, but now all out, effort by the Red Bulls to take Monte Cassino and the town. The 100th soon found themselves pinned down. First, the smoke drifted away from them and they came under fire from Monte Cassino above. Then, clambering up to Point 175, just north of Castle Hill, and on to Point 165, next to the castle near the hairpin, they could get no further. Sergeant Isaac Akinaka spent the next four days scuttling between sangars and foxholes as the Nisei Battalion became stuck and blasted by mortar, shellfire and sniping.

Meanwhile, the attack on Monte Cassino was renewed as well. Ralph Schaps had taken over as Company H medic because there was no one else left to do it. It proved a hellish job. 'The screaming', he noted, 'was hard to take when you were trying to bandage them and stop the blood flowing.' One man he treated had his right leg shattered below the knee and his right arm was also a mess. Schaps really struggled to get the leg to stop bleeding but eventually snipped off the artery, tied it in a knot, applied tourniquets and taped up the other lacerations. Fortunately, he then managed to get some stretcher-bearers to take the wounded man back down the mountain. An aid station was also set up in a farmhouse just over the southern side of Snakeshead Ridge; it was swiftly renamed the 'Doctor's House'. It had been repeatedly shelled but there was a back room that was still intact and offered reasonable protection, so this was where the aid station was. Schaps was hardly properly trained for the task, but used an abandoned German stretcher as a treatment couch and did the best he could. Men screamed and cried, often with horrific wounds. Sometimes it was a question of waiting for a man to die so he could be taken off the stretcher and replaced with the next fellow. One time, he had his canteen shot off his hip as he helped bring in another wounded soldier. By the morning of the 8th, however, fresh medics reached them. Schaps was relieved to get back to his Browning machine gun, although another ordeal was about to begin.

The next two days were nightmarish for him and his fellows. He spent much of the time on the heavy water-cooled Browning machine gun with his closest friend in the platoon, Jesse Tyre, a former paratrooper who had been kicked out on a manslaughter charge. Schaps never quite got to the bottom of what his friend had done, but he didn't care; he reckoned Tyre was the best and toughest soldier he'd ever met and always felt a little more confident when his friend was beside him. The fighting, though, was as relentless as the terrible weather. They were all continually soaked and freezing-cold. Sleep was next to impossible because the sound of battle and continual shelling never seemed to let up. Even in the cold, the growing number of dead now littered over the mountains began to stink; but there was no way they could be buried.

On 9 February, the Red Bulls of Schaps's battalion managed to hold on to Point 593, so that when Oberst Karl Schulz arrived with his 1. Fallschirmjäger battle group, it was to discover that the key position on the massif was now in American hands. This was an embarrassment to Major Rudolf Kratzert, who from his bunker in the Masseria Albaneta had not realized it had been taken. It had hardly been his fault, however. The rocky knoll had only ever been held by a machine-gun team and an observer; the Allies had been kept from it by enfilading fire and by Kratzert repeatedly replacing men on the top from the caves directly behind and beneath it. Late on the 9th, however, he ordered a raiding patrol to go and investigate, but the NCO returned a little later to tell him it was now heavily held by the Americans.

Kratzert now decided to lead a second raiding patrol up there himself, dividing his force into two groups. One was to clear the summit of the bluff, while the second would then hold it. Armed to the teeth with submachine guns, grenades and also a radio to keep in contact with his command post, they set off into the darkness of the night, clambering as quietly as they could up on to the jutting peak of Point 593. Beneath the summit they paused, then crept a little further along a low cliff, a natural stone wall that dropped off the northern side. 'We tossed some hand grenades over the wall without encountering any serious opposition,' noted Kratzert. 'In a relatively short space of time we captured the entire hill.' Then, from his radio set, he sent a message to Schulz's command post that they had been successful. Point 593 was once again back in German hands.

Now heading up to the mountain was the Texas Division, and it had fallen to 141st Infantry to support the Red Bulls up on Snakeshead Ridge. They'd moved up overnight on the 9th, an experience both bewildering and terrifying for Lieutenant Harry Bond and no less so for Captain Roswell Doughty, despite, by this time, being something of an old-timer. This was to be Bond's first real taste of action, and although he'd now been with 3rd Battalion for only just over two weeks he was painfully aware that they were in no state to be sent back into action so soon. 'Who the hell do they think we are?' one of his men had groused. 'Who in Christ's name do they think we are?' Everyone was scared, everyone tense. And edgy and short-tempered. They set off at dusk in trucks through the ruins of Cervaro to Portella, just to the south of Sant'Elia. Bond had ditched his gas mask on the advice of the veterans but had packed extra socks. He had no idea what to expect, but just reaching the mountains seemed fraught with danger. From Portella they had to cross over the upper Rapido Valley to Caira on a single causeway now zeroed by German gunners and which was regularly shelled. Every trip was a game of Russian roulette. Vehicles could not get up into the mountains except by using the one hairpin track that led to Terelle. Most of the supplies had to be brought up by mule, but it took seventy-five fully laden mules to keep a single battalion going for twenty-four hours. It was dawn by the time they reached the village of Caira, but it wasn't until later on the 10th that they began their climb up to the top. The ground was icy and snow was falling as they went. German shells crunched behind them and up ahead. Eventually, they emerged from the steep climb up a gully on to a more open area with ridges on either side. Bond had no idea where he was but they had, in fact, emerged into the mountain valley between Castellone and Phantom Ridge on their right and Snakeshead on their left. An officer told him to set up his mortars at the foot of Snakeshead behind a dry-stone wall that marked out a mountain pasture. Small arms and sporadic shelling continued to crash and stutter around the mountain. It was now late afternoon.

After setting up the mortars, Bond told his men to try and dig out what scrapes in the ground they could then went off to find the 3rd Battalion CP; he and his men had simply been told to fix themselves up and then everyone else had disappeared. Bond had not the first idea what else he was expected to do. Following the direction the infantry column had gone, he found himself on a track that climbed the ridge. Passing groups of soldiers, he eventually emerged on to the summit and was stunned to see the abbey perched only half a mile or so across the saddle beneath where he now stood. 'I was greatly startled,' he noted, 'for I had no idea that our troops were so close to it.'

Now spotting the Doctor's House, where Schaps had spent his time as the stand-in medic, he headed towards it only to stumble over two dead and torn Americans at the end of the trail. Medics loitered outside next to a row of further dead men. Inside, he was hit by the stench of wet wool and mustiness. Not only was the house an aid station, it was also the CP for 3rd Battalion and for 2nd Battalion of 135th Infantry, the men of both divisions now somewhat intertwined. Having found an officer, he was told to get back to his mortars and zero them on Point 593, then fix a phone wire to the CP.

A frantic, bewildering night followed. Twice he laid phone wires to both the CP and an OP from where he could direct mortars, and twice they were cut by enemy shellfire. Eventually abandoning further attempts to get them fixed as darkness fell, he returned to his mortar platoon to discover that his orderly, a replacement even newer than himself, had done little preparation of their foxhole. Fuming, Bond and the orderly then did the best they could in the dark. It was now raining, the snow was melting, and the shallow scrape they'd managed to dig out kept filling with water. A mule had dropped a package of blankets so they all helped themselves to those, but this dividend hardly improved their lot. A pup tent canvas was stretched over their shallow grave of a pit which acted as a windbreak but little more. Then the Germans started to shell the area, each missile screaming in towards them with a long baleful wail before exploding terrifyingly close. 'The ground shook,' he noted, 'and the air was full of flying dirt and shrapnel. There was the frightening smell of gunpowder and crash after crash as the shells roared in and exploded on our position.' Bond and his orderly lay side by side, stupefied, shivering, wondering whether the next screeching shell would be the end of them.

Captain Roswell Doughty had reached Monte Cassino the same day, having left most of his I & R Platoon back down at the Regimental CP in Caira. Like Bond, he soon discovered an atmosphere of confusion and disarray. None of the troops he met seemed to know what the hell was going on or where anyone was. The problem was that the endless breaks in field telephone wire combined with the loss of officers meant the units up there were forever in a state of command flux. Doughty also eventually found the Doctor's House, although not before he'd several times missed being obliterated by a matter of seconds, or before he'd come across an open cave at the side of the ridge in which around thirty dead Americans lay sprawled. He couldn't understand how they'd been hit; but then again, nothing up on the mountain seemed to make much sense.

It also appeared that even Colonel Aaron Wyatt, commander of 141st Infantry, had little idea what was going on. Throughout 11 February, first his 1st Battalion and then his 3rd Battalion tried to push their way back down Snakeshead Ridge to Point 593, but twice Kratzert's men launched counter-attacks of their own. Wyatt now summoned Doughty, who had returned to the CP at Caira earlier that morning, to go and find out where his battalions were. Taking a young officer with him, Doughty set out up the mountain trail, noting the shapes of dead mules and men under the snow as they climbed. Reaching the mountain plain, they then began clambering up on to the left, southern flank of Snakeshead Ridge, only for a bullet to zip past Doughty's head. Both men dived into the snow and hid behind a long stone wall that marked the side of the trail where the slope dropped away. Perhaps 200 yards ahead was the Doctor's House. A second shot hissed past when Doughty's companion shifted position, but they had both spotted movement in a clump of low trees 100 yards or so beneath a rock face to the south-east of them. They fired several shots with their carbines and then ran for the house. Doughty was only a matter of yards from it when he slipped on the ice; a burst of machine-gun bullets hissed and fizzed above his head just where he would have been but for his fall. Another stroke of timely luck.

Later, he managed to make contact with the forward companies, the survivors already traumatized by the day's fighting and the close-quarters nature of the battle up on the ridge; 1st Battalion alone had hurled 1,500 hand grenades that day. Doughty discovered that by 4.45 p.m., 1st Battalion had just ten officers and sixty-six enlisted men still standing, while 3rd Battalion, who had entered the fray later, could muster only twelve officers and ninety-four men. It was proving to be a bloodbath up there.

Across the Monte Cassino massif, that Friday, 11 February, was a terrible day for the Americans and one that should have set off plenty of warning bells for the senior command. In addition to the failure to take back Point 593 there had been other attacks, not least by 168th Infantry. There were fewer than 800 fighting men left in the regiment that morning, but they still attacked over the saddle of Sant'Onofrio between Snakeshead and Monastery Hill. It was snowing, freezing-cold. The mountain was desolate. A rolling barrage opened up, but these artillery shells did little damage to the Germans waiting in their caves and bunkers. As soon as it lifted, Schulz's Fallschirmjäger took to their machine guns and mortars and cut the Americans down. A ferocious counter-attack finished off the offensive for good. Meanwhile, 142nd Infantry attacked towards Albaneta but were similarly repulsed.

General Clark was not afraid to push his men hard. However, the fighting on the massif over the past week should have told the senior commanders now responsible for the conduct of the battle that they were hammering against a bolted door. The nature of the terrain, combined with the strengthening, not weakening, of the German defence, indicated that this was no longer a battle zone in which one last show of strength would unlock the position. The Americans still had no idea about the German figure-of-eight defence system, but they should have twigged that so long as the Germans had machine guns and mortars to pour on to the ridges, the number of companies fed along the ridges and saddles would not make any difference. They would all be cut down in turn – just as meat being fed into a grinder would continue to be turned to mince.

General Clark was suffering from another nasty head cold and now had an army of five corps and two fronts to deal with and manage. General Keyes was exhausted, so too Doc Ryder and Fred Walker. Roswell Doughty reckoned that even Colonel Wyatt, his commander at 141st Regiment, was beginning to lose the ability to make sound decisions. So if none of these men were seeing the situation up on Monte Cassino for what it was, that was probably understandable. The same, though, could not be said for Freyberg, who now had a clear opportunity, with his fresh divisions, to salvage a situation that had finally, after an immense and astonishing demonstration of resolve, determination and, frankly, staying power, run its course. The fleeting chance to clear the massif had now gone. Had any of those senior commanders clambered up on to the Monte Cassino massif they would have realized that. Freyberg, however, had an alternative approach – an approach that, while still challenging, offered a far, far better chance of success than another direct attack on terrain, and in circumstances that entirely favoured the enemy.

CHAPTER 18

The Perfect Storm

MOST OF 1. FALLSCHIRMJÄGER-DIVISION were now heading to Cassino, although because they had been so dispersed and were now only a little over 3,000 men-strong all told, they were arriving very much in dribs and drabs. Next to reach the mountain, however, was 4. Fallschirmjäger-Regiment, moved over from the Adriatic coast, and now partially replenished with a raft of new replacements after the battering they'd taken at Orsogna in the December battles. This had prompted a major reorganization of the regiment, not least II. Bataillon, now back with four companies, albeit understrength ones. And one of the new platoon commanders of the reconstituted 6. Kompanie was Oberjäger Rudolf Donth, twenty-three years old and from Silesia, but by now a veteran paratrooper who had seen service in Russia and Sicily and had been fighting in Italy since the Allies first landed the previous September.

Donth, however, had been one of the lucky ones to be given some leave and, much to his delight, had even been handed a marriage licence, which he'd not asked for, but which had allowed him to unexpectedly marry his long-term fiancée. So, all in all, January had proved a far better month for him than December, when he fought through some of the bitterest fighting imaginable and lost a number of cherished comrades. He'd rejoined the battalion – and taken command of his company – at the end of January at Tollo, a little town to the west of Ortona on the Adriatic. For a few brief days he had revelled in the joy of having a functioning battalion once more and also of being reunited with a number of old friends now back from leave or recovered from wounds.

The battalion reached Cassino over several days because of the shortage of trucks, but 6. Kompanie assembled down in the Liri Valley after a long drive across the mountains and in darkness began clambering up on to the mountain. The men all marched in line, close together because it was so dark. Soon they began to climb up what they realized was a steep and increasingly narrow ravine – they had reached Death Gully. The radio operators, with their heavy loads, were panting heavily; Donth was also struck by the smell of detonated shells and dust and smoke on the air, which suggested that this route was regularly under attack. Just as the Germans had zeroed well-known tracks, roads and crossing points used by the Allies, so had the Allied gunners done the same to German routes up to the mountain. Donth urged his men to hurry.

Suddenly, a whoosh through the air and the crashing of mortar shells, loud and tinny in the confines of the ravine. Everyone hit the ground, but Donth ordered his men to get up and keep moving. People up front and behind shouted, 'Report losses!' and Donth replied, 'No losses!' There was, however, a hold-up, because one of the men up ahead in a different platoon had been wounded and was in a bad way. This was no place to stick around and they quickly moved on, although they had to hit the ground twice more before the mortar shells at last started falling behind them. As they then emerged from the ravine near Albaneta they were met by marshallers who led them to their new positions. These were to be on the south-western side of the southern circle of the figure-of-eight – on the Colle d'Onofrio, the saddle between Snakeshead Ridge and Monastery Hill. All went smoothly; Donth was struck by an eerie silence that night.

Not until the first streaks of dawn did he see where they now were. To their left Snakeshead Ridge rose behind them while to their right there was the abbey, perched on its outcrop. 'The sight fascinated us,' noted Donth. 'It looked huge and imposing – just a few hundred metres away.' Their positions were on a low ridge between the two – this was the Colle d'Onofrio – from where they could look out to the Rapido Valley beyond and to Monte Trocchio and the mountains that had held the old Bernhard Line. Immediately behind them the ground dropped into fields, already chewed up by shells and now renamed 'Death Valley'. Individual placements were built up with rocks and stones with embrasures left between them. These forward positions could be seen from Point 593 and a little way along Snakeshead. 'To loosen things up,' noted Donth, 'we pulled some of the rifle positions back to the rear slope. This gave us a certain depth and more freedom of movement.'

A big advantage for the Germans reinforcing Monte Cassino was their better accessibility compared with the Allies. They might have been short of trucks and just about everything else, but when fresh troops arrived they could drive down the Via Casilina largely unhindered – at night or during bad-weather days when no Jabos were about – and then climb the comparatively short trail up Death Gully. The Allies, by contrast, had to cross the flooded upper Rapido Valley. The one road was badly chewed up and corduroy roads made of wooden logs were repeatedly hit by shellfire and wrecked through overuse. A large number of engineers were now spending much of their time on road-building and road repairs in order to keep up the increasingly demanding supply effort.

Among these was Frank Pearce, a twenty-eight-year-old combat engineer from Sulphur Springs, Texas. He'd worked in the automobile business before the war, but with some friends had joined the Texas National Guard to earn a few extra bucks. Before he knew it, however, the division had been activated and he was in the army full-time and for the duration. Part of 111th Engineer Combat Battalion, he'd landed at Salerno back on 9 September and been with the division ever since, and while most of the rifle companies had been replaced twice over already, he'd had a comparatively less life-threatening time of things, although not without its fair share of danger too. He had, though, avoided any of the mine-clearing or bridge work at the Rapido because he'd been waiting in the wings to construct roads on the far side once the infantry got across. As they never formed a coherent bridgehead, he'd been spared the carnage.

Since then, however, he and his fellows had been spending much of their time in the upper Rapido Valley, clearing endless mines and mainly helping to construct much-needed roads – much of which had to be done at night under the supposed safety of darkness. In the wet and the mud and the dark this was a terrible, frustrating and back-breaking task. 'Out all last night,' he noted in his diary on 8 February. 'Really was cold and miserable. Where we were, there was dead everywhere, all ours. Lots of tanks etc buried in mud.' One of the men in 2nd Platoon stepped on a mine that hadn't been cleared and blew off a foot. Pearce was out the next night too. The dead were mostly Red Bulls from two weeks earlier yet to be picked up. 'Pitiful sight,' he noted then added, 'German shells going over our area tonight.' They were landing only about 500 yards away. On the 10th, it was raining again and his tent was leaking. From his bivouac area he could look out and see the abbey, which seemed to be mocking them. 'Germans using for observation etc,' he jotted. 'It has cost us heavily in men as they can see all activity.'

Pearce was far from alone in believing that the abbey was being used by the Germans. Its prominence had unwittingly turned it into a German strongpoint in the eyes of many Allied troops. There were still no German troops in the abbey, but they didn't need to be: its position, perched on the outcrop at the edge of the Monte Cassino spur, gave the troops around it the elevated position they needed both for observers and for machine-gun and mortar nests; there were even some panzers and assault guns up there, hidden round the back of it. The monks' desperate pleas to uphold the 300-metre zone had been completely ignored.

Whether the abbey was now a legitimate target or not was to miss the point entirely, however. What mattered was whether destroying it would help the Allied efforts to break the Gustav Line or whether it would be far better to forget about Monte Cassino as a line of attack and consider alternative approaches, as Tuker had suggested. On the very same day, 9 February, when General Freyberg had presented his plans, the Red Bulls finally got themselves on to Point 593, only to lose it again. In a nutshell, they were a continuation of the current battering-ram approach: a direct assault on the Monte Cassio massif, with 4th Indian simply taking over the Red Bulls' positions. Tuker was desperate to get out of hospital and put a stop to this nonsense but he could barely move, his joints badly swollen and his body racked with pain. Last time he had seen the corps commander, Tuker had stressed that a direct assault should be used as a last resort only, but this was what his men were now being asked to do.

He was, though, still in touch with his division from his hospital bed and, on learning of Freyberg's decision, and with the full agreement of his brigade commanders and the acting divisional commander, Brigadier Harry Dimoline, made it clear that if his division was to make a direct assault on Monte Cassino, the area would have to be flattened first. Truly, he thought, a frontal attack of this nature was a terrible mistake. His point was this, however: if Fifth Army and Freyberg were insisting on continuing the attack in his hare-brained manner, then there was only one way to do it, and that was by obliterating the massif first. A highly cultured and artistic man – as was Alexander, for that matter – Tuker had no desire to destroy the abbey, but while he fervently believed such a drastic measure was the only way the Allies could prevail up there, he was also hoping that so drastic a decision would make Freyberg and the senior commanders think again.

He also told Freyberg that 4th Indian would need comprehensive information about the entire Monte Cassino spur, including details of the construction and size of the abbey. To his astonishment, however, he was told that neither Corps nor Fifth Army HQ had any information about the abbey building at all. He then dispatched a subaltern post-haste to Naples to scour the bookshops there. Eventually, the young officer discovered two books, one published in 1879, the other in 1920, that described the construction of the abbey in some detail, and which confirmed that it had been rebuilt and strengthened as a fortress in both the fourteenth and seventeenth centuries, with further additions in the early nineteenth century. There were vast, deep cellars, walls at least 10 feet thick and only one means of entry. 'Monte Cassino is therefore a modern fortress,' he dictated from his hospital bed, 'and must be dealt with by modern means. No practicable means available within the capacity of field engineers can possibly cope with this place.'

So worried was Tuker that the evolving plan was a disaster waiting to happen, he dragged himself from his hospital bed on 12 February and had himself driven to Freyberg's HQ. 'I did see Freyberg,' he noted, 'and at least twice thumped into him that there must be no compromise in the air etc bombardment . . . ALL or nothing and no direct attack.' In a series of memos also issued that same day, he spelled out what he and his divisional staff had in mind. He pointed out that a series of attacks had already been put in and, at considerable cost, had made almost no progress; there was therefore no reason to expect that a further attack along the same lines would be any different. 'Success will only be achieved in my opinion,' he wrote, 'if a thorough and prolonged air bombardment is undertaken with really heavy bombs a good deal larger than "Kitty-bomber" missiles.' In a second memo he stressed that the Allies had overwhelming aerial supremacy, with both tactical and strategic air forces in Italy and a considerable arsenal of guns. Artillery, he stated, had so far done little to help the infantry. Smothering the entire Monte Cassino spur with the heaviest bombs available followed by an immediate attack was the only way he could see the position being unlocked. 'The 1,000 lb bomb,' he told Freyberg, 'would be next to useless to effect this.'

What he was asking for were what were officially termed 'high-capacity' bombs, and within MASAF's arsenal there were a number of 2,000lb bombs as well as 4,000lb high-capacity bombs, better known as 'cookies', both of which could have been dropped by MASAF's bombers. As it happened, they also had supplies of 1,900lb and 2,000lb general-purpose bombs. Tuker made it clear that the bombardment from both the air and artillery and the subsequent infantry attacks all needed to be closely coordinated. 'The essence of the bombardment', he noted, 'should have been its obliterating weight, suddenness and duration and the immediate continuance of the bombing by artillery bombardment and infantry attack early in the night under the artillery bombardment.'

His final memorandum concluded with a terse admonition. 'When a formation is called upon to reduce such a place,' he wrote via his divisional Chief of Staff, 'it should be apparent that the place is reducible by the means at the disposal of that Div or that the means are ready for it, without having to go to the bookstalls of Naples to find out what should have been fully considered many weeks ago.' Freyberg and his staff may have blanched at such a comment, but it was a fair point all the same.

So not only had Tuker staggered off to see Freyberg in person, he had also written down everything he'd told him verbally in this series of memos. His proposal could not have been any clearer. That evening, Freyberg, his resolve once again stiffened by Tuker's direct intervention, called General Al Gruenther to relay his request for the intervention of the air forces.

'I desire that I be given air support tomorrow in order to soften up the enemy position in the Cassino area,' Freyberg told him. 'I want three missions of twelve planes each; the planes to be Kittybombers, carrying 1,000 pound bombs.' In other words, the very opposite of what Tuker had proposed. It is hard to fathom what on earth Freyberg was thinking. Kittybombers were single-engine P-40 fighter planes adapted to carry bombs but were fighters first and bombers second. Tuker had been specific: no Kittybombers, no 1,000lb bombs; these would not be able to do the job required. Three dozen adapted fighter planes were hardly going to pulverize the entire Monte Cassino massif. Why would Freyberg assure Tuker he was completely in line with all he was suggesting then so massively dilute those specific instructions? It was as though he'd not read the memos properly, which was unforgivable. Or perhaps Freyberg was simply all at sea, his mind scrambled, unable to think clearly.

In Tuker's final missive that day, 12 February, he once again, however, urged Freyberg to reconsider the entire plan. A much better option, he said, repeating what he'd outlined from the outset, was to use II Corps' gains around Monte Cairo as a firm base and attack north of Monte Castellone, where enemy defences were weaker and the ground easier over which to fight, and at the same time to launch an attack across the Rapido. Then he'd made a last point: 'To go direct for the Monastery Hill now without "softening" it properly is only to hit one's head straight against the hardest part of the whole enemy position and to risk the failure of the whole operation.' Freyberg ignored Tuker's final exhortation, however. Instead, he demanded the destruction of the abbey with a woefully insufficient weight of bombs and no follow-up plan whatsoever for the deployment of 4th Indian.

Gruenther relayed Freyberg's request to Clark, who did not consider the bombing of the abbey was necessary. Rather, the Fifth Army commander considered that the Red Bulls were within an inch of victory and that only exhaustion and casualties had prevented them from the vital breakthrough. Therefore, with fresh troops – mountain-trained troops to boot – this final furlong should be eminently achievable. He had not appreciated, as Tuker had understood, that the geography and nature of the German defence massively predicated against this for several reasons. First, the Germans were dug into prepared positions which made artillery fire against them comparatively ineffective. That meant the hard yards had to be undertaken by infantry, and they were finding themselves advancing on a very narrow front. Second, battle space really did dictate how many troops could be flung into a fight at any one time and this area of the Monte Cassino spur was comparatively small. Monte Castellone to the abbey, for example, could have been walked in an hour or so, the length of Snakeshead in fifteen to twenty minutes. From Point 593 to the abbey was a little over half a mile. The Americans had been advancing along narrow ridges on which no more than platoons and companies could be pushed forward at any one time. These comparatively few numbers would find themselves horribly exposed to machine-gun, mortar and artillery fire as they emerged from their places of cover. Each wave was being ruthlessly cut down in turn. It was not the exhaustion or freshness of the troops that was the issue. It was the nature of the terrain and the German defences around that terrain.

Freyberg pressed the point about the bombing, however, insisting it was a military necessity. He also made it clear that if Clark refused, then the Fifth Army commander would have to take responsibility if the attack proved a failure. Alexander had already warned Clark to tread carefully with Freyberg; the New Zealanders were Dominion troops and had no formal obligation to fight. In other words, there were politics at play in these polyglot Allied forces to which Alexander and Clark had to be sensitive. When Harding spoke to Gruenther about the bombing request, he made it clear that Alexander regretted the decision but trusted Freyberg's judgement. Still believing that the destruction of the abbey would be a mistake, Clark insisted the decision should be Alexander's, not his. 'If it were an American commander,' Gruenther noted of Clark's view, 'his decision would be an easy one and he would not bother General Alexander about it.'

'Our abbey is completely ruined,' noted Dom Martino on Saturday, 12 February, 'holed and shattered.' He reminded himself of the abbey's motto: *succicsa, vivrescit – cut them down and they will become stronger*. Errant shells had been crashing into the abbey for days now as the battle raged beyond. No German troops were within the abbey walls but there were plenty around it and on the hill on which it was perched. These men were attracting a lot of Allied fire. Two babies were born that day, their mothers giving birth in the Santa Rosa Chapel, yet as new lives were beginning, Dom Eusebio, so ill for weeks now, was facing the end of his life's journey despite being only thirty-two years old. That night he was struck with severe abdominal pains and was becoming greatly distressed. 'Our Reverend Father Abbot,' noted Dom Martino, 'who has not been to bed for the last few nights, spent the whole night at his bedside, to support him.'

More shells hit the abbey overnight but, as Dom Martino reported, there were now a lot of Germans near the abbey walls, and at the Fortino, within a stone's throw, they had built shelters. There were further MG and mortar pits in the bank between the road and the walls – all part of the second circle of the figure-of-eight. Because the Germans were using Monastery Hill and the Allies knew this, the abbey was inevitably getting hit in the crossfire. So many shells were now landing inside that simply moving about the abbey was fraught with risk. They also now had hundreds of civilians sheltering with them, but feeding everyone was becoming difficult. So too was tending the sick, now that they were largely cut off from the outside world.

Through the morning, Dom Eusebio's condition worsened. Dom Martino had been tending him and just after 1 p.m. he offered him the Sacraments; when the Father Abbot then joined him it was to administer to Dom Eusebio Extreme Unction and make the Sign of San Mauro. Most of the monks now gathered round him while the Father Abbot gave him the Apostolic Absolution and recited Prayers for the Dying. The end came at 2.45 p.m. 'The Lord has taken from us in this terrifying hour one of our young brothers who loved this House so much and had worked so hard for the benefit of the Basilica at Cassino,' wrote Dom Martino. 'The illness which carried him to the grave must have been easily picked up through the help he gave to the sick.' After dressing the dead man in his monastic robes they laid him in the second corridor of the shelter, near the window. It had been a sad day for the monks, for Dom Eusebio had been much loved.

That same day, Sunday, 13 February, as Dom Eusebio lay dying, Alexander and Clark had a strained conversation about Freyberg's bombing request. Clark pointed out that there was no indication that any German troops were using the abbey, that previous attempts to bomb a specific building had invariably failed, and neither Keyes nor Ryder had thought its destruction necessary. After speaking with Alexander, Clark immediately made notes of the conversation. 'For religious and sentimental reasons,' Clark noted, 'it is too bad unnecessarily to destroy one of the art treasures of the world. Besides, we have indications that many civilian women and children are taking shelter therein.' Alexander, though, was determined to back Freyberg, his New Zealand corps commander, even if it meant doing so over his American army commander. He also felt strongly that a commander, if faced with the choice between risking a single soldier's life and destroying a work of art, or even an important religious symbol such as the Abbey of Monte Cassino, should only make one decision – and that should be to protect that man's life. Alexander clearly believed this profoundly, a sentiment that had been endorsed back in December by Eisenhower when the latter had been Supreme Allied Commander. They had to believe this; it was why they'd been able to sanction the bombing of cities and towns, and the relentless shelling of villages or any object that got in the way and hindered the progress of the young men trying to help the forces of democracy win the war. Hundreds of churches in Italy had already been flattened; whole villages and towns razed. Only just a few miles away lay the wreckage of San Pietro, San

Vittore and Cervaro, to name but a few – all peaceful, vibrant places largely untouched for centuries until the war came along.

Yet although Alexander's justification was arguable, there was no denying that these discussions over the abbey's bombing belied a terrible calamity about to happen. Neither Alex nor Clark were asking themselves the right questions at this critical moment. They had completely failed to understand the nature of the challenge facing any attacking infantry up on the Monte Cassino massif, as had Keyes and now Freyberg. The opportunity for clearing the massif of enemy troops had been there, fleetingly, at the start of the month – but that had now passed. None of these generals had been up on to the mountain. They were guilty of misunderstanding lines on a map that showed how close – in terms of physical distance – the Allies were to a breakthrough. In terms of winning they were not remotely close, however. It seems that Juin understood this and so did Tuker. What Freyberg was proposing was a shoddy, badly presented air plan that was way, way short of what Tuker had proposed; already, in the conversation between Clark and Alex, the focus was now purely on destroying the abbey rather than smothering the entire massif with high-capacity blockbusters. No one at the senior level, Tuker aside, appeared to have given any analysis to the fighting up there. By 12 February, the 155mm long toms had fired 12,000 rounds, the 240mm howitzers 900, and the 105s a staggering 100,000 – all in just two weeks of fighting. And yet, for the past week, the Americans up on the massif and down in the northern end of the town had made no progress whatsoever. That should have told them, as clear as day, that firing endless numbers of shells was not working and that a different approach was needed.

Confronted with Freyberg's ultimatum – for that was what it was – they should have asked themselves whether there was another way, or least examined properly what was being asked. But they did not. Alexander was backing Freyberg, who had completely failed to grasp or understand what Tuker had told him. Clark, on the other hand, was supporting his commanders, who had also singularly failed to comprehend the nature of the challenge that was now before them on the Monte Cassino massif. And the commander of the division now poised to order his infantry into the fray had neither the experience nor the knowledge of how to fight any infantry battle, let alone one of such a challenging magnitude. It was a perfect storm.

CHAPTER 19

The Destruction of the Abbey

UNDETERRED, THE ALLIES CONTINUED preparing for Freyberg's battle plan, which called for 7th Indian Infantry Brigade, who were to lead the attack, to take over from the Americans on Monte Cassino on the night of 12–13 February and for the attack to go in two nights later with a sweep down from Snakeshead and Point 593, across the Colle d'Onofrio saddle, towards Monastery Hill. The Germans, however, counter-attacked towards Monte Castellone on the night of the 12th–13th, and so the 7th Indians had to postpone taking over from the otherwise engaged Americans until the following evening. When they finally attempted this, they discovered two things. First, Point 593 was not in American hands as they had been led to believe. In fact, it had not been in American hands since the night of the 9th–10th, when Kratzert's men had recaptured it; that this vital piece of information had not been relayed to 4th Indian underlined the confused nature both of the fighting and of the command up there. Not only had junior officers been killed and wounded, but more senior ones as well: on 13 February, Colonel Wyatt, commander of 141st Infantry, was killed by a shell outside his CP. If there had been a breakdown in the smooth flow of information from up on the massif it was hardly surprising.

The other problem was that some of the Americans were so exhausted they could not physically move. The bombing, originally planned for the 14th, had to be postponed while the Americans extricated themselves from their forward positions; a number had to be stretchered down, which took time. Among those finally coming down off the mountain was Ralph Schaps, miraculously still in one piece. 'We had started up the hill with 42 men in our platoon,' Schaps noted. 'We came down with 7 men.' After being taken to the rear assembly area, they were given their first hot meal in two weeks.

Captain Roswell Doughty was another of the comparatively few survivors of 141st Infantry still standing by 14 February, albeit only just. Four days on the mountain, in which he'd repeatedly cheated death by seconds and by inches and been exposed to freezing temperatures, rain and snow and surrounded by death, decay and destruction, had more than taken their toll. Somehow, he'd staggered back down and reported to the Regimental CP. He'd not shaved, lost a lot of weight just in that time and looked a mess. He'd also been popping Benzedrine pills to keep himself going the past few days. This drug, taken in tablets, was a form of speed. The trouble was, although Benzedrine kept a man awake, it did not relieve the body of exhaustion. Now, at the CP, this caught up with him in dramatic fashion. Soon after his arrival, Doughty collapsed unconscious and had to be taken to a field hospital in San Pietro, to the rear of Cervaro.

There was to be no relief for Lieutenant Harry Bond or the rest of the Texas Division, however. Bond had remained in his post at the foot of the northern edge of Snakeshead Ridge until 14 February. With each passing day, he'd noticed a gradual sapping of energy and spirit. Sleep was hard to come by, despite their growing exhaustion. And each day, mule trains carrying the dead and wounded traipsed past. At night enemy shelling continued, mostly sporadic but relentless. Then word arrived that they were to be moving to the north, up towards Monte Castellone and the ridge that ran from it in the direction of Colle Sant'Angelo. Up there, the battered T-Patchers were to carry out a holding role while 4th Indian moved in on to the Monte Cassino spur.

A guide led Bond and his men 2,000 yards to their right that same afternoon. The remnants of the 141st were to man the southern slopes of Monte Castellone down towards Point 706, which marked the start of Phantom Ridge, but the mortar platoon, much to their relief, were sited in a gully that offered excellent protection. 'It was behind a steep cliff,' noted Bond, 'and we thought it very unlikely that any artillery fire could fall in here.' That was all to the good, but Bond needed an OP where he could see both the battlefield and direct fire. Their guides were from the outgoing Red Bulls, who led them up on to the Castellone Ridge, past a number of dead who had yet to be collected. Suddenly, Bond could see the entire battleground: the abbey, further away now, perched on its outcrop, the clear line of Snakeshead and its rocky end point at 593; Albaneta, the Colle Sant'Angelo and, beyond, the Liri Valley. To his right the ground climbed again up to the monstrous, all-dominating peak of Monte Cairo. Really, this was such a very small corner of Italy – a tiny mountain spur of bluff, ridges and ravines; it seemed incredible that it had become the site of such intense and brutal fighting.

The order to bomb Monte Cassino reached General Ira Eaker's Fifteenth Air Force HQ at Caserta through General Wilson at Allied Forces HQ. Immediately, Eaker contacted Wilson's deputy, General Jacob Devers, and suggested they both go and have a look themselves. Flying from the airstrip at Caserta, they took an L-5 Courier plane, which Eaker piloted himself, with three fighter planes to escort them. The flight didn't take long and Eaker brought the Courier in low over the abbey. Both Eaker and Devers saw Germans around the abbey. 'I could have dropped my binoculars into machine-gun nests,' Eaker noted, 'less than 50 feet from the walls.' Even so, he had little enthusiasm for the task although he accepted the directive, which was specifically to destroy the abbey rather than obliterate the entire Monte Cassino spur as Tuker had detailed. Yet again, this underlined the ever-widening gulf of understanding about what they were trying to achieve.

Eaker made his preparations on the basis of the instructions given to him, although there would not be three dozen Kittybombers as Freyberg had so bizarrely specified to Clark. Rather, there were to be successive waves of heavy bombers, then medium bombers and finally fighter-bombers sent over. Among those earmarked for the task were B-17s of the 2nd BG, which included Lieutenant Michael Sullivan and the crew of *Sad Sack*. In all, 142 heavies were due to take part, and Sullivan and the rest of the 2nd BG were briefed at 4 a.m. on Tuesday, 15 February. Rather than being loaded up with heavy high-capacity ordnance, however, *Sad Sack* was given twelve 500lb bombs. This was the bomb load issued to all the heavies that morning. Not one four-engine bomber would be carrying anything bigger than a 500-pounder. Again, Tuker's very precise instructions were ignored, lost in Freyberg's nonsensical interpretation.

On the day that Tuker had staggered from his sickbed to see Freyberg, the latter had promised that he would not let 4th Indian launch an attack without 'the full orchestra.' Freyberg had already reneged on that by muddling up Tuker's bombing instructions in his discussions with Clark. Now other factors were conspiring against Brigadier Harry Dimoline's plans for the battle that would follow hot on the heels of the bombing. As

Tuker had also specified, such an assault would only be likely to work if the infantry went in straight after the bombing, before the enemy had time to recover. American ammunition and stores could not be used by the 4th Indians, however, as they were mostly incompatible, so the division had to build up its own supplies. Unfortunately, despite the best efforts of Frank Pearce and the engineers, the one road across the upper Rapido was now impassable to their lorries because it was still waterlogged and churned up by overuse. US six-wheel trucks came to the rescue, but it meant a delay in the build-up. Pearce was out again on the night of the 11th, for example, working on the road. 'Terrible traffic jam,' he noted, 'as Indian troops were moving up. Mules, vehicles and men. What a mess.' A further logjam was created by the need to unload trucks and transfer almost everything on to mules. Some 1,500 of these beasts of burden were brought in, but it was mayhem in Caira until these animals could all be properly organized. Nor was getting them loaded and up on to the massif easy with the amount of snow and ice about.

Dimoline had earmarked Brigadier Osmond Lovett's 7th Indian Infantry Brigade to lead off the attack, as it was considered that there was not enough space for any more infantry up there. In fact, only a single battalion, the Royal Sussex, were to start the attack, with the 4th Rajputana Rifles in reserve. In other words, a division-sized attack would be carried out by fewer than 800 men. However, because of the German counter-attacks and the issues of extricating the Americans, Lovett's troops weren't able to take over the forward positions until the night of 13–14 February. Worse, a number of the American wounded could not be evacuated until the following night, 14–15 February. Because of all the delays and setbacks, Dimoline suggested making an assault on Monastery Hill across the d'Onofrio saddle from Snakeshead the evening after that, so 16–17 February. These plans were based on the assumption that the bombing would take place on the afternoon of 16 February; he intended to pull all his forward troops back 1,000 yards while this occurred, then sweep down from the ridge and assault Monastery Hill.

The bombing itself, however, was dependent on a gap in the weather, which had been filthy on the 14th but which promised to be followed by a day of much-improved conditions. What's more, the air forces were on standby for Anzio, where a major German counter-attack was expected any day now – so the sooner they bombed the abbey, the better. And so the operation was set for 9.30 a.m. on Tuesday, 15 February. No one, however, thought to relay this to Brigadier Lovett and his 7th Indian

Infantry Brigade. Since the whole point of the attack was to launch it by stealth and surprise, bombing early on the 15th was a disaster – Lovett's men would not be ready to follow up across the open ground towards Monastery Hill so soon, especially not in broad daylight. Operations were planned at specific times because that was when the troops would be ready and when conditions best suited them; it wasn't possible to click one's fingers and advance an assault to fit in with the weather and the busy schedule of the Fifteenth Air Force. It was one of the challenges of bringing in the Strategic Air Forces to support a tactical operation.

How very attractive an attack to the south of Monte Cairo must have suddenly seemed: weak German troops, no configured defensive system, no bunkers. No determined Fallschirmjäger dug in. And no need for a coordinated bombing assault. It was too much to expect Freyberg to call the whole thing off at this point; if he'd not shown any grasp of what he was undertaking so far, these last-minute additional cock-ups weren't going to make any difference. And Dimoline was too junior, too inexperienced and lacking authority to call a halt to the whole sorry mess. Yet to men like Brigadier Osmond Lovett, whose men were now up on the mountain, it was horribly apparent what was about to unfold.

On 14 February a truce had been agreed, instigated by the Germans, to give both sides a chance to recover the dead that now littered the mountain battleground. Bodies of 165 Germans were collected and carried back down the mountainside by the Americans along with hundreds of their own. Lieutenant-Colonel Harold R. Reese, an aide to General Walker, acted as special envoy to the Germans and found himself standing on the hillside talking to his German counterpart. 'It is such a tragedy, this life,' the German said to him in faltering English. 'Today we laugh, tomorrow we kill.' Reese found his determination to wipe out every last Kraut weakening somewhat. The truce lasted six and a half hours. Then the shelling began all over again.

Allied bombers also dropped leaflets on to Monte Cassino that same day. At around 2 p.m., some civilian youths brought a collection of them to Dom Martino in the abbey shelter and he then immediately showed them to the Father Abbot. The leaflets were addressed to 'Italian Friends'. 'Until now,' one read, 'we have sought to avoid the bombing of Monte Cassino. But the Germans have known how to take advantage of this. Now the battle is even more fiercely joined around the sacred site. With heavy hearts, we are forced to deploy our weapons against the Abbey itself. Leave the monastery immediately; save yourselves. Our warning is urgent. It is given for your benefit.'

Their hearts were full of terrible foreboding at this; down in the shelter, where Dom Eusebio's body still lay, there were a large number of civilians now asking what they should do. Some boys went out to try and make contact with the Germans but they were fired on and scuttled back. A second attempt was made, this time with a white flag, but the same happened again. Meanwhile, Dom Eusebio was placed in a coffin and carried by several volunteers down the College stairs and buried in the main grave of the chancel. Later, a teenager named Morra and his friend braved leaving the abbey once more and this time managed to speak to a German tank driver who was with his panzer behind the San Giuseppe Chapel. The German told him to come back at 5 a.m. to speak to their officer; as Dom Martino was the only German speaker now among them, it was agreed he should go with them. In the meantime, they all packed a suitcase each. That evening the Father Abbot wept openly at their plight.

In fact, the German officer came to them and with Dom Martino's help, at 5 a.m. on the morning of Tuesday, 15 February, spoke with the Father Abbot. The officer told them that the leaflet was intended to intimidate and that they could not allow anyone to pass through their lines. In any case, to do so would be a huge risk; in his experience, he told them, about a third could expect to lose their lives on the roads. However, they would, he conceded, allow anyone who wanted to leave to take a mule track down to the Via Casilina between midnight and 5 a.m. the following morning. After the German had gone, Dom Martino relayed this information to the monks and then to the civilians, of whom there were now as many as 1,000 sheltering there. Not a single person, however, had left since the leaflets had been dropped.

General Clark wanted no part in the bombing of the abbey and so remained in his hut, but the formations flew over Presenzano and for some reason sixteen bombs were dropped early right on top of his CP. Clark was certainly having his fair share of close calls, but once again luck was with him. Shrapnel lacerated tents and hit vehicles, but by great fortune not a single person was hurt. This error aside, the rest of the bombers found the target without a hitch and bombed from only around 1,000 feet, which was extremely low for heavies. It meant a ringside view for the many men up on the mountain and for those further back too at the various rear assembly areas around Cervaro.

Harry Bond, now up at his OP on Castellone, had heard the talk about the bombing and, like all his men, was glad. They all hoped it might finally bring about the end of the battle. Bond himself had no doubt the abbey was useful to the Germans and he reckoned that with so many Allied troops getting killed anything that might save lives and help crack the line should be done. Yet at the same time he recognized that the abbey symbolized much of what they were fighting for – a belief in human dignity and individual worth. 'But war is brutalizing,' he noted. 'The primitive desire to survive soon overcomes our painfully acquired cultural inhibitions, and what is civilized and humane, what is generous and fine in man, can be as quickly destroyed.'

It was a fine morning but there was an icy wind blowing from the east. Just before 9.30 a.m., Bond saw the first formation approaching, lots of them, the drone of their engines filling the air. He could not hear any other guns firing, not even German flak; it was as though everyone was watching. Closer they came, and then they were over, and Bond could actually see the bombs falling, like little black stones. The ground all around them shook as the bombs exploded and the abbey became shrouded in clouds of rolling smoke. Another formation arrived and another, the bombs continuing to fall, the mountain ripped apart, it seemed, by the sound of the explosions, the blasts convulsing through the rock beneath them. The smoke drifted and he saw the abbey fleetingly reappear before being shrouded again.

It was 9.25 a.m. precisely when the first bombs fell. Lieutenant Michael Sullivan was among the crews of thirty-seven Flying Fortresses from the 2nd BG, but three other bomb groups were involved, with 135 of the 142 due to take part reaching the target. 'Target 100 yds in front of our lines,' jotted Sullivan later. 'A real pinpoint job . . . Blew it all to hell.' Then he was banking and turning back to Foggia. One of the easiest missions he'd undertaken so far.

The monks were gathered in the Father Abbot's room off the shelter for Sext and Nones and were all kneeling to recite the final Antiphon of the Madonna when there was a sudden terrifying explosion. Others followed immediately. The Father Abbot now gave them absolution while Dom Martino and the others prayed for what they assumed would be the moment of death. The room shook, smoke and dust came in through the narrow windows and they saw the flames of explosions as they struck the side of the College. Miraculously, they were still alive, and so they all stuffed wadding in their ears as ever more bombs rocked the abbey.

At the 6. Kompanie positions in the Colle d'Onofrio, Oberjäger Rudolf Donth and his troops were now well positioned, he reckoned, with stone sangars built up by the men using the broken ground to hide themselves well. Oberjäger Christl Wöhrl and Obergefreiter Gustl Weber were carrying out machine-gun training for the new men, as they did every morning; Fallschirmjäger were issued with two MG42s per ten-man Gruppe, rather than the one that was standard throughout the rest of the army, and it was seen as their most important weapon. Nowhere was it more important than up here on the mountain, with them now in defensive positions. Suddenly, though, there was a huge roar in the sky and someone shouted, 'The bombers are coming!' Moments later, a formation of heavies appeared directly over them and the bombs started falling in front of them and behind them. Donth and his men lay there, behind and between their stone shelters, pressing themselves as close to the ground as possible, although with each impact they were physically lifted up and slammed back down again.

Obergefreiter Kurt Müller, one of Donth's new men in the company, was struggling badly with a particularly virulent dose of diarrhoea and was at the 6. Kompanie command post that morning when the first bombs landed. In moments, half the roof of the little stone house had been ripped off, but despite his proximity to the blast he was once again gripped by the need to relieve himself. Getting up, he dashed to the latrine 10 yards away. With his trousers down and squatting there, he looked up as a bomber flew right over him, bomb bays open, and then dropped a chain of bombs. His comrades were taking cover behind their sangars 50 yards away and now yelled at him. Hastily pulling up his trousers again, he dashed and dived for cover just as the next wave of bombs exploded. He'd so very nearly been caught with his trousers down.

Brigadier Harry Dimoline was holding a planning conference on the morning of 15 February when Osmond Lovett, commander of 7th Indian Brigade, told him that Point 593 was not, after all, occupied by the Americans but was still held by the Germans. Dimoline's plan had been to have machine guns and mortars up on Point 593 to provide cover as the infantry then swept down over the Colle d'Onofrio, with the rocky bluff as his firm base, so this rather put his plan into disarray. As Lovett pointed out, it would be impossible to get across to Monastery Hill until Point 593 was firmly in their hands and so he recommended this be a separate operation. Dimoline accepted his point and they agreed that the Royal Sussex would capture the outcrop that evening, 15–16 February, and then plan to launch their main attack the following night, 16–17 February.

At that moment, the heavies came over and started to bomb the abbey.

Although Freyberg had not known the truth about Point 593 he did learn from Clark himself on the afternoon of 14 February that the bombing operation was to take place the following morning. He also knew about Dimoline's plans not to attack until the night of the 16th. His battle plan was already going horribly awry even before it had begun and he must have known that there could only be one way the battle would now go. It was nothing less than sending good men to be slaughtered. Admittedly, political pressure from London and Washington was intense and nerves were running high about the prospective German counter-attack at Anzio, yet a battle that failed to achieve its aims would not help those at the beachhead. But rather than put the kibosh on the whole sorry enterprise there and then, Freyberg returned to his HQ and told Dimoline that the bombardment would take place the following morning and that was all there was to it.

The second wave of bombers arrived at around 10.35 a.m. and for the next two hours medium bombers continued to pummel the abbey with 1,000-pounders. Finally, a further wave came over at 2 p.m., which proved the most accurate of all. In all, 576 tons had been dropped on the abbey and surrounding mountainside.

In their shelter beneath the College yard, the monks and the Father Abbot had once again survived; those thick bastions that Tuker had carefully noted had proved impervious, although the retaining wall on the north side had been destroyed and damage from this had partially blocked the shelter's entrance. Despite the Father Abbot's age, he managed to crawl out with the help of the younger monks, and, clutching the suitcases they had packed the previous evening, they clambered up the staircase, also now littered with rubble, and out into the College yard. 'The saddest sight imaginable greeted our eyes,' noted Dom Martino, 'the devastation was total.' All around them lay ruin and desolation, but also many wounded and dying. Some had chosen to flee as the first bombs had fallen, but most had remained. The monks tried to see what they could do for these civilians, but accessing many of the areas where they had been sheltering was now impossible. Dom Martino and Dom Agostino found a door to the lower chapels of the Torretta that was not blocked and, opening it, heard screaming from a woman in the postroom whose feet had been blown off. They carried her into the Torretta but on the stairway of the lower chapel they found several hundred people, some injured but most mercifully unhurt.

Dom Martino felt utterly dazed, barely able to comprehend what had happened and the scale of the ruins and devastation he now saw all around him. At around 8 p.m. a German officer arrived bearing a missive from none other than Adolf Hitler, who was promising to ask for a brief truce with the Allies to allow the Father Abbot, monks and civilians in the abbey to be able to leave; the monks were to be taken to the Vatican, he assured them. 'Feldmarschall Kesselring will request the truce tonight,' he told them. 'Let us hope that the Americans will grant it, otherwise the blame will fall on them.'

That evening, Frank Pearce wrote up his diary after another fraught day trying to rebuild the road over the upper Rapido. 'Saw the prettiest sight I ever expected to see in war,' he wrote. 'Clear day and in groups of 24, 143 Flying Fortresses came over and bombed the Monastery and Mountain above Cassino. Later 36 B25s came in and this evening 36 more. The Monastery just a shell now.'

And in that shell, the monks and some 700 civilians were still cowering in the wreckage. Dom Martino was unable to sleep; he couldn't stop thinking about the terrible events of the day and the horrific situation in which they now found themselves. He wondered whether they really would be able to escape, and if so, how they might get the wounded and sick to safety. He also worried about the Father Abbot, seventy-nine years old, and how he might manage walking down a mountain track to safety in the middle of the night. On the other hand, if they stayed, would they not all end up dead under the rubble? Not for the first time since the war had reached them, he wondered what on earth to do for the best. Suddenly, there was a loud crash and the sound of collapsing masonry; the pharmacy and the ceiling of the Via Crucis Chapel had collapsed. It was about 1.30 a.m. on 16 February.

Elsewhere, around the mountain, it was eerily quiet. Now looming against the night sky was the abbey, no longer the towering edifice it had been earlier the previous morning, but instead a broken mound of rubble and a jagged outline of shattered walls.

CHAPTER 20

FISCHFANG and Monte Cassino Part 1

'THROUGH OUR HEARTS AND minds, resignation and futility crawl like worms,' noted Audie Murphy. 'We cannot advance. And we cannot retreat another yard without adding further peril to the slim security of our beachhead.' Rumours abounded. That the British were pulling out. That a huge gap in the line was about to be created. That the Germans were soon to unleash a wildcat and burst through the middle of their defences and drive them back into the sea. 'We believe nothing,' added Murphy. 'Doubt nothing.'

An air of fearful expectation hung over the bridgehead. An interval of uncertainty. The Allies waiting for the Germans to attack. But there were some causes for cheer: on the morning of 15 February, the sun had been shining on the Anzio bridgehead and Gefreiter Hans Liebschner had been full of wonderment to have heard the dawn chorus. He couldn't understand where all the birds had come from amid this desolation and destruction, yet could hear them well enough, singing their hearts out, a tiny beacon of hope and the sound of normality in this otherwise crazy world. Liebschner was exhausted. After the last fighting around Carroceto, Oberleutnant Weiss's company had been reduced to just sixteen men; the entire battalion had been decimated and had been withdrawn. Liebschner, however, and his friend Horst had been ordered to remain with the Kampfgruppe; good runners were both highly prized and in short supply. And so they'd been transferred to a different company.

Although there were two company runners, in reality either of them could be called at any time. He and Horst shared a dugout and because it was always so cold spent most of the night clasped in one another's arms purely for the extra warmth. Both dreaded the shout, '*Melder!*' – 'Runner!' 'We took it in turns,' noted Liebschner. 'How we hated this dreadful cry, especially in the darkness of a rainy night when the ground was slippery, vision almost nil and mortar and grenades were chasing us from cover to cover.'

Kampfgruppe Gericke were still attached to General Hans-Hellmuth Pfeifer's 65. Infanterie-Division and based in the Moletta Valley. The Moletta ran from south of the Buonriposo Ridge roughly westwards to the sea, and was responsible for many of the wadis that scored this part of the bridgehead like the veins of a leaf. It was disorientating, and especially so for runners like Hans Liebschner because many of the wadis had sides between 10 and 20 feet high but were never very wide – often no more than 5–10 yards, which made them rather like the kind of trenches that had been such a feature of the Western Front in the last war. Since the last attack, Pfeifer's men, which included Gericke's battle group, had pushed on to the Buonriposo Ridge but also further west, into the wadis.

On the 15th there had been much activity because von Mackensen's all-out offensive was due to begin the following morning. Even on a day of comparatively little fighting, however, shells and mortars continued to be fired; risk always lurked for anyone moving about. That day, Liebschner was hurrying towards General Pfeifer's cave command post when he suddenly came across the runner from 2. Kompanie slumped against a tree stump at the edge of one of the wadis. Around him was a large pool of dark blood; he'd been hit by a piece of shrapnel and then bled to death. 'Because one was always alone,' noted Liebschner, 'the fear of getting wounded with nobody to help became one of the runner's nightmares.'

Operation FISCHFANG – 'catching fish' – had been a week in the planning following the reduction of the Campoleone salient. Von Mackensen had two corps surrounding Anzio, General Traugott Herr's LXXVI Panzerkorps and General Alfred Schlemm's I Fallschirmjägerkorps, which amounted to six divisions, forty-five battalions and 452 guns, twenty more than the Allies could muster. All these units were understrength to varying degrees; AOK 14 stood at 91,837 on 12 February, of whom 58,189 were combat troops. More men were also on their way. The 65. Division was getting 900 replacements, 26. Panzer 850 and 3. Panzergrenadier 650. Von Mackensen did, however, now have a battalion of the mighty Tiger tank and another of the Panther and some Hornets – 88mm high-velocity anti-tank guns on a Panzer Mk III chassis. Kesselring had asked Hitler for two more divisions and more armour, but instead the Führer had sent him the Lehr-Infanterie-Regiment, drawn mostly from training instructors and by which he held great store. Also hurriedly sent south for the attack were a number of new weapons, including the Goliath, a small, remote-controlled tracked vehicle full of explosive that was designed to be run forward to blast a path through wire or some other obstacle. There were also now four railway guns – two 210mm and two 240mm. These were mounted on railway wagons and had the range to hit ships out at sea and strike the port facilities of Anzio and Nettuno – and were doing so. The Allies referred to them as 'Anzio Annies', and certainly they were giving the American and British rear areas a taste of their own medicine.

There were some snags in all these accumulated forces, however. First was the usual lack of unit cohesion – there were lots of orphan units temporarily attached to various divisions, which meant unfamiliar commanders. Hitler had also decreed that the Panthers and Tigers – together around 100 of them – should not be needlessly exposed and used very judiciously. And second, while they had amassed nearly 450 guns, von Mackensen's forces had only 7,400 tons of ammunition. That sounded like a lot, but really wasn't for a major offensive. In other words, FISCHFANG looked robust enough on paper but did not have quite the strength in depth required for such a major operation. As the Allies had discovered, going on the offensive in Italy was not easy. Despite this, Kesselring was, as usual, confident of success and already thinking ahead. Once the Allies had been kicked out of Anzio, he intended to turn south, push the British back over the Garigliano, and then fold up the rest of Fifth Army. In the mud and mire of Italy, perhaps it was no bad thing to look at life through sunnier glasses, but Kesselring was getting ahead of himself. Von Mackensen, for one, did not share his confidence, for although the weather had improved, the ground was waterlogged, Tigers and Panthers were over 50 and 40 tons each respectively and his room for manoeuvre was actually comparatively limited despite a seemingly vast and mostly empty plain in front of his troops.

Third, the Allies had already been flexing their muscles the past couple of days with their air power, which was vastly superior to that of the Luftwaffe. Hauptmann Jürgen Harder and his beleaguered fighter pilots in VII/JG53 had been flying relentlessly, often as much as four

General Mark W. Clark en route to Anzio, late January 1944. One of the towering figures of the Italian campaign, Clark commanded the largest force and more multinational troops than any other American Army commander in the war.

Above left: The ruins of Cervaro, the scene of bitter fighting in the first half of January 1944.

Above right: British troops tramp forward through the mud towards the River Garigliano.

Left: One of the bridges successfully put across the Garigliano. The challenges of fighting along this southern end of the Gustav Line were immense.

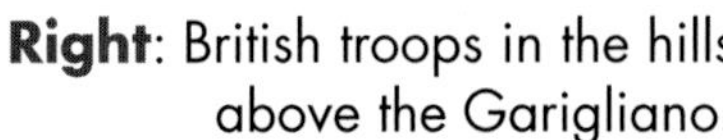

Right: British troops in the hills above the Garigliano.

Below left: T-Patcher stretcher parties dug in along the lateral road that ran along the River Rapido.

Below right: Troops from the 36th Division dug in near the Rapido.

Above: Trucks unloading from landing ships on to hastily emplaced piers and then on to the beaches at Anzio.

Below left: American troops advance inland across the flat expanse north of Anzio.

Above right: The Via Anziate with the Colli Albani in the distance. It was either side of this road that would see some of the heaviest fighting.

Below: The Mussolini Canal, created when the Pontine Marshes were drained in the Fascist era, and a major obstacle no matter which side was attacking.

Left: Landing ships disgorging supplies directly on to Anzio's shattered quayside. This helped the Allies to rapidly build up men and materiel into the bridgehead.

Below left: Anzio Annie – as the Allies called the railway gun. The Germans did not have the numbers of shells the Allies had, but these could reach the coast and beyond.

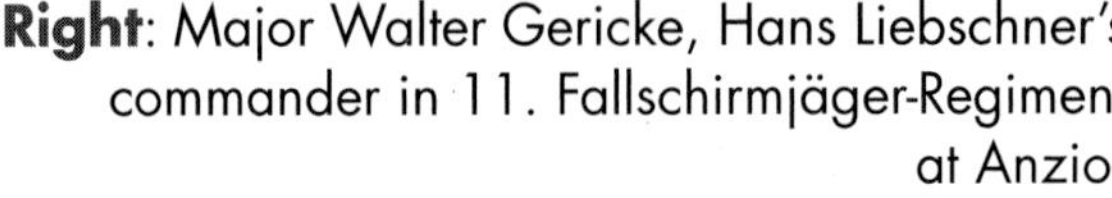

Right: Major Walter Gericke, Hans Liebschner's commander in 11. Fallschirmjäger-Regiment at Anzio.

Below left: A British Tommy crawls along a trench. Anzio often resembled the Western Front of the First World War.

Below right: An American tank destroyer rumbles through Nettuno. General Lucas was woefully slow to bring these and his mass of tanks into the battle.

Above left: General Alexander with his Chief of Staff, John Harding (right) and Général Juin (left) before the CEF's incredible assault of Monte Belvedere.

Above right: French colonial troops of the CEF, entirely equipped by the Americans, preparing to attack.

Above left: Men of the 34th Red Bulls trying to warm themselves near Sant'Elia in the Upper Rapido Valley.

Above right: The conditions in Italy in the first months of the year were appalling: cold and wet and bare on the mountains, with endless mud and flooding in the valleys. It was an additional enemy for the Allied troops.

Right: The town of Cassino under attack, late January, shown in a photograph probably taken from Monte Trocchio. The abbey is perched above, while the 6,000-foot-high Monte Cairo looms beyond.

A soldier of the 142nd Infantry Regiment, part of the 36th T-Patchers Division, having come down from the mountains. His beard, the mud and filth, and the utter exhaustion in his face speak of the brutal conditions and of the huge amount that was expected of these young men.

Left: General Freyberg VC. Brave as a lion but hopelessly out of his depth. His appointment as corps commander at Cassino was a catastrophe.

Right: Gurkhas of 4th Indian Division moving into the line.

Above left: Loading bombs aboard a B-25 Mitchell medium bomber.

Above right: The shattered remains of the old Italian Army barracks just to the north of Cassino.

Left: Fallschirmjäger shelter in a gully and watch the skies above.

Below: The devastated remains of one of the cultural treasures of Europe.

Left: Bombs exploding around the abbey, 15 February 1944.

Below: A column of troops and German armour pause on the wet and mud-slicked Via Anziate at the start of FISCHFANG, 16 February 1944.

Below left: General Eberhard von Mackensen (centre) with General-leutnant Alfred Schlemm (right). Von Mackensen thought fighting so far south in Italy was insane; he had a point.

Below right: An Allied ammunition truck hit and burning at Nettuno.

THE DESTRUCTION OF CASSINO

Above: A Fallschirmjäger looks down over Highway 6 and the Liri Valley from Monte Cassino. Nearly all German press photographs of troops in Italy were of Fallschirmjäger, the poster boys of Nazi propaganda, despite operating at only around 10 per cent strength.

Above: Medium bombers head towards Cassino town, 15 March 1944.

Left: Bombs begin to rain down.

Above left: Cassino being hammered. Huge clouds of smoke, dust and debris rise like a shroud.

Above right: General Clark (top), Al Gruenther and others watching the bombing from Freyberg's command post near San Vittore.

Right: The foot of the Cavendish Road.

Below: The bomb spread marked up on this aerial montage. Cassino town was flattened.

The destruction of Cassino, 15 March 1944.

Left: Nothing like enough troops were sent into Cassino once the bombers had gone and the artillery barrage had ended, and those that were there struggled with both massive piles of rubble and also rain.

Below: 4th Indian Division (**left**) troops advance over the largely bare and rocky mountainside. Incredibly, one company of the 1/9th Gurkhas did reach Hangman's Hill (**right**), just below the ruins of the abbey.

Above left: The desolation of Cassino, seen from the north. The river is the Rapido.

Above right: Oberst Ludwig Heilmann (left), the indefatigable commander of 3. FJR, with the 1. Fallschirmjäger divisional commander, General Richard Heidrich.

Right: The spectral figure of a Fallschirmjäger amid the smoke and ruins of Cassino.

THE FATE OF THE ITALIANS

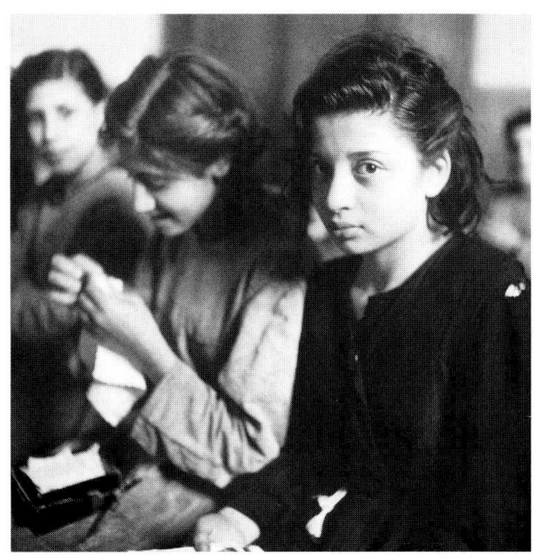

Above: Prostitution was rampant in southern Italy at horrific levels as Italians desperately tried to avoid starvation and destitution. A prostitute in Naples dances on a table in a brothel (**left**), while (**right**) this teenage girl recovers at the Albergo dei Poveri Reformatory having been prostituted by her family.

Above and below: Common scenes in Italy: a young woman with her child eating Allied food, families emerging from the cave in which they'd been living, refugees on the move and an elderly woman outside the ruins of her house. Their suffering was immense.

Above: General Alexander (left) talks to the Eighth Army commander, General Oliver Leese (centre), in the build-up to DIADEM. It opened up (**right**) on the night of 11 May 1944 with more than 1,600 guns – the largest barrage by the Allies of the war to date.

Above: The Poles took over positions on Monte Cassino before DIADEM. Theirs was a truly remarkable story and it was fitting that they finally secured the massif. Polish troops (**right**) in the ruins of the abbey, 18 May 1944.

Above left: A dead Fallschirmjäger lies among the rubble.

Above right: American troops of the 88th 'Blue Devils' in the ruins of Santa Maria Infante, while (**right**) men of the 38th Irish Brigade find themselves halted in the endless jam of traffic beside a knocked-out Nebelwerfer.

Above: US troops of the 88th Division move through Itri, while (**right**) a medic treats a battle casualty.

Below left: No town or village through which the fighting passed avoided the carnage; here a US soldier of the 3rd Division walks past German dead in Cisterna on 25 May.

Below right: A French soldier looks on at the wrecked column of German 71. Division vehicles and troops, blasted by CEF artillery as they tried to escape Esperia on 17 May.

Below: British troops finally retake Aprilia, 'The Factory' (**left**), while American troops corral prisoners in Velletri (**right**). The heat and dust are palpable.

THE LIBERATION OF ROME

General Clark **(top left)** pauses near the edge of Rome on 4 June 1944, and the following day Allied troops poured into the capital. On 5 June, Mark Clark, with his corps commanders Truscott and Keyes, held an impromptu meeting at the Campidoglio in the centre of the city (**below**). The battle for Rome was over.

times a day. This was excessive because flying a fighter plane was extremely draining, both physically and mentally. 'Every day at six in the morning,' Harder wrote to his wife, 'we drive to the airfield, which is 12 kilometres away, and do not return to our "hotel" until evening.' Mostly, they were flying over the Anzio bridgehead and almost always ran into Allied fighters. Harder's trick was to arrive at high altitude and then to dive very fast straight through any enemy aircraft then flatten out, fire rockets at ground targets and scuttle home. On 7 February he'd managed to shoot down a Spitfire, his first confirmed kill of the year. 'It was on my wingman's tail,' he added, 'when I shot it down and I thus saved his life.'

Not all Allied air forces were focused on Cassino on the 15th. Prisoners had revealed to the Allies that a major German attack at Anzio was planned for 16 February, which was the prime reason why Alexander and Clark were somewhat distracted with regard to the Cassino front. Furthermore, reconnaissance planes had seen the build-up behind the lines. Some 700 tons of bombs were dropped on German rear targets in the seventy-two hours leading up to the start of FISCHFANG. Among those flying over the beachhead on 15 February was Lieutenant Smoky Vrilakas, on what was his forty-eighth combat mission. Speeding across the Apennines from Foggia he and his flight had kept low, at only 2,000 feet. It had been a clear day and he'd been able to look down on the Gustav Line front and see the destruction there and to the south of it – ruined and smashed villages and towns marked the route pretty much all the way to Anzio. They were on a bombing job that day, but as they neared their bomb line there was an eruption of German flak. 'The shell bursts were so close we could hear them,' noted Vrilakas, 'and the barrage literally blew our flights apart. We wheeled around and up like a flock of shot-at geese.' His friend Don Kienholz was hit and radioed that his controls were locked and he was heading into a spin. Fortunately, just as he was about to bail, Kienholz managed to regain control. The squadron then dive-bombed their target and headed back home, Kienholz included. Only later, after Vrilakas had landed, did his crew chief find a jagged piece of shrapnel lodged in the landing flap directly behind the cockpit. He'd been lucky.

To the south, from his OP on Monte Castellone, Harry Bond had been astonished that once the bombers had flown away from Monte Cassino, nothing happened. No sudden artillery, no infantry attack, no charge across the ridges. Routine harassing fire, occasional bursts of small arms, but that was it. He couldn't understand it. Nor could the Germans, poised and waiting. Much to his relief, Oberjäger Rudolf Donth had not lost a single man in the bombing, although they were all battered and bruised from being jolted into the air by the explosions. Even Kurt Müller survived, despite being among the closest to the abbey; after his dash from the latrine he had hunkered down in a rocky niche with four others. After the last of the bombers had gone, they all returned to their weapons and readied themselves for the inevitable attack they knew must surely come. 'But nothing happened,' noted Donth, 'and that unsettled us even more. Attack or bombing, that was the question.' They all started to think something must have gone wrong with the Allied plan, but they remained on their guard, on edge, waiting for an attack that never came. No one slept that night, and certainly not Donth, who turned twenty-four as the clock passed midnight. For the first few hours of his birthday he remained awake and alert and expecting an attack at any moment.

In fact, C Company of the 1st Royal Sussex did try and take Point 593 that night, but they had had no time at all to recce the ground and struggled across the boulders and rocks up on the ridge only to be confounded by a narrow ravine they'd not anticipated. They soon came under fire from Rudolf Kratzert's men, who once again emerged from their shelters directly beneath the bluff and manned their machine guns and hurled grenades. The Sussex soldiers threw grenades until they ran out, which was all too quickly. This was the kind of supply shortage that happened when attacks were planned too quickly; or without taking enough consideration of how long it took to get ammunition across a waterlogged, still-mine-infested valley and then up a winding mule track on to a mountain ridge. By dawn, Point 593 was still in German hands and so C Company pulled back. On Snakeshead Ridge there was now nothing but rocks, boulders, smaller stones and jagged crags. And bodies. All around this key feature, a jutting bluff that very obviously marked the end of the ridge, there were thick entanglements of German wire. Not a single tree remained. So while it was possible to pull back, take cover and remain out of sight easily enough, it was incredibly difficult to move forward in any way at all, or even remain forward.

So the Sussex men really had no choice but to pull back, because to have remained exposed on the forward slopes close to the rocky outcrop would have brought very swift annihilation. So, too, would any attempt to advance in daylight – it would have triggered withering machine-gun fire: from Monastery Hill, from Colle d'Onofrio, from Colle Sant'Angelo, from Phantom Ridge and, of course, from Point 593 itself. Even at night, figures were silhouetted against the sky or lit up by flares which hissed into the sky and crackled as they burst and slowly descended, casting an umbrella of light over a wide area so that darkness became light.

The mountain was calm again for much of the 16th, although early that morning most of the civilians remaining in the abbey ruins left. Rudolf Donth and his men watched them, a trail of clearly terrified people – men, women and children – picking their way over the rubble and heading for the trail down Death Gully. Dom Martino and the rest of the monks remained for the time being, however, still unsure what to do for the best. There were also the injured to attend to; they couldn't just abandon them. Dom Martino found an old man dying on the staircase opposite the altar of St Benedict; Dom Agostino gave him absolution and the man died soon after. They also found two little boys and a girl. Their mother had died in the bombing and their father had abandoned them. The boys were crying loudly, but it was clear the girl was badly injured. 'Father Abbot himself helped them and gave them some food,' noted Dom Martino. 'They wrung my heart.' He felt as though all of them left there were now bound together in life and maybe in death too. More aircraft were heard in the afternoon and they all shuddered, but the falling bombs and machine-gunning fell elsewhere. The monks were also waiting for instructions from the Germans; they had been promised safe passage down to the valley but since the bombing there had been no sign of the officer who had visited them before; there had been no sign of any Germans at all.

'It is night,' noted Dom Martino later. 'The shadows increase our despair. We wait for the officer, hoping that he would come at the same hour as yesterday. Our wait was in vain. We believe now that there is nothing to be hoped for from men.'

'Our attack, with the purpose of eliminating the enemy beachhead, began,' noted the AOK 14 war diary on 16 February, 1944. FISCHFANG got under way at 6.30 a.m. in the morning. Von Mackensen had originally planned for the infantry to attack along a wide front all around the bridgehead and then, once they'd broken into the Allied line, to throw in the armour wherever the weak spot emerged. Hitler, however, put the kibosh on this and instead insisted that the main thrust should once again be down the Via Anziate, with the newly arrived Lehr-Regiment in the lead and with 26. Panzer and 29. Panzergrenadier following to exploit the breakthrough. The Führer also demanded a creeping barrage, behind which this main thrust would advance. Neither von Mackensen nor even Kesselring were happy with this meddling, not least because when forces were concentrated in such a manner they made themselves a much easier target for Allied air forces and artillery. Nor was a creeping barrage remotely possible; they simply didn't have the ammunition. Hitler also insisted that all troops were given a copy of his latest pep-talk. The 'abscess' south of Rome was to be destroyed once and for all, and, he promised, the German units that first broke through would be given the honour of escorting the prisoners captured in the battle through the streets of Berlin.

The constraints imposed by Hitler did not auger well. Nor was it a great idea to launch the attack with the first wisps of dawn, although it was thought necessary because the Lehr-Regiment had only just arrived and didn't know the ground well enough for a night attack. Hans Liebschner was part of the combined 4. Fallschirmjäger and 65. Infanterie troops under General Pfeifer, directed southwards across the wadis at 56th Division – newly arrived and holding the British front while the battered 1st Division was now in reserve. Liebschner had become convinced he couldn't possibly survive another major battle and so had sat down to write a farewell letter to his parents, thanking them for their love, care and the gift of the eighteen years he'd been given.

Soon, though, he was busy hurrying from his own battalion to those of Pfeifer with numerous messages. The infantry, meanwhile, managed to infiltrate the British positions but couldn't quite break through as the Tommies made the most of the wadis and undulating terrain. Meanwhile the Lehr-Regiment had begun moving down the Via Anziate, now held by the 45th Thunderbirds. Astride the Via Anziate just to the south of Carocetto was Company E of 157th Regiment, commanded by Captain Felix Sparks, a twenty-six-year-old bull-faced and no-nonsense Texan from San Antonio. The Thunderbirds had only just taken over from the British in this sector and 2nd Battalion of the 157th had been given the forward outpost position, while 3rd Battalion was holding the road in the second line of defence about two and a half miles back. Company E was out front, with Companies F and G either side and a little to the rear. Supporting Spark's riflemen was a Browning machine-gun platoon from the heavy weapons company, two M10 tank destroyers and one 57mm anti-tank gun. It was not a lot with which to defend against the main thrust of FISCHFANG.

The first Sparks knew of the German attack was when their guns thundered for the opening barrage and shells started whistling over and crashing all about them. After being shaken around the foxholes by the earthquake of missiles landing and exploding, there was a brief calm and Sparks peered out of his own hole in the ground. To his horror, he saw that three enemy tanks had already penetrated the positions of his 3rd Platoon. Moments later one of them was squeaking and rumbling towards his CP, but then a .50-calibre opened up and Sparks watched the commander of one of the M10s sitting half out of his turret hammering away, skittling a number of German infantry, until suddenly red spray spat out of his back as he was hit by a sub-machine gun across the chest. Sparks reckoned the sergeant's selfless heroics had saved the Company E CP, however. A couple of minutes later, two other M10s were hit and burst into angry fireballs. The battle had not yet been going half an hour.

Sparks didn't have a forward artillery observer but he did have a radio, so performed the job himself, directing artillery fire on to the attacking enemy troops to devastating effect. The Lehr-Regiment was hammered by the Allied gunners and also harassed by Allied Jabos, and it soon cut and ran – an embarrassment for a unit so specifically championed by the Führer. Then, at 11 a.m., an enemy half-track trundled forward to Sparks's CP waving a white flag. A German officer called out and asked for a half-hour truce to evacuate the wounded. Sparks agreed, and then the fighting began again. He was losing more and more men as the day wore on, and when the final M10 ran out of ammunition he told the commander to get out of there, quick, while he had the chance. Sparks watched the tank destroyer pull out and scuttle back. It left him and the rest of Company E in a desperately isolated position. Despite this, he and his surviving men did manage to hold their ground. 'By nightfall,' noted Sparks, 'we still held our position, but less than a hundred men were left in the company.' Taking stock, he reckoned they could hold out longer if they had some tanks. Getting back on to his radio, he put in the request and was told they were on their way.

Elsewhere along the line, the Germans were attacking with varying degrees of strength. The tanks of the HG-Division attacked 3rd Division's lines some miles to the east. That morning, Sergeant Audie Murphy was in the remaining portion of an upstairs room in a wrecked house near Ponte Rotto, just a couple of miles south-west of Cisterna. He had his binoculars to his eyes when he suddenly spotted a German tank. Immediately, his hands started trembling. Another sweep of his binoculars revealed more – and more, until he had counted twenty. Snatching his map, he frantically tried to work out the coordinates, then, grabbing the field telephone, yelled for the artillery. Moments later, the shriek and whine of shells passed overhead but they fell short until, with the phone glued to his head, he was able to correct their fire. One panzer was hit. The crew clambered out and Murphy shot one of them with his rifle. He watched as two of the German's comrades dragged him to safety. He didn't shoot again in case the enemy located him in turn and then trained their big tank guns on him. Eventually the other tanks started moving back, the American artillery following them. 'But I soon lose sight of the Krauts and notify our gunners,' he noted. 'Wasting further ammunition would be senseless.'

Murphy then sat back down, feeling weak, cold sweat on his forehead. His knees shook and his stomach felt leaden. It was the thought of all those tanks out there. Yet those panzers had pulled back – for the time being at any rate.

In fact, all along the line, the Allies held firm on that first day. 'I am being attacked from every direction,' noted Lucas, 'but so far the enemy has made little progress.' Total German casualties had been 324 killed, 1,207 wounded and 146 missing. 'Our heavy losses', noted the AOK 14 war diary, 'were due to insufficient training of troops, heavy enemy artillery fire, frequent fighter attacks, and enemy sniper activity.' That wasn't a summary to instil much confidence. Once again, the difficulty of attacking in Italy in winter was strikingly clear.

CHAPTER 21

FISCHFANG and Monte Cassino Part 2

THESE WERE TESTING DAYS for the men commanding Allied troops in Italy. Two weeks earlier, Fifth Army had been within 400 yards of the abbey and half a mile from the Via Casilina. Since then, that breakthrough had eluded them and now they were facing the major German counter-attack at Anzio. Both Alexander and Clark were hopeful that they could hold this at bay, but they were naturally deeply concerned. A defeat at Anzio was simply unthinkable. Now, as Freyberg was poised to mount his ill-conceived mash-up of a battle, their minds were focused not on Cassino, where victory might be elusive but defeat was not a consideration, but on Anzio, where victory was not, for the moment, a consideration, but defeat was a distinct possibility.

On the morning of Wednesday, 16 February, with news arriving of the German attack at Anzio, Alexander and Clark and their respective Chiefs of Staff met to discuss the current situation. Neither could pretend the front was going well, an enormous frustration having been so tantalizingly close to victory at Cassino and both feeling there had been missed opportunities at Anzio. The two men were under gargantuan amounts of pressure; they were commanding what was the only land campaign against Nazi Germany and all eyes were on them. Expectations from the President and Prime Minister as well as the Combined Chiefs, not to mention the media of the free world, were incredibly high. Alexander was facing regular missives from Churchill demanding greater drive and comparing Anzio to a beached whale rather than the wildcat he'd expected. He also wondered whether Alex was asserting his authority enough. This kind of armchair generalship, conducted from far away and without sufficient understanding of the many limitations imposed upon Alexander's armies, was not helpful.

Alexander had already contacted Brooke and Eisenhower, both now in London, about the delicacy of sacking an American corps commander, but he was disappointed with VI Corps HQ. 'They are negative and lack the necessary drive and determination,' he signalled. 'They appear to have become depressed by events.' He had little doubt that Lucas should go but was worried about who might then replace him. 'It is one thing to command a corps when everything is going in the right direction,' he added, 'and quite another to regain the initiative when lost.' What he really needed, he said, was 'a thruster like Patton'. Eisenhower was actually willing to loan Patton for a month but suggested Truscott was the obvious choice. General Marshall, the United States' most senior soldier, had also questioned whether not only Lucas but Clark too should be fired. Devers spoke to General Wilson about this on Marshall's behalf; both felt Clark was doing well, however, so that was the end of the matter, but the tenure of most generals was results-based and the Americans were willing to be ruthless if it was felt necessary. Yet the truth was this: for all the significant number of men and arms within the bridgehead and within Italy as a whole, it was not nearly enough to win the kind of convincing victory that those beyond the sea thought should be within their grasp. It was all very well looking at maps and examining statistics, but such things did not indicate just how debilitating it was fighting in Italy in winter, when so much was expected of the infantry especially. In no other part of the war so far had Allied infantry spent so much time in the front line and also absorbed such cripplingly high losses.

None the less, Alexander was as disappointed by Anzio as was Churchill and, for that matter, as was Clark. Alex had been urging Clark to sack Lucas for several weeks but now both were in agreement. His lack of drive, his inability to grasp detail and his unwillingness to spend enough time visiting the front had all worked against him. Clark, though, told Alex that while they were having frank discussions about personalities, he felt obliged to say he had little confidence in General Penney, and nor did Lucas, Truscott, Harmon or General William W. Eagles, commander of the 45th Thunderbirds. 'This shocked Alexander,' noted Clark, 'and he replied that he had confidence in him, to which I replied, "Naturally, for you appointed him."' The criticism was also unfair, because Penney's infantry had faced the heaviest German counter-attacks and had not had the armoured support from Lucas he'd asked for. The British battalions had been decimated not because of weak generalship by Penney, but because his men had stood and fought and suffered the consequences. In fact that very day Penney, while out in his jeep at the front, was wounded by shrapnel. Whatever decisions he was making, it wasn't because he was stuck in a bunker at Nettuno. At any rate, they did agree that Lucas had to go and that Truscott should take over, although not until the current battle had played out. In the immediate term, Truscott was to act as Lucas's American deputy, with Major-General Vyvyan Evelegh, the former commander of 78th Division, as his British number two. Bumping up Truscott led to an immediate shuffling of command. John O'Daniel, one of 3rd Division's regimental commanders, took over from Truscott, and Colonel Bill Darby, still commanding the Ranger Force that had survived Cisterna, was to take over 179th Infantry.

With the headspace of Alexander and Clark so fully preoccupied with Anzio, the Cassino battle had been very much left to Freyberg. It was quite some achievement for the bombers to have caused such damage with so little effect. The number of German troops killed or wounded was small – the largest number of deaths were among the 300 or so civilians who had left in panic as the bombers first arrived. The mountain as a whole had not been pummelled with anything like the weight of ordnance Tuker had so very specifically prescribed and the attack by one company of the 1st Royal Sussex Battalion – fewer than 100 men – had been bloodily repulsed for no gain. The message was incredibly clear: this was an awful battle plan that had already gone horribly awry. From his hospital bed, Tuker was tearing his hair out in frustration as he learned what had happened. He'd collapsed again from his efforts to see Freyberg on the 12th but now regretted not directing the ambulance, as it had sped him back to hospital, to go via Alexander's HQ first. Perhaps, he thought, had he had a face-to-face meeting with the Chief he could have put him in the picture a bit better. What terrible timing it had been for him to have been struck down.

There had been repeated opportunities for Freyberg to have stopped the rot, but he had not. Or even Dimoline, had he had a bit more gumption, might have insisted it was time to draw stumps. Brigadier Donald Bateman's 5th Brigade was not being flung into the meat grinder just yet, but he had been with the division a long time, was a disciple of Tuker's, and had commanded the 4th Rajputana Rifles before they'd been moved across to the recently formed 11th Indian Brigade; they were now being sent up as an extra battalion for 7th Brigade, and it angered him greatly that a fine battalion was about to be destroyed for no reason. He had also been appalled to learn that none of the forward troops on Monte Cassino had even been told about the timing of the bombing; the first they'd known about it was when the heavies had flown over.

Dimoline's solution was to attack once more the next night, with the Sussex men trying to take Point 593. Again, because of the narrowness of the ridge, there was space for only one company at a time; C Company had a crack the previous evening, so first up was B Company with help from A Company and they were to be largely on their own. There couldn't be much by way of direct artillery support because the Sussex were still too close to Point 593 even though they'd pulled back a stretch. Also, the crest clearance meant that any German troops behind this rocky bluff couldn't be hit. So Kratzert's men were completely safe while they remained out of the line of fire – which they could until the last minute and then mow down any troops trying to advance along the ridge. For this second attempt, the Allies had managed to salvage some American mortar shells that had been left behind and planned to get the attack going at 11 p.m. to allow the mule train to reach them with more grenades. Perhaps inevitably, there were further delays and so the attack wasn't launched until midnight. Whether this delay made any difference is doubtful, because the result was exactly the same, with the Sussex men losing all their officers, dead or wounded, who were involved in the assault.

Dimoline had agreed with Lovett that Point 593 needed to be in their hands before the main event, yet first the Red Bulls had failed to take and hold it, and then the Sussex men had also been unable to capture it over two successive nights with fresh troops. This really should have told the acting 4th Division commander that continuing in this vein was a recipe for a very quick end to one of his brigades. Yet Dimoline was being urged on by Freyberg, who was planning to attack the town below that night with his New Zealanders, and who was also being pushed to continue by Alexander's HQ. 'Heard attack by 4 Indian Division, which was a preliminary phase of NZ Corps main attack failed last night,' noted General John Harding in his diary on the 17th. 'Most disappointing as we had counted a great deal on it and had been fairly confident of success. Am convinced we must go on with the grim struggle for the Cassino spur which is the key to the whole enemy position.' In this he was reflecting Alexander's own views, but these were unquestionably influenced by the arrows on the map and the belief, being fostered by commanders such as Keyes, Ryder and Freyberg, that a breakthrough really was still within their grasp. When it really wasn't.

General von Mackensen had ordered his men to give the Allies no rest that first night of FISCHFANG, instructions that paid off because German infantry of 715. Division managed to work around Captain Felix Sparks's surviving riflemen in Company E of 157th Infantry. Realizing he was effectively surrounded, Sparks got permission to pull back to a low hill 300 yards to the rear early on the 17th and told the survivors to dig in, creating a circular defence with the one remaining heavy machine gun. He had just twenty-eight men left in his company. Two days earlier he'd had 193.

Meanwhile, German infantry and armour had pressed forward either side, into the 56th Division men on the western side of the Via Anziate but more heavily on the eastern side. Here was the disused railway line behind which the Grenadier Guards had found cover after their escape from the gully during the last German attack. It ran south-eastwards and soon became a dead-straight road, which the Americans had named the 'Bowling Alley', and by dawn had created a dangerous gap between the 157th and the 179th Infantry. Then, at 7.40 a.m., the Luftwaffe appeared, thirty-five fighter-bombers dropping bombs and strafing the Thunderbirds' positions, swiftly followed by a thrust by infantry and armour that had moved up overnight. One company of the 179th was overrun and the rest fell back. A second bombing attack later that morning hit the 179th Regiment's CP and knocked out all radio contact. By midday, a wedge two miles wide and a mile deep had been driven into the Allied lines. With the regiment's comms down and the strongest weight of the German counter-attack bearing down on the rifle platoons, there was no alternative but for the 179th Infantry to fall back further to the final Beachhead Line. For all the American commanders' criticism of Penney, the Thunderbirds were now discovering what it was like to be in the main firing line without sufficient armoured support, most of which, once again, was still waiting in reserve.

Now, though, Lucas did send reinforcements: artillery, tanks and four batteries of 90mm anti-aircraft guns were all hurried up to support what had quickly developed into a big bite in the Allied line. Two cruisers out at sea began firing on German positions, while 1st Division was brought out of reserve and swiftly moved forward into the line alongside the 56th. Overhead, Allied air forces flew over constantly, bombing and strafing and harrying the German attackers. Von Mackensen now committed the reserve of his first wave into the salient his troops had created, but the weight of Allied fire – from out to sea, from the air, and from the massed artillery now lined up behind the forward infantry positions – ensured that the German attack was brutally bludgeoned.

As dusk fell on the second day of the battle, the Allied line held. But only just.

'I am suffering greatly,' noted Dom Martino after a sleepless night. 'I pray that the Lord will show us what to do but I am also preparing myself for the Lord's call.' He worried that if they stayed they would end up buried alive, and even if they weren't they wouldn't be able to provide for all the people still sheltering with them. But if they left the abbey, how would they manage, walking through a battle zone and with many already injured? By dawn, however, he had come to some kind of resolution, helped by his conviction that to stay would lead to being crushed under the rubble, such was the state of the abbey and the ongoing threat of further bombs and shells. 'There is only one way out,' he noted. 'I proposed it to Father Abbot; let us take the sick and injured and go out in God's name in to the line of fire.' Both the Father Abbot and Dom Agostino agreed. It was now 7 a.m. on 17 February, and having made the decision they were anxious to leave swiftly before it became too light. They managed to get everyone together quickly, and after the Father Abbot had given them all sacramental absolution they made their way out, picking their way over the rubble. Dom Martino went to gather up the three children. The girl was dying, but as he picked up one of the boys he saw to his horror that the little lad had lost both his legs. How had they not realized this earlier? It was now nearly two days since the bombing. The thought of these children's suffering was heart-rending. He also knew neither could possibly survive. The other boy was paralysed too, but Brother Pietro picked him up and carried him on his shoulders. Others hobbled out; the woman who had had her feet blown off was carried on a ladder.

'We left the house of St Benedict,' noted Dom Martino, 'destroyed by the wickedness and cruelty of man.' There were about forty of them all told. The little girl died, the baby boy with his legs blown off was dying, but was left; he couldn't be lifted in his state. Those who had died in the abbey were also left behind; Dom Eusebio in the Crypt, buried in rubble. No one stopped them as they traipsed by. They passed an observation post, then three German soldiers, the men watching them. 'I said to them in German that we were under the Führer's protection,' he noted, 'that we were leaving the abbey freely and were therefore asking for safe passage behind the lines.' But none of them said a word. It was a bright, clear day and they were drenched in sunlight; perhaps the combatants around the mountain saw them and realized they were civilians. They eventually made it down to the valley below, even the Father Abbott, reaching a German command post at Villa Santa Lucia. The valley was being shelled and several shells landed worryingly close by. Dom Martino worried that the Father Abbot no longer had the strength to continue, but while they paused at Villa Santa Lucia a German soldier arrived to tell them Kesselring had issued orders that they were to be given safe passage to the Vatican. The refugees were meanwhile sent off in groups, except for the paralysed boy still in the monks' care, then later that afternoon an ambulance took them to von Senger's headquarters at Castelmassimo, where they would rest the night before continuing to Rome.

'*Che triste incontro*,' von Senger said to the Father Abbot as he welcomed them into his villa. A sad meeting it most certainly was. They were, though, now safe.

Harry Dimoline, an artillery brigadier suddenly bumped up to command a division at one of the most challenging moments imaginable, spent the day preparing the 4th Indians to attack yet again over a third successive night, although this time with three battalions rather than one. Brigadier Bateman was, by this time, beside himself at the futility of the ongoing battle, but was assured it was essential to keep the pressure up at Cassino and so prevent the Germans from reinforcing Anzio. This might have been believed by those facing the German onslaught at Anzio, but no matter how serious the situation in the bridgehead, launching another attack on Monte Cassino wasn't going to make a scrap of difference. The idea that XIV Panzerkorps had any troops to spare or that they could be deployed in time to effect FISCHFANG was risible, as the intelligence picture of German forces at Cassino told them. Rather, and as Bateman was well aware, one of the best-trained and most experienced battalions in 4th Indian Division was almost certainly going to be slaughtered and for no good reason whatsoever.

And so it came to pass. The Rajputana Rifles set off along Snakeshead Ridge around midnight on 17–18 February and soon found themselves pinned down. At the same time, the 1/2nd Gurkhas began descending the south-east slope of Snakeshead towards Colle d'Onofrio. The Gurkhas had not had the chance to recce the area at all and had no idea there were Germans dug in on the reverse slope of the low ridge that rose towards Monastery Hill. Aerial photographs also showed what looked like low scrub on the slopes running up to the Colle d'Onofrio Ridge, which was not expected to cause too many difficulties. Unfortunately for the Gurkhas, clambering down there under the cover of night, this shin-high scrub turned out to be chest-high thorns which had also been sown with a devil's garden of tripwires and anti-personnel mines. Soon they were detonating both mines and explosives, which not only killed and wounded a number of them but also alerted the Fallschirmjäger to their presence.

A second Gurkha battalion, the 1/9th, attacked closer to the lower slopes of Snakeshead, towards Death Valley where Oberjäger Donth and his men were. The Gurkhas managed to take the northern end of the Colle d'Onofrio as the circle on the figure-of-eight curled back up towards Snakeshead and Point 593, but they too were soon pinned down and at dusk pulled back. Oberjäger Donth discovered that one of his forward machine-gunners had been killed while trying to change the barrel of his MG42. 'He still had the burnt barrel in his hand,' noted Donth. 'His second gunner was also seriously wounded.' Later, after the attack had been repulsed, Donth reported to the company command post, one of the farm buildings on the Colle d'Onofrio. Much to his surprise, someone was lying in his foxhole, covered by a blanket. Rather astonished, Donth tried to pull the blanket off but the person below pulled it tighter around him. Donth now kicked him hard in the side and the man groaned. Grabbing the blanket, he now saw a Gurkha looking up at him, terrified, and clearly expecting to be killed on the spot. The Germans nicknamed the Gurkhas the 'metre men' because of their generally small stature. 'They must have heard scary things about us!' noted Donth. 'Where on earth did he come from?' Donth and his men burst out laughing, pulled him to his feet and took his kukri, the curved knife carried by every Gurkha. 'A terrible weapon,' jotted Donth, who kept it for himself.

At last the attack was called off. No ground had been gained at all, no bite made into the German defences. Briefly, the Rajputana Rifles had taken Point 593, but once again it had been swiftly snatched back. Until the Allies worked out how the German defences were laid out and then came up with a plan to overwhelm them, Monte Cassino would be safe in the enemy's hands. The Liri Valley beyond might have looked so close that they could almost touch it. But it might as well have been 100 miles away.

PART III

The Seeds of Change

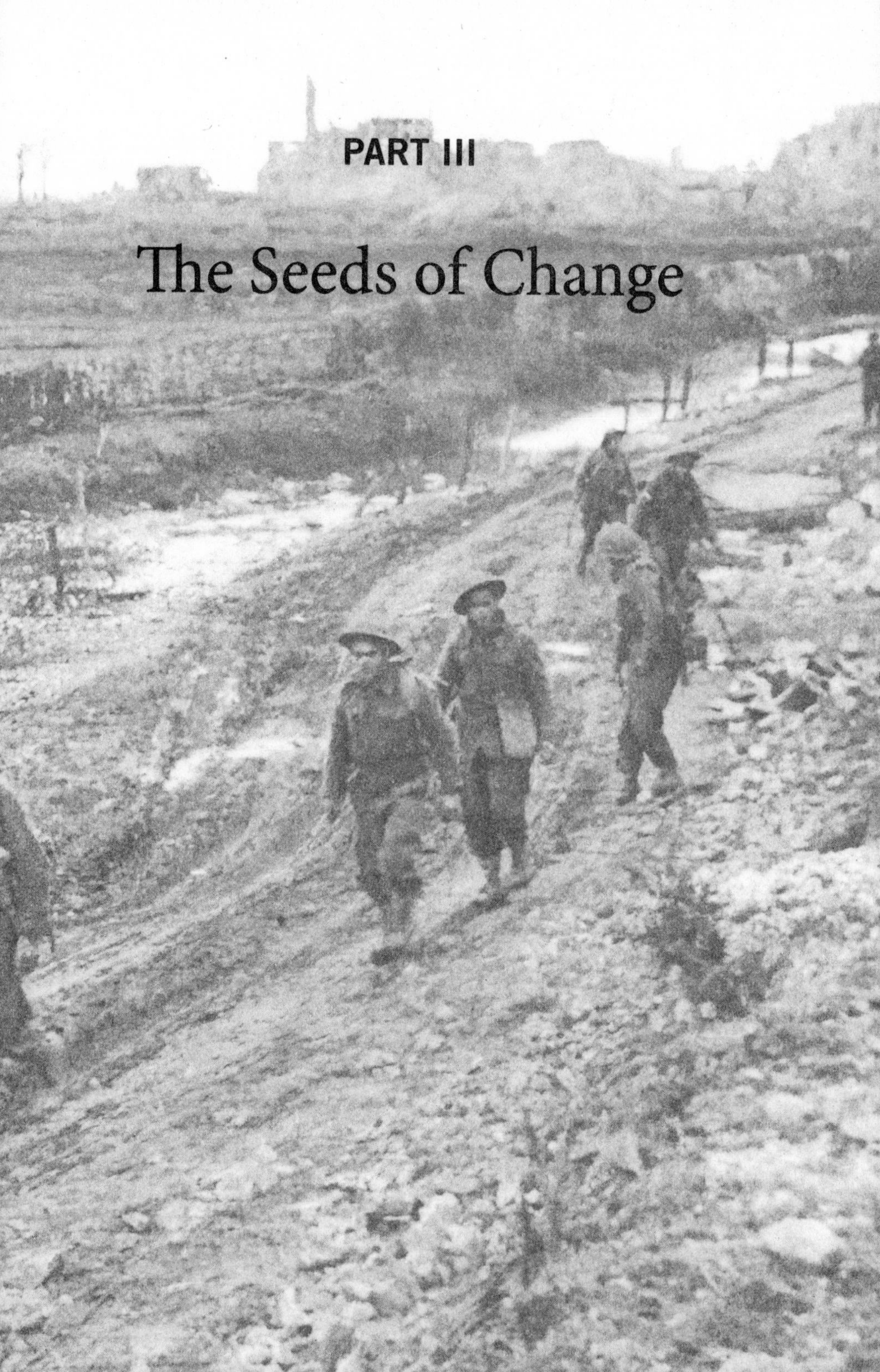

CHAPTER 22

The Tank of Courage

THURSDAY, 17 FEBRUARY, 1944. The London Irish Rifles were now entering the fray; their brigade had been in reserve so far, but on this second day of the German offensive they were urgently needed to help hold the line. No sooner were they reaching their new positions, however, than orders arrived for them to move up to the Buonriposo Ridge and relieve the 7th Oxfordshire and Buckinghamshire Battalion. That meant a daylight advance on a very circuitous route so they could use the web of wadis to cover their advance. Back among them was Captain John Strick, now second-in-command of C Company, but he and his men were struggling through the wadis, which were thick with mud, and they also had to negotiate a number of wide ditches no one had expected because they were not marked on the map. As the leading troops emerged from the wadis they came under very savage artillery, mortar and small-arms fire, and immediately went to ground. A number of officers and NCOs were hit, which caused mayhem; the London Irish had already suffered an 80 per cent turnaround of troops since the Garigliano battles and so there were now a lot of men unfamiliar with one another. Some of the fresh arrivals had been hustled into new platoons and companies and were now flung into action before they'd barely had a chance to meet the men they were commanding. Even John Strick was in this situation to a degree; he'd only been back a few days and C Company was new to him, with plenty of replacements in its ranks. This lack of familiarity – lack of cohesion – was an old problem for the Germans but less so for British battalions. Until now.

Pinned down and taking casualties, they reported their situation to Brigade. It was pretty clear that the Buonriposo Ridge was now in enemy hands and that the Ox and Bucks must surely have been overrun. Orders from Brigade were insistent, though: they were to find the lost battalion; the survivors had to be brought out. This seemed crazy to the London Irishmen: what was the point of doing so if they were to lose half their number in the process? As dusk descended they started sending out patrols, vainly hoping to find some sign of the missing 7th Battalion.

The same night that the 4th Indians were putting in their third night of attacks on Monte Cassino, the New Zealanders were making their attack on the town. Or, rather, two companies of the 28th Māori Battalion were doing so. Brigadier Donald Bateman had earlier very sensibly suggested swamping the town from multiple approaches to the south and east, but instead something altogether more modest had been planned. The Māori were to attack the railway station at the southern end of the town using the railway line as their axis of advance. Sherman tanks were going to support them, but this hinged on whether the sappers could repair twelve breeches in the embankment, all caused by German demolitions. It felt like a tall order to do this overnight and with so few forces, but it was the plan that had been devised and there was no other way the Shermans were going to be able to reach the station with the ground as waterlogged as it was. With the Māori A Company leading and B Company following, they began their attack at 8.45 p.m. It all felt a bit half-hearted and based on hope rather than any real expectation of success.

Meanwhile, a little to the south, between the edge of the town and Sant'Angelo, 24th Battalion were along the banks of the Rapido to cause a diversion; they'd just taken over the positions from the Māori earlier that day – a rough changeover hurriedly carried out.

'They've got a Spandau up there somewhere,' a Māori officer told them, wafting a hand vaguely in the direction of the enemy. 'Gives us a bit of a hurry up sometimes; some mortars down there.' It hadn't sounded too bad, though. 'Oh, there's a lot of dead Yanks around,' he had added, 'but you can't do much about it, the bastards shoot you up if you play round in daylight.'

Among the 24th Battalion men was newly promoted Roger Smith, Platoon Sergeant in A Company. A farm boy from Waikato near Auckland, Smith was something of an old-timer in the battalion; he'd joined back in June 1942 and had fought through the Alamein battles, all across Egypt and Libya and on into Tunisia. The New Zealanders had been sent to Italy the previous autumn and participated in the terrible battles across the River Sangro and Orsogna. Smith had lost a great number of good mates in more than a year and a half of fighting. Mates who had been shot, blown up and tripped mines; he'd even nearly come a cropper himself when he'd felt his foot on a tripwire in Orsogna. He'd got away with that, just as he'd got away with so many other close calls when others had not. And now he was Platoon Sergeant, the somewhat spurious perk of survival, although one not taken by the two others in the platoon who were senior to him in terms of service but who had refused the extra stripe. There had been other changes too, including a new company commander in Captain Sam Schofield. But the battalion had been out of the line for over a month, doing very little on the Adriatic and recovering some of the losses of the November and December battles. Now, though, they were at Cassino and the familiar sounds, smells and fears of front-line action were once more all around them.

Fortunately, this night all they were expected to do was make a lot of noise, and particularly with their Brens. Behind them the sloping hulk of Monte Trocchio loomed. As Smith helped bring up more ammo, one of the men was pissing on a recently replaced barrel to cool it down, the metal sizzling with the touch of bodily fluid. The urine gave the bluing of the metal a curiously mottled effect. One load of ammo dumped, and then Smith was back to the road. Picking up another box of bullets, he hurried over to the next Bren team.

The fighting continued all night. They could hear the Māori and their battle: a cacophony of mortars, explosions and small arms. Earlier, Smith reckoned he'd never seen a bunch of men so well armed with automatic weapons: Brens, Tommy guns, looted German Spandaus and Schmeissers. They'd looked like a bunch of pirates, bandoliers across their chests, balaclavas with tin hats perched atop.

As dawn crept over 24th Battalion's stretch of the front, Smith saw the landscape for the first time; up until the previous evening they'd been bivouacked behind Trocchio, and although they'd watched the bombing of the abbey from one of the mountain's saddles, he'd not seen the ground here before. A scene of desolation. Dead Americans scattered in pitiful heaps, one here, two there; an upended boat riddled with bullet holes, left by the T-Patchers after their disastrous attempt to cross the Rapido a month earlier. It was a quiet morning now, and cold, the faint thud of

25-pounders somewhere a little way off. Isolated houses, most wrecked. All deserted. A door or window creaked in the wind somewhere nearby.

Captain Schofield appeared in a jeep with rations – and news. The Māori had captured the station, also a quarter-circle building known as the Round House, and had cleared several MG nests, despite running into mines, wire and having been mortared from the lower slopes of Monte Cassino. It had felt as though there was an opening there, but while the sappers had filled in ten of the demolitions along the railway and even got a Bailey bridge across the Rapido, they hadn't been able to repair the last two holes in the embankment and that had prevented the Shermans from reaching the Māori at the Round House and the station.

Smith and the rest of 24th Battalion lay up during the morning and into the afternoon. Then further news arrived. The Māori had lost half their number and could no longer hold out until dark. The Germans had got infantry and StuGs and were still firing from the slopes of Monte Cassino, but they were, in fact, far weaker than the New Zealanders realized. Even so, without the Shermans the Māori had become isolated and lacked fire support. Late in the afternoon they pulled back, having suffered 130 casualties of the 200 that had started out. It was worse for the Germans, though; they had lost nearly 200 men and a further attack that night would very probably have done the trick. Another Māori company or even a second battalion being swiftly thrown into the fray might have made all the difference, but General Freyberg was not prepared to risk his men on a battle he reckoned he was no longer going to win. A pause was needed. A reset. A rethink. For the moment, at any rate, the Monte Cassino battle had come to a pause.

Friday, 18 February 1944. At Anzio it was the third day of Operation FISCHFANG and it was now raining again, which was not what General Lucas wanted. Rather, he'd been praying for clear skies so that the air forces could hammer the enemy. It was proving to be a desperate battle, but Lucas was now cautiously optimistic his corps could hold on. Whether it would be his corps for much longer, though, he rather doubted; two deputy commanders thrust upon him was a big clue that his days were numbered. Overnight, however, he had ordered a counter-attack by infantry and armour to push back the unwanted bulge in the line along 179th Infantry's front, but the Germans had stubbornly refused to budge. None the less, the British 169th Brigade was landing that morning, which meant 56th Division was now in the bridgehead in its entirety. Truscott had also been making his presence felt, urging Lucas to counter-attack more heavily that day and to use the significant armoured force amassed in the bridgehead.

General Mark Clark also flew in that morning, landing by Piper Cub, having been escorted all the way in by two Spitfires. Despite the airstrip being under enemy shellfire the Cub landed safely and Clark drove straight to Lucas's CP, where he found his corps commander and deputies planning a counter-attack for that afternoon. Clark, however, felt that was too hasty, and instead suggested they hold the shoulders of the German salient for the rest of the day then counter-attack the following morning with as much strength as they could muster – and that meant with the full weight of armour. Clark then sped off to visit his generals around the battlefront.

'Later,' noted Lucas. 'More trouble. The Navy has closed the harbor until 9:00 tomorrow because of mines which the Germans have sown either by plane or by some other method.' The trouble was, 169th Brigade's equipment was still out at sea in LSTs. 'Have protested,' added Lucas, 'saying it is vital that they be unloaded and worth considerable risk. Hope it works.' It did not, though, because by the time Lucas's request had reached the navy the LSTs had already pulled back out to sea and dispersed. So that was that; they would have to wait until the following day to unload and that meant 169th Brigade could not be sent into the line right away after all. This prompted a further dilemma for the cautious Lucas: should he send Harmon's 1st Armored force without the newly arrived British, or wait for 169th Brigade's supplies and equipment to be landed?

The London Irish still hadn't found any trace of the Ox and Bucks but were now dug in at the edge of the wadis below the Buonriposo Ridge. In fact, the missing battalion was now surrounded and isolated along with the remnants of 2nd Battalion of the 157th Infantry, and were now sheltering in the old Roman caves under the ridge. Also surrounded but still holding out was Captain Felix Sparks and his ever-decreasing band of brothers, valiantly fighting their own Alamo on their isolated knoll off the Via Anziate. The London Irish knew none of this, however; they were pinned down in the wadis, exhausted, wet and covered in mud and making no progress whatsoever. A Company was already down to around thirty-five men and C Company the same. That morning John Strick was resting, having just returned from a patrol, when suddenly a large-calibre shell screamed in. It happened so very quickly: the sucking, shrieking sound that seemed to fill the air, a thunderous crash and then a large hole in the side of the wadi where the captain had been sitting a moment before. CSM David Flavelle was killed, Major Brooks severely wounded. And Captain Strick obliterated. Just like that. Another young life of so much promise, so much vitality, gone in a split second of screeching violence.

The shell that killed John Strick was part of von Mackensen's renewed offensive on this third day of the battle. A little to the east, the full force of the German second wave was now rolling forward as the 29th Panzergrenadier and 26. Panzer divisions were committed to the battle. For a while it looked as though the Germans might well burst through the beleaguered 45th Thunderbirds and British 1st Division. The 179th was almost wiped out: one battalion smashed, another woefully understrength and the third reduced to less than 50 per cent as they fell back to the final Beachhead Line. It was now that Colonel Bill Darby was sent up to take command and he was horrified by what he discovered, so he asked General Eagles if he could pull them back further, to the Bosco di Padiglione. No, Eagles told him. The Beachhead Line was to be held at all costs.

And then there was a stroke of luck, because the Germans now shifted the weight of their attack to the right, using a track the Allies called 'Dead End Road' on the western side of the Via Anziate. They crashed straight into 180th Infantry, who had barely yet been touched, and the Loyals, a British battalion, who were holding the Flyover – that strange concrete bridge without a road that crossed the Via Anziate and the railway line. It was a murky morning and the Lehr-Regiment, backbones stiffened since the first day, emerged through the mist; although they overran the forward platoon of the Loyals they got no further. Once again, Allied artillery pounded the Germans all day, and while the weather was too grim and grey for the bombers the fighters were over in strength, bombing, strafing and harrying the enemy. At one point, 200 British and American guns were directed on to a column of German tanks and infantry just twelve minutes after they had been detected. Five other shoots of concentrated artillery fire also helped blunt the attack: the German infantry ground to a halt as the grenadiers frantically took cover and started digging in. No one could be expected to advance in this kind of steel rain. The fighting over the narrow stretch from Dead End Road to the Flyover had by now been going on for more than fourteen hours, but not another yard had been given to the attackers.

The final Beachhead Line held.

Meanwhile, from his tent near the ruins of Cervaro some fifty miles to the south, Frank Pearce was writing to his wife, Iona, back home in Sulphur Springs, Texas. He was about to be given some leave – five whole days! – and in truth, he felt he needed it. Over the past fortnight he had laid roads, been repeatedly shelled and even watched the dive-bombing of the abbey ruins. On the 16th he was peering through binoculars and could even follow the bombs as they fell. The next night he listened to the 4th Indians' attack up on the mountain. The noise had been quite something.

His wife had been worrying about him as, of course, she would; not just for his safety but also his state of mind. She had thought he sounded so down in his letters sometimes. 'There are times when I am low,' he wrote, 'generally after some experience or certain things I see which is best you don't know about. I used to think I knew war and its results, but one can never know until one actually sees it first-hand. To me it is something terrifying although not in a physical sort of way. It's the mental side that hurts. Physical wounds will heal but the mind retains its injuries.' He couldn't understand why civilized people were trying to kill one another; it made no sense. She had also asked him about promotion – she was ambitious for him – but he'd no desire for that. 'The buck private is the one who will win this war,' he told her. 'I'm only trying to do my part and then get out. To me, the most important thing is to get this over as soon as possible.' But as he'd been scribbling his letter it had got him thinking about things and he now found himself writing to her about the amount of courage each man had in the bank. He'd seen plenty of men run empty. They weren't cowards in his opinion; rather it was a mental injury that had got the upper hand. 'So far,' he wrote, 'my nerves have weathered it all and I still feel no great amount of fear. To say I feel no fear would be an untruth. All men fear something but not the same thing. More heroes are accidentally made than on purpose.' He was satisfied to be one of the majority, he wrote to her, plugging away, trying to get through. He was proud of being in the engineers, and his work was certainly plenty dangerous enough. 'But I still say,' he added, 'the infantry are the ones who bear the brunt of the war. At least I feel I have a better chance to come thru it all.' He signed off by wishing he was back at home, peaceful, happy, with the main street in Sulphur Springs all lit up; he'd had plenty enough of darkness. 'No noise and no worries,' he wrote. 'That is my idea of heaven.'

Harry Bond was still up on Monte Castellone. Everyone in his mortar platoon was cold, usually wet, and fed up. And no one liked being up at the OP because an observation post was always the number-one target for the enemy. Bond allocated the task in shifts in strict rotation between him and his sergeants. But then one of these sergeants was refusing to go. Bond told him he had to: it was his turn. The sergeant pleaded with him, saying he'd been up in too many OPs and just couldn't take any more. The other sergeants were now getting angry with him. They'd been on lots of OPs too; everyone had to do their share. The mood turned angry; the sergeants were cursing him and he was swearing back at them. Bond intervened – enough of this! Then he told the sergeant for the last time: it was his turn. He had to go and that was an order. Then the sergeant broke down in front of him, crying uncontrollably. Nevertheless, he gathered his things together, all the time cursing the war, cursing the army, cursing his fellows. He told them of the many OPs in which he'd served, and when he'd been as brave as any man. Bond felt sorry for him, but he didn't see how he could change his orders. If he let this sergeant off then no one would be willing to head up to the OP.

The sergeant was still sobbing as he set off, shouting, 'I won't go to that OP! I won't go!' And then he disappeared round a bend in the mule track and that was the last they saw of him. He didn't go to the OP. Instead, he headed straight to the battalion CP and was then evacuated as a battle casualty. Another sergeant, just as worn out, took his place. Everyone was very bitter about it but the sergeant's nerve had gone. He'd been bled dry. Bond, who was still only a month into his time at the front, had not yet understood this.

Saturday, 19 February 1944. Allied bombing and artillery had almost entirely wrecked the German system of command and control because command posts had been repeatedly hit, radio sets destroyed and telephone wires cut. This made it hard for the Germans to coordinate their attacks. The planned VI Corps counter-thrust went in at 6.30 a.m., the British advancing down the Via Anziate, and General Harmon's armoured infantry and tanks moving north-west with the Bowling Alley as its axis. It was as cheering a sight for the Allied infantry watching this advance as it was disheartening for the Germans who, after three exhausting days, were now running out of steam. They also had a dangerous salient to uphold; a reversal of the British thumb that had run up to Campoleone, although the German bite was wider and shallower. And Harmon's men were fresh and their tanks new to the battle. They were also supported by eight British artillery regiments and eight of Corps Reserve – that was 384 guns. It was this superior firepower that did for FISCHFANG; even the day before, the Allies were out-firing the Germans by a ratio of between ten and twelve shells to one. Subjected to relentless shelling and an armoured force of fresh troops, the Germans wilted. Harmon's men reached their objective and the British and American infantry moved up out of their positions and advanced north until they got to the line of the Dead End Road. Despite this thrust there were still Allied troops encircled, from the survivors of the 2nd 157th Infantry in the caves, to Felix Sparks's men, to the 7th Ox and Bucks. 'During the day,' noted the AOK 14 war diary, 'strong enemy counter-attacks, supported by tanks, forced partial withdraws from newly gained positions.' This, though, was a euphemism for admitting that FISCHFANG had shot its bolt. Von Mackensen knew it, and for once even Kesselring accepted that his men could go no further. The Germans were left with a salient they could not expand and might well soon find difficult to defend. That afternoon, Kesselring asked permission from Hitler to call the whole thing off for the time being. To his relief, the Führer agreed.

His men were exhausted. Hans Liebschner, for one, had not stopped. Snatches of sleep, but that was all, then the dreaded cry, '*Melder Viertel*', and either he or his friend Horst had to jump up and take whatever message needed delivering, back through the mud, through those winding, disorientating northern wadis, heart pounding, fear coursing through every vein, shells screeching over and the relentless sound of small arms. It seemed to him as though he'd been out and about almost continually these past few days. Often he found himself crouching and crying, through fear, despair and frustration, as heavy shelling pinned him to the ground and stopped him delivering the message he knew his comrades were depending on.

Sporadic fighting continued into the 20th, but FISCHFANG was over. That day, Sherman tanks finally reached the beleaguered 7th Ox and Bucks, who had been cut off for two days on the western edge of the Buonriposo Ridge. At 7.30 p.m. they withdrew through the lines of the

London Irish, who had been sent to rescue them but who until now had not been able to get through. Of the Ox and Bucks who had moved up on 14 February, just three officers and seventy-eight men walked out. It was even worse for 2nd Battalion of the 157th Infantry. Repeated attempts to reach them had failed. Most of the 2nd Battalion men were still holed up in the caves; the Germans had been trying everything but the entrances were easy to defend and they knew that eventually the Americans would have to give up. Or they would have to make a dash for it; water and rations had run out, so too medical supplies. On the night of 22 February, a radio message ordered them to try to break out. By stealth, by luck and by making the most of this strange land of wadis and ditches, 225 men of 2nd Battalion made it back to their own lines. Of Sparks's Company E, just two men got through: Sparks and Platoon Sergeant Leon Siehr. More than 75 per cent of the battalion had been lost. And Company E had been destroyed.

'All quiet on the Anzio front,' noted General Lucas early on 22 February. 'Maybe Jerry has gotten tired. Certainly, he has suffered losses, as Darby, now in command of the 179th Infantry, counted 500 dead in front the battalion of the 179th in the line. That many dead means many more wounded.' One prisoner of war revealed that he'd never seen anything like the slaughter his comrades had suffered over the past few days – not even in Russia. Lucas had good reason to be pleased: a major crisis had been averted and the line had held, yet Clark was less impressed, having spent the day beetling about the front, talking to commanders and seeing the lie of the land for himself. 'I continue to be disappointed with the follow-up by VI Corps of work on their final beachhead position. Apparently, Lucas thought it had been done, but neither himself nor his subordinates had checked.' Certainly, Clark had spent more time scuttling about the front in his jeep than Lucas had done. And while Lucas had as his HQ a bunker dug out of the limestone under Nettuno, Clark's Advanced CP was a tented affair in woods at the edge of the town. A number of times the Fifth Army commander found himself ducking behind a large, vertical map board as shells swooshed over. It was made of plywood, only an eighth of an inch thick and fixed against one side of the tent; this knee-jerk reaction would clearly have done him no good at all. Both tents and vehicles had become increasingly splintered, but so far Clark's luck had held. No one could accuse him of cowering in a bunker, although to have based himself in a deep cellar or hastily carved-out bunker like Lucas might have made more sense. Be that as it may, Clark liked to be out and about and, unhappy with what he'd seen, he now had no further doubts about wielding the axe.

That morning, 22 February, at 8.45 a.m., a message from Clark reached Lucas. 'He arrives today with eight generals,' Lucas noted. 'What the hell.' It was not until 8 p.m., however, that Clark summoned him to his CP in the grounds of the Castello Borghese at the edge of Nettuno, and there Lucas learned that he was being relieved of his command. Clark blamed the decision on both Alexander and Devers. Lucas was not surprised about Alexander but was shocked that Devers should think he was tired. Weren't they all? War was an exhausting business, after all. He had hoped he might have been reprieved after his victory of sorts, but he left Anzio the following day with no small sense of pride that he'd commanded VI Corps in its hour of greatest peril and seen it pull through to fight another day.

Lucas was a good and humane man, but it was the right decision. Fresh eyes and fresh thinking were needed. Greater dynamism, too, and Truscott certainly had that.

These sustained levels of combat and the losses endured had not been experienced anywhere else by the Allies. This made Italy a special theatre, albeit for all the wrong reasons. General Alexander was desperate for a pause now that the crisis at Anzio was over. FISCHFANG might have been a defeat for Kesselring, but it also confirmed – if further confirmation had been needed – that the original aims of SHINGLE would not be achieved, not any time soon at any rate. The Gustav Line was not for breaking just yet. On the other hand, the determination of the Germans not to retreat in Italy did conform to one of the original aims of the campaign when launched the previous autumn: to draw off German troops. The scale of German reinforcement had been extraordinary, and totally at odds with their strategy of the previous summer to retreat to the Pisa–Rimini Line.

And the strategic landscape had now changed for the Allies. General Montgomery and Eisenhower had torn up the original plans for OVERLORD and agreed they needed to be larger and more ambitious. It had also been agreed, back on 4 February, that OVERLORD would now be launched at the beginning of June, not early May. That allowed more time for preparation, for training, for constructing more landing craft. It also took away some of the shipping pressure on Italy. Also, if Italy was drawing off so many German troops, why bother with ANVIL at all? Even

Eisenhower, whose idea the invasion of southern France had been in the first place, was prepared to sacrifice ANVIL to OVERLORD. The British were now in favour of cancelling it altogether, which General Wilson suggested in his appreciation of 20 February – written on the back of the failure at Monte Cassino and the knowledge that Anzio, for the time being, was safe. Wilson and Alexander had different views as to how the campaign in Italy might play out, however. Wilson, Eaker and Slessor believed that continuous intense air attacks on the Germans' lines of supply would compel them within the next couple of months to pull back to the Gothic Line. Alexander, though, was not convinced by this. He reckoned it would need a further, larger offensive in the spring once the ground was firmer and the skies clearer to force the Germans from the mountains. He and Harding were already thinking about plans for this.

Be that as it may, there was, however, no escaping the commitment to Italy now, no matter the arguments for ANVIL. Anzio could not be allowed to fail and had to be further reinforced. So too must the Allied armies in Italy as a whole – Alexander was asking for seven and a half fresh divisions to be transferred to Italy in the next seven weeks. The stronger the Allies became, the more likely they would be able to force the Germans' hand – either by drawing in ever more troops or smashing their armies and forcing them to retreat. Either way, it was surely a win-win for OVERLORD, a point the British Chiefs – and Wilson for that matter – were keen to stress to the Americans.

ANVIL was not cancelled, however, but its scale was reduced and the Combined Chiefs were listening, accepting that there were very good reasons for continuing the campaign in Italy. Ironically, the twin failures of Anzio and Cassino to achieve all that was hoped were now increasing the Allied commitment to this theatre. Those battles had been fought and planned on assumptions about how the enemy might respond. And they had responded differently than expected, by dramatically reinforcing Italy and taking untold casualties to keep the Gustav Line intact. Yet now, with OVERLORD looming in a little over three months' time, the battle in Italy was proving increasingly helpful to Allied plans and chances. On 26 February, the Combined Chiefs signalled Wilson. 'The campaign in Italy must,' it read, 'until further orders, have overriding priority over all existing and future operations in the Mediterranean and will have first call on all resources, land, sea and air in that theatre.'

General Clark was impatient and wanted to keep hammering away at the Gustav Line – to send the French to Atina, the newly arrived 88 Division across the mountains at Terelle, to keep going and not stop. But General Jumbo Wilson and Alexander had recognized that the time had come to pause, rebuild strength and stop operating at the frenetic pace at which they'd been battering the Germans so far this year. They were surely right: arguably, the lack of planning time had been at the root of the setbacks they'd experienced these past two months.

Certainly, many of the men at the front were in desperate need of rest, both German and Allied alike. It was as though they'd been fighting ten rounds and both boxers barely had the strength to stand any more. At Anzio, Hans Liebschner was still at the front, the line in his sector having barely moved, except that now they were a little further into the wadis, an area the British were starting to refer to as 'The Fortress'. Somehow, both Liebschner and his friend Horst had survived February's battles; the farewell letter he had written to his parents could remain unsent for a little while longer.

A fresh sack of mail, that most precious of front-line gifts, had just arrived and Liebschner was ordered to go and fetch it from the cookhouse area where the regimental quartermaster was also based. Liebschner reached the battalion rear area without incident and the quartermaster added some chocolate, cartons of cigarettes and dry socks to the sack as well. Liebschner also managed to get a fresh pair of trousers and socks and filled his stomach with hot potato and sausage stew. For the first time in weeks, he felt like a new man.

With the sack on his shoulder, he set off back to the lines. It was just before dusk and to begin with progress was good; he was also cheered by the thought of how popular he was going to be when he arrived. But as he entered the wadis, the going became harder; first there was thick mud and then there was the water of one of the offshoots of the River Moletta, although he was managing to keep to the banks. Suddenly there was a salvo of shells, screaming in, crashing around him. Liebschner jumped for cover and landed waist-deep in water. The current was stronger than he was expecting and he had a job on his hands just keeping hold of the sack. By the time he managed to crawl back he was once again soaked, covered in mud and shivering. And he sat down and wept, from exhaustion, from anger, from frustration.

When he eventually reached the company, the cigarettes were sticking to the butter, many of the letters were unreadable and the socks sodden.

No one cursed him, but the disappointment in everyone's eyes was crushing.

'Enemy firing shells with delayed-action fuses,' noted Major Georg Zellner. 'It's getting more and more unpleasant. Politics in the evening. Future and family. Cassino is hell.' Zellner and the shattered remnants of his battalion were still in the Secco Valley, holding a very narrow stretch of the line that crossed through Belmonte beneath the mountains which towered above. His command post was in a wine cellar. None of them could move outside this bunker in daylight; it was simply not safe. The cellar, though, was windowless and pitch-black, so they were living like rats by candlelight. His men were in shattered shot-up houses on either side of his command post. There were now about eighty in all, as he'd had a few replacements arrive. 'Our bunker is damp,' he wrote, 'and when it rains it's full of groundwater. We have mice, lice, ants, and even more vermin as flatmates.' What a terrible year it had been for him already: just three days of out the line, his battalion destroyed, not once, but twice, and living in conditions of perpetual danger and unspeakable discomfort. Worse, Regensburg had been bombed twice; he didn't know it but the US Eighth Air Force and RAF Bomber Command, operating from England, had launched Operation ARGUMENT, an all-out, week-long assault of the German aircraft industry and the Luftwaffe. Regensburg was a key target. 'Heavy worry weighs on me for my loved ones,' he wrote. 'Our daily prayer is a curse on those guilty of the war. But they don't die. Innocent people do.'

Despair was eating away at him – at all his half-dozen battalion staff with whom he was sharing the cellar bunker. Shellfire sucked the air above them. Another crash, some close, others further away. The building shook, the cellar shook. Dust and grit fell from the ceiling and walls. They passed the time by playing cards and trying to write poetry. They even wrote a song which began, 'At Cassino and Belmonte in the valley full of blood and pain . . .'. It had done little to cheer them. The food they got was awful and so they smoked a lot; it took away the taste of the food and was something to do. 'You are happy when the day is over,' he jotted in his diary, 'you are happy when the night is over. You want to forget, you don't want to think anymore, you don't want to hope and you don't want to despair. Eternal restlessness torments you. If it's quiet, you want noise, if it's noisy you want it quiet. Day and night creep along and you don't know why. We know each other better than we know ourselves. We know every idiom, every joke, every curse, every idiosyncrasy, indeed every thought. Only the food carriers bring variety and mail, the only joy of the day.'

Back up at Anzio, a young leutnant in Hans Liebschner's company had been awarded the German Cross of Gold for gallantry. It was a big deal and everyone was pleased for him; medals mattered and reflected well, not just on the recipient but on the unit as a whole. Liebschner had been ordered to fetch the leutnant and take him to Gericke's headquarters, which he'd done without any hitches. The award ceremony was carried out by the light of some candles. Everyone stood to attention while the Führer's commendation was read out, which was followed by the opening of several bottles of wine and a further announcement from Gericke that the leutnant had also been given two weeks' home leave.

After the wine had been drunk it was time for the leutnant to be taken back. '*Melder Vierte!*' someone shouted, and Liebschner appeared from the shadows at the back of the cave where he'd been waiting. The two men set off. It was now night-time and dark outside, but there was intermittent moonshine between racing clouds. Then a salvo of shells whined over and they were forced to take cover as the missiles crashed round about. Once the firing stopped and the smoke had drifted away they got going again, but the shelling had disorientated the young officer and he believed Liebschner was taking him the wrong way. This made Liebschner doubt his own judgement and so he allowed himself to be swayed by the leutnant, who was, after all, his superior and now a winner of the Cross of Gold. They took a different path. It soon became clear they'd gone the wrong way. The British were just up ahead; neither wanted to end up running into enemy lines with the prospect of being killed or taken prisoner. The leutnant became increasingly agitated and argumentative, his earlier cheerful chatter about going home replaced by increasingly desperate panic. Eventually he stopped and refused to move another metre. Suddenly, more shells screeched over and in the dark and the mud they had to take cover. Lying there, hands over their heads, the leutnant broke down completely and sobbed like a child, so Liebschner held him tightly in his arms. Nothing Liebschner said could persuade him to budge, however. Only at daylight did the leutnant finally agree to move off. 'We find our way all right,' noted Liebschner.

Meanwhile, Kesselring and von Mackensen were readying themselves for the next round at Anzio, aware that the Allies would probably reinforce and that the window to push them back into the sea was fast diminishing. Time was not on Kesselring's side. Shattered units were pulled out, fresh new divisions, such as 362. Infanterie-Division, brought south. Kesselring suggested striking hard with LXXVI Panzer-korps in the centre of the line, but once again Hitler intervened, micromanaging from East Prussia. He'd never been to this part of Italy and knew only what he could see on maps and from reading reports, yet told Kesselring they must attack south of Cisterna, on the eastern side of the bridgehead, where, he pronounced, the going would be better for the panzers. Yet the reason why von Mackensen had not attacked this part of the line so far was because of the lack of roads in the soggy plain and because this was the area of the Mussolini Canal with its embankments, in places 30 feet high. They were the best anti-tank obstacle imaginable. Hitler had no idea; and, as if to cast further doubt on the wisdom of this decision, there was torrential rain on the 26th and 27th. Operation SEITENSPRUNG – 'Cascade' – had to be postponed.

Von Mackensen agreed to launch this new battle on 29 February – 1944 was a leap year. He had nine divisions against the five now in VI Corps and had massed five of those against the US 3rd Division. On paper it looked like an overwhelming advantage, but it was certainly not as clear-cut as that because, except for 362. Division, von Mackensen's units were all badly understrength after five weeks of heavy fighting, while the Americans, expecting the attack, had reinforced 3rd Division with two tracked field artillery battalions and a mass of further artillery. And, of course, they had the barrier of the Mussolini Canal on their side too.

On the afternoon of 28 February the Germans laid a heavy smoke-screen to hide the movement of troops forward for the start of the attack. It was not fooling Truscott or John O'Daniel, the new 3rd Division commander. They knew full well what was coming and they were ready. At 4 a.m. on Tuesday, 29 February, SEITENSPRUNG began.

It was the Germans' last chance at Anzio.

CHAPTER 23

Disease and Desertion

SERGEANT ROSS CARTER HAD just reached the battered farmhouse that served as Company CP after a night on outpost duty and was tucking into some breakfast when the air was suddenly filled with an ear-splitting scream of shells, followed by a ripple of ground-shaking explosions. Frank Dietrich rushed into the house. 'Run like hell to the canal bank,' he said breathlessly, 'the Krautheads are only two hundred yards from it.'

Carter and his fellows grabbed their weapons and hurried out. A large number of shells continued to screech over, spewing up huge geysers of dirt and creating craters around them big enough to sink a jeep. Fortunately, shellfire here was significantly less effective than it was in the mountains because there was soft, waterlogged clay to absorb much of the blasts. There was still plenty of shrapnel flying around, though, and Carter, for one, reckoned he'd rather take a chance swimming the Niagara Falls than darting through this. He was still running when a shell exploding nearby knocked him to the ground. Side numb, leg numb, foot numb. Lying there, he massaged his leg and foot and then hobbled to the banks of the Mussolini Canal to his outpost foxhole. Miraculously, not a single man was lost in this dash across the plain.

The 504th PIR were still holding the eastern part of the line where the Mussolini Canal ran south. From his position near the top of the embankment, Carter looked out towards the small town of Sessano and could barely believe what he saw: only 400 yards or so away, marching in four skirmish lines, were nearly 1,000 enemy troops, men from 16. SS Panzergrenadier-Division 'Reichsführer' in their first major action. 'Their bright metal belt buckles glimmering in the sunlight,' he noted, 'high, soft-polished jack boots and gray-green uniforms contrasted strikingly with the brown fields behind and in front of them. Noncoms or officers giving orders in loud, guttural-bradded tones, walked just in front of each wave to keep it in perfect alignment'. Carter couldn't believe that the Krauts could be quite so stupid. So dumbfounded were he and all in his platoon that for a moment they simply gawped, open-mouthed. Then, reactions sharpening once more, they opened fire.

Dietrich was on the .30-calibre machine gun. Mowing them down. Then his barrel got so hot he had to pause. All of them were firing their automatic weapons. Enemy shells still whooshing over, the air thick with smoke. The yells of German officers urging their men forward. More men falling. Carter now oblivious to the enemy shells and full of murderous intent. A minute or so passed, then the American artillery opened up, missiles whooshing through the air, screaming, exploding, fragmentation shells crashing all around the advancing enemy troops. Carter couldn't see how even a fly or cockroach could survive this. He saw one German lead his men from a ditch, turn, wave to the others to follow, then was hit, his rifle flying from his hand, his body spinning and toppling to the ground. Ten minutes was all it took to stop the attack in its tracks. 'Every enemy soldier participating in that brave, foolhardy attack,' noted Carter, 'lay on that brown meadow shattered or ripped or decapitated or torn in half.'

Elsewhere, the attack made a small dent in 3rd Division's line but got no further, just as German troops had made little impact against the 504th PIR's positions. The low quality of the attacking troops, the woeful lack of training, as well as the rain, the mud and the flat, open ground all combined to make advancing next to impossible against American troops now well dug in and with considerably greater ammunition for their artillery than those of the German gunners. Low cloud had kept Allied air forces grounded in the morning, but the skies cleared a little in the afternoon and suddenly 247 Jabos and a handful of medium bombers were over, hammering German armour and troops now horribly exposed in the open. In the evening, 3rd Division counter-attacked and regained all the ground they'd lost earlier. Day one of SEITENSPRUNG had been a disaster for the Germans.

Although von Mackensen's men had suffered badly that day, he was compelled to keep going with Kesselring and, from East Prussia, Hitler looking over his shoulder. In truth, SEITENSPRUNG had already run its course and continuing the attack was as senseless and the results as inevitable as had been 7th Indian Brigade's continued assaults on Point 593.

Considerably weakened by the first day's fighting, his troops made even less progress on the second, their difficulties compounded by yet more driving rain. Finally, that evening, Kesselring told von Mackensen to halt the battle, but the following day, 2 March, the weather cleared and the Strategic Air Forces came over – some 300 heavy bombers pounded the German rear areas with 349 tons of fragmentation bombs, while more than 175 fighter-bombers attacked the forward positions. Later, a further 260 fighter-bombers swept along Highway 7 up to Albano, dropping bombs and strafing anything that moved. SEITENSPRUNG had cost von Mackensen 3,000 casualties for no gain. These losses were worse than those suffered by the Allies in two weeks on the summit of Cassino. The following day, von Mackensen, with Kesselring's approval, placed his AOK 14 on the defensive.

After six weeks of fighting, there was now stalemate at Anzio.

There was stalemate too, of sorts, up on Monte Cassino, as both sides became ever more firmly entrenched, the sounds of picks and blasts of dynamite ringing out across the mountain as holes in the ground and caves were dug out and stone wall sangars built. It rained incessantly, the temperatures were freezing and a new kind of misery descended on all those unfortunate enough to be stationed up there. Casualties continued too, from patrols, from desultory shellfire, but most of all from illness and disease. Men deprived of sleep or any comfort, constantly sodden and cold, could not remain healthy. Fires couldn't be lit unless in caves and out of sight and there wasn't much to burn anyway. It was astonishing that anyone should be expected to exist up there, let alone fight.

Lieutenant Harry Bond's dehumanizing and demoralizing introduction to front-line junior command continued with his mortar platoon still stuck in their gully beneath Monte Castellone. He'd not lost a single life yet, but everyone was wretched, nerves were strained and the mood of all of them was darkening. When it was his turn to head up to the OP he went with one of his men, Stevenson, although by the time they set off Bond was already struggling with severe stomach cramps and diarrhoea. On the route up, he had to stop three times and crouch behind a rock. Their first port of call was the Company CP for instructions, by which time Bond could feel a fever sweeping over him. On the final leg to the OP he had to stop yet again.

It was, inevitably, an exposed position. Bond began shivering, and even with a blanket wrapped around him couldn't stop. He felt terrible, his head heavy with fever, his body weak. Stevenson said nothing. 'I don't know if I can last the night out here,' Bond said eventually, to which Stevenson just looked glumly at his carbine.

They spent the next half-hour directing mortar fire on to where they thought some German MG positions were, but all the time Bond's chills were getting worse. 'I'm going to go back, Stevenson,' he said at last. 'I'm afraid I'm pretty sick.'

Stevenson was not sympathetic. He didn't want to be left alone up there; it had happened before and he'd been abandoned to man an OP on his own. It wasn't fair. 'For Christ's sake,' Bond snapped, 'what kind of a man do you think I am? I'll either come back here myself after I get some medicine, or I'll send someone else out.'

With that, he staggered out of their rocky hole in the ground and stumbled back to the CP where the medics checked him out. It turned out he had a temperature of 103 degrees and was clearly suffering from dysentery. He wouldn't be heading back to the OP; rather, he was escorted back down the mountain to the regimental aid station. As he stumbled along the mule track he saw the ruins of the abbey through the mist and rain, just visible in the fading light of dusk. He felt as broken as the abbey. At the aid station he collapsed on a bench then fell asleep, only to be woken again and carted off by an ambulance. Back over the upper Rapido Valley they drove, the driver struggling to see through the rain and the truck jolting and bumping jerkily, but speeding in the hope they would avoid German shellfire. Then they passed an American long-tom battery, the flashes from the muzzles briefly lighting the rain-drenched landscape. Eventually they stopped, and Bond was led into a warm tent with a stove in the centre and given some pyjamas and a camp bed with fresh sheets and blankets. For the time being, ill though he felt, Bond was safe.

Disease, 'neuro-psychiatric' cases and low morale were just some of the many problems and challenges facing the Allied commanders in Italy, and not least the Fifth Army commander, whose men had shouldered almost all the fighting since the start of the year and plenty more besides in the back end of 1943. The number of men suffering from STDs showed no sign of abating, while combat fatigue cases were on the rise. General Devers wrote to Clark on 24 February airing his concerns. 'Records indicate that the present rate of neuro-psychiatric cases in the 5th Army is 66 per 1000 per annum. This is much too high and although continued strain of combat has a cumulative effect which causes men to break, it is believed that careful supervision on the part of surgeons will do much to reduce this figure. More attention must be paid by unit commanders and unit surgeons to the recognition of exhaustion and to anticipate cases before they actually occur.' But how was Clark supposed to resolve this when the Combined Chiefs of Staff had been urging a rapid breakthrough of the Gustav Line and repeatedly stressing the importance of getting to Rome ahead of OVERLORD? More to the point, how could surgeons possibly supervise troops stuck in the rain and cold on the top of Monte Cassino, or in a sodden irrigation ditch at Anzio, especially when there had been such a large turnover of officers, the very men expected to anticipate cases of combat fatigue? Such problems couldn't be resolved by a memo written from the dry surrounds of the palace at Caserta.

Morale, though, was an ongoing problem. How a GI from a small town in Texas, such as Ralph Schaps, for example, kept going was in many ways hard to fathom. Being shelled on, shot at, seeing friends blown to bits and men's guts spilling out was hard to take; but being up a mountain in Italy, or the wadis at Anzio in winter, with freezing temperatures and snow and rain falling made the experience even more wretched. Sergeant Audie Murphy had taken out a night patrol to investigate German troop movements ahead of SEITENSPRUNG but on their return discovered that one his men, Thompson, had disappeared. Murphy had checked with the aid station but he was not among the reported wounded. Then, three days later, Thompson was discovered cowering in an abandoned hut far to the rear. 'A deserter,' noted Murphy. 'He is placed under arrest and confined in the prison stockade.' Murphy guessed that his nerve had gone and that he simply couldn't face the guns again. Thompson was court-martialled and Murphy was called to testify. In the makeshift court, Murphy was brief and factual. Thompson was given twenty years' imprisonment. Afterwards a jeep took the deserter back to the stockade, and since it was heading in Murphy's direction he took a ride. Sat beside Thompson, he told him he felt sorry for him. 'Sorry for me? I'm sorry for you,' Thompson told him. 'I got only twenty years. If I serve the whole sentence, I'll be just thirty-nine when I get out. But what happens to you? Why, you poor sonofabitch, you go back into the lines. You attack. If you live, you attack again. And you keep attacking until you're dead. What's twenty years compared to a corpse?'

It was with the growing numbers of desertions in mind that Alexander had written to Wilson on 18 February about the possibility of reintroducing the death penalty, something that had been abolished in the British armed forces after the last war. A prison sentence for desertion, he argued, was ineffective. 'Firstly, because the man knows that it is likely to be suspended after he has served a short term, secondly, because he counts on a general amnesty at the end of the war.' At the time there were some 450 cases in Naples alone waiting for court martials. He was not suggesting a return to the very harsh approach of the last war but only for 'aggravated desertion'. The abolition of the death penalty, however, was unlikely to be overturned, as he was aware; after all, it had been considered again by the War Cabinet back in June 1942 and swiftly kicked into the long grass. He did, though, urge Wilson to announce far stricter punishments for desertion and let these be known.

As a recent study had shown, however, the most common reasons for desertion were that men believed they had had too much continuous fighting, or they'd been posted to an unfamiliar regiment or battalion in which they had no mates. The first two months of 1944 had seen unprecedented scales of fighting on Fifth Army's fronts in appalling conditions. One way to reduce desertions, as Alexander was also well aware, was to give his troops a respite. Now, with the rain consistently sleeting down and with stalemate descending on both fronts – and with increased support for the theatre from the Combined Chiefs – a breather seemed a very good idea.

Among other recent headaches for General Clark was an article written by the *New York Times* correspondent Cy Sulzberger, which had been passed by the press censor despite roundly criticizing the quality of American weapons when compared with those of the Germans. The Sherman tank, Sulzberger claimed, was manifestly inferior not only to the Tiger tank but also the Panzer IV. He also wrote that the latest German anti-tank gun had 'at least double' the muzzle velocity of the best American weapon. 'And', he had continued, 'we have no weapon of the caliber of the enemy's machine-pistol.'

Sulzberger also highlighted the widespread exhaustion of the front-line troops and their disenchantment with the weapons and their lot in general. 'This dispatch', Sulzberger concluded, 'may sound gloomy. It is meant to. It is necessary to realize what these soldiers are up against and although they are advancing, why is it such a slow and costly process against tough obstacles and a determined, skilful enemy.'

The article reached General Marshall in Washington, who was incensed. He then brought it to the attention of General Devers, who passed it on to Clark. 'Practically everything in this article', noted Devers, 'is untrue.' He was absolutely right about this; the only bit that was correct was the notable exhaustion of the troops with whom Sulzberger had talked. The truth was, Sulzberger had been flitting around the front talking to lots of GIs, most of whom were grumbling and grousing to him – which was entirely understandable in the circumstances. He had not, though, done any kind of fact-checking.

The soldier on the ground was actually very often an unreliable source on matters such as the quality of enemy weaponry. Throughout the history of warfare, soldiers have bemoaned their lot and weapons envy has been a part of that. The Sherman did not have as big a gun or armour as thick as that of a Tiger but possessed many other advantages. It could fire more quickly and effectively on the move, it was easier and more nimble to manoeuvre, there were considerably more of them than their German counterparts, and in truth, in any tank-on-tank engagement, which was incredibly rare, whoever shot first tended to win out. This was because the moment a tank was hit the commander retreated into the turret and, despite periscopes, was then effectively blind and so easy prey. Tanks didn't need to be destroyed to be made ineffective; they just needed to stop working or for the crew to bail out. Tigers were as susceptible to this as Shermans. Nor was there anything between German sub-machine guns and those built in the United States. The German MP40 was better engineered but the Thompson – the Tommy gun – was more robust and its equal over 30 yards or so, the ideal range for such weapons, and even at further ranges. American artillery was more numerous and accordingly more effective; the 57mm anti-tank gun had a velocity of 3,300 feet per second, which was better than that of the Pak 40 75mm anti-tank gun and that of the dreaded 88mm. Sulzberger's line about the velocity of anti-tank guns was simply plain wrong.

His article was grossly irresponsible and shoddy journalism, but because he was the son of the scion of the *New York Times*, one of the United States' most highly regarded newspapers, Sulzberger was both untouchable and his piece of greater influence back home than many others might have been. So despite what was effectively a stab in the back of Fifth Army, Clark could only lightly admonish him and had to ensure he kept him on side. Clark, like all American generals, understood that he now lived in a media age and that keeping the Italian campaign and

Fifth Army's part in it at the forefront of newspapers, radio bulletins and film newsreels was very important. Public opinion mattered. Clark gave as much time as he could to newspapermen but the demands on his attention were immense, he lacked the ready, easy charm of Alexander and had a habit of referring to Fifth Army as though it was his. This got around the correspondents and they then all started to pick up on it. When Cy Sulzberger was hauled in to be told off about the article, Clark then followed the dressing down by putting a placatory arm on his shoulder. 'Cy,' Clark told him, 'when we make our breakthrough I want you to ride in a jeep with me. I'll see to it when we get there that you can tell the world just how Mark Clark took Rome.' For Sulzberger, who had been spending his time with the front-line troops in the mud and mire, this seemed like unbridled vanity. And so it was, but it was also Clark's way of trying to be chummy and conspiratorial at the same time. It just missed the mark. Nor did it help that Clark had been quite ill himself recently, struggling with severe sinusitis. A lack of charm with war correspondents was, however, not the most serious shortcoming, and for the most part Clark came across quite well in the American media: tall, youthful, good-looking and always fearlessly wearing his side cap rather than a tin helmet in photos, and resolute and equally fearless in interviews. 'I decry some of the armchair strategists who publish their views as to how things should have been done,' he wrote to his mother at the end of February, 'without knowing any of the surrounding conditions.' It was hard not to feel some sympathy for him.

On the Adriatic front, meanwhile, the line had remained static. On one level this seemed rather odd given that both sides were fighting so viciously on the western half of the peninsula, and yet neither side had enough troops to mount an offensive in this area; the Allies had decided that the full weight of their offensive capability needed to be hurled at the Gustav Line and into the Anzio bridgehead. The Germans, on the other hand, were equally throwing what troops they could into defending the Gustav Line and, at Hitler's urging, trying to fling the Allies back into the sea at Anzio.

Kesselring was once again shuffling troops hither and thither. He'd hurriedly posted LXXVI Panzerkorps to Anzio from their holding position on the Adriatic, which had meant shifting them from one army to the other. In their place had come LI Gebirgs-Armeekorps, commanded by Generalleutnant der Gebirgstruppen Valentin Feurstein. Until it had been rushed south, Feurstein's mountain corps had been part of von Mackensen's AOK 14; why they couldn't have been sent to Anzio and LXXVI Panzerkorps remain where they were was not clear, especially since Feurstein was friends with von Mackensen and the two had a very good working relationship. Feurstein was a forty-nine-year-old Austrian, full-faced with greying hair and a trim moustache; in many ways he had the look of a typical British general about him. A career soldier, he'd served through the last war and had remained in the Austrian Army after the armistice, then joined the Wehrmacht after the Anschluss back in 1938. Whatever enthusiasm he had had for Hitler and the Nazis, however, had long since gone. Like von Mackensen, Feurstein had become deeply disillusioned by the ongoing war. He also had family back home about whom he was deeply concerned; his wife and children were at Innsbruck, in the Austrian Alps, but even that town had been hit by the Allied bombers in December and 170 people were killed. Fortunately for Feurstein none of his family had been among the dead, yet his second son, Günther, had recently been called up for anti-aircraft defence duty, despite still being in his teens. 'It's hard not to become despondent,' his wife had written to him, 'when your children are taken away from you. You may see it differently than I do. But perhaps you remember that at the beginning of the war you sent an eighteen year-old volunteer back home because he was too young. And Günther is fifteen.'

Yet, like von Mackensen and von Senger, Feurstein was not willing to take any kind of stand against the regime, not even resign. And so he accepted his posting to AOK 10, just as he also accepted losing yet more units from his corps. The 65. Infanterie-Division had been taken from him, sent south and destroyed on the Sangro at the end of November the previous year, partially rebuilt and now badly hammered again at Anzio. Since arriving on the Adriatic his divisions had been further butchered and chopped up: 1. Fallschirmjäger, for example, had been sent over to XIV Panzerkorps and its component units were being posted bit by bit. 'We were the army's piggy bank,' he noted, 'and had to pull ourselves apart like a rubber band after such cuts.' It meant there was no chance of his putting his depleted troops on to the offensive – none at all.

Nor was there any chance of Eighth Army doing so either. General Oliver Leese's troops had discovered that the ridges along the coastline here, which ran roughly west–east above rivers that flowed from the

Apennines out to the sea, were every bit as easy to defend as they had been difficult to attack over the previous autumn. Taking advantage of these ridges, as well as scattered farmhouses and liberal use of wire, mines and occasional artillery stonks, the British and German troops along this front had reached an impasse made easier for both sides to maintain by the abominable weather. Leese had had it in mind that in mid-February his divisions might attack again, but with Alexander's decision to move the New Zealanders and 4th Indian Division such plans were kicked into the long grass.

So while some units were being decimated on Monte Cassino or on the Via Anziate, others were having a comparatively easy time of things, not least 8th Indian Division – which might so easily have been sent to Cassino. Instead it had been stretched further and had taken over the old positions of the New Zealanders, which was why, back on Tuesday, 8 February, 8th Indian Division HQ had been moved to Castelfrentano. It had originally been captured by the New Zealanders at the very end of November. Like so many in this area, it was a small town perched on a ridge, some miles north of the River Sangro but south of the Moro Valley. From up there, Orsogna, still in German hands despite multiple efforts in December to prise it from them, winked defiantly from a distant ridge-line. Beyond that were the mountains again, vast, snow-covered, immutable. Corporal Harry Wilson, still part of the cipher team at 8th Indian HQ, thought Castelfrentano a strange mixture of hope and despair. 'Many homes are still in ruins and many are vacant,' he noted, 'and while some people are quitting to find safer accommodation, others are returning with bundles on their shoulders and their kids trotting behind them to re-occupy their houses if still standing.'

He had, though, spotted a very beautiful Italian girl while out scouting for a billet with his colleague, Tom Sayers. They had noted this Venus, with her long, dark hair, pout and striking red sweater, and Wilson's pining for one of the girls living near their old HQ had immediately evaporated.

'Did you see what I saw,' Wilson asked his friend, 'or was I dreaming?'

'If ever there was such a thing as a come-hither look,' Tom replied, 'hers was one.'

Retracing their steps, Wilson, who by now could speak half-decent Italian, talked to the girl. She explained that she had no rooms to spare in her house but next door did. This house was owned by Toni and his young wife, Filomena, and their four children. They had a twin room, fully furnished, that Wilson and Sayers could use. The two men took it on the spot and Wilson immediately determined that his life's quest was to win the heart of the beautiful girl in the red sweater who lived next door. It turned out that she was eighteen, called Adelia, and related in some way to Toni. 'My heart began to throb', wrote Wilson, 'like so many dynamos.'

Wilson had arrived in Italy in October with an indifference verging on contempt for Italians which was shared by many Allied troops reaching the country for the first time. Remaining in one position, however, had led to him increasingly conversing with the locals and making friends. Suddenly, Italians were not all Fascists who had brought their plight on themselves but, he had discovered, highly localized and mostly very warm-hearted and family-orientated people. Katie, the farmer's daughter with whom he had been flirting for some weeks at their old HQ, had even burst into tears when they'd packed up and left.

For the ensuing days, however, Wilson's heart was devoted entirely to Adelia, and he spent most of his waking hours wondering how he could win her heart. On 12 February it had been snowing and he had spent most of the afternoon trying to keep warm by sitting near Toni's charcoal burner. Later that evening, Tom Sayers joined them and before either of them knew it they were part of quite an evening. First, another Toni – who had spent time in America – arrived with his wife, and then so did Adelia. Wilson found himself sitting with this gathering in a wide circle around the brazier, boots off and his feet warming. Adelia's mother then joined them – her husband had died some years earlier – and they all began to sing songs. Eventually, Adelia and one of the daughters began singing, just the two of them. Wilson was mesmerized. 'So they sang,' he noted, 'Concetta and Adelia together, and I shall never forget that song, and the sweet pathos they put into it. As they sang, they looked dreamily in the dwindling fire as if remembering the false hopes and happiness of former years.'

He was only able to enjoy just a few more conversations with Adelia before the cipher office moved once again. Wilson cursed the war, cursed life, cursed everything. On Monday, 14 February he bid her – and the family – farewell. '*Parti?*' she asked. Wilson nodded and they both said how sad they were. 'And we both went on saying it for quite a while,' he noted, 'until parting became such sweet sorrow that our farewells were in danger of being distasted with the salt of broken tears. In truth, the words of Shakespeare did flash through my mind, and I felt like Troilus leaving

Cressida.' But it was wartime, the cipher office could wait no longer, and so at last, miserably, regretfully, he left her.

There was another reason for keeping things quiet on Eighth Army's front and that was because Alexander was now planning his major offensive for the spring, which he and Harding had been working up and which became the basis of the new appreciation of the situation he submitted to General Wilson on 22 February. His aim was to force the Germans to commit the maximum amount of forces in Italy at the time OVERLORD was launched. A firm date for the cross-Channel invasion had still not been set, but he was working on the assumption that it would be early June and that his spring offensive would need to be launched at least three weeks beforehand. While he recognized that Fifth Army was exhausted and that all those units fighting on the Cassino front and at Anzio would need a chance to rebuild, he also assumed the Germans were exhausted too – the number of casualties, the intelligence gathered from prisoners and the rate at which divisions were being split up and recycled all indicated this. Not unreasonably, he reckoned that the enemy would be unable to launch a major new offensive any time soon.

His aim, he wrote, was not just to push the enemy back up the leg of Italy but to destroy as many of their forces as possible so that, unless rapidly reinforced, they would be completely routed. This, he made clear, was how to most effectively help OVERLORD, and the best place to draw off enemy troops from France was here, in Italy. Gaining ground was no longer to be the prime objective; instead, it was destroying the Germans.

To achieve this, three things needed to be accomplished. First, he had to have a three-to-one superiority in manpower – and by that he meant numbers of divisions. Second, he wanted good weather and the ground to dry out so they could bring to bear their advantages in vehicles and air power. Third, he wanted time to rest, refit and retrain the divisions so battered by the winter's fighting. Lessons learned from the recent battles this year had also shown that it was important not to mix up formations equipped by the British and those by the Americans if at all possible, for while there were crossovers, for the most part the two nations used different weapons, ammunition and uniforms as well as rations and other basic supplies. So the two Canadian divisions would remain in Eighth Army and the French in Fifth Army, for example. However, the only way in which sufficient weight of arms could be brought together was by bringing over Eighth Army to the west for the first time and moving them side by side with Fifth Army. In other words, there were a lot of moving of parts, and much untangling and straightening needed to be done if Alexander was to have two armies match-fit and ready for mid-April when he imagined he would launch his battle.

They would then attack along a broad front into the Liri Valley and through the mountains to the coast at Minturno. Meanwhile, Anzio would have to be reinforced and supplies built up; then it could be a huge asset to his battle plan. Alexander envisaged VI Corps striking out from the bridgehead at a key moment and cutting off the Via Casilina, which he assumed would be the key route of retreat for AOK 10. This was to be called Operation DIADEM.

Before DIADEM, however, there was to be Operation DICKENS, the latest attempt to clear both Cassino and Monte Cassino, which Alexander thought would be a huge advantage before he launched the main battle; on this matter Clark was in agreement. He was less sure about Freyberg's battle plan for this next assault, however. Despite the failure of the New Zealand Corps' attempt to unlock the Cassino position, Freyberg was full of fight and determined not to be beaten. Ever since the last battle was called off on 19 February, he and his staff had been thinking about alternative approaches. Having ignored Tuker's advice, he had immediately revisited those very same plans: a crossing of the Rapido in force at Sant'Angelo with the New Zealanders and 4th Indians striking further north between Monte Cairo and Monte Castellone. The fate of the T-Patchers, though, had left a deep scar, and the pace had been so frenetic that few commanders had had the chance to forensically analyse where Walker's attack had gone so badly wrong.

Tuker had argued that it wasn't the concept that was the problem with 36th Division's attack but the execution. He was quite right, but Tuker was still in hospital and, away from the front, could no longer influence battle plans. There were also concerns that an attack north of Monte Castellone would require more mules than were available. This, however, was nonsense and exposed both a lack of corps staff and Dimoline's lack of experience. Tuker's point had been that further north the German defences were weaker, and that it would be easier to manoeuvre there because the narrow ridgelines that were such a feature of the end of the Monte Cassino spur were not a part of the topography at the base of Monte Cairo. What's more, there the ground was more open and so more men than a single company would be able to advance at one time. Barriers to these suggestions that did not necessarily exist – or rather, barriers that could be overcome – had once again been allowed to creep in, and for the second time Tuker's plan had been too quickly abandoned. The Cassino position, more than just about any the Allies had yet come up against in this war, required imagination, vision, daring and clarity to unlock. There was a solution; there was just not the leadership to champion it, prepare for it and then deliver it.

So instead Freyberg proposed an alternative plan. The New Zealand Division would attack Cassino from the north, using the same route that 133rd Infantry had used; the Americans still held the northern edges, so this, he reasoned, would provide a useful jump-off point. In any case, there was no viable approach because of the waterlogged ground all around the town other than the railway embankment, and that was narrower than a ridgeline on Monte Cassino and the Māori attack had not got very far. The northern route also offered two roads which could be used by tanks.

And although he'd not admitted this to anyone, Freyberg clearly realized he had got the aerial bombardment on Monte Cassino terribly wrong. He should have listened to Tuker, but now thought to apply overwhelming saturation of bombs to Cassino town instead. It had a kind of logic to it, because buildings got in the way of clear fields of fire. Also, Cassino had been empty of civilians for some months and was already a shell-damaged shattered wreck, but obliterating an Italian town very ruthlessly and deliberately didn't sit easily with Clark, for one, and especially not after the wanton destruction of the abbey.

Meanwhile, for the second time, it was 4th Indian Division who would be getting the raw deal in this latest plan. Instead of clambering up on to a wide, open stretch of mountain north of Monte Castellone they would attack Castle Hill, which overlooked the town, and then push on up to the summit of the massif from the southern end of the spur. A key objective was to be the old cable car pylon on the last knoll before the abbey. The Germans had dismantled this the previous autumn, but the pylon remained, bent-backed, silhouetted against the sky like a gibbet. It had been renamed 'Hangman's Hill' by the troops. In other words, the Indians would have to scale Monte Cassino at its steepest part. It would be Belvedere and Abate all over again, except that instead of being defended by the weakened and badly trained units of the 44. Hoch-und Deutschmeister-Division, the slopes and the summit would be covered by German paratroopers armed to the teeth with machine guns and mortars. The quality of German troops by this stage of the war varied wildly and there were certainly young, undertrained Fallschirmjäger who were wet behind the ears now manning prepared pits and bunkers; but there were also enough veterans laced through these units to provide experience and leadership. This put the Fallschirmjäger holding the Monte Cassino spur at the higher end of the quality spectrum.

Freyberg was doggedly haranguing Clark to ensure he was given the full weight of heavy bombers he reckoned his plan needed. 'We have bent all our energies in arranging for air bombardment of Cassino,' noted Clark on 24 February. 'I told him I would take no further steps because I have satisfied myself, as had General Alexander, that this is an air matter – they were the experts and putting enough on it to do the job, in their opinion.' At Clark's reply, Freyberg told him he was going to write a letter in order to have his request for the level of heavy bombing Tuker had suggested for Monte Cassino on record. Clark, in turn, also let Alexander know of this somewhat charged exchange. 'The more I see of Freyberg,' Clark noted in his diary, 'the more disgusted I am with his actions. He may be an extremely courageous individual, but he has no brains, has been spoiled, demands everything in sight, and altogether is most difficult to handle.' Clark was spot on. Yet while Alexander could demand the sacking of Lucas, Clark was in no position to fire Freyberg. Alex's decision to create a New Zealand Corps, whatever the good intentions back at the end of January, was unravelling horribly as Freyberg's shortcomings were becoming ever more apparent.

On one point, Alexander was not to be budged. No matter how much Freyberg was now champing at the bit, there was to be no further assault on the Cassino position until there had been three whole days of fine weather. That, however, was proving as far off as Rome, as the rain continued to sleet down, making everyone's life a misery. Cassino, for the time being, had been given a stay of execution.

But Armageddon was coming.

CHAPTER 24

Thoughts of Home

OBERLEUTNANT HANS GOLDA AND his men in the 7. Batterie of Werfer-Regiment 71 had been having a pretty quiet time of things for the past month – at least, certainly when compared with other stretches of the line. They were still based at Pignataro, where they were protecting the mouth of the Liri Valley and the River Rapido but were not really in range for Monte Cassino or the town, which was hidden behind the end of the massif. The area ahead of them was completely devastated but they had enlarged their bunkers, worked on improving them with a few creature comforts and established a routine that, frankly, suited Golda just fine. After the frenetic and relentless fighting of the previous year and then the battles of January he reckoned he'd earned the right to live a quieter life for a while. Days were spent drinking wine and listening to a gramophone they'd purloined and rigged up in the bunker. Often, he'd wander over and visit other bunkers, pausing for a drink and a chat. 'There was good wine,' he noted, 'cognac and liqueur.' They'd keep their eyes on the Tommies holding the line up ahead, on the far side of the river. 'It was especially fun,' he wrote, 'when a Tommy sat in the field with his pants down.' They'd fire off a salvo and roar with laughter watching him pull his trousers up and run for his life.

Now, though, at the beginning of March, Golda was unexpectedly called back to Germany and then posted to a battery leader training course near Le Mans in France. It wasn't just individuals who were on the move, however. At the beginning of March 1944 it seemed that although the fronts were not shifting there was still plenty of movement behind the lines. Despite the failure of AOK 14's counter-attacks, Hitler had no intention of allowing his forces to budge an inch in Italy and Kesselring, ever his willing accomplice, was determined not to disappoint his Führer further. Hitler even insisted that a delegation of AOK 14 officers visit him for a personal interrogation to help him prepare for future operations at Anzio. He was still determined to rid himself of the Allied abscess. General Walter Fries, the commander of LXXVI Panzerkorps, duly arrived at the Wolf's Lair with a delegation of fellow officers on 7 March. Fries and co. were unable to add much to what Kesselring and von Mackensen had already reported. They were all, though, unanimous in telling the Führer that superior Allied artillery and overwhelming air power lay at the root of their failures. These were two things Hitler was powerless to do anything about.

Although the intention remained to kick the Allies back into the sea, Kesselring was still mystifyingly anxious about further outflanking amphibious assaults and so moved the HG-Division to the Tuscan coast north of Rome. It does not seem to have occurred to him that if the Allies had enough shipping for such an operation they would use that first and foremost to substantially increase the scale of Allied forces at Anzio. Nor does he appear to have considered that maintaining a bridgehead that far north would cause insurmountable problems of supply. At any rate, the policy at Anzio was for von Mackensen's forces to keep up the pressure with aggressive patrolling and shelling and allow the Allies there no rest.

Meanwhile, more reserves from the north and from the Adriatic were being sent to the Cassino front. On 28 February, Generalleutnant Feurstein had seen von Vietinghoff, his AOK 10 commander, and pointed out that his depleted corps could not be stretched any further. 'Vietinghoff listened to my arguments with quiet humour,' noted Feurstein, 'although he couldn't promise me much relief because there were always urgent holes to be filled at Cassino.' In any case, Feurstein's troops were struggling simply to exist in the winter conditions that seemed to get worse now that March had arrived. What had been driving rain on the western side of Italy had turned to snow once it crossed the Apennines. At times, units were entirely cut off from one another and were suffering particularly badly because although greatcoats had been issued, no special winter clothing had been delivered. Feurstein had to resort to skis and sledges to get around to see his troops.

At Cassino most of 1. Fallschirmjäger-Division had now assembled, so much so that on 26 February Kesselring had withdrawn 90. Panzergrenadier into reserve and General Richard Heidrich, the division commander, had taken over command of the Cassino sector from Baade, setting up his headquarters at Roccasecca. That day he could call upon just 1,780 men – a mere 10 per cent of its proper strength. His 1. Regiment, with just 610 men, was moving from Point 601 – Colle Sant'Angelo – up to Monte Cairo; 4. Regiment, with 880 men and which included Rudolf Donth's 6. Kompanie, held the middle of the spur around Point 593, Albaneta and Colle d'Onofrio, while Oberst Ludwig Heilmann's 3. Regiment, with 775 men, was in and around the abbey, Monastery Hill and the town. Also given to Heilmann was the MG Bataillon, some engineers, an anti-tank gun company and five StuGs.

Among the last of the division's units to arrive was the Pionier-Bataillon, and of these men it was 2. Kompanie that was the final unit to leave the Adriatic. On 2 March the orders arrived for them to move out that night, the men and their equipment loaded up on to lorries and beginning the long and torturous journey with its many climbs, descents and hairpin bends, all the time with the mountains looming darkly above them. Unteroffizier Jupp Klein and his comrades finally reached Cassino in the early hours, bid farewell to their Henschel truck for the time being and, loaded with all the equipment they could carry, began the climb up the mountain. It was hard to make out much of the surrounding countryside but they were heading up Death Gully, the sides of the gorge closing either side of them the higher they climbed.

Their final positions were up on Phantom Ridge, below Monte Castellone, and as Klein and his platoon moved into their sangars he was struck by how lively it was up there even though there was no specific action under way: machine guns barked and chattered seemingly incessantly, the crack of snipers' rifles rang out, and mortar fire continued to scream in throughout the remainder of that first night. Klein watched these pyrotechnics for a while, but when a mortar round crashed nearby he realized it would be a foolish man who kept his head above the parapet, especially once daylight came. Instead, he and his men built up the stones round them then pulled over a tarpaulin in an effort to protect themselves from the rain.

They had only been there a day, however, when orders arrived for 2. Kompanie to improve the mule track up through Death Gully, which was being relentlessly shelled. The gully was very narrow and steep-sided just before it emerged at Albaneta, then dog-legged after dropping a few hundred yards and widened appreciably until it emerged by a collection of stone houses and a small church and joined the Via Casilina. The real danger area for the German troops using it was at this lower, more open end, as shells were being fired from behind Trocchio, six miles away, over the southern end of the Monte Cassino spur and landing in the mouth of the gully. The task of Klein and his fellow engineers was to clear the unexploded shells lying there, improve damaged parts of the track, and also create better caves and trenches along the way so that those using it had places of cover should they suddenly come under shellfire. Very quickly, Klein realized this vital supply route deserved its name. 'Pioneering in the gorge was no easy task,' he noted, 'starting with the reconstruction of the trenches in the valley and the maintenance of the track up to the ridge under almost constant artillery fire.' What's more, the repair of the track had to be carried out mainly in daylight so as not to hinder the night-time supply chain. It was tense work and the men were constantly on edge, praying they wouldn't get caught out in the open and that if a shell screamed in they would have time to take cover.

After a few days working on the Death Gully track, however, Klein's platoon was ordered to improve the defences in Cassino town itself and particularly along the Via Casilina, from the Hotel des Roses, a palatial villa on the road at the southern edge of town, to the 90-degree turn in the centre. Reinforcing bunkers in cellars, laying mines and tripwires, and especially blasting underground connecting tunnels between cellars were their prime tasks, but they were also ordered to create further MG posts on the lowermost slopes of Monte Cassino as it rose up from the town. The idea was that connecting tunnels would run under the road, and from cellar to cellar between houses, so that MG teams could shelter then emerge unseen and man their weapons. While Cassino was a shattered ghost town above ground, an underground labyrinth of bomb-proof tunnels and connecting passages was being prepared.

Alexander was determined to build up Anzio as strongly as possible, both to ensure that there were ample men and supplies to see off any future German attack, but also to have VI Corps prepared for Operation DIADEM when it was launched. Shipping, as always, was the biggest headache, because although up until the beginning of March they had survived with an average daily delivery of 2,000 tons, he estimated that this needed to be doubled. The Royal Navy, however, who were running the naval effort at Anzio, told him they could not guarantee more than 2,500 tons a day, and to make matters worse, thirteen British LSTs had left for the UK on 29 February and a further twenty-eight were due to sail back on 1 April. A solution was available but would mean using LSTs earmarked for ANVIL and delaying landing ships earmarked for OVERLORD until the last minute. It was the kind of decision that could have been agreed with the stroke of a pen but instead became another sticking point between the British and American Staff and Eisenhower, whose team were still finalizing plans for the cross-Channel invasion.

While decisions on landing ships hung over the supply plans for Anzio, there were still an average of six LSTs reaching Anzio every day, mooring, bow first, directly on to the quayside, from where fifty trucks would drive off, each one double-loaded with 50 tons of supplies, roughly divided into 60 per cent ammunition, 20 per cent rations and 20 per cent fuel. Incredibly, VI Corps was now burning through a staggering 60,000 gallons of fuel per day. Merchant vessels were also arriving in small convoys every ten days into Naples and were then shipped forward to Anzio, where a fleet of more than 500 DUKWs would scuttle back and forth in ant lines from the ships now anchored offshore. Arguments over landing ships aside, Anzio had by now long gone past the twenty-eight days the planners of SHINGLE had argued over back at the beginning of January. From a limited operation with the aim of unseating the Gustav Line, Anzio had become both a major commitment and also key to the future battle plans for DIADEM.

There were also new troops arriving too, including replacements especially for the decimated 45th Thunderbirds. During the four days of FISCHFANG the Thunderbirds' casualties were 400 dead, 2,000 wounded and a further 1,000 missing, either obliterated or now prisoners of war. The cold, the wet and the exhaustion had snatched a further 2,500 from the front line, men suffering variously from exposure, fever, trench foot and combat fatigue. The main fighting component of an infantry division was its nine infantry battalions, which at full strength amounted to 7,839 men, so the Thunderbirds taking losses of nearly 6,000 meant they had suffered German levels of punishment. Captain Felix Sparks, for example, had been sent back to the rear area, where he'd been given 150 new recruits and told to shape them into a new Company E. In just a few days he had to choose company commanders, platoon and squad leaders and try to lick them into shape.

Captain David Cole and the 2nd Inniskillings were still on the Garigliano front, although they had moved about a bit. In the second half of February they'd spent ten days and nights on Monte Damiano, where the weather had been as much an enemy as the Germans, before being moved to

Tremonsuoli, a shattered village atop a small ridge a mile inland from the sea and overlooking Highway 7, the Via Appia. The men had set themselves up amid the ruins, which now resembled little more than a giant rockery. A large number of graves, mostly belonging to Guardsmen before the brigade had shipped up the coast to Anzio, lay scattered around the village and hillside and were a persistent reminder of the sacrifices that had already been made here.

On 2 March, Cole wrote to his parents telling them he was still in the line although things were quieter – there was now just machine-gunning and shelling to contend with. This would have been quite enough for most people, but after the battles over the river and into the hills it had become commonplace. His CP, he told them, looked just like a Hollywood film set of the front line. 'Sandbag walls; roof made of railway lines, sleepers and sandbags,' he wrote, 'bunks round the inside walls; table and chairs in the middle; stove in one corner; and, at the far end and separated by a curtain of blankets, my signals centre with its wirelesses, telephones and switchboards; and outside more wires than the GPO.' Enemy shellfire frequently broke the telephone lines, so they were forever scrambling out and repairing them. Nor were they devoid of danger. Cole's friend Captain Jock Crawford was shot, having only just returned after being treated for a previous wound. It was dusk and Cole had been running up a track from the forward companies when he'd seen him staggering rather groggily. Cole hurried over to him and Crawford explained he'd been hit in the shoulder. 'I escorted him back to the Doc,' wrote Cole. 'Unfortunately, the Jerries seemed to have a machine-gun targeted on the track and twice we had to throw ourselves flat as their bullets whished over us. The trouble with bullets is they come in such swarms.'

A couple of days later, however, the brigadier showed up with several American officers, all wearing British helmets so as not to give the game away to the Germans that they would soon be taking over this stretch of the line. The US 88th Infantry Division had been in Italy since the first week of February and had been variously earmarked for Anzio and the Cassino front; but now, as part of the giant reorganization of the two armies, it had been allocated 5th Division's front and would be part of II Corps for the coming DIADEM battle. In the meantime, it was to hold the line while 5th Division was withdrawn and posted to Anzio instead. Meanwhile, 56th Division would be pulled out of Anzio and Italy altogether and sent to the Middle East for refitting and retraining.

The 2nd Skins moved out from Tremonsuoli on 7 March, although no sooner had they done so than David Cole began to feel feverish, and by the time they had pulled into their next resting place, Frignano, near Caserta, he had a raging temperature. 'I was billeted in an Italian house,' he wrote in a letter home, 'and the kindness of the whole family was most touching. They put me on their best bed, enveloped me with hot water-bottles, sprinkled me with cologne, brought me some cognac and coffee and all but gathered round to pray for me!' A day later an ambulance turned up and whisked him off to hospital in Caserta. The doctors diagnosed a malarial relapse.

One of those now moving into 5th Division's positions – and wearing a Tommy helmet – was twenty-seven-year-old Captain Klaus Huebner, the Assistant Battalion Surgeon in 3rd Battalion, 349th Infantry Regiment, part of the 88th 'Blue Devils' Infantry Division. This was the division's first time at the front. Huebner had been born in Bavaria in 1916 but his family had moved to the United States after the last war and he had grown up speaking both languages; however, he felt American through and through. He'd joined the medical reserve Officers' Training Corps while still a freshman at medical school and after graduating had further undergone two Medical Field Service School courses. As a result, when he was finally called up the previous September, he had felt reasonably well prepared for service. The title 'surgeon', though, was something of a misnomer, for although he was expected to carry out emergency surgery if required, his task was to be the first medical port of call for the front-line troops in 3rd Battalion, whether he was needed for treating wounds, illness or battle exhaustion.

He was certainly apprehensive as they began the move to the front on 1 March. This in itself was quite a challenge. Huebner was in his jeep, driving with the windshield down flat on the bonnet as per orders, but it was raining and then it had begun to sleet. 'Wind and rain beat my face,' he noted. 'We are on Highway 7 leading north to the front. We pass through many small villages, mostly all rubble. British camps are scattered along the road.' Nor was he feeling in perfect health himself, having discovered that he was suffering with pinworms in his gut. Doses of Epsom salts and laxatives to flush them out had now given him chronic diarrhoea. At dusk the column paused, and he watched the infantry load into British trucks to maintain the deception about their deployment. On they rumbled, Huebner in his jeep, past signs that said, 'Lights Out – Under Enemy Observation'. Military police along the road further yelled instructions. Up ahead, mountains loomed in the darkening light beyond the coastal plain, and then bright flashes and deafening explosions either side of the road told him there were artillery batteries firing nearby. Occasionally, a screeching whine would follow and some short distance behind him there would be an explosion as the enemy fired back. Despite this unwanted welcome, the convoy kept going.

Then they left the highway and turned down a track that ran along a railway line until they reached a pontoon bridge across the Garigliano. The infantry clambered down and tramped over on foot but Huebner was allowed to remain in his jeep; much to his relief, he made it across without a hitch, but doing this at night, with almost no lights and while under enemy shellfire, was a nerve-jangling experience. 'It is an eerie feeling,' he noted, 'wondering how soon the next shell will come in.' Up ahead the bulk of the mountain loomed ever larger and as they drew closer, so the artillery fire increasingly landed behind them. Eventually, a British corporal stopped them and directed them down a track to a stone farmhouse tucked in against the foot of Monte Damiano. The 349th were on the right flank of the division's new position, which, as had been the case with 5th Division, ran all the way from Damiano to the coast. Parking outside the farmhouse, Huebner and his seventeen men were told that this was to be their aid station. Over a yard thick with mud he reached the house, and after passing through a series of blackout curtains he entered a candle-lit room filled with British medics ready to move out. The subsequent handover only took them a matter of minutes. 'We are finally at the front line,' noted Huebner, 'and on our own.'

The 2nd Royal Horse Artillery were now in Italy but yet to be posted to the front, which certainly suited Captain Mike Doble just fine. The regiment had last seen action in Tunisia but, having been in the thick of the fighting since their posting to Egypt back in December 1940, an extended break was probably owed to them. Despite their name they had no horses and were, to all intents and purposes, equipped like any other Royal Artillery field regiment, with three batteries of eight 25-pounders and all the accompanying trucks and gun tractors. After a long sojourn in North Africa, however, they had finally been posted to Italy in February, and Doble, for one, had been very unimpressed. 'One of the most unpleasant days I have spent in 4 ½ years' total warfare,' he had written in his diary on 20 February. 'After the chaotic business of disembarkation we had to march 10 miles to the transit camp, which was well outside Naples. Arrived latish and was given a totally mundane meal of chaf bread and

MV. Went straight to bed.' Then added, 'Apart from this hell we can now say that we have seen the sea off Capri, Vesuvius and Naples.'

Doble was twenty-three and from Hertfordshire, to the north-west of London, and despite the long years of front-line service and hard drinking in between he remained fresh-faced, youthful-looking and as quick to laugh as he was to become vexed by the discomforts of army life. He was also by now extremely experienced, having served in France, Egypt, Greece, Crete and all across North Africa – and was decorated too, having been awarded an MC in Tunisia. Yet like many young men of his age he enjoyed boozing, cards and sport and over the past nine months had spent a huge amount of energy on those activities, mostly in the heat and sun. Italy was a shock, as was having to walk ten miles in the rain; these past nine months he'd barely walked anywhere. That's what jeeps were for. 'Up at 0830 and had breakfast in bed, it was bloody,' he noted the next day. 'Spent the morning entertaining the troops with semaphore, PT etc. Shall be delighted when our vehicles arrive and we can live fairly comfortably.' Over the next few days he managed to get the Mess up and running, and spent the ensuing evenings drinking and playing poker with his fellow officers.

At the beginning of March they were posted to Benevento, a dismal town forty miles from Naples that had been largely flattened by Allied bombers a year earlier. They were near the airfield, which meant the ground was flat but also a quagmire. Getting the tents up in the driving rain had been a nightmare. A small river had been running through the mess tent. 'Not at all like a Sunday,' Doble noted on 5 March. 'Working like slaves all day.' It was still raining but at least the camp was starting to take some kind of shape. That evening Doble went into the town with a friend before dinner and both had rather too much gin. 'Arrived back in the mess,' he noted, 'and were greeted with howls of derision rather like the family when I used to come home from The Cock.' This had been his local pub back home. Being half-cut did not stop him from boozing some more after supper, however. 'Drank Scotch,' he added, 'with the Canadian officers until midnight.'

The arrival of artillery units such as the 2nd RHA allowed others to depart the theatre, however. 'Out of action 0600 and clear by 1200 hrs, moving to TEANO,' noted Captain Leonard Garland on 4 March. 'Amazing – it's really happened!' Despite the brutal pace and relentlessness of the fighting all along the Cassino front, the Allies were far better at rotating troops than the Germans and now, on 4 March, it was the turn of the 70th Field Regiment, who were to be leaving Italy along with the rest of 56th Division and heading to Palestine. Garland was still missing his wife, Ann, as much as ever. On 18 February it had been the second anniversary of their engagement – a night they had spent together at The Foley Arms at Claygate in Surrey. 'This happened two years ago,' he'd written in his diary, 'the only time I can remember being completely exalted by a woman's "YES"'. He'd written to her the following day from his CP, letter No. 63. By that time, his battery was no longer out on the mountain but based in a village in the hills overlooking the Garigliano not far from Sant'Apollinare. Much to his delight they now had a roof over their heads and, even better, when they'd pulled into the village there had been a mass of letters awaiting him, many of which were in response to letters he'd sent and gifts he'd posted her. The gifts, he explained, had been bought in one of the many bashed-about Italian towns he'd passed through. 'From Salerno onwards,' he wrote, 'it is as if a giant with a hammer had run amok, bashing, breaking, uprooting, and tearing apart all man's works. Italy is indeed paying a price.' He recalled their engagement, then the doubts she had had, but actually, he told her, it was the happy memories of them being together that were most painful. Their wedding night, especially. 'Looking back,' he wrote, 'it seems to have been "a moment out of time", on another planet, an Elysium. And I suppose these present trials are but the fare that has to be paid to regain it – rent in advance on a plot in Paradise. You need not ask me to love you, my darling. Every part of me, mind and body, cries out for you day and night.'

Now, a fortnight later, he was at least away from the danger. Sailing to Palestine would take him further away from, not closer to, Ann. But he would be safe. There would be warmth and sunshine and he would be away, a far cry from the oppressive misery and destruction he had found in Italy.

Oberst Wilhelm Mauss was also missing his wife, Elly, and their children, and was worried sick about them now that Allied bombers were pounding Germany round the clock. On 25 February, however, much to his delight he had managed to speak to his wife on the telephone for the best part of a quarter of an hour – all the way from their home in Barsinghausen near Hanover. They also had a home in Berlin, and Elly was able to tell him that it was still standing; that had been a relief to hear. His wife also spoke of the large aerial battles that had been taking place that week as Operation ARGUMENT had been running its savage course. Then, at the start of March, the American Eighth Air Force turned its attention on the German capital – Berlin had already been heavily hit by the RAF's Bomber Command, operating by night, but this had been the first time the Americans had bombed the capital by day. They had then struck three times in quick succession – on 6, 8 and 9 March. 'Naturally, I am worried about my family,' he noted, 'because the inflight corridor to Berlin goes just over the Deister near Barsinghausen and there is already talk of strong aerial battles in the area of Hanover.' Meanwhile, it was suddenly very quiet on the Cassino front – almost too quiet for Mauss. 'It is almost frightening,' he noted. 'What are the intentions of the opponent?'

Thoughts of home were never far away for Lawrie Franklyn-Vaile, now promoted to acting major and commanding C Company of the 1st Royal Irish Fusiliers, and particularly so on Thursday, 9 March. 'My Dearest Olive,' he wrote to his beloved wife, 'Nine years ago today, we were married and what a lot has happened since. I think this is only the second time that we have spent our wedding anniversary apart, the other being 1940 when I was at the ITC Bedford. I certainly hope that next year we will be together again.' What a lot of lives had been tossed into the wind in this war, leaves swept off to distant places.

Franklyn-Vaile had had a somewhat frustrating time because he'd been acting commander of B Company, the company with which he'd mostly served since arriving in Sicily back in the summer, but then had been pipped to the post by the arrival of another officer who was senior to him in terms of length of service, despite having less combat experience. Worse, he'd also been bumped back down to captain and company second-in-command. The CO, however, was both fond of him and rated him, so when command of C Company surfaced Franklyn-Vaile was reinstated as a major and given this promotion instead. He'd left his B Company men with no small regret but his new second-in-command was Dicky Richards, of whom he was very fond, while Douglas Room, another friend in the battalion, was one of his platoon commanders. He was also genuinely delighted to be given command again, something he relished and enjoyed; he was evidently a natural leader.

After starting the year in the snow-clad mountains near Castel di Sangro in the centre of the line, the Faughs had moved back first to Campobasso in Molise and then to Capua in the coastal plain north of Naples; at the time when the New Zealand Corps had come back into being, Alexander had also had 78th Division, to which the Faughs and the Irish

Brigade were attached, earmarked for this new formation too. They'd accordingly been brought over to the west, ready for deployment, although had remained on the Volturno, thirty miles to the south of the Cassino front. The Faughs had been training there for the rest of the month, although on 5 March training had stopped because it was Barossa Day – marked each year by the battalion in memory of the French Eagle that had been captured at the Battle of Barrosa in the Peninsular War in 1811. 'Barrosa Day was quite a big success,' Franklyn-Vaile told Olive. 'The Officers and Sgts football match was quite a hilarious affair and about the best ever. It was contested on a field about an inch deep in water and we were certainly a sight at the end.' This was followed by a dinner in the town hall in Capua along with a speech by the junior subaltern, Second Lieutenant Hansson, and the passing of the Barossa drinking cup. 'Afterwards,' he added, 'the evening assumed a fairly hectic note and ended up in some fierce scrums and a few thick heads the following morning.'

While this had proved a welcome distraction and a lighter moment for the entire battalion, Franklyn-Vaile worried a good deal about his wife and his daughter, Valerie, who turned two on 11 March. He also felt anxious about money, constantly, for they were not well off; this was one of the reasons why he was so keen to receive the extra pay from being a major rather than a captain. He'd even encouraged Olive to mate their dog, Sadi, in order to make a few extra shillings. Valerie, like most little girls, was often sick with some bug or other, and as a father Franklyn-Vaile felt rather helpless at such a distance. Olive had sent him a photo of her with which he was very pleased, although he was taken aback by how much she had grown and developed since he'd last seen her the previous summer; he was missing a great deal while he was away. 'I would certainly like to be at home with you today,' he wrote on the 11th, 'sharing in Valerie's second birthday. I expect she is now able to realise the significance of the day and is having quite a good day.' He'd sent her a doll, but it was yet to reach home. It was hard for all soldiers being away for such long periods of time, but especially so for those with wives and children back home to worry about.

This included many of the generals, and not least Alexander, who had three children. Rose, Shane and Brian were eleven, nine and four, and so still very young; Alex had been forty years old when he'd married Lady Margaret Bingham, the daughter of the 5th Earl of Lucan, and because he had missed so much of their childhood already with his army career and, over the past few years, the war, he liked to write regularly and fill his letters with stories, jokes and amusing cartoons; he was an accomplished artist, in addition to his many other skills. Alexander might be commanding great armies but he was a loving father to his three children too. 'It's about time we have another baby, as you are all growing up,' he wrote in a letter at the end of February. 'Ask Mummy what she can do about it, but tell her not do anything until I get back.' On 1 March he wrote to them with a number of cartoons woven into the letter – including a slavering fox crawling around a duck coop on the right of the page, with a rifle firing a bullet on the left. 'Bang! Hello! There goes the bullet,' he wrote. 'Do you think Mummy will hit him? I hope she doesn't miss and kill poor Mrs Duck instead.' On the next page was a picture of a grave and cross with the words, 'Mrs Duck' written on it. 'Dear, oh dear!' he added. 'What bad luck, but accidents will happen sometimes, you know.' That was ever the truth.

General Clark also made time to write to his family. 'Renie darling,' he wrote on 8 March, 'just a V-mail note to tell you I love you.' V-mails were a means of getting letters home more quickly: a single page was photographed and the reels flown back to the States, developed and then posted through the domestic mail system. It meant they could be delivered in days rather than weeks, and while generals could give letters and packages to any fellow commanders or VIPs heading back to the United States, they otherwise had to use the same mail system as the troops. 'My problems get no less worrisome as the days go on,' he added. 'However, things will work out, and I am waiting for the day when I can lead my Fifth Army into a victory.'

Much had changed for the Allies in Italy. The theatre's greater commitment by the Combined Chiefs, the defeat of the German counter-attack at Anzio, the pause now – so welcome after the frenetic, almost manic pace of the fighting in the first two months of the year – and the evolution of a far weightier, balanced battle plan for the spring all augured well.

First, though, there was to be one more attempt to turn the Cassino position.

CHAPTER 25

The Destruction of Cassino Town

THE MEN OF THE New Zealand Corps were having a frustrating time. They'd been brought across the upper Rapido back on the night of 21–22 February, had swapped places with the Americans of 133rd Regiment and then found themselves crammed together in rocky gullies and blasted hillsides, waiting for the battle to begin. Every time the sun came out, the men would all agree the battle was bound to begin the following day and then it would rain again. They were in a state of semi-permanent pre-battle tension. It wasn't good for the nerves.

On that first night, Sergeant Roger Smith and the men of A and D Companies had been led to the narrow valley that ran between the barracks and Hill 213 and which was the foot of the main trail up to Monte Cassino. They quickly renamed it 'Mud Valley' and although the two companies were supposed to be comparatively safe and sheltered there, during their first day they had come under shellfire from German artillery in the Secco Valley which was clearly directed from Monte Cifalco. Smith had felt that being attacked by the Germans from behind had been a little unsporting, but more than that it was deeply unnerving because it meant they were not safe. Two lads in his platoon had been badly wounded, and he had just helped get them off the slopes near the foot of the gully when another salvo had screamed in as a bunch of men were collecting their clobber and bringing it back down to the safety of the gully floor. Smith had been clear of the blasts but he saw men tossed and flipped by the explosions. As soon as the shelling stopped, he had clambered up to see if he could help. 'Most were bashed into hideous broken carnage,' he noted. 'I turned over one lad whose heart still beat, to find only a mush of brains where his face should have been.'

After this sobering episode, they all made sure they were as well dug in as possible or protected by sangars, but the area was horribly overcrowded, with Gurkhas from 4th Indian above them further up the gully and the 1/4th Essex, also from 5th Indian Brigade, packed in waiting for the battle to start. Behind, in and around the village of Caira were more men plus a mass of Sherman tanks, carriers and other vehicles. Smith and his platoon commander, Lieutenant Jeff Armstrong, managed to dig out a two-man trench deep enough for them to sit down in and with a crawl-hole at one end. They then covered it with branches and bits of wood, placed a canvas bivvy over it, and then topped it with a further foot of soil. Armstrong named it the 'Doover'. It wasn't comfortable, but they felt reasonably safe and made sure that after that first day's tragedy they cut any further daylight movement to a bare minimum. It made for a very tedious and morale-sapping three weeks, however, in which they all had too much time to think, feel bored and fed up, and were mostly soaking wet.

Certainly, Brigadier Donald Bateman was once again tearing his hair out in frustration, not least because his 5th Brigade, spared during the February fighting on the mountain, were now poised to lead 4th Indian's attack. 'Keeping 5 Bde sitting on the "touch line" for three weeks,' he wrote, 'in spite of my emphatic protests was a constant drain of needless casualties.' These had come from desultory German shelling but also from illness and trench foot. Nor had it helped sanitation to have so many men crammed into such a narrow space. There were dead mules round and about and many of the men began slinging defecation over the side of foxholes and sangars. Unsurprisingly, cases of dysentery quickly rocketed. One night, 12 March, it sleeted down and rainwater running off the mountain coursed through their makeshift encampment in a torrent, sweeping away bivvies and filling trenches. As preparation for a major battle went, this was about as bad as it got.

The next day, all of A and D Companies were pulled out for one night for showers and fresh clothes. By this time they'd been in Mud Valley for nigh on three weeks; Smith was not alone in having become indescribably filthy, but also extremely browned off by the terrible combination of appalling conditions and inertia. The shower, haircut and change of clothes did them good but there was also a feeling of being dressed up for the slaughter. 'I'd like to meet the man who did not have a sinking feeling in his stomach', noted Smith, 'as we trudged once more up the rugged track to our sordid gully, feet already heavy and cold in sodden boots, and thinking of the damp welcome of filthy blankets on the floor of a slimy hole.'

Given the cards General Alexander had been dealt since the start of the Italian campaign, it was hard to criticize him or many of his decisions. Salerno had paid off, three of the four objectives for the campaign had been quickly secured the previous autumn and, considering the weather, the terrain and the levelling of the playing field these factors had caused, his armies had done well, capturing a third of the country, crossing innumerable rivers, scaling mountains and smashing through successive lines of German defences. Even Anzio, which had not fulfilled its original objectives, had drawn in more German troops than they had ever imagined – all to the good of OVERLORD – and now stood as a thorn in the enemy's side and a base for a key part of his DIADEM plan. He had also handled the complicated political challenges of commanding a multinational coalition with deft diplomacy.

Yet there was one decision that had not worked well, and that was the creation of the New Zealand Corps. The 2nd New Zealand Expeditionary Force had fought throughout the Mediterranean, fighting in Greece and North Africa and now in Italy. Despite a population of only 1.5 million, 19 per cent of its adult population had joined the army, a significant proportion of them volunteers. That was a very impressive contribution. However, trouble had begun brewing late the previous summer when censorship reports on mail home from soldiers in 2nd Division picked up a big dip in morale and rising resentment at the lack of leave given to many of the troops, a number of whom had not only been fighting for well over two years but were also a long way from home. This led the New Zealand government to allow 6,000 men furlough; these were shipped back home in two batches, the Ruapehu and Wakatipu drafts. Each of these provided the furlough men with what was swiftly extended to a four-month break. Yet while the furlough scheme was drawn up with the very best intentions, it quickly created all manner of problems. First, those not eligible were left wondering why they had not been granted leave as well, and so little was done for the morale of those remaining in the ranks. And although the scheme was staggered, the NZEF had collectively lost 20 per cent of its number and the 2nd New Zealand Division about a third.

On arriving back, these men were shocked to discover everyday life in New Zealand carrying on as normal, as though the war was barely taking place. Worse, there were some 35,000 'category A' men at home who had been granted exemptions because of jobs in reserved occupations. To the furloughed men this looked like class exemption for the better off; 'No man twice before every man once,' became their refrain. When the time came for them to be sent back to the front, which by now meant Italy, most refused to go. Because of the Furlough Mutiny, only 13 per cent of those who had been due to be posted back actually did so.

News of this mutiny inevitably crept back to Italy, while the replacements were slow to arrive and were, for the most part, poorly trained. Letter censors had noted a steady decline in morale within the 2nd New Zealand Division. It was estimated that 25 per cent of troops were showing signs of war-weariness and homesickness by the beginning of January. By the middle of the month the figure had risen to 50 per cent. This only worsened by the time the New Zealand Corps was created and they were posted over to the Cassino front. Freyberg had warned of the psychological effect on men as leave periods approached. 'We have to face the fact', he noted back in December, 'that once a man knows his turn is coming he ceases to be such a good soldier.' That Roger Smith was now platoon sergeant was because of the catastrophic losses they'd suffered in the fighting in November and December and because two men senior to him were fed up and didn't want the added risk and hassle that came with promotion; all previous sergeants in his platoon had been killed or wounded. In December battle exhaustion rates had been a comparatively modest 9 per cent, but in February, once back at the front, they rose dramatically to 36 per cent, and this despite the men playing a very limited role in the fighting at Cassino.

Freyberg was very alive both to the problems caused by the furlough scheme and to the state of his 2nd Division, which was not only understrength but now undertrained too. During the February battles, only two companies had fought an aggressive action – those from 28th Māori Battalion at the railway station on the edge of Cassino. The Māori were all volunteers, their companies based on tribal allegiances, and generally they had an esprit de corps and cohesion that trumped those of the Pakeha – white – battalions. While the Māori had fought their way to the station, the rest had had a holding role only. The plan now with Operation DICKENS was to try and continue this policy of limiting New Zealand casualties to a bare minimum. If all went well, the saturation of the town would enable his lead companies to walk through and clear an imaginary line just beyond the Via Casilina as it ran east–west called 'Quisling' and a further line, half a mile beyond the town to the south and code-named 'Jockey', by 6.30 p.m. on the same day. That was his hope, at any rate.

When Alexander had created the New Zealand Corps he had expected them to be bursting out into the Liri Valley through a hole punched by II Corps, not battering their way up the mountain or fighting the kind of battle DICKENS looked set to be. There was, though, a whiff of misfortune now clinging to this new corps because on 2 March the division commander, Major-General Howard Kippenberger, stepped on a mine which blew off one leg and then, as he hopped around, stood on a second mine and lost the other. Incredibly, he survived, but it meant that yet again another divisional commander was suddenly needed on the cusp of battle. Although Brigadier Graham 'Ike' Parkinson was commanding the New Zealand 6th Brigade, he was, like Dimoline, a gunner by trade and had a reputation for adequate competence without any of the long experience and flair that Kippenberger possessed. Around the same time, Major-General Alex Galloway was also brought in to take over from the beleaguered Dimoline at 4th Indian. Galloway had made a name for himself as an excellent staff officer – he'd been Jumbo Wilson's Chief of Staff in 1941 – but had very limited combat command experience. Nor was he Indian Army. This meant that both divisions were now commanded by men lacking the kind of dynamism, drive and determination that was urgently needed.

While it is easy to be wise in retrospect, even at the time there had been very good reasons to have left the New Zealanders where they were on the Adriatic. All formations needed the chance to rest and refit and it was down to the generals to know when a formation had shot its bolt. Withdrawing 56th Division, for example, was a case in point. It had fought relentlessly, first at the Garigliano then at Anzio. The New Zealanders had experienced similar levels of intense fighting at the back end of 1943 yet had been left at the front. They too needed a stint in Palestine – some sun, some heat, a chance to build up strength, train up newly arriving recruits and give the veterans local leave. Instead, they'd been flung into Cassino. Now, at the end of the second week of March, morale had dropped even further. Cases of sickness had risen by 96 per cent among the ranks and a staggering 162 per cent among officers. It was no wonder the New Zealanders were browned off.

There had been plenty of alternatives. There were officers of a higher calibre than Freyberg and his new subordinates in Italy. In terms of manpower, the 78th Division had avoided the worst of the December battles, for example. The 8th Indian Division had also had an easier time of things than either the New Zealanders or the Canadians, despite being involved in the fighting on the Adriatic. Almost certainly, Alexander would have opted for the New Zealanders because of Freyberg's seniority of rank: he was a lieutenant-general rather than a major-general, as befitted a divisional commander, and had past form in which he'd twice been temporarily bumped up to corps commander; this must have elevated him, and his division, above the others. It had been a mistake, however. That had been apparent in the first weeks of February, but now, as the skies suddenly cleared at long last in the middle of March, it was looking even more startlingly so.

With spring approaching, the days lengthening and the full twenty-one bomb groups scheduled for deployment around Foggia now in place, it was only natural that the revitalization of the Allies' overwhelming air superiority in the theatre should come to the forefront once more. General Wilson had even begun to believe that air power might be the panacea that could finally unlock the Gustav Line. 'Operations in Italy must be conditioned mainly by the air factor,' he wrote to Alexander on 25 February. 'My general plan for Italy is to use the air to deprive the enemy of the ability either to maintain his present positions or to withdraw his divisions out of Italy in time for OVERLORD.' Depending so heavily on air power, however, did not wash with either Alexander or the Combined Chiefs, and DIADEM became the basis of the immediate strategy in Italy. None the less, a major air operation was brewing, not least thanks to a report made by Professor Solly Zuckerman, a former British zoologist who had become something of a guru to many of the leading airmen – Eaker and Slessor included – for his pioneering analytical work on bombing results. Zuckerman had recently headed a bombing survey team that had carefully studied the air interdiction operations in Sicily and southern Italy the previous summer, and they had concluded that, in order to disrupt German attempts to supply the front, the prime targets should be railway marshalling yards and other rail centres. Attacking bridges, Zuckerman and his team concluded, was a waste of time.

The Target Section at Twelfth Air Force, the tactical air force, strongly disagreed, pointing to plenty of evidence of destroyed bridges hampering German supply efforts. There were forty-eight major marshalling yards in Italy and 100 further hubs with at least ten tracks or more – a huge amount – and enormous numbers of bridges. The solution, of course, was to strike both Zuckerman's targets and also bridges in a massed and sustained assault on the transportation system in German-occupied Italy, about which all Allied commanders, no matter what side of the doctrinal debate they stood, were enormously enthusiastic. Operation STRANGLE, which was 'to reduce the enemy's flow of supplies to a level which will make it impracticable for him to maintain and operate his forces in Central Italy', was due to be launched in the third week of March.

General Hap Arnold, C-in-C of the USAAF, meanwhile, was equally enthused by Freyberg's plan to obliterate Cassino. 'We are all very greatly disturbed here by the apparent "bogging down" of the Italian campaign,' he had written to Eaker at the end of February. He suggested massing as many bombers as they could. 'Utilizing all this assembled air power,' he added, 'break up every stone in the town behind which a German soldier might be hiding. When the smoke of the last bombers and fighters begins to die down have the ground troops rapidly take the entire town of Cassino.' Eaker, however, while greatly enthused by STRANGLE, was less optimistic about plans to pulverize Cassino, and replied to Arnold warning him that it was unlikely the army would be able to follow through sufficiently swiftly to win a quick victory. 'Personally,' he wrote, 'I do not feel it will throw the German out of his present position completely or entirely, or compel him to abandon the defensive role, if he decides and determines to hold on to the last man.'

Up on Monte Cassino there was an air of nervous apprehension and a palpable sense that this lull was a calm before the storm, and yet while the Fallschirmjäger were aware that the Allies were preparing for another attack, they too had received a number of replacements – not many, but enough to make a difference to these horrendously depleted units. In 6. Kompanie of Fallschirmjäger-Regiment 4 the new boys had been just that – seventeen- and eighteen-year-old lads and volunteers, rather like Hans Liebschner, who had been in Luftwaffe field units and opted to cross over to the Fallschirmjäger. 'As small as the little guys were sometimes,' noted Rudolf Donth, 'some looked like full-grown schoolboys and they were real blokes.' Donth and his NCOs were glad of them but also made sure they did all they could to give them the benefit of their experience and some crash-course training. There were other changes too; Leutnant Reimar Gütschow, the company commander, was given leave to get married. The boys all had a whip-round, and as he'd left had handed over a savings book of 100 Reichsmarks for his firstborn. Unfortunately for Donth, Gütschow's replacement was Leutnant Stahl, with whom he'd had a run-in at Battipaglia during the Salerno battle the previous September. Back then, Donth had been an NCO and during a fraught moment at the height of the fighting he had told Stahl – who had been in 1. Bataillon – to 'lick my arse.' 'When he greeted me at the command post,' noted Donth, 'he didn't recognise me and I didn't let on.' At any rate, the incident at Battipaglia was not mentioned. 'So that was all right!' added Donth, with relief.

An impressively large Allied force had been assembled for the launch of DICKENS. In addition to the 2nd New Zealand and 4th Indian Divisions, Freyberg could call upon the British 78th Division and Combat Command B. Also assembled were some 900 guns. Astonishing feats of engineering had been undertaken. A goat track, for example, leading from the back of Caira up to the mountain pastures between Castellone and Snakeshead Ridge, now renamed by the 4th Indian men as the 'Madras Circus,' had been substantially widened. It had originally been the idea of Lieutenant-Colonel Edward Stenhouse, commander of the 4th Indian sappers, to try and improve it to take, first, increased numbers of mules, and then also jeeps. The route was about two miles and wound its way around the folds of the mountain's spurs and in places had a gradient of one in four, but despite this the Indian sappers had completed it in nine days between 16 and 25 February. Freyberg then suggested widening it further to take tanks; he had it in mind to use it as the second prong to a pincer movement from Monastery Hill once the Indians had taken the abbey. To this end, a makeshift armoured force was created, made up from 4th Indian's Recce Squadron, a further New Zealand Sherman squadron and a company – the equivalent of a squadron – of American light Stuart tanks, so around forty in all.

At any rate, the track, named the 'Cavendish Road' after an earlier commander of the 4th Indian's sappers, was further widened in the first half of March; its entire creation was an extraordinary feat, not least because the sappers were, in a number of places, under the eyes of the Germans while constructing it.

*

One day during the long wait, Roger Smith and Lieutenant Armstrong did venture out of their 'Doover' and make their way to the barracks to scavenge some American rations that had been left there, then took a mule path up on to the higher ground above, where back on 24 January 44. Division had had their outposts. They made their way through a wood of skeleton trees, now just jagged stumps, and then found the body of a dead Gurkha. After rolling him under a rock, covering him and marking his grave, they continued clambering up the side of the slopes until they were level with Castle Hill, three-quarters of a mile to the south. The castle was a ruin but still more or less in one piece, with high walls standing sentinel over the town below. As for the town, it was a bit battered but still pretty much intact: buildings looked like the houses, palaces, churches and public buildings they were. From the east, the Via Casilina ran dead straight then was consumed by the town; they couldn't see its 90-degree dog-leg in the heart of Cassino, or how it ran, almost due south, hugging the foot of Monte Cassino until turning westwards into the Liri Valley and on, all the way to Rome. A shoulder of the ridge they were on obscured that view. They could, though, see the ruins of the abbey, perched on its outcrop, far above the town and even the castle, the bastion walls still intact, but above a heap of rubble. 'We sat for some time in the screen of the bush,' noted Smith, 'smoking and gazing at the panorama.' The mountain and the town appeared deserted, sickening, but frozen in a moment of brief calm.

Now it was Tuesday, 14 March, the second day in a row of fine, clear weather; there had even been a ground frost that morning. Wednesday the 15th – the Ides of March – looked set to be clear again. The wait was almost over.

General Mark Clark, with Al Gruenther in tow, left his HQ at Presenzano at 7 a.m. and drove to Freyberg's CP near the ruins of San Pietro, getting there at 8.20 a.m., just ten minutes before the bombers were due to arrive. From there, on a saddle on the lower slopes of Monte Sammucro, there was a clear view across to Monte Cassino. Perched on the end of the massif and still white in the morning light was the rubble of the abbey, and from there the massif gradually rose, up to Snakeshead Ridge, then Monte Castellone and then, towering over them, Monte Cairo with its gentle but immense sides, and the route to the Liri Valley that might have been had there been a bit more imagination and clear-headedness.

And beneath, also pale against the dark slopes of the mountain that rose above it, lay Cassino, still, in this morning light, identifiable as a town even though the only living souls were a few hundred paratroopers of Oberst Heilmann's 3. Fallschirmjäger-Regiment, mostly hiding out of site in the labyrinth of tunnels, vaults and reinforced cellars.

Also already at Freyberg's CP were Generals Alexander, Harding, Eaker and Devers, and they were now led to an OP, a battered stone house around which they could all watch the bombing of the town. The destruction of the town. The view from the stone house was pretty good but Clark thought it might be better from the roof, and so, with Eaker and Gruenther following, they clambered up on to the ridge and sat there, waiting for the bombers to arrive.

It did seem as though little had been left to chance. The town, castle and Monastery Hill were about to receive the greatest concentration of firepower ever unleashed. For every German soldier in Cassino, the New Zealand Corps planners had reckoned 3,000 lbs of bombs would be dropped. In addition there were a staggering 890 artillery pieces ready to follow up after the bombers, firing a mixture of concentrations and a creeping barrage. Behind the attacking infantry were 400 Sherman tanks, including those from New Zealand 4th and 19th Armoured Brigades, ready to push through the town with the infantry and clear the last shell-shocked survivors, and also the armour of Combat Command B, the infantry of 78th Division, and, with one RCT, the 36th T-Patchers, poised to push through and secure a lodgement on the western side of the Rapido.

Among the bomber crews, Lieutenant Michael Sullivan wasn't on the roster for the day's attack, so was left behind at Foggia. 'The boys pulled a milk run today,' he noted in his diary. 'Cassino City'; it might have been an operation of enormous significance in the history of aerial warfare, but to Sullivan and his fellows it was just another mission and a straightforward one at that. Frank Pearce and most of the rest of the Texas Division were now camped near Caserta and had been the past three weeks, out of the line, thankfully, at long last. That morning, Pearce had been out early lecturing the infantry about mines when they'd heard the roar in the sky. 'Hundreds of big bombers going over,' he jotted. 'Must be headed for Cassino.' Up at Cassino itself, the New Zealand Infantry, which had been holding the northern part of the town, had been pulled back 1,000 yards. As the first heavies headed towards them, however, that didn't feel like nearly enough; in Mud Valley, Roger Smith looked up and prayed for the courage to watch, rather than cower. Also watching and ready to move in with the armour when called upon was Frenchy Bechard, who as an armoured engineer was on standby to move. That the town was about to be obliterated didn't wash with him. Frankly, he was terrified. He'd been told he was part of a 'flying column' that would sweep through the town once it had been cleared and then burst out into the Liri Valley. 'We are to penetrate through the enemy lines with everything we got,' he noted. 'Hand grenades and extra belt of ammunition have been distributed to the men.' The chaplain had even come over to say a few words of comfort – which hardly instilled confidence. 'Looks more like a suicide mission,' he added. 'It's a frightening feeling to know we're going to attack head-on, at a heavily fortified enemy, with less than 50 per cent chance of coming back.' Memories of the Rapido were at the forefront of his mind, but before they moved out the New Zealanders had to clear the town. And before them, the bombers had to pulverize it.

They were now right over, and Roger Smith could see the bomb bays open of the first there, 72 B-25 twin-engine Mitchells. On the bombers streamed, twinkling silver in the morning sun. The air was full with the heavy drone of their engines as they flew in at between 8,000 and 10,000 feet, not a Luftwaffe plane in sight. Then the bombs began to fall and the thunder of the explosions rose like a volcanic eruption, the ground shook, a constant rumbling ripple as more and more struck the town. A vast cloud of dust billowed upwards, climbing until it turned and rolled and burst out on itself. 'The pall of dust thickened and spread,' noted Smith, 'obliterating and enlarging the target area until we were peering apprehensively upward from under the rim of a giant mushroom cloud.' Occasionally, above the ear-shattering din, a screaming whine could be heard as bombs fell wide and punctured the side of the mountain, worryingly close. Yet no one in A Company, at any rate, was hurt.

From his perch atop the stone house on the slopes of Sammucro, General Clark was mesmerized. 'When the bombs hit,' he noted, 'they sent quick, stabbing flashes of orange flame, and this was followed by a joint eruption of smoke and debris. By the time the first wave of bombers had passed over Cassino, the town was almost obliterated by smoke and dust.' Then came the B-17s, 114 of them, and now the little stone house began to shake violently from the mass of detonations six miles away.

*

Unteroffizier Jupp Klein was with the rest of the 2. Kompanie men in the vaulted cellars of the Hotel des Roses on the Via Casilina at the southern end of the town; this was their command post and shared with a number of Jäger from Heilmann's 3. Fallschirmjäger-Regiment. Klein had only just settled down for some kip after a night's work when a Jäger rushed in from the rear entrance and shouted, 'They are attacking the abbey again!' Moments later, one of the first bombs to fall hit their palazzo. Above, the building crumbled, the din immense, as stone and timbers crashed in an ear-shattering cacophony of destruction. Dust and grit falling and the walls and ground shaking like an earthquake. Klein tried to keep calm. The cellar would hold, he was sure, the rubble above strengthening the vaulted ceilings. But then, what if they were cut off, hermetically sealed in their tomb? Suffocating would not be a pleasant death – he remembered all too clearly his comrades lost in the collapsed bunkers at Tollo.

More bombs falling, and yet more. Clearly, the Tommies meant to kill them all, but Klein was determined not to die; they all were. Think clearly. Think calmly. After the bombardment, the Tommies would attack and the paratroopers needed to be ready. So they got to work, making sure the entrances were kept clear and trying to keep any tormenting thoughts clear of their minds. Not easy, with Armageddon playing out above and the cellar dark and the air thick with dust. Klein now remembered that when he was young, his father, who had been a coal miner, had told him about a time when a shaft had collapsed; he had prayed to God and made sure he kept calm, making every breath count. That had saved him. By keeping calm and breathing steadily, Klein was determined to survive too.

On and on the bombs fell; there would be a pause, the men would cough and gasp and splutter and think it was over, only for more to arrive. Klein and his comrades asked themselves who else it was, other than paratroopers, that the Americans and British were trying to kill. The Fortresses had been followed by 164 Liberators. There were also some errors – one bomber dropped its load only a mile from the gaggle of Allied generals, killing several men in a New Zealand artillery battery. Others unleashed bombs on San Michele and Venafro, tragic mistakes that killed ninety-six Allied troops and 140 civilians. Most, though, found Cassino; 47 per cent of the bombs dropped landed within a mile of the centre of the town and 50 per cent near or on Monastery Hill. Not until midday did the last bomber turn and drone away, leaving behind a still-swirling cloud of black and yellowish smoke and dust that covered the town like a thick blanket. This, however, was not the end of Cassino's ordeal, because now the 890 guns opened fire, from 312 25-pounders to 48 240mm-calibre pieces. While some of the artillery fired prepared concentrations – not only on the town but on known enemy strongpoints on Monte Cassino – the men of the New Zealand 25th Battalion began moving south towards the town behind a creeping barrage and with the Shermans of the New Zealand 19th Armoured Regiment following behind.

The leading companies were met by scenes of indescribable destruction. Cassino had been obliterated just as Freyberg had intended it should be, a manifestation of the Allies' huge destructive power, and despite Eaker's reservations there was no doubting that using air power in this way was what General Jumbo Wilson had had in mind back in February. Since North Africa, the Allies had been following a policy of 'steel not flesh', or rather, 'steel not *our* flesh'. The hope was to use air power as one of the primary tools with which to defeat the enemy and, in the process, minimize the number of young lives that had to be sacrificed to achieve victory – and specifically the lives of front-line troops, especially the infantry.

Now the leading 25th Battalion men began picking their way across vast bomb craters, over immense piles of rubble, through mud. Cassino was no longer a town, it was just an immense plateau of stone, brick and shattered glass. Not a single building was left intact, except perhaps a few stubbornly standing walls. Cassino was now a hellish wasteland, the air choking with the lingering stench of explosive and mortar dust. The men needed gas masks, although these had not been worn – or even carried – in an age. The weather had turned – it wasn't raining, but cloud had built up by the afternoon, which meant no further heavy bombers would be coming over. Instead a succession of fighter-bombers roared in, dive-bombing targets mostly on Monte Cassino and other objectives and supply lines in the Liri Valley, while the infantry pushed on into the wreckage.

Freyberg had imagined that the German defenders would be as obliterated as the town and that the New Zealanders would soon be through and out the other side; but the going was far slower than planned – a 100 yards' advance every hour rather than every ten minutes. The barrage ceased abruptly at 3.30 p.m., by which time a staggering 195,969 rounds had been fired. By dusk they had almost reached the Via Casilina as it ran straight from the east, but were meeting increasingly heavy resistance from the usual cocktail of mortars, machine guns and snipers. They were still some way short of the Quisling Line. Meanwhile, D Company managed to scale Castle Hill, Point 193 on their maps, and capture it; but already the battle was unravelling despite two-thirds of the ruined town being in New Zealand hands by nightfall. Only ten Shermans had managed to get into Cassino – often by means of the crews getting out and hand-clearing rubble with picks and shovels. Some crews even resorted to charging piles of debris like a battering ram. Bulldozers were due to follow but had yet to do so; the rest of the armour was still languishing behind on the two parallel roads that ran from the north.

In the pre-battle plan, the New Zealanders had been due to be at the 90-degree dog-leg of the Via Casilina at the Hotel Excelsior and Piazza Ciano by 2 p.m., and out the other side entirely by dusk. By that time, Brigadier Donald Bateman's 5th Indian Brigade were expected to be holding the key points of the road up to the abbey and Hangman's Hill. None of this had happened; the schedule had slipped badly, and instead of a phalanx of dozers and engineers sweeping into the town, chronic congestion on the two roads from the north had meant that only one of the four field companies planned had reached the ruins.

To make matters worse, it had then begun to rain again, and not lightly but heavily. Operation DICKENS had been based upon smashing the town and its defenders with unprecedented violence, and the infantry, engineers and armour then swiftly sweeping through in the wake of this enormous hurricane; if there had been any survivors, these dazed, stupefied men were to have been swept aside in a tidal wave of concentrated all-arms power. Instead, congestion and a palpable lack of drive had overwhelmed the entire assault. That day, the New Zealanders suffered just forty-one casualties. By the standards of the campaign, those were very light indeed. It suggested that the infantry had been very quick to hit the ground the moment enemy fire opened up, or had taken cover rather than pressing on with the attack. A lack of training could be soaked up if all that was being expected was for the men to defend; but training, experience and, above all, leadership were essential in an attack. No one wanted to be in the vanguard of an assault – the Forlorn Hope, it had been called in Wellington's time – but actions that might save lives on one day could easily cause rivers of blood on the next.

Certainly, DICKENS, conceived as a short, sharp overwhelming roll of the ball that would knock down all the skittles in one go, had fallen badly short.

CHAPTER 26

Battle in the Ruins

ONCE THE BOMBING AND bombardment was over, Generalleutnant Fridolin von Senger decided to head to Heilmann's 3. Fallschirmjäger-Regiment command post, which he knew Heidrich was also visiting. The afternoon had clouded over but it was still not raining, and for the Germans that made being out and about a dangerous business; one never knew when Jabos might be swarming about, even after such a heavy bombardment as Cassino had been subjected to earlier. If one did need to venture out in daylight, however, the safest way to move from A to B was alone and on foot, in von Senger's case with a staff officer following a little way behind. It wasn't quite a mile from his advanced command post near Aquino to Heilmann's, which was in a farmhouse next to the railway line as it hugged the southern side of Monte Cassino. As he picked his way he gazed at the shattered ruins of Aquino, another ghost village in this now-cursed corner of Italy, then followed a zigzag course across a landscape pitted with craters, doing his best to follow the remains of the track. The entire landscape looked utterly ravaged; not a tree still stood, not a building was untouched. He suddenly remembered back nearly thirty years to the Battle of the Somme and the wrecked landscape there, in northern France. This looked much the same. 'There was a smell of freshly torn earth,' he noted, 'and of red-hot iron mingled with gunpowder.'

He reached the command post safely, conferred with both Heidrich and Heilmann and agreed to move 1. Bataillon of 4. Fallschirmjäger-Regiment, which was holding the reasonably quiet sector on Colle Sant'Angelo, down into the town. Heidrich also wanted the help of the

Luftwaffe; von Senger promised to ask. He then made his way back again, and on his return immediately rang von Vietinghoff.

'Heidrich's demand is for a show of strength from the Luftwaffe tomorrow,' he told his army commander. 'Although rain is better than our own air support. Hopefully nothing now happens overnight; the defence appears to be in good hands, and the men reasonably equipped and supplied with enough ammunition.' Von Senger felt reasonably certain that this time, at any rate, they could hold the Allied attack.

The Allied commanders had been dumbfounded that any German troops could have survived such a bombardment, and yet Jupp Klein had been right: those vaulted ceilings in the cellars of the Hotel des Roses had held, just as he'd told himself they would. So had plenty of others, which they'd reinforced with railway girders and steel cages. Commanding 2. Bataillon in the town was Hauptmann Ferdinand Foltin, who had managed to lead first eighty, and then a further twenty-five men into a cave behind the Excelsior Hotel; together with the Pioniere of Klein's 2. Kompanie this meant that he had around 150 men who had survived. On the other hand, twenty-five had been killed and a further forty from the northern half of the town swiftly captured. Foltin was determined to defend the ruins to the last man, but by any reckoning 150 was not a big number – not against two divisions and 400 tanks. Up on Monastery Hill, meanwhile, was Major Rudolf Böhmler's 1. Bataillon; his command post was now in the Crypt of the shattered abbey. Again, he could only call upon a comparatively small number of men – perhaps 200 – without drawing on 4. Fallschirmjäger-Regiment, who still held the figure-of-eight on Colle d'Onofrio, up to Point 593 and down to Albaneta and beyond.

There was no question that by so swiftly taking Castle Hill, the New Zealanders had had a golden opportunity to cut down behind the Via Casilina as it turned south and led out of the town. Those MG posts were pointing in the direction of the town, not back up the hill, and there were only around fifty men defending the lower slopes of Monastery Hill. The 3. Kompanie of the Pionier-Bataillon had been sent to recapture the castle, but had been repulsed; this counter-attack, perhaps, deterred the D Company men from doing more than consolidating the ruined castle, but a more aggressive commander might well have hurried further troops up on to Castle Hill and used it as a springboard to attack down behind the Excelsior Hotel and even the Hotel des Roses. After all, with the castle in their hands, they now had a crucial bit of high ground, which should have been a big help.

Instead, the night's fighting had seen Bateman's 5th Indian Brigade begin their assault on Monastery Hill, an attack made in three stages. Every Indian infantry brigade was split into one British battalion, one Indian and one Gurkha, and it was the English battalion, the 1/4th Essex, who had been supposed to take over from the New Zealanders on Castle Hill early in the afternoon as well as take the first hairpin on the abbey road – Point 165 on the map. In fact, they had only begun their climb up the hill at 6.15 p.m., by which time it was dark. The ascent was steep and they were being spat at by machine guns and bombarded with mortars. So although they reached the castle, it wasn't until around 3 a.m. on the 16th that Point 165 was reported to be in their hands. And by then it was raining hard. The idea had been for the 1/6th Rajputana Rifles to seamlessly pass through and then secure the second hairpin directly above Castle Hill, Point 236. Instead, the Rajputana Rifles made good progress before being caught in a savage crossfire from paratroopers below in the town and from above. As dawn neared, the Rajputanas fell back to the safety of the castle.

By this time the entire attack was hopelessly behind schedule. In the pre-battle plan, Castle Hill and then the second hairpin were to have been taken in daylight and made secure, and then the 1/9th Gurkhas were to have used these as a springboard to cut diagonally across the steep southern face of Monte Cassino and take Hangman's Hill. Instead, the battalion had been stuck in the New Zealanders' traffic and that of the armour, and it had taken them five hours just to get to their jump-off point from the northern edge of Cassino. Progress had been inevitably slow, but then, amid the rain and the mayhem, the company commander had realized that his C Company were entirely missing. In fact they'd become separated and had actually reached Hangman's Hill, having met no enemy troops other than one outpost which they had cleared with grenades. Because Hangman's Hill was a rocky, jutting knoll, not entirely unlike Point 593, it was quite possible for them to shelter among the rocks and overhangs and emerge only when they had to.

The success of the Gurkhas in reaching their objective indicated several things. First, that they could slip through, albeit at night, without being noticed suggested that the surviving Fallschirmjäger on Monastery Hill and in the town were both thin on the ground and had their hands full. Second, it clearly implied that a far, far heavier swamping of objectives by the infantry would have made much greater sense than the staggered, piecemeal attack that had been planned. Herein lay the rub with DICKENS, for while it was supported by the full weight of the Allies' resources of air power, artillery and armour, the plan for the infantry was fundamentally flawed. Armour and bulldozers, obviously, could only advance along raised roads, but that was not the case with the foot-sloggers; they could move over still-waterlogged ground if need be and scurry over rubble more easily than tanks. Armoured support was helpful – even important – but nothing trumped sending in large numbers of troops from multiple directions. Freyberg had planned to attack with two battalions but only with one, the 25th, up front, and that with just a brace of companies. What the bombing and artillery had given the attackers had been a chance – a comparatively narrow window – in which to sweep into the town before the dazed defenders could recover their wits and balance and suss out what the heck was going on. Even if a number of Hauptmann Foltin's men had managed to quickly man their machine guns, they couldn't be everywhere; there simply weren't enough of them.

Nor did the attack have to be canalized by the two roads heading into the town from the north. Rather, the Allies would have done well to send in a brigade along the railway line. The men could have been brought up overnight to a mile or so south-east of Cassino, then scampered along using the railway embankment as their axis. The Māori might have needed tanks back on 17–18 February, but that was because the town still existed, it was comparatively full of troops, and the Germans had assault guns and other weapons to hand. As it was, the two companies of Māori had penetrated quite a way. But tanks would not have been essential immediately after the bombardment and artillery barrage. There was no reason why two battalions, for example, could not have moved either side of the railway behind a barrage. They had enough guns for this. Had the German defenders been facing enfilading attacks from the north and south-east they would almost certainly have been overwhelmed.

The same approach applied to the 4th Indians. Knowing his brigade would be in the van of the attack, Donald Bateman had begged first Dimoline and then, after his arrival, Galloway to allow him to put in his entire brigade that first afternoon; he wanted them massed and ready on Point 175, the low knoll to the south of the barracks from where his men could scramble across the lower slopes overlooking Cassino and sweep straight on to their objectives. He also begged for the New Zealanders to put at least a brigade into the town too. 'It seemed so obvious', he noted, 'that 5 Bde would never have a chance unless its base – Cassino town – was clear; and a brigade could have done it in those first few hours.' But Dimoline lacked the authority to challenge the plan that had evolved from the Corps HQ, and Galloway, really a desk wallah, was new and hardly in a position to start challenging his corps commander. And so the plan had stood.

Now, on the morning of 16 March, Bateman was once again left scratching his head in wonder. He had huge respect for both Alexander and Harding and couldn't understand how they'd let a second terrible plan be put into action. 'We had', he noted, 'lost the initial advantage of surprise and the air bombardment by plain stupidity.' That was true enough. All surprise had gone. The Germans now knew the Allied plan and could ready themselves. Which they did, and very effectively too.

General Mark Clark was as frustrated as Bateman. He'd asked the New Zealand Corps for updates about numbers of tanks and troops now in the town and, getting only vague answers, had then headed up to the front to see for himself. At the bridge across the Rapido on the Via Casilina he'd discovered just one tank, whereas Freyberg had told him there were two squadrons – around forty – over. With his anger rising, he'd then gone to see Freyberg and suggested sending 78th Division along Highway 6 to attack the town from the east – a very sensible idea. Clark had also understood that the Cavendish Road was to have been used as part of a joint attack on Monte Cassino, so was dismayed to learn that no such armoured thrust had been undertaken. What Clark had envisioned was swamping Cassino and Monte Cassino with a mass of troops and armour, all of which had been made available to the New Zealand Corps; he had been assured that this was indeed the plan. To learn, this second morning, that no such thing had happened was infuriating to say the very least. 'Freyberg's handling of the ensuing attack', he noted tersely, 'has been characterised by indecision and lack of aggressiveness.' Nor had Clark been impressed with Galloway, who he thought seemed hopelessly defeatist. Repeatedly, throughout the day, Clark spoke with Freyberg, urging him to commit more troops and also put in the armoured thrust round the back of Monte Cassino. Galloway had five battalions at his disposal yet they were being used piecemeal. 'I told Freyberg the tanks to be employed were American,' Clark added, 'and he could lose them all and I would replace them within 24 hours.' But Freyberg refused to do as Clark suggested; there was no armoured assault from the north and 78th Division were not brought into the fray. 'If he were an American corps commander with American troops, I would have no hesitancy in giving such an order,' he noted. 'I have just now telephoned to General Alexander, whom I would never go to on such a move if it were not for the delicate international relations involved here.'

And just as General Tuker had wanted to weep with frustration from his hospital bed a month earlier, now it was Kippenberger's turn. Legless but with a mind as sharp was ever, he had learned of the faltering attack with no small amount of anguish. 'We smashed the town, destroyed half the garrison and then Ike Parkinson entirely disregarded my plan,' he noted, 'for swamping the defence with infantry before it had recovered.'

At least Frenchy Bechard was happy. 'Early in the morning, platoon leaders came round and told us to turn in grenades and ammo,' he scribbled in his diary. 'The attack has been called off! A great relief fell upon the men. Guess the Brass had second thoughts about this mission. Thank God for that!' In the meantime, very little attempt had been made by the infantry in the town to infiltrate through the night. By nightfall they had held around two-thirds of it, but were still short of the Quisling Line. During those long, wet hours of darkness, while Bateman's men were scrambling up and round Monastery Hill, the New Zealanders were doing very little except feeling wretched and miserable.

The contrast with the defenders could not have been more stark, for while the German forces in Italy had many shortcomings, they were supreme at deploying troops with both speed and decisiveness. It was this, rather than the quality of the troops involved, that was the crucial factor, for if the Fallschirmjäger were 'elite' it was only really in their mindset; the majority were undertrained and lacked sustained experience. Kurt Mueller was in his first proper combat action up on Monte Cassino and he was far from alone; most new arrivals had barely had a month of formal training. Roger Smith, on the other hand, had far greater knowledge, experience and understanding of warfare than the vast majority of German paratroopers. However, within the Fallschirmjäger units were backbone troops around whom these young, impressionable and still motivated young teenagers and new boys could coalesce. Men like Jupp Klein, who had served in Russia, Sicily and now Italy. He'd developed a sixth sense – a soldier's instinct – and a resilience that helped him face any new scenario. Or men like Hauptmann Ferdi Foltin, the kind of tough, decisive and aggressive young battalion commander who was worth his weight in gold. It meant that while the New Zealanders, given a poor battle plan and with morale seeping away with every passing hour, lacked the motivation to put themselves at risk in this hellish place, the Fallschirmjäger had given themselves a stiff shot of defiance and had spent the night beetling about working out how best to stop these Tommies from making any further progress. While Jupp Klein and his Pioniere were ordered to stay put and hold the Via Casilina at the Hotel des Roses, Foltin had sent fourteen others to recce the south of the town. They were astonished to discover that the station, Round House and Hummocks – a series of small knolls – were all unoccupied. Foltin was so surprised to hear this that he initially refused to believe the reports. After all, he reasoned, what was the point of such a bombardment if the infantry had not swamped the area afterwards? It made no sense to him at all. Needless to say, by first light German troops now held all these locations.

Other reinforcements were swiftly brought up, including a company of anti-tank guns. These had been dismantled and then carried over the piles of rubble and set up again around the Hotel des Roses. This kind of ingenuity was entirely absent from the Allied battle plan. General Heidrich had also released 3. Bataillon of 3. Fallschirmjäger-Regiment – Kratzert's battalion – although after his heroics on and around Point 593, he'd been sent home on leave as part of his reward for winning the Knight's Cross up there. The battalion had been pulled off Monte Cassino with just sixty-five men left, but thanks to an influx of teenagers its ranks had risen again to 170. Kratzert's men were now being temporarily commanded by an Oberleutnant and the companies by NCOs. All the new boys were green and badly undertrained. Yet there was still a spine of experience and all they were being asked to do was obey orders and man machine guns and mortars. No one was expecting them to attack, have to use their initiative or make decisions. Effectively they were young automatons. And right now, that was enough. The 3. Bataillon had been out of the line but it was a case of needs must. After being given a hot meal the men had been driven up towards the front and that night, while the New Zealand troops were doing very little, they were rushed forward. Meanwhile, as had been agreed with von Senger, 1. Bataillon of 4. Fallschirmjäger-Regiment would swap positions with a battalion from 15. Panzergrenadier while 1/4 FJR moved down into the town. Logistically, it made more sense for the grenadiers to go straight into Cassino, but Heidrich wanted only one chain of command operating in the town.

So by dawn there were now around 300 Fallschirmjäger in the town, bolstered with anti-tank guns, one StuG that had survived the bombing, artillery they could call upon and Nebelwerfer batteries further back, facing a similar number of New Zealanders – because although there were thousands of troops backed up to Caira and hundreds of tanks, very few of them were actually in the rubble of the town. In truth, Freyberg might as well have called the entire battle off right now, this second morning. If anything had been learned from the fighting so far up on Monte Cassino, or from the German counter-attacks at Anzio, it was that offensives like this really were one throw of the dice. The opportunity for a breakthrough lay on the opening day, if not the first hours. All that effort, all that terrible destruction, the eradication of what a year ago had been a peaceful, vibrant rural market town largely unchanged in centuries had been pointless because the battle plan had been so abjectly terrible: badly planned, badly thought through and badly executed. It wasn't the fault of the troops involved; rather, the blame lay squarely with those who had planned it, who had been too short-sighted, too stubborn to listen to subordinates like Bateman, who'd implored them to think again, or Kippenberger, whose original plans for his division had been thrown out, or even Clark, whose exhortations to Freyberg had been repeatedly ignored.

It was a tragedy of the highest order. Yet while, ultimately, it was the men at the top who were responsible for success or failure, there was a limit to how much Alexander could influence the tactical flow of a battle, and Clark's hands were so badly tied in his dealings with Freyberg. What a very challenging position Clark was in for a still-young American army commander: effectively commanding two armies made up of units from the United States, Britain, Canada, India, New Zealand and France. No other US general was in charge of so many foreign troops in battle – and over two fronts. Alexander's role was to provide firm direction, to coordinate plans and ensure that his subordinates had the right tools for the tasks they were given. Alex's great mistake had been creating the New Zealand Corps under Freyberg, but while both he and Clark had the right to sack underperforming corps and divisional commanders, such decisions were necessarily rare and never taken lightly. In any case, the theatre was hardly awash with dynamic replacements.

Rather, blame for the failures at Cassino, especially, needed to be laid at the doors of the corps and divisional commanders. Fifth Army's battering of the Gustav Line had played witness to untold scales of courage, yet the poor bastards made to carry out this fighting had repeatedly been badly served by men devoid of inspiration, creativity or chutzpah: Fred Walker, Geoffrey Keyes, Harry Dimoline, Alex Galloway, Ike Parkinson and, especially, Bernard Freyberg had let down their men badly. The missions given them had been tough, but none of them impossible to overcome. The Rapido could have been crossed; the Monte Cassino position could have been turned in the first half of February; and Cassino town could and should have been a walkover on 15 March. The Allies had been dealt a terrible hand in Italy, but in these first ten weeks of 1944 they'd not helped themselves.

And so the New Zealanders renewed their attack on the morning of 16 March with all the aces they'd held the day before now lost to them. It had finally stopped raining as the attack in the town resumed, which was carried out by two platoons of B Company of 24th Battalion, A Company of 25th Battalion and 11 Platoon of 26 Battalion. In other words, about 240 men all told. The attack very quickly ground to a halt as they came under fire; at this point, casualties in B Company of 24th Battalion, for example, were just three killed and seven wounded. The infantry were helped by a few tanks that had managed to enter the rubble from the north-east; that they'd done so had been because American engineers had built a bridge across the Rapido overnight and culverts were covered with Valentine bridging tanks. The tanks weren't able to get very far, however, because now the craters were filled with water, and dozers brought forward found themselves being sniped at and were struggling with both the mountains of rubble and craters that had now become ponds.

Meanwhile, the Rajputanas again tried to take the second hairpin and were once more cut down by enfilading fire; to make matters worse, a mortar shell hit the battalion CP, wounding the CO and four other officers. Only at around 2 p.m. was it realized that C Company of the 1/9th Gurkhas were clinging to Hangman's Hill. Bateman now decided to send the rest of the Gurkhas up to try and reach them after dark, and the Rajputanas were to make the most of the darkness to have another crack at the second hairpin. Bateman yet again urged the New Zealanders to commit more infantry into the town, which was relayed via Galloway, but Freyberg rejected this request. As far as he was concerned, there were already quite enough operating within the confined spaces there. If

Freyberg wasn't listening to the army commander, he certainly wasn't going to take heed of a brigadier.

That night the artillery fired concentrations on to the Germans on Monastery Hill, and behind this the Rajputanas took the second hairpin and the rest of the Gurkhas managed to reach Hangman's Hill – getting there at around 5 a.m. on the 17th – and in the nick of time, too, to help C Company beat off a German counter-attack. Dawn saw the Rajputanas counter-attacked yet again; the second hairpin was turning into a rematch of Point 593 and, as had happened on the massif, the pattern was the same now, with the Rajputanas forced back to the castle once more. It meant the Gurkhas were now isolated high above the rest of the brigade, hanging on to their positions by the old cable car mount. The battle as a whole, however, was stuttering badly, although on the morning of the 17th the New Zealanders' 26th Battalion, with the help of a number of tanks, did finally manage to push over the Via Casilina as it ran into the town from the east, past what had been the Chiesa del Carmine, the Convent of the Stimmatine Sisters, and on a further 700 yards or so to the station. This they had managed to capture along with the Hummocks.

With this comparative success, Freyberg now finally authorized the feeding in of more infantry, which, at long last, included A and D Companies of 24th Battalion. It was late morning when the two companies were sent forward. Sergeant Roger Smith felt wretched. Shoulders hunched against the biting cold wind, his stomach knotted with fear. Fear and the shame of feeling fear. 'That merciless enemy born of memory and imagination,' he noted, 'that can twist your mind until your body shrinks with the tingle of apprehension. Your palms sweat. Your arm involuntarily flinches at a remembered vision, flashed on your inner retina, of a gory sleeve with a severed arm beside it, still twitching on the sand. Is any man immune? Can anyone face the imminent danger of violent death or deformity with complacency?' He knew he couldn't.

They marched down the Caruso Road that hugged the foot of the massif, a road now littered with the debris of smashed stones, wrecked vehicles and other detritus. Next to the road ran the Rapido, a couple of feet deep and low in its watercourse, which still had much of its retaining walls despite the battle damage. In the distance loomed Monte Trocchio, but before that was the upper Rapido Plain, a scene of desolation, churned-up ground and blackened, skeletal tree trunks; and then there up ahead was Cassino: a lone, wonky tower, part of a church that had not entirely collapsed, a jagged skyline of rubble and butchered walls, light glimpsed through gaping gaps. Armageddon had turned this town into Hades. Smoke rose from the ruins and out on the plain as yet more shells landed.

They reached the northern edge of the town at around 2.30 p.m., still shocked by what they saw: a vast jumble of masonry, totally devoid of life. A town utterly ravaged. A number of walls and abutments still stood, but not a single roof that they could see. Beams lay awkwardly skewed where they'd fallen. It was a wasteland. As they neared the first piles of rubble bullets fizzed and zipped around them. Smith assumed they were being sniped from the castle, but the bullets must have been coming from the lower slopes; a number of Foltin's men were in the ruins of houses built up on to these lower parts of Castle Hill. At any rate, they hit the deck and crawled forward on their stomachs, past bodies of New Zealanders only recently killed. Smith was at the back, still scared but glad that the waiting was over and that they were now at least engaged.

They now had to cross the culvert that ran across the top of the town roughly west–east, but bomb damage had blown the road, a dyke and the concrete culvert all into one. The men kept crawling, but as Smith joined one of his mates down in a part of the culvert that was still in one piece they heard voices, then realized they were German. Two, perhaps three, one louder than the others and frantic, crying, mad with panic. Clearly, they'd been covered by concrete and masonry just a bit further along. But there was at least 15 feet between them and huge blocks that not even ten men could lift, let alone two. 'So we had to abandon them to madness and death,' wrote Smith, 'crouched in a black vault through which water still moved in a stream two feet deep.'

After crawling clear they were now, mercifully, out of sight of the enemy on the hill and could walk upright again among the smashed remains around the old jail. From here it was less than 500 yards to the eastern stretch of the Via Casilina, but as they moved forward through the part of the town that was now in their hands they passed three more bodies, this time close together. Two were face-down, but the third was on his back with a complete head, shoulders and arms but otherwise nothing left other than a gleaming white spine and set of ribs. Their column now checked again, and so Smith and the others at the back of the line sat down for a smoke. But the dead man's head, arms and shoulders depressed him so he quickly moved. There was firing rattling across the afternoon air – Spandaus, Brens, mortars crashing, the crack of a rifle. Incessant. Relentless. And they were now heading towards it.

On they moved, weaving around craters, past piles of rubble and along a narrow path cleared by the dozers. The stench from the remains of one building was gaggingly grim – a pile of German bodies that now rose to the ground-floor windows. They crept on, scampering across gaps, pushing deeper into the wreckage. 'It was like another world,' noted Smith, 'a sepia world without colour, a dead world of muted sounds.'

It was not until around 9 p.m. that they reached the Via Casilina. On the northern side was what had been the Botanical Gardens and the remains of what appeared to have been municipal buildings. Smith, still keeping the tail, followed the rest into what had become a dank cavern under the sagging remains of a collapsed first floor and there they all took shelter. Only then did Smith realize that not half the platoon was with him and there was no sign of Lieutenant Armstrong, so he clambered out and dashed over the road to the remains of the Stimmatine Convent, which was now being used as an aid station. There he learned that the rest of A Company and B Company were further along the road in the remains of the Chiesa di Sant'Antonio.

The task of these three of the battalion's four companies now in the heart of Cassino was to launch an immediate attack from the Excelsior Hotel down past the Hotel des Roses to the Baron's House and the Colosseum beyond the southern edge of the town. The Baron's House was another large palazzo, the Colosseum an architectural gem from the Roman era, but one not spared by the bombers. However, Major Sam Turnbull, the B Company commander, after consulting with Captain Schofield, decided to call off the attack. D Company had not yet arrived – they'd been held up by snipers – and Turnbull felt that without his full complement of troops and without tanks the attack would be hopeless and doomed to fail. Instead, Armstrong told Smith to head back to the rest of the platoon and hold the building on the far side of the Via Casilina until morning. Smith then spent the night in a cellar, and having munched some cold bully beef and drunk some tea he got his head down. While he was sleeping his picquets captured two Germans who inadvertently scuttled into the cellar during a heavy salvo of shells.

Armstrong picked up Smith and the rest of the platoon early on the morning of the 18th and they scurried back across the Via Casilina and joined the rest of the company. A firefight was in full flow in the remains of a building further up the street on the left. Machine guns, Tommy guns, Schmeissers, grenades exploding. As they reached the company area, Captain Schofield was brought in with two others, all three badly wounded in the firefight. It was around 6.15 a.m. Smith went with several comrades to help with the casualties and they managed to scamper forward, stumbling over several dead at the next building, which was now held by their men. Four Germans were captured and brought in soon after, one unharmed but the others badly wounded and clearly dying.

Suddenly the fighting died down again, but then four Germans came sneaking down alongside the building the A Company men now held, clearly unsure where the New Zealanders were. Pausing for a moment, they looked around and then the Bren-gunner next to Smith opened up. Smith watched his head judder against the stock of the machine gun as it fired, the bullets cutting down all four men into a heap on the mud and debris of the road.

'No word of D Coy,' reported Captain Turnbull by radio around the same time, 'should be somewhere left of A Coy. Town literally full of enemy snipers and Spandaus. They inhabit rubble and ruined houses. We are being as aggressive as possible. Have advanced as far as possible without losing most of my fighting strength. Until MONASTERY Hill is in our hands sniping problem will continue. It is NOT to be underrated.'

Here was the problem of fighting with too few troops and with infantry who, understandably, felt disinclined to risk their necks for another 100 yards of rubble. The moment they ventured forward, enemy machine guns spat out a stream of bullets or snipers picked off the officers and anyone else who passed their crosshairs. None of the troops in the New Zealand 6th Brigade had much experience of fighting in towns, whether still standing or reduced to piles of rubble. On the Adriatic at the back end of the year it had been the Canadians who had fought through Ortona, and while the New Zealanders had attacked the small hilltop town of Orsogna they'd never managed to get much further than the approach roads.

There was no getting away from the harsh reality, however: that on the morning of 18 March, the fourth day of the battle, the New Zealand Corps was still far short of objectives it had been expecting to reach in just a few hours two days earlier. Incredibly, though, New Zealand casualties in the town amounted to only 130 men and twelve tanks knocked out. It wasn't a lot in the big scheme of things. That day, Freyberg once again considered whether he should commit more troops and once again concluded he should not. But Freyberg had no experience of urban fighting either. Rather, 6th Brigade, he felt, still had enough strength to push on through and take the rest of the town. Only Galloway, now convinced by Bateman's urgings, remained a dissenting voice. It was a voice that was not heard.

Roger Smith, for one, wished the brass had been listening as a day of confused, difficult, frequently terrifying fighting continued. 'It was impossible to define any area as safe,' he noted, 'as the Hun was continually infiltrating our line and occupying houses behind us. We were too thin on the ground to garrison all the captured houses, and had the everlasting task of retaking them over and over again.' Several tanks arrived but one was shot up right in front of the building where Smith had spent the previous night, destroyed by a Panzerfaust. Several men tried to help get the crew out but enemy bullets stopped them; they eventually got them clear later that night, when they discovered that four of the crew were uninjured but that the driver had had his head spattered all over the front compartment; the co-driver had had to sit there, covered in his mate's gore, all day.

Stalemate had descended on the town as the fourth day ended with little progress. Freyberg was determined to give the entire operation a renewed sense of impetus so he planned a series of further attacks for the following day, 19 March. The Māori Battalion, notably more aggressive than the Pakehas in other battalions, were attached to 6th Brigade and thrown into the battle early that fifth morning. Inexplicably, though, only two companies – just over 200 men – were sent forward and they made as little headway as the others. Meanwhile, the 4th Indians were finally ordered to use the Cavendish Road, four days too late; its use had always been conceived as being part of a two-fisted attack on the abbey, not a single thrust all on its own. Yet it was in this latter role, and with all other ideas rapidly diminishing, that Freyberg ordered the armoured force to strike up the Cavendish Road while Bateman's men had another shot at taking the abbey from the jump-off point of Hangman's Hill.

Brigadier Bateman's plans for this latest attack on Monastery Hill were to once again make the most of the hours of darkness. The two battalions of Rajputanas in 4th Indian Division had now been brought together into a composite force; two companies had also been used to help resupply the Gurkhas the previous night, 17–18 March. This new amalgamated battalion was then to take over the castle the next night, 18–19 March, while the 1/4th Essex clambered up to join the Gurkhas on Hangman's Hill. The Essex men were already understrength when they set off, late because of difficulties of handing over the castle to the Rajputanas, and so it wasn't until 5.30 a.m. on the 19th that they finally got going. No sooner had they done so, however, than men from 1. Bataillon 4. Fallschirmjäger-Regiment hurtled down the hill in a planned counter-attack against the castle. A ferocious close-quarter fight ensued, the Rajputanas falling back into the castle itself and holding their ground while the Essex men tried to extricate themselves and push up, first in darkness, then in gradually growing light, to Hangman's Hill. About seventy of them made it.

There was now absolutely no chance of then further attacking the giant bastions of the abbey and clearing it of Germans. The entire plan had been fairly crackpot in the first place, but the moment the town had failed to fall on the first day of the battle, the chance of any success here, with the Allies still completely unaware of the figure-of-eight defence system on the massif, was slim to say the very least. Despite this, the armoured assault up the Cavendish Road was still, inexplicably, given the go-ahead. Again, the moment to have launched this was immediately, on the first day, or certainly within the first twenty-four hours, as Clark had repeatedly urged. Above, on Monte Castellone and Snakeshead, the men of 7th Indian Brigade were still clinging to the positions that had been originally won by the Red Bulls, but the attack had not been coordinated with Lovett's men, nor had any other infantry been allocated to the armoured force – despite the whole of 78th Division and most of Combat Command B twiddling their thumbs in the valley below. And so the armoured force was sent up alone. This, frankly, was a schoolboy error of the highest order, although in a little over three hours the armoured column managed to rumble up, push on through the Madras Circus out towards Albaneta and even start crawling around the cliff face beneath Point 593. But without any infantry to support them they began to be picked off by Fallschirmjäger armed with Panzerfausts. Nineteen of the forty-four tanks sent up were destroyed or knocked out, almost half the force. In the fading light they then pulled back through the bottleneck to the Madras Circus for the night. They'd got to within 1,000 yards of the abbey but the figure-of-eight had barely been dented, and once the last of the tanks had gone German engineers began laying tank mines around the bottleneck and track beneath Point 593. Tanks on Monte Cassino were another one-trick throw of the dice that had also failed.

That day the fighting continued in the town, but now almost no progress was being made at all. New Zealanders were killing and capturing Fallschirmjäger and the Germans were killing and capturing New

Zealanders. A house would be taken then lost again, then won again. Dying in this hell of rubble and wretchedness was so very pointless because the Allied attack had clearly shot its bolt. That day, Roger Smith had been in the Company CP beside one of his boys who was keeping watch from the remains of a window. Suddenly there was a burst of fire and the sound of bullets hitting flesh. 'The lad toppled from his seat onto his face,' noted Smith, 'a string of wet marks up his back, his head flattened into a red pulpy mess.' Two further men were wounded by a second burst. Overnight some Fallschirmjäger had crept into the building between them and the Church of Sant'Antonio, awaiting their chance to fire.

Later that day the rest of the building suddenly, and without any warning, collapsed. Smith had been lucky to get clear; a number of others hadn't. And others still were only freed after frantic digging through the rubble and by cutting through an iron grille. They'd gained very little that day; simply surviving had become the biggest achievement. They very nearly weren't alive the following morning, however, when, heading to the new Company CP to draw rations, they were fired on again; the building had been reoccupied by the Germans in the night. 'Lack of manpower to occupy every house after it was taken and prevent infiltration,' noted Smith, 'was one of the major curses.'

DICKENS had already gone way past the point where anything meaningful could now be achieved. Really, it needed to be called off right away. Tragically for all involved, however, Freyberg had no intention of calling a halt just yet.

CHAPTER 27

Via Rasella

THE FIRST COUPLE OF weeks of March had been an especially demoralizing time at Anzio because, as at Cassino, it had rained incessantly. 'We were soaking wet,' noted Hans Liebschner, 'cold, often hungry and utterly exhausted from lack of sleep.' He and the depleted troops of Kampfgruppe Gericke were now dug in to the west of the Buonriposo Ridge, along the northern stretch of the wadis, which they were now referring to as the '*Schwalbennest*' – the swallows' nest. The British called it The Fortress. In this strange maze of gullies and narrow earthen passageways, the Tommies were sometimes only 50–75 yards away. Liebschner could often hear English voices, especially at night, when it was quieter. The stench was also getting worse. They were all filthy and each man was giving off an increasingly ripe odour, but worse was the build-up of excrement; both sides would hurl it in tins at the other and it lay out in no-man's-land along with the dead. Collecting the corpses was impossible, because as soon as anyone put their head above the parapet machine guns opened up and snipers' rifles immediately cracked, and so the dead remained where they were, their youthfulness extinguished and instead quietly rotting and adding to the terrible stench that hung heavily over the battleground. Several dead, blown up and shredded, lay trapped on wire and in the mud just ahead of their positions; Liebschner thought they looked like sacks of flour hanging there. He was still one of the 4. Kompanie runners, so was expected to know his way around this maze better than most. In this the scattered corpses were still able to help their comrade. 'The dead of no-man's-land,' he noted, 'with their eyes open and their teeth sticking out like a row of fence posts, became my orientation markers.'

A number of men in Audie Murphy's platoon had started to get trench foot. He'd send the worst cases to the rear for treatment. Most were given cans of foot powder and fresh socks, and sent back again. Then he suffered another malarial relapse; he had tried to keep going but eventually his legs buckled underneath him and he collapsed unconscious in the mud. He'd been carried back to one of the field hospitals on an old door. There he made friends and flirted with a nurse called Helen before heading back again to the front, by which time there was a touch of spring in the air. 'On the ruined land,' he wrote, 'new green glistens in the sunlight. When the guns are quiet, we can hear the song of birds.' A cherry tree that had survived burst into bloom. Murphy's great friend Martin Kelly even felt inspired to compose a new song:

> We've got cherries on Anzio;
> Cherries, yes; but women no.
> Don't ask me how, but it sure is so.
> That's the hell with Anzio.

A little way from 15th Infantry, the 504th PIR were still in the line, although just after SEITENSPRUNG Company C of 1st Battalion were ordered into reserve, which meant pulling back from the Mussolini Canal by about a mile and a half and encamping near the artillery. Neither Ross Carter nor any of his fellows thought much of this, because it was the Allied artillery that seemed to attract a lot of the enemy's heavy guns. 'Many of us bitched long and viciously,' he noted, 'because we preferred the battle up front to shells in the rear.'

While they were out of the line they got a number of replacements, mostly young kids still very wet behind the ears. Carter couldn't help feeling sad to see them, because he would have to lead them into battle at some point soon and a good proportion would inevitably get themselves killed before they'd had the chance to develop a sixth sense or learn some of the tricks that helped a man survive. In Carter's platoon they found space for the new men in the stone house they'd taken over, but in another, seven young replacements decided to bed down in a small wooden barn with a straw roof. Seeing this, Carter strongly recommended they get out of there right away. It was too soggy to dig trenches so instead he suggested they build themselves log shelters close to the ground and then cover them with soil. That way, he told them, they'd be protected from shrapnel and anything other than a direct hit. 'Filled with the bravado born of ignorance,' noted Carter, 'the youngsters didn't think the danger justified the trouble and continued to make coffee and be homesick.' The very next day, a mortar shell crashed through their thatched roof. Carter and others rushed out at the sound of the explosion only to find all seven boys dead or dying.

A little while later, Carter went back over to get some straw to make a palliasse and walked past a trooper as he tried to match up the boots and legs with the bodies. 'Let's see now,' the trooper was muttering to himself, 'this is a size eight boot for the right foot. Yeah, it fits him. Cut off at the same place. Here's his left foot. Now what about this blond kid? His leg is missing at the knee . . . '. As Carter listened to this, he pulled some straw, only to discover it was slick with blood. 'I got my straw elsewhere,' he noted.

Meanwhile General Truscott, the new corps commander, was planning for a new, but limited, offensive to straighten the line and push back the salient south of Carroceto, which was being urged upon him by Alexander especially but with Clark's support too. Truscott felt reasonably certain the Germans were unlikely to try anything any time soon and in this appreciation he was quite right. Rather, von Mackensen had begun the process of rotating divisions out of the line to rest and refit at long last; the HG-Division had been sent to Livorno, 114. Jäger to Feurstein's LI Gebirgs-Armeekorps, and 26. Panzer and 29. Panzergrenadier pulled back towards Rome. Replacement units had also arrived, including two battalions from Mussolini's new Italian divisions.

Changes were being made in VI Corps too, with not only 56th Division being packed off to Palestine but also the Guards Brigade, who had originally been attached to that division and who had suffered particularly badly during nearly eight weeks of fighting. Edward Danger and the Grenadier Guards left on 8 March, although he, for one, had not felt safe until he set foot back on shore in Naples; as they'd pulled out of Anzio on an LST he'd seen German gun flashes winking from the Colli Albani until they had been quite far out to sea. 'Our casualties since landing on 22 January', he noted, 'had been 35 killed, over 200 wounded and over 300 missing, mostly prisoners of war.' In a battalion of 845 men, that amounted to 63 per cent.

On the other hand, replacements had arrived for Penney's 1st Division and 5th Division was also reaching the bridgehead. Truscott had been thinking of launching Operation PANTHER to reduce the German salient and with these reinforcements now thought it was worth undertaking, but only if he was assured of adequate air support, which had been notably reduced since he'd taken over. Air power, as he well knew, was a significant force multiplier, and as he was aware that VI Corps needed to be at peak strength by the middle of the next month when DIADEM was due to be launched, Truscott was anxious not to undertake costly offensive operations. Heavy support by Allied air forces would, he reckoned, be the difference between a comparatively easy operation and one that might quickly get bogged down.

As if to underscore the dangers, on 14 March Penney launched a limited attack near the Flyover to seize a better jump-off point for PANTHER and lost almost three infantry companies in the process. Truscott had originally intended to launch his attack the following day, but the focus for the air forces had been switched to Cassino. He then reset for the 19th, having been promised by Clark that he would have the air support he needed. That promise, however, had been made when Clark had expected Cassino to be a quick job, but with the battle there dragging on it became clear that Truscott would be getting only a fraction of the air support he'd demanded. On 18 March PANTHER was quietly shelved. Life in the bridgehead resumed its recreation of the grimmest days of trench warfare in the last war.

Meanwhile, the fighting continued at Cassino. Another night of fighting on Monastery Hill on 20–21 March saw an attempt by the 6th Royal West Kents to break through. They'd been brought in from 11th Indian Brigade to bolster Bateman's troops, and attempted to reach the abbey by climbing the ravine beneath the Colle d'Onofrio while the Gurkhas attacked from Hangman's Hill. At the same time, German paratroopers launched another attempt to retake Castle Hill. Both sides, once again, discovered just how difficult it was attacking rather than defending. Neither side got very far; a night of very confused fighting stretched into the morning, by which time a load more men from both sides had been killed and wounded and not very much achieved. The Gurkhas still on Hangman's Hill were dropped ammunition, food and water by fighter-bombers, although a number of the packages also fell on the lower slopes and were gratefully picked up by Jupp Klein and his men, delighted to have had the far better Allied rations land in their laps.

Part of the New Zealand 21st Battalion was sent into the town the same night, the 20th–21st; it was supposed to coordinate with the Indians' attack on the south face of Monte Cassino, but the assault made only the smallest of dents in the line. The next morning, Tuesday, 21 March, General Clark drove up to the New Zealand Corps OP near San Pietro. Waiting for him were Freyberg, Ike Parkinson, Galloway and Major-General Charles Keightley, the 78th Division commander. Freyberg told him that in his experience mountain fighting was generally slow going, which was not the language used before DICKENS had been launched. 'He was not pessimistic about the eventual outcome,' Clark noted, 'and definitely stated that he was not in favour of calling off the attack.' Clark then turned to Galloway and asked him straight how many men he reckoned he'd need to take the abbey. 'General Galloway', noted Clark, 'estimated three brigades.' That was an entire division with no infantry in reserve. Keightley's division had so far done very little because Freyberg had ignored Clark's suggestions that it be thrown from the east. Using it now was a possibility. Before Clark left, Freyberg again told him he thought the attack should continue and that the present situation did not seem at all hopeless.

A conference with Alexander was planned for that afternoon, but before heading to Caserta Clark called in on Général Juin to gauge his opinion on the situation at Cassino. Juin told him frankly it was time to call it off, and yet at Alex's conference later the number of German prisoners taken – close to 300 – made them all agree that the enemy must be at the point of collapse. New Zealand casualties had been just 120 the previous day and so it was agreed to keep going for a further twenty-four to thirty-six hours. No one wanted all this effort to end with the Cassino position still in the enemy's hands.

Had they had a chance to speak to the men embroiled in the bleak wreckage of Cassino they might have drawn different conclusions, however. Admittedly, Freyberg still did not have a properly functioning corps staff, but there were plenty of reports emerging from the fighting, all of which would have told him and Parkinson that there was no sign of the enemy weakening; rather, Heidrich had continued to feed in more troops. A day earlier, on the morning of the 20th, the 24th Battalion had just 144 men left; A and B Companies were amalgamated under Major Sam Turnbull and now held a line across the Via Casilina and over the wreckage of the Chiesa di Sant'Antonio. They could look across the open ground through which the start of the Garigliano flowed and see Highway 6 as it ran southwards, and also gaze across at the remnants of the Hotel des Roses, where Jupp Klein and his Pioniere still held out. The distance was no more than 300 yards. But it was as out of reach as ever.

Nor were the front lines remotely clear; the fighting had continued its asymmetric pattern, with the piles of rubble and basements of wrecked buildings repeatedly changing hands. Roger Smith and his platoon were trying to mop up an area around the church and asked three Māori whether a neighbouring building was clear. They told him it was, and to prove the point bounded up the steps that still led to the entrance – and were promptly gunned down, tumbling back down the steps in a heap. Smith and his men then hammered the wreckage in retaliation and captured nearly thirty enemy troops, for once with no loss to themselves. Around the same time, Jupp Klein was taking charge of a similar number of Tommies from 4th Indian who had been captured in the night. Because he spoke reasonable English he had been asked to interrogate them; he'd then begun a lengthy debate with the Tommy captain about the future of the war.

The morning of Thursday, 23 March dawned bright and with more than a hint of spring in the air, yet the front lines had still barely moved in over a week's fighting. 'Chief went up to Fifth Army and NZ Corps to examine situation in detail,' noted General Harding. 'Held army commander meeting and decided to call Cassino battle off.' This, Harding noted, was disappointing but the right decision. 'Reasons,' he added. 'Too much reliance on bombing. Insufficient infantry to start with. Loss of time and lack of real drive when things get sticky. Must now go all out for major offensive later.' It was hard to argue with this pithy wash-up. At least now they could all pause again, take a deep breath and ready themselves for a battle that would be better prepared, better planned, better coordinated and, perhaps most importantly of all, would be fought during longer days and with the ground dry at long last. That way the Allies could finally bring their vastly superior materiel strength to bear, as they had last done in the heat of the previous September's Indian summer. What an age ago that seemed now. Yet with this decision it was as though a line had now been drawn in the ground.

The long, brutal winter was over.

Rome beckoned still but would have to wait a little while longer, which was very tough on the majority of Romans struggling to survive in a city starved of food and amenities and in which there was now a perpetual air of menace no matter which side one was on. None the less, it was also a city bathed in spring sunshine that fourth Thursday in March, and with temperatures to match. The endless rains had gone and there was now the promise of summer in the air. This, however, was the last thing Carla Capponi – Elena – wanted, for she was starting to feel conspicuous in her raincoat on such a beautiful day. She felt her fingers clasped round the pistol in her pocket and her heart thumping heavily in her chest. A couple of hours before, she had been too nervous to have any of the beer and potatoes on offer for lunch. Instead, she and Paolo and two other partisans of GAP Centrale had left their meal and hurried over to the hideout near the Colosseum. There Paolo had collected the old dustcart that had been stolen the day before – in which was now hidden a home-made bomb of 18 kilos of TNT topped by a fifty-second fuse. While the bomb was big enough to destroy an entire building, the Gappisti had planned to bolster their attack with mortars and gunfire. It had been Elena's job to pick up four mortars, specially adapted so that they could be ignited with a three-second fuse lit by a cigarette. She had collected them from the hideout and delivered them to Francesco, another partisan, waiting in the Via del Traforo. Carrying the mortars in nothing more than a shopping bag, she had, much to her relief, safely delivered them to Francesco and then, as she walked past, glanced down the Via Rasella, a comparatively narrow street perhaps 250 yards long, lined by high office buildings and apartments and running up to the gardens of the Palazzo Barberini. The street had been quite deserted; Paolo, with his heavy bomb-laden dustcart, had not yet reached his appointed mark.

Passing the bottom of the Via Rasella, she had continued up the Via del Traforo and was now waiting by the offices of the *Il Messaggero* newspaper. She spotted Pasquale, another fellow partisan, standing by a newsstand. Perhaps he could sense her nerves by the taut expression in her face, because he looked across at her and gave her a reassuring wink.

At last they were both in position; Pasquale was due to give Elena the signal to let her know that the German troops were on their way. She would then turn right on to the Via del Tritone, a main thoroughfare that ran roughly parallel to the Via Rasella, and after 200 yards turn right again on to another main street, the Via delle Quattro Fontane, until she reached the entrance to the Palazzo Barberini gardens. There she would wait for Paolo with the raincoat – the overcoat that was to cover up his dustman's uniform as they attempted to make good their escape. That was the plan at any rate, but this operation, the biggest they had yet attempted, involved a number of people being in a particular place at a particular time; if any one part of the plan went awry it was highly possible that the entire operation would quickly unravel too. And there was always the unexpected to factor in: a delay, some other event or random happenstance. What's more, Rome was a very different place now than it had been when she and Paolo had headed to Centocelle back in January. The triumvirate of Obersturbannführer Herbert Kappler, Pietro Koch and the Questore, Pietro Caruso, had made life increasingly hard for the partisans of Rome. The Gappistis' major bomb-making plant had been raided and a number of key partisans caught, tortured and executed. Koch had then closed down the Partita d'Azione's underground newspaper, *L'Italia Libera*, with a number of further arrests and a series of raids that had led to yet more people being rounded up.

With stalemate at Anzio and no immediate prospect of Rome being liberated, Paolo and Elena had returned to the centre of Rome and to GAP Centrale at the end of February. Elena had been shocked by the change in just a month. 'Growing fear and despair,' she noted, 'hunger and sickness were wasting people away.' Running water was no longer available; it was hard to wash and the population was becoming overrun by a lice epidemic. 'You could smell the nauseating lice medicine on the passengers on a bus, in public bathrooms, and on the people standing in lines for rations.' She had got noticeably thinner; everyone was suffering the same. Hunger, increasingly hollow eyes, clothes that once fitted perfectly now hanging loosely. Rome was not as beaten up as Naples but the lack of food, lack of amenities and lack of personal freedom were taking their toll. On the other hand, one could still get the finest food and wine, drive cars and live it up, but only if one was a German, Fascist or prepared to collaborate with both. 'The city had two categories of citizens,' noted Elena, 'a minority who fraternized with the enemy, and the rest of the Romans, the vast majority, who suffered and died hoping for their liberation.'

Then, on 1 March, SS police troops had carried out another round-up of able-bodied young men to be used as forced labour, whisking them off to the military barracks along the Viale Giulio Cesare. Word got out about where the men had been taken and so the GAP partisans decided to hold a demonstration outside the barracks. Elena, despite struggling with a recurrence of the pleurisy she had contracted over the winter, helped organize it and was there on the morning of 3 March, along with hundreds of women armed with illegal leaflets addressed to the 'Women of Rome', bundles of which they would surreptitiously throw into the air. Suddenly a pregnant women, a child in tow, ran through the crowd, the women parting to let her through. She had spotted her husband leaning from one of the barracks windows and, after breaking through a gap in the police barricade, paused beneath him and tried to lob a parcel of food up to him. Unfortunately, it caught on a ledge and then fell back to the ground. The crowd was chanting her name over and over: Teresa, Teresa, Teresa. Bending down, she collected the package and made ready to lob it again. Elena watched it all; she also saw a German soldier on a motorcycle roll forward towards her. In that moment, Elena knew the German was going to shoot her. The German now grabbed the woman but she pulled free, only for him to grab her again by the clothing on her chest. Her son picked up the package and then there was a loud crack; the German shot her dead. Teresa Gullace had been a mother of five and was pregnant with her sixth child. A collective howl rose up from the crowd and Elena found herself pulling her Beretta from her pocket and aiming at the German.

Before she could fire, she was pounced on by Fascist police and hauled off to the guardhouse in the barracks. There she produced faked ID and explained that she was a member of the Honour and Combat Group, a Fascist organization, and had been there to try and keep the women calm and encourage them to go home. After showing her card and flirting with her interrogator she'd been allowed to go. She'd been lucky.

A few days later she single-handedly destroyed a German fuel truck on the Via Claudia. Some 2,500 gallons of fuel had gone up in a massive explosion. It was easier, in many ways, to carry out such an attack on her own. Now, though, an even bigger operation was under way, and as she waited for the signal she paused by a glass display case with a copy of the day's *Il Messaggero* pinned inside, hoping to catch Pasquale's reflection. Nearby, far too close for comfort, were two men, very obviously plain-clothes policemen. Her heart hammered in her chest. The newspaper was full of news about the eruption of Mount Vesuvius, but as her eyes flickered over the newsprint she was conscious that too much time was going by. Something had gone wrong. The planned attack had been built around the Germans' unvarying Teutonic routine: every day, without fail, the same column of around 160 men of 11. Kompanie of the 3. Bataillon SS-Polizei-Regiment Bozen would march through the centre of the city on their way back to their barracks after a morning's training at a shooting range near the Ponte Milvio. And as they marched, singing

'*Hupf, Mein Mädel*', they passed up the length of the narrow and enclosed Via Rasella.

A quarter past two came and went. Then 2.20. 2.30 p.m. passed. 2.45 p.m., and still no sign of the troops. She wondered what had gone wrong. And what she should do. Loitering by the newsstand was courting trouble. As if to prove the point, the plainclothes policemen approached her, and as they did so Elena felt her fingers once more tighten around the pistol in her pocket. 'Excuse me, signorina,' one of them said to her, 'Are you waiting for someone?'

For a split second she froze, then said, yes, she was waiting for her fiancé, who, she explained, worked at the Palazzo Barberini. She then began talking to them about the eruption of Vesuvius and the potential disaster this might cause for Naples. This seemed to work. She felt calmer suddenly, so that when one of them asked her sharply why she was carrying a raincoat on such a hot day she told them that it was her fiancé's and that she had had a stain removed for him and was going to give it back to him.

She then saw Pasquale start towards her, and so asked the policemen the time. It was 2.47 p.m., she was told. In that case, she said, it was time for her to go. Hurrying away from them she passed Pasquale, who muttered something she could not hear, but she knew she could not look back; hoping Pasquale's message had been the signal for her to move, she turned into the wide Via del Tritone, walked up the hill towards the Piazza Barberini and then turned right, up the Quattro Fontane, to take up her position for the attack.

At the top of the Via Rasella Elena was relieved to see Paolo sweeping the road halfway down the street, the dustcart nearby. She had been expecting to see the SS column marching into the bottom of the street but there was still no sign of them. She could not think what had gone wrong.

The growing dangers and the palpable sense that Kappler and Koch were tightening a noose around Rome's partisans had done little to deter the Gappisti, but all of those in GAP Centrale, Elena included, knew that their planned attack in the Via Rasella was the most daring strike they had attempted yet. The night before, lying next to Paolo in their hideout, she had needed to remind herself why she was taking part in such an action. In the silence and the dark she had thought about how terrible and unjust the war was and the destruction it had caused – and the devastation across the country. She thought of her companions who had already been horrifically tortured and shot, and of all those who had been deported and who had not been heard of since; and she thought of all those friends of hers who had already died in the fighting in Russia, in Greece, in Yugoslavia; she remembered her cousin, Amleto, killed at Alamein. But while such thoughts helped stiffen her resolve, they did nothing to erase her fears. If they were caught, she knew they could expect no mercy.

It was now well after 3 o'clock. Some children were playing football in the gardens of the Palazzo Barberini. Imagining the horrors of them being hit by the blast of the bomb, she crossed the street and shouted at them, 'You can't play football in this garden. Go home and do your homework!' They obviously recognized something in her tone, because they all immediately scurried off.

The minutes ticked by. Still nothing. Something had clearly gone wrong. Waiting by the gates of the Palazzo Barberini, the same two plainclothes policemen approached her once again. It was now just after 3.30 p.m., more than an hour and a half after the bomb was supposed to have gone off. 'You still here?' they asked her. Elena had always been smart, but she had developed quick wits and an ability to remain flawlessly cool in such moments, and so without a moment's hesitation told them her fiancé was at the Officers' Club in the Palazzo, while desperately hoping they would not see Paolo and his dustcart 100 yards in front of her. She couldn't go in there, she explained, as it was men only, and so had to wait. 'We'll wait with you,' they told her.

Now increasingly terrified that everything was going badly wrong, Elena was beginning to inwardly panic when she saw her chance to get away from the policemen, for across the road on the other side of Via delle Quattro Fontane she spotted an elderly friend of hers. Excusing herself, she hurried across the road and after a very brief conversation warned the lady to get away as quickly as possible.

It was at that moment that she saw one of the other Gappisti walking down the street towards Paolo. As he passed, Elena finally spotted the head of the column of SS men turn into the bottom of the Via Rasella. Her heart in her mouth, she watched them gradually fill the entire street, tramping rhythmically – but not singing as usual – towards Paolo and the dustcart until he was lost from view, engulfed by the marching column.

She was still straining to see him when he suddenly and miraculously appeared by her side. The front of the column was now near the top of the Via Rasella. He hastily put the raincoat over his overalls just as Elena saw the two plainclothes policemen, who had not stopped watching her, begin to cross the street. She pulled out her pistol but a passing bus came between them.

And then the bomb detonated.

Such was the scale of the explosion, it rocked the entire city centre. A violent blast of hot air followed, pushing Elena and Paolo forward and knocking the bus, directly in front of the Via Rasella, across the street. Elena spotted the policemen fleeing the scene and now she and Paolo hurried in the opposite direction, sprinting uphill, bullets and slivers of stucco and stone pinging and ricocheting around them as the troops at the head of the column opened fire at anyone they saw. Behind them, more explosions – the mortars detonating – but they both kept on running, sprinting for their lives until the sounds of the inferno at last began to die down.

CHAPTER 28

STRANGLE

Roger Smith and the rest of A and B Company were relieved on the afternoon of 23 March, at first gingerly pulling back only 300 yards to the Chiesa del Carmine. Changeovers could be fraught and dangerous so were undertaken at night, which meant that for a few hours Smith was able to sit in the ruins, a sanctuary not because it had been a house of God but because its thick walls remained standing. 'There was', he noted, 'still good protection in that desecrated nave.'

Exhausted men sat down either side of the transept amid broken roof tiles and fragments of coloured glass. Smith felt relief and exhaustion sweep over him like a wave but was conscious of the theatricality of the scene, with shafts of thin sunlight shining through holes in the parts of the roof that still stood, dust motes swirling idly and caressing the weary faces of the men below. 'Sleeping forms', he wrote, 'that still twitched and flinched from the constant menace of shellfire outside.'

That night they moved back again, marching to the left flank to the south-east of the town, where they took over foxholes near the station and the Hummocks. The Gurkhas and parties of 1/4th Essex, some of whom had been up on Hangman's Hill for nine days, were brought down under cover of darkness that same night, so that by dawn on the 24th there was now a new front line, as issued in orders from Freyberg that same day, which ran from Point 175 north of Cassino, through Castle Hill, across the northern two-thirds of the town down to the Botanical Gardens and to the station and the Hummocks – so almost north–south. All posts were to be laced with wire entanglements and sown with wire. Offensive action would be limited to vigorous patrolling. The 78th Division took over the positions of the 4th Indians, who were pulled into reserve and back to V Corps on the Adriatic, and, for the time being at any rate, the New Zealanders continued to garrison the shattered wreckage of the town. Two days later, on 26 March, the New Zealand Corps – only ever intended as a temporary organization – was dissolved. Freyberg's second stint as a corps commander was over, and frankly not before time.

Meanwhile, to the north in Rome, the reaction to the Via Rasella bomb was swift, although the perpetrators were still very much on the loose. Elena and Paolo had barely been able to believe they were still alive that first night after the attack, and it had also seemed like something of a miracle that the other dozen Gappisti involved had also made good their escape. From what had looked like disaster at 3.30 p.m. that day they had managed to successfully pull off their most devastating attack yet. Twenty-eight SS men had been killed immediately and by the following day, 24 March, that figure had risen to thirty-three. Two civilians – a middle-aged man and a thirteen-year-old boy – had also been killed. The street itself was now wrecked by a massive 30-foot crater and littered with debris from the dead and the surrounding buildings.

Kesselring had learned of the terrorist attack at around 7 p.m. that night on his return to Monte Soratte following a visit to the Anzio front. By this time, however, General Kurt Mälzer, the German Commandant of Rome, had already informed a staff officer at Kesselring's OB Süd, Oberst Dietrich Beelitz. Without waiting for his chief's return, Beelitz had then informed the German High Command in Berlin, the OKW, who in turn relayed the news to Hitler, who, predictably, was incensed. He would, he vowed, destroy an entire quarter of the city with everyone in it; a moment later he demanded the shooting of at least thirty Italians for every German killed. During the same rant this figure rose to fifty.

Hitler's reaction reached Beelitz before Kesselring and Westphal's return and so he rang Generaloberst von Mackensen. Mälzer, Beelitz and von Mackensen all recognized that the Führer's demands were excessive, but they also accepted that they had to respond both emphatically and swiftly. Partisan actions in Rome had been on the rise, and while they had not yet prompted reprisals, only renewed efforts to hunt down the perpetrators, there was a feeling that the Via Rasella attack had crossed a line and that previous anti-partisan measures had been too soft and ineffectual. What might constitute a ruthless but reasonable response was hard to gauge, however. Mälzer suggested shooting Italians at a ratio of ten to one. At the time of their conversation that meant executing 280 Italians; von Mackensen accepted this, but stipulated that they should shoot only those already sentenced to death and awaiting execution. Beelitz duly reported this decision back to OKW in Berlin, who in turn presented the proposal to Hitler.

When Kesselring finally reached his headquarters at Monte Soratte at seven o'clock that evening he was quickly put in the picture. He then spoke with Obersturmbannführer Kappler and asked him whether he had enough people awaiting execution to fill the ten-to-one criteria. Both Kesselring and Beelitz, who was listening in, heard Kappler say that yes, he did have enough prisoners already condemned to death. Kesselring then received a call from the OKW in Berlin confirming that Hitler wanted ten Italians executed for every German killed that afternoon in Rome; this was a direct order. The OKW later reconfirmed this and informed General Westphal, Kesselring's Chief of Staff, that the round-ups and executions were to be carried out by the SD under Kappler's supervision. 'The Führer wishes that thorough action should be taken this time,' Jodl told Westphal. 'Tell that to your Feldmarschall.' Soon after this conversation, Kesselring confirmed the order: ten Italians would be executed for every German soldier killed in the Via Rasella, and the executions were to be carried out immediately, within twenty-four hours.

The problem for Obersturmbannführer Kappler was that despite his earlier claim, he had nothing like 280 prisoners awaiting execution; in fact there were just three. This prompted a panicked readjustment: those condemned would now be 'worthy of death', but this only gave them sixty-five Jews and a handful of known Communists. They were still way off the total needed – one that was rising through the night and morning as more SS men died from their wounds. Frantically, Kappler and his men rounded up other criminals, but also a number of men from the Italian armed forces who had been detained ever since the fighting in and around Rome at the time of the armistice the previous September. Throughout the day, as the death toll rose to thirty-three, more men were recklessly added to the list, including a priest and a number of people detained by Neo-Fascist authorities on largely spurious charges.

The prisoners, most increasingly confused then terrified, were taken in butchers' trucks to the Ardeatine Caves, just south of the city near the ancient Roman catacombs on the Appian Way. The first arrived shortly before 3.30 p.m. on Friday, 24 March. The men, in groups of five, were then taken into the dark, dank caves, told to kneel and turn their heads to one side. And then they were shot.

To begin with, the executions were carried out with some semblance of order, but as the bodies began to mount and the caves filled with bloody corpses, discipline, made worse by the amount of drink the executioners had taken to help steel themselves for the ordeal, began to waver. It took a long time to kill more than 300 men. The firing grew wild; moreover, most of the executioners were clerks rather than soldiers, and members of the SS and SD who, like Kappler, had only limited military training. Nearly forty of those killed were completely decapitated. Others were beaten to death, while a number were not killed outright; the executioners were becoming increasingly cack-handed as the evening wore on and so the victims were left to die through suffocation and loss of blood. At the end of the slaying they also discovered they'd rounded up five more than had been needed. Of course, as witnesses to the executions they could not be spared, and so they too were shot. These men ensured that the final tally of those murdered that afternoon was 335.

While these terrible events were playing out in Rome, the front was, for the most part, reasonably quiet with spring most definitely in the air. The Faughs had just moved up into the line along the Cassino front two days earlier and were now in the area east of the Rapido, the same stretch the T-Patchers and then the New Zealanders had held. There was no doubt, however, that their extended break from front-line action and the chance to refit and retrain had done the battalion a great deal of good, not least Major Lawrie Franklyn-Vaile, who found himself feeling quite cheered that day. 'I am writing this letter in the sun,' he scribbled, 'It is a beautiful day, clear blue sky and the countryside is beginning to look very pleasant. The mountains, some of them now snow-topped, present a magnificent sight. It is very much a case of "All prospects please and only man is vile". The thunder of our guns, the drone of our planes and the heavy AA fire of the enemy all seems strangely incongruous under such surroundings. What a life.' He supposed there would come a day when the war was over and normal life returned; it was a most senseless, brutal and bestial business. There had been moments of terror and he'd lost his greatest friend, Johnnie Glennie, the previous autumn, who had died in his arms; there had been disappointments, frustrations and certain things that had annoyed him, but he had rarely been bored and on the whole felt he'd got on pretty well. He was certainly now enjoying being a company commander and all the responsibility that came with it.

And he was also glad that his finances were a little better, something that had given him much cause for worry; he'd hated the thought of being over in

Italy, risking his life, while his wife and young daughter were struggling to find a half-decent house to rent and struggling with the bills. That situation had improved, not least because of his increased pay due to promotion, and he told Olive that he had instructed Lloyds bank to pay her £40 in April and thereafter £30 a month. He spent very little out in Italy and was anxious that they should try and save for when the war was over. 'Look after yourself, precious,' he signed off. 'Remember I love you far beyond everything in the world. Give my little daughter a great big kiss and hug from her Daddy. All my love and kisses to you both. Lawrence.'

The full twenty-one heavy bomb groups that had been planned for Foggia were now operating out of a mass of airfields. Poor weather continued to hamper operations, but there were growing signs that spring had arrived and longer days and clearer skies were on their way. And whenever the skies were clear, hundreds of bombers could be seen flying north, twinkling silver in the sunlight, streams of contrails following behind. For the Germans below it was a demoralizing sight. Oberst Wilhelm Mauss had been given some leave and drove north with a colleague all the way to Verona then on, north, into the Alps. The journey increasingly became a tour of destruction. 'Bozen has been much beleaguered by aerial attacks,' he noted, 'in the railway station quarter one sees only wreckage and ruins.' Later, as they went through the Brenner Pass, they had to stop again because of a fresh air raid alarm. There was more destruction at Innsbruck. There was bomb damage all the way, in fact.

From Austria he took a series of trains. 'Hanover looks desolate,' he noted with shock. 'The railway station is a field of ruins; through the fractured walls one looks on to the blackened remains of the Ernst-August Square, and then looks right through into the city centre. Just ruins everywhere, debris and destruction.' He felt consumed with hatred and anger. One more train ride and he was in Barsinghausen and reunited with his family, all of whom seemed well; happiness at being home diffused the anger.

During his leave he visited their flat in Berlin; the building had survived but because the window had been blown in there was an inch of dust and dirt on everything; he spent the night there fully clothed on the sofa. 'Here one can walk through wide streets of houses even in the inner centre, which were once areas of busy business life, but now are only fields of wreckage,' he noted. 'Often one hardly knows where one is at all. There has indeed been clearing, and the roads are freely passable, but the empty faces, the heaps of rubble, the stonewalls of piled-up bricks talk a more eloquent language. There is a sweet smell of smoke over everything, which somehow reminds one of decomposing corpses.' This was the reality of Germany's ongoing war, and as the Allies tightened the noose and prepared for the invasion of France and the Soviets were getting closer from the east, the fate that had befallen Cassino and so many other towns and villages in Italy could be expected in the Reich too. It was the reason why many men felt they had no choice but to fight: to make a vain effort to protect their homes and families.

The heavy bombers of the Fifteenth Air Force continued to hammer both POINTBLANK and STRANGLE targets. On 16 March, Lieutenant Michael Sullivan had parted company with the rest of his crew, all of whom were posted to England and to Eighth Air Force. As a bombardier, however, and by now a very experienced one, he was not allowed to go with them; the 'ground bastards', as he called them, wanted him to remain at Amendola. As it was, he'd already flown a number of extra missions – with new crews, when *Sad Sack* had been out of action, and on other occasions when a crew had been missing their bombardier and Sullivan's crew had not been flying. 'It breaks my heart to lose the boys,' he noted. 'We had the best combat crew in the business.' He was also sore as hell about it and in need of a break; he'd been flying with the 2nd Bomb Group since October and, as for every other serviceman in Italy, the winter had been long and the privations many. Frankly, he'd had enough; it wasn't the combat – he could cope with that – it was the brass and endlessly living in a tent, and the rain and lack of anything much to do when one wasn't flying.

Yet within a few days of his crew leaving, his dark mood began to lift; there was a new club on the base for starters, which he reckoned was really OK, and although he had felt lonely for a couple of days that feeling hadn't lasted long. After all, he was still only twenty years old and there were plenty of people his age coming through on this base. And he was busy, too: a POINTBLANK target on 19 March, the ball-bearing plant at Steyr in Austria. That had been a fraught trip; they'd been jumped by forty enemy fighters, but despite their P-38 escorts he'd seen two Fortresses collide mid-air, two get shot down by flak and two more knocked out by fighters. 'Lost Marshall,' he noted, 'a good buddy.'

On the next two days his missions were cancelled due to the weather, but on 22 March he flew his first STRANGLE operation, which had been launched on the 19th. The objective was the marshalling yards at Verona and he'd managed to drop his six 1,000lb bombs right on the target. A few days later he was given some leave and headed off to Naples.

The 504th PIR left Anzio on 24 March, shipping out the way they'd arrived, by LST. They were heading to England to join the rest of the division ready for OVERLORD. As they were waiting to board at the transportation company mess hall, Sergeant Ross Carter heard a GI grousing about their departure. 'Oh, I wish I were a paratrooper!' the man grumbled. 'You guys fight a few days at a time and then you get relieved.' Paratroopers didn't fight much, he said, but got an extra fifty dollars a month. Carter felt like ramming his rifle butt into the man's mouth. They'd been in Anzio two months and that had cost the regiment 120 dead, 410 wounded and thirty-five missing, amounting to 35 per cent of the strength with which it had arrived. In any case, they'd been in action a lot since landing in Italy. 'Sicily, Salerno, Shrapnel Pass, Plains of Naples, the Volturno, Cassino,' Carter said to him instead of whacking him, 'and sixty-three days on Anzio. Now go goof your guns on a clam, you silly bastard!'

The 504th were taking landing ships that had just delivered part of the 34th Red Bulls, including Sergeant Ralph Schaps and the rest of 2nd Battalion of 135th Infantry; the flow in and out continued. The Red Bulls had spent the last five weeks mostly rebuilding and training the new boys, but one look at Anzio harbour told Schaps that their new assignment was going to be no picnic. Half-sunk vessels, collapsed buildings, piles of rubble and a palpable air of doom greeted all new arrivals. They took over positions from 3rd Division and quickly realized that moving around by day was not a good idea because there was barely a square yard within the bridgehead that couldn't be seen by prying eyes up in the Colli Albani. Shelling continued throughout the day, mostly fairly desultory but regular enough. Snipers and machine-gun posts were also a problem, and while the Allied gunners were firing considerably more shells than the Germans, the enemy were sending over sufficient amounts to make everyone keep their heads down. The four German railway guns made the biggest impression because of the size of each shell, the ferociously loud, air-sucking whoosh each made as it hurtled over, and the considerable damage it caused. All troops soon learned to fear 'Anzio Annie.'

Captain David Cole had his first experience of these railway guns soon after arriving into Anzio at the end of March. From a distance, he'd thought Anzio looked a rather attractive Mediterranean port, but then he'd noticed the barrage balloons floating above the town and then, as they docked and disembarked, saw the wreckage all around: hardly a building intact along the seafront, rubble bulldozed into huge piles, wires dangled loosely everywhere. There was not an Italian to be seen. Cole had just disembarked and was walking down the quayside when he heard a strangely prolonged and escalating whine that filled the air. Suddenly there was a massive explosion and a cloud of smoke and dust slowly rose up above a group of already crumbling buildings. 'Gee, Annie's on target today,' a GI told him.

Soon after, he was speeding away in a battalion truck to rejoin the battalion, now dug in along the western side of the beachhead south of the River Moletta in the heart of the wadi country. He knew he'd reached the British sector when he started spotting signs pointing to 'Ealing Broadway' and 'Park Lane'. Somewhere near 'Edgware Road' was the battalion Rest Area and also where B Echelon were based; the companies were all a little way further forward. The CP, when he reached it, was surprisingly sophisticated despite being dug out of the ground, with an outer hall area, a kitchen and then an inner sanctum; the heart of it was lit with electric lights and there was a table, chairs, even cupboards and a wireless. Cole thought it seemed a bit like the snug bar of a country pub. His own dugout was almost as impressive; the officer who had taken his place since the Garigliano had been recently captured, which was why Cole could return to his job as Signals Platoon commander once again, but had left him a proper dugout with timbers lining the walls and a roof made of wood and an old door. There was a stool, some shelves and a space for his sleeping bag, and sandbags lining the walls. 'I couldn't stand upright and could barely turn around,' he noted, 'but it was home.'

Among the Messerschmitts which Lieutenant Michael Sullivan and others from Fifteenth Air Force had been encountering had been those of I/JG53, now commanded by Hauptmann Jürgen Harder. Losses had been mounting – in the case of I Gruppe, Major Quaet-Faslem was killed in a flying accident; by this stage of the war, the Luftwaffe fighter arm was losing more pilots and aircraft to accidents than in the air, which was saying something, and was a direct result of over-flying the veterans and under-training the new boys. Harder had been dumbfounded to have been promoted but it had meant being posted to Maniago, near Udine in the north-east of Italy, where they could intercept the Allied bombers attacking Verona, Trieste, Bolzano and the Brenner but also those heading into the southern Reich. Harder had been busy since the move, flying whenever the weather allowed and adding to his personal tally. His Gruppe had been substantially reinforced too. 'All 50 machines always serviceable,' he wrote to his wife, 'and we are leading in victories. In another month I hope to have it at the level toward which I have been striving for a quarter of a year.' Harder shot down his forty-fifth enemy plane on 28 March, which made him the leading ace in the Gruppe by some margin.

Most of the fighters they were coming up against were long-range P-38s and P-47s, but Smoky Vrilakas was no longer among them. He'd finally finished his tour on 25 February, his last combat sortie escorting bombers as they returned from Georg Zellner's home city of Regensburg. That had been one of the last missions of Operation ARGUMENT, during what had become known as Big Week, and which had been the first time Fifteenth Air Force had flown as part of a joint operation with the Eighth Air Force and Bomber Command operating from England. Vrilakas had survived that trip and then been on his way. 'Put the pot on the stove,' he had written to his family, 'am on my way home.'

The USAAF could enforce limited flying tours because of the smooth flow of highly trained pilots constantly heading across the Atlantic. The clear skies – both of cloud and enemy aircraft – over many parts of the United States ensured that pilot training could continue all day every day of the year, a luxury the Luftwaffe could only envy. The USAAF also had plentiful amounts of fuel to boot; the USA was, at this time, the largest oil producer in the world. Among this steady stream of pilots now arriving into Italy was twenty-four-year-old Lieutenant Ralph 'Luke' Lucardi, a chemistry graduate from the American International College in Springfield, Massachusetts. Lucardi had passed out of flight training Class 43-J and then converted to P-47s at Dothan, Alabama, before being shipped over to North Africa and winding up at Châteaudun-du-Rhumel near Constantine in Algeria. For young men like himself who had never left the States before and were used to living in the most technologically modern country in the world, it had been startling. This, combined with the sudden separation from his family and especially his fiancée, Jane O'Malley, was proving a terrible jolt. Châteaudun was just an earthen runway and the whole place was dirty as hell. He wished he'd had some letters, but there had been nothing so far. 'Miss Jane,' he scribbled in his diary on 25 March. 'Gee, hope I get some mail soon.' The next day he was still anxiously waiting. 'Gee, I miss my mail!' he wrote. 'Dreamed I was home with Jane last night. Gosh – I think of her so much!' He was anxious to get flying and start his missions; the sooner he got going, the sooner he could get home to her and his folks back in Massachusetts.

A couple of days later he'd still not had any letters, but he and a number of other replacements were on their way to Italy. They were due to leave at 9 a.m., but as was so often the way were delayed and finally got going at 1 p.m., by which time they'd already been allocated their units. Lucardi was to join 57th FG, which was fulfilling a ground-support role. A number of the men were disappointed; they had imagined they'd be flying as fighters rather than fighter-bombers. Lucardi wasn't bothered. 'What the hell,' he noted, 'it's combat! That's all I care about.' It felt strange to him to be flown – in a C-47 – rather to be flying himself, but as they took off and flew east across Tunisia he saw plenty of bomb-damaged airfields, wrecks still scattered around the edges from the previous year's fighting. Then, as they crossed over the tiny island of Pantelleria, he looked down on the remains of the island's smashed town. The destruction grew as they flew over Sicily and landed for the night at Catania. 'Wrecked buildings and wrecked planes,' he jotted, 'especially at airport.' Following the twister of destruction across the sea, they finally reached Capodichino near Naples on Wednesday, 29 March. 'Quite a day!' he wrote. 'Naples is a beat up place!' Mount Vesuvius, the destroyer of Pompeii back in AD 79, was erupting again and causing yet more devastation nearly 2,000 years later. The 57th FG had left Arcola airfield in a hurry on 24 March as molten lava 6 feet deep swept down on to the airfield. They managed to move out to their new base in Corsica, the French island off the western Italian coast, in the nick of time, but a number of B-25s on the eastern and northern slopes had been wrecked. It was still smouldering as Lucardi and his fellows landed.

Only three of them were posted to the 57th, the first USAAF fighter unit to be shipped to the Mediterranean back in the summer of 1942. Sent to Egypt, the fighter group had been attached to the RAF's Desert Air Force, learning the ropes and going on to play a key role not only in the Battle of Alamein but throughout the remainder of the North African campaign. They had also been the largest fighter unit present at what became known as the 'Palm Sunday Turkey Shoot' on 18 April the previous year, when sixty-nine Axis aircraft were shot down or crash-landed. The 57th had been in the thick of it ever since and still had some personnel from those early days sprinkled among its number. Now attached to Twelfth Air Support Command in the Twelfth Air Force, they had just been posted to Corsica, liberated by Juin's CEF the previous September. And it was to Alto airfield, just inland on the central east coast, that Lucardi flew on 30 March, a slightly hair-raising journey at wave-top height in bad weather. Attached to 'A' Flight in 64th Fighter Squadron, he was pleased to discover that his flight commander was Captain Mike 'Mac' McCarthy, also from Massachusetts; that connection was a small thing but one that helped a new boy like Lucardi feel a little more at home. 'Seems like a nice guy,' he wrote, 'on the ball.' The airfield was a bit rough and ready and the facilities were sparse; they slept in four-man tents, but that was par for the course in the Mediterranean. During the first couple of days he dug himself a slit trench, which produced blisters on both hands, made an effort to get himself better acquainted with the rest of the boys, and had a chance to check out his new plane, No. 25, which he was sharing with Lieutenant Paul Rawson. The Thunderbolt, as the P-47 was called, was a 7-ton beast: it had a large radial engine, elliptical wings like a Spitfire but was quick to climb and dive, was armed with six .50-calibre machine guns and could carry both extra fuel tanks and bombs. It had a reputation for being one of the most rugged fighter aircraft flying, which was good news for Lucardi because 57th FG were also involved in some of the more dangerous operations being undertaken: their task was to bomb at low level and then follow up by strafing enemy targets at both low altitude and speed. This meant the margins for error were very narrow; if one was hit, there was often little opportunity to then climb and bail out. There were also a lot of other obstacles the closer one flew to the ground.

'Well, this was the day!' jotted Lucardi on 1 April. 'My first combat mission is over. What a thrill. We dive-bombed two railroad bridges at Arezzo, Italy!' Having dropped their bombs they then went tearing down to treetop height and opened fire at a train, strafing both the locomotive and its wagons. One of the other new boys went so low he flew straight into the top of some trees, bending back the wings, but, incredibly, was still able to fly and was nursed by Mike McCarthy all the way back to Alto, where he touched down safe, but was left severely traumatized by the experience. For all the pilots, the episode underlined just how robust the Thunderbolt was proving. For Lucardi, however, the entire flight had been an adrenalin-charged thrill; he'd not felt scared except when taking off, and thereafter had felt tense but no fear. 'I forgot a lot of little things,' he noted, 'but I stayed on my leader's wing and next time I'll do a better job on bombing.' No one could expect to be the finished article right away; but he'd opened his account, survived, and had the wit to recognize he still had much to learn despite nearly 400 hours in his logbook by this time. What's more, he had joined the 57th FG at a critical time in the air war in Italy with STRANGLE now in full flow.

Although the Fifteenth Air Force were involved in STRANGLE, it was, however, primarily a job for MATAF, and although the operation began on 19 March it was not until the Cassino battle was called off that MATAF was dramatically freed up to focus all out on STRANGLE. The idea was to smother the Italian transportation network with multiple attacks all along the main rail routes but also road routes from the Po Valley all the way south to Rome and on to Cassino. The term being used was 'simultaneous interdiction'. So instead of directing missions primarily against bridges, they were also bombing tunnels, cuttings and even open stretches, trying to cut the rail routes, especially, as many times as possible. This was being undertaken by a combination of twin-engine medium bombers and fighter-bombers such as the Thunderbolts of 57th FG. Lucardi flew his third mission on 10 April. 'Whew!' he scrawled in his diary. 'Going "balls out" now. Today we bombed a railroad just north-west of Siena. Guess we got four good hits out of the bunch – not too bad.' A couple of days later he flew his fourth mission, clobbering Montalcino in southern Tuscany, knocking out a bridge, then strafing a number of freight wagons.

And STRANGLE was starting to pay off because by the middle of April, twenty-seven bridges had been destroyed along the key central route and innumerable wagons and locomotives shot up. By 4 April, Kesselring's two armies at the front were receiving just 1,357 tons of supplies per day rather than the minimum daily requirement of 2,261 tons; at Anzio alone, the Allies had received, on average, more than 5,000 tons a day in March. From 22 March the eastern rail route was almost impassable, while large parts of the central and western routes were also almost continuously blocked. STRANGLE was most certainly strangling German lines of communication, although whether it would cut the air supply entirely and to what degree this would affect plans for DIADEM was, at this stage in early April, not yet apparent. None the less, one thing was abundantly clear: when those thousands of aircraft in the MAAF could actually fly, Allied ground operations became that much easier. And life for the Germans became considerably tougher. For all the disappointments of the winter, Alexander was now looking to the future with renewed confidence.

PART IV

The Battle for Rome

CHAPTER 29

Spring in the Air

One of General Alexander's most useful characteristics was his imperturbability. Through his long military career he'd experienced plenty of triumphs but many disappointments too. In this war alone, not only had he been the last British soldier to leave Dunkirk, he'd overseen the retreat of the Burma Corps across the Irrawaddy River and back into India. In Tunisia, he'd arrived as Army Group commander at the very moment fortunes had taken a turn for the worse; he'd deflected the contrary demands of Prime Ministers, Chiefs of Staff, prickly subordinates and taken the disappointments of the winter in Italy very squarely on the chin. Battles, let alone wars, rarely, if ever, went according to plan, and one of the greatest challenges of generalship was how one dealt with setbacks.

Despite his current workload, he was still finding time to send his children letters with more cartoons and waggish stories, and he also made sure he was as welcoming and charming as always when visitors called at his Caserta HQ. There was never so much as a whiff of irritation or frustration, and when, on 26 March, Harold Macmillan came to dinner he found the Chief on as predictably good form as ever despite his disappointment at not breaking through at Cassino – to which he readily confessed. 'He is never downcast,' noted Macmillan, 'but merely led by temporary failure to study more deeply and carefully the means of obtaining success in the future. He is an extraordinarily balanced character, drawing strength from a combination of modesty, disinterestedness, a remarkable grasp of main principles, and a deep religious faith. Each time I see him I find him more attractive.'

Alex was also energized by the prospect of DIADEM. Back in September, the last time the sun had shone consistently, his armies had achieved a great deal, and he had always been convinced that once the days lengthened and the ground improved they would triumph once more. The pressure of time had not gone away, but while the prospect of ANVIL had been hovering over him and threatening to upend plans in Italy, that debate had, at long last, come to a head. Not only had Wilson submitted an appreciation recommending cancelling it outright, Eisenhower had also expressed his 'firm opinion' that it would be impossible to launch an invasion of southern France concurrently with OVERLORD. While the British Chiefs were very much in line with Wilson and Eisenhower, the Americans agreed only to a postponement to a target date of 10 July. So ANVIL hadn't entirely gone away, but it had for the time being, and certainly for long enough to allow Alexander the forces he needed for DIADEM. That was one major hurdle overcome.

Yet while Alexander appeared as charming and assured as ever when dining convivially with Harold Macmillan, his Fifth Army commander was unquestionably feeling the heat. Clark had to shoulder gargantuan amounts of responsibility and at every turn had demonstrated more vision, drive, aggressive spirit and tireless determination than any of his subordinates. Now, though, it was clear that seven months at this furious pace were starting to affect him negatively. He was exhausted, repeatedly suffering from sinusitis and head colds, and becoming short-tempered and peevish. The frustrations of coalition warfare were also taking their toll; he hated his impotence when dealing with Freyberg and Galloway. That the Cassino battle had flopped was a particularly bitter disappointment, especially when a breakthrough had been within their grasp. He was also convinced that the March battle for Cassino could and should have brought a victory. 'It has been a most difficult situation that I have been in,' he noted. 'The New Zealanders and Indians have not fought well. Freyberg, whereas he is a courageous and co-operative commander, is woefully deficient in intelligence. His British subordinates do not admire his leadership, and it has been an unhappy situation since Alexander created Freyberg's provisional corps. Freyberg is not qualified to command it, nor does he have the staff to implement his instructions.' That was nothing less than the truth, yet Clark also worried that the New Zealand Corps debacle, entirely of Alexander's creation, would end up being blamed on him. Clark often succumbed to paranoia and believed Devers had not backed him enough in dealings with Marshall and the War

Department. 'In fact,' he added, 'I'm convinced of that.' And actually he was right to be worried, because there were conversations about removing him. As it happened, these were fairly swiftly put to one side, but there was no doubt Clark needed a break, especially if he was to be leading Fifth Army in DIADEM and, with a fair wind, his troops into Rome itself – the prospect of which had motivated him ever since landing at Salerno the previous September.

Clark drove down to Caserta for the major DIADEM planning conference on a very springlike 2 April, then went on to the rest camp at Sorrento for four much-needed days before, on 9 April, being suddenly summoned to Washington – not to be fired but so that General Marshall and the President could hear his plans for the capture of Rome and his frank and honest appreciation of the situation in Italy. Clark, always assiduous and with the kind of grasp of detail that had made him such a good military planner, had done his homework and once in Washington was able to swiftly cast aside any doubts at all as to his suitability to command such an enormous and complex enterprise as the multinational two-fronted Fifth Army. The trip also gave him a chance for a reunion with his wife, Renie, although Marshall had insisted his visit be kept secret; even his mother, who lived in Washington, had not been allowed to know of it. First Sorrento, then Washington, did much, at this vital time, to help recharge Clark's batteries and also his confidence. Both would be needed in the battle to come.

Alexander had also left Italy for a visit to London to present the DIADEM plan in person to the Chiefs of Staff, and also to placate the Prime Minister, who was horrified that the launch date had been now pushed back to May. It had become clear that mid-April had been too optimistic, partly because of the weather but primarily because of the huge logistical challenge of getting his armies ready. Five divisions – three British, two American – were only reaching Italy in April and then required deployment. Two further divisions and two brigades were not due until early May. Moving units across the peninsula took time as well. The logistics were mind-boggling in their complexity. It seemed likely that Fifth Army would have completed its various moves by 23 April and Eighth Army by the 25th, so a launch date of 10 May allowed time for the troops to familiarize themselves with their new locations, build up stockpiles, and also enable them to make the most of a full moon on 8 May. Alexander's presence in London helped considerably in easing Churchill's concerns; both the PM and the Chiefs of Staff were persuaded by his arguments. As he pointed out, it was the rushed nature of the battles so far this year that had contributed to their shortcomings. It was far better to ensure that the conditions were right, that balance could be maintained at all times, even if plans deviated as the battle unfolded, and that no stone had been left unturned. Back in the late summer of 1942, Alexander had rightly argued that more time would be gained by waiting to launch Alamein until they were ready. It had paid off then and he was certain it would pay off again.

Now back at the front was Oberleutnant Hans Golda, fresh from his course in France to discover his battery had been busy during the Cassino battle. 'They still looked pretty good, my boys,' he noted, despite their ordeal. 'The bunkers had suffered a little. Only the landscape was even more tattered and torn. There was not a green growth to be seen, nor a tree or shrub. The ruins of houses had been levelled.' Despite this, he was pleased to be back with his men, although he'd only been with them a few days when he was told he was going to be transferred to 8. Batterie. They'd lost a number of troops captured up on Monte Castellone and several more killed, and needed to be rebuilt and licked back into shape. Golda was told he was just the man for the job. It was a compliment, of course, but he was devastated to be leaving the men he'd been with, through thick and thin, since Sicily. 'What was left,' he noted, 'but to follow orders?'

The Germans were also undergoing large troop movements and the rotation of front-line units. At Anzio, Hans Liebschner and the rest of Kampfgruppe Gericke were now out of the line, although just making the changeover had been fraught enough. No matter how quiet they tried to be, the British seemed to know something was up and so plastered the lines with a rain of mortar- and shellfire. Liebschner was already out of the front line when another salvo of shells whooshed in and so jumped into the nearest shell-hole and found himself next to one of the new infantry boys taking over. While they waited for the shelling to calm down the two got talking. It turned out that the new arrivals had just been posted from a village near Meissen in Saxony, where they'd been recovering from a stint in Russia. Liebschner then discovered they'd actually been based in the very village where one of his uncles ran a *Gasthaus*. 'Liebschner?' said the young man. 'I was billeted with him.' He then paused and said, 'Have you heard that Walter was killed in Russia? They received the telegram while we were there. Their only child too.'

Liebschner had not heard this tragic news and was very sorry too, as

Walter had been his favourite cousin; they'd spent many summers together. What a place to hear of it, he thought – in a shell-hole in Anzio. And yet, sad though he was, he realized his prime concern was to get out of there and away to safety as quickly as possible. It was in the early hours that he finally reached the 'Tross' – the rear area – where they could finally walk around upright, without crouching. They were also paid – two months' worth plus front-line bonus pay. Liebschner and his comrades went for a quick exploration, found a huge wine barrel on the back of a wagon and managed to fill as many of their empty water bottles as they could. With another hot meal in their bellies they spent the night in a barn, sitting on ammunition boxes, surrounded by straw and lit by candles. It was quite a *gemütlich* atmosphere as they drank, sang and played cards. Liebschner lost his entire pay thanks to his increasingly drunken gambling. But he couldn't have cared less. He was alive. No one could shout, '*Melder Vierte!*' and he was warm and dry. What did money matter now?

Having been sent back into Cassino on the night of 27–28 March to relieve the Māori, 24th Battalion in the New Zealand Division spent only a further week there before they, too, were pulled out for good. They'd been holding the northern side of the Via Casilina, the 'Mad Mile' as it had come to be called. And a tough week it had been. The smell of the dead grew increasingly overwhelming, combined with a permanent stench of explosives, dust and destruction – that's what it was: the all-pervading odour of devastation and desolation. For the most part they'd been able to keep their heads down, but at dusk each night there was always a 'hate' – a sustained salvo of artillery, Nebelwerfers and mortars – before their own 25-pounders joined in by way of returning the compliment. The air filled once more with the whine of shells, of explosions, crumbling masonry, the ground trembling, the worry that more walls would collapse on top of them, smoke, dust – and that stench, sharp, gagging, grating the back of the throat.

The biggest risk each day was sending out the collection party for company rations and ammunition from the Chiesa del Carmine Crypt, which could be an awkward trek. One night, Roger Smith and his mates lost their bearings and he stepped straight over an 8-foot drop. 'It was awful,' he noted, 'like being hit in the face by a sledgehammer.' Apart from cuts and bruises he was all right, but the experience left him feeling deeply on edge and strangely overwrought.

Relief came on the night of 2–3 April as their positions were taken over by the 1st Guards Brigade, part of the British 4th Infantry Division. Smith and his fellows had simply walked straight on down the Via Casilina, back towards Trocchio and the far side of the Rapido Valley. They'd paused at some barns where, with straw on the ground, they'd got their heads down. Nightmares, however, plagued Smith's sleep and he woke with a chill at the nape of his neck and feeling frozen by fear. Memories threatened to overwhelm him. 'Memories of friends that were and are no more,' he noted. 'Memories of sights and sounds unbelievable in terror. Memories of deeds done with viciousness undreamed of.' He looked around and realized that two of his mates were also awake; they agreed they'd all get blind drunk that night. Drunk for forty-eight hours at least and then, perhaps, he thought, it wouldn't be so bad.

While the New Zealanders were escaping Cassino and heading a little way to the north to take over the line from the CEF, the Fallschirmjäger were still very much there, holding both Monte Cassino and the southern third of the ruined town. Jupp Klein and his company of Pioniere remained rooted in and around the Hotel des Roses, while 2. Bataillon of 4. Fallschirmjäger-Regiment had first moved to Roccasecca to take on more replacements and undergo some training, and then, in the second week of April, had taken over the town from Heilmann's 3. Fallschirmjäger. Oberjäger Rudolf Donth had found it unsettling being up on the Colle d'Onofrio during the March battle, waiting constantly to be bombed or attacked but with no sign of either. They'd all felt on edge all the time. The awful weather hadn't helped; the kind of weather to make men ill. A lot of the men hadn't looked after their personal hygiene well enough, which had exacerbated the number of cases, whether trench foot, dysentery or infections. 'We Russians,' he noted, using the term they used for Eastern Front veterans, 'had to look after the lads like wet-nurses.'

A couple of weeks in Roccasecca had done them the world of good, however: hot meals, a chance to rest, and freedom from the relentless artillery fire. On Easter Sunday they'd even been treated to a performance by the 44. Division concert party. 'There was no large room available,' noted Kurt Müller, 'so the "theatre" took place in a destroyed church.' One of the performers had been so convincing as a female singer that several of the young lads had made a pass at him afterwards. 'After the unmasking,' jotted Müller, 'there was disappointment and shame on one hand and great *Schadenfreude* on the other.' Later that Easter night, Müller and some of the veterans began recalling the Christmas Eve they'd had in the ruins of Ortona. 'How differently,' he added, 'we had experienced these holidays!'

They moved into the town on the night of 12–13 April, taking cover a number of times as Tommy machine guns spat out. Rudolf Donth found it a deeply unsettling experience. There was a heavy fog, adding a spectral feel to the ruins. It was also very dark, they could see little, and had no real idea of where they were. The outgoing troops briefed them but Donth had no sense of what to expect amid all the rubble. In some confusion they staggered around, often hitting themselves as they tried to make sense of the buildings that were no longer really buildings at all. Just before the outgoing Leutnant left, Donth found himself standing in front of a dark chasm – the entrance to his new command post. Was there always this fog, he asked? 'Yes,' came the reply. 'Sometimes more, sometimes less. But you get used to it. The main thing is that it's quiet. You can hear each other coughing we're so close together.' He meant the Tommies. Mamma mia, thought Donth, but they'd got themselves into something.

'The general public are tired,' noted Filippo Caracciolo. 'The pressing problems are literally those of the bed, of bread, of the street.' He was feeling pretty tired himself, exhausted by his role as something of an arbitrator amid the politicking going on; most of his colleagues lacked his natural charm, patience and calm good sense amid the wranglings. He was in a rather unique position: a prince and an aristocrat, a former diplomat, supremely well connected yet also part of the Partita d'Azione which was actively lobbying to get rid of the King. At the end of February, he'd heard that Vittorio Emanuele might consider handing over his powers to a lieutenant, possibly his son, Prince Umberto. This was nothing less than a mealy-mouthed compromise for his party but also for most in the CLN, yet he felt that compromise was probably the way forward. It was a step in the right direction, after all, and that was better than standing still, with all the political machinations and uncertainty that came with doing nothing.

Unsurprisingly, however, nothing happened for another month until, on 1 April, the leader of the Italian Communist Party, Palmiro Togliatti, arrived in Naples, newly returned from eighteen years in exile. In what proved to be a sensational press conference, he announced that the Partito Comunista d'Italia – PCI – would now be willing to join a government with anyone professing to share the same goal: winning the war and ridding Italy of both Fascists and Nazis. And that meant even a government headed by Badoglio and the King remaining as Head of State. Togliatti had been persuaded to make the move by the Russians, and it had been a canny one, as Caracciolo was well aware. 'The situation now becomes heavy with unknowns,' he noted. 'The Partita d'Azione draws much of its strength from the rigidity of its moral standpoint. We cannot follow these waltzes with ease.' On the other hand, if they didn't step in line with the stance of the Communists they would be in severe danger of becoming politically isolated. With the Communists in government and taking plum ministerial jobs, that would only further their ambitions to become the dominant post-war party. It was a dilemma.

It was also one to which Harold Macmillan was very alive, as was Robert Murphy, his old friend and his direct American equivalent as the senior US diplomat in Italy. The two men had worked very closely together in the Mediterranean for eighteen months but Murphy had been back in the States since December; his return now, looking, Macmillan reported, fit, well, ten years younger and on great form, was most welcome. Both Macmillan and Murphy agreed that the time had come to force the hand of the King. Clearly, the Communists could not be allowed to dominate the Badoglio government.

The resolution that was put forward by Murphy and Macmillan and voted on by the Advisory Council – albeit with Soviet abstention – was for the same solution Caracciolo had heard suggested a month earlier: for the King to abdicate his powers immediately to his son, Prince Umberto, but not yet his title. This they put to the King in person on 10 April, Easter Monday. Vittorio Emanuele affected to be surprised although he had, in fact, been warned beforehand. He demanded forty-eight hours to make up his mind, but then announced on the following day that he would renounce his powers as proposed; however, this would take effect only once the Allies were in Rome. Whether this fudge would be accepted by the remaining parties of the CLN was not yet clear.

Caracciolo had been entirely right, however, in assuming that the vast majority of Italians were more concerned about food and survival than about the Allies ceding power, or the slow reintroduction of democracy. In Eboli, Lina Caruso was still living in the broken remains of the town and daily confronting the challenge of how to survive – and she and her family were among the more fortunate ones. In the third week of March the natural disaster of Vesuvius's eruption added to the misery; Cercola and San Sebastiano became yet two more towns to be destroyed during the war, while much of the surrounding area was smothered in volcanic ash. Even in Eboli it rained sand, covering much of the town in a layer several centimetres thick. Lina Caruso's father was, as a middle-class civil servant of the state railways, earning 4,000 lire a month, but with butter priced at 500 lire a kilo and a pair of new shoes costing the same as he was earning, such a salary didn't stretch very far, especially not with a family of seven. 'We are starving!' wrote Lina in her diary. 'If I even spend 10 lire, I cry about it.' What's more, prices were only rising still, not falling. 'Today,' she added, 'only the smuggler lives!' She was right about this. As was the time-honoured way, it was the black marketeers who thrived in this vacuum.

Lina Caruso had not yet been forced to succumb to prostitution but as spring arrived in southern Italy there was no sign at all of this terrible pandemic of poverty abating in any way. Sergeant Norman Lewis was still working as a field security officer in Naples and despaired of the lack of any will, it seemed to him, on the part of AMGOT to straighten things out. Colonel Charles Poletti was now the head of Civil Affairs in Naples, having first held that post in Palermo in Sicily the previous summer. There he had employed the services of Vito Genovese as a translator and fixer. Genovese was a notorious gangster and the former right-hand man of the even more notorious New York hood, Lucky Luciano. That Poletti, who was also Italian-American and who had been Governor-General of New York, was not aware of who Genovese was stretched credulity. Rather, it seemed likely that Genovese had been in touch with American secret intelligence services before the invasion of Sicily. Whatever the truth, when Poletti had been transferred to Naples, so too had Genovese, and it was now widely known by the man on the street – as well as Lewis – that he was running most of the Mafia-Camorra syndicates. 'Yet nothing is done,' noted Lewis. 'However many damaging reports are put in about the activities of high-ranking AMGOT officials, they stay where they are.' And in Naples, this was happening on Poletti's watch.

Meanwhile, the population struggled on, battling black-market crime as well as criminally high prices, and all too often succumbing to criminal activities themselves. At the end of March, Lewis was accosted at the top of the Via Roma near the Piazza Dante by a lady with a kindly enough looking face. She wanted to show him something, she told him, and he found himself following her to a typical Neapolitan side-street. In her single, windowless room there was a young girl standing in the corner. The woman explained that the girl was thirteen years old and her daughter and she wanted to prostitute her to him. The woman offered him a scale of fees for various services; for example, the girl would strip and show him her pubescent organs for just 20 lire. Disgusted, Lewis told her that he would report her to the police and the woman began to make a great play of weeping, although these were all too obviously crocodile tears. Both Lewis and the woman also knew his threats were idle ones. 'There are no police,' he noted, 'to deal with the thousands of squalid little crimes like this committed every day in the city.'

Lewis found himself confronting prostitution on a daily basis. At the beginning of April he had to investigate twenty-eight prospective brides for Allied servicemen, of whom twenty-two were prostitutes. He would go to their houses and discover that while they were surrounded all around by abject poverty, their homes were clean and tidy with tins of food in the larder and their children, if they had them, reasonably well turned out. In every instance, Lewis asked them where they got the money to live so much better than their neighbours. 'My uncle sends me some,' was the stock answer. At this Lewis would then ask for a name and address, at which point the game was up. The girl in question then always asked for his personal help. 'I didn't ask to live like this,' they told him. 'Give me the chance to get away from it and I'll be as good a wife as anybody else.'

Such matters were hardly the concerns of those at the front, however, who were understandably mostly absorbed by their own experiences, anxieties and by what was directly either side of them and, more to the point, in front of them. Captain Klaus Huebner and 349th Infantry had spent barely ten days at the front before being pulled out to Caserta for a brief rest to make way for the 85th 'Custer' Division, newly arrived and new to combat and in urgent need of some front-line experience. Ten days later, however, Huebner and the 349th Infantry were back, the Custermen shifting to the south as there were now two divisions holding the line where there had been just one during X Corps' stint. From Castelforte northwards to the southern edge of the Liri Valley the CEF were moving into position and now with four, not two divisions. So where there had been three divisions in January along this stretch of the front, there were going to be six, while opposite them remained the beleaguered 94. Division, given some replacements but nothing like enough to fill their depleted ranks.

At the end of March, Huebner was back in the same stone house at the foot of Monte Damiano, to which he'd actually become quite attached. Firing continued all day and throughout the night, mostly from their own side. Huebner learned that the 88th Division was firing 1,500 artillery rounds per day, which amounted to one every minute, as well as 400 tank destroyer rounds – high-velocity anti-tank shells – and 700 mortar rounds. That was a lot of ordnance being fired at the enemy. Although it wasn't expected of him, Huebner had been keen to learn the lie of the land and so took to regularly climbing up Damiano and heading to the battalion OP. Here, he discovered, he could see quite a lot of enemy activity if he waited around long enough. At one point, he watched a barrage of mortar rounds pound an unremarkable knoll, only for boards and branches suddenly to fly in all directions from the blast; it seemed they'd scored a direct hit on an MG post. Moments later, Red Cross flags were being waved and several German medics emerged to gather the wounded.

By night the battalion undertook vigorous patrolling and the men frequently reappeared with prisoners, most of whom were Poles only too happy to have been captured. The Americans also lost a few men, though, not least Lieutenant John A. Liebenstein, who, on the night of 11 April, carried out a raid and after fierce close-quarter fighting dragged a frightened German from his foxhole. Unfortunately, as the lieutenant stepped back with the prisoner he tripped on a wire, triggering a mine that wounded him severely. Worse, the detonation prompted a furious reply from German mortars. Realizing that his men would be in danger themselves if they tried to rescue him, he ordered them all to abandon him and head back to their lines. Later that night, Huebner's medics made an attempt to rescue him but could find no trace. 'Have the Germans carried him off dead or alive?' Huebner wondered. 'He was only a young kid, small, thin, and blond, yet ordered his men to leave him dying to save themselves.'

Meanwhile, the 56th Heavy Regiment had finally moved from the Garigliano area with two batteries posted more than 150 miles to the south for rest and refit, while the other two were sent north of Cassino. RSM Jack Ward had headed south with the rest of RHQ at the end of March, passing through many of the places where they'd fought the previous autumn, then on to Naples and past the still-erupting Vesuvius. 'What a view,' he noted. 'Lava was still coming down in the sides and the roads and tracks were covered in ash, in some places to a depth of two feet. We got choked with it.' He was impressed to see an army bulldozer clearing the road and astonished to discover that ash was still covering buildings and fields many miles further to the south.

A few days later, on 3 April, it was his wife's birthday. 'Many happy returns of the day, Else,' he jotted, 'have been thinking about you, and about us, and as I write I have some daffs stuck in a bottle which I picked up in the grounds of this place and which, of course, keep reminding me of Easter, home, and your birthday.' Yet while Ward was only too happy to be out of the line for a while, there was not much rest for him as he then had to drive to Barletta on the Adriatic coast to collect some NAAFI supplies, then three days later, after Easter, head back north again to join the two batteries in the line at Cassino. They'd taken over positions from the French, who were now pretty much where the 56th Heavy Regiment had been, so it really was all change; they found themselves 3,000 feet above sea level, which had not been an easy location to lug the big guns. Ward immediately went up to the lines and helped build a new CP. 'Weather very nice,' he wrote, 'have been digging myself today, and now I ache like the devil.'

The Faughs, meanwhile, were up on the massif between Monte Castellone and Monte Cairo. They had moved up there at the end of March without a glitch and also without overtly straining the mule trains, which rather suggested they could have done so back in February or March. Lawrie Franklyn-Vaile was wondering whether his wife Olive had heard the BBC's 8 o'clock news that day, 8 April. They regularly managed to tune in on their radio set at Company CP. That evening, however, there had been a report from Cassino in which the broadcaster had pointed out that 'Nothing to report' gave completely the wrong impression. He had described the mule trains, jeeps coming forward loaded with rations, water and mail, unloading in the dark, the almost continuous rattle of machine guns, incessant artillery and mortar duels. Patrols going out each night. 'All this occurs every night,' noted Franklyn-Vaile, 'even when the official communique says, "Nothing to report," and it is always a time of anxiety, excitement and strain.'

On the other hand, he wrote, he was feeling really very calm. In the past he had always been a terrible worrier, but since arriving in Italy he had learned to be a little more philosophical. 'The CO has two great sayings,' he added. '"Nothing is ever as bad as it seems," and "Everything comes right in the end" and it is surprising how right he is.' He was also more confident – in his job, in his ability to lead his men, in understanding this business of being an infantryman. He ended this latest letter by asking for some paperbacks, a toothbrush, writing paper and Brylcreem. 'I miss you both very much indeed,' he signed off. 'All my love and kisses, it will be grand when we are together again.'

Also now at the front was Captain Mike Doble and the rest of the 2nd RHA. They had taken over positions from the New Zealand gunners and would be supporting the British 4th Infantry Division in the upcoming battle. Doble had moved up on 2 April to take up position in a new OP on Monte Trocchio. 'After a terrific struggle, I got out of bed and later made my way to the OP,' he jotted in his diary on 3 April. 'A wonderful view out over Cassino and Monastery Hill.' He spent the morning being shown around by the New Zealand officer he was taking over from. It all seemed fairly straightforward to him, but he was still marvelling at the sight before him; there were few better vantage points than atop Trocchio. 'Cassino is a remarkable sight,' he wrote. 'There is not a building left intact in the town and for the most part is just a vast pile of rubbish with an odd wall standing out of the middle.'

A couple of days later he had what he considered a rude shock when he was asked to go into Cassino with the 1st Guards Brigade as a forward liaison officer. Crossing the causeway he was staggered by the amount of wreckage – abandoned machine guns, blown-up tanks, other detritus, and dead on the roadside all the way. The stench had been nauseating. He was led to the Crypt of the Chiesa del Carmine, where the brigade now had its CP, and managed to establish comms with the regiment fairly easily. He was relieved the following night.

Once safely back behind Trocchio, the rhythms of daily life in an artillery regiment at the front soon settled down and he returned to his more leisurely morning routine, although the nights of relentless drinking were now over. The one exception was Sunday, 16 April, which was his twenty-fourth birthday. The party began at 6 p.m. and went on until 2 a.m. and included not only a lot of drinking but also cards. 'Hangover this morning,' he jotted the following day, 'did not get up till after 0800 but got round the guns by 0900, just finished, and the Major called, had tea cakes after discussing register points.'

Meanwhile, the machinations over the future of the King and the government in the south had continued, for while Macmillan, Murphy and the Advisory Council accepted Vittorio Emanuele's compromise, his terms had prompted considerable squirming among some of the CLN parties, not least the Partita d'Azione. Filippo Caracciolo was sent as their representative to negotiate with Badoglio at Salerno on 18 April, who demanded the names of three men from the party to join his government – a minister and two undersecretaries. This, however, prompted yet more internal wrangling, heart-wringing and long, highly charged meetings. Eventually, though, on 21 April a deal was done, not just within the Partita d'Azione but the CLN as a whole. 'I think Italy will be brought safely to bed of a "democratic government",' noted Macmillan. He felt rather as though he were the putative father and Noel Mason-MacFarlane one of the midwives. 'But the labour', he added, 'has been long and painful.' Filippo Caracciolo felt equally worn down by the months of uncertainty and, more recently, long days of feverish negotiation. He'd reluctantly agreed to be one of the Partita d'Azione's two undersecretaries, and while he knew they'd very probably conceded too much, and although it stuck in his gullet that Badoglio was still Prime Minister, he was relieved – as everyone was – that a deal had been agreed and that a multi-party government would now be in power. 'Let us all exude a sweet honey of concord,' he wrote in his diary as they'd emerged from the Municipio in Salerno to face the press, 'let us radiate handshakes, applause, congratulations. Finally: an aura of fraternal cordiality, flashes of magnesium and questions from reporters.' Two days later, the first session of the new government took place in Salerno. Slowly but surely, a new democratic Italy was emerging from the wreckage.

Meanwhile, Operation STRANGLE continued, bridges, marshalling yards, trains, motorized columns all bombed, strafed and harried relentlessly. The 57th FG, still based at Alto, Corsica, were there so they could better attack targets in the northern part of the Apennines, mainly between Bologna and southern Tuscany. It was seventy miles or so to the Italian coast, which took fifteen to twenty minutes' flying time, depending on where they crossed. Alto itself had a single steel-plate runway, a mile long and wide enough for two Thunderbolts to take off side by side. A wooden-framed control tower had been constructed and huge numbers of stores and equipment built up, and although their ships looked a little rough and beaten about, neither Luke Lucardi nor any of the other pilots ever had cause to worry about the airworthiness of their Thunderbolts. The American genius for shifting vast amounts of materiel and construction anywhere, any place, any time was quite extraordinary.

Lucardi was swiftly racking up the combat sorties, sometimes flying twice a day. On Wednesday, 12 April he had been part of a mission to Montalcino in southern Tuscany. 'We clobbered a railroad bridge and some railroad tracks,' he noted. 'Then we went down and strafed a bunch of freight cars.' In fact they managed to cut the tracks in multiple places, destroyed three locomotives and shot up twenty-five carriages. 'One very successful mission,' noted Captain Earl Lovick in the squadron war diary. Later in the day, the squadron also destroyed a three-span railway bridge. Two days later they attacked the railway near Arezzo and, having encountered very heavy flak, then ran into more than thirty enemy fighters. 'It was the biggest dog-fight the squadron's had!' noted Lucardi in his diary. 'And I'm disappointed in myself – my part in the fight, that is, and feel kinda low because my buddy Gundy went down.' Lieutenant Gunderson had been seen with two Me 109s on his tail, but at the same time Lucardi thought he'd heard someone call out, 'Duck, Luke!' and so he'd immediately split-essed, escaped the fray and hurtled after what he thought was an enemy aircraft only to discover it was a Thunderbolt. He was cut up about his friend but also wished he'd been able to do something to help him. 'He's been with me all through flying school,' he scribbled. 'Shucks! I still hope he bailed out or crash-landed safely in enemy territory. Damn! Damn this war!'

By the end of the month, Lucardi had chalked up sixteen missions and was starting to feel a little more confident. He hoped his luck would hold and that, with God's help, he would be able to make it back to his folks and to Jane. The following day, Monday, 1 May, he flew missions seventeen and eighteen. 'Boy, oh boy,' he jotted, 'up by Arezzo at a railroad bridge they covered the sky with 88mm stuff.' Black puffs of exploding flak burst all around him while as he dived tracer whipped past him. Hurtling down at more than 400 mph with that amount of anti-aircraft fire was a heart-stopping business, but his luck held and after dropping his bomb he pulled up and, together with the rest of the squadron, headed for the safety of the mountains.

By the end of April the central rail route had been cut in sixty-nine places, and by the end of the first week of May 155 more had been added. Allied air forces had flown an average of nearly 1,500 sorties a day – each sortie a single-aircraft combat mission – which was a staggering amount; their efforts had brought a catalogue of destruction and damage. Yet with the kind of logistical efficiency that was such a feature of Kesselring's command, the Germans managed to repair large parts of track and numerous bridges, while also making good use of lesser roundabout routes and moving goods between trains across damaged parts of track. Overseeing this work was a 'General with Special Responsibility for the Maintenance of Rail Communications in Italy' newly appointed by Kesselring. German engineers provided the skills, and the Organisation Todt press-ganged Italians into labouring for them. It also helped that Kesselring had built up considerable stocks at the front during the winter, and that, with a stagnant front, he had been using up little of his reserves of fuel and ammunition. Furthermore, the Germans had managed by moving greater volumes of traffic by road and by sea, using coast-hugging lighters at night, and by taking what they could from the land. So STRANGLE had failed in its very lofty aims of crippling German supply lines and forcing the enemy to pull back, but had none the less caused untold damage and ravaged Kesselring's supply lines. The help this enormous air effort had given the DIADEM plans was considerable.

General Alexander had arrived back in Italy on 20 April. 'Chief returned,' noted Harding, 'looking better than when he left.' Clark was back three days later, similarly refreshed and reinvigorated, and based at a new CP at San Marco Evangelista, near Caserta; his HQ had moved there at the end of March. Waiting for him was a new, specially adapted trailer, with which Clark was thrilled. That night, bottles of whisky and bourbon were opened and shared with several of his staff. Ever since Fifth Army had reached the Bernhard Line at the beginning of November, it had felt as though his forces were battling against immense challenges, of which the Germans had been just one. No one was suggesting that DIADEM would be easy, but there was a palpable sense of confidence in the air. Rome, that elusive prize, beckoned.

CHAPTER 30

Preparations

'THE COMMANDING GENERAL,' NOTED the AOK 10 war diary on 18 April, 'before departing, transferred command to General Hartmann.' Now that the front was so quiet, von Senger had been summoned to the Berghof, Hitler's home in the Obersalzberg in the Bavarian Alps, to personally receive the Oak Leaves to his Knight's Cross. Von Senger had felt reasonably confident that the Allies were not planning anything major imminently, although he reckoned the weak point in his line was in the south, along the Garigliano, where 94. Division was still very understrength. He'd ordered his corps reserves of artillery down there but that had not amounted to much. That part of the line, especially, remained a worry.

None the less, pulling him and General Baade, who was to receive the Swords to his Knight's Cross, away at this time was far from ideal. And lovely though the Obersalzberg was, both von Senger and Baade were deeply unimpressed with their Führer, who had timed the ceremony to coincide with his fifty-fifth birthday on 20 April. Von Senger thought he looked frail and melancholic: his handshake was clammy, his skin flabby and wan, and his eyes had a glassy, faraway look. The two generals were among a number of guests, most of whom were young men being decorated for their gallantry, and Hitler sat them all down at a round table and gave them one of his monologues. Inspiring, it was not: the situation on the Eastern Front was dire, the Allies were about to invade across the Channel, the Battle of the Atlantic was all but lost. There was little mention of Italy and none at all of the much-vaunted secret weapons that were soon to be unveiled. 'The only encouragement this man was able to give the soldiers from the front', noted von Senger, 'was a half-mumbled admonition to overcome all these difficulties through "faith".' Nor was von Senger hurrying back to the front; rather, both he and Baade had been ordered to Ordensburg in North Rhine-Westphalia, the Nazi Party educational centre set up in 1936 for future National Socialist leaders. It was now being used for indoctrination courses to remind senior commanders such as von Senger about the values and aims of National Socialism. So in the XIV Panzerkorps commander's absence, General Hartmann was at the helm, a man who, the year before when in Russia, had been considered unsuitable for front-line command.

Incredibly, though, General Heidrich had also been at the same award ceremony, like von Senger to be given the Oak Leaves to his Knight's Cross. He had not, however, been sent to Ordensburg and so was back at the front in the last week of April. He visited Jupp Klein and 2. Kompanie Pionier-Bataillon, who were now resting and refitting at Castrocielo, eight miles to the north-west of Cassino at the foot of the mountains on the Via Casilina. Heidrich talked to Klein and all the men in turn and then, much to their amazement, invited all of the veterans to join him for dinner. A long table had been set up under some olive trees with plenty of food and wine. 'We were all thunderstruck,' noted Klein, 'because we'd not expected this at all.' After the meal they moved and sat under the trees in a circle round Heidrich while he told them about his visit to the Berghof. Heidrich was remarkably frank; like von Senger, he'd been shocked at Hitler's physical and mental decline. 'Heidrich called on us to support Germany and the Führer,' noted Klein, 'in the difficult situation they found themselves and to bravely fulfil our duty as soldiers.'

Heidrich's challenges were certainly considerable because of the elevated status his division had. The Fallschirmjäger remained the darlings of Nazi propaganda and much was expected of them, despite dwindling manpower and, more to the point, ever-decreasing numbers of hardened veterans. His depleted division was horribly stretched. On 22 April he sent an appreciation, guessing that the next likely attack would be on the Monte Cassino massif with the Allied *Schwerpunkt* – main point of assault – towards Albaneta. His 1. Regiment was now only 500-strong and he had also been stripped of the entire 3. Bataillon from 3. Regiment; Major Kratzert and his men had been posted back to Germany as instructors, which was as stark an admission of how thin this arm of the Wehrmacht was becoming as any. Heilmann had around 730 left in his regiment and they were now taking over the main positions around

Monastery Hill, Point 593, Albaneta and up on to Colle Sant'Angelo, while Schulz's 1. Regiment had been reinforced into a battle group with two battalions from 15. Panzergrenadier-Division. In all, Heidrich now had around 2,000 men. It wasn't a lot.

While von Senger, Baade and Heidrich had been receiving their awards, other medal ceremonies were playing out on this latest Führer birthday. Also on 20 April, Hans Liebschner was presented with the Iron Cross First Class, although he received it with very mixed feelings. He was happy to have something to tell his parents and his father, especially, who'd served in the trenches in the last war, but on the other hand he'd been lined up along with nine other medal recipients while being watched by fifty or so men who'd been awarded nothing. When he turned and faced them, he felt ashamed. 'I could think of no reason why I had been selected,' he noted, 'except that I had been lucky.' He wasn't at all sure he should have been given the Iron Cross just for surviving; it had not occurred to him that as a company runner he had faced considerably greater danger than most infantrymen, or that it was in this very role that Hitler himself had won his Iron Cross in the last war.

His battalion were still out of the line, but now at Pratica, not far from the sea and west of their old positions. He'd turned nineteen the day before Easter and on reaching their new camp had received a mass of mail that had stacked up and been waiting for him. Not all the news had been good. His brother, Arnim, had been wounded a third time in Russia; his neighbour's son had been shot down and killed in his Messerschmitt; their local grocer, aged sixty, had joined up. Many others, though, had far worse news waiting for them. While American and Commonwealth troops, for the most part, had families living peacefully at home despite the war, the same was not the case for the Germans, and front-line troops often opened letters with trepidation, hoping it would not be their turn to hear that their homes or worse, family, had been destroyed by the Allied bombing. 'Such news affected everyone in the company,' noted Liebschner, 'and convinced us even more that we were fighting for a just cause.'

The British 5th Division, meanwhile, had now been dug in among the maze of wadis for several weeks. The front line ran roughly west–east and along the course of the River Moletta, but from this there were various offshoot wadis of different depths and sizes, most of which were now inhabited by British infantrymen. The central part of this network was The Fortress, but there was also the 'Lobster Claw' and, a little behind,

'The Cutting', which was where the east–west lateral road – a dirt track – ran. One of the 2nd Inniskillings' companies was dug in behind The Cutting and two others in The Fortress. Getting in and out of the latter was another game of Russian roulette, because the approaches were across open land covered by enemy machine guns and snipers. When Captain David Cole had first headed down the slope into The Fortress he had immediately thought of his Virgil, '*Facilis est descensus Averno*' – 'easy is the descent into Hell'. Although the men were largely safe from shell and mortar fire in these gullies, just existing day to day was hellish: they were damp, it was dark because of the tattered vegetation clinging to the sides, and rats, flies and all kinds of bugs and other insects made life a misery. For much of the time, Cole, however, was glad to be based at the battalion CP in The Cutting, with dugouts hacked into the embankment. Even here, though, they were far from immune. In fact, a feature of the Anzio bridgehead was that nowhere was out of range of the German guns, one of the very good reasons for having pushed further out in the early days of the SHINGLE operation.

One evening, Cole had just finished talking to his batman and walked a few yards back towards the CP when a cluster of shells, with almost no warning, whammed in and exploded all around them. One killed Cole's batman immediately. 'I heard someone say that they would need a shovel to pick him up,' noted Cole. 'I could not bring myself to look.' Cole was particularly cut up about his death; it seemed more personal to him than many others and for some time he sat alone in the CP, unable to stop himself shaking.

In Cassino, Rudolf Donth had been promoted to Feldwebel – staff sergeant – now that he was commanding his 1. Zug, and was promptly ordered to lead a raiding party to capture some British troops as they now had no idea who was in front of them. This had come direct from Heidrich himself and with the promise that for every Tommy captured they'd get a day's leave. Donth was told to organize the assault party himself, and although not expected to lead he decided he should and would do. Gathering twenty men together, he split them into two groups of ten, with his great friend Oberjäger Christl Wöhrl taking one group and Oberjäger Werner Rudolph the other, with himself leading. They set off at 5.30 a.m. on 25 April. No speaking, just nods and hand signals from Donth. Within a few yards they were already in hand-grenade range, such was the close-quarter nature of the fighting in the town.

They lay down and paused on a pile of rubble, near the dog-leg of the Via Casilina, beyond which were the Tommy lines. Almost immediately, they heard the first sounds of the enemy – a Tommy snoring loudly.

Donth quickly spotted a series of possible enemy strongpoints, one of which had sandbags stacked beside what looked to be an entrance of some kind. Now eschewing quiet stealth and caution, the Rudolph Gruppe dashed across and hurled a couple of Teller mines over the sandbags and down into the entranceway. Moments later there was a loud detonation, screams and immense amounts of swirling smoke, dust and grit that enveloped the whole area. Despite enemy machine guns opening up now the hornet's nest had been poked, Donth and his men used the thick smoke and dust to mask themselves as they scampered across a narrow stretch of open ground to better cover. As Donth crouched beside the half-standing walls of a house he saw a row of smashed buildings on the northern side of the Via Casilina, each with cellar windows looking on to what had been the road. He was sure the Tommies would be in these but reaching them without being seen was the challenge. Then, to the side of one of these houses, he spotted a still-intact archway into the remains of the building, and in the early-morning light spied a shadow cast on to the far side of the entranceway. He could even make out the shape of a British steel helmet. Whoever was standing there could only be a sentry.

One of his men now lowered his Panzerfaust towards the archway but Donth shook his head, worried they might be heading into a trap. A moment later, though, he saw smoke rising from the narrow, low cellar window next to the archway and now his mind was made up: clearly, Tommies were in that building and holding the cellar; the smoke he'd seen was probably from a cigarette. He'd be unlikely to find a better opportunity to take prisoners and so now ordered the Panzerfaust to be fired straight at the archway. One of his men scuttled forward, crouching, aimed and fired, the missile whooshing across the street and hitting the archway with a load explosion, yet again prompting eruptions of thick smoke and dust; this was what one got when fighting in a town of rubble. Now Donth ran forward, flinging in a grenade through the low window. To his right the archway was collapsing, while cries, yells, choking and coughing could be heard from the cellar. As more of his men ran across the open ground to the building, each man a spectre covered head to toe in dust, Donth stood by the remains of the archway and, looking down the steps that led to the cellar, called out in his best English, '*Komm aut!*' 'Come in!' a British soldier yelled in return, which prompted another grenade to be thrown inside. Only then did one Tommy after another start crawling out through the cellar window.

'Christ, it's like a vending machine,' Donth called out to Wöhrl. 'You put something in the back and another thing comes out of the front.' In all, eleven men emerged coughing and spluttering, and while Donth and the Rudolph Gruppe gave cover, Wöhrl and his men ran back with the prisoners through the still-swirling smoke and dust. 'We secure all sides,' noted Donth, 'because there's wild shooting everywhere.' Only as they were about to make a run for it themselves did they realize that Obergefreiter Oswald Luft was missing. There was no sign of him; frantically, Donth looked around but he'd vanished and the Tommy fire was getting increasingly heavy. It was time to swiftly get the hell out of there. With everyone firing manically they scampered away, saved by the combination of their own fire and the blanket of dust and smoke. 'Our joy at our success,' noted Donth, 'was even greater when we learnt that we had captured an enemy company command post.' The prisoners consisted of an officer and ten men. One of the Tommies was treated for light chest wounds but soon after they were taken away, although not before captors and prisoners all shook hands. 'Great attack, great attack,' one of the Brits told them as they were shuffled off. Donth decided that this would be their clarion call from then on. The only depressing note had been the loss of Luft. Back in Ortona the previous December, Luft had saved his life; Donth felt terrible that he'd not been able to protect his comrade in this otherwise gratifyingly successful raid.

Meanwhile, taking over the positions of 78th Division up on Monte Cassino were the men of the Polish II Corps, two divisions and an armoured brigade 48,000 men-strong in all. They'd begun moving to Italy in December, but apart from holding a quiet stretch of Eighth Army's line were new to combat and something of an unknown quantity. Despite this, early on in his planning General Oliver Leese had earmarked the Poles for the key role of capturing the Monte Cassino massif. The reasons for this thinking were twofold. First, up on the massif the Poles would be out on something of a limb compared with the operations down in the Liri Valley. This was no bad thing, because few of them spoke English. Fighting effectively in isolation from the rest of Eighth Army ensured there would be less risk of confused lines of communication. Second, and perhaps most importantly, Leese had sensed a fire and pride in the bellies of the Poles that suggested they might be more willing to take on this toughest of nuts than other units in Eighth Army. Visiting General Władysław Anders, the Polish corps commander, on 24 March, Leese coated his proposal in very clear terms: that what he was offering would be immeasurably challenging, but was also a singular honour and indicative of the respect he had for the general and his men.

Anders was well aware that the abbey had not been taken in two months of bitter fighting and that it had eluded the efforts of battle-hardened and highly experienced troops. 'The stubbornness of the German defence at Cassino and on Monastery Hill was already a byword,' Anders noted. 'I realised that the cost in lives must be heavy, but I realised too the importance of the capture of Monte Cassino to the Allied cause, and most of all to that of Poland.' Victory would strengthen the resolve of the resistance movement in Poland and would bring glory to his corps and all Polish troops now serving alongside the Allies. 'After a short moment's reflection,' he noted, 'I answered that I would undertake the task.' Like the French before them at Belvedere, capturing Monte Cassino was about Poland's national pride, and about showing the world that this most horrifically treated nation could still, after all its suffering, fight back. And win. So of course Anders had accepted Leese's challenge.

Among those who would be in the firing line up on Monte Cassino was twenty-seven-year-old Lejtnant Władek Rubnikowicz of 2nd Squadron, 12th Podolski Reconnaissance Regiment. They had been designated part of 3rd Carpathian Rifle Division. The regiment had been trained as cavalry, but for the coming battle they'd left their armoured cars behind with the rear echelons and become infantry, foot-sloggers like almost every soldier that had fought across this now accursed stretch of mountain.

Rubnikowicz's journey to this blighted corner of Italy had been an astonishing and truly epic one, just as it had for the majority of those in II Corps – Anders included; rarely in history had a single fighting force collectively overcome quite so much before its first major battle. Born in the small north-eastern Polish town of Głębokie in 1916, Rubnikowicz had been an officer cadet in the Polish Army when the Germans had invaded from the west on 1 September 1939, and had soon found himself caught up in the fighting. Then, seventeen days later, the Soviet Red Army had crossed the Polish border from the east, forcing the Poles to fight on two fronts. By the end of September, Poland had been erased from the map, split between these two invading forces. Rubnikowicz had been wounded in the final days of the campaign, but had managed to make his way home, although Głębokie was now part of the USSR. With no jobs and no hope, he left his parents and made for Warsaw, but was arrested trying to get across the now German-controlled border. Managing to escape, he eventually reached the wreckage of Warsaw but discovered that prospects there were little better than they had been in Głębokie. Soon after, he began working for the Polish Underground, but a few months later was arrested a second time at the border as he tried to get back into Soviet Poland and was taken to Białystok prison. Conditions were unspeakably brutal; Rubnikowicz was flung into a cell designed for eight men into which fifty-six had been crammed. Beatings, torture and hard physical labour were his daily fare. He remained at Białystok Prison for thirteen months until in June 1941, at the time of the German invasion of the Soviet Union, he and 500 others were loaded on to wagons and sent to Siberia, eventually to the Mar Gulag in the Bolshezemelskaya Tundra in the Arctic Circle. The conditions were appalling. Rubnikowicz became so deprived of vitamins and other nutrients that he found himself repeatedly losing his sight. After a day's hard labour he had to depend on others to help guide him back to the camp each night.

It was towards the end of 1941 that he was eventually released, along with some 850,000 other Poles – part of a deal brokered between General Władysław Sikorski, the head of the Polish government in exile in London, and Stalin; after all, they were now allies of sorts. Rubnikowicz and his fellow prisoners were expected to join a mass migration to Uzbekistan, where General Anders was mustering a new Polish Army. Somehow he survived, pilfering food along the way and even, at one point, eating a dog. None the less, by the time he'd travelled several thousand miles to Guzar he was critically ill with typhoid. More than 93,000 Poles died on this trek, but miraculously Rubnikowicz was not one of them. With the help of a Russian nurse who took a shine to him, he pulled through.

It had initially been Sikorski's plan for his reborn army to fight on the Eastern Front against Nazi Germany, but Stalin wanted to be rid of the Poles and when Churchill let it be known that Britain would like them fighting alongside his DUKE forces in the Middle East, Sikorski agreed to evacuate Anders's fledgling army to Iran. While waiting to be transported into Persia, Rubnikowicz met, by chance, a friend of his sister who told him that his parents had been sent to a collective farm in the Soviet Union. Part of the deal with Stalin was that those in Anders's army could take their next of kin with them, so Rubnikowicz did all he could to arrange for their release in the hope they might be able to join him.

Before he could learn any more, however, he was sent to Persia, where he next contracted malaria and nearly died a second time. Again, however, he recovered and was sent to northern Iraq, where training began in earnest. Given a commission, he was allocated to 12th Podolski Uhlan Regiment – the Polish Lancers. It was while he was near Kasil Rabit that he learned his parents had made it to Tehran. Given three weeks' leave, he was finally reunited with them; they were not a demonstrative family, but on the day he saw them again he hugged them and they all wept tears of both joy and despair.

Once his leave was over he rejoined the regiment in Kirkuk, where they trained some more and carried out border patrols. The bedraggled, malnourished, disease-ridden skin-and-bone wrecks that had staggered into Guzar now looked like the fit and healthy young men they should always have been. From Iraq they were posted to Palestine, where training continued. Fully equipped by the British, they wore British uniforms, British helmets and, in the case of the 12th Recce Regiment, operated British AEC armoured cars. In November 1943 they moved once more, this time to Egypt and to Alexandria, where in December they boarded a troopship and sailed to Taranto. Rubnikowicz was excited to be in Italy. 'We all felt anxious to get to the front,' he noted. 'That may sound strange, but it was true.'

His astonishing journey, his terrible, shattering ordeal of more than four years, was unique to him but also very similar to those of almost all the 48,000 men now in II Corps. A burning desire to live and for the chance to avenge Poland's plight motivated Rubnikowicz, just as it motivated most of his comrades. Now here they were, as April gave way to May 1944, at Cassino. And soon to attack, in their very first action since 1939, a mountain that had defied all previous Allied troops. Rubnikowicz was proud, just as Anders had been proud, to have been given this task. 'We all wanted to be able to fight for our country,' he noted. 'All of us, a hundred per cent and a hundred per cent more, felt a sense of honour at going into battle for Poland.'

The Poles began moving up on 24 April. By day they squeezed into cramped sangars, caves and gullies, on cold rations and just four pints of water per man every twenty-four hours. Their nights, meanwhile, were dominated by endless supply trails, across the Rapido Valley by vehicle then by mule and foot up into the mountain. Anders's plan was to attack along two thrusts, one on either side of Snakeshead Ridge, the other along the ridgeline extending from Monte Castellone, which meant they would be using the well-trod routes already tried by the Red Bulls and 4th Indians. Anders, though, wanted to attack along both simultaneously, although he still didn't know about the German figure-of-eight defence system. His divisions were also only two brigades strong, rather than three, so to ensure the largest number of troops possible in the opening attack he planned to use all his infantry battalions at once, with none left behind in reserve. Władek Rubnikowciz's 12 Recce Regiment was normally part of the Corps Troops but had been attached to 3rd Carpathian Division as an extra infantry battalion because of this foot-slogger shortfall. He and his platoon now found themselves digging in on the lower southern slopes of Snakeshead, overlooking the Colle d'Onofrio. Waiting for the attack to begin.

CHAPTER 31

DIADEM

All along the line, troops were getting ready. Corporal Harry Wilson had now reached the Cassino front. The 8th Indian Division were to be playing a key role in the DIADEM battle; the infantry would be leading the way in crossing the Rapido and pushing on into the Liri Valley. The divisional headquarters had moved on Sunday, 23 April, and Wilson thought it a much smoother and well-organized move than previous ones. As they neared Venafro he quickly realized they were getting close from the sudden plentiful road signs that had sprung up, all helpfully written in English, French and Polish too. 'No halting on road!' 'Bailey bridge two hundred yards ahead', then, added underneath, 'No overtaking! No double-banking! Transporters – unhitch trailers before crossing and use winch!' All were orders, lightened by the liberal use of exclamation marks. Division HQ was staged at Presenzano, where Clark had been for a while. It was suddenly hot, which made Wilson and everyone else feel more flustered than they otherwise might have done as they set up the cipher truck once more. Two days later, word reached them on the QT that a big push was due on this front and that 8th Indian would be playing a prominent part.

'May Day,' wrote Lawrie Franklyn-Vaile, 'and we still seem to have a long way to go to finish the war.' He'd just been given a week's leave at the rest camp near Sorrento but on his return had found the battalion had been relieved by the Poles and that they were also now at Presenzano, readying themselves for the offensive. Despite this break, his equanimity of a few weeks earlier had since deserted him. Looking around, he wondered how they had ever advanced at all. 'You would agree with me,' he wrote to Olive, 'if you saw the country, hills and mountains with a few rivers thrown in, until one is absolutely sick of the sight of them.' There had been much grumbling from the men recently who felt they'd more than done their bit. 'There is also a strong feeling', he wrote, 'that the Second Front is being so glamourised that, when it does commence, people will forget all about this campaign and will be saying afterwards, "What, were you not in the Second Front, oh Italy, that was nothing," forgetting all about the terrain, the stern German resistance and the fact that we have not got the advantage the people in France have of being able to get home early.'

Meanwhile, summer kit had been issued to Eighth Army troops in the first days of May, so the serge battledress uniforms were swapped for denim and Airtex and cotton summer shirts, but also included new underwear. 'The American underpants were dainty little things,' noted Harry Wilson. 'The brigadier called them ladies' drawers.' Three days later, on the afternoon of 6 May, the Chief Clerk at 8th Indian HQ gathered the cipher team together for a briefing. They would all be under enemy observation at the front and from two directions, he told them. If bivvies had to be erected they were to be done after dark and taken down before dawn. Movement was restricted by day. Vehicles were also only to be moved by night, and rations would, from now on, arrive only by night. One of the cipher team asked the Chief Clerk whether he had anything cheerful to say. 'Yes,' he replied. 'It won't last much longer – only another five years.'

By evening, Wilson and the rest of Division HQ had moved up to the front and were now behind Monte Trocchio. He felt an intense yearning for peace and freedom but viewed the coming battle with calm resignation. 'I repeated to myself,' he jotted, 'what Francis Thompson wrote about death: "It seems to me, That we rehearse too much, For such a mean and single scene," and derived a kind of melancholic comfort from it.'

Oberst Wilhelm Mauss, now back near the front, found the strange hiatus between battles rather eerie. 'When will it suddenly be interrupted, when will the artillery guns' muzzles open again and pour out their ominous salvos?' he wondered. 'We do not know how this will continue; it is extremely possible that they are planning a landing further to the north in order to cut us off.'

What they were not expecting was a two-army attack across a fifteen-mile front. For all the movement of troops that had been both heard and spotted by the German command, and been observed and commented on by men at the front line such as Rudolf Donth and his comrades, yet again their intelligence had failed them, just like it had before SHINGLE.

Thursday, 11 May 1944. That night, DIADEM was due to begin. At 8th Indian Division HQ, Harry Wilson read the two orders of the day with apprehensive interest, the first from Alexander, the second from General Leese. They were to go forward with the light of battle in their eyes. They outnumbered the enemy and had considerable superiority in guns and armour. The Allies were now ready for the great assault on Nazi-occupied Europe, and in Italy they had the honour of striking the first blow.

After dinner, the division's brigade major gathered the HQ together outside the officers' mess tent and, having spread out a large map against a tree, told them all what was going to happen. 'Tonight,' he said, 'we're attacking the Gustav Line across the River Rapido here. We'll have the Poles and the 4th Div on our right and French troops on our left. The Fifth Army are making a push at the same time. This is the first blow of the second front. It will be closely followed by the invasion of Western Europe and a general attack by the Russians.' Wilson listened attentively as he then went through the details of their own part in this massive assault, the number of guns, the timings of the barrage and their attack across the river into the 'Liri Appendix', a narrow finger of land at the southern side of the valley where the Liri and Garigliano ran parallel to one another. Vickers heavy machine guns would be dug in ready to keep the enemy's heads down. 'So if you hear close machine-gun fire,' the brigade major added, 'you'll know it'll be our fellows pumping lead into this Appendix. You'll hear Bofors, too.' At daylight, they would also have a mass of aircraft overhead, many flying standing patrols and linked by radio to forward controllers on the ground. This was a comparatively new development and these RAF ground controllers, operating with an army forward observation officer, were known as 'Rover Davids'. The brigade major paused, looked at his map, and then, with a dry smile, said, 'We hope that will do the trick.'

For the Allied commanders it was a time for last-minute checks, visits to see the troops – and to wait. General Clark worked on dispatches until 9 a.m. then flew off in his Cub to visit the 36th T-Patchers at their encampment at Qualiano near Naples, where he faced over 1,000 men from the division, all lined up for his visit. He was there to present a number of gallantry medals and not least the Distinguished Service Medal to his former War College teacher, General Fred Walker – the man who had been privately blaming Clark for the fiasco of the Rapido crossing in January. Now, though, the T-Patchers were Clark's army reserve, to be committed whenever and wherever he felt they were needed in the coming battle.

If Clark was nervous, he wasn't letting on, but there were signs that he was feeling a little on edge. His prickliness tended to come to the fore when the pressure was on. Back on 5 May – four days after his forty-eighth birthday – he'd become riled after Alexander had made a visit to the Anzio bridgehead, from where the US-led VI Corps was to make its breakout once the southern front had been sufficiently broken in the forthcoming battle. There Alexander had spoken with Truscott, and after hearing the VI Corps commander's plans had suggested he should be concentrating on only one course of action, namely to spearhead north-eastwards towards Cisterna, Cori and Valmontone, as had been previously agreed with Clark and all concerned. Truscott then informed Clark of this conversation. Outraged, Clark rang Alexander's HQ and demanded to speak to the C-in-C. 'I told Alexander', noted Clark in his diary, 'that I resented deeply his issuing any instructions to my subordinates.'

Alexander, by now used to these flare-ups of oversensitiveness, assured him he had not intended to undermine his authority in any way, and that he had merely made the point lightly in the course of his conversation with Truscott, gently reminding Clark that he was only telling Truscott what had already been agreed. It seemed to be what the American wanted to hear. 'This is a small matter,' Clark noted later, his honour sated and his feathers smoothed once more, 'but it is as well that I let him know now, as I have in the past, that he will deal directly with me and never with a subordinate.' Neither this tendency to overreact nor his ambition mattered particularly – that is, so long as it did not cloud his military judgement.

At his Tactical HQ, an encampment near Venafro, General Oliver Leese was understandably apprehensive as this was his first battle since taking over Eighth Army; he was impatient for the battle to begin, but none the less quietly confident. He had more than 253,000 men under his command. Ammunition and petrol were ready in dumps at the front line. Every participating soldier had been briefed on the battle and the role they were expected to play. And from his manic tours around the front, his men all seemed to be in good heart. 'It has been a vast endeavour and it will be a huge battle,' he wrote to his wife. 'All we want is fine weather and a bit of luck.'

As the evening shadows lengthened, infantrymen along the front furtively began to move up to their start lines and forming-up positions. In the Liri Valley men were uncovering assault boats and bridging parties were moving trucks of Bailey bridge sections forward, while other sappers were reeling out long lines of white marker tape that would guide the troops in the dark towards specific river crossings.

Dusk soon gave way to the darkness of night, and the first desultory shelling of Cassino began just as it had every night for weeks. Partly as cover, and partly to give the impression that this was just like any other evening along the front, it gradually died out, so that at ten o'clock, when General Leese sat down to write to his wife, the front seemed eerily quiet. 'In sixty minutes,' he scrawled on the thick blue writing paper which Margie had sent out to him, 'hell will be let loose, the whole way from Monte Cairo to the sea. At 11 p.m., 11 May, 2,000 guns will burst forth.' There were, in fact, 1,600 guns: 1,000 supporting Eighth Army in the Liri Valley and 600 for Fifth Army. It had, Leese added, been a lovely day, and was now a glorious night. A sweeping, crushing victory promised untold riches, yet defeat would not only be a blow to Allied chances of success when they shortly launched the invasion of northern France but would also wreck the future of the Italian campaign, and with it British credibility in particular. No wonder General Leese was counting down the minutes.

That same day, 11 May, was Major Georg Zellner's thirty-ninth birthday. Still in his basement bunker in Belmonte, it had not been a joyous one, although his staff had tried their best, showing him a lot of warm-heartedness and, touchingly, bringing him some mountain flowers.

No post had arrived for him that evening, which depressed him. 'Already I'm really sad,' he jotted. 'The whole day I've felt a strange tension.' The ration cart had delivered two bottles of Sekt, however, so they'd just opened them and were about to take their first drink when the sky erupted. 'Is the enemy attacking?' he wondered. 'Companies are alerted. It's weird. The firing is increasing. The mule is supposed to go back, but how? We are nervous about everything but composed. We drink the Sekt anyway.'

A little to the south, in the ruins of Cassino and at just before 11 p.m.,

Jupp Klein had been standing beside the remains of the Hotel des Roses talking to a corporal. Now back from their rest at Castrocielo, they had returned to much ribbing from the paratrooper infantry sharing this dubious billet about having been fattened up at their expense. Now, standing outside in the night air, Klein was discussing the latest tunnelling they were to undertake when suddenly the sky lit up as bright as day and a moment later shells screamed overhead. Immediately he understood that the sheer scale of the barrage could only mean one thing: the offensive had started – and sooner than any of them had expected.

Watching the barrage from the safety of Monte Trocchio, behind the Allied lines, was Lieutenant Ted Wyke-Smith, a sapper in the 281st Field Park Company of 78th Division Royal Engineers. Commanding a bridging unit, his job was to be among the division's spearhead as they advanced once the initial breakthrough had been made by the 4th Infantry and 8th Indian Divisions, and build Bailey bridges over the numerous rivers and anti-tank ditches that barred the Allied progress. Wyke-Smith had been sitting in his tented dugout listening to nightingales in the trees nearby when the guns opened fire. 'It was terrific,' he commented 'The noise was incredible and even where we were several miles behind the lines, the ground trembled.' Curiously, however, the nightingales began singing again shortly after. 'It was most extraordinary,' said Ted, 'a concerto of nightingales and cannons.'

'11pm – H-Hour of D-Day,' noted Captain Klaus Huebner at the foot of Monte Damiano. 'Huge leaping sheets of bright flashes illuminate the entire Garigliano Valley and are followed by the thunderous roar of a thousand cannons.' Their stone house was rocking from the blast and the roar of the guns was so loud that Huebner found himself shouting at the man standing next to him and still couldn't be heard. Venturing out of the house, he saw sheets of flame from a little way to the east down by the river, while the hills to the north were spattered with phosphorous bursts that lit up the entire horizon. He really didn't see how the Germans could possibly withstand much of this.

His division, the 88th Blue Devils, were among the first attacking alongside the 85th Custermen, even newer to the front and now heading into battle for the first time. None of the French and American troops of Fifth Army had any rivers to cross but they faced the formidable obstacles of the mountains none the less, while barrages, no matter how devastating to hear and witness, were never quite as effective as hoped.

The 349th Infantry were attacking through the centre, along the Ausente Valley, although Klaus Huebner's 3rd Battalion were in reserve, ready to be thrown in when needed. He had finally got his head down at 4 a.m. for a couple of hours' sleep, the guns still booming in his half-consciousness. At 7 a.m., he clambered up to the OP. 'We have spectator seats,' he noted. 'Through field glasses I can clearly see French tanks rumbling into Castelforte on our right.' These were with the 3ème Division Algérienne, attacking from the south-east while the mountain-trained 4ème Division Marocaine de Montagne tried to work their way round through the mountains and attack from the north. The plan was to pinch out this long-standing thorn in the Allies' side in a large pincer move. With his binoculars glued to his face, Huebner saw a tank fire, hitting a building which burst into flames. Then a self-propelled gun began burning too. Infantry rushed forward, surrounding the next objective, until disappearing behind the fog of war. 'We sit and wait,' he jotted. 'I do nothing. All the mountains in front of us are enveloped in a haze of smoke. Artillery fire never stops. I have no idea how our troops are progressing.'

In fact, they were not progressing quite as well as hoped. All along the southernmost part of the front the Americans and French were coming up against a wall of enemy fire and finding it almost impossible to make much headway. The 2ème Division Marocaine had managed to take the heights of Monte Faito, but other objectives had not been won, as they had been confronted with German flamethrowers as well as the usual cocktail of heavy mortar and machine-gun fire.

Meanwhile, in the Liri Valley, barely anything had gone right. After the warm day and suddenly cool night, river mists had developed along the River Garigliano – just as they had done when the T-Patchers had made their crossings – and then mingled with the intense smoke caused by the biggest barrage yet of the war. Despite weeks of endlessly practising river crossings over and over, incredibly, and especially since there was the precedent of the T-Patchers, no one in Eighth Army had considered the effect the smoke from the guns might have on visibility in this river valley surrounded by mountains. Equally incomprehensible was the planners' failure to appreciate just how strong the current would be in the Rapido. Many of those crossing in assault boats were swept away, while others were sunk by machine-gun fire and mortars. Nor had there been any close fire support from the armour. As Tuker had pointed out back in February, the main reason for failing to get across the river successfully in January had been the want of the right plan; history was repeating itself now. The sappers who had been due to lay six all-important Bailey bridges under the light of the moon had found the fog as thick as the worst kind of London pea-souper. Only by enormous ingenuity was the first Class 40 bridge, code-named 'Oxford', successfully built by 7.30 a.m. on the morning of the 12th. Another, 'Plymouth', a Class 30, was open for business by 10 a.m., but attempts to build the others failed amid appalling fog and enemy fire.

Nor had the Poles fared much better. They had not launched their assault until 1 a.m., two hours after the barrage had opened up and some time after 8th Indian and 4th Divisions had attacked in the valley below. As a result, the Fallschirmjäger were fully alert to what was going on. Although the Poles reached their first objectives, they were soon pinned down by positions that had been substantially improved since February. What's more, although few in number, the Fallschirmjäger were now equipped with more machine guns, mortars and flamethrowers than they had had three months earlier. And, like the Red Bulls and 4th Indians before them, the Poles were struggling to get reinforcements and further supplies forward quickly enough.

Lejtnant Władek Rubnikowicz and the 12th Podolski Recce Regiment, from their positions looking across the Colle d'Onofrio towards the abbey, had been given the task of sending out reconnaissance parties across no-man's-land, while the main force attacked towards Albaneta and along the Snakeshead and Castellone Ridges. It was the first time they had ventured from their positions, and although they were not part of the main attack they had still come under heavy enemy machine-gun and mortar fire, while on the ridges above them casualties had begun to mount. Worryingly so.

CHAPTER 32

Breakthrough in the Mountains

No matter how much the fog of war was hindering Eighth Army in the Liri Valley, the Germans were even more in the dark. At 9.15 a.m. on the morning of 11 May at AOK 10 headquarters, Generalmajor Fritz Wentzell, von Vietinghoff's Chief of Staff, spoke to Kesselring. 'There is', he told the field marshal, 'nothing special going on with us.' Later that morning, Oberst Dietrich Beelitz, one of Kesselring's staff officers at Armeegruppe C, repeated the line. 'We have nothing special to report,' he told his opposite number at AOK 10, before they discussed Kesselring's conviction that the Allies appeared to be planning landings as far north as Livorno on the Tuscan coast.

Certainly, AOK 10 remained in a parlous state after the pummelling and battering it had received so far this year. Only 1. Fallschirmjäger-Division was considered fit for any offensive task, even though at just 8 per cent of its strength it self-evidently was no such thing. Five divisions were deemed fit for limited offensive tasks and a further three, including the 44. H-und-D, now in the Liri Valley, were reckoned capable of defensive operations only. The Germans' fighting strength on 10 May was just 81,932, while that of AOK 14 was 76,873. The Allies now had 602,618 fighting troops, with both Fifth Army and Eighth Army sharing 300,000 each. This gave Alexander an advantage of more like 3.8 to one, rather than the three to one he had originally demanded. In terms of the number of artillery pieces and armoured fighting vehicles the ratio was considerably higher, while Allied air forces dominated the skies with overwhelming superiority. DIADEM was, by some margin, the largest single operation yet mounted by the Allies in the war. And it was about to swing into German forces ill-trained and ill-prepared for such an immense weight of fire.

It was also Allied air superiority that had prevented the Luftwaffe from carrying out anything but the sparsest of aerial reconnaissance, while carefully executed deception plans, including amphibious assault exercises in the Bay of Salerno, had convinced Kesselring of his view that more Allied amphibious assaults further up the peninsula were in the offing. There were a number of reasons for Alexander now to be very grateful for the Anzio operation, but one of them was that it had played into Kesselring's paranoia about Allied outflanking operations from the sea; the German commander had also thought the Allies might try an airborne assault in the Liri Valley near Frosinone. German intelligence further suggested that the Allies had far more troops in reserve and less at the front than was the reality, which had convinced Kesselring that a major Allied attack was not imminent.

This total misreading of Allied intentions had had two major consequences. The first was the absence of a number of senior commanders all at once. Not only was von Senger away, so too was his Chief of Staff, Oberst Hans-Georg Schmidt von Altenstadt, an astonishingly crass decision. Incredibly, though, so too was von Vietinghoff, the AOK 10 commander, who had also gone on leave and left Wentzell holding the fort. Even if the Allies hadn't been launching DIADEM, to have had three such important men absent from the front at the same time was incredibly reckless. The second consequence lay with Kesselring's deployment of his forces. He'd instigated a fairly major regrouping at the beginning of May, partly to give battered divisions a chance to draw breath but mainly to ensure that he had enough reserves should the Allies launch more landings as he suspected they would. As a result, the Gustav Line was relatively thinly defended, with most of his reserves either to the north or around Rome. The Cassino front had also seen a major shift of forces. Feurstein's LI Gebirgs-Armeekorps had taken command of both the Cassino and Liri Valley sectors, with the 44. H-und-D and 1. Fallschirmjäger switched into his corps, while von Senger retained only 71. Division and 94. Division to the south, with 15. Panzergrenadier in reserve. Von Vietinghoff had one regiment of Baade's 90. Panzergrenadier in reserve, while the rest of the division was in AOK 14's reserve. Even those units in and around Rome were split up too. The result was that von Senger, by far the most experienced corps commander in the theatre and with intimate knowledge of the Cassino sector, now had a much-reduced command. Nor had these regroupings finished: because of the Allied mastery of the air movement by day had been all but impossible, so moving his units about had taken far longer than would have been the case a short while earlier when the skies had been leaden and flying at a minimum.

The 71. Werfer-Regiment, for example, had been withdrawn from the front line at the end of April and sent to Supino, a small village nestling at the foot of the Lepini Mountains thirty-five miles down the Liri Valley from Cassino. They'd been taken out of 15. Panzergrenadier-Division and attached to Baade's AOK 10 Reserve. Oberleutnant Hans Golda and his fellow officers had set themselves up in a decent apartment, old uniforms had been replaced or repaired, plenty of drink, cigarettes and food had been provided, and during the day they had carried out training drills and other exercise. 'The jaded Cassino fighters', he noted, 'became happy soldiers again!'

The previous evening, 11 May, Golda had heard a dull crumping to the south and the sky was lit up and flickering. He went to bed feeling restless and sure enough, in the middle of the night he was rung by the CO, Major Timpke, who told him the battle had begun and that they were to get going to the front right away. 'Calmly and seriously we got ready to march,' he noted. 'Our recovery time had been cut short abruptly after two weeks.' They were back near Pignataro by dusk on Friday, 12 May; there could be no movement in the middle of the day. Enemy shells were screaming over as Golda reported to the command post. There he was issued with fresh maps and told to set up his battery in new positions between the village and the town of Pontecorvo, which lay on the Hitler Line. Back they clambered into their vehicles and off they went. 'We were driving into a boiling witches' cauldron,' noted Golda. 'The night was pitch-dark. Only the flash of the artillery broke through. The crashing, roaring, screaming was in front of us at first then all around us.' At one point they had to drive round an enormous crater and Golda was thinking that if their ammunition was hit there wouldn't be a piece of any of them left. 'We'd be blown to pieces,' he added. 'That must be a nice death.' But they made it in one piece, the gunners taking up their positions, the ammunition safely stored, and prepared bunkers pretty well constructed.

How long they'd be there, Golda wasn't sure. Before morning, reports had reached him that the enemy were across the Liri and that tanks were now in Pignataro. He and his men were in the very heart of the storm.

Yet while Golda and 71. Werfer-Regiment had received their orders and moved swiftly without a hitch, chaos had reigned across the German command, partly because of missing commanders but also because of the dislocation caused by Allied air forces. Flying Fortresses hammered Kesselring's headquarters at Monte Soratte causing extensive damage, while further heavies from Foggia plastered AOK 10's headquarters at Avezzano, destroying the Operations Branch offices and cutting all telephone lines in and out. For most of the 12th and into 13 May, AOK 10 was cut off and blind. An advanced headquarters was hurriedly sent to Frosinone to share digs with XIV Panzerkorps, but this was far from ideal. Heidrich's headquarters was heavily bombed too, as were those of the 44. Hoch-und Deutschmeister-Division and 15. Panzergrenadier-Division, now in the Liri Valley even though Zellner's battalion was still at Belmonte to the north. Signals at all these headquarters were severely disrupted.

In Cassino, meanwhile, the Fallschirmjäger had felt somewhat cut off from the battle raging on the mountain above and to the south. The town, for the moment, had been spared. Feldwebel Rudolf Donth found the waiting quite nerve-racking; they'd been expecting an attack but nothing came except ever more smoke mortars, which covered the shattered remains in a ghoulish shroud of smoke. Behind Monte Trocchio, however, where the largest proportion of British guns were dug in, Captain Mike Doble had been up all that first night, walking from gun pit to gun pit. As far as he was concerned, it had all gone very well. At 5.30 a.m. he'd returned to his room in the farmhouse where he was billeted, washed and shaved, then headed back to the CP, where the gunners were continuing to blast the Liri Valley. News trickled in. 'Infantry did not get on as expected,' he noted, 'but one or two bridges established.'

None the less, progress was being made. General Alexander sent his first signal back early on the afternoon of 12 May. 'I saw both army commanders this morning,' he told General Brooke, 'and they are reasonably satisfied with the opening stages of the battle, but there is no doubt that the Germans intend to fight for every yard and that the next few days will see some extremely bitter and severe fighting.'

Leese was fairly sanguine and that morning found a moment to write a note to his beloved wife, Margie. 'There is a vast smoke screen like a yellow London fog over the battle field,' he scribbled, 'and drifting back to Tac HQ.' The Poles were fighting well, he told her, but he was worried about Anders. 'I shall have to ensure that Anders gets to bed tonight,' he added. 'I suspect he was up most of last night.' Leese was very much a disciple of his predecessor, Montgomery, who strongly believed that no matter what was going on, generals needed their sleep to ensure their minds were kept keen and fresh. Leese had served under Montgomery in North Africa and Sicily – and Italy – as one of his corps commanders and had observed his chief closely. Informality with the troops, the personal touch, as well as a carefully cultivated image that made him stand out – these were all lessons Leese had absorbed. His appearance, for example, was often most unbecoming for an army general; unlike the sartorial Alexander, he tended to wear baggy corduroy breeches and big sweaters, the effect of which was exaggerated by his large frame; like Clark, he was a tall man, some six foot three. Although prone to brief outbursts of bad temper and irritability, for the most part he was good-humoured, informal, and took great care of his men. His Tactical HQ was always a lively and entertaining place to be. A cricket-obsessed Old Etonian, Leese was also known for his mild eccentricities of behaviour and for his love of the ridiculous. He had recently introduced 'Eighth Army French', which also helped lighten the atmosphere. He'd developed this during his conversations with General Anders, who spoke English poorly, while Leese spoke no Polish at all. The solution was for both of them to speak bad French. When Anders had asked for more guns, Leese told him there was '*non beaucoup de chambre*' – not enough room. At this, Anders had fallen about laughing.

In the early evening of 12 May, however, Leese needed all his charm to calm the Polish commander down after their disappointing start at Monte Cassino. The Carpathian Division had captured Point 593 swiftly but had been unable to push much further; the attack on Albaneta had also been bloodily repulsed. A troop of Sherman tanks that had climbed up the Cavendish Road had also all been knocked out by mines, and twenty minesweeping engineers killed or taken prisoner. Anders had initially planned to renew his attack at 3 p.m. on the 12th but it became increasingly obvious to him that he needed to pause and regroup first. 'It was easier to capture some objectives', he noted, 'than to hold them.' That was nothing less than the truth up on Monte Cassino. When Leese saw him that evening, Anders was planning to have another crack that night, but Leese told him to hold off for twenty-hours to allow more supplies – and manpower – to reach the mountain. Reluctantly, Anders agreed. So far the attack had cost the Poles 1,800 casualties. 'It is tough country,' Leese had added in his letter to his wife, 'and it will take time.'

Time, however, was not a luxury they had much of. Operation OVERLORD was due to launch on 5 June, so in just three weeks' time. The cross-Channel invasion had been towering over the Italian campaign ever since it had been launched the previous September and was still casting a shadow now, because the psychological advantage of taking Rome before D-Day was enormous. Battles very rarely went to plan, as Alexander was well aware, and the start was often the hardest part because that was when the enemy's defences were strongest. Patience – and faith – was needed, but the clock was ticking inexorably. Balance was a vital ingredient too: sufficient weight of arms across the attacking front to be able to swiftly respond to the unexpected. Alexander, just as he'd planned, had that balance, which augured well. None the less, in Eighth Army's sector the news on the morning of 13 May was only slightly more encouraging. By great endeavour, another Bailey bridge, 'Amazon', a Class 40, had been built across the Rapido just to the south of Cassino. The three bridges now open were not enough, but it did mean that bridgeheads were being slowly but surely established on the far side of the river. Progress, albeit slow, was being made.

At 8th Indian HQ, Harry Wilson had been furiously deciphering messages and picking up snippets of news as they trickled in. 'Phew!' a signalman reported from the Liri Appendix where the 8th Indians were crossing. 'It's fair hell down there – mortar bombs falling like hailstones. We crossed with the Argylls. Jerry was waiting for them – the place was a nest of MGs. They've lost thirty men already.' Wilson could hear the 'moaning minnies' of Hans Golda's Nebelwerfers and the never-ending boom of their own 25-pounders. More news: the Guards were pushing on at Cassino. Plenty of Allied fighters had been over, as promised; that had been encouraging. At the end of the day, though, Wilson was aware that progress was not being made as swiftly as had been hoped. 'We're suffering', he noted waggishly, 'from a bad dose of appendicitis.'

General Mark Clark, meanwhile, had spent the first half of the morning of 13 May reading reports and studying maps, then set off to tour his units along the front. Visiting the CP of 85th Division, he learned that in the first thirty-six hours of battle the new boys had suffered 956 reported casualties – a heavy toll for one division. The Blue Devils, meanwhile, had been attacking north of Minturno and south of the Ausente Valley – the triangular-shaped mass of hills that 5th Division had never quite managed to clear earlier in the year. Captain Klaus Huebner and 3rd Battalion of the 349th had been ordered to move up to the village of Tufo, just to the west of Minturno, on the evening of the 12th. Huebner had headed up in his jeep to find the single road thick with American traffic. Ammunition trucks, water jeeps, ambulances, mules and infantry all competed for space. He and his team had spent the night there, then on the morning of the 13th had taken the single road towards Santa Maria Infante, following it as it wound its way along a low ridgeline towards the village. The 351st Infantry were fighting there, and Huebner could hear the sounds of fierce combat, although he was curious as to why there appeared to be no German shellfire coming over. The reason was the breakdown in communications: German radios were struggling to function properly and so the infantry was unable to call in the artillery. As in Tufo, the single-track road was clogged. Jeeps loaded with wounded sped by, showering them with clouds of dust. Columns of dishevelled prisoners tramped past, dusty, wounded and exhausted.

It was midday when 3rd Battalion's column stopped by a walled cemetery a couple of miles south of Santa Maria Infante. The battalion was told to disperse into the fields opposite, but almost immediately the men began detonating mines; they had not realized they'd been deployed into a minefield. Huebner was called to treat a man who'd just had his foot blown off at the ankle. Morphine, an emergency dressing, then the wounded man was strapped to a jeep which sped off. Huebner narrowly missed standing on several mines himself, noticing the detonators sticking up in the nick of time. Orders arrived: they were not to push on into Santa Maria Infante but instead cross down into the valley to the west of the ridgeline and then start to climb Monte Civita, a 1,600-foot-high first peak in the mighty Petrella massif of the Aurunci Mountains, a chain that ran south from Esperia to the coastal plain west of Minturno. On Monte Civita the Germans had brought up a regiment of pack artillery, and these were now firing down on to Santa Maria Infante and the road that ran along the ridgeline. While the second team of medics followed the infantry, Huebner and his men were to stay where they were for the time being.

Later in the afternoon, Shermans rumbled forward only to come under intense fire from enemy guns on Monte Civita. Huebner watched one get hit and then burst into flames, killing all inside. Then the rest were hit too, one tank after another; jammed toe-to-tail on the road they were sitting ducks. 'A passing jeep receives a direct hit and disintegrates in a cloud of smoke and dust,' wrote Huebner. 'Whining shrapnel fills the air, and chunks of hot metal land in my gully. We are swamped with casualties occurring directly in front of us. Wounded jump out of burning vehicles and run to us. Others crawl.' Huebner and his team had never been busier; there were more wounded than they could cope with. Later, another barrage of shells screamed in on the ridge as he'd been trying to head up the road to use a radio to contact the battalion. With each one, Huebner hit the deck then scrambled to his feet again. Then he heard another one coming so loud it seemed to be heading directly for him. Thinking his last moments had arrived, he leaped off the road and on to the sloping meadow as a hiss and a blast of heat fizzed over him and exploded, knocking him to the ground. To his amazement, he'd not been touched. Bracing his hands to get up again, he then very nearly pressed down on a mine buried directly in front of him. He'd been very lucky.

While Klaus Huebner had been dicing with death, General Clark had hurried over to see Général Juin at the CEF's HQ. There, however, the news was dramatically better, as 2ème Division Marocaine had captured the vital Monte Maio, which towered over the Ausente Valley and the town of Ausonia, first targeted by X Corps back in January. Generalmajor Wilhelm Raapke, the commander of 71. Division, and his staff had considered this area of high peaks completely impassable to infantry and so it had been only lightly held. But, using pack mules, the Moroccans had not only climbed straight up but had done so with impressive speed. The Germans had been stunned, their confusion made worse because radio links between division and troops in the mountains were still faulty and so artillery support could not be effectively brought down on the French. The CEF's triumph on Monte Maio, however, was a reminder, once again, of what might have been had Fifth Army attacked between Castellone and Monte Cairo back in February.

Even better for Fifth Army, the French 1ème Division had pushed northwards and looked set to take Sant'Ambrogio and Sant'Apollinare; the Germans had not even been aware that this purely French division existed. Juin's staff reckoned they'd have more than 1,000 German prisoners in the bag by nightfall. Castelforte, the stubborn thorn that had plagued the Allies since January, had also been pinched out.

This meant that on the evening of 13 May, Clark was in a position to act swiftly and decisively. Having realized that the Germans opposite the French were in complete disarray, the moment he got back to his CP he issued orders to Keyes to speed up attacks regardless of previous plans or casualties; he'd not been impressed with the meal 88th Division was making of capturing Santa Maria Infante, and told Keyes to impress upon the Blue Devils the needed for aggressive and determined action. He wanted them to attack Monte Civita that night, two miles west of Santa Maria Infante, from where the enemy artillery was being directed at the village. Taking Civita would also give the Blue Devils a springboard to push on to the village of Spigno, a few miles to the north.

Captain Huebner had meanwhile reached the rest of his battalion on the other side of the valley, having eventually found his guide to take him across. The young GI had been in a terrible state, however. 'The poor fellow', noted Huebner, 'shakes all over, sobs, and is in a severe state of anxiety.' Huebner eventually managed to calm him down and they set off on foot, down the side of the ridge from the cemetery and across the couple of miles of open valley. They'd dash and dodge a short stretch, take cover, pause and suss out the next stretch, then make another run for it. By skipping and ducking their way, they safely made it to the far side and to the foot of Monte Civita. No sooner had he reached the forward troops than Huebner began frantically tending the wounded once more as air-bursts exploded above and around them. Clark's orders to Keyes had been relayed all the way down to their battalion: they were to climb Monte Civita that night and surprise the enemy at dawn. Huebner wasn't part of the assault; instead, he tended the wounded until midnight. Finally, at 1 a.m., with litter crews having collected all the patched-up men, he dug a slit trench and was so exhausted he almost fell into it. 'My first day of actual fighting lies behind me,' he jotted. 'I shall never forget it.'

After the previous day, on which 88th Division had allowed themselves to become bogged down at Santa Maria Infante, they successfully stormed Monte Civita that morning, Sunday, 14 May, surprising the troublesome German mountain artillery unit and capturing twenty-eight enemy guns. That afternoon, Santa Maria Infante, the latest village to have been utterly obliterated, was taken too. On the Americans' right the French were also continuing their extraordinary advance. On the 14th they broke into the Ausente Valley and captured Ausonia, a key town, before pushing on towards Esperia, which nestled beneath Monte d'Oro at the southern edge of the Liri. And as they retreated, 71. Division became more and more separated from 94. Division, opposing the Americans. For possibly the first time since landing in Salerno, the Italian landscape was working to the Allies' advantage, for dividing the retreating Germans was the giant Petrella massif. At its heart was Monte Petrella itself, 4,500 feet high and surrounded by similar-sized giants. These formed the central block of the Aurunci Mountains and were around ten miles wide and eight deep; to the north was the Liri Valley, while to the south was the shallow coastal plain along which the Via Appia, Highway 7, ran. The Germans had not had the time or manpower to prepare any positions up there, but the east-facing ridge, overlooking Spigno and the Ausente Valley and running roughly north–south, had been earmarked as the so-called Dora Position. By dusk on the 15th, the only German troops on the Petrella massif were half a company of pioneers and an Ost-Kompanie – conscripts from eastern Europe. Oberst von Altenstadt, Chief of Staff of XIV Panzerkorps, had earlier asked AOK 10 whether any Gebirgsjäger – mountain troops – could be hurriedly sent over, but was told that evening that a decision about this had yet to be made. In the meantime, General Steinmetz of 94. Division had been ordered by Kesselring to hurriedly send some of his other troops up, but this was impossible because all his units had their hands full fighting the Custermen along the coast and the Blue Devils at the southern end of the massif.

In fact, Monday, 15 May proved to be an even better day for Clark's forces. Realizing that the initiative now firmly lay with his men, he recognized that the situation had to be exploited at full throttle. 'I have directed Keyes', Clark noted in his diary, 'to push with all the energy and speed he can muster from Spigno directly across the mountains to Itri.' The town was eight miles from Monte Civita and divided by the southern wall of the Petrella massif. Once again, the French and the new boys of the 88th Blue Devils were making a nonsense of those earlier concerns about operating around the high peaks of Monte Cairo.

The entire right-hand, southern flank of AOK 10 had now been blown right open, the Gustav Line smashed, and the two German divisions, 71. and 94., left in total disarray and split wide apart. There was no doubt now that the battle along this stretch of the front had been lost by AOK 10; it might grind on for some days longer, but with the collapse of the southern flank, whatever action they fought in and around Cassino would only delay the inevitable and lead to further catastrophic casualties. Rather, as the Allies were showing only too clearly, it was better to fight with two armies side by side than have them split up into penny packets. The time had come to pull AOK 10 and AOK 14 back together behind the Caesar position, where they could regain their balance and hold a continuous line once more.

Needless to say, however, Kesselring was entirely blind to such a suggestion. He'd discovered that General Steinmetz had not sent troops up on to the Petrella massif and was furious when he found out that his orders had been disobeyed; but he was not on the spot and by 15 May, 94. Division had already been reduced to 40 per cent of the numbers it had had on 11 May, and it had been badly understrength even then. 'I always say,' Oberst Beelitz, one of Kesselring's staff officers commented on 11 May, 'you can prepare for 100 cases and then, when you step out of the commander's tent, the 101st case is given.' He'd pithily put his finger on the nub of the matter. Because Kesselring zealously adhered to Hitler's demand never to give a yard, his troops were far too thinly stretched. His response to crises had always been to plug gaps and take from Peter to feed Paul. At 11.30 p.m. on the 15th Kesselring spoke with von Vietinghoff, who was now back at the front. Von Vietinghoff told him he had already ordered 5. Gebirgsjäger-Division to hurriedly send five rifle and two Pionier companies south to help in the Aurunci Mountains. Another battalion from 15. Panzergrenadier had also been ordered to Esperia. None of these moves made any military sense whatsoever. Allied command errors and misjudgements had papered over this strategy in the battles around Cassino earlier in the year, but Kesselring was facing a different opposition now: one reinvigorated and with all assets being brought to bear.

Quite sensibly, General Hartmann, von Senger's stand-in, had, the previous day, 14 May, ordered 71. and 94. Divisione to pull back to the Dora Position, with the mighty Petrella massif as its ramparts. At the same time, he asked to be allowed to withdraw the rest of XIV Panzerkorps behind the Hitler Line, now renamed the Senger Line in case it was eventually overrun; after all, no defensive position bearing the Führer's name could be allowed to be lost to the enemy. Kesselring, predictably, refused to allow either withdrawal, although by the 15th it was already too late to save either of the two divisions facing the Americans and the French. Instead, Kesselring began splitting up his reserve divisions and placing them in penny packets all along the line. The reconnaissance battalion of

15. Panzergrenadier was hurriedly flung against the French and so too was a Panzergrenadier regiment of 90. Division, thrown in against the 2ème Division Marocaine. The grenadiers did manage to briefly push the Moroccans back but were not strong enough to exploit this brief success. In other words, it was a complete waste of time. And lives.

Meanwhile, the British XIII Corps were still struggling to make much headway in the Liri Valley. Only by nightfall on the 14th was the full quota of nine pre-planned Bailey bridges fully completed, but even these represented major bottlenecks through which men and materiel had to pass – bottlenecks that provided rich pickings for enemy fire. While it had been 8th Indian and 4th Division that had been given the job of leading the assault across the river, the 78th Battleaxe and 6th Armoured Divisions had been held in reserve. On Monday, 15 May, however, Leese and his XIII Corps commander, Lieutenant-General Sidney Kirkman, decided the time had come to send 78th Division into the breach in an attack to be combined with the Poles' second assault on Monte Cassino. Unfortunately, though, traffic congestion, along with German mines and concentrated shelling, ensured that 78th Division was unable to cross the river in time – and so the attack was postponed until the morning of 16 May. The Poles were to launch their renewed attack on the morning of the 17th, while also reaching the line was the Canadian Corps, recently created from the Canadian 5th Armoured Division, which had reached the Mediterranean back in November, and 1st Infantry Division, which had been in Italy since September the previous year. They were due to pass through 8th Indian Division on the southern side of the Liri Valley, most likely on 17 May like the Poles.

Among those now arriving at the front were the Seaforth Highlanders of Canada, who, even as late as 12 May, had still been training in the mountains of Molise near Campobasso, far to the south and a part of southern Italy they'd fought through the previous October. Major the Reverend Roy Durnford, the Seaforths' padre, had rather enjoyed the journey, except for an hour's wait after the truck he'd been in had broken its rear axle; they'd eventually been towed the last stretch to Caserta. There they'd remained for a further four days until moving up to the front on the 16th. 'Off at 10am,' noted Durnford. 'Lovely valleys and mountains and rivers. Shades of green. Wild flowers. Endless traffic of the Big Push.' They'd also passed vast ammunition dumps and mountains of stores and then, as they neared Venafro and were now within shouting distance of the front, the tempo of war began to dramatically increase. The new Battalion HQ near Mignano was reached at about 6 p.m. Durnford pitched his tent, ate some supper then retired, busily writing letters 'on soldiers' problems.' As padre, he didn't just deliver church services but also provided solace, pastoral care and spiritual guidance. 'The roar of guns and aeroplanes is terrific,' he jotted in his diary between letters. 'Cassino is near at hand.'

This pause while Leese brought up reinforcements was a welcome breather for the Germans, one appreciated not least by Oberleutnant Hans Golda and his battery, although he had been reprimanded by one of his men, Gefreiter Dink. During a moment of comparative peace, Golda had spotted a rabbit hopping about not far from their position. Taking a rifle, he drew a bead and shot it dead, then proudly showed his men their next meal. Dink, however, had been appalled. 'He explained to me that I had killed one of his rabbits that he had been fattening up with a lot of effort,' noted Hans, 'and that it had been completely tame.' Needless to say, they ate the dead bunny all the same, and much enjoyed it too. That evening, 15 May, however, their position was once again under fire from heavy-calibre shells. He and his men could only cower in the corners, staring at the roof. 'After every hit', noted Golda, 'the whole bunker shook like a ship.'

A few miles to the north at Belmonte, Georg Zellner and his battalion were still holding their narrow stretch of the Secco Valley. Opposite them were the New Zealanders, now in X Corps, and although this stretch of the line was not part of the main thrust of the attack the Kiwis were still keeping up the pressure. 'Planes and crashing of bombs,' noted Zellner. 'We can't get out of our bunker.' Every time a shell whistled through the air towards them he wondered whether it was their turn to get a direct hit. His nerves were stretched, and he was feeling as miserable as he had done four days earlier on his birthday. The early sounds of summer – the nightingales singing, insects buzzing – had gone. 'Death is creeping over everything,' he scrawled in his diary. 'Tonight they carried the dead down to the valley. It looked ghostly and we stood in front of our bunker watching the sad procession with heavy hearts.' Nearby, a badly wounded soldier was screaming horribly. Zellner could barely stand it any more. And to make matters worse, he'd still not received any post from home for weeks.

Meanwhile, on the Allied side of the line, it was Lieutenant Ted Wyke-Smith and his team of sappers' turn to construct their first Bailey bridge – in preparation for 78th Division's attack the following morning. Wyke-Smith had been expecting to move soon after the battle had started, so, having felt somewhat pent-up in anticipation, was relieved to finally get going. The place they needed to bridge was the River Piopetta, a tributary of the Rapido, near the hamlet of Piumarola, just north of Pignataro. Getting there was no easy matter, however. Taking his jeep, Wyke-Smith had behind him several lorries full of bridging gear, but rather than heading over 'Amazon', the nearest of the newly built bridges, they were sent on a fairly lengthy route and ended up crossing over 'Oxford' south of Sant'Angelo. Eventually, despite the detour and despite the night-time darkness, they reached the right spot. As they began unloading, shells screamed overhead and small-arms fire chattered nearby. On the far side of the river – which was only 20 yards wide – infantry had been clearing the far banks of enemy troops and laying down smokescreens to protect Wyke-Smith and his men.

Bailey bridges were a comparatively new and ingenious invention which had only been introduced the previous autumn. Prefabricated, they were transported in steel panels that could be carried by six men and which could be easily fixed together. The panels, each 10 feet wide, made up the walls of the bridge. Stood on rollers on their sides, the two walls were added to side by side, with 19-foot transoms – girders – strung between them. Once several panels had been constructed, these were pushed forward until the front began to tip over the edge of the riverbank. Then two more panels were added at the back and more transoms between them and the men pushed again, repeating the process until the bridge spanned the river. Wooden planking was then placed across the structure and the bridge was ready: a 12-foot-wide roadbed. Each type of Bailey was classified to the tonnage it could take: a Class 40 could cope with 40 tons on it at any one time; a Sherman was 30 tons, for example. By morning on the 16th, and despite a night of being almost constantly under fire, Wyke-Smith and his men had completed the task and the bridge was open to traffic. 'It was', Wyke-Smith confessed, 'very exciting, frankly.'

With this and other crossings now made, 78th Division finally launched their attack. The idea was to push through the bridgeheads made by 4th Division then wheel round northwards and cut the Via Casilina – Highway 6 as the Allies called it. This, they hoped, would isolate Cassino and give the Poles the opportunity to renew their assault on Monte Cassino itself. Meanwhile, the 1st Canadian Division, which had, like 78th Division, been held back for the second wave of the assault, also joined the battle, passing through 8th Indian Division further to the south. Slowly but surely, the Allies were now pushing the Germans back in the Liri Valley as well.

That day, Tuesday, 16 May, Unteroffizier Jupp Klein and the rest of 2. Kompanie were finally ordered out of the Hotel des Roses, just one small unit among many of Kesselring's firefighting forces hurriedly rushed forward to plug gaps. The bulk of 90. Panzergrenadier was on its way but had not yet reached the Cassino front; moving at all was extremely fraught in these days of clear skies dominated by Allied Jabos. Klein and his comrades had been ordered to accompany a section of StuGs and protect them once they had dug in. Mid-morning on the 16th, Klein led the thirty-eight men still standing in 2. Kompanie down the Via Casilina out of Cassino and towards Pignataro. The renewed Allied assault had already begun, with their artillery pounding the German positions. Despite the heavy enemy fire, he found an isolated farmhouse on a slight, shallow hill that was still held by a few infantry and which had been reinforced and converted into a kind of redoubt. The windows had been filled in to become nothing more than loopholes, the lower walls strengthened and the cellars converted into a passable bunker. Zigzagging away from either side of the house were trenches. The whole thing, Klein thought, seemed like a kind of fortress.

Even so, how much they would be able to achieve against a concerted enemy attack was uncertain. As Klein crept forward that afternoon to recce the British positions he saw, on the hill opposite just over half a mile away, a whole tank brigade boldly pointing towards them. Without further ado, he hurried back to the gunners and asked them to send an urgent message to Heidrich's headquarters warning them that his company had no anti-tank weapons whatsoever, and would be defenceless if and when the British tanks attacked. Fortunately for him and his men, the British armour did not attack either that afternoon or evening. Even better, at dusk an anti-tank crew with three Ofenrohre arrived and reported to Klein. Ofenrohre were hand-held anti-tank rocket launchers and very effective at short ranges. The men knew them as 'stovepipes'. Then, during the night, a further infantry battalion of reinforcements also joined them. These were men who had been posted from Yugoslavia, where they'd been fighting partisans, and had little battlefield experience. As if to prove a point, the battalion major immediately insisted on placing a troop of machine-gunners in a shed to the front of the farmhouse, facing the enemy. 'But the attacking tanks will cut them down at once,' Klein warned him, 'and they'll have no chance of pulling back.' The officer insisted, however. Klein could only feel sorry for these MG teams. He knew they were dead men.

The Faughs had moved up to the river, ready to cross in the early hours of 14 May and then, at 5.30 p.m. on the 16th, orders were issued: they were to attack alongside the 16th/5th Lancers and one troop of the 234th Anti-Tank Battery, with D Company on the left and Major Lawrie Franklyn-Vaile's C Company on the right. That day, Franklyn-Vaile had managed to write a note to Olive, albeit in pencil because his fountain pen had run out of ink. The weather was now suddenly very hot, he told her. All that mud had turned to dust, making driving around in an open jeep rather nightmarish; they were all covered, head to toe. Unsurprisingly, the dirt roads were becoming horrendously churned up with this colossal weight of traffic.

He had been having problems with a new officer who was a bit shaky and had struggled when they'd come under heavy shellfire. This had quickly spread to the men, so he'd felt compelled to sit openly at the side of a ditch, not once flinching as more shells screamed over; it seemed the only thing to do to try and steady the morale of the men. Despite this, later that day four men deserted, so he decided it was time for a stern talk. Gathering his entire company around him, he spoke of the 'white-livered gutless skunks' who had deserted their comrades and painted a very grim picture of what would happen to them. He told them: 'I would rather die and know my wife and daughter could hold up their heads for the rest of their lives knowing I had done my job than live disgraced and bring shame and misery on my family.' It seemed to do the trick; the NCOs told him it had hit the spot and he certainly had no more trouble. Even so, now, as they were about to go back into battle, it was a worry.

He told Olive he was looking forward to hearing more of her news and wondered how their dog Sadi was getting on. He was also now wearing the ribbon of the newly issued Italy Star medal. 'Of course, it does not mean much out here,' he added, 'but it will be nice to have when I return home.' He was feeling well and rested, he assured her. 'All my love and kisses, darling wife, to you and Valerie,' he signed off. 'Your ever devoted husband, Lawrence.'

CHAPTER 33

Monte Cassino

IN RIPI, IN THE Liri Valley, Viviana Bauco had been woken up by the opening barrage to the south. What a terrible spectacle it had seemed to her: the distant sound of the guns, the sky flickering as though sheets of lightning were crossing it and the ground trembling; they could feel it, even all these miles away. News reached them the following day, the 12th, that the great battle had begun. She prayed the Allies would be successful, but also that Ripi might be spared. It was worrying, terrifying; the uncertainty and not knowing what was really happening or what to expect gnawed at them all. 'Lord,' she wrote, 'do not abandon us!'

Yet while Viviana and her family had witnessed falling bombs and German troop movements, and were keenly aware that their village might well lie directly in the line of fire before too long, there were communities round and about that had so far been largely untouched by the fighting. In the Ausoni Mountains, for example, there were a number of small villages and farms that were still very cut off from the rest of the world and whom the terrible events that had been playing out at Cassino, thirty miles away, had passed by entirely. It was up on the verdant 1,600-foot-high mountain plain of Monte Rotondo, for example, that Pasua Pisa farmed with her family. She was twenty-eight, and had lived on the mountain all her life. They were a small community – just a few farmhouses of around ten families – although unlike most *contadini*, Pasua's family owned their own farm. This scarcely made their life any easier, however, and like most peasant farmers, everyone had to help and work long and physically demanding hours.

They were, though, largely self-sufficient up on the mountain. They grew crops, made their own wine, and reared buffalo from which they had milk and made mozzarella cheese. Once a week they went down the mountain with their donkeys to the small market town of Amaseno, a journey that took a little over an hour on the way down, but more than an hour and a half on the way back up. They didn't sell much – only what they needed to allow them to buy a few staples such as salt. Down in Amaseno, they would also take their grain to the mill and get it milled, and their grapes pressed. There was no electricity up on the mountain, nor drains. Water was collected when it rained or could be drawn with the help of a donkey from a nearby spring. On feast days they would sometimes go down into the valley; more often, they would stay on the mountain and hold a dance there.

Pasua was a beautiful young woman and had married at twenty-three, which was quite late for country girls like her. Her son, Lorenzo, had been born in her first year of married life. It was a simple existence, yet happy enough; she had known no different. For the most part, Mussolini, Fascism and national and international affairs had passed her by. Only when war arrived did she take notice, for with it came conscription: being a farmer was not a reserved occupation. Suddenly, the young men on the mountain were gone, her husband included, leaving her with their only child. Her husband had been posted to North Africa, where he had been taken prisoner by the British. Pasua had heard nothing except for a telegram informing her that he was now a prisoner of war in Canada. He might as well have been sent to the moon.

Without the young men around, life had been considerably harder: it had meant even longer hours and more work for everyone, but there had been no point complaining. Pasua, like everyone else, simply got on with the task of getting by and making sure the farm kept running. She was also lucky that her father was still alive and there to help her. Furthermore, little four-year-old Lorenzo adored him and followed him everywhere. 'He was his grandfather's shadow,' commented Pasua. Yet now, in the middle of May, even she and her small community were aware that war was coming. Distant guns boomed across the mountains. Distant guns that were getting closer by the day.

Tuesday, 17 May. The Faughs finally began their attack that morning, part of Leese's next phase of offensives in the Liri Valley and following a fifteen-minute barrage. Major Lawrie Franklyn-Vaile and his men in C Company had been lying in a sunken track for much of the night when their guns opened up. Walking between the platoons, tin hat on the back of his head and Tommy gun slung over his shoulder, he exuded calm, the morale issues of a couple of days earlier now gone, it seemed. At 7.16 a.m., with the barrage now ended, they moved off. Half an hour later, Franklyn-Vaile was walking back towards Lieutenant Douglas Room, one of his platoon commanders. He grinned at Room reassuringly and then suddenly a shell screamed in and cut him down. Room was only 5 yards from him and rushed to him immediately, but there was nothing he could do. 'I am certain he was not conscious after he had been hit and suffered no pain,' Room wrote to Olive. 'He died in a few minutes.' Everyone in the entire company was devastated; Franklyn-Vaile had seemed one of those untouchable types who would always somehow come through. 'I'm still numb about it and am very grieved,' wrote Room. 'He was such a wonderful officer and the men loved him. He understood them so well and was so wholehearted in his genuine liking for them, cheered them up and gave them courage. When things were difficult, they knew he would be there.' This war really was a brutal business.

Although the Germans in the Liri Valley were fighting stubbornly, the biggest brake on Eighth Army's advance was congestion and the canalization of troops and vehicles due to the numbers of rivers and bridges and the increasingly churned-up state of the roads and tracks being used. None the less, not only was 78th Battleaxe Division now in the battle, the Canadian 1st Division was also being moved up from the Mignano Gap. Padre Roy Durnford spent the early part of the morning checking on the companies. The boys seemed to be in good fettle. It had been December that they'd last been in battle but here they were again, about to be committed into the maelstrom once more, and Durnford knew exactly what that would mean. 'My prayers are all for them just now,' he noted. 'God give them courage to face the foe and fitness to answer the Last Call if it comes for any one of them. Amen.'

Just before 9 a.m., he clambered into a jeep and followed the men as they trundled up to the front line in trucks, already in full battle order, magazine pouches full, grenades hanging on belts and clutching weapons. Cub observation planes swept remarkably low above them, while up ahead, beyond Trocchio, the battle appeared to be one vast cloud of dust, swirling low across the mouth of the valley. The road was choked full of traffic. Jeeps weaved in and out between tanks and trucks. As they slowly rumbled forward, Durnford's eyes swept over the scenes of desolation.

'Cemetery blasted, coffins askew and at rakish angles,' he jotted. 'Cedars just stumps. Walls, church all smashed. German dead on the roadside badly mutilated and badly decomposed.' They reached the front and almost immediately Durnford was asked to go and help bury the dead on the far side of the river in the Liri Appendix – most of whom were German. With a burial party, they spent hours collecting and digging shallow graves for fifty-two who had been lying out to their immediate front. 'What a ghastly job!' he jotted. 'More about too, I'm sure.' Not until quite late did he finally manage to get some rest for the night. 'At long last,' he added, 'the stars are left to shine alone and the earth ceases to shudder. I sleep in my hollow.'

Meanwhile, General Fridolin von Senger was back in command of 14. Panzer Corps that Tuesday, 17 May. He had been shocked by what he had found. AOK 10 was still sharing his headquarters at Castelmassimo near Frosinone, so after getting himself up to speed with the situation he had hurried down to the southern part of the front towards Itri. Before he had even reached there, he came across the MG-Bataillon from the 44. Hoch-und Deutschmeister-Division frantically pulling back from yet another enemy penetration. This battalion, although part of the division holding the Liri Valley and so no longer in his corps, had been another gap-filler sent by Kesselring. He also learned that the Americans had reached Formia, ten miles further along the coast from Minturno, while that same day disaster had struck 71. Division and its reinforcements. A line of assault guns, trucks, half-tracks and panzers were pulling out of Esperia and winding their way through the valley road out of the town below Monte d'Oro. An Allied Cub spotter plane saw this tightly packed column, billowing dust as it hurriedly tried to escape; that it was being forced to do so in daylight was entirely because withdrawal had been refused earlier. Had it not been so, they could have pulled out in good order and under the safety of darkness. Instead, the spotter plane swiftly reported the nose-to-tail column and within minutes the massed artillery of 3ème Division Algérienne, some eighty-four 105mm field guns, fired concentrations directly on to the fleeing German armour. With a terrace wall on their left and a steep drop on the right, the column had nowhere to go. A holocaust followed. In moments, fifty tanks, assault guns and other armoured vehicles and trucks were annihilated and the road was left strewn with burning, mangled vehicles and a mass of incinerated corpses.

Von Senger was also dismayed to learn that his only reserve unit, 15. Panzergrenadier, which he'd earmarked for exactly the kind of split in the line that had happened between 71. and 94. Divisione, had instead been broken up and funnelled in piecemeal rather than as a whole. These penny packets had been horribly mauled already and were now streaming back to the Dora Position. Von Vietinghoff was of exactly the same mind. 'These reserves could have been used to far better effect,' he noted, 'if, instead of launching scattered and therefore useless counter-thrusts, they had been given the opportunity to prepare, without any interference, the defence of the position to which they now had to return.' This was the price being paid for having been away at such a vital time. At a conference with Kesselring and senior commanders that day, von Senger pointed out, quite reasonably, that the Gustav Line had been blown wide open and that the only course now was an orderly retreat. This could only be achieved by holding a continuous line in successive phases to the Caesar position, and possibly even beyond. Kesselring was deaf to this, however, although he had, finally, agreed with von Vietinghoff to pull back behind the Senger Line over three successive nights.

'Then we shall have to give up Cassino?' Kesselring had asked in a telephone conversation the previous evening.

'Yes,' had been von Vietinghoff's one-word reply.

That was all it had taken for the fate of this blood-soaked and accursed corner of Italy to be finally settled.

A three-night withdrawal, however, rather than over one night, made little sense, because while 1. Fallschirmjäger still held the town and Monte Cassino, most of the troops in the Liri Valley had been pushed back and were now having to fight in front of the Senger Line rather than behind it, to keep a continuous line with the troops at Cassino. The last time German soldiers had been ordered to fight in front of a defensive line, in the first half of January, they had been slaughtered. It had been the Hoch-und Deutschmeister-Division then, as it was now. And because the withdrawal from Cassino had been so pointlessly delayed, men like Oberleutnant Hans Golda had found himself stuck in open ground rather than safely behind the Senger Line. On the night of the 16th, Golda and his 8. Batterie had been ordered to move back – but only about a mile, between the Gustav and Senger Line defences. As dawn broke on the 17th they had found themselves standing in the middle of a cornfield. Their command post was an old Italian Army post, but this was no more than a poorly camouflaged shed with a shallow dugout. Sure enough, they'd not been there long when they heard an enormous crash; suddenly it was dark and they were covered in dirt and dust. Golda soon realized they had been buried alive. Frantically he and the three men with him had begun digging themselves out with such fury that their fingers bled. They had been fortunate – no one had been seriously hurt, and later that evening they had, along with the rest, moved behind the Senger Line.

As it happened, Generalleutnant Feurstein had initially ordered Heidrich to pull out on the night of 16–17 May, which was the right and sensible decision. He then, however, told him that he could continue to hold Monte Cassino for longer provided casualties were minimal. This made no sense: not for his men in the Liri Valley, now forced needlessly to fight in front of the Senger Line defences, nor for the beleaguered paratroopers. What could possibly be achieved by remaining there any longer? Before being deployed to Cassino, Heidrich had been pleading for his division to be sent back to France for a sustained rest and refit. Since Cassino, however, his 'Green Devils' had become Germany's pin-up boys, ruthlessly exploited by Nazi propaganda as the most elite, celebrated division in the Wehrmacht, heroes to a man for their extraordinary defence at Monte Cassino. Heidrich had begun to believe this hype despite having fewer than 2,000 men still standing, many of whom were insufficiently trained teenagers. So instead of leaving Cassino and the mountain in orderly fashion right away in a move that would have significantly helped their comrades fighting in the Liri Valley, they remained where they were – and consequently faced the full weight of the Polish Corps when they attacked at around 7 a.m. on the morning of the 17th.

Since the end of their first attack, Władek Rubnikowicz and the 12th Podolski Recce Regiment had remained dug in along the meadow below Snakeshead Ridge, but although they had been unable to move by day, they had patrolled aggressively by night, as had the rest of the Polish troops on Monte Cassino. What had made their life marginally easier had been the amount of mines around the abbey that had been detonated by relentless Polish shell and mortar fire, which rained over the narrow battlefield day and night. On one occasion, Rubnikowicz had been standing behind three men. 'A shell came over and exploded right on top of them,' he commented. 'Two of the men disappeared into thin air. There was nothing left. But on a bush nearby I saw the ammunition belt and the stomach of the third. That was all that was left.' Soon after, he spotted a soldier sitting down close by, simply staring into space. The man was covered in dust and had a glazed expression on his face. Rubnikowicz bent over and touched his back and saw that it was covered in blood. The man, he realized, was dead.

Since their first attack, however, the Poles had learned some very important lessons. Their night patrols had finally revealed the nature of the German defences and Anders now realized that his men would have to overwhelm more than half of both rings of the figure-of-eight simultaneously in the first part of their renewed attack if they were to break the entire position. The rub was that the terrain naturally restricted the frontage of any such assault. The solution, he reckoned, was for the infantry to attack in waves, a battalion at a time, down the ridges. Overwhelming the enemy was what he had in mind, and this would be launched following a barrage and a series of artillery and mortar concentrations. Anders's men had also had a stroke of luck when a company-size patrol had captured the entire German forward positions on Phantom Ridge the night before the attack. By 11 p.m., the Lwowska Rifle Battalion were already firmly holding what they'd taken in the night.

The battle began, as planned, the following morning. The fighting was brutal. 'It was often a case of kill or be killed,' commented Rubnikowicz. 'Bullets were flying everywhere. One simply had to pray the angels made those bullets go around you.' Point 593 yet again changed hands several times that day, but despite dramatically increasing the weight of their attack the Poles were unable to overrun more than half of both circles as had been planned. While there were enough Germans to man machine guns and mortars, it was very difficult, over that bare, rocky, open ground, to make much headway, no matter how many men were flung into the fray. By nightfall, the Poles held Point 593 and nearly half of two circles of the figure-of-eight – but not enough to overwhelm the entire position. Anders issued fresh orders at 9 p.m. The attack would resume early the following morning, 18 May.

Meanwhile, at their redoubt near Pignataro, Unteroffizier Jupp Klein and his small band of men had been up before dawn that day, 17 May. Having made some coffee, they then chewed what they believed must surely be the last meal of the condemned. Klein was concerned about the NCO in charge of the Panzerfausts. He had looked nervous on his arrival the previous evening, but now appeared even more terrified. All of them, though, felt forebodings of the worst kind.

But the morning passed quietly, his men keeping under cover while the inexperienced reinforcements that had arrived the night before busied themselves in front of and around the farmhouse. Klein could hear the sounds of fighting nearby, but directly opposite he saw shirtless British tank men sunning themselves on top of their machines. It frustrated him, watching them. His sharpshooters itched to use their long-range telescopic-sighted Mauser rifles, but they knew they had to keep hidden for the time being and preserve ammunition.

Midday came and went, then the afternoon. Not until seven in the evening did the screams and explosions of British shells start to fall around them, followed soon after by the telltale grinding and squeaking of approaching tanks. Suddenly they emerged, around twenty Shermans cresting a slight ridge in front of them. Behind were considerable numbers of infantry. Immediately, the heavy machine gun in the shed in front of the house opened fire. With horrible inevitability, moments later the inexperienced machine-gunners were hit by enemy tank fire.

Klein looked around for the Ofenrohr men but could no longer see them. By now the forward tanks were rolling right next to their farmhouse. A shot rang out, followed swiftly by one more – two of the Shermans had been hit; Klein need never have doubted the stovepipe team. At the same time, his men opened fire with their own machine guns. The Ofenrohr men continued to fire – and with good accuracy at these very short ranges. More tanks had been knocked out while the remainder began hastily retreating. Klein watched as the crews of the burning tanks piled out of the wrecks, running wildly, a number of them ablaze. And as the tanks departed so, too, did the British infantry, who disappeared back behind the ridge ahead.

This tiny German force – fewer than fifty men in total – had beaten off a concerted Allied assault. 'We stormed out of our command post', noted Klein, 'and hugged our stovepipe men.' Klein noticed that the fear in the eyes of their NCO, so palpable the previous evening, had gone; he was now a picture of insouciance. As they counted the burning Shermans, they realized they had knocked out no fewer than thirteen, more than half the force. Then they saw the mangled remains of the machine-gun crew. 'A senseless death,' wrote Klein, 'for these young soldiers.'

*

Orders for the retreat had not reached Klein and his men in their now-isolated farmhouse redoubt, but the rest of 4. Fallschirmjäger-Regiment, who had remained in Cassino town, had received theirs. Feldwebel Rudolf Donth and his 1. Zug had been struggling a little in the ruins. His friend Christl Wöhrl had been suffering from a relapse of malaria and all had gone hungry as the ration cart had been unable to reach them for several days. Finally, though, emergency rations got through overnight on 16–17 May and a feeding frenzy began as they all gorged themselves. Then, early in the morning of the 17th, orders arrived for them to pull out of Cassino that night. They were to head out to the Baron's House to the south of the town between 8 p.m. and 10 p.m. and then wait for the code-word 'Munich II', wait a further half hour and then move out.

The Baron's House presented a ghostly sight as they reached it at dusk that night: the ruins silhouetted against the darkening sky while within, down in the cellars, candles flickered and there were rations left lying about. It was like the *Mary Celeste*. Outside, guns boomed while British loudspeakers blared out over the shattered remains: 'German soldiers, come along the Via Casilina and throw away your weapons. The war is over for you. Save your lives!' Over and over, in German. None of them took this seriously. Instead, they watched the battalion tramp past and disappear round the bend into the Liri Valley, only to be followed by the sounds of heavy fighting. 'So the enemy was already on our retreat route!' noted Donth. 'A bad situation.' When more retreating paratroopers approached, Donth and his men warned them about the fighting they'd heard and so the troops immediately switched direction and began heading up the mountain. 'Over the mountain in this darkness?' thought Donth. 'Mamma mia! But what the hell. We'll just have to do it.'

At 11.45 p.m. it was their time to go. The town appeared quiet despite the blaring of the loudspeaker still repeating its exhortation for them to give up. From the Liri Valley, the sounds of battle were still going; presumably, the same attack Jupp Klein and his men had been trying to repel. 'We immediately began an extremely arduous march over the rocks and through undergrowth,' he noted. 'We felt our way forward, step-by-step, and laughed cautiously when someone fell over a boulder.' The laughter soon stopped, however, as they began to tire. Long days and nights with insufficient sleep, food and water had taken their toll. And leading his platoon in the pitch-dark was, Donth discovered, proving a very hard slog. Everyone was struggling. As they paused at one point, Donth had the men throw away anything they didn't absolutely need;

they were to hang on to one magazine per sub-machine gun and twenty rifle rounds each and ditch everything else. 'Some of those who were giving up were brutally pushed on,' he noted. 'A good slap in the face did for the rest.' They reached the ruins of the abbey, worked their way round it and eventually descended via Death Gully. As the first streaks of dawn spread over the Liri Valley now ahead of them their journey became easier, and they made swifter progress as even the most tired found new reserves of energy as they neared safety. Donth found his spirits rising to see greenery either side of them as they emerged at the bottom of Death Gully – the first signs of resurgent nature they'd seen in a long time. 'And it was fragrant everywhere,' he jotted. 'What a wonderful world. The grass almost chest-high and a sea of lights from fireflies swarmed around us.'

It was around 7 a.m. when they reached the Via Casilina. The road was under fire but the shelling seemed fairly regular, so they timed their move, made a run for it, and all of them managed to make it through unscathed. Safety at last. The fraught hours swiftly forgotten, the men wide awake again. Rejoining the rest of the battalion at around 9 a.m., Donth learned that his platoon was the only one to have survived the escape from the town unscathed. Losses had been heavy; 2. and 3. Zug had lost roughly half their number. 'A short sleep made us temporarily forget all the misery,' noted Donth. 'Joy and sorrow were so close together.'

It was now Wednesday, 18 May. Overnight it wasn't just Cassino town that the Fallschirmjäger had evacuated, but the entire Monte Cassino massif. Early patrols ahead of the planned assault discovered that Albaneta had been abandoned. Just three Germans were found beneath Point 593. No fire came from the abbey at all, so at 8 a.m. a patrol of thirteen men from Lejnant Władek Rubnikowicz's regiment, the 12th Recce, picked their way carefully across the Colle d'Onofrio and approached the ruins. They found only thirty wounded German paratroopers and two medics left in the remains of the abbey, who all surrendered without firing a shot. The Poles, unable to find a Polish flag, attached a 12th Lancers pennant to a branch and stuck that into the rubble instead. It was 10.20 a.m. and the Battle of Monte Cassino was finally over.

It was a triumph for the Poles but came at a bitter cost. 'Of course, we were thrilled to have taken Monte Cassino,' commented Rubnikowicz. 'When we captured it, we all felt as though we had shown everyone what we were capable of. But a lot of people died.' Polish casualties were

3, 779 – and most of those were men who had, like Rubnikowicz, already suffered immensely. They'd lost their homes, their families and their country; they'd been imprisoned, beaten and starved, endured untold hardships and privations and had then travelled thousands of miles in order to continue the fight for their freedom. Their victory on Monte Cassino had been a triumph that spoke of so much more than the capture of a much-bludgeoned mountain.

Two miles to the south, Lieutenant Ted Wyke-Smith had been watching the abbey on Monte Cassino through his binoculars and saw the Polish pennant now flying above the rubble. 'Have a look, boys,' he told his men, passing round his binoculars. A profound sense of relief swept over him that the fighting for the mountain and town was, at long last, over.

'We suddenly felt,' he commented, 'as though the abbey, Cassino, the Rapido – none of them mattered any more. They were all done with. Our problems now lay up ahead.'

Later that day, Captain Mike Doble was among those who met Polish troops as they descended down Death Gully and reached the Via Casilina. Much to his chagrin, Doble had been attached to B Squadron, the Derbyshire Yeomanry, as a forward observation officer. It meant that, rather than being tucked safely behind the lines, he was in the thick of the action, closeted in a Sherman tank. 'Had one shoot during the afternoon,' he noted, 'and am said to have knocked out two guns.'

A little to the south, the Canadians were now in action and that afternoon Padre Roy Durnford was reminded of just how dangerous it was operating a tank, having been called out to bury a five-man Sherman crew. 'Tank holed by Jerry anti-tanks and blown up in intense heat,' he jotted. 'Condition of lads beyond description.' They were halfway through this grisly task when they were suddenly called away as the battalion was on the move once more. Trying to notify the Graves Registration Unit before they left, he then sped off in his jeep, moving forward about five miles. 'Dead Jerries all over and boys being captured.' They told their Canadian captors they'd not eaten for three days.

Kesselring and his commanders were now frantically trying to find further reinforcements for a front that was crumbling badly. His manic determination to keep fighting as far south as possible made no military sense whatsoever. The time to defend the Senger Line had already passed; as the position's namesake had pointed out, a measured withdrawal to the Caesar position was their best course and the one most likely to delay the fall of Rome. Only by lining up there, side by side, could Kesselring's two armies come together as a whole and regain the high ground. Really, it was amazing how the Germans repeatedly shot themselves in the foot with crass command decisions and the grotesque misuse of manpower. This, though, had Hitler's stamp all over it, and those of his lackey commanders who slavishly insisted on carrying out his maniacal will. And so, with the Führer's backing, more troops were hurrying to the rescue – which was good news for OVERLORD and terrible for those German troops about to be flung into the fray. Two divisions had been ordered from the Adriatic coast, while another from the Trieste area was also sent south. In the meantime, 26. Panzer, which had been in the Colli Albani south of Rome since SEITENSPRUNG, had been sent to rejoin AOK 10 and was hurrying to block the CEF in the mountains; the intention was to withdraw the broken 71. Division through them before the French achieved another catastrophic breakthrough.

Furious fighting continued in the Liri Valley that same day as the Germans struggled to get behind the Senger Line, which began at Piedimonte, a couple of miles west of Cassino, and cut across the valley at 45 degrees in a south-westerly direction to the little town of Pontecorvo, perched above the River Liri. The Senger Line was actually fairly well developed. There were a number of concrete bunkers as well as fixed MG positions and also 'Tobruks' – tank guns and turrets fixed into the ground. Also, of course, minefields, wire entanglements and connecting zigzag trenches. Feldwebel Rudolf Donth and his men in 1. Zug had barely had a chance to have the briefest of kips before they were roused and ordered to go and retake a position that had been overrun early that morning. Donth was furious. 'We were to help a completely desolate bunch of infantry,' he railed, 'who had hastily abandoned their positions.' Sleep-deprived and grumpy, they marched off. 'What a shitty assignment!' he added. They were so angry about this that they charged the position like berserkers, fired all their weapons, hurled lots of grenades and swiftly drove off the enemy. Again, not a single man in his platoon had suffered so much as a scratch.

It was inconceivable that Allied troops in their situation would have been expected to fight such an action or to head straight back into combat later that day. The German Army, however, was a different beast, and with a collapsing front Kesselring was determined to keep plugging the gaps. And so, quite independently from the rest of his company, let alone his battalion and division, Donth and his platoon were ordered to head over to Pontecorvo, seven miles away, and support a platoon of Tiger tanks in an attack to push back the enemy and buy time. They trudged across the valley and finally reached the Tigers, which impressed them all with their size and power, and were then told that the attack had been cancelled. Donth and his men dug in along the Aquino–Pontecorvo road and slept; they'd barely had more than a couple of hours' sleep in the last thirty-six hours. Monte Cassino, from where they'd walked the previous night, glinted in the distance across the far side of the valley.

Then, once again, they were shaken awake and told the attack was on after all. 'All you have to do is follow up and keep the Tommies at bay,' the panzer commander told them. 'Stay about twenty-five metres behind, otherwise the sound of our cannons will shatter your eardrums.' They set off soon after, Donth and his men following behind the eight Tigers as they slowly inched forward in a staggered formation. Nothing much happened, then all of suddenly everyone was firing: the Canadians, the Tiger tanks, mortars crashing down, the 88mm guns on the panzers booming, machine guns blasting. Donth remembered the fireflies they'd seen coming down from Monte Cassino. The fireflies now were tracers and star-shells.

The Tigers were soon halted, however, and after a while they began pulling back until finally the firing died away. Donth had been rather amazed by this new experience of fighting alongside the mighty Tigers, and miraculously once again he and all his men had lived to tell the tale.

'Too bad,' the panzer commander told him once they were back behind the Aquino–Pontecorvo road, 'the attack should have been better prepared, and artillery was sorely lacking. But you are dashing fellows. I wish you continued luck in the war!' And then that was that. The panzers moved off, rumbling and squeaking, and at long last Donth and his men dug in and got their heads down. Despite his exhaustion, though, Donth struggled to sleep, his mind reeling from all he'd experienced over the past twenty-four hours.

Across the other side of the valley, Unteroffizier Jupp Klein and his men were still in their farmhouse redoubt near Pignataro, having received no orders whatsoever. In other words, they were still in front, not behind, the Senger Line. That same day, 18 May, they watched British tank crews and infantry busying themselves. Klein couldn't understand why they weren't attacking. Not until that afternoon, 18 May, did the British tanks open fire, their shells whooshing over and smacking into the upper walls of the farmhouse. Klein and his men hurried down into the bunker below the house, listening to the muffled tumbling of roof and walls above them.

Suddenly rubble crashed down into the entrance of the cellar, blocking them in. The air was filled with fine dust. One of the men called for a match, but Klein stopped him. 'It'll use too much oxygen,' he told them. 'Everyone will sit quietly in one place, breathe gently and behave sensibly.' Quietly, Klein then called out the names of all his men – they were all there. Then he told the strongest to start clearing away the rubble. 'Think about what you're doing,' he told them, 'be prudent and we will survive this and not suffocate all together like guys in a coffin.'

The men were still clearing the debris when he realized they could no longer hear the sounds of battle around them: no shells crashing, no machine-gun fire. 'What this meant no one had to tell us,' noted Klein. 'We had been overrun by the enemy.'

It was dusk by the time they were clear and able to clamber outside the house. The roof had collapsed entirely, as had several of the walls, but the observation platform that they had used on first reaching the house, and the wall in front of it facing the British, still stood, 10 feet high. Klein was just about to clamber up on to it when he saw a number of infantry moving towards them. With his Italian Beretta machine gun already on his shoulder, he opened fire. This was enough to make the Tommies drop to the ground and take cover. In the meantime, his men hurriedly joined him on the platform and prepared for a fight.

Between them they had six machine guns, rifles with telescopic sights, sub-machine guns, pistols and hand grenades, so a reasonable arsenal for thirty men. From an embrasure in the wall, Klein looked out towards Cassino. He could see enemy infantry and vehicles advancing and realized that their only chance was to try and wait for darkness then head back through the enemy lines to their own positions. He had not, however, been conscious of a young Tommy approaching his loophole. Evidently, the soldier must have climbed a pile of rubble, for now they stood no more than a metre apart. For a moment they stared at each other. Klein hoped the Tommy would drop down and out of the way but, after a brief moment, the young man instead reached for his rifle. Tearing out his Beretta, Klein was quicker, fired first, and riddled the young man with bullets. He felt considerably shaken by this exchange, although he did not let his men see it. He'd looked that young man in the eyes, then cut him down. It was quite a thing to take a life in such a way.

An eerie quiet descended for a while until as many as 200 British troops appeared up ahead. Almost immediately the six machine guns opened fire. 'The last time I had seen the effects of this weapon was during our operations in the Soviet Union, and I had observed them with horror,' noted Klein. 'This time was no different and in a few seconds it was all over.' The survivors still moving were finished off by the Pionier sharpshooters until Klein called for them to stop.

They eventually made their escape after midnight, working their way quietly back through what were now enemy lines, using the narrow gap between the road and the railway to both hide and guide them. As the gap widened, they suddenly heard a British soldier call out to them.

Klein froze then shouted back in English, 'Polish soldiers.'

'All right,' the Tommy replied, and on they continued.

Three hours later, having seen what appeared to be German flares, they began to think they must have successfully reached their own lines. When they saw a group of soldiers they felt bold enough to call out. 'They answered us in German,' noted Klein. 'In the next moment each man was yelling for joy and all the tension was released.' Incredibly, not a single one of his men had been either wounded or killed. The only man missing was a medic, who had been captured at the farmhouse.

When Klein later reported to his battalion commander he expected congratulations. Instead, the major merely looked at him and said, 'I'd expected you much earlier, for there are 2,000 anti-tank mines to be laid, and I don't have any other Pioniere available.' For the Fallschirmjäger, the battle was still far from over.

CHAPTER 34

Death in the Mountains

On the afternoon of the 18th, General Alexander along with his Chief of Staff, John Harding, arrived at General Mark Clark's HQ. Clark, by now delighted with the progress of Fifth Army, told them with no small amount of satisfaction that Formia was in the bag, that he expected the town of Itri to fall the following day, and that Esperia had also fallen. 'General Alexander showed great elation,' noted Clark, 'as he should.'

Alex then raised the subject of the US 36th T-Patchers. This now battle-hardened division had been deliberately kept in Fifth Army reserve, ready to be deployed wherever Alex saw fit. He had, in fact, always intended to send it to the Anzio bridgehead to play its part in the eventual breakout, but until now had kept it behind the southern front just in case. It was all part of maintaining balance. Now, however, with the Gustav Line smashed, the time had clearly come to send them on a short sea voyage north to Anzio. Moreover, Alexander, like von Senger, was by now convinced that the Senger Line could not possibly hold. 'I agree,' noted Clark, 'but the only reason it will not is because of the flanking action of the Fifth Army.'

By nightfall the following day, Clark's optimism had proved justified. The French had captured another key feature, Monte della Mandrone, which overlooked both Pontecorvo to the north-east and Pico to the north-west. Ahead of them lay the Liri Valley and the strongest defences of the Senger Line. Further to the south, the Americans of II Corps were also continuing to make tremendous strides. That day, Gaeta, on the coast, fell to the Custermen, while the Blue Devils of the 349th RCT reached Itri around 3 p.m.

It was a little while later, however, that Captain Klaus Huebner and his medical team reached the town. They'd been following behind the battalion as it crossed directly over the mountains – an eight-mile trek as the crow flies but many times more on foot. The 349th had been temporarily attached to the 85th Custermen on their flank, who were advancing along the coast road but had moved through the southern end of the Aurunci chain. Here, huge mountain spurs sloped down to the coastal plain, but between these spurs was one ravine after another. The retreating Germans, although thin in number, 1,500 feet above sea level, would wait for their pursuers to reach each ravine and then fire several salvos of mortars. Unfortunately, civilians from the coastal towns and villages had fled up there and were sheltering in a number of these ravines; shrapnel and shards of rock were killing and wounding GIs and civilians alike. 'The opposing sides of the ravine give each exploding shell an echo,' noted Huebner, 'which adds to the fright of all the civilians. Women and children scream and soldiers curse.' Huebner was busy, doing what he could, patching up men – and civilians – giving them plasma and sending the walking wounded down into the plain below to warn the stretcher-bearers of the more serious cases left up on the mountain. Then one mortar round managed to fell ten men; it was night and dark and Huebner couldn't see the wounded, only hear their moans. Again, he did what he could, but halfway up a mountain, in the pitch-dark, and with the limited medical supplies that could be carried on foot there was a limit to what could be done for these latest casualties.

By the time they finally reached Itri after a four-day trek through the mountains it was dark and all the men were exhausted, but there was to be no stopping; the Krauts were on the run and needed to be licked. They could rest tomorrow. 'Aching backs, blistered feet, hunger and thirst must be ignored,' noted Huebner. 'After all, there's a war on, so says the colonel.' Huebner had finally caught up with his jeep and was inching through town when several mortar rounds crashed in close by, shrapnel clattering against the vehicle. Instinctively, he leaped from it but straight into a moat some 8 feet deep, cutting and bruising himself and his team. Realizing they'd be no good to anyone without getting some rest, he and his team then decided to put up a red cross outside a shot-up church and inside found a back room with a sofa. In moments, they were all asleep.

He awoke at 6 a.m. to discover he'd been bitten alive by bugs. His jaw was swollen, one of his eyes had closed and his hands were cut and scratched; he looked a sight. 'When not plagued by the Krauts,' he noted, 'we are victims of vermin.' Getting going again, they soon caught up with the foot-slogging battalion five miles further along the Via Appia towards Fondi. The retreating Germans had cratered and mined the roads and the numbers of men felled by Schü-mines soon mounted. Usually, the man's foot was blown loose and, if still attached at all, then only by shredded tendons. Dirt and grit embedded themselves into the shattered stump and there were always further wounds from splinters up the legs and to the groin. There was no time to properly clean the wounds. 'All I can do,' noted Huebner, 'is administer morphine for the pain and apply a thick padded dressing.' Splints were useless since there was never any chance of saving the foot. On the other hand, the stumps tended to bleed little because the blast usually cauterized them quite effectively. Once they had had their morphine and the stump was dressed, they would be left where they were to be picked up by ambulances, which tended to arrive in pretty quick order; Huebner's role was simply to stem catastrophic bleeding, provide pain relief and patch them up until they could be treated and operated on properly.

Meanwhile, their next objective, Fondi, was reached at 3 p.m. on Saturday, 20 May and prompted a short but vicious street battle. Huebner set up his aid station in a bakery, he and his men working rapidly as the number of wounded quickly mounted. By 7 p.m., however, the fight was over. Another town had fallen, the Germans were once again on the run and the Americans almost halfway to Anzio.

Progress had not been anything like as rapid in the Liri Valley, however. Now entrenched behind the Senger Line was Oberleutnant Hans Golda and his 8. Batterie, who was quite impressed by these latest fortifications; they were certainly an improvement on the almost non-existent defences between the two lines. Now near Pontecorvo, his command post was a decent bunker and on either side were further well-covered bunkers for the Nebelwerfers, with ramps down which they would run when not firing. His only complaint was that the concrete stands outside the entrance to the bunkers did not allow enough movement to swivel the Werfers. 'Our first job therefore', he wrote, 'was to blow up the beautiful Werfer stands in order to get enough turning space.'

Also now behind these defences were the sparse remainders of 1.

Fallschirmjäger-Division, as well as 90. Panzergrenadier, which was at last fully involved with the battle. Reaching the front too was 305. Infanterie-Division from the Adriatic, as was 26. Panzer, now coming to the rescue of 71. Division. That so much of AOK 10 was now massed behind the Senger Line in the Liri Valley gave the Allies an opportunity to rout the Germans there and then. Leese's plan was an extension of what it was already doing: XIII Corps attacking along the Via Casilina, the Canadians further south towards Pontecorvo. Meanwhile, the Poles, still flushed with their success on Monte Cassino, would try and outflank the northern edge of the Senger Line through the village of Piedimonte.

Thanks to the bridge-laying efforts of the sappers – Ted Wyke-Smith had completed his third bridge in as many nights – Eighth Army began storming the Senger Line on 19 May. Captain Mike Doble was still with the Derbyshire Yeomanry. They'd planned to push through the village of Melfa. 'They found the place stiff with Bosche,' he noted. 'We were waiting to go through when the squadron was heavily shelled by anti-tank guns. Three brews. My tank alight, fore and aft, bailed out.' Only then did they discover they weren't as badly hit as they'd thought, so clambered back in and hastily reversed, crushing a truck in the process. 'Did nothing all day as felt we could not take Aquino, shelled wherever we went,' he added. 'Leagured in a wood. More again tomorrow.'

Feldwebel Rudolf Donth and his 1. Zug had been among those desperately trying to block Eighth Army's path. They were now part of the Kampfgruppe Schulz, yet another hastily cobbled together battle group made up from a dizzying number of units drawn from no fewer than three different divisions. There were four other such battle groups, each with a jumble of units now stretching across the Liri Valley and up into the mountains beyond. Donth had no idea who was in the line with him and his platoon; all cohesion had gone entirely. He'd been shaken awake at 6 a.m. and had scrambled to his feet to see what he reckoned must be at least 100 enemy tanks almost on top of them. They were there so suddenly that his platoon barely had a chance to get to their positions. Donth jumped into a ditch with two signalmen and realized there was an enemy tank in front of just about every position and that the mass of the platoon had been captured. 'It was horrible to watch,' noted Donth. Dismayed, he and the signallers and a handful of others cautiously scuttled back into a cornfield. They were crouching there when two Shermans pulled up almost in front of them and swung their guns, fired several rounds then raked the area with machine guns. 'I lay there,' jotted Donth, 'face pressed to the ground, clutching myself with impotent rage.' It seemed to be an age before the tanks moved off again. From his cornfield hideout he saw Canadians corralling his comrades. Carefully moving back, he then came across the two signalmen, shredded by bullets. Donth pulled back further and eventually found several others who had managed to escape and were hiding out in a small house. It was clear, though, that this was not safe either, so they agreed to make a run for it. While trying to escape, however, Obergefreiter Hubert Divok was wounded; they dragged him back and then made a makeshift stretcher for him. 'In his pain,' noted Donth, 'he screamed so loudly that I had to cover his mouth so we wouldn't be betrayed.' For much of the rest of the day they scuttled from one place to another, trying to avoid the enemy and reach their own lines. Some time in the afternoon they stumbled into some of their own infantry – presumably another element of Kampfgruppe Schulz – but when the Gruppe commander tried to deploy them, Donth punched him to the ground. He'd had enough and wanted to sleep. All his comrades in 6. Kompanie did – or, rather, the dozen survivors still standing.

When Donth later awoke it was dark, the infantry had pulled back and the fighting had died down. So began a long and fraught night as they desperately tried to make their way to their own lines once more, but still feeling tired, disorientated and increasingly at their wits' end. At first light on the 20th they reached the Arce road and ran into an infantry recce unit who told them the Fallschirmjäger were a little way further along. 'In the meantime,' noted Donth, 'I remembered that today was Crete day. What a fucking game!' That had been three years earlier and had been a costly but great victory. The current battle was proving even costlier, but this time they were emphatically losing. Donth, though, was, against all odds, still alive and in one piece. 'You have been transferred to the Führer Reserve,' he was told as he reported to Hauptmann Heinz Schmücker, the battalion commander. 'Now I don't need to write to your wife, you can do that verbally!' Donth's battle was over. After an extraordinarily difficult few months, he was going home.

Despite Donth's experiences the previous day, Leese's attempt to rush the Senger Line defences before the Germans had properly established themselves had failed. Resistance had been too strong and Leese was not prepared to take the kind of casualties necessary to bludgeon his men through. To the south-west, however, lay the main chance. There was a clear geographical gap between Pontecorvo and Pico, which lay around six miles due west. This axis marked the boundary between the mountains and the Liri Valley. If the Allies could get sufficient forces through this gap and push on to the town of Ceprano on the Via Casilina, then they would be able to cut in behind the bulk of AOK 10 now in the Liri Valley and holding the Senger Line there. During Alex's meeting with Clark on the afternoon of the 20th the Fifth Army commander had suggested just this. 'If the Eighth Army will attack the Hitler Line in the Pontecorvo region in the next days,' he told Alexander, 'we hit it north from Pico all-out with all our forces and the bridgehead the next morning, we will fold up the German Army in Italy.' Understandably, Alexander was very enthusiastic about this.

In his caravan that evening, 21 May, Leese was jotting down a letter to his beloved wife, Margie. They had, he admitted, underestimated the strength of the Senger Line, and the will of the Germans to defend it. 'All along the line we came up against strong defences with barbed wire, ditches and with boxes and anti-tank guns. It will be a tough nut to break.' Frustratingly, it had also rained that afternoon, causing problems for the flow of traffic that depended so heavily on dirt tracks for quick movement. Overnight it rained some more, making the situation worse.

Leese still hoped that Fifth Army might come to the rescue, but so far only two French divisions had been thrown into the breach between Pontecorvo and Pico, and they had come up against stiffer opposition than they had been used to so far in the battle. Aware that Alexander had hoped for a quick breakthrough at the Senger Line – they all had – Leese none the less believed that small, piecemeal attacks would cost a lot of lives with no guarantee of success. Far better, he argued, would be to make thorough preparations for a set-piece attack against the line. That meant bringing up more men, more ammunition, more artillery and more tanks. And that was not going to happen overnight. Zero hour for the renewed assault on the Senger Line was accordingly set for 6 a.m. on 23 May.

There may have been a pause in the fighting in the Liri Valley, but Kesselring was conscious that his southern flank was still continuing to be overrun at an alarming speed. True, the French were now being halted south of Pico, but that was only two divisions. The rest of Juin's force were continuing to make great strides through the mountains to the southwest. US II Corps' drive was also gathering speed, so much so that they had now begun to overtake the French on their right flank. Here, in the mountains and along the Tyrrhenian coast, Kesselring's forces were in as much disarray as they had been several days before. He had still not banished his fears of an Allied seaborne landing north of Rome, which was why he had continued to keep two of his best divisions coast-watching there. However, by the 19th he had accepted that the more pressing crisis was on the southern front, and so at long last ordered Generaloberst von Mackensen to release 29. Panzergrenadier-Division from AOK 14. This done, he fully expected the Panzergrenadiers to have been in position and able to stem the flow of the French and Americans by the following morning. However, when he reached his command post on the 20th, he was shocked to discover that von Mackensen had objected to the decision, believing the greater threat lay with an Allied breakout from Anzio, which he felt sure was imminent, and so had disobeyed the order. Incensed, Kesselring, immediately altered the boundary between the two armies so that the southern section of the line now came under AOK 14's jurisdiction and reiterated his original order for 29. Panzergrenadier to move south immediately.

By the following day, however – 21 May – it was already too late. Although 29. Panzergrenadier were now on the southern front, the positions to which Kesselring had originally ordered them to deploy had already been overrun; the Blue Devils were now in Fondi, which had been taken after a three-hour battle that afternoon. 'An area ideally suited for defence had been given away,' noted Kesselring bitterly, 'and an almost impregnable position had been opened to the enemy between Terracina and Fondi.'

'Hit Anzio about 8am,' noted Frank Pearce that same Sunday, 21 May. 'Nice size town and not badly torn up but ruined, of course.' The whole of 36th Division was now landing in preparation for the breakout from Anzio, for which Pearce and the rest of his fellow engineers were briefed almost the moment they'd dug their first foxholes: some 2,000 guns would get the ball rolling – even more than had kicked off DIADEM – and then 3rd and 45th Divisions were to start the drive towards Cori and Velletri. The T-Patchers would be part of the follow-up. 'Will be a noisy, bloody battle,' he added.

Also now ashore was Lieutenant Harry Bond, fully recovered from his illness caught atop Monte Cassino and no longer commanding the mortar platoon of 1st Battalion of 141st Infantry but second aide-de-camp to Brigadier-General Robert I. Stack at Division HQ. Stack had joined the T-Patchers from 1st Armored Division back in February and was now Executive Officer of the 36th under Fred Walker. Each regiment had been asked to nominate a junior officer for the job of Stack's aide and from 141st Infantry that had been Bond, presumably because he was a college man from Dartmouth. Bond had duly presented himself for interview and thought it had gone very badly so had been amazed to discover he'd got the job; apparently, his ability to speak French had clinched it. Bond had left his comrades in the battalion with a few regrets but knew he'd been given a lifeline: his brief time at the front had told him that junior infantry officers could at best expect a wound bad enough to get them sent home, but were just as likely to wind up dead.

At any rate, now he was in Anzio and had been left in charge of ensuring that General Stack's caravan and equipment was safely disembarked and delivered to the new Division HQ, based around a large villa at the edge of Nettuno. Bond placed Stack's caravan under some oak trees, now in full leaf, and pitched their pup tents nearby. By early afternoon their camp was well organized, while a war room had been set up in the villa, complete with an outsize map on the wall showing everything that was known about enemy dispositions. The following day, Bond saw General Clark when he arrived in a convoy of jeeps and a cloud of dust to confer with Walker and ensure the division had settled in. The T-Patchers were now back at full strength and fully rested, having been out of the line for the best part of three months.

Nor was Bond the only casualty back at the front – so too was Captain Bob Spencer, recovered from the head wound he'd suffered at the Rapido and now commanding Company G. Captain Roswell Doughty was also back commanding the I & R Platoon in 141st Infantry and frantically preparing for a multitude of different deployments depending on how the breakout panned out. 'Some eleven alternative plans,' he noted, 'with appropriate map overlays and operations instructions were developed for standby use.'

Certainly, General Mark Clark was very occupied with the planning of the breakout. From the outset, this had always been expected to be a key moment in Alexander and Harding's plans for the battle, but its execution was a Fifth Army show, and Clark was determined to oversee every part of its preparation. Truscott might have been VI Corps commander, but Clark was determined not to leave anything to chance: every command decision was to go through him. Nothing was to happen without his stamp of approval.

This included the timing of the breakout. Clark and Alexander had been in almost constant communication over the past few days, including several face-to-face meetings. When Alex had visited Clark on 18 May they had agreed to launch the breakout 'when timing seems appropriate'. With news reaching him that Kesselring had thrown more divisions south into the Liri Valley, Alex felt, on the evening of 19 May, that that time had come and so issued orders to Clark to begin the breakout on the night of 21–22 May or on the morning of 22 May, whichever the Fifth Army commander felt was more appropriate.

This prompted Clark to succumb to another of his fits of umbrage. 'I was shocked', he confessed to his diary, 'when I received it – to think that a decision of this importance would have been made without reference to me. I sent that word back to General Alexander.' Alex, that most patient of men, replied calmly that he felt they had discussed it for the previous three days. At any rate, a new date for the breakout was agreed: 23 May, the same as Eighth Army's attack on the Senger Line.

Meanwhile, Unteroffizier Jupp Klein and his small company of Pioniere had been promised a spell out of the line by the battalion commander, Major Frömming, the moment they had finished laying 5,000 mines in front of the remainder of 3. Fallschirmjäger-Regiment, now dug in on the Senger Line. With the task completed, Frömming was as good as his word, sending Klein's men all the way back to Arce, a few miles behind the lines on the Via Casilina. Klein, however, had remained behind at battalion headquarters in order to write up a report about the previous few days' fighting. It was a rare luxury, but when he finally went to join the rest of his company, Frömming gave him a Kübelwagen and a driver. It was, of course, tempting fate to drive during the day, and sure enough Klein and his driver were creeping round a mountain road when they were attacked by an American P-38 Lightning. The driver was hit, the car swerved from the narrow mountain road and began tumbling down the slopes. Klein was flung out of his seat, rolling several yards until bushes and a fir tree checked his fall. There was a piercing pain in his arm – his collarbone had broken. He crawled over to the remains of the car and saw that the driver was dead, with several shots in the head and chest, then staggered back up to the side of the road, sat down, pain searing through his body, and wondered what he should do. Luck was now on his side, however. He'd not been waiting long when a lorry full of mountain troops trundled towards him. A medic treated him by the side of the road and from there he was taken to hospital. For the time being, at any rate, the war for Klein was over.

Captain Klaus Huebner was still closely following his battalion of 349th Infantry. Having taken Fondi, they'd pursued the retreating Germans overnight up across another mountain to the north-west, the Cima del Monte, and were still slogging their way up on the afternoon of Sunday, 21 May. The lead companies were nearing the summit when suddenly the Germans opened up with that familiar combination of artillery and mortar fire. Exposed on the bare, open rock, Huebner discovered that the only cover was found by crouching behind the biggest boulder he could spot. 'The terrain is constantly in the enemy's favor,' he noted, a complaint echoed by almost every Allied front-line soldier since landing in Italy the previous September. 'I always feel as though I am being led to slaughter. Most of the boys are.' Inevitably, casualties soon mounted. He and his team could only scuttle from one wounded man to another, try and stem the flow of blood, then direct stretcher-bearers to each and get them out of there as quickly as possible. As dusk fell the fighting died down, but with the summit still in German hands. Huebner had lost his blanket earlier in the day and was forced to spend the night out in the open, shivering at the dramatic dip in temperature up there, but none the less grateful still to be alive and able to shiver.

The following morning, 22 May, the mountain was quiet; the Germans had once again pulled out during the hours of darkness. Casualties were still very numerous and so he and his team went back down the mountain a little way to a mountain hut where his superior, Captain Felts, had established the battalion aid station. Felts, however, was in a bad way and asked Huebner to check him out. 'My examination reveals that his heart is fibrillating and he is on the verge of heart failure,' noted Huebner. 'I write out his emergency medical tag with great remorse.' With Felts packed off to hospital in quick order, Huebner was left in full command – and a man down. Nor had the mountain been taken after all, and another bitter fight broke out that afternoon. Huebner set up a new aid station by a rock ledge but twice had plasma bottles shattered by shrapnel and rock splinters. 'We start all over with new infusions,' he jotted. 'Metal whirs through the air and bounces off the rocks. The casualties in the saddle increase.' Not until dusk was the mountain finally theirs.

Captain Mike Doble had greatly appreciated the pause in the Liri Valley; he'd had a bout of gyppy tummy, was utterly exhausted, suffering from a bad back and had been in dire need of a chance to catch up on sleep. On the morning of 22 May, he treated himself to breakfast in bed and allowed himself a leisurely rise, then toddled over to RHQ, where he was told to take it easy for a day or two. Well, that wasn't going to happen, because they were to be back in action the following day and he'd be needed. He was also disgusted to learn that it had taken nearly a week for one of his men, Sergeant Jones, to learn that his mother had died back home in England. 'One is willing to give one's life for one's country but it does not even ease up for one minute,' he scribbled angrily in his diary. 'The British soldier gives all and receives nothing. I have seldom felt so disgusted with my government as I have this moment.'

A few miles to the north, however, Sergeant Roger Smith was now out of the line for the immediate future. He and the rest of the New Zealand 24th Battalion had been holding positions up at Terelle, just beyond Belvedere, captured by the French and 142nd Infantry at the beginning of February and sadly never exploited any further. The New Zealanders had not progressed much either once DIADEM began and then, on the night of 16–17 May, 24th Battalion had been relieved by their old friends the 28th Māori, and that had been it for them for the time being; Smith and the survivors in the 24th were back in the upper Volturno Valley near Venafro, their part in the battle done and dusted for the moment.

RSM Jack Ward was still up in the mountains, 56th Heavy Regiment's guns continuing to hammer the Secco Valley and up around Monte Cifalco. It had been so cold up on the mountains – and wet – on the 21st that he'd put his serge battledress back on again. The following day, 22 May, he drove down to Cassino to confer about the firing plan for the renewed Eighth Army attack on the Senger Line. Like everyone who passed through this hellscape, he was shocked. 'Never have I seen anything like it,' he wrote in his diary, 'the town was just a heap of rubble.' Corporal Harry Wilson was also shocked by the scale of the desolation. 'I've seen wreckage many a time,' he noted, 'but this was wreckage wrecked over again and again. It was destruction itself destroyed. It took an effort to reconstruct in imagination the scene that had once existed – to see a bridge in a pile of twisted girders and a house in a heap of pulverised rubble.' He couldn't help thinking of Sodom and Gomorrah and the destruction of ancient Babylon.

Not far from 56th Heavy Regiment's CP as the crow flies, the beleaguered 134. Regiment were still holding out at Belmonte in the Secco Valley, although the village had been largely obliterated in the four months since Major Georg Zellner had been posted there. He was aware that the front line had shifted enormously in recent days, although not where he was. 'Now the enemy is a long way behind us on our right wing,' he noted, 'but we are holding out.' Outwardly, he knew he had to be strong and look after his men, but to his diary he confessed his true feelings of misery. 'I'm overcome with homesickness,' he scribbled. 'I think of my little one, of the kids, and there's only death all around us. It's enough to make you crazy. The world could be so beautiful but for a few criminals . . . In the meantime we fight on to the last battalion or the last man. Only laughing and swearing helps. Swearing at the people who order this idiocy. I want to get back to my life. My family is my life's dream – I don't care about anything else.'

Zellner was finally about to move, however, because the following morning, Tuesday, 23 May, Eighth Army launched its renewed assault on the Senger Line. It began at 6 a.m. and, in time-honoured fashion, with another immense barrage. Padre Roy Durnford thought it incredible – 792 guns firing for two and a half hours. The night before he'd seen the men go off, heading up to the start line alongside the Churchill tanks of the North Irish Horse. The new lads had looked obviously fearful and nervous, trying to hide it with quick smiles, while the old campaigners had that familiar faraway look. 'It is the hardest thing to watch,' he noted, 'without breaking into tears.'

Corporal Harry Wilson might have been a cipher clerk at 8th Indian Division HQ, but he and his fellows were hardly avoiding the action. They'd been pulled back and were expecting leave when that was promptly cancelled and they moved back into the line under shellfire. Now, as Eighth Army assaulted the Senger Line, his cipher team came under the most sustained shelling he'd ever experienced. Wilson was surprised to discover a kind of spiritual calm sweep over him; shells were falling either side of them and their truck, and the law of averages suggested one would soon hit them. He realized, though, that this new-found calm was down to his acceptance of his inevitable demise. 'The odds were so much against it,' he noted, 'that hope was slim; and without hope there is no agony of mind, no fear.' His equanimity was increasingly tested as the day wore on, however, because he felt an overwhelming urge to relieve his bowels; but the shells kept screaming over and one landed right next to the latrines. 'We couldn't have it both ways,' he noted, 'it was either death or constipation.' Eventually, it began to rain and he decided that while the Jerries were fetching their raincoats he might risk a dash for it. He managed to run and empty his bowels in record time.

'Sixty seconds!' exclaimed one of his fellows on his return. 'What did it feel like?'

'Sixty years,' Wilson replied.

The Seaforth Highlanders, meanwhile, had got to within 300 yards of their objectives by 8.30 a.m. that morning, but casualties had already been heavy; four hours later, they'd helped break the Senger Line. Padre Durnford had been back at RHQ when prisoners started to be brought in. 'Pale, dirty and utterly exhausted, they stagger down the line,' he jotted. 'I make tea endlessly and soup.' Plenty of their own casualties arrived back at the RAP too. 'Some bomb happy, some terribly broken and shell-shocked,' Durnford added, 'some with limbs torn off and some almost gleefully with light wounds.' Later that afternoon he saw the CO, Lieutenant-Colonel Sid Thompson, looking indefatigable but understandably strained.

'How are things going, Sid?' Durnford asked him.

'Don't know, Pad,' Thompson replied, 'but I've one hundred men left in all rifle companies and three officers.' That was just a fifth of its fighting strength.

Despite the forward infantry battalions suffering similar casualties across the line, the attack had none the less prevailed; clearly, a methodical and carefully planned assault with overwhelming firepower was the only way to crack a German fixed defensive position such as the Senger Line. 'A great day!' General Leese wrote to his wife that evening. 'It was a very hard fight all the morning but after lunch we broke in deeper with tanks and infantry.' There had been more rain, which, frustratingly, had prevented them from pushing through further tanks and armour before dark, but he could not feel too disheartened. 'The Germans are in complete chaos: units mixed up everywhere and nearly all serving under command of any division except their own,' he added with no small amount of truth, 'whereas we are all tidy and present and the army is eager to get on.'

Of Fifth Army's effort to cut in behind the Senger Line, however, there was little sign.

This fear of being trapped at the Senger Line was precisely why its architect, General von Senger, had so forcefully suggested to Kesselring and von Vietinghoff that they fall back to the Caesar Line right away. Instead, by 23 May, a significant part of AOK 10 had been crammed into the Senger Line in the Liri Valley, not to mention 26. Panzer and 29. Panzergrenadier now on AOK 10's front. However, there was little room to manoeuvre substantial numbers of troops into the gap between Pontecorvo and Pico, and in any case Juin already had half his corps fighting alongside the Blue Devils further to the north and about to burst down into the Amaseno Valley. Divisions could not easily break off fighting and pivot more than 90 degrees through mountains in quick order – as Juin's men had discovered at Belvedere at the end of January. As a result, there had still been only two French divisions available to try and cut into the Liri Valley; that was not enough, although it was sufficient, in combination with the Eighth Army battering ram, to force the Germans to retreat. That night, 23 May, Generalleutnant Feurstein ordered 90. Panzergrenadier to pull back several miles and for the artillery to retreat back over the River Melfa. At 11 p.m., even Kesselring accepted that the game was up along the Senger Line.

The Blue Devils were now on one part of Monte Rotondo and overlooking the Amaseno Valley, close to Pasua Pisa's family farm. Klaus Huebner had spent the morning of 23 May tagging the dead, including an officer he'd known well back in the States, and pondering the utter futility of war when he'd paused to watch a column of Goumiers approaching. These were Berbers, mostly tribal Moroccans from the Atlas Mountains, and structured in a slightly different way to the rest of the CEF. Rather than being attached to battalions they were placed in 'tabors' with three tabor per 'groupe de tabors'; in effect, such a group was similar to a brigade of a regiment. They were a comparatively small component of the CEF but were, however, very distinctive, because while most of the French Armée Coloniale were dressed and equipped like any other French troops, the Goums wore striped ponchos, had beards, carried long knives and looked as though they belonged to an earlier century. There was a culture among these Goums of cutting off the ears of slain enemy troops and lacing them into necklaces. They had a deserved reputation for terrifying brutality.

Pasua Pisa had heard the guns getting closer and as that Tuesday, 23 May, wore on, she and her tiny community found themselves on the boundary between the French and the Americans and the retreating Germans. Shells began landing nearby, then troops appeared, using the piles of freshly cut hay as cover. 'They were shooting over our heads,' she commented, 'there were aeroplanes too. We were scared.' That afternoon, her four-year-old son Lorenzo found an unexploded mortar shell. Still glued to his grandfather, the boy and old man picked it up and took it to back to the house where they all now lived. Neither had the slightest idea what it was – they'd never seen anything like it before. Had Pasua known what they were up to she would have warned them, but she had been busy. With her husband gone and so few men about she was working flat-out from dawn until dusk, despite the proximity of the fighting.

As soon as Pasua heard the explosion she rushed back, but on entering the house found both her father and her adored son dead.

CHAPTER 35

Breakout and the Big Switch

GENERAL MARK CLARK HAD spent 22 May beetling about the Fifth Army front and urging II Corps to push on towards Terracina on the coast and the Lepini Mountains to the north, and to link up with VI Corps just as quickly as possible. He then flew to Anzio, reported progress to Alexander, and that evening gave a briefing to war correspondents at 8 p.m., telling them, off the record, about plans for the breakout. Called Operation BUFFALO, it would begin at 6.30 a.m. the following morning, with US forces striking straight for Cori and Valmontone. Clark made it clear that the aim was to cut the Via Casilina and then push troops north and south to destroy as many German forces as possible. He also stressed that while this was the current plan, he wanted to maintain flexibility and had several other plans up his sleeve which he could put into action depending on the reaction of the Germans.

The following morning he rose at 4.30 a.m., had a quick breakfast and then went forward in his jeep to join Truscott at a forward OP to watch the attack begin. It was a quiet morning, a bit hazy and with some drizzle. Little had been left to chance. Some 150,000 fighting men were ready. Daily barrages had been fired in the run-up, each day targeting different parts of the enemy's lines so that now, as Operation BUFFALO was launched, the enemy would not necessarily think it meant the start of a major attack.

But then, at 5.45 a.m., more than 500 guns of varying calibres opened fire, supported by tanks and tank destroyers hammering forward enemy positions with their main guns and machine guns – in precisely the way Walker should have done at the Rapido but had not. Even though the men on the ground had been prepared for such a barrage, it was unlike anything Sergeant Ralph Schaps, for one, had ever heard or experienced before – and he was hardly a stranger to front-line combat. 'The concussion,' he noted, 'was so great it felt like your ear drums were about to burst.' His 2nd Battalion of 135th Infantry had been temporarily detached from the rest of the 34th Red Bulls and instead attached to Combat Command A – CCA – of 1st Armored Division, who were attacking in the centre of the bridgehead with the 45th Thunderbirds on their left flank and 3rd Infantry to their right. Soon after the guns opened up, much of the plain and the mountains behind disappeared in the smoke and morning haze. 'Little could be seen,' noted Clark, 'but through the din and roar of the gunfire, tanks could be heard moving up into position ready to attack.' Then, at 6.26 a.m. medium bombers and fighter-bombers thundered over, and bombed and strafed Cisterna and enemy positions all around. At 6.30 a.m. the attack jumped off.

Minefields were, as always in any fresh attack, a perennial problem, but the Allied troops were now moving behind a new device called an 'M2A1 Snake'. Frenchy Bechard, now with the complete 1st Armored Division, had been helping to prepare these devices ahead of the attack. The idea was ingenious in principle: a 400-foot-long tube, filled with 3,200 pounds of explosive that was pushed forward by a Sherman tank. Eighty feet ahead, the snake detonated any mines to clear a path 320 feet long and 16–20 feet wide.

Also leading the advance alongside the 1st Armored on their left and Special Service Force on their right were the 15th Infantry of 3rd Division. As shells hurtled over and tanks fired their rounds and spat bullets, Staff Sergeant Audie Murphy and his platoon clambered out of the foxholes they'd held for the best part of four months and headed across no-man's-land towards the enemy. Up ahead were 362. Infanterie-Division in the centre of the line and 715. Infanterie to the east, on the right of the line where the Special Service Force were attacking. Both were the new 1944-model two-regiment divisions, poorly equipped, lacking decent transport and filled with what was effectively cannon fodder: undertrained men, many older Germans or conscripts from eastern territories. That either could be expected to put up much resistance against this storm of steel being hurtled at them was very optimistic. Frenchy Bechard and his fellows in Company A of 16th Armored Engineer Battalion were up front in general support, mostly clearing mines. 'Our attack is going well,' he jotted that day. 'We cleared about 1,500 anti-tank and personnel mines, one-and-a-half miles deep.' While moving forward they overran a trench in which two wounded Germans from 362. Division were still cowering, both badly wounded. They looked terrified and clearly feared that the Americans would shoot them on the spot. One had a bad stomach wound, while the other had one of his feet attached by only a few strands of tendon. 'This one got on his feet and dropped to his knees,' noted Bechard. 'How he managed that is beyond us. Guess fear can overcome anything if you're begging for your life.' Bechard and his fellows did not shoot either; rather, their medic gave them each some morphine and had them picked up and taken back to the rear.

Sergeant Ralph Schaps also found they were overwhelming enemy positions with comparative ease and taking large numbers of prisoners. 'They were in a state of shock,' he noted. 'Some said they had been on the Russian front but had never experienced a barrage such as we had laid down.' By the end of the first day, Schaps and his fellows had reached the railway line that ran across the front between Cisterna and Campoleone Station, their objective. Combat Command B, which had not used the Snakes as liberally as CCA, had not made quite such good progress, nor had 3rd Division as it attacked Cisterna; as the Allies had discovered time and time again in the Italian campaign, attacking an enemy who was well dug in and equipped with plentiful amounts of mortars and machine guns was a very hazardous business, whether over open plain or up a mountain. Nor did manning either of these lethal weapons require excessive training.

Audie Murphy was lucky to escape with his life that day when they had to pass across a deep cutting. To do so they needed to slide down the first bank, cross the bed of the cutting, then scramble up the opposite slope. One of his men was killed as he paused a fraction too long clearing the opposite bank, but the rest got across until it was Murphy's turn. Sliding down the first bank, his entrenching tool became wedged between two rocks so that he was suspended there, bullets spattering all around him. He saw the panic on his friend Martin Kelly's face, felt panic himself but managed to free himself with a great heave and bolted across the track.

'You ignorant bastard,' Kelly cursed him, 'are you hurt?'

'No,' Murphy replied. 'Just a slight heart attack and a nervous breakdown.'

Later that day, as they approached Cisterna from the south-east, Murphy and his men witnessed Sergeant Sylvester Antolak of 2nd

Platoon of Company B single-handedly charge the first of two MG posts that was holding up the entire attack. Hit repeatedly, he kept getting back to his feet and continuing his charge, knocking out the first MG position and capturing ten men. He then charged the second position and was finally cut down just before reaching it. His actions were enough to inspire his men to continue the assault and finish the job.

By the end of the first day, Truscott's men had pushed forward around two and a half miles but had suffered 1,626 casualties, including 107 dead. On the other hand, German losses had been catastrophic. AOK 14 reported losing 50 per cent of 362. Infanterie-Division, while two of the Panzergrenadier regiments in 715. Division also lost 40 per cent of their fighting strength.

There had been no let-up for the Allied air forces, which had continued to bomb and strafe German positions and anything that attempted to move during the day. On 24 May, MATAF alone flew nearly 2,000 sorties, the biggest effort in a single day since the start of the battle. Roads and motor transport north of Rome were attacked; enemy artillery was heavily pasted in the northern sector of the Anzio bridgehead. The Via Casilina was repeatedly sprayed with bombs and bullets as German forces hurried south from the north of Rome, with the fighter-bombers claiming as many as 563 enemy vehicles south of Valmontone. Sixty-one P-40 Kittyhawks and 35 P-47 Thunderbolts blasted the towns of Lanuvio and Cori in support of VI Corps.

Lieutenant Luke Lucardi had flown his 36th mission on the 23rd and now, on 24 May, flew two more. The second was an attack on the HG-Division, which had been up near Livorno on the coast and which had been urgently ordered south to the Anzio front. Even Kesselring had by now accepted that the greater risk lay south of Rome rather than from some Allied amphibious outflanking operation for which there was no sign or evidence whatsoever. This ludicrous paranoia of Kesselring's had led him to place HG-Division some 200 miles north of Rome, a huge distance, but because of the urgency at the front they now had to travel south during the hours of daylight, a high-risk undertaking to say the very least. Lucardi and his fellows in 64th Fighter Squadron had been attacking a factory at Pomarance near Pisa when they heard from the boys in the 66th FS that they were targeting long columns of the HG. 'So, we joined them,' noted Lucardi. 'Whew, what a lot of trucks, tanks and half-tracks!! We just made a gunnery pattern on them – made about 10 passes.' Lucardi reckoned they got at least twelve to fifteen 'flamers'. Later, Lucardi's squadron sent out a further nine Thunderbolts and bombed and strafed the column again. They reckoned they'd got a further twenty to thirty vehicles.

The 57th FG had struck the HG-Division's main artillery column although all parts were struggling to reach the front; their lead units only reached Lake Bolsena, fifty miles north of Rome, by the night of the 24th, and not until the following night did the first elements reach Artena, south of Rome and a few miles from Valmontone. And by then they'd already been reduced to a shell of what they were before.

Meanwhile, General Clark had reason to be pleased with progress in the Anzio bridgehead. Despite continued heavy fighting, the Germans were falling back, especially in the centre of the line, through which the main thrust was being directed. Although the 36th T-Patchers had not been brought into action yet, all available combat engineers had been roped in to deal with the abundant mines and booby traps, and that included Frank Pearce and the rest of the 111th Engineers. On the evening of the 24th, he and a number of others were called out to clear mines for the artillery that was moving up, and they soon found themselves pushing north from the beachhead plain. 'Rolling country full of deep ditches full of Germans,' he noted. 'Dead scattered, some buried, feet sticking out, theirs & ours alike. Bad smell.' Shellfire seemed relentless and they managed to get lost with fighting going on all around them. He finally reached the right area at around 1.30 a.m. but it was clear that they were doing well. 'We are winning!' he added.

They most certainly were, and that same evening of the 24th, Colonel Hamilton Howze, whose 13th Armored Regiment had been in reserve on the opening day, was given command of 'Howze Force', principally his own regiment, less one company, and placed directly under divisional control. Cisterna was now all but surrounded, but Howze's specific job was to push on past the town towards the long valley that led directly to Valmontone, while CCA pressed on across the valley in the direction of Velletri and the Colli Albani.

Having assembled during the night, Howze Force got going early the following morning, 25 May. Almost immediately one of the light reconnaissance tanks received a direct hit, killing all its crew instantly, but, pushing on, the other tanks managed to encircle one of the fearsome Ferdinands, a German self-propelled 88mm gun, and incredibly, forced the crew to surrender despite the gun's phenomenal 7.5-inch-thick armour. Shortly after, Howze took the opportunity to clamber over the abandoned gun. 'I looked at it closely later,' he noted. 'Our little 37mm guns had hardly dented it.' Later that day they finished off a German column of the HG-Aufklärungs-Bataillon – reconnaissance force – that had been shot up by the air forces, and then further saw off an attack by enemy panzers. When Howze reached the remains of the column he was met with a scene of utter carnage. 'Bodies and pieces of bodies,' he noted, 'strewn among the scores of wrecked and burning vehicles.' His force continued to make good progress all day, with his Sherman tanks reaching the key road that linked Cori with Valmontone, the town that was VI Corps' ultimate goal.

That same day, elements of US II Corps and VI Corps met up, and in so doing Fifth Army became whole again after 125 days of separation between the two fronts.

Directly to the south, the left wing of the CEF had continued pushing through the mountains, albeit at a slower pace now than US II Corps on their southern flank. On 25 May, Pasua Pisa's father and her son Lorenzo were being buried in Amaseno. Everyone from the tiny mountain-top community had gone to the funeral – everyone but Pasua and her mother. 'My mother and I stayed behind in the house,' she commented. 'My grief was too great.'

Suddenly there were soldiers at the door: strange-looking men, French colonial troops – Goums – wearing striped woven ponchos over their uniforms and with knives tucked into their belts. One of them grabbed Pasua, dragged her out of the house and in the courtyard brutally raped her. Then they left, sparing Pasua's mother. 'The Moroccans', commented Pasua, 'stole my life away.'

They had done spectacularly well during the eighteen-day battle, but the behaviour of the Goums in the Groupement de Tabors had been reprehensible; Pasua Pisa was far from alone in being brutally raped. On 24 May, Juin issued a warning that such behaviour had to stop. 'However strong our feelings may be against a nation which treacherously betrayed France,' he wrote, 'we must maintain an attitude of dignity.'

It had not been much of a reprimand and the raping and pillaging continued unchecked. 'The Italians are raising the devil because of a large number of rape cases by Goums,' Al Gruenther scribbled in a brief memo to Clark on 27 May. 'Money stolen, men and women beaten and generally a series of disgraceful incidents.' Gruenther promised to take this up with Juin, who issued a further, tougher, note threatening 'punishment without mercy'. Even after this there was little effort to curb the frenzied spree of rape, murder and pillaging by the Goums. As one French officer explained, Moroccans were recruited 'by way of a pact which granted them the right to sack and pillage'. The reaction of the senior Civil Affairs officer was certainly complacent in the extreme. 'If native African troops are to be used in Europe,' said one report, 'more of these outrages must be expected than would be expected from a similar number of British, American or white French troops; that it is impossible to suppress these outrages altogether; and that in any event the reports are greatly exaggerated.'

This latter point, especially, was appallingly ill-judged. If anything, the number of rapes reported was far less than the reality, for many Italian victims never told of such abuses. Rather, the Allies were sweeping under the table a barbaric episode, largely because they feared it would cause awkwardness with the French and because it was far easier to brush it to one side when the victims were disempowered Italians.

Sergeant Norman Lewis was still based in Naples but witnessed the effects of this mass rape and pillage. 'It is reported to be normal for two Moroccans to assault a woman simultaneously,' he noted, 'one having normal intercourse while the other commits sodomy. In many cases severe damage to the genitals, rectum and uterus have been caused.' On 28 May he visited Santa Maria a Vico, a village far south of the line near Caserta, to see a girl who had reportedly gone insane as a result of an attack by a large party of Goums. He found her living alone with her mother – who had also been gang-raped – in abject poverty and unable to walk because of her injuries. Mentally, however, there was little sign of madness. Rather, it had been the local Carabiniere who had tried to commit her to an asylum. Only the lack of a bed had prevented them. As Lewis observed, she would now be most unlikely ever to find a husband. 'At last one had faced flesh-and-blood reality of the kind of horror that drove the whole female population of Macedonian villages to throw themselves from cliffs rather than fall into the hands of the advancing Turks,' he wrote. 'A fate worse than death: it was in fact just that.'

In Lenola, a village north of Fondi, for example, fifty women were raped and children and old men also violated. The priest of Morolo, a village just south of the Via Casilina not far from Frosinone, claimed that there was not a single family in the parish who had not suffered some form of physical or psychological damage. 'All the women who were caught alone in the countryside or up the mountains were forced to undergo the shame of the feral instincts of those inhuman beings. As if this wasn't enough, the Moroccans finished what they had started by stealing money, precious objects, linen and even kitchen utensils.' The doctor of the mayor of Frosinone heard witness to, and saw with his own eyes, the evidence of countless such acts. Females of all ages were taken, from innocent peasant girls as young as twelve to elderly women. 'They forced them to submission with threats and gunshots – some wounding them; they dragged them into the cornfields or into sheds. Mothers were disgraced on their own beds before their crying children and their husbands held at bay by the butt of a rifle pointed at their chests. Old ladies of more than seventy were not spared. Some spouses were killed while defending their loved ones. Gold, linen and livestock which had been left by the Germans was taken away by the Moroccans.'

In the Liri Valley the Germans had begun to fall back, even the Fallschirmjäger-Division, who, until ordered to retreat, had continued to hold up the Poles at the village of Piedimonte. On the 24th, Hans Golda and his battery of Nebelwerfers had fought a valiant rearguard action while infantry streamed past, but had been stuck while they were waiting for their vehicles to arrive. Eventually, as tank shells began falling all around, they appeared. After quickly loading up, they headed north through the night towards Arce on the Via Casilina and into new positions on the northern banks of the River Melfa, a tributary of the Liri that cut the road at right angles and provided an obvious natural line of defence. 'Retreating along the Via Casilina at high speed under shellfire,' scribbled Golda. By the road was a pile of horses, torn to pieces, still in harness with the gunners lying next to them. 'Jabos all around,' he added. 'Charged through. An infantryman sitting in a motor cycle side car, burning. A horse shaking in the middle of the road. We drive straight over it.'

Facing Golda's men had been the Canadians, who continued to advance that day. The 3rd Infantry Brigade reached all their objectives, as did the battalion of Princess Patricia's Canadian Light Infantry on the Seaforth Highlanders' right. The Seaforths, meanwhile, had another day of heavy casualties. 'Conway gets his hand blown off by a grenade,' noted Padre Roy Durnford. 'Hentig dies. McLaughlin dies. Allen wounded. McBridge missing. Jack McLean wounded three times and carried on.' More wounded streamed back to the RAP. When Durnford later went forward to retrieve the dead he was sniped at. 'The battlefield', he added, 'is an indescribable carnage.'

In XIII Corps' sector along the Via Casilina, Captain Mike Doble had been back operating with the Derbyshire Yeomanry for the Senger Line assault. On that Wednesday, 24 May, he had just been relieved by an officer from the 128th Field Regiment and was heading back to rejoin the 2nd RHA when a stray shell killed him outright. Really, it was very often just a matter of luck and chance whether one lived or died. There was usually little rhyme or reason to it. 'The Regt mourned a first-class officer', noted the regimental diarist, 'and a very good friend.'

Roy Durnford buried forty-two in the dark in a hastily squared-off cemetery on the 25th. 'Bodies keep coming in,' he jotted, 'mute testimony to awful victory.' When he eventually got to bed he struggled to sleep, his mind whirring and then kept awake by a Luftwaffe raid mounted that night. The house he was in shook as bombs fell, plaster falling off the walls. 'Three deaths in B Coy,' he added. 'I can't sleep tonight.'

In the face of this mayhem and carnage, Eighth Army struggled to follow up with any kind of speed. The Poles, still unencumbered by their tanks and motorized transport, would have been a good option for continuing the chase to the Melfa, but Leese, recognizing that they were a spent force after battling through possibly the hardest fighting of the offensive to date, and having sustained horrendous casualties, withdrew them from the fight. Instead it was left to XIII Corps on the right and the Canadians on the left to make their way through the now empty Senger Line, over the Forme d'Aquino – another Liri tributary – and then get across the Melfa, which ran across the Liri Valley at 90 degrees to the axis of the Allied advance.

The river had been reached by forward Canadian units on the 24th, but it had been impossible to get any further because of the hopeless congestion behind. 'The Canadian Corps are a bit rusty', wrote Leese, 'in their staff work, inter-communication and traffic control.' Certainly, bridging equipment and bulldozers, so crucial for their advance, were not given the kind of priority they should have had. XIII Corps was unable to move at all that day because of the jams.

The rate at which vehicles arrived into a bottleneck was far greater than the speed with which they could pass through. Armoured divisions such as 5th Canadian and 6th British, now vying for the few tracks, crossings and roads that would enable them to push forward, were made up of 366 tanks and 3,048 other vehicles, while an infantry division would have has many as 3,375 vehicles. This made for an awful lot of traffic.

Lieutenant Ted Wyke-Smith and his sappers were still busily building new bridges every night. In XIII Corps, priority was always given to his lorries and their bridging equipment, but this meant other vehicles in their way would have to pull off the road and let them pass, which, of course, caused further hold-ups. During the day, Wyke-Smith would be travelling around in his jeep or in an armoured car, carrying out reconnaissance work for the next night's bridging. On the night of the 22nd, for example, he had driven to a conference with the CO at 11 p.m. It had been raining and was pitch-black. No headlights could be used, so it was both hard and slow going. In such conditions, and with shell- and potholes dotting all the roads, accidents were common. On that occasion, he had helped tow an ambulance out of a ditch. 'When a vehicle got wrecked,' he commented, 'everyone had to gather around and get it off the road; get it out of the way as quickly as possible to keep the traffic moving.' But inevitably such incidents caused even more delays. Then there were also the vast numbers of mines and intricate booby traps which the Germans were past masters at laying and preparing. This made the leading elements of any columns of vehicles, whether tanks or trucks, understandably nervous and cautious.

Casualties were mounting at Anzio too. Sergeant Ralph Schaps and 2nd Battalion of 135th Infantry were still advancing hand in glove with the tanks of CCA and were helping to clear a series of large tunnels, also dating from Roman times and similar to the old quarries beneath the Buonriposo Ridge. Schaps and his men managed to capture twenty-five Germans, who swiftly put up their hands. They lined them up, searched them, then Schaps and Private Smithe were detailed to lead them back to the nearest POW cage, about a mile to the rear. All of the prisoners were compliant enough except for their officer, who was acting surly and uncooperative; Smithe was all for shooting him, but Schaps ordered him to leave him be.

After a little while they reached the railway, which lay in a shallow cutting. Schaps went over first and all the prisoners crossed without any issues until the officer brought up the rear. As he struggled up the far embankment, Schaps held out a hand to help him, but instead of taking it the German pulled out a pistol, clearly hidden when they'd searched him earlier. Schaps reached for his own weapon, but the German shot him in the throat. Before he collapsed Schaps fired back with his carbine, the officer taking a full clip of bullets in the chest. Schaps lost consciousness soon after, although he'd been lucky that the single shot had not pierced an artery. The POWs carried him back to the aid station, where he was patched up and then hurriedly dispatched to a field hospital, his part in the battle for Rome over.

Audie Murphy and his platoon, meanwhile, were involved with the capture of Cisterna on Thursday, 25 May, then found themselves pausing in a wood to reorganize themselves. They sensed that the enemy was beaten, but even in retreat the Germans continued to harass them with machine guns and sniper rifles and fire salvos of mortars and artillery. Murphy and his men were dog-tired and hungry too as their sudden rapid advance had outpaced the supply lines, but they knew they had to keep going. Murphy was sitting in a German foxhole, his helmeted head between his knees in rest, when Abraham 'Horse-Face' Johnson slid in beside him. He looked ashen and asked Murphy for some water. Murphy handed him his canteen but Johnson dropped it.

'What the hell is the matter with you?' Murphy asked.

'Think I strained my back,' Johnson replied.

He then slumped forward and Murphy ripped off his shirt to see a small, ugly wound under his shoulder blade. Johnson insisted it was only a scratch but Murphy reckoned he needed a medic.

'No. Keep down,' Johnson told him. 'You wouldn't get two yards. Shells are thicker'n whores at an Elks convention.'

Murphy realized his old friend was in trouble, however, and when Johnson next spoke, blood bubbled at his mouth. Murphy couldn't believe it. *Not Horse-Face*, he thought. Scrambling out of his foxhole, he hurried to find a medic, but by the time they got back Johnson was dead. The two friends had been together since North Africa. Soon after, the shelling lifted. 'We climb out of our holes,' noted Murphy, 'regroup, and plod towards a flaming town.'

Despite heavy losses, by the evening of 25 May the situation in the Anzio bridgehead looked very promising indeed. A large hole had been punched forward from the bridgehead, but although fighting had continued to be fierce to the north, Howze Force had clearly found a soft spot, and fortunately it was in precisely the direction of VI Corps' objective. Valmontone, Howze felt sure, would fall the following day, and with it they would cut the Via Casilina. Sensing that a great victory was now within their grasp, Howze reported this to Brigadier-General Frank Allen, commander of CCB, imploring him to try and get the whole of 1st Armored Division diverted into this gap as soon as possible. Allen agreed wholeheartedly with Howze's appreciation and relayed this to Division. The divisional commander, General Harmon, also agreed, and in turn urged General Truscott, the VI Corps commander, to order such a move. Truscott needed no convincing – it was, after all, the obvious course of action. 'By the following morning', he wrote, 'we would be astride the German line of withdrawal through Valmontone.'

Truscott returned to his HQ late that evening, only to find Major-General Donald Brann, Clark's Chief of Operations, waiting for him with some stunning and at first incomprehensible news. There would be no all-out drive on Valmontone the following day, Brann told him. Instead, the main axis of the attack was to switch north, through the Colli Albani – and directly towards Rome.

Life for Carla Capponi – 'Elena' – and her boyfriend, Rosario Bentivegna – 'Paolo' – had become almost unbearable since the end of April. Having survived the aftermath of their bomb attack on the Via Rasella, they had then been betrayed by Guglielmo Blasi, a partisan of GAP Centrale whom Elena had had doubts about even before the bomb on 23 March. Struggling to keep himself and his family alive, Blasi had offered himself to the notorious Pietro Koch, Fascist commander of the vigilante Koch Gang. Remaining with the partisans but working as Koch's spy and informer, Blasi had since then almost single-handedly brought about the end of GAP Centrale.

Fortunately for Paolo and Elena, one of their fellow partisans managed to escape from Koch's new headquarters and so was able to warn them of the betrayal. Even so, Koch now knew all about Paolo's key role in the attack and declared him Public Enemy Number 1. Now hunted like wolves, they were forced to change their place of refuge daily and frequently went days without any food.

They had known the offensive was coming thanks to American agents in Rome working with the partisans, and it had been a relief to hear news that the battle had begun. But Carla began to seriously doubt whether they would still be alive when the Allies finally reached the Eternal City at long last. Since the beginning of the Allied air offensive, Operation STRANGLE, food shortages had risen dramatically. Rome had begun to starve and civilians were now dying as a consequence. And as the battle continued to rage the situation only worsened. Top priority for the Germans now was supplying the front – with men, food, equipment and ammunition. With so many roads and bridges destroyed, with railway lines cut and marshalling yards wrecked, and with Allied fighter planes strafing and bombing anything that moved by day, that was hard enough. Feeding Rome was nigh on impossible. But Elena was not only starving, she was also stricken with a lung infection and coughing up blood. She was saved by the CLN, who helped her and Paolo to smuggle themselves out of Rome altogether and head for Palestrina in the hills to the east of Rome. There, protected by the local partisans, she lay low, happy to hear the guns getting closer and praying the Allies would reach them soon.

On Eighth Army's front, the remnants of AOK 10 were starting to slip away. Von Vietinghoff and his senior commanders, von Senger included, had, since the collapse of the Senger Line, been doing their best to persuade Kesselring that a deep withdrawal was their only course of action, and had not only made plans but begun to act on them in anticipation of approval. Kesselring's hands, however, continued to be tied by Hitler and the German High Command, and so he continued to forbid such a retreat. Nor was there any talk of giving up Rome. Rather, Kesselring intended, at the moment he was finally authorized to pull back, to fall in behind the Caesar Line.

The Allies had been aware of the C-Position before the battle, and its existence was another reason why Alexander and Harding had favoured blocking off AOK 10 with a strike from the Anzio bridgehead before the enemy could reach it. Yet although this thrust towards Valmontone had been an integral part of Alex's battle plan, Clark had never been so convinced that it was the one and only course of action. Always the most assiduous planner, he was not willing to leave anything to chance, and so had prepared three possible lines of attack from the bridgehead. One was towards Valmontone as Alex envisaged; the second was south-east towards Sezze, in case the attack in the south had not gone as well as hoped; and the third was north to Rome via the Appian Way – or Highway 7 – to the west of the Colli Laziali in the Colli Albani. Clark had briefed his commanders on 5 May outlining all these plans, but later in the day Alex visited him and told him to concentrate on only one line of attack. 'He said that the only attack he envisages from the beachhead,' noted Clark, 'is the Cisterna-Cori-Valmontone attack.' Three days later, on 8 May, and three days before DIADEM's launch, the two men had a further conference, when Alex directly expressed his concerns that Clark was not 'all-out' for the attack towards Valmontone and that he felt he was not in agreement with his plans. 'I told Alexander that I wanted to attack out of the beachhead with everything I had,' noted Clark, 'that if conditions were right I wanted to attack towards Cori (and Valmontone) but that what I was guarding against was pre-conceived ideas as to what exactly was to be done.' Clark agreed that they potentially had a big opportunity for a great victory but was wary of over-optimism. In light of his experiences so far in Italy, this was understandable. 'He kept pulling on me the idea that we were to annihilate the entire German Army,' continued Clark, 'and did it so many times that I told him that I did not believe that we had too many chances to do that; that the Boche was too smart.' Clark insisted that he wanted to maintain his flexibility, although his biggest concern before DIADEM's launch had been that the main attack along the southern front might be stalled and that Alex would then order a premature breakout from Anzio. At their meeting on 8 May he had also made it clear to Alexander that striking straight across the front of the Colli Albani towards Cori and Valmontone was his first priority.

Clark had still been expressing this desire for flexibility even once it was clear that the main attack in the south was going well. During his meeting with Alexander on 18 May he raised the issue of the direction of VI Corps' attack from the bridgehead once more. Alex was again adamant that an attack in the direction of Valmontone was the only course of action. When Clark pointed out the mountains he might have to fight through in order to take Valmontone, Alex 'brushed this aside'. The following day, during a meeting with Truscott, Clark once again stressed that he wanted to maintain flexibility, regardless of Alexander's orders. The plan to thrust towards Valmontone would be carried out as directed, but Truscott should be prepared to change the line of attack north-west towards Rome. 'Much depended', added Clark, 'upon the German reaction to the attack on the main Allied front.'

What concerned Alexander was less his suspicion that Clark had ulterior intentions than what he perceived as over-caution. Yet Clark did have some reasons for this. The attack on Cori and then on to Valmontone meant funnelling VI Corps from the flat plain around Anzio into a comparatively narrow stretch of softly undulating low ground of about twenty miles. To their right were the Lepini Mountains, with Cori, and further on Artena, lying on the lower slopes of the edge of this range. On their left, as they advanced, were the Colli Laziali and the Colli Albani, across which, and looking down on the valley below, was the Caesar Line. Velletri, like Cori opposite, lay on the lower slopes overlooking the low ground. Before the battle, Clark would have been aware that, potentially, he could have enemy troops in the high ground either side of him. He was also aware that making a flank march across two fronts of an undefeated force was a classic military sin. The threat to his southern flank had all but gone – although not entirely – by the evening of 25 May as the leading troops of the Blue Devils had, on 23 May, reached Roccasecca, a village high in the Lepini Mountains that overlooked the entire Anzio and VI Corps battleground. None the less, the threat to his flanks from the Colli Albani was very much still there because by the evening of 25 May much of AOK 14 now lay dug in along the Caesar Line, looking down on any VI Corps troops crossing below. From Clark's point of view, there was no guarantee the enemy would not counter-attack and assault his vulnerable left flank and rear. There was no way Clark was going to risk a major setback now. To his mind, AOK 14 had to be faced, and that meant continuing the pressure on Velletri.

Furthermore, Fifth Army intelligence reports suggested on 25 May that the remnants of the German 362. Division had withdrawn towards Valmontone to the east of Velletri. On the evidence of the way the Germans had fought the battle so far, Clark also suspected that von Mackensen would shift units from the Colli Albani into the Valmontone Gap. The Via Casilina ran beneath Valmontone and continued north through a saddle in the hills to the north – and right – of the Colli Albani. This pass, or gap, was why the Via Casilina had been built through there in the first place by the Romans. Because it was the main axis northwest to Rome, it stood to reason that the Germans would reinforce it as strongly as possible. This, though, would in turn then thin out the German forces along the Caesar Line in the centre of the Colli Albani. Nor was Clark convinced that much could be achieved by pushing across to Valmontone as it seemed that very few, if any, German troops from AOK 10 were using the Via Casilina to retreat. In any case, beyond the town lay more mountains, an enormous barrier blocking any further advance north.

As it happened, although Kesselring and his commanders were worried about such a threat to Valmontone, their concern was for the right wing of AOK 10 only, and they certainly did not envisage the whole of AOK 10 being destroyed there. In fact, the Via Casilina that passed through Valmontone was just one of five escape routes von Vietinghoff and his two corps commanders planned to use for their withdrawal. The other four all concertinaed northwards out from the narrow southern front, and so further away from Valmontone with every mile. The next route to the east of Valmontone, for example, led through Genazzano, eight miles by a rough track road across mountains; north of that lay another route, through Subiaco, fourteen miles as the crow flies, but barred from Valmontone by further mountains and tracks. The fifth route was more than forty miles as the crow flies, and many more on the ground. VI Corps did not have trained mountain troops; some American paratroopers dropped in to block these escape routes might have been put to good use, but Clark did not consider using the 509th Airborne Combat Team – who were out of the line but theoretically available – for this. At any rate, there was absolutely no chance whatsoever of heavily motorized US troops being able to speed over mountains and across rivers – there were a minimum of five that would have to be crossed to reach Subiaco, for example – and cut off the retreating Germans, who were lightly motorized and mostly passing down existing valley roads.

What's more, in the pre-DIADEM plan it had been assumed that Eighth Army would take the lead with the Fifth Army lagging behind on its right flank. This, it had been assumed, would push AOK to the west, so that with VI Corps cutting the Via Casilina at Valmontone, the bulk of the German army would be caught in a massive trap. But the opposite had happened: Fifth Army had taken the lead, with Eighth Army lagging behind and so pushing much of AOK 10 to the north-east on the four escape routes beyond the Via Casilina. In fact, German troops were now not planning to use the Via Casilina as a line of retreat at all. In other words, the opportunity to fold up much of AOK 10 by cutting the Via Casilina at Valmontone had already passed.

At any rate, on the morning of 26 May the Fifth Army commander issued orders which split his forces into two lines of attack rather than one. The 34th Red Bulls and 45th Division were now thrown north-west of Velletri through the Colli Albani, with almost all 1st Armored supporting them, and with 36th Texas Division ready to attack northwards too. This way his army could deal with the threat to his flank by turning and attacking it face on; it was also his judgement that it was the best and quickest way to take Rome, with the chance of destroying a large part of AOK 14 in the process. The other half of his forces – 3rd Infantry, Howze Force and 1st Special Force – were to carry on driving towards Valmontone, with the CEF continuing to push through the Lepini Mountains towards the Via Casilina, and II Corps also sweeping north.

Truscott, however, was dumbfounded by the decision and protested vociferously. Even once he had heard Clark's reasons for the switch he still believed the change of attack was mistaken, although did his best to fall in line. General Harmon, commander of 1st Armored, was also deeply gloomy about the change of plan, as was Colonel Hamilton Howze. 'It was a dreadfully bad decision,' noted Howze. 'It is a cardinal battle principle that in attack one should reinforce success.' The move also caused organizational difficulties – Howze Force, for example, was now seconded to 3rd Division, with the accompanying change of command structure. His main gripe – shared by Truscott and Harmon – was not the missed chance to annihilate AOK 10, but rather that Clark was losing out on a golden opportunity to capture Rome quickly by using the Via Casilina as the main axis of advance. Clark's concern, however, was that the bulk of his forces would be pushed into a comparatively narrow front if they pursued this option and that the original reason for the all-out drive to Valmontone had gone because there was no longer any chance of destroying the bulk of AOK 10 by doing so. He preferred to attack on a broad rather than a narrow front that he believed the Germans might find easy to block. What's more, the congestion on Eighth Army's front suggested that trying to put too much traffic through limited axes of advance was problematic, to say the least. Clark had a broader picture of what was going on than men like Howze, Harmon and even Truscott. The point was this: his decision to split his force and turn up into the Colli Albani was both arguable and entirely reasonable now that the situation on the ground had changed. In any case, his troops *were* still driving towards Valmontone – but now only a proportion rather than all of them.

At the time, Alexander accepted Clark's judgement, believing that VI Corps was attacking northwards in support of the main drive to Valmontone. Later that same day, 26 May, Alexander even visited the VI Corps front, and although he did not see Clark he did spend time with Gruenther. Having been fully briefed, Alexander told him, 'I am for any line of action which the Army Commander believes will offer a chance to continue his present success.' A few minutes later Alex added, 'I am sure that the Army Commander will continue to push towards Valmontone, won't he?' Gruenther assured him he was continuing to do so. 'I am certain that he left with no mental reservations as to the wisdom of your attack,' Gruenther wrote later in a message to Clark. 'He stated that if you are able to capture the high ground north of Velletri it would put the enemy at a serious disadvantage and would practically ensure the success of the bridgehead attack.'

At any rate, Clark had made his decision. Fifth Army would begin attacking the Caesar Line the following day, his combined army hammering together against AOK 14. Less than twenty miles away was Rome, the elusive prize that his army had been trying to reach for the past eight months. It was now so close, almost within the Allies' grasp. It looked likely, though, as dawn rose on Friday, 26 May, that hard fighting still remained until this glittering jewel could be finally taken.

CHAPTER 36

Rome

To BEGIN WITH IT looked as though Clark's change of plan was going to bring a sweeping and rapid success, with the thrust towards Valmontone continuing to surge forward. As Colonel Howze's tanks rumbled onwards they encountered plenty of still-burning German vehicles, but almost no resistance. Travelling in his armoured car, Howze saw only signs that the Germans had given up the fight. At one point he watched the tank ahead of him fire three rounds into a field of wheat. 'I thought this was imbecilic,' he noted, 'but went ahead to see an imploded 50mm German anti-tank gun with its crew strewn bloodily around. What had it been waiting for? It could have destroyed two or three of our tanks. The crew must have been exhausted – and asleep.'

As the day progressed they swept past Artena, where 3rd Infantry had surrounded the town, and by late afternoon the leading tanks of Howze Force were just a tantalizing mile from Valmontone and the Via Casilina. As Howze approached in his armoured car he could see three of his tanks burning. When he eventually caught up with his leading tank commander, Lieutenant-Colonel Bogardus Cairns, he learned that they were now being engaged by large numbers of German infantry coming from the east, as well as tanks from the north. Howze ordered his tanks to fall back for the night, but the following morning his outposts along the railway track to the north-west of Artena reported infantry advancing through wheat fields in front of them. The infantry were moving so brazenly that Cairns wondered whether they might be Americans.

'Hell, no,' Howze retorted, 'shoot 'em up!' He then hurriedly left his CP in his own tank and, reaching the front line, could hardly believe his eyes:

running and crawling through the wheat just 300 yards or so in front of them were Panzergrenadiers from HG-Division. 'We slaughtered them,' noted Howze. 'I imagine I killed half a dozen or more with my own tank gun.' The German attack collapsed.

In fact, Kesselring had told the HG commander, Generalleutnant Wilhelm Schmalz, not to deploy any more of his division other than the reconnaissance battalion until the rest had reached the front. That restriction had been lifted the previous evening, 26 May, and Schmalz had intended to attack first thing the following day, the 27th. The weight of American artillery fire had persuaded him to delay until later that evening to allow more troops entering the fray to catch up. Clearly, however, the changed orders had not reached the Panzergrenadiers now being cut down. It had not been a good start for Schmalz's division.

They then counter-attacked again that evening as Schmalz had planned but made little progress. They did, however, knock out two of Howze's tanks and bring down a concentration of artillery on 160 replacements arriving to join 6th Armored Infantry; half were killed or wounded before they'd been more than an hour at the front. Earlier that same day, 27 May, Artena fell, taken by Audie Murphy and 15th Infantry, and from the slopes above the town American artillery was now able to direct fire on to the Via Casilina. But, just as Clark had suspected, the Germans were pouring troops into the gap between Valmontone and the Via Casilina to the north of the Colli Albani. The secondary thrust of VI Corps, Howze Force and 3rd Infantry included, was now facing not only HG-Division but the recently arrived 334. Infanterie-Division from the Adriatic as well as the newly formed 92. Infanterie-Division, and the remnants of 715. Division who had joined them having retreated from the French. Suddenly, from having faced almost no opposition at all, there was now a sizeable German force offering a solid wall through which the exhausted Americans simply could not punch a hole.

In fact, by 28 May Truscott's entire attack had already started to run out of steam, and it became clear to Clark that he was now going to have to bring all units available into the battle. This meant that the Custermen and Blue Devils were to be brought up on the left flank of 3rd Infantry, the T-Patchers, so far still in reserve, would be sent into the centre of the line, and the two British divisions still holding the western edge of the Anzio bridgehead would also be ordered into the attack.

Meanwhile, on the 28th Truscott decided to move the 34th Red Bulls round to the west of Lanuvio, at the base of the Colli Laziali, and finally commit the T-Patchers into the centre of the line. The 45th Thunderbirds were to make a renewed effort on the Red Bulls' left flank. That same day, the two British divisions, the 5th and 1st, were also put on notice to attack the following morning. The 2nd Inniskillings were still only at 50 per cent strength and Captain David Cole, for one, was not relishing the attack at all. Confidence, however, was bolstered that evening when two Germans deserted and, hands raised, nimbly made their way to the Skins' lines. Interrogated, they freely spilled the beans on enemy dispositions opposite the British and revealed that 4. Fallschirmjäger-Division was starting to pull back behind the Caesar Line. Hans Liebschner was not among them: as a young survivor with an Iron Cross pinned to his chest, he'd been sent to train as an NCO at a school near Rome and so was out of the battle.

At any rate, when Captain David Cole and the rest of the battalion finally moved out of their gullies and dugouts early on the morning of 29 May they discovered that the Germans had already left. 'The fiery hell-hole of the beachhead', he noted, 'was ending not with a bang but a whimper.' Cole found it extraordinarily unsettling to now find himself standing upright, in plain sight, across a desolate landscape that even twenty-four hours earlier would have meant certain death. A faint breeze swept over from the sea, bringing no sweet smell of summer but only the sour stench of death. Unburied corpses lay everywhere, some reduced to skeletons shrouded in faded uniforms and straps of leather, while others were still quite new, their flesh waxy-white. And while some were shredded and in pieces, others were so complete as to appear as though they were asleep. From no-man's-land they anxiously probed their way through the enemy wadis and trenches – where one man was killed by a booby-trap – and then beyond, past rows of graves and churned-up ground that mirrored their own side of the line, until they reached the old German artillery lines. 'Everywhere there was evidence of hasty departure,' noted Cole, 'signs and notice-boards not removed, ammunition abandoned, half-finished meals and even men lying dead on stretchers in casualty clearing stations.'

Meanwhile, on the Eighth Army front, German rearguards, demolitions, mines, congestion and far too many river crossings were grinding the massed armour of XIII Corps and the Canadian Corps almost to a halt, much to the frustration of everyone concerned, from Alexander and General Leese down to those fighting on the ground. None the less, Eighth Army was on the move, just at a slow pace. The constant moving wasn't washing with Harry Wilson, however. 'I'm cheesed off hole-hopping from one spot to another,' he noted. 'War is a stupid business when you come to think of it – it turns men into moles and earthworms and throws their souls into the muck.' On 26 May he ended up being the lead truck in the lead convoy of 8th Indian Division HQ as they reached Castrocielo, the town near Frosinone where so many Germans had earlier experienced a brief leave. He felt rather proud to have successfully brought the convoy into their allotted new camp in order and without hiccup, but was put out not to have received a word of praise or acknowledgement for this. 'How inconsistent the Army is!' he jotted. 'At times it treats you as a child and plans everything for you; at other times it piles responsibility onto your shoulders and leaves you to fend for yourself.'

The Seaforth Highlanders were now at camp near the wreckage of Pontecorvo but out of the line; they were expecting to remain where they were with the rest of their brigade now for a week. Padre Roy Durnford had helped lead a dedication service at the new brigade cemetery on the 26th but spent most of the next day, 27 May, finding and burying yet more dead. He saw men still sitting up in their tanks, faces towards the enemy but with sightless eyes and bodies riddled by bullets or charred by flames. 'It is impossible to describe the inside of a tank after an explosion,' he noted, 'in which all ammo bursts and everything is torn to bits and shreds and jagged steel.' He buried a lone artilleryman he discovered by a ditch and also a dead German, then visited the engineers to collect another fifteen wooden crosses. What a service padres like Roy Durnford performed.

Eighth Army was now moving forward at a rate of around five miles or so a day. The Liri Valley narrowed as it ran further to the north-west, and was criss-crossed with numerous tributaries of the Liri. As such, it was no longer really suitable country for armoured warfare and congestion only increased. The Via Casilina was repeatedly blocked by mines and German demolitions, while the secondary roads and tracks were too narrow and often steep-sided, making it impossible to deploy off them at all and ensuring that any advance could only be made with a line of tanks one behind the other. Setbacks such as a bridging failure at Ceprano ensured that units were forced to pass through one another. No fewer than five divisions – two of which were armoured – were vying for space in this maze of narrow tracks, streams and gullies. As everyone involved could see, it was utter mayhem.

Leese could have perhaps left some of his vehicles and armour behind and continued advancing more or less on foot, but he would need his motor transport once they emerged into the more open rolling countryside to the east and north of Rome. He wished he had been sent a division of mountain troops as he'd requested – troops trained in fighting in mountains and who were able to carry pack artillery and equipment by using mules and limited motor transport. But the best-trained mountain division, the 52nd, had been earmarked for Normandy; and OVERLORD, of course, was the priority. Even so, they reached Ceprano, twenty miles north-west of Cassino, on the 26th and by the following day were only a few miles from Ripi, where Viviana Bauco and her family lived. She had been watching the German retreat for days. She thought the Germans looked increasingly desperate, crazy even. This moment, she was keenly aware, was very possibly the most dangerous they had yet faced: the front about to pass through, frustrated and angry Germans hastily leaving. On 26 May her father was angrily grabbed by a German soldier and thrown to the ground; landing badly, he fractured his right leg. He was now immobile and bed-bound, but her mother wanted their children to flee and hide in a shelter until the fighting had passed. 'How could I go there safely,' Viviana scribbled in her diary, 'leaving them in danger?'

On 28 May, four German soldiers burst into their house, yelling at them to leave; all civilians were supposed to have evacuated Ripi, it seemed. At the time, Allied planes were roaring overhead, shells whistling, whining and crashing around their battered village. Viviana and her mother and sister clung to her father, expecting to be killed at any moment either by the Germans or by Allied bombs and bullets. Eventually left alone, they moved their father to the cellar and the rest of the family took shelter in the caves underneath the village as their mother had urged, while the battle raged above them and they listened to the crash of shells and tumble of falling buildings. Not until just after midnight on 31 May was Ripi finally liberated. 'Night of jubilation!' she wrote. 'Festive hurrahs announced the English had arrived.' As soon as it was light, Viviana ventured out to see what had become of their little village. 'What a terrible sight!' she noted. 'Stones, tiles. Beams, crumbling windows, electric wires in the streets, shell damage in almost every house – this is what war brought to Ripi.'

Kesselring had finally ordered the general retreat of AOK 10 on 28 May, by which time it was far too late to bring these shattered forces back in an orderly manner alongside AOK 14 on the Caesar Line. While units of von Senger's XIV Panzerkorps were holding the Allies at bay either side of the Via Casilina, the rest of AOK 10 was now rapidly disappearing down the four other escape routes. Georg Zellner and his 3. Bataillon of 134. Regiment had been ordered to pull back on 24 May, along with other units of the LI Gebirgs-Armeekorps. Carrying out a fighting retreat, they fell back down the fourth escape route in the direction of Sora. Following them hard were the New Zealanders of X Corps. 'Night march,' noted Zellner on 28 May. 'Command post Santa Capello.' Two nights later his command post was at Vallefredda, more than twenty miles from Belmonte and near the town of Sora. They'd marched on foot and by night to reach here, but even now the New Zealanders were hard on their tails.

A huge shift was suddenly taking place in the front line, all of which had been caused initially by the rapid advance of the CEF and of II Corps. With the southern half of the front all the way to Anzio now firmly in Allied hands, not only was the bulk of AOK 10 retreating through the valleys to the north, Juin's CEF was gradually being squeezed out between Eighth Army on their right and US II Corps on their left. Juin therefore suggested that his troops sweep out of the Lepini Mountains and cut across the Via Casilina towards the town of Ferentino, ten miles north of Frosinone, and then head up the Via Casilina towards Valmontone. A better idea might have been to hurriedly push on north from Ferentino and try and block the road to Fiuggi, one of AOK 10's escape routes. However, the CEF had slowed its pace dramatically and by the time the French were entering Ceccano on the southern side of the Liri Valley on 30 May, the Canadians were finally reaching the town themselves. For the time being, the French were played out.

Meanwhile, on the main battlefront, the Allied attack was faltering. For four days, VI Corps could make no impression on the Germans' defences of the Caesar Line, while Eighth Army continued to struggle slowly northwards at a rate of between three and four miles a day. In London, Churchill was beginning to fret. Looking at the arrows on his map, he could see the advance appeared to have stalled, and that Clark was not bringing maximum pressure on Valmontone. 'I feel I should be wanting in comradeship,' he signalled to Alex, 'if I did not let you know that the glory of this battle, already great, will be measured, not by the capture of Rome or the juncture with the bridgehead, but by the number of German divisions cut off.' What the maps did not tell him, however, was that even by travelling mostly at night to avoid Allied air attacks, the retreating divisions of AOK 10 could walk down their escape routes considerably faster than Eighth Army could follow in their motorized transport. Nor was any part of AOK 10 actually using the Via Casilina as a line of retreat.

Meanwhile, VI Corps was attacking against fortified positions in which the enemy had the advantage of height. Even at the main point of Clark's thrust, to the west of the village of Lanuvio, the ground was still hilly and running against the line of attack. Clark did, though, now have huge forces arraigned against the Caesar Line, with the British 5th and 1st Divisions in the south-west, the Thunderbirds on their flank, then the Red Bulls and 1st Armored, the T-Patchers entering the fray in the centre, and then finally 3rd Division, Special Service Force and Howze Force. Also waiting in the wings were the two divisions of II Corps. Realistically, there was simply no way Clark could have sent this immense force to Valmontone; in fact, his only course really had been to do exactly as he'd done: to turn and face the Germans on a broad front and for them all to attack at the same time to exert the maximum amount of pressure. If there was one criticism to be thrown at Clark's plans to assault the Gustav Line back in January, it had been that the various assaults had all been launched in succession rather than concurrently. Not so now: von Mackensen's forces were being battered all along the line.

It was just that, so far, the German line showed no sign at all of crumbling. Fifth Army appeared to have hit another solid wall of enemy defences. Then, for some reason, the gods of fortune played into Clark's hands. For just as it seemed as though a bloody and bitter stalemate might grip the front once more, the Germans let down their guard.

It was on the afternoon of 28 May that Captain Roswell Doughty was passed a report that had come in from an air force sergeant attached to the regiment, in which he claimed that a significant gap in the line had been discovered up on Monte Artemisio. It turned out that the seconded USAAF sergeant had been part of a patrol and taken command when the patrol leader had been killed. They'd stayed out on the slopes of Artemisio for two days and two nights and, apart from the death of the original patrol leader, had met very little opposition. This report not only reached Doughty but made it all the way to Major-General Fred Walker, who had begun to have a sinking feeling that his division was about to be slaughtered all over again. Now, though, it seemed as if there was a gap in the Caesar Line that it might well be possible to exploit.

The Colli Albani and the Colli Laziali were a rather unusual geographical feature based around a giant but extinct volcano. There was an inner ring, at the heart of which was a plugged crater, and an outer ring, with farmland between the two. It was this outer ring – a long, semicircular, continuous and very pronounced ridgeline – that overlooked the plain down to Anzio and the coast but also the valley and the next chain of mountains, the Lepini, to the south-east and also to Valmontone and the Via Casilina. The highest point in this outer ring was Monte Artemisio, just over 3,000 feet high.

On the 28th, Walker made a personal recce of Monte Artemisio and also ordered detailed aerial reconnaissance. 'I saw almost no field works,' he noted. 'Nor did I see any entrenchments or gun positions.' Air reconnaissance photos revealed nothing either. That afternoon, he made another personal recce and saw there was a track that led to the summit. Perhaps, he wondered, it might be possible to widen this to take artillery and armour up there. The division's Chief Engineer felt certain that it could be done. Truscott was initially dubious, but after cross-examining the divisional Chief Engineer gave Walker the go-ahead to try and capture the ridge. Walker might have approached the Rapido crossing back in January with a singular lack of imagination and tactical skill, but he was certainly thinking creatively for this latest attack. Armed with an extra regiment of engineers and a number of powerful bulldozers, the Texas men began their assault on the night of 30 May.

Feldmarschall Kesselring, on one of his regular visits to the front, had also noticed this gap in the line between 362. Infanterie-Division – positioned between Velletri and Lanuvio – and the now almost complete HG-Division, now in the line between the eastern side of Monte Artemisio and Valmontone. Immediately giving the order to fill the gap and to do so with all speed, he was horrified when, a day later, the gap was still not closed. 'I personally spoke sharply to the Commander of Fourteenth Army,' noted Kesselring, 'and drew his attention to this inexcusable failure to take prompt action, pointing out to him that what could be accomplished easily with one battalion today might be impossible with a division tomorrow.'

Von Mackensen had called for the gap to be closed, but such was the shortage of men that the only battalions available were two from the HG-Division, at that stage still reaching the front and unable to move up on to Monte Artemisio in time to stop the Texas men's assault. Despite Kesselring's rebuke, von Mackensen had still not sufficiently closed the gap, and the Texans were able to infiltrate first 142nd Infantry and then 143rd on to Monte Artemisio along with the 751st Tank Battalion.

Among those now back in action was Captain Bob Spencer, leading Company G of the 143rd Infantry. Almost immediately, he was hit in the back by pieces of shrapnel that got lodged all round his spine. That he had been so swiftly wounded again rather underlined just how dangerous it was to be an infantry officer. On one level he was unlucky; on another, he'd the luck of the devil because he wasn't paralysed and he wasn't dead. But he was once more rushed back to hospital and, for the time being at any rate, out of any further action.

Such casualties aside, the T-Patchers had done exceptionally well; by sunset on 1 June they had won total control of the entire Monte Artemisio Ridge, by which time the 111th Engineers had bulldozed and blasted a twenty-five-mile track to the summit. The engineering feats of the Allies were simply astonishing. Meanwhile, 141st Infantry, using part of the new mountain route, slipped in behind Velletri, cutting off the German retreat in that part of the line. Suddenly, a massive hole had been blown in the Caesar defences.

When Kesselring heard of the American infiltration, he wasted no time in recommending to Hitler that von Mackensen be sacked immediately. To his mind, his troublesome army commander had disobeyed two major orders: first, when he initially refused to move 29. Panzergrenadier-Division south, and now with his failure to close a gap in the line that should never have existed in the first place. 'It was no longer possible,' noted Kesselring, 'after four years of war, to reply on the strict execution of an order.' Kesselring's gross mishandling of his men and slavish adherence to Hitler's demands never to retreat were far more responsible for the catastrophic defeat his armies were now facing than von Mackensen's lack of enthusiasm for wantonly sacrificing ever more troops, but loyalty to the Führer outweighed sensible military judgement by this stage of the war. A counter-attack by the HG-Division tried to unseat the Texas men, but failed; the Americans were by then too entrenched. Kesselring's worst fears had been realized.

Clark, on the other hand, now recognized that a great opportunity had suddenly and inadvertently arrived to smash the Caesar Line once and for all. He had also completely regrouped, with his two British divisions brought up to the line in the west and II Corps, with 3rd Division, Howze Force and 1st Special Force attached, also brought into line between the

Texas men and Artena. Aware that VI Corps had suffered no small amount of casualties, Clark was none the less never afraid to throw men into the breach if he felt it was a risk worth taking. Moreover, all across AOK 14's front he now had both sustained and wide pressure – his favoured policy. The night before the renewed assault Clark gave another press conference, an 'off-the-record' briefing about the next phase of the battle, in which he once again emphasized that capturing Rome was not the primary objective. Rather, he stressed, the main aim was 'to kill and annihilate as many of the Germans as possible' on Fifth Army's front, although he had not lost sight of the fact that Rome might be taken as a result; this was very much in line with Alexander's original aims for DIADEM.

He spoke to the press men with confidence but was hiding an anxiety he felt keenly. Back at his Anzio HQ, he sat down to dictate a letter to his wife Renie, his pet dog, Pal, on his lap as he spoke. 'We are in as desperate a battle as Fifth Army has ever been in,' he wrote. 'If it were only the battle I had to worry about and not many other matters, it would be easy, but I am harassed at every turn on every conceivable subject – political, personal and many others.' He again reiterated his hope that they would annihilate much of AOK 14, and prayed for early results. 'I am on the go every minute,' he added, 'trying to visit my commanders to get the latest information and buoy them on to greater effort.'

But now, as May gave way to June, the final act in the battle was about to be played out.

Audie Murphy and his platoon were now south of Valmontone; they'd moved forward overnight and although they woke to enemy shellfire, they discovered they were dug in amid a cherry orchard. The branches above Murphy were thick with plump, ripe cherries and they were wondering whether to risk getting out of their foxholes when Tattie Lipton had a good idea. 'He lies on his back and with bursts from his Tommy gun, clips off branches of the tree,' noted Murphy. 'They fall in our hole; and we eat.'

Also surrounded by cherry trees was Oberleutnant Hans Golda, whose 8. Batterie was now dug in among the foothills overlooking Valmontone and Artena. They'd been there a number of days since the collapse of the Senger Line, although had reached this new position only after a hellish journey that had seen them pass slaughtered horses, exploding ammunition trucks and endless close shaves as they'd been harried by

Jabos. Since then, however, he'd had a chance to catch up on sleep in a proper bed in the farmhouse they'd taken over and fill his belly with fruit and wine. Golda's soul had been nourished too by the beauty of the landscape, so different from the desolation of the Cassino front: the corn high in the fields, the fecundity of the cherry orchards and the sun beating down. For one whole day he simply lay back on his bed in the farmhouse and idly plucked cherries. He felt consumed with joy.

The peace and beauty were shattered with the beginning of the American assault the following day, 1 June. Enemy artillery pounded their position. A direct hit obliterated the first floor of the farmhouse. They fired back for as long as they could, then, with evening arriving, and even heavier shelling from the enemy, they retreated into their cellar. They felt safe there until there was an enormous explosion and fire could be seen in the cellar entrance. 'There was screaming, groaning and pushing,' noted Golda. 'Finally the smoke cleared and I saw the entrance to the cellar had half caved in.' He tried to calm his men, but, looking down at the tangle of bodies, realized some would not survive. 'One of my radio operators was lying there with his left ear missing,' he noted. 'He looked at me without a word. I gave him solace then he slowly shut his eyes and lost consciousness.' Another radio operator was dead, his chest torn open. A further man was ashen and groaning, his hip bleeding profusely. Those, like Golda, who were unharmed did their best to tend the wounded. Later that evening, once it had become dark and the shelling had died down, they loaded the injured men on to one of their vehicles and took them to the dressing station. 'The cellar floor was covered in blood, which stuck to our boots,' scribbled Golda. 'We shovelled earth over it and slept on top, although the whole night I hardly shut my eyes.'

Meanwhile, advancing towards Hans Golda and the German lines around Valmontone were the tanks of Task Force Howze. Its commander, Colonel Howze, had been in a tank himself and glad to have the chance for some shooting. 'We knocked out a few anti-tank guns,' he noted, 'killed a number of infantry, captured a fair bag of prisoners and received a lot of enemy artillery fire.' By nightfall they were abreast of 3rd Infantry Division, but to Howze's disappointment had been unable to penetrate further.

Also back in action that day was 349th Infantry of the Blue Devils Division, now to the west of Valmontone in the foothills of the Alban chain and with their old friends, the Custermen, on their left. Their advance had begun the previous evening but by the morning of 2 June they'd still not met any enemy. They were now closing in on the hills west of the Via Casilina and Valmontone, which meant crossing open fields first. As the infantry swept forward the fighting began again and Captain Klaus Huebner found himself frantically looking round for somewhere to set up his aid station. Unfortunately, the last building he'd seen had been a mile back, which he felt was perhaps too far behind. Spotting a small, dense grove of trees, he decided to hurry there instead, only to find a number of abandoned German foxholes in the little copse. He and his men had not been there long, however, when he realized he'd made a terrible mistake. German shells were bursting against the trees and raining not only shards of white-hot metal but pieces of wood as well. One piece of shrapnel passed straight through his trouser leg without touching him but he certainly couldn't count on such luck continuing. 'Every few seconds during treatment of a casualty,' he wrote, 'I am forced to jump back into my hole, and the poor fellow lying wounded is left exposed for additional injury.' Soon after, he realized that the better part of valour was to get himself and his team out of there as quickly as possible and head back to the house he'd spotted a mile further back, catching a ride with an ambulance that had come forward to collect several stretcher cases. They moved into the cellar of a farmhouse, jeeps bringing in new cases every few minutes, among whom were a number of Germans, all from HG-Division and a lot of them pitifully young. After dark they moved forward again, following the infantry and pausing for the night at a shot-up railway station.

Captain Roswell Doughty, meanwhile, moved into Velletri that day, now in the hands of the T-Patchers, to help supervise the disposition of more than 200 prisoners. He thought they looked like some of the sorriest examples of soldiers he'd ever seen. 'They were crumby, dirty, smelly creatures,' he noted, 'so worn out and tired from the pummelling we'd given them that they looked like sleepwalkers.' Doughty's task was to pick out the ones most likely to talk and interrogate them. He'd become a bit of an expert at this; he reckoned he could pretty much always tell, just by looking at them, which were most likely to break.

Later that evening, his work over for the day and the POWs packed off in trucks, he returned to the battalion CP in the schoolhouse on the road into the town. Doughty had seen enough death and destruction to last a lifetime since reaching Italy the previous September, but nothing had prepared him for the sight he discovered in a yard behind the CP. The building had evidently been used by the Germans before them and clearly by their equivalent of the graves registration units, for there, abandoned in a hurry, was a 15-foot-high pile of corpses, most not complete: torsos, heads, arms, legs and hands that had been scraped off the battlefield and were yet to be buried. Hurrying past the pile to a different outhouse, he nearly tripped over another body. There was, it seemed, nowhere to hide, but there were other GIs milling about, most eating rations, and Doughty was hungry too. Finding a tree stump, he sat himself down and began to eat.

One man caught his eye: a GI who got up, a sandwich clamped between his teeth, and went over to the pile of body parts, rummaged around and, using his bowie knife, cut a German belt buckle from a corpse then, with the knife back in its sheaf, carried on eating. Doughty watched this aghast, but then realized that despite his horror he'd carried on eating his own rations himself. This is what this brutal war had done to them all.

That same day, Friday, 2 June, Hans Golda and his Werfer team continued to keep firing from their now devastated position, but the German front was crumbling and in the afternoon they were ordered to withdraw north to Palestrina. In the light of this German withdrawal, Task Force Howze had a far easier day and reached their original objective of Lábico, astride the Via Casilina, while battered Valmontone, Alex's original goal for VI Corps, finally fell to 3rd Infantry.

There was now no question of pushing on north, beyond the town and over the mountains, however. If any retreating AOK 10 troops were to be caught it would have to be by Eighth Army, and only by pursuing them down the routes through the valleys that spread out, like spokes on a wagon wheel, to the north and north-east. The Canadians of 5th Armoured Division might have been able to catch and overwhelm the last of the rearguards – mostly the remnants of 1. Fallschirmjäger-Division – now that the traffic congestion was at last thinning out. General Tommy Burns, however, the Canadian Corps commander, chose this moment to pull them back and let the infantry division take over the lead. The changeover was supposed to be gradual – one brigade at a time – so as not to impede the advance, but it was still not the best time to risk momentum or lose firepower. At any rate, von Vietinghoff's rearguards managed to keep them at bay while the rest of AOK 10 continued to slip away into the hills.

The Germans were now on the run across the front: the breakthrough at Valmontone had presaged the collapse of the whole of the Caesar Line along AOK 14's front. On 3 June, Colonel Hamilton Howze had the strange experience of receiving an order by air when General Keyes, the II Corps commander, buzzed over him in his Piper Cub and dropped a package with the words, 'Howze – get these tanks moving!' Now alongside the 88th Blue Devils, Howze and his Task Force set off immediately. Initially, he felt his tanks were not progressing fast enough, cautiously approaching every new bit of terrain. So he ordered a platoon of Shermans to rush on down the road at ten miles per hour. Inevitably, every so often the lead tank would hit a mine or be knocked out by enemy fire, but it ensured their rapid progress. Such an advance also meant that they were not stopping to mop up any enemy troops, so that as the infantry followed more slowly behind they often found themselves involved in heavy firefights. Even so, the Germans were in disarray. Howze's tanks made short work of several enemy columns, including a battery of horse-drawn artillery. At one point, Howze's jeep driver paused to relieve himself. Armed with only his pistol he disappeared into some scrub and returned with around twenty Germans, all with their hands up. Later a German colonel was captured and spent the rest of the day travelling with Howze in the jeep.

By the following morning, 4 June, they were closing in on the capital. Howze was now placed under the command of 1st Special Force. It was agreed that the assault on the suburbs was an infantry job, so Howze and his tanks spent a frustrating morning waiting for the go-ahead to follow on behind. Eventually, at 3.30 p.m., his Task Force began its final drive for Rome. They lost two more tanks but knocked out five of the enemy's and captured a further large number of prisoners. 'Between strongpoints', noted Audie Murphy, who was following up the road, 'the German retreat turns into practically a rout.'

Captain Klaus Huebner had barely stopped, following close on the tails of the battalion as they surged forward towards Palestrina. On the morning of 4 June they were cautiously probing forward when the enemy once again opened fire. Huebner had set up his latest aid station near a large birdbath in the middle of a vineyard. Casualties quickly began mounting and he was still busy dealing with the wounded when a completely naked German soldier ran manically up the track towards him, lacerated in the abdomen, legs and lungs by shrapnel fragments. Huebner couldn't understand how he could stand, let alone run, but he gave him a shot of morphine and calmed him down before more German casualties were brought in. The pace was quickening, however, and later that afternoon they moved their aid station forward again, this time to a small, thick-walled stone shed at the edge of a cemetery.

Later that afternoon the stretcher-bearers brought in another HG-Division man in a terrible way. 'On pulling back the blanket,' jotted Huebner, 'I see several feet of gut spilled out over his abdomen and laying between his legs; every time he coughs, more bowel spills out; to make matters worse the bowel is perforated in numerous places and fecal material pours out of the holes.' The German told him he'd been hit eight hours earlier, but despite the appalling nature of his wounds seemed quite calm. Huebner was conscious that nothing was sterile any more, but after setting up an intravenous drip of morphine he tied off the perforated loops of bowel with black silk string and stuffed all the loose gut back into the man's abdomen, then stitched him up enough to ensure there were no more spillages and put a binder around his stomach. 'He receives two units of plasma and smokes several cigarettes,' noted Huebner. 'Not once has he complained.' Then he was loaded off on to an ambulance and taken away. Whether he survived, Huebner had no idea.

In Rome itself, the Germans had been leaving all that day, Sunday, 4 June. Any remaining cars and vehicles had been requisitioned, but there were no detonations, no mass destruction of roads and buildings. Kesselring had, as promised, spared the Eternal City. Back in Rome and feeling largely recovered were the Gappisti, Elena and Paolo. They had returned a few days before to monitor the German retreat. By 4 June they were even wearing partisan armbands: red, white and green with CLN spelled out. They were not alone – there were now hundreds of partisans, most armed, marking the German withdrawal.

Not that Colonel Hamilton Howze saw them. As dusk began to fall, he and his leading company were nearing the centre of Rome. In contrast, the streets were completely empty, with doors and windows shuttered tight. Howze called a halt with his company of tanks, waiting for the rest of his column to catch up. Some Italians clearly heard him and his driver talking, because suddenly a window opened and someone shouted '*Americano!*' Soon, hundreds of Romans were emerging, throwing themselves upon Howze and his men, the women showering them with kisses. 'It was,' he noted, 'both gratifying and annoying.'

Just to the south of the city, on the Via Casilina, General Clark and his small entourage of jeeps pulled off the side of the road while the Fifth Army commander conferred with his generals – Keyes of II Corps and Frederick of 1st Special Service Force. They were standing at the foot of a shallow hill, on the top of which was a large sign inscribed 'ROMA.' For Clark this was a proud moment, and he was particularly keen to get a photograph of himself standing by this sign – a shot he knew would make for a great news picture. There had been some shooting going on nearby, but when it died down Clark, Keyes and Frederick gingerly scrambled along a ditch and up towards the sign. When it seemed safe, they stood and no sooner had the camera shutters snapped than a bullet smacked into the sign next to them. 'I doubt that anybody ever saw so many generals duck so rapidly,' noted Clark. 'We crawled back down the ditch to safer ground, but later Frederick had someone get the sign and eventually brought it to me as a souvenir.'

Captain David Cole and the 2nd Skins also reached Rome that evening, having broken through the German defences north of Ardea, near the coast. By dusk they'd reached the River Tiber and camped in a wood nearby, then Cole and his friend, Sam Irving, took a jeep and drove on into the city, speeding past the Colosseum and Piazza Venezia, where, on 10 June 1940, almost four years earlier, Mussolini had declared war on Britain and France. Italians cheered and mobbed them. 'The Italians all said, "We are so happy to see you at last,"' Cole wrote in a letter home. '"Why did it take you so long?"'

Rome had fallen, and the following day, Monday, 5 June, the Eternal City was awash with Americans, the streets swarming with overjoyed Italians who believed that at last their salvation was at hand. Klaus Huebner was among the men of the Blue Devils now entering the city. The outskirts were a shambles, with overturned and blasted German vehicles lining the roads and the rumble of artillery fire still heard to the north. But as they neared the centre the signs of battle diminished and suddenly they found themselves being cheered by huge crowds of people. 'Our vehicles barely have room to pass,' he noted, 'and we ride at a snail's pace.' People threw flowers, cheered and shook their hands. Huebner was agog – at the beautiful buildings, and a city that was intact rather than a pulverized wreck. A number of Italians, he noticed, wept quite openly. Children jumped on to the jeep for a brief ride. 'Our trip through Rome,' he noted, 'is fantastic and seems like a dream.'

In the middle of the morning, Clark and his entourage of jeeps drove into the centre of the city too. The Fifth Army commander certainly wanted to savour the moment, but he also wanted to waste as little time as possible pursuing AOK 14 north of Rome, and so one of his staff officers suggested he meet his corps commanders for a quick conference at the Campidoglio on Capitoline Hill. Neither Clark nor any of the entourage had been to Rome before, and they lost their way; not that the Fifth Army commander minded too much – after all, it was good to see the sights and to bask in the adulation of the near-hysterical Roman crowd. When they eventually reached the Campidoglio they then discovered that the town hall was locked. After banging on the door several times, Clark pulled out his map and laid it out on the balustrade. Juin, especially, looked bewildered, but his corps commanders gathered round him. There was a pressing mob of reporters and photographers. 'Well, gentlemen,' said Clark, glancing up at the assembled correspondents, 'I didn't really expect to have a press conference here – I just called a little meeting with my corps commanders to discuss the situation. However, I'll be happy to answer your questions.' Then he added, 'This is a great day for the Fifth Army.' It was also a great day for all the Allied armies in Italy – the largest single victory by the Allies so far in the war.

The Battle for Rome was over.

A British Sherman loaded with infantry rumbles forward in the heat and dust, late May 1944.

Postscript

THE VERY NEXT DAY after General Mark Clark drove through Rome, the Allies launched their cross-Channel invasion of Normandy. D-Day, 6 June, 1944 immediately took over as the most dominating single event of the Western Allies' war, and Italy and the campaign that followed receded somewhat into the background. In truth, Operation OVERLORD had overshadowed the Italian campaign from its conception, yet, psychologically at least, it was good for all Allied forces involved in Italy that they had at least one entire day to bask, centre-stage, in the glory of their remarkable triumph.

The casualties, of course, had been horrendous. Between 11 May and 4 June the Germans suffered 51,754, dead, wounded and missing; the Allies, 43,746. For the Germans, this represented around a third of their total fighting strength and, needless to say, it was the infantry units that bore the largest burden of the losses. Entire battalions had been annihilated. The German capacity to rebuild these units – these phoenix divisions – from scratch at breakneck speed was astonishing, but every time they did this the replacements arriving were just that bit younger and older and less well trained; and with every battle, especially such a sustained one as DIADEM, the pool of veterans was diminished just a little bit more. Germany was paying dearly for Hitler's insistence on fighting south of Rome and for this Kesselring, so assiduously following the Führer's orders, was also culpable. It had been Kesselring who had thrown everything at Salerno the previous September – and whose failure had been rewarded with supreme command and the poisoned chalice of fighting for every yard of Italian soil.

It was also on Kesselring's watch that the horrific Ardeatine Massacre had taken place on 24 March 1944, and it had been his decision – albeit under pressure from Hitler and the OKW – to execute ten Italians for every soldier killed in the Via Rasella. He could have avoided sanctioning such a terrible massacre; and he could also have decided not to make the ten-to-one policy a hard-and-fast rule, yet he did so because he believed it was the best policy to deter further partisan activities. In this he was entirely mistaken. Young Italians took to the hills and mountains because of oppression, because the alternative offered even less hope, and if anything the brutality of the German policy made the situation considerably worse. Partisan bands swelled dramatically with the onset of summer and by the time the war in Italy was finally over, at least 30,000 German troops had been killed and many more wounded at their hands. Many more civilians would pay the ultimate price too. From the Massacre of San Terenzo to that of Monte Sole and Sant'Anna – and countless more – the story of the German retreat up the leg of Italy was also one of untold civilian suffering. People were left dangling from streetlamps in towns, shot while tied to fenceposts, and entire villages and mountain communities were razed. It was a brutal reign of terror.

Historical reputations are fascinating in the way they evolve and take hold, and it is astonishing really that for so many years opinions on the Italian campaign have remained so largely consistent despite plenty of evidence to suggest that should not have been the case. Generally speaking, Kesselring has emerged rather better than he should have done. He was tried for war crimes and found guilty but avoided the death sentence, in part due to lobbying by Field Marshal Alexander – as he had become – and others who viewed him as a soldier first and foremost and a stout-hearted if misguided opponent, and so a man worthy of respect. He was given a life sentence instead of the noose, but was freed very early in 1952 after just five years in prison and lived out his days peacefully.

While he was unquestionably guilty of war crimes, his reputation as a military commander has, for the most part, remained high. As an operational commander he was superb, but tactically and strategically he deserves far less credit. In thrall to Hitler, he made a series of terrible decisions from the moment the Allies landed in Italy and his handling of his troops was appalling. It made no military sense to fight in front of the Gustav Line, for example, and repeatedly driving his beleaguered units until they were operating as skeleton formations was cruel as well as senseless. The counter-argument is that it was because of this that it took the Allies nine months to reach Rome, but to what purpose has rarely been questioned. The Italian campaign might have sucked in ever more Allied resources, but the Allies could better afford these than could Nazi Germany. Sacrificing one division after another, and then again – and again – achieved very little when the terrain over which they were fighting was of limited strategic importance for Germany. Fighting so maniacally south of Rome ended up drawing in more troops from elsewhere, which particularly played into Allied plans for OVERLORD. Pulling back to the Pisa–Rimini Line would have cost fewer lives, shortened very stretched lines of supply, and saved a large swathe of Italy from the brutal storm of war that so devastated much of the country.

The reputation of the German troops in Italy, and especially that of 1. Fallschirmjäger-Division, has also remained extraordinarily high, not least because of the credit given to them by Allied commanders at the time. It has been fascinating to read of the contempt and surprise expressed by Allied troops on the ground when they came face to face with prisoners. Most, like Roswell Doughty or Klaus Huebner, for example, were shocked at how dishevelled and physically unimpressive they were; it was as though they'd been sold a lie. In many ways they had been. The number of seasoned veteran German troops in Italy was increasingly small and they played a disproportionally large role. These few undoubtedly kept the show on the road, but equally, as I hope I've shown, defending was considerably easier than attacking, and while discipline was vital, training was less so. It was not especially challenging to fire their machine guns or mortars, while remaining at their posts was about discipline rather than any skill. The 1. Fallschirmjäger-Division might have been all-German, better motivated, and with an esprit de corps lacking in other units, but the notion that they were an elite unit of highly trained special forces was absurd.

In contrast, while historians have been kind to the Allied troops being flung into battle, the commanders have emerged as donkey-like figures to the lions they commanded. The notion of 'lions being led by donkeys' is a ridiculous analogy, not least because donkeys have a traditional role as hard-working beasts of burden and lions as being notoriously lazy. The reality is that the Allied army commanders were dealt an incredibly tough hand: expectations were, from the outset, very high, while materially the Italian campaign was massively under-resourced for what was being demanded. Alexander has been accused of lacking 'grip', of not having the intellect to manage such a challenging command and of depending too much on Harding. Such criticisms are unfair. In fact, he handled the grand strategy with tact, charm and with a streak of Machiavellian cunning and managed his polyglot forces with considerable skill. The moment he was given the backing to fight the battle on his terms, the result was the triumph of DIADEM; the enormity of that victory, which was the Allies' greatest up to that point, should not be underestimated or lost in the excitement and prioritizing of D-Day that followed.

Furthermore, DIADEM might well have turned into an even greater victory had Operation ANVIL not raised its head once more almost the moment Rome had fallen. Rather than exploit success and drive home the Allies' victory, the decision was made to mount an invasion of southern France after all. It morphed into becoming Operation DRAGOON and was launched on 15 August 1944; much of its forces were stripped out from Alexander's Allied armies in Italy and also from the MAAF. At the very moment when the all-out pursuit of Kesselring's shattered forces made the most immediate military sense, seven divisions were taken away, including the T-Patchers, Thunderbirds, 3rd Infantry and the entire CEF, as well as a mass of air forces. As always, it was about choices and priorities. The Allies, for all their materiel wealth, could not be everywhere.

Yet no single figure in the Italian campaign emerged with such a consistently lambasted reputation as General Mark W. Clark, something I have always found utterly mystifying and even more so having researched and written this book and *The Savage Storm*. I first looked at the Italian campaign many years ago and remember standing in the valley beyond the bridgehead at Anzio, roughly between the towns of Cori and Artena. Behind me were the Lepini Mountains, and across the way were the Colli Albani and the great ridgeline of Monte Artemisio. I thought then, and continue to think the same thing every time I visit, that had I been General Clark, I would have been very reluctant to send the bulk of my forces across the flanks of those mountains.

That initial visit made me wonder why Clark had been so criticized time and again for his decisions in the Italian campaign, but particularly this one: to turn his troops to face the AOK 14 dug in behind the Caesar Line in the Colli Albani. The well-worn argument is that Clark was so desperate to get to Rome first that he flagrantly disobeyed Alexander's direct orders. In so doing he placed personal ambition over the greater need to destroy the enemy, and as a direct consequence allowed much of AOK 10 to escape. To make matters worse, such was his rampant

Anglophobia that he gave orders to shoot any British soldier who was seen in Rome ahead of his own American troops.

All of this is utter nonsense, yet it is incredible how well rooted it has become. On the other hand, Clark is hardly the only victim of misconceptions, misinformation and conspiracy theories.

There's no doubting he saw Rome as a great prize, not for the Allies but for Fifth Army – a force that he had nurtured since its formation in North Africa – and also for America. Sure, he was happy to take some of the glory that came with such a victory, but this should not cloud the fact that Clark recognized how important the capture of Rome by an American army would be viewed back home in the United States and around the world, both in terms of future operations in Italy but also in giving Fifth Army the credit he believed they were due. After all, it had been Fifth Army that had absorbed the bulk of the fighting since the previous September, and especially since the start of 1944. And it was only right that Fifth Army should take the glory of being first into Rome. It's also important to remember that the US Fifth Army was, like Eighth Army, a polyglot force that included French, British, Canadian, Indian and New Zealander units as well as American.

Without question, though, he had harboured suspicions that the British – and Eighth Army in particular – were trying to steal his show whenever possible; it's also hard not to overstate how frustrated Clark had been during Freyberg's brief but disastrous command of the New Zealand Corps, and how impotent he had felt to do anything about the catastrophic decisions that were being made. What became known as the Second and Third Battles of Cassino, in February and March, marked some of the lowest points of generalship by British and DUKE forces in the entire war and Clark, for much of that six-week period, had had his hands tied by the delicate politics of having an over-promoted and hapless Dominion general over whom he had little influence or control. What's more, since January he'd had two British generals above him in Alexander and Jumbo Wilson.

So if Clark was a little paranoid about potential British ambitions it was not altogether surprising. 'Clark was always very sensitive about the taking of Rome,' said Alex after the war. 'I assured Clark that neither I nor Leese wanted the Eighth Army to participate in its capture; we felt it fell naturally into the Fifth Army's area.' That might have been Alexander's intention, but Leese would have jumped at the chance to pip Clark for

Rome if the opportunity had arisen. A few days before the battle began, one of Clark's periodic paranoias began to develop over the matter. 'I know factually that there are interests brewing for the Eighth Army to take Rome,' he vented in his diary, 'and I might as well let Alexander know now that if he attempts anything of the kind he will have another all-out battle on his hands; namely, with me.' Peevish, certainly, but at that time he knew that Fifth Army's role in the battle was due to be secondary – until the Anzio breakout at any rate – with Eighth Army's effort down the Liri Valley expected to be the main push. Before DIADEM, he sensed Eighth Army might storm ahead and reach Rome first despite reassurances to the contrary.

As the battle developed, however, and Fifth Army raced ahead of Eighth, so his worries began to subside. Never one to hold back from ranting to his diary, his anger, when it surfaced, was directed at other matters once the battle began. Indeed, his concern about reaching Rome was barely mentioned again.

And if his motives for changing Alex's plan from the Anzio beachhead were to get to Rome quickly, then he was certainly taking a massive risk, as events subsequently showed. It was good fortune that Walker and his Texans had discovered the potential opening on Monte Artemisio; without that breakthrough, Clark could well have faced a far more protracted and costly battle. What's more, had Fifth Army become unstuck, Eighth Army might have taken Rome after all, something that would never have occurred had he stuck to Alex's original plan and pressed his main effort up the Via Casilina. Certainly, by the beginning of June Leese was rubbing his hands in glee at the prospect of stealing Clark's thunder. 'AL [Clark]* is making desperate efforts to get to Rome on his own,' he wrote to his wife on 1 June. 'I only hope he will do and we can then go north on our own business, but I'm afraid he'll bungle it like Cassino and then we shall have to clear it up. I believe it would have been much better if he would wait for us to help but he was terrified we might get to Rome first.' Then, with mounting relish, he added, 'I only hope it does not warp his military decisions if he does fail now and we have to go. I shall race him to it all out and beat him.' So Clark's suspicions had been entirely justified.

Interestingly, however, Leese never criticized Clark for the change of

* Leese used a number of code letters to represent people in his letters home. Clark was 'AL,' although why he chose these particular letters is not clear.

attack, even though he knew Alex's battle plan as well as anyone. On the contrary: 'The American effort from the bridgehead was extremely good,' he admitted in a letter to General Montgomery, 'the troops fought magnificently with great dash.' Nor did Kirkman, the XIII Corps commander, in his diary complain about Clark's switch; and neither did Harold Macmillan in his, despite being a close friend of Alexander's – and despite spending considerable time with the C-in-C throughout the battle. Yet all three were quite happy to complain about people and to gripe to their diaries whenever they felt the need. Indeed, nor even was there any criticism from Harding, the co-architect of DIADEM, in his diary. 'Battle has gone well,' he noted on 4 June, 'and as planned. Everyone very thrilled and pleased.'

After the war Clark was repeatedly grilled over his decision by interviewers, and always he gave much the same answers: that his overriding reasons were of a military nature. Later, he claimed that on his brief return to the United States in April, Roosevelt himself had told him he had to take Rome before D-Day. Yet by turning to face AOK 14 at the Caesar Line head on, it is reasonable to argue – as Hamilton Howze maintained – that the path to Rome took longer than it would have done had he exploited through Valmontone and headed up the Via Casilina. But in so doing he almost certainly destroyed more of AOK 14 than he would have done otherwise. Rather than annihilating AOK 10, as had been Alex's original plan, the Allies seriously mauled the former and virtually annihilated the latter. On balance, that was a better outcome than had been originally envisioned.

Certainly, it is unfair to suggest that the Allies failed to annihilate AOK 10 south of Rome because of Clark's decision to change his line of attack, and it is a myth that should be firmly kicked into the long grass once and for all. Nor did Clark ever issue any orders that British troops in Rome were to be shot. Of course he did not. Needless to say, there is no evidence whatsoever for it. In any case, the British troops in Fifth Army entered Rome straight away; David Cole was a case in point. In 1981, Raleigh Trevelyan, a former British second lieutenant who had served in Anzio, wrote a book called *Rome '44* in which he cited a claim by Harold Macmillan that Alexander had been furious when he'd heard that Clark had turned away from Valmontone. This single quote has been repeated by almost every historian who has written about this period over the course of the intervening years. Interestingly, there was no footnote for the source of this quote, a matter I raised with Trevelyan some years ago before he died. He was rather embarrassed about it but assured me he'd interviewed Macmillan in the 1960s, by which time the entire mythology around this episode had taken root. Alexander was famous for never losing his temper; neither Harding nor Macmillan nor anyone else mentioned any fury on Alex's part at the time. Nor did Alexander express any concern either. In any case, Clark did send troops to Valmontone, it was captured, US forces did use the Via Casilina to advance on Rome and the city fell before D-Day. It was just that no German troops were cut off here – because none of them were using it as a route of escape.

Clark's reputation also took a beating because of the Rapido fiasco when, in 1946, the 36th Infantry Division Veterans' Association, stoked up by Fred Walker, demanded a Congressional Inquiry into Clark's actions. It was a ludicrous charge on every level and dismissed in quick order, but the damage had been done. Suddenly, a post-war case against Clark's generalship was mounting. An alternative view, and one that I hope I've demonstrated, is that it was up to the army commander to provide the means, which he most certainly did, and the responsibility of the divisional commander to use those assets in the best possible way. If anyone let the side down at the Rapido it was Walker, not Clark, which is why it was so brilliant that it was the T-Patchers' commander who unlocked the Caesar before Rome.

While Clark could be vain, prickly and quick-tempered, he was also physically courageous as well as having the courage of his convictions; he was a tough, aggressive commander with an extraordinary eye for detail, a meticulous planner, and, for the most part, got the big decisions right. No other US Army commander in the war had such a challenging brief or such an immense force, made up from multinational troops and spread over two entire fronts. The responsibilities resting on his shoulders and the demands laid upon him were gargantuan. He was certainly not without flaws, but like all the very best commanders he understood the strategic, operational and tactical levels of war equally well – something not shared by all given such high command – and his grasp of the fundamentals and ability to learn were impressive considering his age and comparative lack of experience when he landed at Salerno back in September 1943. And when Alexander was bumped up to Supreme Allied Commander in the autumn of 1944 it was Clark, not a British general, who he recommended should take over as Army Group commander. The final Allied offensive in Italy had been Clark's conception and had led to the complete implosion of German forces there. Their unconditional surrender on 2 May 1945 was the first such capitulation of German troops. General Mark Clark, one of the more interesting characters to have emerged from the war, certainly deserves a far better reputation.

The characters I've followed through this book are just a snapshot – a handful only of the many hundreds of thousands – or millions in the case of the Italians – who fought, died or survived this terrible period in Italy's long, rich history. It's hard not to feel pained by the scale of destruction. The awfulness – the terrible folly – of destroying the abbey still stabs at the heart, but plenty of other communities were obliterated too. The town of Cassino was 100 per cent destroyed – that is, not a single building remained intact – but the surrounding villages and towns hardly fared better. Nearby Pignataro, for example was 93 per cent destroyed. Belmonte Castello, close to where Major Georg Zellner was dug in, had been 95 per cent destroyed. Esperia, in a valley beneath the Aurunci Mountains, had not been evacuated until the last minute but lay 92 per cent destroyed. The village of San Giorgio, halfway between the Gustav and Senger Lines, was 89 per cent utterly destroyed. So it went on, and so it would continue as the battle rumbled northwards. After the war the abbey was painstakingly reconstructed, the work completed largely by German prisoners of war, and reconsecrated by Pope Paul VI on 24 October 1964, yet most of the surrounding towns and villages were not rebuilt with quite the same care and attention to detail. Today it is hard to tell that the abbey was ever flattened in February 1944, so perfectly has it been rebuilt. The same cannot be said for Cassino, which is a larger, more bustling town than it ever was, but certainly lacks its former charm. Hidden, though, behind trees on the lower slopes of Castle Hill one can still see the remains of some of the original houses, blasted on 15 March 1944. It is an eerie, haunting place to wander around.

Elsewhere in the surrounding mountains one can still find the remains of old sangars and foxholes. On Belvedere and Abate, for example, there are a number. Monte Cassino has been tidied up; Albaneta had been partly rebuilt and is now home to a micro-brewery. Baby oaks, acacia and other trees cover the ridges that once were bare and ghastly killing zones. On Point 593 one can climb under the lip and find the remains of German positions; just off the summit there are German wire entanglements still to be tripped over. Atop this bluff stands a memorial cross to the Polish Corps, while the Colle d'Onofrio, where Rudolf Donth and his men were dug in, is now the very striking and beautifully laid out Polish Cemetery. General Anders, when he died in 1970, chose to be buried here, among so many of his men. It remains a place of pilgrimage to many Poles – and other visitors besides – to this day.

Yet, it is the people, above all, that live long in my own thoughts. Most, I'm glad to say, survived the war. Audie Murphy, Felix Sparks, Roswell Doughty and Frank Pearce all headed off to France that August and fought through the long campaign that led them up from the south all the way into Germany. Some lived out long lives, others did not. After becoming the most decorated US serviceman in the war, Audie Murphy became a movie star but was tragically killed in a plane crash in May 1971, aged only forty-five. Many of the rest of the characters featured here fought on in Italy. I don't know what happened to them all. Harry Wilson left his superbly vivid and often very witty diary to the Imperial War Museum in London but with no notes, no forwarding address, nothing. What happened to him remains unknown. Jack Ward appears to have made it back to his wife, Else. I picked up his diary when it came up for sale in Blackwell's Rare Books. It's sad to think there's no one in his family – if any of his family remain – who wanted it. On the other hand, it's wonderful to read and I will certainly continue to treasure it and think about him and his experiences often.

Of the Germans, I also know little about Georg Zellner, Rudolf Donth or Hans Golda, to name but three. What remarkable testimonies they left behind, however. I found it impossible not to care deeply for these men. Jupp Klein I was lucky enough to meet and get to know reasonably well; a tough, fiercely intelligent but delightful old man he was too. I'd certainly not have wanted to fight against him. He did, I know, remain haunted to his dying day by the face of the young Tommy he'd killed at point-blank range in the Liri Valley. I will also never forget talking to Pasua Pisa in her farmhouse kitchen on Monte Rotondo. Silent tears ran down her face that day as she recalled the death of her son and father and the brutal rape she suffered. She told me she could never sleep with a man again after that. Once the war was over she visited Rome, went to an orphanage and picked out a baby that looked strong and well and smiled at her happily. She took him home and he became her son. When I visited, he was still farming there. They gave me a glass of their buffalo milk. It was delicious.

What a terrible, tragic fate befell all these people, though. All in their contemporary jottings betray a combination of hope, regret, despair, exhaustion, resignation, fatalism, longing and deep sadness: for what they were missing, for what they were witnessing. For what they'd become. This was their lot. Their burden. But oh so vividly do their characters emerge from the words they noted at the time. The novelist L. P. Hartley famously wrote that the past is a foreign country, but these characters do not seem foreign or in any way alien. To me they feel very real, and it has been a privilege to bring them back to life, in a way, in the pages of a book. As I write this, soldiers and civilians alike in too many corners of the world are going through many of the same experiences so many of these characters suffered. Will we never learn? It seems not, for while history never repeats itself, patterns of human behaviour most certainly do. Despots, warped ideologies, the thirst for power, anger and intolerance continue to blight the world, so that new generations face devastation, desolation and slaughter. It is so tragic.

It has been humbling to write about these brave men and women but profoundly upsetting too. I can vividly remember the feeling of shock and deep sadness when I first read the diaries and letters of John Strick, Dom Eusebio, Mike Doble and Lawrie Franklyn-Vaile and realized all had died during these brutal months in Italy. And I can also just as clearly recall visiting the Commonwealth War Graves Cemetery at Cassino, a lovely haven at the southern edge of town. It was a beautiful late-April day, the surrounding trees already in full, fecund leaf, and the sun warm. Looming above it were the mountains and there, looking down, and shining in the sunlight, was the rebuilt abbey. I found the grave of Mike Doble, paused then wandered on and stopped before Lawrie Franklyn-Vaile's headstone. '*Semper paratus*' was inscribed underneath his name, regiment, date of death and age. 'Always ready.' It was ridiculous, really, to feel so choked up, but I couldn't help myself. And then suddenly, from a tree at the southern edge of the cemetery, a nightingale began bursting into song: strange, haunting, but immeasurably melodic and beautiful. A reminder that life had returned here to this place that had once been so very desolate.

And with it, I felt a renewed sense of hope.

A British Tommy and his German captive. Many of the German replacement troops were young teenagers like this fellow.

APPENDIX I

Timeline of Events

1944

January

SATURDAY, 1
Heavy storm at Cassino front

SUNDAY, 2
Alexander orders SHINGLE to be launched on 21 January

WEDNESDAY, 5
US attack out of Mignano Gap – San Vittore and Cervaro

THURSDAY, 6
The Father Abbott refuses to leave the abbey – more civilians taken away

SATURDAY, 8
General Sir Henry 'Jumbo' Maitland Wilson takes over as Supreme Allied Command Mediterranean
Count Galeazzo Ciano on trial in Verona

SUNDAY, 9
VI Corps leaves front to prepare for SHINGLE
Monte Maio captured for good by Special Service Force

TUESDAY, 11
Ciano executed by firing squad

WEDNESDAY, 12
Directive for Allied winter offensive issued by Alexander
Harold Macmillan hosts Anglo-US conference about Italy

SATURDAY, 15
Fifth Army reaches Gustav Line

MONDAY, 17
British X Corps crossings of River Garigliano near Castelforte

WEDNESDAY, 19
46th Division failed crossing of River Garigliano

THURSDAY, 20
US 36th Division's abortive attempt to cross the River Rapido
German 90., 29. and HG-Divisione counter-attack X Corps around Castelforte
Georg Zellner opposite Texan attacks

FRIDAY, 21
River Rapido crossings

SATURDAY, 22
Operation SHINGLE: Allied landings at Anzio
German counter-attacks stopped by X Corps on River Garigliano

SUNDAY, 23
German LXXVI Panzerkorps moves to Anzio beachhead

MONDAY, 24
CEF attacking towards Belvedere and Abate
Hitler orders destruction of Anzio 'abscess'

TUESDAY, 25
34th Red Bulls cross Upper Rapido
French attack Monte Belvedere

SUNDAY, 30
VI Corps attack at Anzio

MONDAY, 31
British 1st Division reaches Campoleone Station
US Rangers caught in trap and destroyed near Cisterna

February

TUESDAY, 1
Kesselring puts Heidrich on notice to move 1. Fallschirmjäger-Division to Cassino

THURSDAY, 3
German preliminary counter-attack at Anzio
Major Rudolf Kratzert and 3./3. FJR move up on to Cassino
Kampfgruppe Schulz of 1. FJR pulled out of Cisterna and sent to Cassino

FRIDAY, 4
Halt of CEF attack
British salient at Anzio destroyed
2nd NZ Division and 4th Indian Division formed into the New Zealand Corps
Tuker falls ill

SATURDAY, 5
FJR MG Bataillon moves to Cassino from Cisterna – only 125-strong

SUNDAY, 6
Kratzert's 3./3. FJR retakes Point 593

MONDAY, 7
Second German attack at Anzio
The Factory captured by German troops
Kampfgruppe Schulz reaches Cassino
X Corps put on defensive at River Garigliano

WEDNESDAY, 9
Texans move up to Monte Cassino overnight 9–10
Kratzert's men retake Point 593

FRIDAY, 11
New Zealanders start taking over at Cassino

SATURDAY, 12
Tuker leaves his hospital bed to visit Freyberg
Freyberg submits plans for Monte Cassino to Clark

SUNDAY, 13
Debate over bombing of abbey

MONDAY, 14
Order given to bomb abbey following day

TUESDAY, 15
Bombing of Abbey of Monte Cassino
Night: attempt by Royal Sussex Battalion to retake Point 593

WEDNESDAY, 16
Germans at Anzio launch Operation FISCHFANG
Renewed attempt to take Point 593 by Royal Sussex Battalion fails

THURSDAY, 17
Day 2 of Operation FISCHFANG
Fighting on Monte Cassino
Night: 3rd attempt to take Point 593 by 4th Rajputana Rifles and also 1/9 Gurkhas and 2/4 Gurkhas
Night: 28 Māori Battalion attacks Cassino Station

FRIDAY, 18
Day 3 of Operation FISCHFANG

SATURDAY, 19
End of FISCHFANG – Kesselring given permission to pause by Hitler

SUNDAY, 20
King Vittorio Emanuele agrees to retire

TUESDAY, 22
Gen John Lucas relieved of command – Truscott takes over

THURSDAY, 24
Tentative start date for Operation DICKENS

SATURDAY, 26
Heavy rain
Heidrich takes over from Baade as commander of Cassino – headquarters in Roccasecca
1./3. FJR = 610 men; 3./3. FJR = 775; 4./3. FJR = 880

SUNDAY, 27
Heavy rain

Priority for Fifteenth Air Force now supporting ground operations in Italy, not OVERLORD

TUESDAY, 29
Germans launch Operation SEITENSPRUNG at Anzio – fails

March

WEDNESDAY, 1
Kesselring orders 14. Armee on to defensive at Anzio
US 88th Division move to front near Castelforte

SATURDAY, 4
Von Mackensen orders 14. Armee on to defensive at Anzio

WEDNESDAY, 15
8.30 a.m. bombing of Cassino town
Operation DICKENS – New Zealanders attack

THURSDAY, 16
Fighting in Cassino

FRIDAY, 17
Fighting in Cassino

SATURDAY, 18
Fighting in Cassino

SUNDAY, 19
Fighting in Cassino

MONDAY, 20
Fighting in Cassino
Vesuvius erupts

TUESDAY, 21
Fighting in Cassino

WEDNESDAY, 22
Fighting in Cassino

THURSDAY, 23
Battle for Cassino halted
GAP partisan attack in the Via Rasella
34th Red Bulls posted to Anzio

FRIDAY, 24
Massacre in the Ardeatine Caves – 335 killed
85th Division sails from Algeria to Italy
Postponement of Operation ANVIL

SUNDAY, 26
XIII Corps relieves New Zealanders

April

SUNDAY, 9
Easter Sunday

MONDAY, 10
Abdication: King Vittorio Emanuele III agrees to hand over powers to his son once the Allies are in Rome

MONDAY, 17
Alexander authorized to prepare for Operation DIADEM

May

MONDAY, 1
Mark Clark's forty-eighth birthday

THURSDAY, 11
Launch of Operation DIADEM

FRIDAY, 12
Poles fail to take Monte Cassino

TUESDAY, 16
Canadian 1st Infantry Division into action again

WEDNESDAY, 17
Night: Fallschirmjäger abandon Monte Cassino

THURSDAY, 18
Poles capture Abbey of Monte Cassino

FRIDAY, 19
Alex authorizes move of US 36th Division to Anzio
Gaeta falls

TUESDAY, 23
Breakout from Anzio begins
Eighth Army attacks Senger Line

WEDNESDAY, 24
German forces ordered to fall back to Caesar Line
Hitler orders four more divisions to be sent to Italy

FRIDAY, 26
Clark changes direction and moves towards Rome through the Colli Albani

TUESDAY, 30
Start of final drive for Rome

June

FRIDAY, 2
Caesar Line collapses

SUNDAY, 4
Fall of Rome
King Vittorio Emanuele hands over remaining powers to his son, Umberto
Von Mackensen sacked and replaced by Joachim Lemelsen

MONDAY, 5
Mark Clark in Rome

TUESDAY, 6
Operation OVERLORD – D-Day

Ironic humour was often all the troops had left during the long, grim battle of attrition at Anzio.

APPENDIX II

Order of Battle: Allied and Axis Armies, 22 January 1944

Allies

US FIFTH ARMY
General Mark Clark

Anzio force
US VI Corps
British 1st Infantry Division
US 3rd Infantry Division

Army reserve
US 1st Armored Division
US 45th 'Thunderbird' Infantry Division

Gustav Line front
Corps Expéditionnaire Français
2ème Division d'Infanterie Marocaine
3ème Division d'Infanterie d'Algérienne

US II Corps
34th 'Red Bulls' Infantry Division
36th 'T-Patchers' Infantry Division

British X Corps
5th Infantry Division
46th Infantry Division
56th Infantry Division

BRITISH EIGHTH ARMY
General Oliver Leese

V Corps
Canadian 1st Infantry Division
8th Indian Division

XIII Corps
4th Indian Division
78th 'Battleaxe' Infantry Division

Arriving in army area
3rd Carpathian Infantry Division
Canadian 5th Armoured Division

German

ARMEEOBERKOMMANDO (AOK) 10
General Heinrich von Vietinghoff

Gustav Line front
LXXVI Panzerkorps
1. Fallschirmjäger-Division
26. Panzer-Division
334. Infanterie-Division
305. Infanterie-Division
3. Panzergrenadier-Division

XIV Panzerkorps
5. Gebirgsjäger-Division
15. Panzergrenadier-Division
29. Panzergrenadier-Division
44. 'Hoch-und Deutschmeister' Infanterie-Division
71. Infanterie-Division
94. Infanterie-Division
Hermann Göring Fallschirm-Panzer-Division

I Fallschirmjägerkorps
4. Fallschirmjäger-Division
90. Panzergrenadier-Division
92. Infanterie-Division

ARMEEOBERKOMMANDO (AOK) 14
General Eberhard von Mackensen

Northern Italy
162. 'Turco' Infanterie-Division
16. Waffen-SS Panzergrenadier-Division

LI Gebirgs-Armeekorps
362. Infanterie-Division
278. Infanterie-Division

LXXVI Panzerkorps
356. Infanterie-Division
65. Infanterie-Division

Army reserve
114. Jäger-Division
188. Gebirgsjäger-Division

APPENDIX III

Order of Battle: Allied and Axis Armies, 11 May 1944

Allies

US FIFTH ARMY
General Mark Clark

Anzio beachhead
US VI Corps
British 1st Infantry Division
US 1st Armored Division (less Combat Command A)
US 3rd Infantry Division
British 5th Infantry Division
US 34th 'Red Bulls' Division
US 45th 'Thunderbirds' Division

Gustav Line front
Corps Expéditionnaire Français
1ème Infanterie Division
2ème Division d'Infanterie Marocaine
3ème Division d'Infanterie Algérienne
4ème Division Marocaine de Montagne

US II Corps
85th 'Custermen' Infantry Division
88th 'Blue Devils' Infantry Division

Army reserve
US 36th 'T-Patchers' Infantry Division

BRITISH EIGHTH ARMY
General Oliver Leese

British X Corps
New Zealand 2nd Infantry Division

British XIII Corps
4th Infantry Division
6th Armoured Division
8th Indian Division
78th 'Battleaxe' Infantry Division

Canadian I Corps
1st Infantry Division
5th Armoured Division

Polish II Corps
3rd Carpathian Infantry Division
5th Kresowa Infantry Division

Army troops
South African 6th Armoured Division (main front)

V Corps (Adriatic)
4th Indian Division
10th Indian Division

German

ARMEEOBERKOMMANDO (AOK) 14
General Eberhard von Mackensen

Anzio beachhead
715. Infanterie-Division
362. Infanterie-Division
26. Panzer-Division

I Fallschirmjägerkorps
3. Panzergrenadier-Division
65. Infanterie-Division
4. Fallschirmjäger-Division

Army reserve
29. Panzergrenadier-Division
92. Infanterie-Division

ARMEEOBERKOMMANDO (AOK) 10
General Heinrich von Vietinghoff

Gustav Line front
LI Gebirgs-Armeekorps
5. Gebirgsjäger-Division
44. 'Hoch-und Deutschmeister' Infanterie-Division
1. Fallschirmjäger-Division

XIV Panzerkorps
71. Infanterie-Division
94. Infanterie-Division
15. Panzergrenadier-Division

Army reserve
90. Panzergrenadier-Division (main front)

Armeeabteilung von Zangen (northern Italy)
Hermann Göring Fallschirm-Panzer-Division
162. 'Turco' Infanterie-Division
356. Infanterie-Division
278. Infanterie-Division
188. Gebirgsjäger-Division

A Canadian Sherman and infantry move on through the Liri Valley, May 1944.

Notes

Abbreviations used in the Notes

BA-MA	Bundesarchiv-Militärarchiv, Freiburg
FMS	Foreign Military Studies, US Army Heritage and Education Center, Carlisle, PA
IWM	Imperial War Museum, London
LHCMH	Liddell Hart Centre for Military Archives, King's College London
SWWEC	Second World War Experience Centre, Otley, West Yorkshire
TNA	The National Archives, Kew
USAHEC	US Army Heritage and Education Center

Prologue

1 'Have my camp . . . ': Mark Clark letter to Renie Clark, 23/10/1943, Mark W. Clark Papers, The Citadel, Charleston, South Carolina
2 'Am having a portable . . . ': ibid.
3 'Wish you could see . . . ': Mark Clark to Renie Clark, 19/10/1943
9 'That's one reason . . . ': Mark Clark to Ann Clark, 23/12/1943
9 'misconduct in the face . . . ': Mark Clark Diary, 10/12/1943
10 'The mission of our forces . . . ': memo to Brigadier-General Raleigh R. Hendrix, Mark Clark Papers, 12/12/1943

1 The Storm

17 'The new year . . .': Viviano Bauco Diary, 1/1/1944
18 'May this day . . .': Wilhelm Mauss Diary, 1/1/1944, in *The War Diary of Dr Wilhelm Mauss*
18 'Happy New Year': Jack Ward Diary, 1/1/1944
20 'I have never seen . . .': Lawrie Franklyn-Vaile letter to Olive, 2/1/1944
21 'Tell them there's a bloody blizzard . . .': Harry Wilson Diary, 31/1/1944
21 'Only the elements . . .': ibid.
21 'About fifty breezes . . .': ibid., 1/1/1944
22 'Flatulence, heart and lung . . .': Georg Zellner Diary, 27/12/1943
22 'We were seized . . .': ibid., 1/1/1944

23 'Although we already knew it . . .': ibid.
23 'Reidl reads . . .': ibid.
23 'Storms which assume . . .': BA-MA RH/24/14
26 'Consensus here': Mark Clark Diary, 1/1/1944

2 A Cunning Plan

27 'All hell is breaking loose . . .': Georg Zellner Diary, 2/1/1944
27 'We huddle in the corners . . .': ibid., 3/1/1944
28 'Abandon all hope . . .': ibid.
28 'I take my diary . . .': ibid.
37 'I urgently request . . .': Mark Clark Diary, 2/1/1944
37 'had a difficult time . . .': ibid., 4/1/1944
38 'light-heartedly': ibid.
38 'Certain factors have . . .': cited in Winston S. Churchill, *The Second World War*, Vol. V, p. 395
38 'Even if this does . . .': ibid.
39 'I love you, Darling . . .': Leonard Garland Diary, 1/1/1944
39 'They have seen . . .': ibid., 2/1/1944
40 'This sort of job . . .': ibid., 4/1/1944
40 'Nothing left there . . .': Maurice Bechard Diary, 4/1/1944
41 'He was shaken up . . .': ibid.
41 'Sometimes . . . it felt like . . .': ibid., 5/1/1944
42 'I deploy another . . . ': Georg Zellner Diary, 5/1/1944
43 'Nothing is achieved . . .': ibid., 7/1/1944

3 The Tragedy Waiting to Happen

45 'May God forgive . . .': Dom Eusebio Diary, 31/12/1944, in Eusebio Grossetti and Martino Matronola, *Monte Cassino Under Fire*, p. 61
46 'It is impossible . . .': Dom Eusebio Diary, 5/1/1944
46 'All were weeping': ibid., 6/1/1944
46 'It is a real Noah's Ark': ibid., 9/1/1944
47 'We are still very fearful . . .': ibid., 10/1/1944
47 'Howard Maughan killed . . .': Leonard Garland Diary, 4/1/1944
47 'Tony Gray killed outright': ibid., 7/1/1944
47 'Cleared a lot of trails . . .': Maurice Bechard Diary, 8/1/1944
48 'Young lads . . .': Georg Zellner Diary, 8/1/1944
49 'Despite his coarseness . . .': ibid., 9/1/1944
49 'So the madness . . .': ibid., 13/1/1944
49 'First, I take a deep breath . . .': ibid.
49 'They are the ones . . .: ibid.

4 Meddling Madness

54 'The superiors have no . . .': Georg Zellner Diary, 14/1/1944
54 'The higher commanders . . .': Wilhelm Mauss Diary, 11/1/1944

56 'Shelled all night . . .': Roy Durnford Diary, 3/1/1944
59 'Nothing can be changed . . . ': Joseph Klein, *Fallschirmjäger*, p. 135

5 The Garigliano

61 'Has been a grand day . . .': Jack Ward Diary, 8/1/1944
62 'Jerry country': ibid., 11/1/1944
62 'Think that is going . . .': ibid.
63 'We often discussed . . .': Leonard Garland Diary, 11/1/1944
64 'Operation SHINGLE is on! . . . ': Mark Clark Diary, 8/1/1944
66 'He did not wish . . .': ibid., 9/1/1944
66 'I'm frightfully keen . . . ': ibid.
68 'Advise action taken': ibid., 11/1/1944
69 'We lost very many . . .': John Strick letter to his mother, 21/12/1943
70 'Drink has been his problem . . .': ibid., 31/12/1943
70 'I have only time . . .': David Cole, *Rough Road to Rome*, p. 136
73 'In the distance . . .': John Strick Diary, 22/1/1944
73 'Time is now . . .': Jack Ward Diary, 17/1/1944
76 'Good. Good . . .': Cole, *Rough Road to Rome*, p. 147
77 'A pretty scruffy lot . . .': ibid., p. 154
77 'Battle in progress . . .': John Harding Diary, 18/1/1944

6 The Plight of the People

81 'He saw things as they were . . .': von Senger in FMS C-95b, USAHEC
82 'He was, after all . . .': ibid.
82 'I am convinced . . .': AOK 10 Kriegstagebuch, 18/1/1944, Mark Clark Papers
84 'I shot about eight foot . . .': ibid.
84 'My nerves were in pieces . . .': John Strick letter to his mother, 22/1/1944
85 'I kept breaking into tears . . .': John Strick Diary, 22/1/1944
85 'Have no news of the Sgt . . .': John Strick letter to his mother, 22/1/1944
85 'It is terrible . . .': John Strick Diary, 22/1/1944
85 'Discipline tightens . . .': Audie Murphy, *To Hell and Back*, p. 60
87 'Already shadows dance . . . ': ibid., p. 72
88 'I kiss her full . . .': ibid., p. 77
88 'Mother accommodated . . .': E. P. Danger, Diary and Reflections, IWM 4465
90 'Economically in Italy . . .': Pasqualina Caruso Diary, 5/1/1944
92 'As usual, the small people . . .': Norman Lewis Diary, 12/1/1944, in *Naples '44*, p. 72
92 'Be nice to get back . . .': ibid., p. 73
92 'Starving cats, rats . . .': ibid.
92 'He was suffering . . .': ibid., p. 74
93 'So Priore would be . . .': ibid.

7 The Largest Air Force in the World

95 'At 8 o'clock . . .': cited in James Parton, *Air Force Spoken Here*, p. 355
99 'Flak heavy . . .': T. Michael Sullivan Diary, 15/1/1944
99 'Completely destroyed target . . .': ibid., 16/1/1944
99 'They are going to hit us . . .': ibid., 17/1/1944
99 'Easy mission . . .': ibid., 18/1/1944
100 'We would often start . . .': Robert A 'Smoky' Vrilakas, *Look Mom – I Can Fly!*, p. 146
100 'The opponent's aircraft . . .': Wilhelm Mauss Diary, 21/1/1944
101 'Extensive enemy movements . . .': AOK 10 Kriegstagebuch, 17/1/1944
101 'Faithful as a child . . .': Hans Golda, BA-MA MSg 2/4335, p. 43
102 'He was completely torn . . .': ibid.
103 'Personal life creeps . . .': Georg Zellner Diary, 16/1/1944
103 'When do you actually . . .': ibid.
104 'Outrageous luck': ibid., 18/1/1944
104 'What a shame . . .': ibid.
107 'Everything tickety-boo . . . ': Leonard Garland Diary, 17/1/1944
108 'The failure of the attack . . .': Mark Clark Diary, 20/1/1944
108 'We are still doing well . . .': Jack Ward Diary, 20/1/1944
108 'News has just . . .': ibid.

8 The Rapido

112 'There were no satisfactory answers . . . ': Major-General Fred L. Walker, 'Comments on the Rapido River Crossing', USAHEC
115 'We heard machine-gun bullets . . .': Roswell K. Doughty, *Invading Hitler's Europe*, p. 106
116 'We can't stay awake . . .': Georg Zellner Diary, 20/1/1944
116 'We help him . . .': ibid., 21/1/1944
116 'Strong enemy assault . . .': AOK 10 Kriegstagebuch, 21/1/1944
117 'I have talked with Keyes . . .': Mark Clark Diary, 21/1/1944
117 'It would have been . . .': General Hamilton Howze, Senior Officers Debriefing Program, USAHEC
117 'It was an ideal place . . .': ibid.
118 'Imagine my consternation . . .': Robert F. Spencer, Veterans History Project, Library of Congress
120 'Lost one officer . . . ': Maurice Bechard Diary, 21/1/1944
121 'Slowly, he walked away . . .': ibid., 22/1/1944
121 '1) We had 50% . . .': cited in Robert L. Wagner, *The Texas Army*, p. 121
121 'He came back . . . ': Doughty, *Invading Hitler's Europe*, p. 107

9 SHINGLE

123 'I learn from the radio . . .': Filippo Caracciolo Diary, 11/1/1944, in *43/44 Diario di Napoli*, p. 106
124 'I recall my relations . . .': ibid.

125 'We are not sure . . .': Harold Macmillan Diary, 3/11/1944, in *War Diaries*, p. 276
127 'I am hopeful . . .': ibid., 20/1/1944
127 'Everything was agreed': ibid.
128 'Very depressing . . .': John Harding Diary, 19/1/1944
128 'It's a difficult gamble . . .': ibid., 20/1/1944
128 'Whole 5 Army plan . . .': ibid., 21/1/1944
128 'SHINGLE set off OK . . .': ibid.
129 'We were horrified . . .': E. P. Danger Diary, 14/1/1944
130 'We have every confidence . . .': John Lucas Diary, 10/1/1944
131 'I think we have . . .': ibid., 21/1/1944
131 'The Fifth Army is attacking . . .': ibid.
133 'I had laughingly . . .': William O. Darby, *Darby's Rangers*, p. 180
134 'FOGGIA NEW YORK . . .': Mark Clark Diary, 22/1/1944
135 'All those who could lift . . .': E. P. Danger Diary, 20/1/1944
135 'You look extremely scruffy': cited in William Sugden Papers, SWWEC
136 'Wet, cold, miserable . . .': Ross S. Carter, *Those Devils in Baggy Pants*, p. 117

10 Rapid Response

138 'Her brain was leaking . . .': Dom Eusebio Diary, 18/1/1944
138 'Only God can save us': ibid., 19/1/1944
139 'A diabolical noise . . . ': ibid.
139 'You've had a slight fracture . . .': Robert F. Spencer, Library of Congress
140 'At first I was inclined . . .': John Strick Diary, 22/1/1944
140 'How terrible if . . .': ibid.
142 'A dead Kraut . . .': Harry L. Bond, *Return to Cassino*, p. 24
142 'You know, the three . . .': ibid., p. 26
142 'But I'm a good swimmer . . .': ibid., p. 32
142 'You don't know . . .': ibid.
143 'What in Christ's name . . .': ibid., p. 42
143 'Like a lion it crouched . . .': ibid., pp. 44–5
143 'The cable railway . . .': Wilhelm Mauss Diary, 21/1/1944
144 'Yesterday passed full of tension . . .': ibid., 23/1/1944
145 'We have a problem . . .': cited in Lloyd Clark, *Anzio*, p. 99
148 'No idea, Liebschner . . .': Hans-Paul Liebschner, *Iron Cross Roads*, p. 68, IWM 9011
149 'a prime tank trap': cited in Martin Blumenson, *Salerno to Cassino*, Office of the Chief of Military History, U.S. Army, 1969, p. 385

11 The Distant Hills

156 'Today it can be stated . . .': cited in Richard Lamb, *War in Italy*, p. 205
157 'The hour has arrived . . .': DORER No. 1256
158 'Some blood had to be spilled . . .': Mark Clark Diary, 23/1/1944
159 'I must keep in motion . . .': John Lucas Diary, 24/1/1944
160 'a) To seize and secure . . . ': ibid., 12/1/1944

161 'As I write . . .': Jack Ward Diary, 22/1/1944
161 'The battle is still fierce . . .': ibid., 24/1/1944
161 'I'm sitting in an ambulance . . .': Spike Milligan, *Mussolini: My Part in His Downfall*, p. 279
161 'Familiarity bred not contempt . . .': Cole, *Rough Road to Rome*, p. 173
162 'I tried to pull him up . . .': Liebschner, *Iron Cross Roads*, p. 68
163 'As far as I could make out . . .': ibid.
163 'What are we looking for . . .': Carter, *Those Devils in Baggy Pants*, p. 121
164 'Obviously, someone . . .': ibid., p. 122
164 'Lieutenant, are we . . .': ibid., p. 123
164 'OK. Lead off . . .': ibid.
164 'We German-stepped . . .': ibid., p. 124
164 'By God, we'd done . . .': ibid.
165 'Four ships knocked out . . .': John Lucas Diary, 25/1/1944
165 'Now I have things . . .': Jürgen Harder, letter to his wife, 26/1/1944, cited in Jochen Prien, *Jagdgeschwader 53*, p. 762
166 'They were very difficult . . .': ibid.
166 'Unfortunately, we have too few . . .': ibid.
167 'And behind that . . .': TNA WO 170/1350
168 'I made a start . . .': E. P. Danger Diary, 25/1/1944
168 '6 Corps virtually . . .': John Harding Diary, 24/1/1944
168 'Lucas must be aggressive . . .': Mark Clark Diary, 23/1/1944
168 'He apparently feels . . .': ibid., 25/1/1944
169 'One after another . . .': C. L. Sulzberger, *A Long Row of Candles*, p. 227
169 'Nevertheless, the Germans . . .': ibid., p. 228
169 'I asked him why . . .': ibid.
169 'What a splendid piece of work . . .': John Lucas Diary, 25/1/1944
170 'I must keep my feet . . .': ibid.

12 Belvedere

173 'Storming the Belvedere!': cited in René Chambe, *Le Bataillon de Belvedere*, Éditions J'ai Lu, 1965, p. 29
174 'The battalion is morally . . .': Paul Gandoët Diary, 24/1/1944, cited in Serge Douceret, *Paul Gandoët: Général*, Lavauzelle, 1987, p. 106
175 'Honour is engaged.': ibid.
175 'Decision: one big meal . . .': ibid.
175 'This is demented! . . . ': ibid., p. 30
176 'I will succeed . . .': ibid., p. 107
176 'My friends . . .' ': cited in Chambe, *Le Bataillon de Belvedere*, p. 43
178 'This is a mission of trust . . .': ibid., p. 47
179 'Already departed . . .': ibid., p. 70
179 'Oh, the bastards!': ibid., p. 57
180 'I'm screwed . . .': ibid., p. 58
180 'This is Denée . . .': Paul Gandoët Diary, 26/1/1944, cited in Douceret, *Paul Gandoët: Général*, p. 108

180 'So quickly, fire the flare . . . ': cited in Chambe, *Le Bataillon de Belvedere*, p. 61

13 Cisterna

183 'God is waiting for you . . .': cited in Chambe, *Le Bataillon de Belvedere*, pp. 110–11
184 'In small groups . . .': Paul Gandoët Diary, 261/1/1944, cited in Douceret, *Paul Gandoët: Général*, p. 100
184 'Lower your head . . .': ibid.
185 'Firing, bursts . . .': ibid.
185 'Men would like to eat . . .': ibid., p. 111
186 'Trying to put some ginger . . .': John Harding Diary, 27/1/1944
186 'I am too . . .': Mark Clark Diary, 27/1/1944
187 'Considerable damage done . . .': John Lucas Diary, 28/1/1944
187 '11.14. A bomb . . .': ibid..
188 'I think more . . .': ibid., 29/1/1944
189 'The commander of the 44 . . .': von Senger in USAHEC FM C-095b, p. 67
191 'We set off dead tired . . . ': Georg Zellner Diary, 26/1/1944
191 'It's a mess . . .': ibid.
192 'Of 320 men . . .': ibid., 28/1/1944
194 'Prisoners say that in front . . .': Paul Gandoët Diary, 29/1/1944, cited in Douceret, *Paul Gandoët: Général*, p. 117
194 'Food and ammunition . . .': ibid., 20/1/1944, cited in ibid., p. 117
197 'They seemed too dazed . . .': Carter, *Those Devils in Baggy Pants*, p. 125
197 'In the heat of battle . . .': Murphy, *To Hell and Back*, p. 96
198 'But the question . . .': ibid.
198 'The bodies writhe . . .': ibid., p. 100
198 'Where are our goddam tanks . . .': ibid.
198 'My brain whirls . . .': ibid., p. 102
199 'Some of the fellows . . . ': Darby, *Darby's Rangers: We Led the Way*, p. 202
199 'The strain of a thing like this . . .': John Lucas Diary, 24/1/1944
199 'Cheerless rumours have spread . . .': Murphy, *To Hell and Back*, p. 105

14 So Close Yet So Far

201 'My dear love . . .': www.anpiroma.org
202 'The harbingers of the Congress . . .': Filippo Caracciolo Diary, 25/1/1944
202 'The thankless task . . .': ibid., 26/1/1944
202 'Words so far . . .': ibid., 28/1/1944
202 'A breath of grandeur . . .': ibid.
203 'All those called . . .': ibid., 29/1/1944
203 'How to describe . . .': Viviana Bauco Diary, 29/1/1944
203 'The sad events . . .': ibid., 6/2/1944
203 'We pray that the wrath of God . . .': Dom Eusebio Diary, 25/1/1944
204 'This story made . . .': ibid.

204 'A night broken . . .': Dom Martino Matronola Diary, 2/2/1944
204 'Our former "neutral zone" . . .': ibid., 3/2/1944
204 'My head will probably fall . . .': John Lucas Diary, 2/1/1944
205 'Lucas is an old woman . . .': John Harding Diary, 1/2/1944
205 'I have been disappointed . . . ': Mark Clark Diary, 30/1/1944
205 'This was a definite . . .': ibid., 1/2/1944
207 'If we succeed in dealing . . .': cited in Walter Warlimont, *Inside Hitler's Headquarters*, p. 411
208 'These are put forward . . .': Harold Macmillan Diary, 29/1/1944
210 'The terrain was . . .': Ralph B. Schaps, *500 Days of Front Line Combat*, p. 97
211 'Bastards! . . .': ibid., p. 98
213 'The area was strewn . . .': ibid.

15 The Battle of the Thumb

214 'I only hope . . .': John Strick Diary, 1/2/1944
214 'Life in those days . . .': ibid.
215 'I only missed . . .': ibid., 4/2/1944
215 'Life, if it goes on . . .': ibid.
217 'Have not yet taken . . .': Jack Ward Diary, 1/2/1944
218 'But the town has yet . . .': ibid., 4/2/1944
218 'Nostalgia not nearly . . .': Leonard Garland Diary, 28/1/1944
218 'Wonder why . . .': ibid., 3/2/1944
219 'Poor scarf . . .': Leonard Garland letter to Ann, 6/2/1944
219 'By stepping outside . . .': ibid.
220 'The fields below us . . .': Cole, *Rough Road to Rome*, p. 175
220 'The battle must be . . .': cited in Walter Warlimont, *Inside Hitler's Headquarters*, p. 411
223 'And this was the last . . .': Michael Gordon-Watson Report, General Ronald Penney Papers, LHCMH
224 'This acted as a . . .': ibid.
224 'So, with this news . . .': ibid.
226 'About this time . . .': ibid.
226 'No one was more surprised . . .': ibid.
226 'This little episode . . .': ibid.
227 'The battle became . . .': ibid.

16 Point 593

231 'Sir, let's run . . .': Gandoët Diary, 4/2/1944
232 'Take it, my commander . . . ': ibid.
234 'There was a lot . . .': Schaps, *500 Days of Front Line Combat*, p. 99
234 'Finally, the Krauts . . .': ibid., p. 100
235 'He was a gung-ho type . . .': ibid.
235 'This proposal . . .': FM C-095b, USAHEC
237 'Heavy fighting continues . . .': Mark Clark Diary, 6/2/1944
238 'A doomlike quality . . .': Murphy, *To Hell and Back*, p. 109

238 'With their arms . . .': Liebschner, *Iron Cross Roads*, p. 73
238 'They were all huddled . . .': Hans-Paul Liebschner, IWM 9011
239 '3.10am . . .': John Lucas Diary, 7/2/1944
240 'Do you realise . . .': TNA WO 170/1350
241 'Every time our gun . . .': cited in Clark, *Anzio*, p. 168
241 'At daylight, Jerry . . .': E. P. Danger Diary, 9/2/1944
241 'There is nothing worse . . . ': cited in Clark, *Anzio*, p. 163
242 'There is a fucking great German tank . . .': ibid., p. 171
243 'Life is a rod . . .': John Strick Diary, 10/2/1944
243 'I have lost the old keenness . . .': ibid.

17 The Meat Grinder

244 'At one point . . .': Dom Martino Diary, 5/2/1944
244 'Among the refugees . . .': ibid.
245 'A waste of breath!': ibid.
245 'We gave him . . .': ibid.
245 'The Anglo-American . . .': ibid., 9/2/1944
245 'That well will be . . .': ibid.
245 'Have spent the morning . . .': John Lucas Diary, 9/2/1944
246 'Lucas does not . . .': Mark Clark Diary, 7/2/1944
247 'I feel you can stop . . .': ibid., 9/2/1944
247 'No operational appreciation . . .': General Ronald Penney Papers, LHCMH
249 'We considered this . . .': Lieutenant-General Sir Francis Tuker, 'Monte Cassino Memories', Tuker Papers, IWM 14075
252 'The screaming was hard . . .': Schaps, *500 Days of Front Line Combat*, p. 100
253 'We tossed some . . .': cited in Ben Christensen, *The 1st Fallschirmjäger Division in World War II*, Vol. II, p. 392
254 'Who the hell . . .': Bond, *Return to Cassino*, p. 77
254 'I was greatly startled . . .': ibid., p. 91
255 'The ground shook . . .': ibid., p. 100

18 The Perfect Storm

259 'The sight fascinated us.': BA-MA BW57/128
260 'To loosen things up . . .': ibid.
260 'Out all last night . . .': Frank Pearce Diary, 8/2/1944, in John A. Pearce, *A Private in the Texas Army*, p. 85
261 'Pitiful sight . . .': ibid., 9/2/1944
261 'Germans using for . . .': ibid., 10/2/1944
262 'Monte Cassino is therefore . . .': TNA WO 204/12508
262 'I did see Freyberg . . .': Tuker Papers, IWM 14075
262 'Success will only . . .': TNA WO 204/12508
263 'The essence of the bombardment . . .': Tuker Papers, IWM 14075
263 'When a formation . . .': TNA WO 204/12508
263 'I desire that I be given . . . ': Mark Clark Diary, 12/2/1944

264 'To go direct . . .': TNA WO 204/12508
265 'If it were an American . . .': Clark Papers, memo from Gruenther, 12/2/1944
265 'Our abbey is . . .': Dom Martino Diary, 12/2/1943
265 'Our Reverend Father . . .': ibid.
266 'The Lord has taken . . .': ibid., 13/2/1944
266 'For religious and sentimental reasons . . .': Mark Clark Diary, 13/2/1944

19 The Destruction of the Abbey

268 'We had started . . .': Schaps, *500 Days of Front Line Combat*, p. 102
269 'It was behind . . .': Bond, *Return to Cassino*, p. 121
270 'I could have dropped . . .': cited in Parton, *Air Force Spoken Here*, p. 364
271 'Terrible traffic jam . . .': Frank Pearce Diary, 11/2/1944
272 'It is such a tragedy . . .': cited in Wagner, *The Texas Army*, p. 148
272 'Until now . . .': cited in Dom Martino Diary, 14/2/1944
274 'But war is brutalizing . . .': Bond, *Return to Cassino*, p. 135
274 'Target 100 yds . . .': T. Michael Sullivan Diary, 15/2/1944
276 'The saddest sight . . .': Dom Martino Diary, 15/2/1944
277 'Feldmarschall Kesselring . . .': ibid.
277 'Saw the prettiest . . .': Frank Pearce Diary, 15/2/1944

20 FISCHFANG and Monte Cassino Part 1

278 'Through our hearts . . .': Murphy, *To Hell and Back*, p. 116
278 'We believe nothing . . .': ibid., p. 117
279 'We took it in turns . . .': Liebschner, *Iron Cross Roads*, p. 74
279 'Because one was always . . .': ibid.
281 'Every day at six . . .': cited in Prien, *Jagdgeschwader 53*, p. 766
281 'It was on my . . .': ibid.
281 'The shell bursts . . .': Vrilakas, *Look Mom – I Can Fly!*, p. 154
282 'But nothing happened . . .': BA-MA BW 57/128
283 'Father Abbot himself . . .': Dom Martino Diary, 16/2/1944
283 'It is night . . .': ibid.
283 'Our attack, with . . .': 'The German Operation at Anzio', John P. Lucas Papers, Box 9, USAHEC
285 'By nightfall . . . ': cited in Emajean Buechner, *Sparks: The Combat Diary of a Battalion Commander (Rifle) WWII*, Thunderbird Press, 1992, p. 85
286 'But I soon lose sight . . .': Murphy, *To Hell and Back*, p. 122
286 'I am being attacked . . .': John Lucas Diary, 16/2/1944
286 'Our heavy losses . . .': *Operations at Anzio*, p. 55

21 FISCHFANG and Monte Cassino Part 2

288 'They are negative . . .': doc. 1553, Chandler, *The Papers of Dwight D. Eisenhower*, Vol. III, p. 1730
288 'It is one thing . . .': ibid.
288 'a thruster like Patton': ibid.
288 'This shocked Alexander . . .': Mark Clark Diary, 16/2/1944

290 'Heard attack by 4th Indian . . .': John Harding Diary, 17/2/1944
292 'I am suffering greatly . . .': Dom Martino Diary, 17/2/1944
292 'There is only one . . .': ibid.
292 'We left the house . . .': ibid.
293 'I said to them . . .': ibid.
293 '*Che triste incontro*': ibid.
294 'He still had the burnt . . .': BA-MA BW57/128
294 'They must have heard . . .': ibid.
294 'A terrible weapon . . .': ibid.

22 The Tank of Courage

300 'They've got a Spandau . . .': Roger Smith, *Up the Blue*, p. 175
303 'Later. More trouble . . .': John Lucas Diary, 18/2/1944
303 'Have protested . . .': ibid.
305 'There are times when . . .': Frank Pearce letter to Iona, 18/2/1944
307 'During the day . . .': 'The German Operation at Anzio', John P. Lucas Papers, Box 9, USAHEC, p. 60
308 'All quiet on the Anzio front . . .': John Lucas Diary, 22/2/1944
308 'I continue to be . . .': Mark Clark Diary, 24/2/1944
309 'He arrives today . . .': John Lucas Diary, 22/2/1944
310 'The campaign in Italy . . .': C. J. C. Molony, *The Mediterranean and the Middle East*, Vol. V, p. 751
312 'Enemy firing shells . . .': Georg Zellner Diary, 22/2/1944
312 'Our bunker is damp . . .': ibid., 25/2/1944
312 'Heavy worry weighs . . .': ibid., 24/2/1944
312 'You are happy when . . .': ibid.
313 'We find our way . . .': Liebschner, *Iron Cross Roads*, p. 76

23 Disease and Desertion

315 'Run like hell . . .': Carter, *Those Devils in Baggy Pants*, p. 138
315 'Their bright metal . . .': ibid., p. 139
316 'Every enemy soldier . . .': ibid., p. 140
318 'I don't know . . .': Bond, *Return to Cassino*, p. 118
318 'I'm going to go back . . .': ibid.
318 'For Christ's sake . . .': ibid.
318 'Records indicate . . .': General Jacob Devers memo to Mark Clark, 24/2/1944, Mark Clark Papers
319 'A deserter . . .': Murphy, *To Hell and Back*, p. 133
319 'Sorry for me?': ibid., p. 134
320 'Firstly, because the man . . . TNA WO214/62
320 'aggravated desertion': ibid.
320 'And we have no weapon . . .': Mark Clark Papers, cited in letter from General Jacob Devers, 11/2/1944
320 'This dispatch may sound gloomy . . .': Mark Clark Papers, Letters and Reports, Devers to Clark, 11/2/1944

321 'Practically everything . . .': ibid.
322 'Cy, when we make . . .': cited in Sulzberger, *A Long Row of Candles*, p. 229
322 'I decry some . . .': Mark Clark letter to mother, 27/2/1944
323 'It's hard not . . .': Valentin Feurstein, *Irrwege der Flicht*, Welsermühl Verlag, 1963, p. 208
323 'We were the army's . . .': ibid., p. 220
324 'Many homes are . . .': Harry Wilson Diary, 10/2/1944
324 'Did you see . . .': ibid.
325 'My heart began . . .': ibid.
325 'So they sang . . .': ibid., 12/2/1944
325 '*Parti?*': ibid., 14/2/1944
329 'We have bent . . .': Mark Clark Diary, 24/2/1944
329 'The more I see of Freyberg . . .': ibid.

24 Thoughts of Home

330 'There was good wine . . .': Golda, BA-MA MSg 2/4335, p. 45
331 'Vietinghoff listened . . .': Feurstein, *Irrwege der Flicht*, p. 221
333 'Pioneering in the gorge . . .': Klein, *Fallschirmjäger*, p. 151
335 'Sandbag walls . . .': Cole, *Rough Road to Rome*, p. 187
335 'I escorted him back . . .': ibid., p. 188
336 'I was billeted in . . .': ibid., p. 189
336 'Wind and rain . . .': Klaus H. Huebner, *Long Walk Through War*, p. 40
337 'It is an eerie feeling . . .': ibid., p. 41
337 'We are finally . . .': ibid., p. 42
337 'One of the most unpleasant . . .': Mike Doble Diary, 20/2/1944
338 'Up at 0830 . . .': ibid., 21/2/1944
338 'Not at all . . .': ibid., 5/3/1944
338 'Arrived back in the mess . . .': ibid.
338 'Out of action 0600 . . .': Leonard Garland Diary, 4/3/1944
339 'This happened two years ago . . .': ibid., 18/2/1944
339 'From Salerno onwards . . .': Leonard Garland letter to Ann, 19/2/1944
340 'Naturally, I am worried . . .': Wilhelm Mauss Diary, 9/3/1944
340 'It is almost . . .': ibid.
340 'My Dearest Olive . . .': Lawrie Franklyn-Vaile letter to Olive, 9/3/1944
341 'Barrosa Day . . .': ibid.
341 'I would certainly like . . .': Lawrie Franklyn-Vaile letter to Olive, 11/3/1944
342 'It's about time . . .': General Alexander letter to children, 02/44, Private Papers of Field Marshal the Earl Alexander
342 'Bang! Hello!': General Alexander letter to children, 1/3/1944
342 'Renie darling . . .': Mark Clark letter to Renie Clark, 8/3/1944

25 The Destruction of Cassino Town

344 'Most were bashed . . .': Smith, *Up the Blue*, p. 183
344 'Keeping 5 Bde sitting . . .': Bateman Papers, IWM 13122
345 'I'd like to meet . . .': Smith, *Up the Blue*, p. 190

346 'We have to face the fact . . .': No. 290, in *Documents Relating to New Zealand's Participation in the Second World War 1939-45*, Vol. II
348 'Operations in Italy . . .': Molony, *The Mediterranean and the Middle East*, Vol. V, p. 836
349 'to reduce the enemy's . . .': Craven and Cate, *The Army Air Forces in World War II*, Vol. II, p. 373
349 'We are all very greatly . . .': cited in Parton, *Air Force Spoken Here*, p. 372
349 'Personally, I do not feel . . .': cited in Molony, *The Mediterranean and the Middle East*, Vol. V, p. 779
349 'As small as . . .': MA-BA BW 57/128
350 'lick my arse': BA-MA
350 'When he greeted me . . .': ibid.
352 'We sat for some time . . .': Smith, *Up the Blue*, p. 185
352 'The boys pulled . . .': T. Michael Sullivan Diary, 15/3/1944
352 'Hundreds of big . . .': Frank Pearce Diary, 15/3/1944
353 'We are to penetrate . . .': Maurice Bechard Diary, 16/3/1944
353 'The pall of dust . . .': Smith, *Up the Blue*, p. 191
353 'When the bombs hit . . .': Mark Clark Diary, 15/3/1944
354 'They are attacking . . .': Klein, *Fallschirmjäger*, p. 158

26 Battle in the Ruins

358 'There was a smell . . .': FMS C-095b, USAHEC
359 'Heidrich's demand . . .': BA-MA RH20-10/105
362 'It seemed so obvious . . .', Donald Bateman letter to Francis Tuker, 24/2/1959, Bateman Papers, IWM 13122
362 'We had lost the initial . . .': 'A Note on the Operations of 4th Indian Division at Cassino', Bateman Papers, IWM 13122
362 'Freyberg's handling . . .': Mark Clark Diary, 17/2/1944
362 'I told Freyberg . . .': ibid.
363 'If he were an American . . .': ibid.
363 'We smashed the town . . .': cited in Matthew Wright, *Freyberg's War*, Penguin, 2005, p. 194
363 'Early in the morning . . .': Maurice Bechard Diary, 16/3/1944
367 'That merciless enemy . . .': Smith, *Up the Blue*, p. 192
368 'So we had to abandon . . .': ibid., p. 195
369 'It was like another world . . .': ibid.
370 'No word of D Coy . . .': 24th Battalion War Diary, 18/3/1944, cited in Pete Connor, 'Finding Ways to Survive', MPhil thesis, Massey University, p. 134
371 'It was impossible . . .': Smith, *Up the Blue*, p. 198
373 The lad toppled . . .': ibid., p. 200
373 'Lack of manpower . . .': ibid., p. 204

27 Via Rasella

374 'We were soaking wet . . .': Liebschner, *Iron Cross Roads*, p. 83
374 'The dead of no-man's land . . .': ibid.

375 'On the ruined land . . .': Murphy, *To Hell and Back*, p. 146
375 'We've got cherries on Anzio . . .': ibid.
375 'Many of us bitched . . .': Carter, *Those Devils in Baggy Pants*, p. 150
376 'Filled with the bravado . . .': ibid., p. 154
376 'Let's see now . . .': ibid.
376 'Our casualties . . .': E. P. Danger Diary, 8/3/1944
376 'He was not pessimistic . . .': Mark Clark Diary, 21/3/1944
379 'Chief went up to . . .': John Harding Diary, 23/3/1944
381 'Growing fear and despair . . .': Capponi, *Con cuore di donna*, p. 184
381 'The city had two . . .': ibid.
383 'Excuse me, signorina . . .': cited in Robert Katz, *Fatal Silence*, p. 221
384 'You can't play football . . .': cited in ibid., p. 222

28 STRANGLE

386 'There was still good . . .': Smith, *Up the Blue*, p. 212
386 'Sleeping forms . . .': ibid.
388 'The Führer wishes . . .': TNA WO206/4622
389 'I am writing this letter . . .': Lawrie Franklyn-Vaile letter to Olive, 24/3/1944
390 'Look after yourself . . .': ibid.
390 'Bozen has been . . .': Wilhem Mauss Diary, 19/2/1944
390 'Hanover looks desolate . . .': ibid., 25/3/1944
390 'Here one can walk . . .': ibid., 8/4/1944
391 'It breaks my heart . . . ': T. Michael Sullivan Diary, 16/3/1944
391 'Lost Marshall . . .': ibid., 19/3/1944
392 'Oh, I wish . . .': Carter, *Those Devils in Baggy Pants*, p. 159
392 'Sicily, Salerno . . .': ibid.
393 'Gee, Annie's on target . . .': Cole, *Rough Road to Rome*, p. 195
393 'I couldn't stand . . .': ibid., p. 193
393 'All 50 machines . . .': Jürgen Harder letter to wife, March 1944, cited in Prien, *Jagdgeschwader 53*, p. 781
394 'Put the pot . . .': Vrilakas, *Look Mom – I Can Fly!*, p. 158
394 'Miss Jane . . .': Ralph Lucardi Diary, 25/3/1944, www.57thfightergroup.org
394 'Gee, I miss my mail . . .': Ralph Lucardi Diary, 26/3/1944
395 'What the hell . . .': ibid., 28/3/1944
395 'Wrecked buildings . . .': ibid.
395 'Quite a day!': ibid.
396 'Seems like a nice guy . . .': ibid., 31/3/1944
396 'Well, this was the day!': ibid., 1/4/1944
396 'I forgot a lot of little things . . .': ibid.
397 'Whew! Going '"balls out"': ibid., 10/4/1944

29 Spring in the Air

401 'He is never . . .': Harold Macmillan Diary, 26/3/1944
402 'It has been a most . . .': Mark Clark Diary, 24/3/1944
403 'In fact . . .': ibid.

404 'They still looked pretty good . . .': Golda, BA-MA MSg 2/4335, p. 45
404 'But what was left . . .': ibid.
404 'Liebschner? I was billeted . . .': Liebschner, *Iron Cross Roads*, p. 85
405 'It was awful . . .': Smith, *Up the Blue*, p. 217
406 'Memories of friends . . .': ibid., p. 223
406 'We Russians . . .': BA-MA BW57/128
406 'There was no large . . .': ibid.
406 'After the unmasking . . .': ibid.
407 'How differently . . .': ibid.
407 'Yes. Sometimes more . . .': ibid.
407 'The general public . . .': Filippo Caracciolo Diary, 28/2/1944
408 'The situation now becomes . . .': ibid., 1/4/1944
409 'We are starving!': Pasqualina Caruso Diary, 28/3/1944
409 'Yet nothing is done . . .': Norman Lewis Diary, 18/4/1944, p. 110
410 'There are no police . . .': ibid., 28/3/1944, p. 100
410 'I didn't ask to live . . .': ibid., 5/4/1944, p. 105
411 'Have the Germans . . .': Huebner, *Long Walk Through War*, p. 59
411 'What a view . . .': Jack Ward Diary, 31/3/1944
411 'Many happy returns . . .': ibid., 3/4/1944
412 'Weather very nice . . .': ibid., 14/4/1944
412 'All this occurs . . .': Lawrie Franklyn-Vaile letter to Olive, 8/4/1944
412 'The CO has two great sayings . . .': ibid.
412 'I miss you both . . .': ibid.
413 'After a terrific struggle . . .': Mike Doble Diary, 3/4/1944
413 'Hangover this morning . . .': ibid., 17/4/1944
414 'I think Italy will be brought . . .': Harold Macmillan Diary, 21/4/1944
414 'Let us all exude a sweet honey . . .': Filippo Caracciolo Diary, 21/4/1944
414 'We clobbered . . .': Ralph Lucardi Diary, 12/4/1944
415 'One very successful mission': War Diary 64th Fighter Squadron, Month of April 1944, 57thfightergroup.org
415 'It was the biggest dog-fight . . .': Ralph Lucardi Diary, 14/4/1944
415 'Duck, Luke!': ibid.
415 'He's been with me . . .': ibid.
415 'Boy, oh boy . . .': ibid., 1/5/1944
416 'Chief returned . . .': General Harding Diary, 20/4/1944

30 Preparations

417 'The commanding general . . .': FMS C-095b
417 'The only encouragement . . .': ibid.
418 'We were all thunderstruck . . .': Klein, *Fallschirmjäger*, p. 182
418 'Heidrich called on us . . .': ibid.
419 'I could think of no reason . . .': Liebschner, *Iron Cross Roads*, p. 89
419 'Such news affected . . .': ibid., p. 90
420 'I heard someone say . . .': Cole, *Rough Road to Rome*, p. 204
421 '*Komm aut!*': ibid.

422 'Christ, it's like a vending machine . . .': ibid.
422 'We secure all sides . . .': ibid.
422 'Our joy at our success . . .': ibid.
422 'Great attack, great attack . . .': MA-BA BW 57/128
423 'The stubbornness of the German defence . . .': W. Anders, *An Army in Exile*, p. 163
425 'We all felt anxious . . .': Władek Rubnikowicz, notes to author
425 'We all wanted . . .': ibid.

31 DIADEM

427 'May Day . . .': Lawrie Franklyn-Vaile letter to Olive, 1/5/1944
427 'You would agree . . .': ibid.
428 'There is also a strong . . .': ibid.
428 'The American underpants . . .': Harry Wilson Diary, 3/5/1944
428 'Yes. It won't last . . .': ibid., 6/5/1944
428 'I repeated to myself . . .': ibid.
428 'When will it suddenly . . .': Wilhelm Mauss Diary, 5/5/1944
429 'Tonight we're attacking . . .': Harry Wilson Diary, 11/5/1944
429 'All this information . . .': ibid.
430 'I told Alexander . . .': Mark Clark Diary, 5/5/1944
430 'This is a small matter . . .': ibid.
431 'It has been a vast . . .': Oliver Leese letter to Margie Leese, 10/5/1944, IWM 19548
431 'Already I'm really sad . . .': Georg Zellner Diary, 11/5/1944
432 'It was terrific . . .': Ted Wyke-Smith, author interview
432 '11pm – H-Hour of D-Day . . .': Huebner, *Long Walk Through War*, p. 61
433 'We have spectator seats . . .': ibid., p. 62
433 'We sit and wait . . .': ibid.

32 Breakthrough in the Mountains

435 'There is nothing . . .': BA-MA RH 20-10/119
437 'The jaded Cassino . . .': Golda, BA-MA MSg 2/4335, p. 48
437 'Calmly and seriously . . .': ibid., p. 49
437 'We were driving . . .': ibid.
437 'We'd be blown . . .': ibid.
438 'Infantry did not get on . . .': Mike Doble Diary, 12/5/1944
438 'I saw both army commanders . . .': TNA CAB 121/594
439 'There is a vast . . .': Oliver Leese letter to wife, 12/5/1944
439 'It was easier . . .': Anders, *An Army in Exile*, p. 176
440 'It is tough country . . .': Oliver Leese letter to wife, 12/5/1944
440 'Phew! It's fair hell . . .': Harry Wilson Diary, 12/5/1944
440 'We're suffering from . . .': ibid.
442 'A passing jeep . . .': Huebner, *Long Walk Through War*, p. 66
443 'The poor fellow . . .': ibid., p. 67
443 'My first day . . .': ibid., p. 68

444 'I have directed . . .': Mark Clark Diary, 15/5/1944
445 'I always say . . .': BA-MA RW 20-10/119
446 'Off at 10am . . .': Roy Durnford Diary, 16/5/19944
447 'The roar of guns . . .': ibid.
447 'He explained to me . . .': Golda, BA-MA MSg 2/4335, p. 49
447 'After every hit . . .': ibid.
447 'Planes and crashing . . .': Georg Zellner Diary, 15/5/1944
447 'Death is creeping . . .': ibid.
448 'It was very exciting . . .': Ted Wyke-Smith, author interview
449 'But the attacking tanks . . .': Klein, *Fallschirmjäger*, p. 191
450 'I would rather die . . .': Lawrie Franklyn-Vaile letter to wife, 16/5/1944
450 'Of course, it does not . . .': ibid.

33 Monte Cassino

451 'Lord, do not abandon us!': Viviana Bauco Diary, 12/5/1944
452 'He was his grandfather's . . .': Pasua Pisa, author interview
453 'I am certain . . .': Douglas Room letter to Olive Franklyn-Vaile, 18/5/1944
453 'I'm still numb . . .': ibid.
453 'My prayers are all . . .': Roy Durnford Diary, 17/5/1944
454 'Cemetery blasted . . .': ibid.
454 'What a ghastly . . .': ibid.
454 'At long last . . .': ibid.
455 'These reserves . . .': FMS C-025
455 'Then we shall have . . .': BA-MA RH 20-10/119
456 'A shell came over . . .': Władek Rubnikowicz, author interview
457 'It was often a case of . . .': ibid.
458 'We stormed out . . .': Klein, *Fallschirmjäger*, p. 189
458 'A senseless death . . .': ibid.
459 'So the enemy was . . .': BA-MA RW57/128
459 'Over the mountain . . .': ibid.
459 'We immediately . . .': ibid.
460 'Some of those . . .': ibid.
460 'And it was fragrant . . .': ibid.
460 'A short sleep . . .': ibid.
460 'Of course, we were . . .': Władek Rubnikowicz, author interview
461 'Have a look, boys . . .': Ted Wyke-Smith, author interview
461 'Had one shoot during . . .': Mike Doble Diary, 18/5/144
461 'Tank holed . . .': Roy Durnford Diary, 18/5/1944
461 'Dead Jerries . . .': ibid.
462 'We were to help . . .': BA-MA BW 57/128
463 'All you have to do . . .': ibid.
463 'Too bad . . . ': BA-MA BW57/128
464 'It'll use too much oxygen . . .': Klein, *Fallschirmjäger*, p. 195
465 'The last time I had seen . . .': ibid., p. 200

34 Death in the Mountains

466 'General Alexander . . .': Mark Clark Diary, 18/5/1944
466 'I agree, but . . .': ibid.
467 'The opposing sides . . .': Huebner, *Long Walk Through War*, p. 70
467 'Aching backs . . .': ibid., p. 71
468 'When not plagued . . .': ibid., p. 72
468 'All I can do . . .': ibid., p. 73
468 'Our first job therefore . . .': Golda, BA-MA MSg 2/4335, p. 52
469 'They found the place . . .': Mike Doble Diary, 19/5/1944
469 'It was horrible . . .': BA-MA BW57/128
469 'I lay there . . .': ibid.
470 'In his pain . . .': ibid.
470 'In the meantime . . .': ibid.
470 'You have been transferred . . .': BA-MA BW57/128
471 'If the Eighth Army . . .': Mark Clark Diary, 20/5/1944
471 'All along the line . . .': Oliver Leese letter to wife, 20/5/1944
472 'An area ideally suited . . .': FMS C-064
472 'Hit Anzio about 8am . . .': Frank Pearce Diary, 21/5/1944
472 'Will be a noisy . . .': ibid., 22/5/1944
473 'Some eleven alternative . . .': Doughty, *Invading Hitler's Europe*, p. 12
474 'when timing seems . . .': Mark Clark Diary, 18/5/1944
474 'I was shocked . . .': ibid., 19/5/1944
475 'The terrain is . . .': Huebner, *Long Walk Through War*, p. 77
475 'My examination reveals . . .': ibid., pp. 78–9
475 'We start all over . . .': ibid., p. 79
476 'One is willing . . .': Mike Doble Diary, 22/5/1944
476 'Never have I seen . . .': Jack Ward Diary, 22/5/1944
476 'I've seen wreckage . . .': Harry Wilson Diary, 19/5/1944
477 'Now the enemy . . .': Georg Zellner Diary, 20/5/1944
477 'I'm overcome with homesickness . . .': ibid., 21/5/1944
477 'It is the hardest . . .': Roy Durnford Diary, 23/5/1944
477 'The odds were so much against it . . .': Harry Wilson Diary, 21/5/1944
478 'We couldn't have it . . .': ibid., 23/5/1944
478 'Sixty seconds!': ibid.
478 'Pale, dirty and utterly . . .': Roy Durnford Diary, 23/5/1944
478 'Some bomb happy . . .': ibid.
478 'How are things going?': ibid.
478 'A great day!': Oliver Leese letter to wife, 23/5/1944
478 'The Germans are . . .': ibid.
480 'They were shooting over . . .': Pasua Pisa, author interview

35 Breakout and the Big Switch

482 'The concussion . . .': Schaps, *500 Days of Front Line Combat*, p. 112
482 'Little could be seen . . .': Mark Clark Diary, 23/5/1944
482 'Our attack is going well . . .': Maurice Bechard, 22 [*sic*] /5/1944

483 'This one got . . .': ibid.
483 'Some said . . .': Schaps, *500 Days of Front Line Combat*, p. 113
483 'You ignorant bastard . . .': Murphy, *To Hell and Back*, p. 152
484 'So, we joined them . . .': Ralph Lucardi Diary, 24/5/1944
485 'Rolling country . . .': Frank Pearce Diary, 24/5/1944
486 'I looked at it . . .': Hamilton Howze, *Thirty-Five Years and Then Some*, Ch. IX, p. 3
486 'Bodies and pieces . . .': ibid.
486 'My mother and I . . .': Pasua Pisa, author interview
486 'The Moroccans stole . . .': ibid.
486 'However strong our . . .': Juin memo to CEF, 24/5 /1944, Mark Clark Papers
487 'The Italians are raising . . .': Al Gruenther memo to Mark Clark, 27/5/1944, Mark Clark Papers
487 'punishment without mercy': Juin memo to CEF, 27/5/1944, Mark Clark Papers
487 'by way of a pact . . .': cited in Tomasso Baris, *Tra due Fuochi*, Laterza, 2003, p. 94
487 'If native African . . .': TNA WO 204/9945
487 'It is reported . . .': Norman Lewis Diary, 28/5/1944
487 'At last one had . . .': ibid.
488 'All the women . . .': DORER No. 1303
488 'They forced them . . .': ibid. No. 1317
488 'Retreating along the Via Casilina . . .': Golda, BA-MA MSg 2/4335, p. 52
489 'Conway gets his hand . . .': Roy Durnford Diary, 24/5/1944
489 'The Regt mourned . . .': TNA WO 170/916
489 'Bodies keep coming . . .': Roy Durnford Diary, 25/5/1944
490 'The Canadian Corps . . .': Leese Papers, IWM 19548
490 'When a vehicle . . .': Ted Wyke-Smith, author interview
491 'What the hell . . .': Murphy, *To Hell and Back*, p. 155
491 'No, keep down . . .': ibid., p. 156
492 'We climb out of our holes . . .': ibid.
492 'By the following . . .': Lucian K. Truscott, *Command Missions*, p. 375
494 'He said that the . . .': Mark Clark Diary, 5/5/1944
494 'I told Alexander . . .': ibid., 8/5/1944
494 'He kept pulling . . .': ibid.
494 'brushed this aside': ibid., 18/5/1944
495 'Much depended . . .': ibid.
497 'It was a dreadfully . . .': Howze, *Thirty-Five Years and Then Some*, Ch. IX, p. 6
498 'I am for any . . .': Mark Clark Diary, 26/5/1944
498 'I am certain . . .': ibid.

36 Rome

499 'I thought this was . . .': Howze, *Thirty-Five Years and Then Some*, Ch. IX, p. 8
499 'Hell, no . . .': cited in Ernest F. Fisher Jr., *United States Army in World War II: Cassino to the Alps*, p. 169

500 'We slaughtered them . . .': Howze, *Thirty-Five Years and Then Some*, Ch. IX, p. 13
501 'The fiery hell-hole . . .': Cole, *Rough Road to Rome*, p. 221
501 'Everywhere there was . . .': ibid., p. 223
502 'I'm cheesed off . . .': Harry Wilson Diary, 26/5/1944
502 'How inconsistent the Army is!': ibid., 26/5/1944
502 'It is impossible . . .': Roy Durnford Diary, 27/5/1944
503 'How could I go . . .': Viviana Bauco Diary, 26/5/1944
503 'Night of jubilation . . .': ibid., 31/5/1944
504 'Night march . . .': Georg Zellner Diary, 28/29/5/1944
504 'I feel I should be . . .': message of 28/5/1944, cited in Churchill, *The Second World War*, Vol. V, p. 536
506 'I saw almost no . . .': cited in Wagner, *The Texas Army*, p. 160
506 'I personally spoke . . .': FMS C-064
507 'It was no longer . . .': ibid.
508 'to kill and annihilate . . .': Mark Clark Diary, 31/5/1944
508 'We are in as desperate . . .': Mark Clark letter to Renie Clark, 31/5/1944
508 'He lies on his back . . .': Murphy, *To Hell and Back*, p. 161
509 'There was screaming . . .': Golda, BA-MA MSg 2/4335, p. 57
509 'One of my radio . . .': ibid.
509 'The cellar floor . . .': ibid.
509 'We knocked out . . .': Howze, *Thirty-Five Years and Then Some*, Ch. IX, p. 18
510 'Every few seconds . . .': Huebner, *Long Walk Through War*, p. 87
510 'They were crumby . . .': Doughty, *Invading Hitler's Europe*, p. 133
511 'Howze – get these tanks . . .': Howze, *Thirty-Five Years and Then Some*, Ch. IX, p. 19
512 'Between strongpoints . . .': Murphy, *To Hell and Back*, p. 161
512 'On pulling back . . .': Huebner, *Long Walk Through War*, p. 90
513 'He receives two units . . .': ibid.
513 'It was both gratifying . . .': Howze, *Thirty-Five Years and Then Some*, Ch. IX, p. 24
514 'I doubt that anybody . . .': Clark, *Anzio*, p. 364
514 'The Italians all said . . .': Cole, *Rough Road to Rome*, p. 231
514 'Our vehicles barely . . .': Huebner, *Long Walk Through War*, p. 97
514 'Our trip through Rome . . .': ibid.
515 'Well, gentlemen . . . ': cited in Eric Sevareid, *Not So Wild A Dream* (Athenaeum, 1976), p. 409

Postscript

521 'Clark was always . . .': Alexander interview with Sidney Matthews, USAHEC
522 'I know factually . . .': Mark Clark Diary, 5/5/1944
522 'AL is making . . .': Oliver Leese letter to Margie Leese, 1/6/1944
523 'The American effort . . .': ibid., 4/6/1944
523 'Battle has gone well . . .': John Harding Diary, 4/6/1944

Selected Sources

PERSONAL TESTIMONIES

Author Interviews

Berkieta, Stanislav
Bowlby, Alex
Bradshaw, Sam
Calvocoressi, Ion
Dills, Chas
Ellington, Edward 'Duke'
Harris, Reg
Klein, Jupp
Moore, Peter
Ortscheidt, Helmut
Piesakowski, Tomasz
Pisa, Pasua
Potts, Maggie
Pun, Nainabadahur
Reed, James E.
Rubnikowicz, Władek
Saidel, Ray
Walters, Ed 'Bucky'
Wyke-Smith, Ted

Canadian War Museum

Coombs, William D.
Dunn, Hunter
Medd, A. Bruce

Go For Broke National Education Center Oral History Project

Hamasu, Mitsuo
Miyashiro, Takeichi
Sumida, Leighton

Imperial War Museum, London

Harding, Field Marshal Lord John
Hazel, Edmund
Liebschner, Hans-Paul
Nutting, Ivor
Pockson, Maynard

Library of Congress, Washington DC

Sparks, Felix
Spencer, Robert

Matthew Parker Papers

Cunningham, Clare
Eggert, Werner
Langelüdecke, Kurt

National World War II Museum, New Orleans

Dumas, Floyd
Gilbert, Lawrence
Goad, Roy
Hayashi, Shizuya
Hughes, Lowell
Pierce, Wayne
Tweedt, Vernon T.

Rutgers, The State University of New Jersey

Cloer, Russell W.

Second World War Experience Centre, Otley, Lancashire

Bowen, H.
Chaudri, I. A.
Frettlöhr, R.
Ivy, R.
Kaeppner, G. R.
Kingstone, J.
Talbot, G.
Thorman, R.

US Air Force Historical Research Agency, Maxwell, Alabama

Quesada, Elwood R. 'Pete'

US Army Heritage & Education Center, Carlisle, Pennsylvania

Senior Officers Debriefing Program:
Clark, Mark W.
Howze, Hamilton

Sidney Matthews Interviews:
Alexander, Harold
Clark, Mark W.
Keyes, Geoffrey
Lemnitzer, Lyman
Lucas, John
Truscott, Lucian
Walker, Fred

UNPUBLISHED REPORTS, DIARIES, LETTERS, MEMOIRS, PAPERS ETC.

Baranowski, Julian, Papers, Transcribed Oral History, Audio Files
Garland, Leonard, Letters, Diary, c/o Surrey Garland
Moore, Peter, *Khaki And Gown: Memoirs 1940–1949*
Obermeier, Leonard, Letters, c/o Joe Hudgens
Trousdell, Philip J. C., Diary
Ward, Jack, Diary
Woodhouse, W. J., 'Memories of an Old Soldier', c/o Pete Connor

Private Papers of Field Marshal the Earl Alexander of Tunis

Lady Alexander Interview
Letters

Bundesarchiv-Militärarchiv, Freiburg

Personal Testimonies

Donth, Rudolf, *Chronic 6. Kompanie/Fallschirmjäger 4*, BW 57/128
Eggert, Ernst, MSg 2/7283
Franek, Fritz, MSg 1/1398
Golda, Hans, MSg 2/4335
Goldschmidt, Karl, MSg 2/6303
Schmalz, Wilhelm, MSg 2/13109
Sikta, Hans, MSg 2/5520
Zellner, Georg, MSg 1/2816 & 2817

General Papers, Reports, Diaries Etc.

AOK 10, Kriegstagebuch, RH 20-10/93-120; RH 20-10/329
Hermann Göring-Division, MSg 2/13111
26. Panzer-Division Kriegstagebuch, N 10/3
29. Panzergrenadier-Division Kriegstagebuch, MSg 2/4453
XIV Panzerkorps Kriegstagebuch, RH 24-14/140
LXXVI Panzerkorps Kriegstagebuch, RH 24-76/22

Canadian War Museum, Toronto

Durnford, Roy, Diary

Collezione di Gaetano Bonelli, Museo di Napoli, Naples

Vincenzo, Lionitti, Letters

Dwight D. Eisenhower Presidential Library, Abilene, Kansas

Bedell-Smith, Walter, Papers

57th Fighter Group Website (57thfightergroup.org)

Lucardi, Ralph 'Luke', Diary

82nd Fighter Group Website (82ndfightergroup.org)

Abberger, Tom, Diary

Imperial War Museum, London

Awdrt, R. J., Letters, Papers
Bateman, D., Letters, Papers
Baxendale, J., Diary
Clark, Norman, 'War Dispatches'
Cowles, B. R., Diary
Danger, E. P., Diary
Deane, D. H., Diary
Doble, M. L., Diary
Drury, K. R., 'One Man's Memories'
Harper, E. R., Diary
Holworthy, A. W. W., Diary
Kirkman, S., Papers
Leese, Oliver, Papers
Lovett, P. J., Memoir
Montgomery, Bernard, Papers
Morgan, K., Letters
Oakley, A. G., Diary
Parkinson, J. E., Diary
Strick, John, Diary, Letters, Papers
Tomlinson, J. B., Diary
Tuker, F., Papers
Turner, Rev. E. A., Diary
Wilson, H. A., Diary
Windeatt, J. K., 'A Very Ordinary Soldier'
Wrigley, V. J., Diary

Irish Brigade Website (irishbrigade.co.uk)

Franklyn-Vaile, Lawrence, Letters
War Diaries, 1st Royal Irish Fusiliers

Library and Archives Canada, Toronto

Vokes, Chris, 'Crossing of the Moro and Capture of Ortona'

War Diaries

Hastings & Prince Edward Regiment
Three Rivers Regiment
Seaforth Highlanders of Canada

Library of Congress, Washington DC

Patton, George S., Papers

Liddell Hart Centre for Military Archives, King's College, London

Alanbrooke, Alan, Papers
Green, Henry, Diary
Howson, John, Papers
Kirkman, Sidney, Papers
McNeil, John, Papers
Nelson, John, 'Always a Grenadier'
Penney, Ronald, Papers
Sprot, Aidan, Memoir

McMaster University Library, Ontario

Mowat, Farley, Papers

National Archives, Kew

War Diaries

AMGOT War Diary
1st Battalion, Royal Irish Fusiliers
2nd Battalion, Royal Inniskilling Fusiliers
2/5th Battalion, Leicestershire Regiment
2nd Battalion, Scots Guards
2nd Regiment, Royal Horse Artillery
3rd Battalion, Coldstream Guards
4/16th Punjab Battalion
6th Battalion, Royal Inniskilling Fusiliers
17th Field Regiment, Royal Artillery
30th Field Regiment, Royal Artillery
56th Heavy Regiment, Royal Artillery
185th Infantry Brigade
X Corps War Diary
XIII Corps War Diary
XXX Corps War Diary

Operational Record Books

45 Squadron
74 Squadron
111 Squadron
249 Squadron
324 Wing

Documents

Alexander, Harold R. A., Papers
Bombing of Cassino
British Casualty Figures
JG77 Operations in the Mediterranean
Kappler, Herbert, Interrogation Reports etc., TNA WO 235/366 and WO 175/330
Lessons from the Italian Campaign
Luftwaffe Reports, Sicily
Major Capron's Statement
NATAF Report on Operations
Port of Naples
Special Report on Events in Italy
Training Notes from the Sicilian Campaign
Ultra Decrypts, Italy

National Archives and Records Administration, College Park, Maryland

1st Armored Division Operations Reports
3rd Infantry Division in Sicily Report on Operations
15th Infantry Regiment in Sicily
34th Infantry Operations and Reports
36th Infantry Operations and Reports
45th Infantry Division Operations and Reports
88th Infantry Division Operations and Reports
Training Notes from the Sicilian Campaign
US Wire Monitoring
Weekly Intelligence Summaries

Naval Historical Branch, Portsmouth

Dürchführung Landungsunternehmen
RN Captured German Documents
RN Morale, Efficiency & Organisation
RN Reports on Operation SHINGLE

Papers of Nigel Nicolson

Interviews, Documents, Papers relating to Field Marshal the Earl Alexander

Second World War Experience Centre, Otley, Lancashire

Kingstone, J., Diary
Knowles, S. W., 'Soldier On'
Milnes-Coates, R. E. J. C., Papers

Tagebuch Archiv, Emmendingen

Lemperle, Hermann, Diary and Letters

US Army Heritage Center, Carlisle, Pennsylvania

Memoirs, Diaries, Papers and Veterans' Surveys

Beehard, Maurice, Diary, Veterans Survey
Boyer, Robert H., Memoir, Veterans Survey
Brown, Joseph T., Memoir, Veterans Survey
Chafin, Mitchell, Diary, Veterans Survey
Childers, Ernest, 'The Operations of Company C, 180th Infantry (45th Infantry Division) at Oliveto, Italy, Northeast of Salerno, Italy, 21–22 September 1943'
Cloer, Russell W., 'The Road to Rome', Veterans Survey
Francis, William H., Diary, Veterans Survey
Griffin, Eugene 'Breezy', Veterans Survey, Memoir
Hall, George, 'Ranger Scout', Veterans Survey
Hannum, Thomas, Memoir, Veterans Survey
Harper, George C., Memoir, Veterans Survey
Hooper, Vincent, 'My Favourite War'
Howze, Hamilton, 'Thirty Years and Then Some', 'Breakout from Anzio'
Kunz, William J., Memoir, Veterans Survey
Lindquist, Harold E., Veterans Survey
Lucas, John P., Diary, Papers
MacDonald, Donald E., Diary, Veterans Survey
Maffei, Norman, Papers and Diary, Veterans Survey
Marsh, Robert M., Memoir, Veterans Survey
Moses, Russell T., Papers
Mueller, Gustav, Memoir, Veterans Survey
Pritchard, James, Diary, Veterans Survey
Ridgway, Matthew B., Diary, Papers
Saidel, Ray, Journals, Veterans Survey
Schunemann, Gustave, Memoir

Smith, Stanley, Memoir
Valenti, Isadore, Veterans Survey, 'Combat Medic'
Williams, Warren, Memories
Wilson, Lloyd, Memories

Foreign Military Studies

B-269, *German Rear Area Organization – Italy*
B-270, Kesselring, Albert, *German Strategy During the Italian Campaign*
B-338, Blumentritt, Günther, *German Soldier (Morale)*
C-014, Kesselring, Albert, *Concluding Remarks on the Mediterranean Campaign*
C-015, Kesselring, Albert, *Italy as a Military Ally*
C-025, Von Vietinghoff, Heinrich, *The Campaign in Italy: The Operations of 71 German Infantry Division During the Month of May 1944*
C-031, Kesselring, Albert, *Fortifications in Italy*
C-064, Kesselring, Albert, *The Campaign in Italy*, Part II
C-95b, Senger und Etterlin, Fridolin von, *War Diary of the Italian Campaign*
D-112, Fries, Walter, *29th Panzergrenadier-Division*
D-141, Fries, Walter, *29th Panzergrenadier-Division, February 1944*
D-158, Kuhn, Walter, *The Artillery at Anzio-Nettuno*
D-168, Glasl, Anton, *Mountain Infantry Regiment 100*
D-301, Klinkowström, Graf Karl-Heinrich, *Italy's Break-Away and the Fighting Around Rome*
D-312, Von Luttwitz, Freiherr, *The Employment of the 26th Panzer Division from 15th May 1944 to 12th July 1944 in Italy*
D-314, Mälzer, Kurt, *The Problem of Rome During the Period of the Fighting Near Anzio-Nettuno Until the Evacuation of Rome on 4 June 1944*
D-316, Bernstorff, Graf Douglas, *The Operations of the 26th Panzer-Division in Italy*

Other

Rapido Crossing Enquiry

CONTEMPORARY PAMPHLETS, BOOKLETS AND TRAINING MEMORANDA

Army Life, War Department Pamphlet 21-13, US Government Printing Office, 1944
Basic Field Manual: First Aid for Soldiers, FM 21-11, US War Department, 1943
The Battle of the Atlantic: The Official Account of the Fight Against the U-Boats, 1939–1945, HMSO, 1946
By Air to Battle: The Official Account of the British Airborne Divisions, HMSO,1945

Combat Instruction for the Panzer Grenadier by Helmut von Wehren, 1944, English translation by John Baum
Company Officer's Handbook of the German Army, Military Intelligence Division, US War Department, 1944
Der Dienst-Unterricht im Heer by Dr. jur. W. Reibert, E. S. Mittler & Sohn, Berlin, 1941
The Development of Artillery Tactics and Equipment, The War Office, London, 1951
Field Service Pocket Book, various pamphlets, The War Office, London, 1939–45
German Infantry Weapons, Military Intelligence Service, US War Department, 1943
The German Squad in Combat, Military Intelligence Service, US War Department, 1944
German Tactical Doctrine, Military Intelligence Service, US War Department, 1942
German Tank Maintenance in World War II, Department of the US Army, June 1954
The Gunnery Pocket Book, The Admiralty, London, 1945
Handbook of German Military Forces, TM-E 30-451, US War Department, 1945
Handbook on the British Army with Supplements on the Royal Air Force and Civilian Defense Organizations, TM 30-410, US War Department, September 1942
Handbook on the Italian Military Forces, TME-30-240, Military Intelligence Service, US Army, August 1943
Infantry Training, Part VIII: *Fieldcraft, Battle Drill, Section and Platoon Tactics*, War Office, London, 1944
Infantry Training: Training and War, HMSO, London, 1937
Instruction Manual for the Infantry, Vol. 2: *Field Fortifications of the Infantry, 1940*, H.Dv. 130/11, English translation by John Baum
Instruction Manual for the Infantry, Vol. 2a: *The Rifle Company, 1942*, H.Dv. 103/2a, English translation by John Baum
Instruction Manual for the Infantry, Vol. 3a: *The Machinegun Company, 1942*, H.Dv. 130/3a, English translation by John Baum
Logistical History of NATOUSA & MTOUSA, US War Department, 1945
Pilot's Notes General, Air Ministry, 1943
The Rise and Fall of the German Air Force (1933–1945), Air Ministry, 1948
Shooting to Live by Capt. W. E. Fairbairn and Capt. E. A. Sykes, 1942
Der Schütze Hilfsbuch, 1943 by Oberst Hasso von Wedel and Oberleutnant Pfasserott, Richard Schröder Verlag, Berlin, 1943
Statistics Relating to the War Effort of the United Kingdom, HMSO, November 1944
Tactics in the Context of the Reinforced Infantry Battalions by Generalmajor Greiner and Generalmajor Degener, 1941, English translation by John Baum
TEE EMM: Air Ministry Monthly Training Memoranda, Vols I, II, III, Air Ministry, 1939–45
Truppenführung: On the German Art of War, Bruce Condell and David T. Zabecki (eds), Stackpole, 2009
What Britain Has Done 1939–1945, issued by the Ministry of Information, 1945

OFFICIAL HISTORIES

Aris, George, *The Fifth British Division 1939 to 1945*, The Fifth Division Benevolent Fund, 1959

Behrens, C. B. A., *Merchant Shipping and the Demands of War*, HMSO, 1955

Burdon, R. M., *24 Battalion*, War History Branch, Department of Internal Affairs, New Zealand, 1953

Coakley, Robert W. and Leighton, Richard M., *United States Army in World War II: Global Logistics and Strategy 1943–1945*, Office of the Chief of Military History, U.S. Army Center of Military History, 1968

Cody, J. F., *28 (Maori) Battalion*, War History Branch, Department of Internal Affairs, New Zealand, 1956

Cosmas, Graham A. and Cowdrey, Albert E., *United States Army in World War II: Medical Service in the European Theater of Operations*, Historical Division, Department of the Army, 1992

Craven, Wesley Frank and Cate, James Lea, *The Army Air Forces in World War II*, Vol. II: *Europe: Torch to Pointblank*, University of Chicago Press, 1947

Delaney, John P., *The Blue Devils in Italy: A History of the 88th Infantry Division in World War II*, The Battery Press, 1988

Duncan Hall, H. and Wrigley, C. C., *Studies of Overseas Supply*, HMSO, 1956

Echternkamp, Jörg (ed.), *Germany and the Second World War*, Vol. IX/I: *German Wartime Society 1939–1945: Politicization, Disintegration, and the Struggle for Survival*, Clarendon Press, 2008

Fairchild, Byron and Grossman, Jonathan, *United States Army in World War II: The Army and Industrial Manpower*, Office of the Chief of Military History, U.S. Army Center of Military History, 1959

Fisher, Ernest F. Jr., *United States Army in World War II: Cassino to the Alps*, U. S. Army Center of Military History, 1977

Fitzgerald, D. J. L., *History of the Irish Guards in the Second World War*, The Naval & Military Press, n.d.

Garland, Albert N. and McGaw Smyth, Howard, *United States Army in World War II: Sicily and the Surrender of Italy*, U.S. Army Center of Military History, 1986

Hancock, W. K. and Gowing, M. M., *British War Economy*, HMSO, 1949

Harris, C. R. S., *Allied Military Administration of Italy, 1943–1945*, HMSO, 1957

Hinsley. F. H., *British Intelligence in the Second World War*, HMSO, 1993

Howard, Michael, *Grand Strategy*, Vol. IV: *August 1942–September 1943*, HMSO, 1972

Howe, George F., *The Battle History of the 1st Armored Division*, Combat Forces Press, 1954

Hurstfield, J., *The Control of Raw Materials*, HMSO, 1953

The Institution of the Royal Army Service Corps, *The Story of the Royal Army Service Corps 1939–1945*, G. Bell and Sons Ltd, 1955

Knickerbocker, H. R. et al., *United States Army in World War II: Danger Forward: The Story of the First Division in World War II*, Society of the First Division, 1947

Leighton, Richard M. and Coakley, Robert W., *United States Army in World War II: Global Logistics and Strategy 1940–1943*, Office of the Chief of Military History, U.S. Army Center of Military History, 1955
Militärgeschichtliches Forschungsamt, *Germany and the Second World War*, Vol. V: *Organization and Mobilization of the German Sphere of Power*, Part 1: *Wartime Administration, Economy and Manpower Resources, 1939–1941*, Clarendon Press, 2000
—*Germany and the Second World War*, Vol. V: *Organization and Mobilization of the German Sphere of Power*, Part 2B: *Wartime Administration, Economy and Manpower Resources, 1942–1944/5*, Clarendon Press, 2003
—*Germany and the Second World War*, Vol. VI: *The Global War*, Clarendon Press, 2001
—*Germany and the Second World War*, Vol. VIII: *The Eastern Front 1943–1944: The War in the East and on the Neighbouring Fronts*, Clarendon Press, 2017
Molony, C. J. C., *The Mediterranean and the Middle East*, Vol. V, HMSO, 1973
Morison, Samuel Eliot, *History of the United States Naval Operations in World War II: Sicily-Salerno-Anzio, January 1943–June 1944*, Castle Books, 2001
Naval Historical Branch, *Invasion Europe*, HMSO, 1994
Nicholson, G. W. L., *Official History of the Canadian Army in the Second World War*, Vol. II: *The Canadians in Italy, 1943–1945*, Edmond Cloutier, 1957
Norton, Frazer D., *26 Battalion*, War History Branch, Department of Internal Affairs, New Zealand, 1952
Otway, T. B. H., *Airborne Forces of the Second World War 1939–45*, HMSO, 1951
Palmer, Robert R., Wiley, Bell I. and Keast, William R., *United States Army in World War II: The Procurement and Training of Ground Combat Troops*, Historical Division, Department of the Army, 1948
Parker, H. M. D., *Manpower: A Study of War-Time Policy and Administration*, HMSO, 1957
Pogue, Forrest, *United States Army in World War II: The Supreme Command*, Historical Division, Department of the Army, 1954
Postan, M. M., *British War Production*, HMSO, 1952
—Postan, M. M., Hay, D. and Scott, J. D., *Design and Development of Weapons*, HMSO, 1964
Puttick, Edward, *25 Battalion*, War History Branch, Department of Internal Affairs, New Zealand, 1960
Rapport, Leonard and Northwood, Arthur, *Rendezvous with Destiny: A History of the 101st Airborne Division*, 101st Airborne Association, 1948
Richards, Denis, *Royal Air Force 1939–1945*, Vol. II: *The Fight Avails*, HMSO, 1954
—*Royal Air Force 1939–1945*, Vol. III: *The Fight is Won*, HMSO, 1954
Risch, Erna, *The Technical Services, United States Army in World War II: The Quartermaster Corps: Organization, Supply, and Services*, Vol. I, Historical Division, Department of the Army, 1953
Rissik, David, *The D.L.I. at War: The History of the Durham Light Infantry 1939–1945*, The Depot: Durham Light Infantry, n.d.

Roberts Greenfield, Kent et al., *United States Army in World War II: The Organization of Ground Combat Troops*, Historical Division, Department of the Army, 1947

Scott, J. D. and Hughes, Richard, *The Administration of War Production*, HMSO, 1955

Stevens, G. R., *Fourth Indian Division*, McLaren & Sons, 1948

Wagner, Robert L., *The Texas Army*, privately published, 1972

Wardlow, Chester, *United States Army in World War II: The Transportation Corps: Movements, Training, and Supply*, Office of the Chief of Military History, U.S. Army Center of Military History, 1956

Warren, John C., *Airborne Operations in World War II, European Theater*, USAF Historical Division, 1956

—*Airborne Missions in the Mediterranean, 1942–1945*, USAF Historical Division, 1955

EQUIPMENT, WEAPONS AND TECHNICAL BOOKS

Barker, A. J., *British and American Infantry Weapons of World War 2*, Arms and Armour Press, 1969

Bidwell, Shelford and Graham, Dominick, *Fire-Power: British Army Weapons and Theories of War 1904–1945*, George Allen & Unwin, 1982

Bouchery, Jean, *The British Soldier*, Vol. I: *Uniforms, Insignia, Equipment*, Histoire & Collections, n.d.

—*The British Soldier*, Vol. II: *Organisation, Armament, Tanks and Vehicles*, Histoire & Collections, n.d.

Brayley, Martin, *The British Army 1939–45 (1) North-West Europe*, Osprey, 2001

—*British Web Equipment of the Two World Wars*, The Crowood Press, 2005

Bruce, Robert, *German Automatic Weapons of World War II*, The Crowood Press, 1996

Bull, Dr Stephen, *World War II Infantry Tactics*, Osprey, 2004

—*World War II Street-Fighting Tactics*, Osprey, 2008

Chamberlain, Peter and Ellis, Chris, *Tanks of the World*, Cassell, 2002

Chesneau, Roger (ed.), *Conway's All the World's Fighting Ships 1922–1946*, Conway Maritime Press, 1980

Dallies-Labourdette, Jean-Philippe, *S-Boote: German E-Boats in Action 1939–1945*, Histoire & Collections, n.d.

Davis, Brian L., *German Combat Uniforms of World War II*, Vol. II, Arms & Armour Press, 1985

Davies, W. J. K., *German Army Handbook 1939–1945*, Military Book Society, 1973

Doyle, David, *The Complete Guide to German Armored Vehicles*, Skyhorse, 2019

Enjames, Henri-Paul, *Government Issue: US Army European Theater of Operations Collection's Guide*, Histoire & Collections, 2003

Falconer, Jonathan, *D-Day Operations Manual*, Haynes, 2013

Farrar-Hockley, Anthony, *Infantry Tactics 1939–1945*, Almark, 1976

Fleischer, Wolfgang, *The Illustrated Guide to German Panzers*, Schiffer, 2002

Forty, George and Livesey, Jack, *The Complete Guide to Tanks and Armoured Fighting Vehicles*, Southwater, 2012
Gander, Terry and Chamberlain, Peter, *Small Arms, Artillery and Special Weapons of the Third Reich*, Macdonald and Jane's, 1978
Gordon, David B., *Equipment of the WWII Tommy*, Pictorial Histories, 2004
—*Uniforms of the WWII Tommy*, Pictorial Histories, 2005
—*Weapons of the WWII Tommy*, Pictorial Histories, 2004
Grant, Neil, *The Bren Gun*, Osprey, 2013
Griehl, Manfred and Dressel, Joachim, *Luftwaffe Combat Aircraft: Development, Production, Operations, 1935–1945*, Schiffer, 1994
Gunston, Bill, *Fighting Aircraft of World War II*, Salamander, 1988
Hart, S. and Hart, R., *The German Soldier in World War II*, Spellmount, 2000
Hogg, Ian V. (intro.), *The American Arsenal: The World War II Official Standard Ordnance Catalog of Small Arms, Tanks, Armored Cars, Artillery, Antiaircraft Guns, Ammunition, Grenades, Mines, Etcetera*, Greenhill Books, 1996
—*The Guns 1939–1945*, Macdonald, 1969
Jowett, Philip, *The Italian Army 1940–45 (1)*, Osprey, 2000
—*The Italian Army 1940–45 (2)*, Osprey, 2001
—*The Italian Army 1940–45 (3)*, Osprey, 2001
Kay, Antony L. and Smith, J. R., *German Aircraft of the Second World War*, Putnam, 2002
Konstan, Angus, *British Battlecruisers 1939–45*, Osprey, 2003
De Lagarde, Jean, *German Soldiers of World War II*, Histoire & Collections, n.d.
Lavery, Brian, *Churchill's Navy: The Ships, Men and Organisation 1939–1945*, Conway, 2006
Lee, Cyrus A., *Soldat*, Vol. II: *Equipping the German Army Foot Soldier in Europe 1943*, Pictorial Histories, 1988
Lepage, Jean-Denis G. G., *German Military Vehicles*, McFarland & Company, 2007
Lüdeke, Alexander, *Weapons of World War II*, Parragon, 2007
Mason, Chris, *Soldat*, Vol. VIII: *Fallschirmjäger*, Pictorial Histories, 2000
McNab, Chris, *MG 34 and MG 42 Machine Guns*, Osprey, 2012
Ministry of Information, *What Britain Has Done, 1939–45*, HMSO
Mundt, Richard W. and Lee, Cyrus A., *Soldat*, Vol. VI: *Equipping the Waffen-SS Panzer Divisions 1942–1945*, Pictorial Histories, 1997
Musgrave, Daniel D., *German Machineguns*, Greenhill Books, 1992
Myerscough, W., *Air Navigation Simply Explained*, Pitman & Sons Ltd, 1942
Ruge, Friedrich, *Rommel in Normandy*, Macdonald and Jane's, 1979
Saiz, Augustin, *Deutsche Soldaten*, Casemate, 2008
Spayd, P. A., *Bayerlein: From Afrikakorps to Panzer Lehr*, Schiffer, 2003
Stedmoan, Robert, *Kampfflieger: Bomber Crewman of the Luftwaffe 1939–45*, Osprey, 2005
Suermondt, Jan, *World War II Wehrmacht Vehicles*, The Crowood Press, 2003
Sumner, Ian and Vauvillier, François, *The French Army 1939–1945 (1)*, Osprey, 1998
Sutherland, Jonathan, *World War II Tanks and AFVs*, Airlife, 2002
Trye, Rex, *Mussolini's Soldiers*, Airlife, 1995

Vanderveen, Bart, *Historic Military Vehicles Directory*, After the Battle, 1989
Williamson, Gordon, *Gebirgsjäger*, Osprey, 2003
—*German Mountain & Ski Troops 1939–45*, Osprey, 1996
—*U-Boats vs Destroyer Escorts*, Osprey, 2007
Windrow, Richard and Hawkins, Tim, *The World War II GI: US Army Uniforms 1941–45*, The Crowood Press, 2003
Zaloga, Steven, *Armored Thunderbolt: The US Army Sherman in World War II*, Stackpole, 2008
—*Sicily 1943: The Debut of Allied Joint Operations*, Osprey, 2013
—*US Anti-Tank Artillery 1941–45*, Osprey, 2005

MEMOIRS, BIOGRAPHIES, ETC.

Alanbrooke, Field Marshal Lord, *War Diaries, 1939–1945*, Weidenfeld & Nicolson, 2001
Alexander, Field Marshal Earl, *The Alexander Memoirs 1940–1945*, McGraw-Hill, 1962
Alexander, Mark J. and Sparry, John, *Jump Commander*, Casemate, 2012
Altieri, James, *The Spearheaders*, Popular Library, 1960
Ambrose, Stephen E., *Eisenhower: Soldier & President*, Pocket Books, 2003
—*The Supreme Commander: The War Years of Dwight D. Eisenhower*, University Press of Mississippi, 1999
Anders, W., *An Army in Exile*, Macmillan, 1949
Ardizzone, Edward, *Diary of a War Artist*, Bodley Head, 1974
Arneson, Paul S., *I Closed Too Many Eyes: A World War II Medic Finally Talks*, self-published, n.d.
Awatere, Arapeta, *Awatere: A Soldier's Story*, Huia, 2003
Badoglio, Marshal, *Italy in the Second World War*, Oxford University Press, 1948
Balck, Hermann, *Order in Chaos*, University Press of Kentucky, 2015
Ball, Edmund F., *Staff Officer with the Fifth Army*, Exposition Press, 1958
Bentivegna, Rosario, *Achtung Banditen! Roma 1944*, Mursia, 1983
Binder, L. James, *Lemnitzer: A Soldier for His Time*, Brassey's, 1997
Blumenson, Martin, *Mark Clark*, Jonathan Cape, 1985
Bond, Harold L., *Return to Cassino*, J. M. Dent & Sons, 1964
Booth, T. Michael and Spencer, Duncan, *Paratrooper: The Life of General James M. Gavin*, Casemate, 2013
Bosworth, R. J. B., *Mussolini*, Arnold, 2002
Bradner, Liesl, *Snap Dragon: The World War II Exploits of Darby's Ranger and Combat Photographer Phil Stern*, Osprey, 2018
Bruno, James F., *Beyond Fighter Escort*, Ken Cook Co., 1995
Buchner, Emajean, *Sparks*, Thunderbird Press, 1991
Bull, Peter, *To Sea in a Sieve*, Peter Davies Ltd, 1956
Burgwyn, H. James, *Mussolini Warlord: Failed Dreams of Empire 1940–1943*, Enigma Books, 2012
Burnes, John Horne, *The Gallery*, New York Review Books, 2004

Butcher, Harry C., *Three Years with Eisenhower*, William Heinemann, 1946
Byers, E. V., *With Turbans to Tuscany*, self-published, 2002
Caddick-Adams, Peter, *Monty and Rommel: Parallel Lives*, Arrow, 2012
Capponi, Carla, *Con cuore di donna*, Il Saggiatore, 2000
Caracciolo, Filippo, *43/44 Diario di Napoli*, Vallecchi Editore, 1964
Carboni, Generale Giacomo, *L'Armistizio e la Difesa di Roma*, Donatello de Luigi, 1945
Carter, Ross S., *Those Devils in Baggy Pants*, Appleton-Century-Crofts, 1951
Cederberg, Fred, *The Long Road Home*, General Paperbacks, 1989
Chandler, Alfred D. Jr. (ed.), *The Papers of Dwight David Eisenhower: The War Years*, Vol. II, Johns Hopkins Press, 1970
—*The Papers of Dwight David Eisenhower: The War Years*, Vol. III, Johns Hopkins Press, 1970
Churchill, Winston S., *The Second World War*, Vol. V: *Closing the Ring*, Cassell, 1952
Ciano, Galeazzo, *Ciano's Diary 1937–1943*, Phoenix, 2002
Clark, Mark W., *Calculated Risk*, Harper & Brothers, 1950
Clarke, Rupert, *With Alex at War*, Pen & Sword, 2000
Cole, David, *Rough Road To Rome: A Foot Soldier in Sicily and Italy 1943–44*, William Kimber, 1983
Comfort, Charles Fraser, *Artist at War*, Remembrance Books, 1995
Corrado Teatini, Giuseppe, *Diario Dall'Egeo*, Mursia, 1990
Corti, Eugenio, *The Last Soldiers of the King*, University of Missouri Press, 2003
Corvo, Max, *Max Corvo: OSS in Italy, 1942–1945*, Enigma Books, 2005
Cunningham, Admiral of the Fleet Viscount, *A Sailor's Odyssey*, Hutchinson, 1951
Darby, William O., with Baumer, William H., *Darby's Rangers*, Ballantine Books, 2003
Davis, Benjamin O Jr., *American*, Smithsonian Institution Press, 1991
Davis, Richard G., *Carl A. Spaatz and the Air War in Europe*, Center for Air Force History, 1992
Deakin, F. W., *The Brutal Friendship: Mussolini, Hitler and the Fall of Italian Fascism*, Pelican, 1966
Defazio, Albert, *The Italian Campaign: One Soldier's Story of a Forgotten War*, Merriam Press, 2020
De Grada, Magda Ceccarelli, *Giornale del tempo di Guerra*, il Mulino, 2011
Destefano, Anthony M., *The Deadly Don: Vito Genovese Mafia Boss*, Citadel Press, 2021
De Wyss, M., *Rome Under the Terror*, Robert Hale, 1945
Doolittle, James H. 'Jimmy', *I Could Never Be So Lucky Again*, Bantam, 1992
Doucerte, Serge, *Paul Gandoet, Général*, Lavauzelle, 1978
Doughty, Roswell K., *Invading Hitler's Europe*, Frontline Books, 2020
Dundas, Hugh, *Flying Start*, Penguin, 1990
Durnford-Slater, John, *Commando: Memoirs of a Fighting Commando in World War Two*, Greenhill, 2002
Eisenhower, Dwight D., *Crusade in Europe*, William Heinemann, 1948
Fairbanks, Jr., Douglas, *A Hell of a War*, St. Martin's Press, 1993

Farrell, Nicholas, *Mussolini: A New Life*, Phoenix, 2004
Forman, Denis, *To Reason Why*, Pen & Sword, 2008
Gavin, James M., *On To Berlin: Battle of an Airborne Commander, 1943–1946*, Viking, 1978
Gellhorn, Martha, *The Face of War*, Eland, 2016
Gilmour, David, *The Pursuit of Italy*, Penguin, 2012
Gnecchi-Ruscone, Francesco, *When Being Italian Was Difficult*, Milano, 1999
Goebel, Robert J., *Mustang Ace*, Pacifica Military History, 1991
Gorle, Richmond, *The Quiet Gunner At War: El Alamein to the Rhine with the Scottish Divisions*, Pen & Sword, 2011
Guest, John, *Broken Images*, Leo Cooper, 1949
Gunner, Colin, *Front of the Line: Adventures with the Irish Brigade*, Greystone Books, 1991
Hamilton, Nigel, *Monty: Master of the Battlefield 1942–1944*, Hamish Hamilton, 1983
Hamilton, Stuart, *Armoured Odyssey*, Tom Donovan Publishing, 1995
Hatch, Herbert 'Stub', *An Ace and His Angel*, Turner Publishing, 2000
Hirst, Fred, *A Green Hill Far Away*, Charlesworth, 1998
Horne, Alastair, *Macmillan 1894–1956*, Macmillan, 1988
Horsfall, John, *Fling Our Banner to the Wind*, The Roundwood Press, 1978
Howard, Michael, *Captain Professor: A Life in War & Peace*, Continuum UK, 2006
Huebner, Klaus H., *Long Walk Through War*, Texas A&M University Press, 1987
Jackson, W. G. F., *Alexander of Tunis as Military Commander*, Batsford, 1971
Kemp, Nick, *Ever Your Own, Johnnie – Sicily and Italy, 1943–45*, Nick Kemp Books, 2016
Kennedy, Alex, *The Liberator: One World War II Soldier's 500-Day Odyssey*, Arrow, 2013
Kennedy, I. F., *Black Crosses On My Wingtip*, GSPH, 1995
Kershaw, Ian, *Hitler: 1936–1945 – Nemesis*, Penguin, 2001
Kesselring, Albert, *The Memoirs of Field-Marshal Kesselring*, Greenhill Books, 2007
Klein, Joseph, *Fallschirmjäger*, self-published, 2008
Lewis, Norman, *Naples '44*, Eland, 1983
Macmillan, Harold, *The Blast of War 1939–1945*, Harper & Row, 1967
—*War Diaries: The Mediterranean 1943–1945*, Macmillan, 1984
Mauss, Hans-Jörg and de Rijke, Roger, *The War Diary of Dr Wilhelm Mauss*, Mook Publishing, 2016
McCarthy, Michael C., *Air-To-Ground Battle for Italy*, Air University Press, 2004
McCrum, Tony, *Sunk by Stukas Survived at Salerno*, Pen & Sword, 2010
McIntosh, Charles, *From Cloak to Dagger: An SOE Agent in Italy 1943–1945*, William Kimber, 1992
Meon, Marcia and Heinen, Margo, *Heroes Cry Too*, Meadowlark Publishing, 2002
Miller, Victor, *Nothing Is Impossible*, Pen & Sword, 2015
Millers, Lee G., *The Story of Ernie Pyle*, Viking, 1950
Milligan, Spike, *Mussolini: His Part in My Downfall*, Penguin, 2012

Montanaro, Elena, *Tra le Pieghe della Memoria*, Edizione a cura dell'Amministrazione Comunale di Piedimonte S. Germano, 2004
Montgomery, Field Marshal the Viscount, *El Alamein to the Sangro*, Hutchinson, 1944
—*Memoirs*, Collins, 1958
Moore, Peter, *No Need to Worry*, Wilton 65, 2002
Moorehead, Alan, *Eclipse*, Penguin 2022
Mowat, Farley, *And No Birds Sang*, Douglas & McIntyre, 2012
—*The Regiment*, McClelland & Stewart, 1955
Murphy, Audie, *To Hell and Back*, Picador, 2002
Murphy, Thomas D., *Ambassadors in Arms*, University of Hawaii Press, 2020
Nicolson, Nigel, *Alex: The Life of Field Marshal Earl Alexander of Tunis*, Weidenfeld & Nicolson, 1973
—*Long Life: Memoirs*, Weidenfeld & Nicolson, 1997
O'Brien, Phillips Payson, *The Second Most Powerful Man in the World: The Life of Admiral William D. Leahy, Roosevelt's Chief of Staff*, Caliber, 2020
Orange, Vincent, *Coningham: A Biography of Air Marshal Sir Arthur Coningham*, Center for Air Force History, 1990
Origo, Iris, *War in Val d'Orcia*, Flamingo, 2002
Parton, James, *'Air Force Spoken Here': General Ira Eaker and the Command of the Air*, Adler & Adler, 1986
Pearce, John A., *A Private in the Texas Army*, State House Press, 2021
Peyton, John, *Solly Zuckerman*, John Murray, 2001
Pogue, Forrest C., *George C. Marshall: Interviews and Reminiscences*, Marshall Foundation, 1991
Pyle, Ernie, *Brave Men*, Henry Holt, 1944
—*Here Is Your War*, Forum Books, 1945
Reynolds, L. C., *Motor Gunboat 658*, Cassell & Co., 2002
Richardson, Robert L., *The Jagged Edge of Duty: A Fighter Pilot's World War II*, Stackpole, 2017
Ridgway, Matthew B., *Soldier: The Memoirs of Matthew B. Ridgway*, Harper & Brothers, 1956
Roberts, William F., *Bonus Time: One Pilot's Story of World War II*, Xlibris Corporation, 2002
Robinson, James A., *Alexander*, The Banbridge Chronicle Press, 1946
Robinson, Stephen, *Panzer Commander: Hermann Balck: Germany's Master Tactician*, Exisle, 2019
Ross, Hamish, *Paddy Mayne*, The History Press, 2004
Samwell, H. P., *Fighting With the Desert Rats: An Infantry Officer's War With the Eighth Army*, Pen & Sword, 2012
Schaps, Ralph B., *500 Days of Front Line Combat*, iUniverse, Inc., 2003
Scislowski, Stanley, *Not All of Us Were Brave*, Dundurn Press, 1997
Senger und Etterlin, Frido von, *Neither Fear Nor Hope*, Presidio, 1989
Smith, David A., *The Price of Valor: The Life of Audie Murphy, America's Most Decorated Hero of World War II*, Regnery History, 2015

Smith, Roger, *Up the Blue*, Ngaio Press, 2000
Steinbeck, John, *Once There Was a War*, Penguin, 2000
Stone, James W. F., *World War II Diary*, privately published, n.d.
Stowers, Richard, *Wellingtons Over the Med*, Richard Stowers, 2012
Stoy, Timothy R., *Sharpen Your Bayonets!*, Casemate, 2022
Sulzberger, C. L., *A Long Row of Candles: Memoirs and Diaries, 1934–54*, Macdonald, 1969
Teatini, Giuseppe Corrado, *Diario dell'Egio*, Mursia, 1990
Tedder, Marshal of the Royal Air Force Lord, *With Prejudice*, Cassell, 1966
Tobin, James, *Ernie Pyle's War*, University of Kansas Press, 1997
Tompkins, Peter, *A Spy in Rome*, Simon & Schuster, 1962
Tregaskis, Richard, *Invasion Diary*, Random House, 1944
Truscott, Lucian K., *Command Missions*, Presidio, 1990
Ullrich, Volker, *Hitler: Downfall, 1939–45*, Bodley Head, 2020
Valenzi, Maurizio, *C'è Togliatti!*, Sellerio Editore, 1996
Vrilakas, Robert 'Smoky', *Look Mom – I Can Fly!*, Amethyst Moon Publishing, 2011
Wagner, Bud, *And There Shall Be War: World War II Diaries and Memoirs*, Wilmer Wagner & Lloyd Wagner Press, 2000
Warlimont, Walter, *Inside Hitler's Headquarters 1939–45*, Presidio, 1962
Warner, Oliver, *Cunningham of Hyndhope: Admiral of the Fleet*, John Murray, 1967
Whicker, Alan, *Whicker's War*, HarperCollins, 2005
Winton, John, *Cunningham: The Greatest Admiral Since Nelson*, John Murray, 1998

GENERAL

Allport, Alan, *Browned Off and Bloody-Minded*, Yale University Press, 2017
Alonso, Miguel et al. (eds), *Fascist Warfare 1922–1945*, Palgrave Macmillan, 2019
Anon., *The Rise and Fall of the German Air Force 1933–1945*, Air Ministry, 1948
Anon., *Italy*, Vol. I, Naval Intelligence Division, 1944
—*Italy*, Vol. II, Naval Intelligence Division, 1945
Arthur, Max, *Men of the Red Beret*, Hutchinson, 1990
Associazione Nazionale Combattenti della Guerra di Liberazione Inquadrati nei Reparti Regolari delle Forze Armate, *La Ricossa dell'Esercito: Il Primo Raggruppamento Motorizzato Monte Lungo*, Cassino, 1993
Baedeker, Karl, *Southern Italy & Sicily*, Karl Baedeker, 1912
Ballantine, Duncan S., *US Naval Logistics in the Second World War*, Princeton University Press, 1949
Battaglia, Roberto, *The Story of the Italian Resistance*, Odhams Press, 1957
Bekker, Cajus, *The Luftwaffe War Diaries*, Corgi, 1972
Black, Robert W., *Rangers in World War II*, Ballantine, 1992
Bosworth, R. J. B., *Mussolini's Italy: Life Under the Dictatorship*, Penguin, 2006
Carafano, James Jay, *GI Ingenuity: Improvisation, Technology and Winning WWII*, Stackpole, 2006
Champagne, Daniel, *Dogface Soldiers: The Story of B Company, 15th Regiment, 3rd Infantry Division*, Merriam Press, 2003

Christensen, Ben, *The 1st Fallschirmjäger Division in World War II*, Vol. II: *Years of Retreat*, Schiffer, 2007
Citino, Robert M., *The German Way of War*, University Press of Kansas, 2005
—*The Wehrmacht Retreats: Fighting a Lost War, 1943*, University Press of Kansas, 2012
Clark, Lloyd, *Anzio: The Friction of War*, Headline, 2006
Cook, Tim, *The Necessary War*, Vol. I: *Canadians Fighting in the Second World War 1939–1943*, Allen Lane, 2014
Dancocks, Daniel G., *The D-Day Dodgers: The Canadians in Italy 1943–1945*, McClelland & Stewart, 1991
Daudy, Philippe, *Naples*, Editions Rencontre, 1964
David, Saul, *The Force*, Hachette, 2019
Deakin, F. W., *The Brutal Friendship*, Pelican Books, 1966
De Luna, Giovanni, *Storia del Partito D'Azione*, Feltrinelli, 1982
Dickson, Paul, *The Rise of the G.I. Army, 1940–1941*, Atlantic Monthly Press, 2020
Di Marco, Andrea, *Assolutamente Resistere!*, D'Abruzzo Edizioni Menabò, 2013
Dinardo, R. L., *Germany and the Axis Powers: From Coalition to Collapse*, University of Kansas Press, 2005
—*Germany's Panzer Arm in WWII*, Stackpole, 1997
Doherty, Richard, *Clear the Way! A History of the 38th (Irish) Brigade, 1941–47*, Irish Academic Press, 1993
Edgerton, David, *Britain's War Machine*, Penguin, 2012
—*Warfare State: Britain 1920–1970*, Cambridge University Press, 2006
Ellwood, David W., *Italy 1943–1945*, Leicester University Press, 1985
Eriksson, Patrick G., *Alarmstart South and Final Defeat*, Amberley, 2019
Fennell, Jonathan, *Fighting The People's War*, Cambridge University Press, 2019
Ford, Ken, *Battleaxe Division*, Sutton, 2003
Fraser, David, *And We Shall Shock Them: The British Army in the Second World War*, Cassell, 1999
French, David, *Raising Churchill's Army: The British Army and the War Against Germany 1919–1945*, Oxford University Press, 2000
Gardiner, Wira, *The Story of the Maori Battalion*, Reed, 1995
Gavin, James M. and Lee, William C., *Airborne Warfare*, Infantry Journal Press, 1947
Gooderson, Ian, *Air Power at the Battlefront: Allied Close Air Support in Europe, 1943–45*, Frank Cass, 1998
Gregory, Barry, *British Airborne Troops*, Macdonald & Jane's, 1974
Harrison Place, Timothy, *Military Training in the British Army, 1940–1944*, Frank Cass, 2000
Harris Smith, Richard, *OSS: The Secret of America's First Central Intelligence Agency*, The Lyons Press, 2005
Heaton, Colin D. and Lewis, Anne-Marie, *The German Aces Speak*, Zenith Press, 2011
Holland, James, *Heroes: The Greatest Generation and the Second World War*, Harper Perennial, 2007

—*Italy's Sorrow: A Year of War 1944–45*, Harper Press, 2008
—*The Savage Storm: The Battle for Italy 1943*, Bantam Press, 2023
Howard, Michael, *The Mediterranean Strategy in the Second World War*, Greenhill Books, 1993
Hoyt, Edwin P., *The GI's War*, Cooper Square Press, 2000
Irving, David, *The Rise and Fall of the Luftwaffe: The Life of Luftwaffe Marshal Erhard Milch*, Weidenfeld & Nicolson, 1973
Jackson, W. G. F., *The Battle for Italy*, Harper & Row, 1967
Joseph, Frank, *Mussolini's War*, Helion, 2010
Katz, Robert, *Fatal Silence*, Cassell, 2004
Knox, MacGregor, *Hitler's Italian Allies*, Cambridge University Press, 2000
Kogan, Norman, *Italy and the Allies*, Harvard University Press, 1956
Kurowski, Franz, *The History of the Fallschirm Panzerkorps Hermann Göring*, J. J. Fedorowicz Publishing, 1995
Lamb, Richard, *War in Italy 1943–1945: A Brutal Story*, John Murray, 1993
Leccisotti, Tommaso, *Monte Cassino*, Abbey of Monte Cassino, 1987
Linklater, Eric, *The Campaign in Italy*, HMSO, 1951
LoFaro, Guy, *The Sword of St. Michael: The 82nd Airborne Division in World War II*, Da Capo, 2011
Lopez, Jean et al., *World War II Infographics*, Thames & Hudson, 2019
Macintyre, Ben, *SAS Rogue Heroes*, Viking, 2016
Malatesta, Saverio, *Orsogna 1943*, D'Abruzzo Edizioni Menabò, 2016
Mallinson, Jennifer, *From Taranto to Trieste: Following the 2nd NZ Division's Italian Campaign, 1943–45*, Fraser Books, 2019
Marlantes, Karl, *What It Is Like to Go to War*, Atlantic Monthly Press, 2011
McGaw Smyth, Howard, *Secrets of the Fascist Era*, Southern Illinois University Press, 1973
McManus, John C., *American Courage, American Carnage: 7th Infantry Chronicles 1812 Through World War II*, Forge Books, 2009
—*Deadly Sky: The American Combat Airman in World War II*, Presidio Press, 2000
—*Grunts: Inside the American Combat Experience World War II Through Iraq*, Dutton Caliber, 2011
—*The Deadly Brotherhood: The American Combat Soldier in World War II*, Presidio Press, 2003
Mead, Richard, *Churchill's Lions: A Biographical Guide to the Key British Generals of World War II*, Spellmount, 2007
—*The Men Behind Monty*, Pen & Sword, 2015
Midson, Harold John 'Peter', *The Thomas Cook Division*, self-published, 2022
Mortimer, Gavin, *Stirling's Men: The Inside History of the SAS in World War II*, Cassell, 2005
Murray, Al, *Command*, Headline, 2022
O'Brien, Phillips Payson, *How the War Was Won*, Cambridge University Press, 2015
O'Connor, Garry, *The 1st Household Cavalry, 1943–44*, Pen & Sword, 2013

Pahl, Magnus, *Monte Cassino 1944*, Brill Ferdinand Schöningh, 2021
Parker, Matthew, *Monte Cassino*, Headline, 2004
Plowman, Jeffrey and Rowe, Perry, *The Battles for Monte Cassino Then and Now*, After the Battle, 2011
Pond, Hugh, *Salerno*, William Kimber, 1961
Prien, Jochen, *Jagdgeschwader 53: A History of the 'Pik As' Geschwader May 1942–January 1944*, Schiffer, 1998
Quilter, D. C. (ed.), *'No Dishonourable Name'*, William Clowes & Sons Ltd, 1948
Reynolds, Leonard C., *Dog Boats At War*, The History Press, 1998
Roskill, Stephen, *The Navy At War 1939–1945*, Wordsworth Editions, 1998
Saunders, Anne Leslie, *A Travel Guide to the World War II Sites in Italy*, Travel Guide Press, 2016
Schmitz, Günter, *Die 16.Panzer-Division 1938–1945*, Podzun-Pallas-Verlag, n.d.
Shores, Christopher and Massimello, Giovanni et al., *A History of the Mediterranean Air War 1940–1945*, Vol. IV: *Sicily and Italy to the Fall of Rome, 14 May 1943–5 June 1944*, Grub Street, 2018
Short, Neil, *German Defences in Italy in World War II*, Osprey, 2006
Solly, Major A. E. (ed.), *The 'Faugh-a-Ballagh': The Regimental Gazette of The Royal Irish Fusiliers, 1943–1949*, Combined Services Publications Ltd, 1950
Stargardt, Nicholas, *The German War: A Nation Under Arms, 1939–45*, Bodley Head, 2015
Steinhoff, Johannes, Pechel, Peter and Showalter, Dennis, *Voices From the Third Reich: An Oral History*, Da Capo, 1994
Thompson, Julian, *Ready for Anything: The Parachute Regiment at War 1940–1982*, Weidenfeld & Nicolson, 1989
Todman, Daniel, *Britain's War: Into Battle, 1937–1941*, Allen Lane, 2016
—*Britain's War: A New World, 1942–1947*, Allen Lane, 2020
Tompkins, Peter, *Italy Betrayed*, Simon & Schuster, 1966
Tooze, Adam, *The Wages of Destruction: The Making & Breaking of the Nazi Economy*, Penguin, 2007
Weal, John, *Jagdgeschwader 53 'Piks-As'*, Osprey, 2007
Werthen, Wolfgang, *Geschichte der 16. Panzer-Division*, Podzun-Verlag, 1958
Whiting, Charles, *Hunters From the Sky*, Cooper Square Press, 2001
Whitlock, Flint, *The Rock of Anzio: From Sicily to Dachau – A History of the US 45th Infantry Division*, Westview Press, 1997
Zambardi, Maurizio, *Memorie di Guerra*, Edizione Eva, 2003
Zuehlke, Mark, *Ortona*, Douglas & McIntyre, 2003

PERIODICALS, JOURNALS, MAGAZINES AND PAMPHLETS

After the Battle, No. 13, *Cassino Battlefield Tour*
After the Battle, No. 52, *Anzio*
After the Battle, No. 142, Rowe, Perry, *Faking Monte Cassino*
Varsori, Antonio, 'Italy, Britain and the Problem of a Separate Peace During the Second World War: 1940–1943', *The Journal of Italian History*, Vol. 1, No. 3

An American soldier with a young Italian child near Pico, 25 May 1944.

Acknowledgements

Books like this one might end up with one name on the front cover, but I have to admit I've been given a huge amount of help along the way from a number of people and in many different capacities, most of whom probably don't really get the credit they deserve.

I've been lucky enough to visit a number of archives and at every turn, those who look after and work at these places have been unfailingly helpful. My thanks to all the staff at the Imperial War Museum in London, but particularly Jane Rosen, also to the staff of The National Archives at Kew, the Liddell Hart Archives for Military History at King's College, London, and to Glyn Prysor and the gang at the National Army Museum in Chelsea. In the United States, my thanks to the staff at the National Archives and Records Administration at College Park, Maryland, and to the brilliant team at the United States Army Education and Heritage Center at Carlisle, Pennsylvania – and especially to Tom Buffenbarger, who could not have been more helpful during my time there. Thank you to Tessa Updike and the team at The Citadel in Charleston, South Carolina, for being so helpful and for making me so welcome. The team at the National World War II Museum in New Orleans are now firm friends as well as unfailingly helpful, and special thanks are due to the brilliant Sarah Kirksey, Becky Mackie and Jeremy Collins. In Germany, I'd like to thank the staff of the Bundesarchiv-Militärarchiv at Freiburg and also the staff of the Tagebuch Archiv at Emmendingen.

In Italy, numerous people gave incredible help, and I owe particular thanks to the following: Dr Gaetano de Angelis-Curtis at the Centro Documentazione e Studi Cassinati; Costantino Jadecola, who helped considerably with researching the Collelungo massacre; Cristina Cangi at the Archivio Diaristico Nazionale at Pieve Santo Stefano; John Simkins of the Monte San Martino Trust; Berniero Barra, the Director of the Centro Culturale Studi Storico; to Giuseppe Caucci of the Associazione Linea Gustav Fronte Garigliano, who gave me a guided tour of his superb museum there in Castelforte; to Alberto Turinetti di Priero and Valentino Rossetti for their help with the Collelungo research; to Anna Balzarro at the IRSIFAR Istituto Romano per la Storia d'Italia dal Fascismo all Resistenza, Roma; Antonella at the Archivio di Stato, in Chieti; Mario Renaudi at the Museo Specialistico della Linea Gustav in Castel di Sangro; Don Mariano Dell'Omo at the Archivio di Montecassino; Gaetano Bonelli at the Museo di Napoli Collezione Bonelli; Monica Sperabene at the Sala Collezioni Speciali at the Biblioteca Nazionale Centrale di Roma; and Kate Wilcox at the Institute of Historical Research at the University of London. My special thanks, however, go to Dr Damiano Parravano, who has become a good friend and who has been unfailingly helpful at every turn.

A number of other people have helped along the way. I am hugely grateful to brothers Richard and Eddie O'Sullivan, who do incredible work keeping the flame alive for the 38th Irish Brigade and who helped get permission for me to use the extraordinary wartime letters of Lawrie Franklyn-Vaile. Joe Hudgens has been incredibly kind in compiling and sending me the wartime air graphs of his wife's great-uncle, Leonard Obermeier, who served with the 36th Division. Henry Wilson has very kindly shared with me his great-grandfather's wartime letters. Earl Alexander has, over many years, been incredibly generous with sharing many of his father's papers and letters. Julian Gordon-Watson has kindly shared various photographs of his father, Michael. Surrey Garland has been unfailingly helpful in sending me his father's diary, letters and other information about his father; it has been a great pleasure to get to know him. John Baranowski has also very generously shared the oral histories and papers of his father, Julian Baranowski, a member of the Polish II Corps at Cassino. Among others who have sent me material, photos and shared details of their various relations who served in Italy are the following: Wolf von Kumberg, Paul Reed, Julian Gordon-Watson, Patrick Bogue, Erik Albertsen, Séan Scullion, Tom Petch, Jake Haywood, Andy de Rosa, Philip Trounsdell, Arturo Bugaon, Athol Forbes, Rod Whitamore, Thomas Bone, Jay Lowrey, Konrad Harandon, Simon Kovach, Richard Willan, Ray Moroney, Patrick Herring, Emma Howard, Charlie Barne, Oliver Davey and Frank Barnard. Others who have helped in various ways are Alex Garrick in Canberra, Jenny Isted and Lorraine Davidson at Traveller's World in Salisbury, Joanne Muhammad, Jane O'Hara and Hugh Alexander.

I am enormously grateful to General Sir Mark Carleton-Smith for reading through some key chapters of the manuscript, and to Matt Doncaster and Paul Davis for adding their beady eyes to the page proofs. There are also a host of fellow historians and other friends who have helped along the way with material, advice and lending an ear. I'm very grateful to Matthew Parker for sharing his archive with me, and also Saul David, a great friend, who has kindly shared material. Mike Neiberg has been a tremendous help as well as brilliant company along with his wife, Barbara, while in Carlisle, PA. Huge thanks to James Scott and his family for their company and for putting me up in Charleston. Jonathan Fennell, a brilliant historian, has also been incredibly helpful, as has Paul Reed in sharing his father's account of his experiences in Anzio and also maps and photographs. Peter Caddick-Adams is another great old chum who has offered a number of incredibly useful pointers, thoughts and suggestions; conversations with Peter are always invaluable and he has, as ever, steered me in various directions and given me much over which to ponder. Thank you, Peter. Stephen Fisher has been very helpful with the naval aspect of the campaign, as has Steve Prince, another great pal and sounding board. My thanks, too, to Kate Brett and Steve's team at the Naval Historical Branch. Thanks also to Jonathan Fennell and John Tregoning.

Huge thanks to the History Hit team: the brilliant Dan Snow, Joe Greenway and Bill Locke and the amazing posse with whom I toured southern Italy and who gave me the chance to have one more look at the battlegrounds before signing off the manuscript – to Mark Edger and Laura McMillen, massive thanks and especially for such brilliant company, enthusiasm and professionalism.

A couple of people have given special help with archival work and translations. Pete Connor in New Zealand has been very generous with sharing his own research into the New Zealanders' experience in Italy and especially his work on the 24th Battalion. Thank you, Pete. Brad St Croix has done a terrific job in Canada – huge thanks, Brad. Will Senior, Ollie Senior and Harry Thomas have also been enormously helpful in scanning various Italian, French and German books and documents – thank you, lads. Dorothee Schneider is an old friend but also a great travelling companion in Freiburg and Emmendingen – Dorothee, thank you, as always. Charlie Mitford has not only been a brilliant and tireless help with translations but has also been a great addition to the History Hit team in Italy – Charlie, I cannot thank you enough for all your immense help. Laura Bailey has helped out at Kew, the IWM, transcribing and generally being incredibly helpful at every turn – Laura, thank you. Thanks, too, to Ollie Senior, neighbour and fellow cricketer, who was roped in to help with translations and my ever-growing archive. Merryn Walters has also been brilliant transcribing diaries, offering pointers and extra documents. Merryn – thank you.

I am extremely fortunate to be published by such brilliant teams either side of the Atlantic. At Grove Atlantic in New York, I am enormously grateful to all the team – to Deb Seager, the ever-supportive head man, Morgan Entrekin, and most of all to George Gibson, a brilliant editor, friend and a man whose judgement I have come to trust and value immensely. Thank you. In London, huge thanks as always to the brilliant Bantam Press team: to Melissa Kelly, Nicole Witmer, Katrina Whone, Phil Lord, Tony Maddock, Tom Hill and especially Bill Scott-Kerr, a great friend and colleague and simply a brilliant editor and publisher. I always feel in such incredibly safe hands and know you'll always have my back – I cannot thank you enough. I also owe enormous thanks to Linden Lawson, who has copy-edited the book with immense care, sensitivity and, above all, skill. Thank you, Linden – truly. Huge thanks, too, to Cora McGregor and all the team at PEW Literary, and especially Patrick Walsh, an extraordinary agent and great friend.

I have also been lucky to have had the opportunity to share the progress of this book as it has progressed on the podcast I co-host with Al Murray, 'We Have Ways of Making You Talk', and also, once a week, John McManus. John has been an enormous help – patiently listening to my theories and proving an invaluable sounding board. Huge thanks, John. The team at Goalhanger who produce the podcast are all owed huge thanks – so, to Tony Pastor, Joey McCarthy and Laura Bailey, especially, but also Jon Gill, Harry Lineker, Izzy Reid and all the team there, good on you. Thank you, too, to all the listeners and especially the Independent Company members for continuing to listen to our podcasts.

Finally, thank you to my family, Rachel, Ned and Daisy, for putting up with this sometimes all-consuming job, to Ned for joining the History Hit team in Italy, and to all three of you for always being there for me and giving me so much support in every way. And finally, finally, my thanks to my great pal, podcasting partner and now 'Walking the Ground' companion too, Al Murray, to whom this final book of mine about the War in Italy is dedicated. We've discussed and debated this campaign through and through, and Al, your thoughts, contributions and advice – as well as reading the book so beautifully – have been immense. *Grazie mille* for sharing the journey.

Picture Acknowledgements

Plate Sections

Page 1
General Clark en route to Anzio: Mark W. Clark Collection, The Citadel Archives and Museum

Page 2, top left
The ruins of Cervaro: From *United States Army in World War II*, National Archives and Records Administration, USA

Page 2, top right
British troops tramp towards the River Garigliano: Supplied by the author courtesy of the Imperial War Museum

Page 2, 2nd row
One of the bridges successfully put across the Garigliano: Supplied by the author courtesy of the Imperial War Museum

Page 2, 3rd row
British troops in the hills above the Garigliano: Supplied by the author courtesy of the Imperial War Museum

Page 2, bottom left
T-Patcher stretcher parties dug in along the lateral road that ran along the Rapido: From *United States Army in World War II*, National Archives and Records Administration, USA

Page 2, bottom right
Troops from the 36th Division dug in near the Rapido: Mark W. Clark Collection, The Citadel Archives and Museum

Page 3, top
Trucks unloading from landing ships: Supplied by the author courtesy of the Imperial War Museum

Page 3, centre left
American troops advance inland north of Anzio: Mark W. Clark Collection, The Citadel Archives and Museum

Page 3, centre right
The Via Anziate with the Colli Albani in the distance: Supplied by the author courtesy of the Imperial War Museum

Page 3, bottom
The Mussolini Canal: John P. Lucas Collection, United States Army Heritage and Education Center

Page 4, top left
Landing ships disgorging supplies on to Anzio's quayside: Supplied by the author courtesy of the Imperial War Museum

Page 4, centre left
Anzio Annie: From *United States Army in World War II*, National Archives and Records Administration, USA

Page 4, centre right
Major Walter Gericke: Bundesarchiv, Bild 101I-575-1807-31A / Seger / CC-BY-SA 3.0 DE

Page 4, bottom left
British Tommy crawling along a trench: Supplied by the author courtesy of the Imperial War Museum

Page 4, bottom right
American tank destroyer rumbling through Nettuno: Mark W. Clark Collection, The Citadel Archives and Museum

Page 5, top left
General Alexander with John Harding and Général Juin: Mark W. Clark Collection, The Citadel Archives and Museum

Page 5, top right
French colonial troops of the CEF: Mark W. Clark Collection, The Citadel Archives and Museum

Page 5, centre left
Men of the 34th Red Bulls trying to warm themselves: Mark W. Clark Collection, The Citadel Archives and Museum

Page 5, centre right
Appalling conditions in Italy: Supplied by the author courtesy of the Imperial War Museum

Page 5, bottom
Cassino under attack: Mark W. Clark Collection, The Citadel Archives and Museum

Page 6
Soldier (Private Ernest Wilson) of the 142nd Infantry Regiment: United States Army Signal Corps Photograph Collection

Page 7, top left
General Freyberg: Supplied by the author courtesy of the Imperial War Museum

Page 7, top right
Gurkhas of 4th Indian Division moving into the line: Supplied by the author courtesy of the Imperial War Museum

Page 7, 2nd row, left
Loading bombs aboard a Mitchell medium bomber: From *United States Army in World War II*, National Archives and Records Administration, USA

Page 7, 2nd row, right
Shattered remains of the old Italian Army barracks: Mark W. Clark Collection, The Citadel Archives and Museum

Page 7, 3rd row
Fallschirmjäger shelter in a gully: Courtesy the author

Page 7, bottom
The devastated remains of the Abbey of Monte Cassino: The National Archives, Kew

Page 8, top
Bombs exploding around the abbey: Mark W. Clark Collection, The Citadel Archives and Museum

Page 8, centre
A column of German troops and amour pause on the Via Anziate at the start of FISCHFANG

Page 8, bottom left
General von Mackensen with Generalleutnant Schlemm: Dr Stecker/Bundesarchiv, bild 183-2004-1007-500

Page 8, bottom right
Ammunition truck burning in Nettuno: Mark W. Clark Collection, The Citadel Archives and Museum

Page 9, top
Fallschirmjäger looking down over Highway 6 and the Liri Valley: Bundesarchiv, Bild 146-1974-006-62/Czimich/CC BY-SA 3.0 DE

Page 9, centre
Medium bombers head towards Cassino: The National Archives, Kew

Page 9, bottom
Bombs begin to rain down: The National Archives, Kew

Page 10, top left
Cassino being hammered: The National Archives, Kew

Page 10, top right
General Clark and Al Gruenther watch the bombing from Freyberg's CP: Mark W. Clark Collection, The Citadel Archives and Museum

Page 10, centre
Cavendish Road: The Polish Institute and Sikorski Museum, London

Page 10, bottom
The bomb spread marked up on an aerial montage: The National Archives, Kew

Page 11, top
The destruction of Cassino: Mark W. Clark Collection, The Citadel Archives and Museum

Page 11, bottom
The destruction of Cassino: Mark W. Clark Collection, The Citadel Archives and Museum

Page 12, top left
Massive piles of rubbish were left after the bombers had gone: Supplied by the author courtesy of the Imperial War Museum

Page 12, 2nd row, left
4th Indian Division troops advancing: Supplied by the author courtesy of the Imperial War Museum

Page 12, 2nd row, right
Hangman's Hill: Mark W. Clark Collection, The Citadel Archives and Museum

Page 12, 3rd row, left
The desolation of Cassino seen from the north: Supplied by the author courtesy of the Imperial War Museum

Page 12, 3rd row, right
Oberst Ludwig Heilmann with General Richard Heidrich: Bundesarchiv, Bild 101I-577-1920-31 / Zscheile / CC-BY-SA 3.0 DE

Page 12, bottom
Fallschirmjäger amid the smoke and ruins of Cassino: Ullstein bild via Getty Images

Page 13, top left
Prostitute in Naples dancing on a table: Courtesy the author

Page 13, top right
Teenage girl recovers at the Albergo dei Poveri Reformatory having been prostituted by her family: Courtesy the author

Page 13, centre left
Young woman with her child eating Allied food: Supplied by the author courtesy of the Imperial War Museum

Page 13, centre right
Families emerging from the cave in which they'd been living: Supplied by the author courtesy of the Imperial War Museum

Page 13, bottom left
Refugees on the move: Mark W. Clark Collection, The Citadel Archives and Museum

Page 13, bottom right
Elderly woman outside the ruins of her house: Supplied by the author courtesy of the Imperial War Museum

Page 14, top left
General Alexander with General Oliver Leese: Supplied by the author courtesy of the Imperial War Museum

Page 14, top right
Operation DIADEM: Supplied by the author courtesy of the Imperial War Museum

Page 14, 2nd row, left
Poles taking over positions on Monte Cassino before DIADEM: Mark W. Clark Collection, The Citadel Archives and Museum

Page 14, 2nd row, right
Polish troops in the ruins of the abbey: The Polish Institute and Sikorski Museum, London

Page 14, 3rd row, left
Dead Fallschirmjäger among the rubble: Supplied by the author courtesy of the Imperial War Museum

Page 14, 3rd row, right
American troops of the 88th 'Blue Devils' in the ruins of Santa Maria Infante: Mark W. Clark Collection, The Citadel Archives and Museum

Page 14, bottom
Men of the 38th Irish Brigade in a jam of traffic beside a knocked-out Nebelwerfer: Supplied by the author courtesy of the Imperial War Museum

Page 15, top left
US troops of the 88th Division moving through Itri: Mark W. Clark Collection, The Citadel Archives and Museum

Page 15, top right
Medic treating a battle casualty: Mark W. Clark Collection, The Citadel Archives and Museum

Page 15, centre left
US soldier of the 3rd Division walking past German dead in Cisterna: United States Army Signal Corps Photograph Collection

Page 15, centre right
French soldier looking at wrecked German 71. Division vehicles and troops: Mark W. Clark Collection, The Citadel Archives and Museum

Page 15, bottom left
British troops retake Aprilia: Supplied by the author courtesy of the Imperial War Museum

Page 15, bottom right
American troops corral prisoners in Velletri: Mark W. Clark Collection, The Citadel Archives and Museum

Page 16, top left
General Clark pauses near Rome: Mark W. Clark Collection, The Citadel Archives and Museum

Page 16, top right
Allied troops pouring into the capital: Supplied by the author courtesy of the Imperial War Museum

Page 16, centre
Allied troops in Rome: Mark W. Clark Collection, The Citadel Archives and Museum

Page 16, bottom
Mark Clark with Truscott and Keyes at an impromptu meeting with his corps commanders at the Campidoglio: Supplied by the author courtesy of the Imperial War Museum

Integrated Pictures

Page xvii
Wounded Polish solider: The Polish Institute and Sikorski Museum, London

Page xxxi
Taped pathway to the ruins of the abbey: Supplied by the author courtesy of the Imperial War Museum

Page xxxviii
New Zealander heavy-machine crew near Castle Hill: Supplied by the author courtesy of the Imperial War Museum

Page xxxix, top
Cassino and Highway 6: From *United States Army in World War II*, National Archives and Records Administration, USA

Page xxxix, bottom
Cassino, November 1943: The National Archives, Kew

Pages xl–xli
Monte Cassino Panorama: Mark W. Clark Collection, The Citadel Archives and Museum

Page xl, bottom
The Factory and Overpass: The National Army Museum

Page xli, bottom
The Wadis: Courtesy of Paul Reed

Page xlii, top
Sketch map of the Monte Cassino Massif: Cavendish Road: The National Army Museum

Page xlii, bottom
Sketch map of the Monte Cassino Massif: Colle Sant'Angelo from Albaneta: The National Army Museum

Page xliii, top
Sketch map of the Monte Cassino massif in profile: The National Army Museum

Page xliii, bottom
Sketch map of the Monte Cassino Massif: Snakeshead and Monte Cairo: The National Army Museum

Page xliv
B-26 Marauder plane: National Archives and Records Administration, USA

Page 13
US mortar crew: United States Army Signal Corps

Page 151
German Fallschirmjäger POWs north of Cassino: Supplied by the author courtesy of the Imperial War Museum

Page 516
Sherman tank loaded with infantry: Supplied by the author courtesy of the Imperial War Museum

Page 528
British Tommy and his German captive: Supplied by the author courtesy of the Imperial War Museum

Page 536
'Sea View Hotel', Anzio: Supplied by the author courtesy of the Imperial War Museum

Page 544
Canadian Sherman and infantry moving through the Liri Valley: Supplied by the author courtesy of the Imperial War Museum

Page 586
American soldier with a young Italian child near Pico: National Archives and Records Administration, USA

Pages 614–15
British 25-pounder team in action: Supplied by the author courtesy of the Imperial War Museum

Page 616
New Zealander infantryman in the shattered wreckage of Cassino: Supplied by the author courtesy of the Imperial War Museum

Part-opener Pictures

All supplied by the author courtesy of the Imperial War Museum

Gallery of Principal Personalities

Isaac Akinaka: Go For Broke National Education Center

General Sir Harold Alexander, General Mark Clark, Mike Doble, General John Harding, John Strick, Harry Wilson: Imperial War Museum

David Cole: David Cole family

Ira Eaker: National Archives and Records Administration, USA

Lawrie Franklyn-Vaile: Franklyn-Vaile family

Leonard Garland: Surrey Garland

Mike Gordon-Watson: Julia Gordon-Watson

Jupp Klein, Władek Rubnikowicz, Ted Wyke-Smith: author's collection

Ralph 'Lucky' Lucardi: 57thfightergroup.org

General John Lucas: John Lucas Collection

Wilhelm Mauss: Hans-Jürg Mauss

Maps

Lovell Johns Ltd

Index

A British 25-pounder team in action.

A New Zealander infantryman peers through the shattered wreckage of Cassino.